Quick Reference Guide

Cengage Advantage Books

Looking Out
Looking In

Ronald B. Adler
Santa Barbara City College

Russell F. Proctor II
Northern Kentucky University

FOURTEENTH EDITION

WADSWORTH
CENGAGE Learning·

Australia • Brazil • Japan • Korea • Mexico • Singapore • Spain • United Kingdom • United States

**Cengage Advantage Books: Looking Out/
Looking In, Fourteenth Edition**
Ronald B. Adler, Russell F. Proctor II

Editor-in-Chief: Lyn Uhl

Publisher: Monica Eckman

Development Editor: Florence Kilgo

Assistant Editor: Alicia Landsberg

Editorial Assistant: Colin Solan

Media Editor: Jessica Badiner

Executive Brand Manager: Ben Rivera

Senior Market Development Manager: Kara
    Kindstrom

Senior Content Project Manager: Michael Lepera

Senior Art Director: Linda May

Manufacturing Planner: Doug Bertke

Rights Acquisition Specialist: Ann Hoffman

Production Service/Compositor: Lachina
    Publishing Services

Text Designer: Janet Alleyn

Cover Image: Daniel W. Adler

For product information and technology assistance, contact us at
Cengage Learning Customer & Sales Support, 1-800-354-9706

For permission to use material from this text or product,
submit all requests online at **cengage.com/permissions**
Further permissions questions can be emailed to
permissionrequest@cengage.com

ISBN-13: 978-1-285-07056-8

ISBN-10: 1-285-07056-9

Wadsworth
20 Channel Center Street
Boston, MA 02210
USA

Cengage Learning is a leading provider of customized learning solutions with office locations around the globe, including Singapore, the United Kingdom, Australia, Mexico, Brazil, and Japan. Locate your local office at:
www.cengage.com/global

Cengage Learning products are represented in Canada by Nelson Education, Ltd.

For your course and learning solutions, visit **www.cengage.com**

Purchase any of our products at your local college store or at our preferred online store **www.CengageBrain.com**

Instructors: Please visit **login.cengage.com** and log in to access instructor-specific resources.

Printed in the United States of America
2 3 4 5 6 7 17 16 15 14 13

To

Neil Towne

whose legacy continues in these pages.

Brief Contents

Contents

PART I   LOOKING IN

PART II   LOOKING OUT

STUDENT WORKBOOK

CHAPTER SIX

PART III   LOOKING AT RELATIONAL DYNAMICS

Preface

In a world where change seems like the only constant, some truths about education endure. Talented and inspiring professors can transform lives. Learning is best when there's a connection between abstract ideas and the student's own life. Interaction makes learning more effective and exciting. And, we believe, textbooks—whether in print or digital form—continue to play an important role by organizing course material into a coherent whole that reinforces and expands on information presented in class and online.

 ## What's Familiar

This edition of *Looking Out/Looking In* retains the elements that have made it the best-selling interpersonal communication textbook for over four decades, used by over one million students. As always, the user-friendly approach connects scholarship and everyday life. Virtually every page spread contains an attention-grabbing assortment of materials that support the text: articles from print and online sources, poetry, cartoons, photography, and profiles of popular films and television shows. A prominent treatment of ethical issues helps readers explore how to communicate in a principled manner. An extensive package of ancillary resources (described below) aims at helping students learn and instructors teach efficiently and effectively.

Looking Out/Looking In presents communication not as a collection of techniques we use *on* others, but as a process we engage in *with* them. Readers also learn that even the most competent communication doesn't always seek to create warm, fuzzy relationships, and that even less personal interaction usually has the best chance of success when handled in a constructive, respectful manner.

The discussion of gender and culture is integrated throughout the book, rather than being isolated in separate chapters. The treatment of these important topics is non-ideological, citing research that shows how other variables are often at least as important in shaping interaction. The basic focus of the chapters has remained constant, and Chapters 2 through 11 can be covered in whatever order works best for individual situations.

 ## New to This Edition

Users of *Looking Out/Looking In* will find that the new edition has been improved in several ways while remaining true to its approach.

- **Advantage Edition**
  Part of the Cengage Learning Advantage Series, this paperback and black-and-white version of the book offers a built-in student workbook at the end of each chapter

that has perforated pages so material can be submitted as homework. The student workbook was revised by Justin Braxton-Brown, Hopkinsville Community College, and contains a wealth of resources to help students understand and master concepts and skills introduced in the text, including correlated learning objectives for each activity.

- **New chapter on close relationships**
  In response to many requests, the new Chapter 9 focuses on communication in the types of close relationships that matter most: with family, friends, and romantic partners. In addition, this chapter retains information about the various ways intimacy can be expressed. This new chapter concludes with guidelines for managing communication in all types of close relationships.

- **Improved organization**
  Material on self-disclosure is now in Chapter 2, where it fits most logically with the topics of self and identity management.

- **Updated and expanded coverage**
  Most notably, coverage of social media has expanded to reflect the importance of mediated communication in personal relationships. For example, Chapter 1 includes a new section on competence in social media, Chapter 2 expands coverage of online impression management, and Chapter 8 explains how social media both shapes personal relationships and how people misrepresent themselves online. A reading in Chapter 2 describes the tensions that arise when parents try to connect with their children on Facebook. In Chapter 8, a young man with cerebral palsy describes how social media has opened doors for him to create and sustain relationships. In addition to in-text material, a bonus chapter dedicated to mediated communication, written by David DeAndrea of Ohio State University and Stephanie Tom Tong of Wayne State University, provides additional coverage of this important topic. To learn more about including the bonus chapter as part of a custom learning solution, please contact your Cengage Learning sales representative.

  In addition to social media, every chapter describes updated research on interpersonal communication. For example, Chapter 1 updates the relationship between communication and physical health. Chapter 3 explains how expectations influence perception. Chapter 9 contains new material on relational maintenance and support. Chapter 11 includes an expanded discussion of toxic messages that can pollute a relationship. A new bonus chapter on military communication by Brandi Frisby is also available for inclusion as part of a custom learning solution, which you can learn more about by contacting your Cengage Learning sales representative.

- **New examples from popular media**
  This edition is loaded with examples that depict how communication operates in a variety of relationships. Television profiles include comedies like *Parks and Recreation*, *How I Met Your Mother*, and *The Office*; reality shows including *Intervention*, *The Bachelor*, and *Undercover Boss*; and dramas such as *Mad Men*, *Parenthood*, *Glee*, *Downton Abbey*, and *Modern Family*. Many other profiles come from popular films including *The Invention of Lying*, *Easy A*, *The Hangover*, *The Artist*, *Irreconcilable Differences*, *Friends With Benefits*, *The Hunger Games*, and the *Harry Potter* series.

- **Updated sidebar readings**
  Compelling readings have distinguished *Looking Out/Looking In* from the beginning. This edition features a new lineup that shows how principles in the text operate in a wide range of settings and relationships. For example, in Chapter 2, an observant dinner guest

explains how even casual messages can shape the self-concept of young children. In Chapter 4, a self-confident introvert offers insights on—and appreciation of—people who prefer to observe instead of talk. In Chapter 5, a mother explains how labels make a difference for describing her special needs daughter. Chapter 7 includes an essay explaining what messages are—and aren't—helpful when confronting someone grieving over a loss. Chapter 11 includes insights about how "paying it forward" pays in the business world.

- New coverage of diversity
  Throughout the book, *Looking at Diversity* profiles—many new to this edition—provide first-person accounts by communicators from a wide range of backgrounds. In Chapter 1, a man born and raised in Europe describes the challenges of communicating across cultures. Chapter 5 offers the perspective of a healthcare clinician whose job requires her and her associates to translate patients' needs from Spanish to English. In Chapter 7, an intercultural scholar explains how listening responses in South Korea, where he was raised, are different from those in the United States. And Chapter 9 describes the challenges faced by a family in which the parents and children are from different races.

 ## In-Text Learning Resources

Every chapter contains a variety of resources to help students understand and use the principles introduced in the text. These include:

- *Looking at Diversity* **profiles**, many new to this edition, provide first-person accounts by communicators from a wide range of cultural, physical, ethnic, and occupational backgrounds. These profiles help readers appreciate that interpersonal communication is shaped by who you are and where you come from.
- *On the Job* **sidebars** in every chapter highlight the importance of interpersonal communication in the workplace. Grounded in scholarly research, these sidebars equip readers with communication strategies that will enhance career success.
- *In Real Life* **transcripts** describe how the skills and concepts from the text sound in everyday life. Seeing real people use the skills in familiar situations gives students both the modeling and confidence to try them in their own relationships. Dramatized versions of many of these transcripts are featured in the *Looking Out/Looking In* online resources described below.
- **Activities** in every chapter help readers engage with important concepts. They are labeled by type: *Pause and Reflect* (formerly *Invitation to Insight*) boxes help readers understand how theory and research apply to their own lives. *Skill Builders* help them improve their communication skills. *Ethical Challenges* offer wisdom about dilemmas that communicators face as they pursue their own goals.

 ## Other Teaching and Learning Resources

Along with the text itself, *Looking Out/Looking In* is accompanied by an extensive array of materials that will make teaching and learning more efficient and effective. **Note to faculty**: If you want your students to have access to the online resources for this text, please be sure to order them for your course. The content in these resources can be bundled with every new copy of the text or ordered separately. If you do not order them, your students will not have access to the online resources for the start of class. *Contact your local Wadsworth Cengage Learning sales representative for more details.*

- The more you study, the better the results. Make the most of your study time by accessing everything you need to succeed in one place. The **Speech Communication CourseMate** for *Looking Out/Looking In* includes these features.

  - The **Interactive eBook for *Looking Out/Looking In*** provides students with interactive exercises, highlighting and bookmarking tools, search tools, and "In Real Life" Video Activities embedded in the Reader near the associated text.

  - **"In Real Life" Video Activities** feature real-life communication scenarios, which allow students to watch and analyze videos of communication encounters that illustrate concepts discussed in the book. In addition, Interpersonal Simulations ask students to consider the consequences of their choices in hypothetical interpersonal situations.

  - **Video Skillbuilder videos** provide unscripted clips of students talking about their struggles and successes in college. Topics covered include taking notes to improve your grades, time management, and learning styles.

  - **InfoTrac College Edition** is a virtual library featuring more than 18 million reliable, full-length articles from five thousand academic and popular periodicals that can be retrieved almost instantly.

  - **Quizzes**, **Flashcards**, and more.

  Go to CengageBrain.com to access these resources, and look for this icon 🖥 to find resources related to your text in Speech Communication CourseMate.

- The **CengageBrain Online Store**, CengageBrain.com, is a single destination for more than 15,000 new print textbooks, textbook rentals, eBooks, single eChapters, and print and digital tools. CengageBrain.com provides freedom to purchase Cengage Learning Products á la carte—exactly what you need, when you need it. Visit CengageBrain.com for details.

- A comprehensive **Instructor's Resource Manual**, revised by Heidi Murphy, Central New Mexico Community College, provides tips and tools for both new and experienced instructors. The manual also contains hard copy of over 1,200 class-tested exam questions, indexed by page number and level of understanding.

- The **PowerLecture CD-ROM** contains an electronic version of the Instructor's Resource Manual, ExamView® Computerized Testing, predesigned Microsoft PowerPoint® presentations, and JoinIn® classroom quizzing. The PowerPoint presentations contain text, images, and videos of student speeches and can be used as they are or customized to suit your course needs.

- **Communication Scenarios for Critique and Analysis Videos** include additional scenarios covering interviewing and group work. *Contact your Wadsworth Cengage Learning sales representative for details.*

- *Communication in Film III*: *Teaching Communication Courses Using Feature Films* by Russell F. Proctor II, Northern Kentucky University, expands on the film tips in each chapter of *Looking Out/Looking In*. This guide provides detailed suggestions for using both new and classic films to illustrate communication principles introduced in the text.

- *Media Guide for Interpersonal Communication* by Charles G. Apple, University of Michigan-Flint, provides faculty with media resource listings focused on general interpersonal communication topics. Each listing provides compelling examples of how interpersonal communication concepts are illustrated in particular films, books, plays, websites, or journal articles. Discussion questions are provided.

- *The Teaching Assistant's Guide to the Basic Course* by Katherine G. Hendrix, University of Memphis, is based on leading communication teacher training programs and covers general teaching and course management topics, as well as specific strategies for communication instruction, such as providing effective feedback on performance, managing sensitive class discussions, and conducting mock interviews.

- *A Guide to the Basic Course for ESL Students* by Esther Yook, Mary Washington College, is available bundled with the text and assists the nonnative English speaker. It features FAQs, helpful URLs, and strategies for accent management and overcoming speech apprehension.

- *The Art and Strategy of Service Learning* by Rick Isaacson and Jeff Saperstein can be bundled with the text and is an invaluable resource for students in a basic course that integrates a service-learning component. The handbook provides guidelines for connecting service learning work with classroom concepts and advice for working effectively with agencies and organizations. The handbook also provides model forms and reports and a directory of online resources.

- **CourseCare training and support** can help you get trained, get connected, and get the support you need for the seamless integration of digital resources into your course. This unparalleled technology service and training program provides robust online resources, peer-to-peer instruction, personalized training, and a customizable program you can count on. Visit cengagebrain.com/coursecare/ to sign up for online seminars, first day of class services, technical support, or personalized, face-to-face training. Our online and onsite trainings are frequently led by one of our Lead Teachers, faculty members who are experts in using Wadsworth Cengage Learning technology and can provide best practices and teaching tips.

- As part of our **Flex-Text customization program**, you can add your personal touch to *Looking Out/Looking In* with a course-specific cover and up to 32 pages of your own content at no additional cost. Create a text as unique as your course: quickly, simply, and affordably. Two bonus chapters unique to *Looking Out/Looking In* are available now: one about computer-mediated communication, the other about communication and the military.

Acknowledgments

We are grateful to the many people who helped bring you this new edition. Thanks are due to the colleagues whose reviews helped shape this new edition: Ronald Biddle, Clovis Community College; Jack Byer, Bucks County Community College; Jan Caldwell, Asheville-Buncombe Technical Community College; Linda Di Desidero, University of Maryland University College; Donna Ditton, Ivy Tech Community College; Clark Friesen, Lone Star College-Tomball; Laura Garcia, Washington State Community College; Julie Simanski, Des Moines Area Community College; Walt Thielen, Paradise Valley Community College; and Joseph Valenzano, University of Nevada-Las Vegas.

We are grateful to the authors of the bonus chapters that accompany this edition: Brandi Frisby of the University of Kentucky, as well as David DeAndrea of Ohio State University and Stephanie Tom Tong of Wayne State University. We also thank Heather Burns for her suggestions on television programs and films.

Our thanks also go to the hardworking team at Cengage Learning who have played a role in this edition from start to finish: Monica Eckman, Michael Lepera, Jessica Badiner, Colin Solan, Kara Kindstrom, Justin Lacap, and Ben Rivera. In addition, we are grateful to the publishing professionals who helped with this edition: Christopher Black, Jennifer Bonnar, Eric Zeiter, Aaron Kantor, Steven Summerlight, Lucy Campos, and Rita Dienst. We are especially indebted to Janet Alleyn for designing the handsome book you are reading, and to Sherri Adler for selecting the photos that help make it unique.

About the Authors

Since this is a book about interpersonal communication, it seems appropriate for us to introduce ourselves to you, the reader. The "we" you'll be reading throughout this book isn't just an editorial device: It refers to two real people—Ron Adler and Russ Proctor.

Ron Adler lives in Santa Barbara, California, with his wife, Sherri, an artist and photo researcher who selected most of the images in this book. Their three adult children were infants when early editions of *Looking Out/Looking In* were conceived, and they grew up as guinea pigs for the field testing of many concepts in this book. If you asked them, they would vouch for the value of the information between these covers.

Ron spends most of his professional time writing about communication. In addition to helping create *Looking Out/Looking In*, he has contributed to six other books about topics including business communication, public speaking, small group communication, assertiveness, and social skills. Besides writing and teaching, Ron teaches college courses and helps professional and business people improve their communication on the job. Cycling and hiking help keep Ron physically and emotionally healthy.

Russ Proctor is a professor at Northern Kentucky University, where his sons R. P. and Randy both attended. Russ's wife, Pam, is an educator too, training teachers, students, and businesses to use energy more efficiently.

Russ met Ron at a communication conference in 1990, where they quickly discovered a shared interest in using feature films as a teaching tool. They have written and spoken extensively on this topic over the years, and they have also co-authored several textbooks and articles. When Russ isn't teaching, writing, or presenting, his hobbies include sports (especially baseball), classic rock music (especially Steely Dan), and cooking (especially for family and friends on his birthday each year).

Masterfile

A First Look at Interpersonal Communication

After studying the topics in this chapter, you should be able to:

1. Assess the needs (physical, identity, social, and practical) that communicators are attempting to satisfy in a given situation or relationship.

2. Apply the transactional communication model to a specific situation.

3. Describe how the communication principles and misconceptions identified in this chapter are evident in a specific situation.

4. Describe the degree to which communication (in a specific instance or a relationship) is qualitatively impersonal or interpersonal, and describe the consequences of this level of interaction.

5. Diagnose the effectiveness of various communication channels in a specific situation.

6. Determine the level of communication competence in a specific instance or a relationship.

AP Photo/Javier Galeano

Perhaps you played this game as a child. The group of children chooses a victim—either as punishment for committing a real or imagined offense or just for "fun." Then for a period of time, that victim is given the silent treatment. No one speaks to him or her, and no one responds to anything the victim says or does.

If you were the subject of this silent treatment, you probably experienced a range of emotions. At first you might have felt—or at least acted—indifferent. But after a while the strain of being treated as a nonperson probably began to grow. If the game went on long enough, it's likely you found yourself either retreating into a state of depression or lashing out with hostility—partly to show your anger and partly to get a response from the others.

Adults, as well as children, have used the silent treatment in virtually every society throughout history as a powerful tool to express displeasure and for social control.[1] We all know intuitively that communication—the company of others—is one of the most basic human needs, and that lack of contact is among the cruelest punishments a person can suffer.

Besides being emotionally painful, being deprived of companionship is so serious that it can affect life itself. Fredrick II, emperor of Germany from 1196 to 1250, may have been the first person to prove the point systematically. A medieval historian described one of his significant, if inhumane, experiments:

> He bade foster mothers and nurses to suckle the children, to bathe and wash them, but in no way to prattle with them, for he wanted to learn whether they would speak the Hebrew language, which was the oldest, or Greek, or Latin, or Arabic, or perhaps the language of their parents, of whom they had been born. But he labored in vain because all the children died. For they could not live without the petting and joyful faces and loving words of their foster mothers.*

Fortunately, contemporary researchers have found less barbaric ways to illustrate the importance of communication. In one study of isolation, subjects were paid to remain alone in a locked room. Of the five subjects, one lasted for eight days. Three held out for two days, one commenting, "Never again." The fifth subject lasted only two hours.[2]

The need for contact and companionship is just as strong outside the laboratory, as individuals who have led solitary lives by choice or necessity have discovered. W. Carl Jackson, an adventurer who sailed across the Atlantic Ocean alone in fifty-one days, summarized the feelings common to most loners:

> I found the loneliness of the second month almost excruciating. I always thought of myself as self-sufficient, but I found life without people had no meaning. I had a definite need for somebody to talk to, someone real, alive, and breathing.†

Why We Communicate

You might object to stories like this, claiming that solitude would be a welcome relief from the irritations of everyday life. It's true that all of us need solitude, often more than we get, but each of us has a point beyond which we do not want to be alone. Beyond this point, solitude changes from a pleasurable to a painful condition. In other words, we all need relationships. We all need to communicate.

*Ross, J. B., & McLaughlin, M. M. (Eds.). (1949). *A portable medieval reader*. New York, NY: Viking.
†Jackson, W. C. (1978, September 7). Lonely dean finishes "excruciating" voyage. *Wisconsin State Journal*. Retrieved from http://newspaperarchive.com/wisconsin-state-journal/1978-09-07/page-2/. Reprinted with permission.

PHYSICAL NEEDS

Communication is so important that its presence or absence affects physical health. In extreme cases, communication can even become a matter of life or death. When he was a Navy pilot, U.S. Senator John McCain was shot down over North Vietnam and held as a prisoner of war for six years, often in solitary confinement. He and his fellow POWs set up clandestine codes in which they sent messages by tapping on walls to laboriously spell out words. McCain describes the importance of keeping contact and the risks that inmates would take to maintain contact with one another:

> The punishment for communicating could be severe, and a few POWs, having been caught and beaten for their efforts, had their spirits broken as their bodies were battered. Terrified of a return trip to the punishment room, they would lie still in their cells when their comrades tried to tap them up on the wall. Very few would remain uncommunicative for long. To suffer all this alone was less tolerable than torture. Withdrawing in silence from the fellowship of other Americans . . . was to us the approach of death.*

Other prisoners have also described the punishing effects of social isolation. Reflecting on his seven years as a hostage in Lebanon, former news correspondent Terry Anderson said flatly, "I would rather have had the worst companion than no companion at all."[3]

The link between communication and physical well-being isn't restricted to prisoners. Medical researchers have identified a wide range of health threats that can result from a lack of close relationships. For instance:

- A meta-analysis of nearly 150 studies and over 300,000 participants found that socially connected people—those with strong networks of family and friends—live an average of 3.7 years longer than those who are socially isolated.[4]
- A lack of social relationships jeopardizes coronary health to a degree that rivals cigarette smoking, high blood pressure, blood lipids, obesity, and lack of physical activity.[5]
- Socially isolated people are four times more susceptible to the common cold than are those who have active social networks.[6]
- Divorced, separated, and widowed people are five to ten times more likely to need mental hospitalization than their married counterparts. Happily married people also have lower incidences of pneumonia, surgery, and cancer than do single people.[7] (It's important to note that the *quality* of the relationship is more important than the institution of marriage in these studies.)

By contrast, a life that includes positive relationships created through communication leads to better health. As little as ten minutes per day of socializing improves memory and boosts intellectual function.[8] Conversation with others reduces feelings of loneliness and its accompanying maladies.[9] Stress hormones decline the more often people hear expressions of affection from loved ones.[10]

Research like this demonstrates the importance of having satisfying personal relationships. Not everyone needs the same amount of contact, and the quality of communication is almost certainly as significant as the quantity. The key point is that personal communication is essential for our well-being.

IDENTITY NEEDS

Communication does more than enable us to survive. It is the way—indeed, the *only* way—we learn who we are. As Chapter 2 explains, our sense of identity comes from the way we interact with other people. Are we smart or stupid, attractive or ugly, skillful or inept? The answers to these questions don't come from looking in the mirror. We decide who we are based on how others react to us.

*McCain, J. (1999). *Faith of my fathers* (p. 212). New York, NY: Random House.

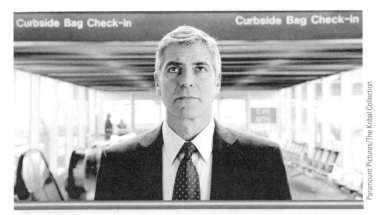

Paramount Pictures/The Kobal Collection

In the film *Up in the Air*, Ryan Bingham (George Clooney) learns the hard way that life without friendship, family, and love is void of meaning. (See the film summary at the end of this chapter.)

Deprived of communication with others, we would have no sense of ourselves. A dramatic example is the "Wild Boy of Aveyron," who spent his early childhood without any apparent human contact. The boy was discovered in January 1800 digging for vegetables in a French village garden. He showed no behaviors that one would expect in a social human. The boy could not speak but rather uttered only weird cries. More significant than this lack of social skills was his lack of any identity as a human being. As author Roger Shattuck put it, "The boy had no human sense of being in the world. He had no sense of himself as a person related to other persons."[11]

Only with the influence of a loving "mother" did the boy begin to behave—and, we can imagine, think of himself—as a human.

Like the boy of Aveyron, each of us enters the world with little or no sense of identity. We gain an idea of who we are from the way others define us. As Chapter 2 explains, the messages we receive in early childhood are the strongest, but the influence of others continues throughout life.

SOCIAL NEEDS

Besides helping to define who we are, communication provides a vital link with others. Researchers and theorists have identified a whole range of social needs that we satisfy by communicating. These include pleasure, affection, companionship, escape, relaxation, and control.[12]

Research suggests a strong link between effective interpersonal communication and happiness. In one study of more than 200 college students, the happiest 10 percent described themselves as having a rich social life. (The very happy people were no different from their classmates in any other measurable way such as amount of sleep, exercise, TV watching, religious activity, or alcohol consumption.)[13] In another study, women reported that "socializing" contributed more to a satisfying life than virtually any other activity, including relaxing, shopping, eating, exercise, TV, or prayer.[14] Married couples who are effective communicators report happier relationships than less skillful husbands and wives—a finding that has been supported across cultures.[15]

Despite knowing that communication is vital to social satisfaction, a variety of evidence suggests that many people aren't very successful at managing their interpersonal relationships. For example, one study revealed that one-quarter of the more than 4,000 adults surveyed knew more about their dogs than they did about their neighbors' backgrounds.[16] Research also suggests that the number of friendships is in decline. One widely recognized survey reported that, in 1985, Americans had an average of 2.94 close friends. Twenty years later, that number had dropped to 2.08.[17] It's worth noting that educated Americans reported having larger and more diverse networks. In other words, a higher education can enhance your relational life as well as your intellect.

Because connections with others are so vital, some theorists maintain that positive relationships may be the single most important source of life satisfaction and emotional well-being in every culture.[18] If you pause now and make a mental list of your own relationships, you'll probably see that, no matter how successfully you interact with at home, with friends, at school, and at work, there is plenty of room for improvement in your everyday life. The information that follows will help you improve the way you communicate with the people who matter most to you.

PRACTICAL GOALS

Besides satisfying social needs and shaping our identity, communication is the most widely used approach to satisfying what communication scholars call **instrumental goals**: getting others to behave in ways we want. Some instrumental goals are quite basic: Communication is the tool that lets you tell the hair stylist to take just a little off the sides, lets you negotiate household duties, and lets you convince the plumber that the broken pipe needs attention *now*!

Other instrumental goals are more important. Career success is the prime example. As the On the Job box on page 8 shows, communication skills are essential in virtually every career. They can even make the difference between life and death. The Los Angeles Police Department cited "bad communication" among the most common reasons for errors in shooting by its officers.[19] The ability to communicate effectively is just as essential for doctors, nurses, and other medical practitioners.[20] Researchers discovered that "poor communication" was the root of more than 60 percent of reported medical errors—including death, serious physical injury, and psychological trauma.[21] Research published in the *Journal of the American Medical Association* and elsewhere revealed a significant difference between the communication skills of physicians who had no malpractice claims against them and those with previous claims.[22]

Psychologist Abraham Maslow suggested that the physical, identity, social, and practical needs we have been discussing fall into five hierarchical categories, each of which must be satisfied before we concern ourselves with the less fundamental needs.[23] The most basic of these needs are *physical*: sufficient air, water, food, and rest, and the ability to reproduce as a species. The second of Maslow's needs is *safety*: protection from threats to our well-being. Beyond physical and safety needs are the *social needs* we have mentioned already. Beyond these, Maslow suggests, each of us has *self-esteem* needs: the desire to believe that we are worthwhile, valuable people. The final category of needs described by Maslow is *self-actualization*: the desire to develop our potential to the maximum, to become the best person we can be. As you read on, think about the ways in which communication is often necessary to satisfy each level of need.

The Process of Communication

We have been talking about *communication* as though the meaning of this word were perfectly clear. Communication scholars have argued for years about communication definitions. Despite their many disagreements, most would agree that at its essence, communication is about using messages to generate meanings.[24] Notice how this basic definition holds true across a variety of contexts—public speaking, small groups, mass media, etc. Before going further, we need to explain systematically what happens when people exchange messages and create meanings in interpersonal communication. Doing so will introduce you to a common working vocabulary and, at the same time, preview some of the topics that are covered in later chapters.

ON THE JOB

Communication and Career Success

No matter what the field, research confirms what experienced workers already know—that communication skills are crucial in finding and succeeding in a job. Communication skills often make the difference between being hired and being rejected. In one widely followed annual survey, employers list the skills and qualities for their ideal candidate. Communication skills always top the list, ahead of technical skills, initiative, analytical ability, and computer skills.[a]

In another survey, managers across the country rated the abilities to speak and listen effectively as the two most important factors in helping college graduates find jobs in a competitive workplace—more important than technical competence, work experience, and specific degree earned.[b] When 170 well-known business and industrial firms were asked to list the most common reasons for *not* offering jobs to applicants, the most frequent replies were "inability to communicate" and "poor communication skills."[c]

Once you have been hired, the need for communication skills is important in virtually every career.[d] Engineers spend the bulk of their working lives speaking and listening, mostly in one-to-one and small-group settings.[e] Accountants and the firms that hire them consistently cite effective communication as essential for career success.[f] One executive at computer giant Sun Microsystems made the point forcefully: "If there's one skill that's required for success in this industry, it's communication skills."[g] Writing in *The Scientist*, a commentator echoed this sentiment: "If I give any advice, it is that you can never do enough training around your overall communication skills."[h]

A LINEAR VIEW

In the early days of studying communication as a social science, researchers created models to illustrate the communication process. Their first attempts resulted in a **linear communication model**, which depicts communication as something a sender "does to" a receiver. According to the linear model in Figure 1.1,

A **sender** (the person creating the message)

encodes (puts thoughts into symbols and gestures) a

message (the information being transmitted), sending it through a

channel (the medium through which the message passes) to a

receiver (the person attending to the message) who

decodes (makes sense of the message), while contending with

noise (distractions that disrupt transmission).

Notice how the appearance of and vocabulary in Figure 1.1 represent how radio and television broadcasting operate. This isn't a coincidence: The scientists who created it were primarily interested in early electronic media. The widespread use of this model has affected the way we think and talk about communication. There is a linear, machinelike quality to familiar phrases, such as "We're having a communication breakdown" and "I don't think my message is getting through." While this is sometimes the case in mediated forms of communication, these familiar phrases (and the thinking they represent) obscure some important features of human communication. Does interpersonal communication really "break down," or are people still exchanging information even when they're not talking to each other? Is it possible to "get a message through" to someone loudly and clearly, but still not get the desired reaction? Here are some other questions to consider about the shortcomings of the linear model:

FIGURE 1.1 Linear Communication Model © Cengage Learning

- When you're having a face-to-face conversation with a friend, is there only one sender and one receiver, or do both of you send and receive messages simultaneously?
- Do you purposely encode every message you send, or do you engage in some behaviors unconsciously that still communicate messages to others?
- Even when you send a message electronically (e.g., through texting or email), is the message's meaning affected by larger factors such as culture, environment, and relational history?

These and other questions have led scholars to create models that better represent interpersonal communication. We will look at one of these models now.

A TRANSACTIONAL VIEW

A **transactional communication model** (Figure 1.2) updates and expands the linear model to better capture communication as a uniquely human process. Some concepts and terms from the linear model are retained in the transactional model, whereas others are enhanced, added, or eliminated.

The transactional model uses the word *communicator* instead of *sender* and *receiver*. This term reflects the fact that people typically send and receive messages simultaneously and not in a unidirectional or back-and-forth manner, as suggested by the linear model. Consider, for example, what might happen when you and a housemate negotiate how to handle household chores. As soon as you begin to hear (receive) the words sent by your housemate, "I want to talk about cleaning the kitchen . . . ," you grimace and clench your jaw (sending a nonverbal message of your own while receiving the verbal one). This reaction leads your housemate to interrupt herself defensively, sending a new message: "Now wait a minute . . . ."

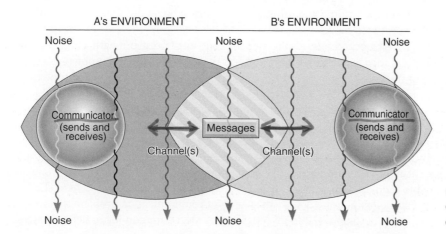

FIGURE 1.2 Transactional Communication Model
© Cengage Learning

A transactional model also shows that communicators often occupy different **environments**—fields of experience that affect how they understand others' behavior. In communication terminology, *environment* refers not only to a physical location but also to the personal experiences and cultural background that participants bring to a conversation.

Consider just some of the factors that might contribute to different environments:

- Person A might belong to one ethnic group and person B to another.
- A might be rich and B poor.
- A might be rushed and B have nowhere to go.
- A might have lived a long, eventful life and B might be young and inexperienced.
- A might be passionately concerned with the subject and B indifferent to it.

Notice how the model in Figure 1.2 shows that the environments of individuals A and B overlap. This area represents the background that the communicators have in common. As the shared environment becomes smaller, communication usually becomes more challenging. Consider a few examples in which different perspectives can make understanding difficult:

- Bosses who have trouble understanding the perspectives of their employees will be less effective managers, and workers who do not appreciate the challenges of being a boss are more likely to be uncooperative (and probably less suitable for advancement).
- Parents who have trouble recalling their youth are likely to clash with their children, who have never known and may not appreciate the responsibility that comes with parenting.
- Members of a dominant culture who have never experienced how it feels to be marginalized may not appreciate the concerns of people from minority co-cultures, whose own perspectives make it hard to understand the cultural blindness of the majority.

Communication channels retain a significant role in the transactional model, as they did in the linear model. Although it's tempting to see channels simply as neutral conduits for delivering a message, a closer look reveals the important role they play. For instance, should you say "I love you" in person? Over the phone? In a text message? By renting space on a billboard? By sending flowers and a card? Via email? In a voice mail? Channel selection matters just as much when sending breakup messages. A study of 1,000 cell phone users found that 45 percent had used their mobile phone to end a relationship (usually by text).[25] Obviously, this way of delivering bad news runs the risk of wounding and infuriating the person being dumped ("She didn't even have the guts to tell me to my face").

The transactional model also retains the concept of noise but with a broader focus. In the linear model, the focus is on noise in the channel—what is known as *external noise*. For instance, loud music or too much cigarette smoke in a crowded room might make it difficult for you to pay attention to another person. The transactional model shows that noise also resides *within* communicators. This includes *physiological noise*, which involves biological factors that interfere with accurate reception: illness, fatigue, hearing loss, and so on. Communicators can also encounter *psychological noise*: forces within that interfere with the ability to understand a message accurately. For instance, a student might become so upset upon learning that she failed a test that she would be unable (perhaps *unwilling* is a better word) to understand clearly where she went wrong. Psychological noise is such an important communication problem that we have devoted much of Chapter 10 to investigating its most common form, defensiveness.

For all the insights they offer, models can't capture some important features of interpersonal communication. A model is a "snapshot," while communication more closely resembles a "motion picture." In real life it's difficult to isolate a single discrete "act" of communication from the events that precede and follow it.[26] Consider the "Zits" cartoon on this page. If you read only the final frame, it appears that Jeremy is the victim of his mother's nagging. If you then read the first three frames, you might conclude that if Jeremy were more responsive to his mother, she might not need to be so persistent. And if you watched the two of them interact over the days and weeks preceding the incident in this cartoon, you would have a larger (but still incomplete) picture of the relational history that contributed to this event. In other words, the communication pattern that Jeremy and his mother have created together contributes to the quality of their relationship.

This leads to another important point: Transactional communication isn't something that we do *to* others; rather, it is an activity that we do *with* them. In this sense, interpersonal communication is rather like dancing—at least the kind of dancing we do with partners. Like dancing, communication depends on the involvement of a partner. And like good dancing, successful communication doesn't depend only on the person who takes the lead. A great dancer who forgets to consider and adapt to the skill level of his or her partner can make both people look bad. In communication and dancing, even having two talented partners doesn't guarantee success. When two skilled dancers perform without coordinating their movements, the results feel bad to the dancers and look foolish to an audience. Finally, relational communication—like dancing—is a unique creation that arises out of the way in which the partners interact. The way you dance probably varies from one partner to another. Likewise, the way you communicate almost certainly varies from one partner to another.

Now we can summarize the definition of **interpersonal communication** that we have been developing. It is a transactional process involving participants who occupy different but overlapping environments and create relationships through the exchange of messages, many of which are affected by external, physiological, and psychological noise. Whether or not you memorize this definition is a matter for you and your instructor to decide. In any case, notice how it reflects a more sophisticated view of the process than you might have had before reading this far. With this definition in

The relationships among the characters on the television show *How I Met Your Mother* illustrate the transactional nature of interpersonal communication. (See the TV summary at the end of this chapter.)

mind, let's look at how interpersonal communication differs from less personal kinds of interaction.

INTERPERSONAL AND IMPERSONAL COMMUNICATION

Scholars have characterized interpersonal communication in a number of ways.[27] The most obvious definition focuses on the number of people involved. A *quantitative* definition of interpersonal communication includes any interaction between two people, usually face to face. Social scientists call two interacting people a **dyad**, and they often use the adjective *dyadic* to describe this type of communication. So, in a quantitative sense, the terms *dyadic communication* and *interpersonal communication* can be used interchangeably. Using a quantitative definition, a salesclerk and customer or a police officer ticketing a speeding driver would be examples of interpersonal acts, whereas a teacher and class or a performer and audience would not.

You can probably see the problems with a quantitative definition of interpersonal communication. For example, consider a routine transaction between a salesclerk and customer or the rushed exchange when you ask a stranger on the street for directions. Communication of this sort hardly seems interpersonal—or personal in any sense of the word. In fact, after transactions like this, we commonly remark, "I might as well have been talking to a machine."

The impersonal nature of some two-person exchanges and the personal nature of others have led some scholars to argue that *quality*, not quantity, is what distinguishes interpersonal communication.[28] Taking a *qualitative* approach, interpersonal communication occurs when people treat one another as unique individuals, regardless of the context in which the interaction occurs or the number of people involved. When quality of interaction is the criterion, the opposite of interpersonal communication is **impersonal communication**, not group, public, or mass communication.

Several features distinguish qualitatively interpersonal communication from less-personal communication.[29] The first feature is *uniqueness*. Communication in impersonal exchanges is determined by social *rules* (e.g., laugh politely at others' jokes, don't dominate a conversation) and by social *roles* (e.g., the customer is always right, be especially polite to senior citizens). Qualitatively interpersonal relationships are characterized by the development of unique rules and roles. For example, in one relationship you might exchange good-natured insults, whereas in another you are careful never to offend your partner. Likewise, you might handle conflicts with one friend or family member by expressing disagreements as soon as they arise, whereas the unwritten rule in another relationship is to withhold resentments until they build up and then clear the air periodically. One communication scholar uses the term *relational culture* to describe people in close relationships who create their own unique ways of interacting.[30]

A second feature of qualitatively interpersonal relationships is *irreplaceability*. Because interpersonal relationships are unique, they have no substitute. This explains why we usually feel so sad when a close friendship or love affair cools down. We know that no matter how many other relationships fill our lives, none of them will ever be quite like the one that just ended.

Interdependence is a third feature of qualitatively interpersonal relationships. At the most basic level, the fate of the partners is connected. You might be able to brush off the anger, affection, excitement, or depression of someone you're not involved with personally, but in an interpersonal relationship the other's life affects you. Sometimes interdependence is a pleasure, and at other times it is a burden. In either case, it is a fact of life in qualitatively interpersonal relationships. Interdependence goes beyond the level of joined fates. In interpersonal relationships, our very identity depends on the nature of our interaction with others. As psychologist Kenneth Gergen puts it: "One cannot be 'attractive' without others who are attracted, a 'leader' without others willing to follow, or a 'loving person' without others to affirm with appreciation."[31]

ETHICAL CHALLENGE

MARTIN BUBER'S *I AND THOU*

Martin Buber is arguably the most influential advocate of qualitatively inter-personal communication, as defined on pages 12–15. His book *Ich und Du (I and Thou)* is a worldwide classic, selling millions of copies since its publication in 1922.[a]

Buber states that "I-It" and "I-Thou" represent two ways in which humans can relate to one another. "I-It" relationships are stable, predictable, detached. In an "I-It" mode we deal with people because they can do things for us: pump gas, laugh at our jokes, buy products we are selling, provide information or amusement. "I-It" is also the approach of science, which attempts to understand what makes people tick in order to explain, pre-dict, and control their behavior. Buber would have regarded advertisers as operating in an "I-It" mode, crafting messages that lead people to buy their products or services. "I-It" relationships exist in personal relationships as well as impersonal ones: On an everyday basis, parents and children, bosses and employees, service providers and customers—even lovers—deal with one another as objects ("I wish she would leave me alone." "Can you pick me up after work?" "How can I get him/her to love me?").

In profound contrast to "I-It" relationships, Buber described an "I-Thou" way of interacting. "I-Thou" relationships are utterly unique. Because no two teachers or students, parents or children, husbands or wives, bosses or employees are alike, we encounter each person as an individual and not as a member of some category. An "I-Thou" posture goes further: Not only are people different from one another, but also they change from moment to moment. An "I-Thou" rela-tionship arises out of how we are now, not how we might have been yesterday or even a moment ago. In an "I-Thou" relationship, persuasion and control are out of the question: We certainly may explain our point of view, but ultimately we respect the fact that others are free to act.

Buber acknowledges that it is impossible to create and sustain pure "I-Thou" relationships. But without this qualitatively interpersonal level of contact, our lives are impoverished. To paraphrase Buber, without "I-It" we cannot exist, but if we live only with "I-It," we are not fully human.

Think of your most important relationships:
1. To what degree can they be described as "I-Thou" or "I-It"?
2. How satisfied are you with this level of relating?
3. What obligation do you have to treat others in an "I-Thou" manner?

Based on your answers to these questions, how might you change your style of communication?

PAUSE AND REFLECT

HOW PERSONAL ARE YOUR FACEBOOK RELATIONSHIPS?

If you're a Facebook user, scroll through your list of friends on that site. Consider how personal (or impersonal) your relationships are with those people:

- How many would you regard to be "highly personal"? How many are "highly impersonal"? (Perhaps you can rank them on a scale of 1 to 10.)
- Which factors noted in this section (unique, irreplaceable, interdependent, disclosing, and intrinsically rewarding) affect your appraisals?
- What percentage of your communication with these people occurs exclusively on Facebook? Through other mediated channels (phone, text, email)? Face to face? How does this ratio affect your friendships?

 You can complete this activity by visiting CengageBrain.com to access the Speech Communication CourseMate for *Looking Out/ Looking In*, and, if requested, email your responses to your instructor.

A fourth feature of interpersonal relationships is often (though not always) the amount of *disclosure* of personal information. In impersonal relationships we don't reveal much about ourselves, but in interpersonal relationships we feel more comfortable sharing our thoughts and feelings. This doesn't mean that all interpersonal relationships are warm and caring, or that all self-disclosure is positive. It's possible to reveal negative, personal information: "I'm really angry with you." The point is, we tend to reserve these kinds of disclosures—both positive and negative—for our more personal relationships.

A fifth feature of interpersonal communication is *intrinsic rewards*. In impersonal communication we seek payoffs that have little to do with the people involved. You listen to instructors in class or talk to potential buyers of your used car in order to reach goals that usually have little to do with developing personal relationships. By contrast, you spend time in qualitatively interpersonal relationships with friends, lovers, and others because you find the time personally rewarding. It often doesn't matter *what* you talk about: The relationship itself is what's important.

Because relationships that are unique, irreplaceable, interdependent, disclosing, and intrinsically rewarding are rare, qualitatively interpersonal communication is relatively scarce. We chat pleasantly with shopkeepers or fellow passengers on the bus or plane; we discuss the weather or current events with most classmates and neighbors; we enjoy bantering with online acquaintances on social networking websites; but considering the number of people with whom we communicate, personal relationships are by far in the minority.

Some observers argue that communicators who strive to acquire a large number of "friends" on social networking websites like Facebook and Twitter are engaging in superficial, impersonal relationships. As one critic put it:

> The idea . . . is to attain as many of these not really-friends as possible. . . . Like cheap wine, "friends" provide a high that can only be sustained by acquiring more and more of them. Quantity trumps quality.[32]

Most relationships aren't *either* interpersonal *or* impersonal. Rather, they fall somewhere on a continuum between these two extremes. Your own experience probably reveals that there's often a personal element in even the most impersonal situations.

You might appreciate the unique sense of humor of a grocery checker or connect on a personal level with the person cutting your hair. And even the most tyrannical, demanding, by-the-book boss might show an occasional flash of humanity.

Just as there's a personal element in many impersonal settings, there is also an impersonal element in our relationships with the people we care most about. There are occasions when we don't want to be personal: when we're distracted, tired, busy, or just not interested. Sometimes all we want to know about certain friends is what they post on social media sites. In fact, interpersonal communication is rather like rich food—it's fine in moderation, but too much can make you uncomfortable.

Most of us don't have the time or energy to create highly personal relationships with everyone we encounter, either in person or via social media. In fact, the scarcity of qualitatively interpersonal communication contributes to its value. Like precious jewels and one-of-a-kind artwork, interpersonal relationships are special because of their scarcity.

Communication Principles and Misconceptions

Now that we've looked at definitions and approaches to communication, it's important to identify some principles of interpersonal interaction—and what communication can and can't accomplish.

COMMUNICATION PRINCIPLES

It's possible to draw several important conclusions about communication from what you have already learned in this chapter.

Communication Can Be Intentional or Unintentional Some communication is clearly intentional: You probably plan your words carefully before asking the boss for a raise or offering constructive criticism. Some scholars argue that only intentional messages like these qualify as communication. Others contend that even unintentional behavior is communicative. Suppose, for instance, that a friend overhears you muttering complaints to yourself. Even though you didn't intend for her to hear your remarks, they certainly did carry a message. In addition to these slips of the tongue, we unintentionally send many nonverbal messages. You might not be aware of your sour expression, impatient shifting, or sigh of boredom, but others view them nonetheless. Scholars have debated without reaching consensus about whether unintentional behavior should be considered communication, and it's unlikely that they will ever settle this issue.[33] In *Looking Out/Looking In*, we will look at the communicative value of both intentional and unintentional behavior.

It's Impossible Not to Communicate Because both intentional and unintentional behaviors send a message, many theorists agree that it is impossible not to communicate. Whatever you do—whether you speak or remain silent, confront or avoid, act emotional or keep a poker face—you provide information to others about your thoughts and feelings. In this sense we are like transmitters that can't be shut off.

Of course, the people who decode your message may not interpret it accurately. They might take your kidding seriously or underestimate your feelings, for example. The message that you intend to convey may not even resemble the one that others infer from your actions. Thus, when we talk about "a communication breakdown" or "miscommunication," we rarely mean that communication has ended. Instead, we mean that it is inaccurate, ineffective, or unsatisfying.[34]

This explains why the best way to boost understanding is to discuss your intentions and your interpretations of the other person's behavior until you have negotiated a shared meaning. The perception-checking skills described in Chapter 3, the tips on clear language offered in Chapter 5, and the listening skills introduced in Chapter 7 will give you tools to boost the odds that the meanings of messages you send and receive are understandable to both you and others.

"We can pause, Stu—we can even try fast-forwarding—
but we can never rewind."

Communication Is Unrepeatable Because communication is an ongoing process, it is impossible to repeat the same event. The friendly smile that worked so well when meeting a stranger last week might not succeed with the person you meet tomorrow. It might feel stale and artificial to you the second time around, or it might be wrong for the new person or occasion. Even with the same person, it's impossible to re-create an event. Why? Because neither you nor the other person is the same person. You've both lived longer. Your feelings about each other may have changed. You need not constantly invent new ways to act around familiar people, but you should realize that the "same" words and behavior are different each time they are spoken or performed.

Communication Is Irreversible We sometimes wish that we could back up in time, erasing words or acts and replacing them with better alternatives. As the cartoon on this page points out, such reversal is impossible. Sometimes, further explanation can clear up another's confusion, or an apology can mollify another's hurt feelings, but other times no amount of explanation can erase the impression you have created. It is no more possible to "unreceive" a message than to "unsqueeze" a tube of toothpaste. The same is true of most electronic messages: Once you hit "send," they can't be taken back. Words said, messages sent, and deeds done are irretrievable.

Communication Has a Content and a Relational Dimension Practically all exchanges operate on two levels. The **content dimension** involves the information being explicitly discussed: "Turn left at the next corner." "You can buy that for less online." "You're standing on my foot." In addition to this sort of obvious content, messages also have a **relational dimension** that expresses how you feel about the other person: whether you like or dislike the other person, feel in control or subordinate, feel comfortable or anxious, and so on.[35] For instance, consider how many different relational messages you could communicate by simply saying, "I'm busy tonight, but maybe some other time" in different ways.

Sometimes the content dimension of a message is all that matters. For example, you may not care much about how the customer service rep feels about you as long as you get a technician scheduled to fix your car. At other times, though, the relational dimension of a message is more important than the content under discussion (consider times when a customer service rep has spoken to you in a tone that seemed dismissive or rude). This explains why arguments can develop over apparently trivial subjects such as whose turn it is to wash the dishes or how to spend the weekend. In cases like this, what's really being tested is the nature of the relationship. Who's in control? How important are we to each other? Chapter 8 will explore these key relational issues in detail.

COMMUNICATION MISCONCEPTIONS

It's just as important to know what communication is *not* as to know what it is.[36] Avoiding the following misconceptions can save you a great deal of personal trouble.

More Communication Is Not Always Better Whereas not communicating enough can cause problems, there are also situations when *too much* communication is a mistake. Sometimes excessive communication is simply unproductive, as when two people "talk a problem to death," going over the same ground again and again without making progress. As one communication book puts it, "More and more negative communication merely leads to more and more negative results."[37] Even when you aren't being critical, too much communication can backfire. Pestering a prospective employer after your job interview or texting too many "call me" messages can generate the opposite reaction from what you're seeking.

Meanings Are Not in Words The biggest mistake we can make is to assume that *saying* something is the same thing as *communicating* it. As Chapter 3 explains, the words that make perfect sense to you can be interpreted in entirely different ways by others. Chapter 5 describes the most common types of verbal misunderstandings and suggests ways to minimize them. Chapter 7 introduces listening skills that help ensure that the way you receive messages matches the ideas that a speaker is trying to convey. As the old saying goes, "Words don't mean—*people* mean."

Successful Communication Doesn't Always Involve Shared Understanding George Bernard Shaw once remarked, "The problem with communication. . . is the illusion that it has been accomplished." This observation may sound cynical, but research (and most likely your personal experience) demonstrates that misunderstandings are common.[38] In fact, evidence suggests that people who are well acquainted may be more likely to misunderstand one another than relative strangers.[39]

Mutual understanding can be one measure of successful communication,[40] but there are times when success comes from *not* completely understanding one another. For example, we are often deliberately vague in order to spare another's feelings. Imagine how you might reply when a friend asks, "What do you think about my new tattoo?" You might tactfully say, "Wow—that's really unusual," instead of honestly and clearly answering, "I think it's grotesque." In cases like this we sacrifice clarity for the sake of kindness and to maintain our relationships.

Some research suggests that satisfying relationships depend in part on flawed understanding. Couples who *think* their partners understand them are more satisfied with each other than those who *actually* understand what the other says and

"My wife understands me."

means.[41] In other words, more satisfying relationships can sometimes come from less-than-perfect understanding. Chapter 2 describes in detail the way we sometimes sacrifice clarity for the sake of maintaining relationships.

Communication Will Not Solve All Problems Sometimes even the best-planned, best-timed communication won't solve a problem. Imagine, for example, that you ask an instructor to explain why you received a poor grade on a project that you believe deserved top marks. The instructor clearly outlines the reasons why you received the poor grade and sticks to that position after listening thoughtfully to your protests. Has communication solved the problem? Hardly.

Sometimes clear communication is even the *cause* of problems. Suppose, for example, that a friend asks you for an honest opinion of the $200 outfit she has just bought. Your clear and sincere answer, "I think it makes you look fat," might do more harm than good. Deciding when and how to self-disclose isn't always easy. See Chapter 2 for suggestions.

Social Media and Interpersonal Communication

As you've read by now, face-to-face conversation isn't the only way people create and maintain personal relationships. The term **social media** collectively describes all the channels that make remote personal communication possible. You're using social media when you text message with friends or coworkers, send a tweet, exchange emails and instant messages, and when you use social networking websites like Facebook. These channels aren't necessarily replacements for in-person communication—in fact, research suggests that the difference between face-to-face and virtual relationships is eroding.[42]

BENEFITS OF SOCIAL MEDIA

A growing body of research reveals that social media isn't the threat to relationships that some critics once feared.[43] For example:

- Social media tools offer "low-friction opportunities to create, enhance, and rediscover social ties that make a difference in people's lives," according to a survey of Internet experts. These benefits of social media significantly outweigh the costs.[44]
- The majority of social media users say that staying in touch with current friends and family members is a primary reason they use social networking sites, while half say that connecting with old friends they've lost touch with is a major reason for using these technologies.[45]
- The text-only format of most online messages can bring people closer by minimizing the perception of differences due to gender, social class, ethnicity, and age. Social media use is associated with having a more diverse social network.[46]
- More than 80 percent of social media users are involved in some kind of voluntary group or organization—significantly more than non-users.[47]
- Facebook users are more trusting, have more close friends, and get more support from their friends than do people who don't use social networking sites.[48]

Electronic communication isn't a replacement for face-to-face interaction. One study of college students who frequently use text-based messaging concluded that "nothing appears to compare to face-to-face communication in terms of satisfying individuals' communication, information, and social needs."[49] Furthermore, there is

Social Networking, Survival, and Healing

If you dig enough, you'll find little bits and pieces of my life scattered across the 'Net. For many people, this sort of transparency is unnerving. For me, it's always been a source of comfort in the storm that has been my life. Throughout 20 years of drinking and drugs, I've always had cyber-friends who, for reasons I can't explain, have stayed up late and saved me more times than I can count.

When I made the decision—or more accurately, when the decision smashed down upon me—to get sober, I was terrified, embarrassed, and angry. I certainly didn't think I needed anyone to help me. Sometime near the end of the third month, the last bits of my sanity were gone. I couldn't function any longer. That's when I turned to the Web. I began to post what I've been told was an ever-increasing series of erratic blurbs—some directly to FriendFeed and others on Twitter, Facebook, and MySpace.

Those messages started a dialogue that took on a life of its own. I began to get e-mails, phone calls, text messages, tweets and other digital notes from people around the world. Some offered kind words. Some offered support. Many people shared their own stories of addiction. In my darkest times, these notes would come. And always, without question, they pulled me back from the brink. Many of these messages were from people I have known for years. Another handful came

from childhood friends and people I'd grown up with. Some I had known well; many I had not. Others came from complete strangers. I have no idea how they found me.

The moment when I knew I'd be okay came one night, during a cross-country drive. The phone rang as I blew through Tennessee, but I didn't recognize the number so I let it go to voice mail. When I pulled into a gas station, I listened to the message. The woman on the phone didn't leave her name, and to this day I have no idea who she was. She told me about her father and his drinking. She told me that she was proud of me for getting sober and that she wanted me to keep trying. Already tenuous with my emotions, I sat on the side of the road crying. I listened to that message dozens of times, over and over.

The encouragement kept coming: strangers leaving messages about their lives, encouraging me to keep going. Throughout the next few months, my life became a 24-hour shower of love. There wasn't one free moment that wasn't taken up by someone making sure that my dumb ass wasn't back at the bar, that I wasn't looking for ways to die, and that I was doing the right thing. I still couldn't bring myself to leave the house. I rarely left my couch. I couldn't communicate with most people. But I was never alone.

AA keeps me sane. But social media got me there. Without that far-reaching network of people—friends and strangers alike—I wouldn't be here today.

Brad K.

From Brad K., "Social Networking, Survival, and Healing." Used by permission of the author.

an interactive relationship between text-based messages, phone contact, and in-person communication. In other words, if you regularly communicate with friends and family online, it is likely that you will also call them and try to see them more often.[50]

PAUSE AND REFLECT

HOW NETWORKED ARE YOU?

The studies cited in this section suggest that social media can enhance interpersonal relationships and networking. See if you agree or disagree by answering the following questions.

Can you identify a relationship that . . .
1. has been enhanced by regular mediated interactions, such as, texting, emailing, or posting on a social network site?
2. was created through mediated channels, perhaps on social networking websites or online dating services?
3. would suffer or perhaps end if mediated channels weren't available?

What do your answers tell you about the impact of social media on interpersonal relationships? Can you think of times when your use of social media has hurt or hindered relationships?

 You can complete this activity by visiting CengageBrain.com to access the Speech Communication CourseMate for *Looking Out/Looking In*, and, if requested, email your responses to your instructor.

There are several reasons why social media can increase both the quantity and quality of interpersonal communication. For one thing, communicating via social media makes it easier to maintain relationships. Busy schedules and long distances can make quality time in face-to-face contact difficult or impossible. The challenge of finding time is especially tough for people who are separated by long distances and multiple time zones. In relationships like this, the *asynchronous* nature of email provides a way to share information that otherwise would be impossible.[51] Communicators can create their own message and respond to one another without having to connect in real time.

Even when face-to-face communication is convenient, some people find it easier to share personal information via mediated channels. Sociolinguist Deborah Tannen describes how email transformed the quality of two relationships:

> E-mail deepened my friendship with Ralph. Though his office was next to mine, we rarely had extended conversations because he is shy. Face to face he mumbled so, I could barely tell he was speaking. But when we both got on e-mail, I started receiving long, self-revealing messages; we poured our hearts out to each other. A friend discovered that e-mail opened up that kind of communication with her father. He would never talk much on the phone (as her mother would), but they have become close since they both got on line.*

Experiences like these help explain why Steve Jobs, the cofounder of Apple Computer, suggested that personal computers be renamed "*inter*personal computers."[52]

*Tannen, D. (1994, May 16). Gender gap in cyberspace. *Newsweek*, pp. 52–53. Copyright Deborah Tannen. Reprinted with permission.

CHALLENGES OF SOCIAL MEDIA

Despite the benefits, communicating through social media also presents several challenges.

Leaner Messages Social scientists use the term **richness** to describe the abundance of nonverbal cues that add clarity to a verbal message. Conversely, **leanness** describes messages that are stark from a lack of nonverbal information. Face-to-face communication is rich because it abounds with nonverbal cues that help clarify the meanings of one another's words and offer hints about their feelings.[53] By comparison, most social media is a much leaner channel for conveying information.

To appreciate how message richness varies by medium, imagine you haven't heard from a friend in several weeks, and you decide to ask "Is anything wrong?" Your friend replies, "No, I'm fine." Would that response be more or less descriptive depending on whether you received it via text message, over the phone, or in person? You almost certainly would be able to tell a great deal more from a face-to-face response, because it would contain a richer array of cues: facial expressions, vocal tone, and so on. By contrast, a text message contains only words. The phone message—containing vocal, but no visual cues—would probably fall somewhere in between.

Because most mediated messages are leaner than the face-to-face variety, they can be more difficult to interpret with confidence. Irony and attempts at humor can easily be misunderstood; so as a receiver, it's important to clarify your interpretations before jumping to conclusions. And as a sender, think about how to send unambiguous messages so you aren't misunderstood.

The leanness of mediated messages presents another challenge. Without nonverbal cues, online communicators can create idealized—and sometimes unrealistic—images of one another. The absence of nonverbal cues allows cybercommunicators to carefully manage their identities. After all, it's a world without bad breath, unsightly blemishes, or stammering responses. This can stimulate both self-disclosure and direct questioning between strangers, resulting in greater interpersonal attraction.[54] Such conditions can lead to what Joseph Walther calls "hyperpersonal" communication, accelerating the discussion of personal topics and relational development beyond what normally happens in face-to-face interaction.[55] This may explain why communicators who meet online sometimes have difficulty shifting to a face-to-face relationship.[56]

Disinhibition Sooner or later, most of us speak before we think, blurting out remarks that embarrass ourselves and offend others. The tendency to transmit messages without considering their consequences can be especially great in online communication, where we don't always see, hear, or sometimes even know the target of our remarks. This **disinhibition** can take two forms.

Sometimes online communicators volunteer personal information that they would prefer to keep confidential from at least some receivers. Consider the example of social networking sites like Facebook. A quick scan of home pages there shows that many users post text and images about

Columbia Pictures/The Kobal Collection

In *The Social Network,* Facebook creator Mark Zuckerberg (Jesse Eisenberg) is handicapped by his disinhibition and the permanence of social media. (See the film summary at the end of this chapter.)

themselves that could prove embarrassing in some contexts: "Here I am just before my DUI arrest"; "This is me in Cancun on spring break." This is not the sort of information most people would be eager to show a prospective employer or certain family members. We discuss the role of social media in identity management—and "reputation management"—in Chapter 2.

Communication via social media can also be highly expressive. A growing body of research shows that communicators are more direct—often in a critical way—when using mediated channels than in face-to-face contact.[57] Sometimes communicators take disinhibition to the extreme, blasting off angry—even vicious—emails, text messages, and website postings.

Permanence Common decency aside, the risk of hostile mediated messages is their permanence. It can be bad enough to blurt out a private thought or lash out in person, but at least there is no lasting record of your indiscretion. By contrast, a regrettable text message, email, or web posting can be archived virtually forever. Even worse, it can be retrieved and forwarded in ways that can only be imagined in your worst dreams. The best advice, then, is to take the same approach with social media messages that you do in person: Think twice before saying something you may later regret.

What Makes an Effective Communicator?

It's easy to recognize good communicators and even easier to spot poor ones, but what characteristics distinguish effective communicators from their less successful counterparts?

Medical professionals, such as those portrayed on *Grey's Anatomy*, must balance being *effective* and *appropriate*. Consider how competently these characters—or medical practitioners you know—handle their interpersonal interactions.

ABC-TV/Picture Desk/The Kobal Collection

COMMUNICATION COMPETENCE DEFINED

Defining **communication competence** isn't as easy as it might seem. Although scholars struggle to agree on a precise definition, most would agree that competent communication involves achieving one's goals in a manner that, in most cases, maintains or enhances the relationship in which it occurs.[58] Put another way, competence seeks to be both *effective* and *appropriate*. You can probably think of people who achieve one of these goals at the expense of the other, such as the high-achieving businessperson who regularly ruffles feathers, or the kind and gracious person who doesn't stand up for her or himself. Competence is a balancing act that requires looking out both for yourself and for others—sometimes a challenging task.[59]

The following characteristics typify a competent communicator.

There Is No Ideal Way to Communicate Your own experience shows that a variety of communication styles can be effective. Some very successful communicators are serious, whereas others use humor; some are gregarious, whereas others are quieter; and some are more straightforward, whereas others hint diplomatically. Just as there are many kinds of beautiful music or art, there are many kinds of competent communication. It certainly is possible to learn new, effective ways of communicating from observing models, but it would be a mistake to try to copy others in a way that doesn't reflect your own style or values.

Competence Is Situational Even within a culture or relationship, the specific communication that is competent in one setting might be a colossal blunder in another. The joking insults you routinely trade with one friend might offend a sensitive family member, and last Saturday night's romantic approach would most likely be out of place at work on Monday morning.

Because competent behavior varies so much from one situation and person to another, it's a mistake to think that communication competence is a trait that a person either has or does not have. It's more accurate to talk about *degrees* or *areas* of competence.[60] You might deal quite skillfully with peers, for example, but feel clumsy interacting with people much older or younger, wealthier or poorer, or more or less attractive than yourself. In fact, your competence with one person may vary from situation to situation. This means that it's an overgeneralization to say in a moment of distress, "I'm a terrible communicator!" when it's more accurate to say, "I didn't handle this situation very well, even though I'm better in others."

Competence Can Be Learned To some degree, biology is destiny when it comes to communication style.[61] Studies of identical and fraternal twins suggest that traits including sociability, anger, and relaxation seem to be partially a function of our genetic makeup. Some research suggests that certain personality traits predispose people towards particular competence skills.[62] For instance, those who are agreeable and conscientious by nature find it easier to be appropriate, and harder to be (and become) assertive and effective. Chapter 2 will have more to say about the role of neurobiology in communication traits.

Fortunately, biology isn't the only factor that shapes how we communicate. Communication competence is, to a great degree, a set of skills that anyone can learn. Skills training has been shown to help communicators in a variety of professional fields.[63] Research also shows that college students typically become more competent communicators over the course of their undergraduate studies.[64] In other words, your level of competence can improve through education and training, which means that reading this book and taking this course can help you become a more competent communicator.[65]

CHARACTERISTICS OF COMPETENT COMMUNICATORS

Although competent communication varies from one situation to another, scholars have identified several common denominators that characterize effective communication in most contexts.

A Wide Range of Behaviors Effective communicators are able to choose their actions from a wide range of behaviors.[66] To understand the importance of having a large communication repertoire, imagine that someone you know repeatedly tells jokes—perhaps racist or sexist ones—that you find offensive. You could respond to these jokes in a number of ways:

- You could decide to say nothing, figuring that the risks of bringing the subject up would be greater than the benefits.
- You could ask a third party to say something to the joke teller about the offensiveness of the jokes.
- You could hint at your discomfort, hoping your friend would get the point.
- You could joke about your friend's insensitivity, counting on humor to soften the blow of your criticism.
- You could express your discomfort in a straightforward way, asking your friend to stop telling the offensive jokes, at least around you.
- You could even demand that your friend stop.

SELF-ASSESSMENT

Assessing Your Communication Skills

How effective are you as a communicator? You can get a clearer answer to this question by taking an online self-assessment. You can find the link to this site by visiting CengageBrain.com to access the Speech Communication CourseMate for *Looking Out/ Looking In.*

With this choice of responses at your disposal (and you can probably think of others as well), you could pick the one that has the best chance of success. But if you were able to use only one or two of these responses when raising a delicate issue—always keeping quiet or always hinting, for example—your chances of success would be much smaller. Indeed, many poor communicators are easy to spot by their limited range of responses. Some are chronic jokers. Others are always belligerent. Still others are quiet in almost every situation. Like a piano player who knows only one tune or a chef who can prepare only a few dishes, these people are forced to rely on a small range of responses again and again, whether or not they are successful.

Many people with disabilities have learned the value of having a repertoire of options available to manage unwanted offers of help.[67] Some of those options include performing a task quickly, before anyone has the chance to intervene; pretending not to hear the offer; accepting a well-intentioned invitation to avoid seeming rude or ungrateful; using humor to deflect a bid for help; declining a well-intentioned offer with thanks; and assertively refusing help from those who won't take no for an answer.

Ability to Choose the Most Appropriate Behavior Simply possessing a large range of communication skills is no guarantee of success. It's also necessary to know which of these skills will work best in a particular situation. This ability to choose the best approach is essential, because a response that works well in one setting would flop miserably in another one.

Although it's impossible to say precisely how to act in every situation, you should consider at least three factors when choosing a response. The first factor is the communication *context*. The time and place will almost always influence how you act. Asking your boss for a raise or your lover for a kiss might produce good results if the time is right, but the identical request might backfire if your timing is poor. Likewise, the joke that would be ideal at a bachelor party would probably be inappropriate at a funeral.

Your *goal* will also shape the approach you take. Inviting a new neighbor over for a cup of coffee or dinner could be just the right approach if you want to encourage a friendship, but if you want to maintain your privacy, it might be wiser to be polite but cool. Likewise, your goal will determine your approach in situations in which you want to help another person. As you will learn in Chapter 7, sometimes offering advice is just what is needed. But when you want to help others develop the ability to solve problems on their own, it's better to withhold your own ideas and function as a sounding board to let them consider alternatives and choose their solutions.

Finally, your *knowledge of the other person* should shape the approach you take. If you're dealing with someone who is very sensitive or insecure, your response might be supportive and cautious. With an old and trusted friend, you might be blunt. The social niche of the other party can also influence how you communicate. For instance, you would probably act differently toward an 80-year-old person than you would toward a teenager. Likewise, there are times when it's appropriate to treat a man differently than a woman, even in this age of gender equity. And one study shows that using casual text language (such as "4" instead of "for") will be less successful when emailing your professor than it might be with your friends.[68]

Skill at Performing Behaviors After you have chosen the most appropriate way to communicate, it's still necessary to perform the required skills effectively.[69] There is a big difference between knowing *about* a skill and being able to put it into practice. Simply being aware of alternatives isn't much help unless you can skillfully put these alternatives to work.

Just reading about communication skills in the following chapters won't guarantee that you can start using them flawlessly. As with any other skills—playing a musical instrument or learning a sport, for example—the road to competence in communication is not a short one. As you learn and practice the communication skills in the following pages, you can expect to pass through several stages,[70] shown in Figure 1.3 below.

Cognitive Complexity Social scientists use the term **cognitive complexity** to describe the ability to construct a variety of frameworks for viewing an issue.[71] To understand how cognitive complexity can increase competence, imagine that a longtime friend seems to be angry with you. One possible explanation is that your friend is offended by something you've done. Another possibility is that something has happened in another part of your friend's life that is upsetting. Or perhaps nothing at all is wrong, and you're just being overly sensitive. Considering the issue from several angles might prevent you from overreacting or misunderstanding the situation, increasing the odds of finding a way to resolve the problem constructively. Chapter 3 discusses cognitive complexity—and ways to improve it—in much greater detail.

SKILL BUILDER

STAGES IN LEARNING COMMUNICATION SKILLS

Learning any new skill requires moving through several levels of competence:

1. *Beginning Awareness.* This is the point at which you first learn that there is a new and better way of behaving. If you play tennis, for example, awareness might grow when you learn about a new way of serving that can improve your power and accuracy. In the area of communication, *Looking Out/Looking In* should bring this sort of awareness to you.

2. *Awkwardness.* Just as you were awkward when you first tried to ride a bicycle or drive a car, your initial attempts at communicating in new ways may also be awkward. As the saying goes, "You have to be willing to look bad in order to get good."

3. *Skillfulness.* If you keep working at overcoming the awkwardness of your initial attempts, you'll be able to handle yourself well, although you will still need to think about what you're doing. As an interpersonal communicator, you can expect the stage of skillfulness to be marked by a great deal of thinking and planning, and also by increasingly good results.

4. *Integration.* Integration occurs when you're able to perform well without thinking about it. The behavior becomes automatic, a part of your repertoire.

FIGURE 1.3 Stages in Learning Communication Skills © Cengage Learning

Empathy Seeing a situation from multiple points of view is important, but there's another step that goes beyond understanding different perspectives. *Empathy* involves feeling and experiencing another person's situation, almost as they do. This ability is so important that some researchers have labeled empathy the most important aspect of communication competence.[72] Chapters 3 and 7 introduce you to a set of skills that can boost your ability to empathize. For now, it's enough to note that getting a feel for how others view the world is a useful and important way to become a more effective communicator.

Self-Monitoring Whereas increased cognitive complexity and empathy help you understand others better, self-monitoring is one way to understand *yourself* better. Psychologists use the term **self-monitoring** to describe the process of paying close attention to one's behavior and using these observations to shape the way one behaves. Self-monitors are able to separate a part of their consciousness and observe their behavior from a detached viewpoint, making observations such as:

"I'm making a fool out of myself."

"I'd better speak up now."

"This approach is working well. I'll keep it up."

Although too much self-monitoring can be problematic (see Chapter 2), people who are aware of their behavior and the impression it makes are more skillful communicators than people who are low self-monitors.[73] For example, they are more accurate in judging others' emotional states, better at remembering information about others, less shy, and more assertive. By contrast, low self-monitors aren't able even to recognize their incompetence. One study revealed that poor communicators were blissfully ignorant of their shortcomings and more likely to overestimate their skill than were better communicators.[74] For example, experimental subjects who scored in the lowest quartile on joke-telling skills were more likely than their funnier counterparts to grossly overestimate their sense of humor.

Whereas low self-monitors may blunder through life, succeeding or failing without understanding why, high self-monitors have the detachment to ask themselves the question "How am I doing?" and to change their behavior if the answer isn't positive. This ability can be useful in both personal and professional settings. The President's Council of Economic Advisers maintains that greater "self-awareness, self-monitoring, and self control" will help students be more successful when they enter the job market.[75]

Commitment One feature that distinguishes effective communication—at least in qualitatively interpersonal relationships—is commitment. In other words, people who seem to care about relationships communicate better than those who don't.[76] This care shows up in at least two ways. The first is *commitment to the other person*. Concern for the other person is revealed in a variety of ways: a desire to spend time with him or her instead of rushing, a willingness to listen carefully instead of doing all the talking, the use of language that makes sense to the other person, and openness to change after hearing the other person's ideas. Effective communicators also care about *the message*. They appear sincere, seem to know what they are talking about, and demonstrate through words and deeds that they care about what they say.

How do you measure up as a competent communicator? Competence isn't a trait that people either have or do not have. Rather, it's a state that we achieve more or less frequently. A realistic goal, then, is not to become perfect, but rather to boost the percentage of time when you communicate in ways outlined in this section.

SKILL BUILDER

CHECK YOUR COMPETENCE

Other people are often the best judges of your competence as a communicator. They can also offer useful information about how to improve your communication. Find out for yourself by following these steps:

1. Choose a person with whom you have an important relationship.
2. In cooperation with this person, identify several contexts in which you communicate. For example, you might choose different situations such as "handling conflicts," "lending support to friends," or "expressing feelings."
3. For each situation, have your friend rate your competence by answering the following questions:
   a. Do you have a wide repertoire of response styles in this situation, or do you always respond in the same way?
   b. Are you able to choose the most effective way of behaving for the situation at hand?
   c. Are you skillful at performing behaviors? (Note that knowing how you *want* to behave isn't the same as being *able* to behave.)
   d. Do you communicate in a way that leaves others satisfied?
4. After reviewing your partner's answers, identify the situations in which your communication is most competent.
5. Choose a situation in which you would like to communicate more competently, and with the help of your partner:
   a. Determine whether your repertoire of behaviors needs to be expanded.
   b. Identify the ways in which you need to communicate more skillfully.
   c. Develop ways to monitor your behavior in the key situation to get feedback on your effectiveness.

 You can complete this activity by visiting CengageBrain.com to access the Speech Communication CourseMate for *Looking Out/ Looking In*, and, if requested, email your responses to your instructor.

COMPETENCE IN INTERCULTURAL COMMUNICATION

Throughout history, most people lived and died within a few miles of where they were born. They rarely had much to do with people from different backgrounds. Today is a different story. To use a familiar metaphor, we live in a global village, our lives intertwined with people from very different personal histories and communication styles.

As our world becomes more multicultural, the likelihood of interacting with people from different parts of the world is greater than ever. Given this fact, it's important to realize that what qualifies as competent behavior in one culture might be completely inept, or even offensive, in another.[77] On an obvious level, customs like belching after a meal or appearing nude in public that might be appropriate in some parts of the world would be considered outrageous in others. But there are more subtle differences in competent communication. For example, qualities like self-disclosing and speaking assertively that are valued in the United States are likely to be considered overly aggressive and insensitive in many Asian cultures, where subtlety and indirectness are considered important.[78]

LOOKING AT DIVERSITY

Igor Ristic: Competent Communication around the World

Photo provided by Igor Ristic

I was born in Bosnia and spent the first ten years of my life in Eastern Europe. I now live in the United States and have visited more than a dozen countries on five continents. The more of the world I experience, the more I'm inspired to learn how to communicate effectively within and between cultures.

Intercultural communication can be challenging. Take something as simple as customer service in restaurants. Waiters and waitresses in the United States make small talk with their customers, check in with them several times during a meal, and go to great lengths to be friendly and helpful. In contrast, most Eastern European servers quickly take an order, never interrupt diners during a meal, and drop off the bill as inconspicuously as possible. When I first came to the U.S., the friendliness of the wait staffs seemed unusual. Now when I return to

Europe, I sometimes perceive their servers as impersonal and curt. Being an effective communicator requires that I remain open-minded and understand the customs of each culture.

This isn't to suggest that Eastern Europeans aren't warm and friendly. In fact, when I talk with family members in Serbia, they often sit right next to me and drape an arm around my shoulder while we chat. After living in the U.S. for more than a decade, I've developed a strong sense of a "personal space bubble"—and I much prefer to sit facing others, at a distance, without touching, while holding a conversation. Those are things I never even thought about while growing up.

What I try to keep in mind is that cultural communication rules aren't "right" or "wrong"—they're simply different. Being a good communicator means I need to be aware of various cultural norms and adapt my communication style as much as possible.

"Competent Communication around the World" by Igor Ristic. Used with permission of author.

Even within a single society, members of various co-cultures may have different notions of appropriate behavior. One study revealed that ideas of how good friends should communicate varied from one ethnic group to another.[79] As a group, Latinos valued relational support most highly, whereas African Americans valued respect and acceptance. Asian Americans prized a caring, positive exchange of ideas, and Anglo Americans prized friends who recognized their needs as individuals. Findings like these mean that there can be no surefire list of rules or tips that will guarantee your success as a communicator. They also mean that competent communicators are able to adapt their style to suit the individual and cultural preferences of others.[80]

National and ethnic differences aren't the only dimensions of culture. Within a society **co-cultures** have different communication practices. Consider just a few co-cultures:

age (e.g., teen, senior citizen)

occupation (e.g., fashion model, long-distance trucker)

sexual orientation (e.g., lesbian, gay male)

physical disability (e.g., wheelchair user, hearing-impaired)

religion (e.g., evangelical Christian, Muslim)

activity (e.g., biker, gamer)

Some scholars have even characterized men and women as belonging to different co-cultures, claiming that each gender's style of communication is distinct.[81] We'll have more to say about that topic throughout this book.

Communicating successfully with people from different cultural backgrounds calls for the same elements of competence outlined in the pages you have just read. But beyond these basic qualities, communication researchers have identified several other especially important ingredients of successful intercultural communication.[82]

Most obviously, it helps to know the rules of a specific culture. For example, the kind of self-deprecating humor that Americans are likely to find amusing may fall flat among Arabs from the Middle East.[83] But beyond knowing the specific rules of an individual culture, there are also attitudes and skills called "culture-general" that help communicators build relationships with people from other backgrounds.[84]

To illustrate the ingredients of culture-general communication competence, imagine you've just been hired to work in a Japanese-owned company in the United States that has manufacturing operations in Mexico and customers around the world. In your new job, you are surrounded by coworkers, supervisors, and clients who come from cultures and co-cultures that are different from your own. You are also required to make occasional trips abroad. How will you handle the communication demands of this position? Ideally, you'll possess the following attributes.

Motivation The desire to communicate successfully with strangers is an important start. For example, people who are high in willingness to communicate with people from other cultures report a greater number of friends from different backgrounds than those who are less willing to reach out.[85] Having the proper motivation is important in all communication, but particularly so in intercultural interactions, because they can be quite challenging.

Tolerance for Ambiguity Communicating with people from different backgrounds can be confusing. A tolerance for ambiguity makes it possible to accept, and even embrace, the often equivocal and sometimes downright incomprehensible messages that characterize intercultural communication.

If you happen to work with colleagues raised in traditional Native American co-cultures, you may find them much quieter and less outgoing than you are used to. Your first reaction might be to chalk up this reticence to a lack of friendliness. However, it may just be a reflection of a co-culture in which quietness is valued more than extraversion, and silence more than loquacity. In cross-cultural situations like this, ambiguity is a fact of life, and a challenge.

Open-Mindedness It's one thing to tolerate ambiguity; it's another to become open-minded about cultural differences. There is a natural tendency to view others' communication choices as "wrong" when they don't match our cultural upbringing. In some parts of the world, you may find that women are not regarded with the same attitude of equality that is common in the West. Likewise, in other cultures, you may be aghast at the casual tolerance of poverty beyond anything at home, or with practices of bribery that don't jibe with homegrown notions of what is ethical. In situations like these, principled communicators aren't likely to compromise deeply held beliefs about what is right. At the same time, competence requires an attitude that recognizes that people who behave differently are most likely following rules that have governed their whole lives. Chapter 3 will offer more guidance on the challenges of viewing the world from others' perspectives.

Knowledge and Skill The rules and customs that work with one group might be quite different from those that succeed with another. For example, when traveling in

Latin America, you are likely to find that meetings there usually don't begin or end at their scheduled time, and that it takes the participants quite awhile to "get down to business." Rather than viewing your hosts as irresponsible and unproductive, you'll want to recognize that the meaning of time is not the same in all cultures. Likewise, the gestures others make, the distance they stand from you, and the eye contact they maintain have ambiguous meanings that you'll need to learn and follow.

Becoming interculturally competent requires *mindfulness*—awareness of your own behavior and that of others.[86] Communicators who lack this quality blunder through intercultural encounters *mindlessly*, oblivious of how their own behavior may confuse or offend others and how behavior that they consider weird may be simply different. When you're in a mindful state, you can use three strategies for moving toward a more competent style of intercultural communication:[87]

1. *Passive observation* involves noticing the behaviors of members of a different culture and using these insights to communicate in ways that are most effective.

2. *Active strategies* include reading, watching films, asking experts and members of the other culture how to behave, as well as taking academic courses related to intercultural communication and diversity.[88]

3. *Self-disclosure* involves volunteering personal information to people from the other culture with whom you want to communicate.

One type of self-disclosure is to confess your cultural ignorance: "This is very new to me. What's the right thing to do in this situation?" This approach is the riskiest of the three described here, because some cultures may not value candor and self-disclosure as much as others. Nevertheless, most people are pleased when strangers attempt to learn the practices of their culture, and they are usually more than willing to offer information and assistance.

COMPETENCE IN SOCIAL MEDIA

All the principles of interpersonal competence described so far apply to online communication. But in addition, communicating via social media calls for a unique set of skills.

Signs of the social networking times.

Think Before You Post Because the Internet never forgets, personal information posted today can haunt you in the future. A society in which everything is recorded will, as one scholar put it, "forever tether us to all our past actions, making it impossible, in practice, to escape them."[89]

Personal information can be especially damaging to your career. According to some surveys, 70 percent of recruiters in the United States have rejected candidates because of information found online—photographs, comments by and about the candidate, and membership in groups.[90]

For one cautionary tale about how your digital indiscretions can haunt you, consider the case of Stacy Snyder. The 25-year-old high school teacher in training posted a photo that showed her in costume at a party wearing a pirate hat, drinking from a plastic cup. The caption read "Drunken Pirate." Snyder's supervisor at the high school announced that the photo was "unprofessional," and officials at the university where she was enrolled said she was promoting drinking in virtual view of her underage students. A few days before Snyder's graduation ceremony, the university denied her a teaching degree.

Stories like this abound. A 16-year-old British girl lost her office job for complaining on Facebook, "I'm so totally bored!!" A 66-year-old Canadian psychotherapist was permanently banned from visiting the United States after a border guard's Internet search found that he had written an article in a philosophy journal describing his experiments with LSD thirty years earlier.[91] While you could make a case that such treatment is unfair, the point is that a little discretion could save a lot of trouble.

Be Considerate "Etiquette" may seem like an old-fashioned term. But whatever label you use, mostly unspoken rules of conduct still keep society running smoothly. The unique nature of social media calls for its own set of civil behaviors, which some refer to as "netiquette." Here are a few.

Respect Others' Need for Undivided Attention If you've been texting since you could master a keypad, it might be hard to realize that some people are insulted when you divide your attention between your in-person conversational partner and distant contacts. As one observer put it, "While a quick log-on may seem, to the user, a harmless break, others in the room receive it as a silent dismissal. It announces: 'I'm not interested.'"[92]

Keep Your Tone Civil If you've ever posted a snide comment on a blog, shot back a nasty reply to a text or instant message, or forwarded an embarrassing email, you know that it's easier to behave badly when the recipient of your message isn't right in front of you. After receiving an abusive, insulting email in response to a piece he had published, one writer described the tendency to be more abusive online than in person:

> The guy couldn't have said this to me on the phone, because I would have hung up and not answered if the phone rang again, and he couldn't have said it to my face, because I wouldn't have let him finish. If this had happened to me in the street, I could have used my status as a physically large male to threaten the person, but in the on-line world my size didn't matter. I suppose the guy could have written me a nasty letter: he probably wouldn't have used the word "rectum," though, and he probably wouldn't have mailed the letter; he would have thought twice while he was addressing the envelope. But the nature of email is that you don't think twice. You write and send.*

One way to behave better in asynchronous situations is to ask yourself a simple question before you send, post, or broadcast: Would you deliver the same message to the recipient in person? If your answer is no, then you might want to think before hitting the "enter" key.

Don't Intrude on Bystanders Everyone has suffered from rude technology use by moviegoers whose screens distract other viewers, restaurant patrons whose phone voices infringe on your conversation, pedestrians who are more focused on their handheld device than on avoiding others, or people in line who are trying to pay the cashier and talk on their cell phone at the same time. If you aren't bothered by this sort of behavior, it can be hard to feel sympathetic with others who are offended by it. Nonetheless, this is another situation where the "platinum rule" applies: Consider treating others the way *they* would like to be treated.

---

*Seabrook, J. (1994, June 6). My first flame. *The New Yorker*, pp. 70–79.

SUMMARY

Communication is essential on many levels. Besides satisfying practical needs, effective communication can enhance physical health and emotional well-being. Communication also creates our identities and satisfies social needs. The process of communication is not a linear one that people *do* to one another. Rather, communication is a transactional process in which participants create a relationship by simultaneously sending and receiving messages, many of which are distorted by various types of noise.

Interpersonal communication can be viewed quantitatively by the number of people involved, or qualitatively by the nature of interaction between them. In a qualitative sense, interpersonal relationships are unique, irreplaceable, interdependent, and intrinsically rewarding. Both personal and impersonal communication are useful, and most relationships have both elements. Qualitatively interpersonal communication can occur in mediated contexts as well as in traditional ones (there are both benefits and challenges to communicating through social media).

Several principles guide how communication operates. Messages can be intentional or unintentional. It is impossible not to communicate. Communication is irreversible and unrepeatable. Messages have both content and relational dimensions. Some common misconceptions should be avoided when thinking about communication: meanings are not in words, but rather in people; more communication does not always make matters better; communication will not solve all problems; communication—at least effective communication—is not a natural ability.

Communication competence is the ability to get what you are seeking from others in a manner that maintains the relationship. Competence varies from one situation to another. The most competent communicators have a wide repertoire of behaviors, and they are able to choose the best behavior for a given situation and perform it skillfully. They are able to understand others' points of view and respond with empathy. They also monitor their own behavior and are committed to communicating successfully. In intercultural communication, competence involves having the right motivation, a tolerance for ambiguity, open-mindedness, and the knowledge and skill to communicate effectively. Communicating via social media calls for a unique set of competencies that helps keep both online and face-to-face relationships running smoothly.

KEY TERMS

channel (8)
co-culture (28)
cognitive complexity (25)
communication competence (22)
content dimension (16)
decode (8)
disinhibition (21)
dyad (12)
encode (8)

environment (10)
impersonal communication (12)
instrumental goals (7)
interpersonal communication (11)
leanness (21)
linear communication model (8)
message (8)
noise (8)
receiver (8)

relational dimension (16)
richness (21)
self-monitoring (26)

sender (8)
social media (18)
transactional communication model (9)

ONLINE RESOURCES

Now that you have read this chapter, visit CengageBrain.com to access the Speech Communication CourseMate for *Looking Out/Looking In* for quick access to the electronic resources that accompany this text. Your CourseMate offers:

- **Study tools** that will help you assess your learning and prepare for exams (*digital glossary, key term flash cards, interactive quizzes*).
- **Activities and assignments** that will help you hone your knowledge, understand how theory and research applies to your own life (*Self-Assessment, Pause and Reflect*), consider ethical challenges in interpersonal communication (*Ethical Challenge*), and build your interpersonal communication skills throughout the course (*Skill Builder*). If requested, you can submit your answers to your instructor.
- **Media resources** that will allow you to watch and critique videos of interpersonal communication situations (*In Real Life, interpersonal video simulations, and interactive video activities*).
- In addition to interactive teaching and learning tools, CourseMate includes an **interactive eBook**. Take notes, highlight, search, and interact with embedded media specific to *Looking Out/Looking In*.

SEARCH TERMS

When searching online databases to research topics in this chapter, use the following terms (along with this chapter's key terms) to maximize the chances of finding useful information:

communication & technology
communication models
communicative competence
information theory

interpersonal relations
quality of life
social networks

FILM AND TELEVISION

You can see the communication principles described in this chapter portrayed in the following films and television programs.

WHY WE COMMUNICATE
Into the Wild (2007) Rated R

Armed with a few books about survival and a fierce streak of independence, 20-year-old college graduate Christopher McCandless (Emile Hirsch) literally turns his back on civilization and heads into the Alaskan wilderness. McCandless dismisses the advice of wiser and more experienced people, convinced that he doesn't need anyone to survive and thrive. As film critic Roger Ebert puts it, "He sees himself not as homeless, but as a man freed from homes."

The last part of the film reconstructs McCandless's final harrowing weeks. More than simply a wilderness adventure, this story provides an extreme example of the human need for contact and support. The self-sufficient loner may be a romantic stereotype, but in real life we can't survive—physically or emotionally—without others.

Up in the Air (2009) Rated R

Ryan Bingham (George Clooney) is a corporate downsizing consultant. He's hired by companies to fly into town and do the grim work of firing their employees. Bingham is good at what he does, and he does it a lot, living out of a suitcase as he jets from city to city. Although he has an apartment in Omaha, Bingham appears to have no real home. Or family. Or friends.

Ironically, Bingham's job is threatened when a new colleague, Natalie Keener (Anna Kendrick), suggests that firings could be accomplished more efficiently online. Bingham decides to prove her wrong, demanding that she accompany him on some in-person dismissals so she can see how heartless computer firings would be. Along the way, he begins to realize how heartless his own life has become. He slowly develops a friendship with Natalie, a romance with a fellow consultant, and a renewed relationship with sisters he had ignored for years.

By the film's end, it's clear that Bingham discovers that a life without meaningful interpersonal connections is a life that's not worth living—not even for all the frequent flyer miles in the world.

TRANSACTIONAL COMMUNICATION
How I Met Your Mother (2005–) Rated TV-14

The framing device for this series is that Ted (Josh Radnor) is in the future, describing to his children how he met their mother. Each episode chronicles the ever-evolving relationships he forges, maintains, or ends while in pursuit of his spouse. His core group of friends includes Marshall (Jason Segel) and Lily (Alyson Hannigan), a married couple who represent stability. Also in the group are Robin (Cobie Smulders) and Barney (Neil Patrick Harris), who are single (in most episodes) and in no apparent rush to settle down.

The dynamics of the group are affected by events in the past. For instance, Robin has dated both Ted and Barney. Not only does that have an impact on Robin's ongoing relationships with these men, but it sometimes causes friction between close friends Barney and Ted. What we see over the course of this series is that every interaction that takes place between the main characters plays a role in how they later relate to each other. This illustrates the irreversible, unrepeatable, and transactional nature of interpersonal communication.

SOCIAL MEDIA AND COMMUNICATION
The Social Network (2010) Rated PG-13

In this character study, Facebook creator Mark Zuckerberg (Jesse Eisenberg) is portrayed as a genius at computer programming and meeting the needs of the marketplace. At the same time, he is a disaster in the domain of personal relationships.

Film critic Roger Ebert called Zuckerberg's character "a heat-seeking missile in search of his own goals." He insults and humiliates his girlfriend Erica (Rooney Mara) and betrays his best friend Eduardo Saverin (Andrew Garfield). He builds an empire but lives in an isolated world of his own creation, indifferent to the feelings of those around him.

The irony of Zuckerberg's successes and failures offer a parable for our times. Mastering communication technology is no guarantee of interpersonal competence. On the relational front, success must come the old-fashioned way. Meaningful relationships can't be reduced to bits, bytes, and dollars.

COMMUNICATION COMPETENCE
House M.D. (2004–2012) Rated TV-14

No one at Princeton-Plainsboro Teaching Hospital would deny that Dr. Gregory House (Hugh Laurie) is an excellent physician. His sharp mind and keen analytical skills help him make diagnoses that often save lives. House's colleagues marvel at his ability to solve baffling medical cases, so they seek out and heed his advice.

On the other hand, House's interpersonal skills leave something to be desired. He is typically gruff, blunt, rude, and condescending. As a result, House often alienates his supervisors, students, and even the patients he's trying to serve. In terms of communication competence, he is long on effectiveness but short on appropriateness. If House engaged in more self-monitoring and expressed more empathy, he would be a better communicator and probably have more friends. But then again, this TV show wouldn't be nearly as entertaining.

35

C H A P T E R   O N E

A First Look at Interpersonal Communication

CHAPTER OUTLINE

Use this outline to take notes as you read the chapter in the text and/or as your instructor lectures in class.

I. WHY WE COMMUNICATE
  A. Physical Needs
  B. Identity Needs
  C. Social Needs
    1. Pleasure
    2. Affection
    3. Companionship
    4. Escape
    5. Relaxation
    6. Control
  D. Practical Goals
    1. Instrumental goals
      a. Influence other's behavior
      b. Career success
    2. Maslow's basic needs
      a. Physical
      b. Safety
      c. Social
      d. Self-esteem
      e. Self-actualization

II. **THE PROCESS OF COMMUNICATION**
  A. **A Linear View**
     1. Sender
     2. Encodes
     3. Message
     4. Channel
     5. Receiver
     6. Decodes
     7. Noise
  B. **A Transactional View**
     1. Communicator is simultaneously sender and receiver
     2. Environments
        a. Physical
        b. Cultural
        c. Experiential
     3. Noise
        a. External
        b. Physiological
        c. Psychological
     4. Transactional communication is done with others simultaneously
  C. **Defining Interpersonal Communication**
  D. **Interpersonal and Impersonal Communication**
  E. **Quantitative Approach to Interpersonal Communication**
     1. Dyad
     2. Impersonal communication
  F. **Qualitative Approach**
     1. Uniqueness
     2. Irreplaceability
     3. Interdependence
     4. Disclosure
     5. Intrinsic rewards

III. **COMMUNICATION PRINCIPLES AND MISCONCEPTIONS**

   A. **Communication Principles**

      1. Communication can be intentional or unintentional

      2. It's impossible not to communicate

      3. Communication is unrepeatable

      4. Communication is irreversible

      5. Communication has a content and a relational dimension

   B. **Communication Misconceptions**

      1. More communication is not always better

      2. Meanings are not in words

      3. Successful communication doesn't always involve shared understanding

      4. Communication will not solve all problems

IV. **SOCIAL MEDIA AND INTERPERSONAL COMMUNICATION**

   A. **Benefits of Social Media**

      1. Low friction opportunities to create, enhance, and rediscover social ties

      2. Maintaining and rekindling relationships

      3. Minimizes perception differences

      4. Increase in "real life" social interaction

   B. **Challenges of Social Media**

      1. Leaner messages

         a. Richness

         b. Leanness

2. Disinhibition
   a. Volunteering of personal information
   b. Highly expressive directness
3. Permanence

V. **WHAT MAKES AN EFFECTIVE COMMUNICATOR?**
   A. **Communication Competence Defined**
      1. There is no ideal way to communicate
      2. Competence is situational
      3. Competence is relational
      4. Competence can be learned
   B. **Characteristics of Competent Communicators**
      1. Wide range of behaviors
      2. Ability to choose most appropriate behavior
         a. Context
         b. Goal
         c. Knowledge of the other person
      3. Skill at performing behaviors
         a. Beginning awareness
         b. Awkwardness
         c. Skillfulness
         d. Integration
      4. Cognitive complexity
      5. Empathy
      6. Self-monitoring
      7. Commitment
         a. Commitment to the other person
         b. Commitment to the message
   C. **Competence in Intercultural Communication**

1. Co-cultures
2. Learn specific cultural rules
3. Motivation
4. Tolerance for ambiguity
5. Open-mindedness
6. Knowledge and skill
a. Passive observation
b. Active strategies
c. Self-disclosure
D. **Competence in Social Media**
1. Think before you post
2. Be considerate
   a. Respect others' need for undivided attention
   b. Keep your tone civil
   c. Don't intrude on bystanders

KEY TERMS

channel

co-culture

cognitive complexity

communication competence

content dimension

decode

disinhibition

dyad

encode

environment

impersonal communication

instrumental goals

interpersonal communication

linear communication model

message

noise

receiver

relational dimension

richness

self-monitoring

sender

social media

transactional communication model

ACTIVITIES

1.1 COMMUNICATION SKILLS INVENTORY

LEARNING OBJECTIVES

- Assess the needs (physical, identity, social, and practical) that communicators are attempting to satisfy in a given situation or relationship.
- Diagnose the effectiveness of various communication channels in a specific situation.

INSTRUCTIONS

1. Below you will find several communication-related situations. As you read each item, imagine yourself in that situation.
2. For each instance, answer the following question: *How satisfied am I with the way I would communicate in this situation and ones like it?* You can express your answers by placing one of the following numbers in the space by each item:

5 = Completely satisfied with my probable action
4 = Generally, though not totally, satisfied with my probable action
3 = About equally satisfied and dissatisfied with my probable action
2 = Generally, though not totally, dissatisfied with my probable action
1 = Totally dissatisfied with my probable action

_____   1. A new acquaintance has just shared some personal experiences with you that make you think you'd like to develop a closer relationship. You have experienced the same things and are now deciding whether to reveal these personal experiences.

_____   2. You've become involved in a political discussion with someone whose views are the complete opposite of yours. The other person asks, "Can't you at least understand why I feel as I do?"

_____   3. You are considered a responsible adult by virtually everyone except one relative who still wants to help you make all your decisions. You value your relationship with this person, but you want to be seen as more independent.

_____   4. In a mood of self-improvement a friend asks you to describe the one or two ways you think he or she could behave better. You're willing to do so, but need to express yourself in a clear and helpful way.

_____   5. A close companion tells you that you've been behaving "differently" lately and asks if you know what he or she means.

_____   6.   You've grown to appreciate a new friend a great deal lately, and you want to express your feelings to this friend.

_____   7.   An amateur writer you know has just shown you his or her latest batch of poems and asked your opinion of them. You don't think they are very good. It's time for your reply.

_____   8.   You've found certain behaviors of an important person in your life have become more and more bothersome to you. It's getting harder to keep your feelings to yourself.

_____   9.   You're invited to a party at which everyone except the host will be a stranger to you. Upon hearing about this, a friend says, "Gee, if I were going I'd feel like an outsider. They probably won't have much to do with you." How do you feel?

_____   10.   A friend comes to you feeling very upset about a recent incident and asks for advice. You suspect that there is more to the problem than just this one incident. You really want to help the friend.

_____   11.   You find yourself defending the behavior of a friend against the criticisms of a third person. The critic accuses you of seeing only what you want to see and ignoring the rest.

_____   12.   A boss or instructor asks you to explain a recent assignment to a companion who has been absent. You are cautioned to explain the work clearly so there will be no misunderstandings.

_____   13.   You ask an acquaintance for help with a problem. She says yes, but the way the message is expressed leaves you thinking she'd rather not. You do need the help, but only if it's sincerely offered.

_____   14.   A roommate always seems to be too busy to do the dishes when it's his or her turn, and you've wound up doing them most of the time. You resent the unequal sharing of responsibility and want to do something about it.

_____   15.   A new acquaintance has become quite interested in getting to know you better, but you feel no interest yourself. You've heard that this person is extremely sensitive and insecure.

By totaling your score for all of the items you can get an idea of how satisfied you are with your overall ability to communicate in interpersonal situations. A score of 68–75 suggests high satisfaction, 58–67 indicates moderate satisfaction, while 45–57 shows that you feel dissatisfied with your communication behavior nearly half the time.

Class _____   Name_____

Another valuable way to use this activity is to make a second inventory at the end of the course. Have you improved? Are there still areas you will need to work on?

1.2 MEDIATED COMMUNICATION

LEARNING OBJECTIVES

- Describe the degree to which communication (in a specific instance or a relationship) is qualitatively impersonal or interpersonal, and describe the consequences of this level of interaction.
- Diagnose the effectiveness of various communication channels in a specific situation.
- Use the criteria in the chapter to determine the level of communication competence in a specific instance or a relationship.

INSTRUCTIONS

Answer the questions below. Then, in small or large group discussion, compare your experiences with classmates.

1. List all the mediated channels you use to communicate interpersonally.

   _____

   _____

2. Describe the reasons you use mediated channels. Consider both *practical* reasons (e.g., to communicate over distance) and *strategic* ones (e.g., to avoid face-to-face confrontation).

   _____

   _____

3. Describe situations in which your communication is more effective using mediated channels and explain why.

   _____

   _____

4. Describe situations in which your communication is less effective using mediated channels and explain why.

_____

_____

5. How do you think relationships are affected when they begin through mediated communication rather than face-to-face?

_____

_____

6. What are the differences in the quantity, frequency, and quality of mediated communication you experience with different generations (parents, grandparents)? Do you use mediated communication more frequently with certain age groups? Why or why not?

_____

_____

7. Your text cites a study that states that mediated communication encourages greater offline interaction with close friends. What is your experience? If you text message more, do you also see each other more?

_____

_____

8. Do you prefer mediated communication over face-to-face to meet some needs for information? Do you prefer email, phone, text messaging, or face-to-face communication with instructors, family, friends, co-workers, supervisors? Does this vary with the person's age, gender, role? How do you let others know your preferences?

_____

_____

1.3 COMMUNICATION BASICS

LEARNING OBJECTIVES

- Describe how the communication principles and misconceptions in Chapter 1 are evident in a specific situation.

- Assess the needs (physical, identity, social, and practical) that communicators are attempting to satisfy in a given situation or relationship.

- Apply the transactional communication model to a specific situation.

INSTRUCTIONS

Use the case below and the discussion questions that follow to discuss the variety of communication issues involved in effective communication. Make notes on this page, add other pages on your own, or prepare a group report/analysis based on your discussion. Add your own experiences to individualize the analysis.

CASE

Kristie and Jacob have been dating one another exclusively for four months. They both have part-time jobs and hope to complete their college studies within two years. Jacob thinks they should move in together. Kristie is reluctant to agree until she has more commitment from Jacob. Jacob doesn't want to make promises he can't keep. Kristie thinks that if they just communicate more they will be able to solve the problem, but Jacob thinks that talking about it more won't help.

1. What needs (physical, identity, social, and/or practical) do Kristie and Jacob seem to have?

_____

_____

2. Identify one element of the communication model that might help explain some of the communication problems they are having and help them communicate more effectively.

_____

_____

3. What communication principles and/or misconceptions described in Chapter 1 may be operating in this situation?

_____

_____

4. What likely role will mediated communication play in the scenario?

_____

_____

5. How would you advise Jacob and Kristie to proceed with their communication practices?

_____

_____

1.4 ASSESSING COMMUNICATION NEEDS

LEARNING OBJECTIVES

- Assess the needs (physical, identity, social, and practical) that communicators are attempting to satisfy in a given situation or relationship.

INSTRUCTIONS

Observe people in two other conversations, either in real life or on television. How did each individual attempt to meet their social, physical, identity, and practical needs during the conversation?Use the checklist below in your analysis.

1. Physical needs: sufficient air, water, food, and rest, and the ability to reproduce as a species

_____

_____

_____

2. Social needs: a link with others, involvement with others, control over the environment

_____

_____

_____

3. Identity needs: deciding who we are

_____

_____

_____

4. Practical goals: which goals (if any) were being met through this interaction?

_____

_____

_____

STUDY GUIDE

CHECK YOUR UNDERSTANDING

TRUE/FALSE

Mark the statements below as true or false. Correct false statements on the lines below to create a true statement.

_____   1. Studies show your physical health may be affected by communication.

_____

_____   2. We learn who we are through communication with others and their reactions to us.

_____

_____   3. Communication skills are usually much less important in getting a job than technical competence, work experience, or a degree.

_____

_____   4. Instrumental goals are the same thing as social needs.

_____

_____   5. Psychologist Abraham Maslow claims that basic needs must be satisfied before people concern themselves with higher order needs.

_____

_____   6. The linear view of communication suggests that communication flows in one direction, from sender to receiver.

_____

_____   7. Disabled people have no repertoire of options available when responding to unwanted offers of help.

_____

_____   8. Richness is verbal cues that add clarity to a nonverbal message.

_____

_____   9. Disinhibition is speaking or transmitting messages without considering their consequences.

_____

_____ 10. Dyadic communication is the earliest form of interaction we experience and the most common type of communication.

_____

_____ 11. What qualifies as competent behavior in one culture might be completely inept, or even offensive, in another.

_____

_____ 12. In order to build a competent relationship, we need to get rid of our need to maintain some space between ourselves and the other person.

_____

_____ 13. Ten minutes per day of socializing improves memory and boosts intellectual function.

_____

_____ 14. Research suggests that face-to-face relationships and virtual relationships are increasingly oppositional.

_____

_____ 15. MySpace, Facebook, and Twitter are just some of the ways that people can communicate through mediated channels.

_____

_____ 16. There is no place for impersonal communication in day-to-day activity.

_____

_____ 17. We can always choose not to communicate if the situation seems too difficult.

_____

COMPLETION

Fill in the blanks with the correct terms chosen from the list below.

instrumental goals	social needs	identity needs	physiological noise
psychological noise	self-monitoring	co-cultures	richness
cognitive complexity	empathy		

1. _____ are the needs we have to define who we are.

2. _____ are the needs we have to link ourselves with others.

3. _____ are the needs we have to get others to behave in ways we want.

4. _____ refers to the forces within a communicator that interfere with the ability to express or understand a message accurately.

5. _____ refers to the biological factors in the receiver or sender that interfere with accurate reception of messages.

6. _____ groups shape our perceptions: ethnic, national, religious.

7. _____ is the abundance of nonverbal cues that add clarity to a verbal message.

8. _____ is the ability to construct a variety of different frameworks for viewing an issue.

9. _____ is the process of paying close attention to your behavior in order to shape the way you behave.

10. _____ is the ability to imagine how an issue might look from the other's point of view.

MULTIPLE CHOICE

Choose the letter of the communication process element that is most illustrated by the description found below. Italicized words provide clues.

a. encode
b. decode
c. channel
d. message/feedback
e. noise (external, physiological, or psychological)
f. environment

_____ 1. The children make a videotape of themselves to send to their grandparents instead of writing a letter.

_____ 2. Marjorie tries to decide the best way to tell Martin that she can't go to Hawaii with him.

_____ 3. Martin decides Marjorie means she doesn't love him when she says she can't go to Hawaii.

_____ 4. It's so hot in the room that Brad has a hard time concentrating on what his partner is telling him.

_____ 5. Linda smiles while Larry is talking to her.

_____ 6. Brooke is daydreaming about her date while Allison is talking to her.

_____ 7. Since Jacob has never been married, it's difficult for him to understand why his married friend Brent wants to spend less time with him.

_____ 8. Whitney says, "I'm positive about my vote."

_____ 9. Richard thinks Jon wants to leave when he waves to him.

_____ 10. Laura winks when she says she's serious and gestures with her arms.

_____ 11. Erin is from a wealthy family and Kate from a poor one. They have a serious conflict about how to budget their money.

_____ 12. Jack has been feeling a cold coming on all day while he has sat through the meeting.

Choose the *best* answer for each of the questions below:

13. The concept of co-cultures is closest to the concept of differing
    a. environments.
    b. relational messages.
    c. self-monitoring.
    d. impersonal communication.

14. Martin Buber's concept of communication that is truly interpersonal is called
    a. I-You.
    b. I-They.
    c. I-It.
    d. I-We.

15. Improving intercultural competence involves all of the following except
    a. motivation.
    b. open-mindedness.
    c. knowledge and skill.
    d. avoiding ambiguity.

16. According to the quantitative definition of interpersonal communication, interpersonal communication occurs when
    a. two people interact with one another, usually face to face.
    b. you watch a TV show about relationships.
    c. you read a romance novel.
    d. large numbers of people communicate.

17. All of the following statements are true <u>except</u>
    a. Communication has content and relational dimensions.
    b. Communication is irreversible.
    c. Communication can be unintentional.
    d. Communication is repeatable.

18. All of the following statements are true <u>except</u>
    a. Meanings are not in words.
    b. More communication is not always better.
    c. Communication can solve all your problems.
    d. Communication is not a natural ability.

19. According to most studies cited in your text, mediated communication
    a. diminishes the amount of face-to-face interaction.
    b. enriches and promotes more social interaction.
    c. leads to more impersonal communication in families.
    d. makes people more aware of gender and age differences.

20. When you are able to perform communication skills without thinking about how you should behave, you have entered the skill stage of
    a. awareness.
    b. awkwardness.
    c. skillfulness.
    d. integration.

21. When we volunteer personal information online that we prefer to keep private from some parties, this is one form of
    a. awareness.
    b. awkwardness.
    c. skillfulness.
    d. integration.

22. Communication competence seeks to be both
    a. loud and clear.
    b. effective and appropriate.
    c. skillful and concise.
    d. intuitive and cautious.

23.   When using social media you should
    a. share your feelings openly and honestly.
    b. include everyone.
    c. think before you post.
    d. upload personal pictures.

24.   In becoming a competent intercultural communicator you should
    a. trust the advice of friends.
    b. remain open-minded.
    c. use a linear communication model.
    d. minimize external noise.

CHAPTER ONE STUDY GUIDE ANSWERS

TRUE/FALSE

1. T	4. F	7. F	10. T	13. T
2. T	5. T	8. F	11. T	14. F
3. F	6. T	9. T	12. F	15. T

16. F
17. F

COMPLETION

1. identity needs	5. physiological noise	9. self-monitoring
2. social needs	6. co-cultures	10. empathy
3. instrumental goals	7. richness	
4. psychological noise	8. cognitive complexity	

MULTIPLE CHOICE

1. c	5. d	9. b	13. a	17. d	21. d
2. a	6. e	10. c	14. a	18. c	22. b.
3. b	7. f	11. f	15. d	19. b	23. c.
4. e	8. d	12. e	16. a	20. d.	24. b.

Communication and Identity: Creating and Presenting the Self

After studying the topics in this chapter, you should be able to:

1. Describe the relationship between self-concept, self-esteem, and communication.

2. Explain how self-fulfilling prophecies shape the self-concept and influence communication.

3. Compare and contrast the perceived self and the presenting self as they relate to identity management.

4. Describe the role that identity management plays in both face-to-face and mediated relationships.

5. Use the social penetration and Johari Window models to identify the nature of self-disclosing communication in one of your relationships.

6. Outline the potential benefits and risks of disclosing in a selected situation.

7. Assess the most competent mixture of candor and equivocation in a given situation.

Who are you? Take a moment now to answer this question. You'll need the following list as you read the rest of this chapter, so be sure to complete it now. Try to include all the characteristics that describe you:

Your moods or feelings (e.g., happy, angry, excited)

Your appearance (e.g., attractive, short)

Your social traits (e.g., friendly, shy)

Talents you have or do not have (e.g., musical, nonathletic)

Your intellectual capacity (e.g., smart, slow learner)

Your strong beliefs (e.g., religious, environmentalist)

Your social roles (e.g., parent, girlfriend)

Your physical condition (e.g., healthy, overweight)

Now look at what you've written. How did you define yourself? As a student? A man or woman? By your age? Your religion? Your occupation? There are many ways of identifying yourself. List as many ways as you can. You'll probably see that the words you've chosen represent a profile of what you view as your most important characteristics. In other words, if you were required to describe the "real you," this list ought to be a good summary.

Communication and the Self

You might be wondering how this self-analysis is related to interpersonal communication. The short answer is that who you are both reflects and affects your communication with others. The long answer involves everything from biology to socialization to culture to gender. We'll begin with a look at two terms that are basic to the relationship between the self and communication.

SELF-CONCEPT AND SELF-ESTEEM

The list you created is at least a partial answer to answer the question "Who do you think you are?" It's likely that the phrases you chose generated some emotional responses—perhaps terms like "happy" or "sad," "confident" or "nervous." Replies like these show that how you *feel* about yourself is a big part of who you think you are. What we think and feel about ourselves are important components of the self that we'll examine now.

Self-Concept Who you think you are can be described as your **self-concept**: the relatively stable set of perceptions you hold of yourself. If a special mirror existed that reflected not only your physical features but also other aspects of yourself—emotional states, talents, likes, dislikes, values, roles, and so on—the reflection you'd see would be your self-concept. You probably recognize that the self-concept list you recorded earlier is only a partial one. To make the description complete, you'd have to keep adding items until your list ran into hundreds of words.

For most people this list dramatically illustrates just how fundamental the concept of self is. Even when the item being abandoned is an unpleasant one, it's often hard to give it up. And when asked to let go of their most central feelings or thoughts, most people balk. "I wouldn't be *me* without that," they insist. Of course, this proves our point: The concept of self is perhaps our most fundamental possession. Knowing who we are is essential, because without a self-concept it would be impossible to relate to the world.

Halfdark/Getty Images

Self-Esteem While your self-concept describes who you think you are, **self-esteem** involves evaluations of self-worth. A hypothetical communicator's self-concept might include being quiet, argumentative, or self-controlled. His or her self-esteem would be determined by how he or she *felt* about these qualities. Consider these differing evaluations:

Quiet	"I'm a coward for not speaking up."
	versus
	"I enjoy listening more than talking."
Argumentative	"I'm pushy, and that's obnoxious."
	versus
	"I stand up for my beliefs."
Self-controlled	"I'm too cautious."
	versus
	"I think carefully before I say or do things."

People with high self-esteem tend to think well of others and expect to be accepted by them. On the other hand, those who dislike themselves are likely to believe that others won't like them either. Realistically or not, they imagine that others are constantly viewing them critically, and they accept these imagined or real criticisms as more proof that they are indeed unlikable people. Sometimes this low self-esteem is manifested in hostility toward others, because the communicator takes the approach that the only way to look good is to put others down.

High self-esteem has obvious benefits, but it doesn't guarantee interpersonal success.[1] People with exaggerated self-esteem may *think* they make better impressions on others and have better friendships and romantic lives, but neither impartial observers nor objective tests verify these beliefs. It's easy to see how people with an inflated sense of self-worth could irritate others by coming across as condescending know-it-alls, especially when their self-worth is challenged.[2]

Despite these cautions, self-esteem *can* be the starting point for positive behaviors and interactions. Figure 2.1 shows the cycles that may begin from both positive and negative self-evaluations. These patterns often become self-fulfilling prophecies, as we'll discuss later in this chapter.

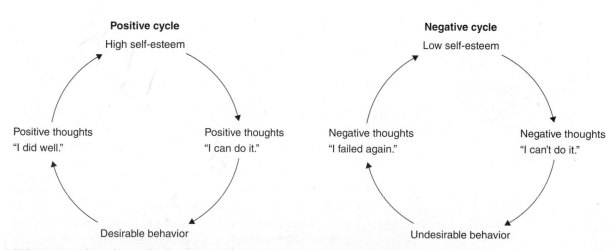

FIGURE 2.1 The Relationship between Self-Esteem and Communication Behavior © Cengage Learning

PAUSE AND REFLECT

YOUR SELF-ESTEEM

Take a self-guided tour of your self-esteem provided by the National Association of Self-Esteem. As you explore, consider how the past and present have shaped your current level of self-esteem. Additionally, speculate about how your current level of self-esteem affects your own communication style and interpersonal relationships. You can find the link to this site by visiting CengageBrain.com to access the Speech Communication CourseMate for *Looking Out/Looking In*. The test will take about 10 to 15 minutes.

BIOLOGICAL AND SOCIAL ROOTS OF THE SELF

How did you become the kind of communicator you are? Were you born that way? Are you a product of your environment? As you'll now see, the correct answer to both of these questions is "yes."

Biology and the Self Take another look at the "Who am I?" list you developed at the beginning of this chapter. You will almost certainly find some terms that describe your **personality**—characteristic ways that you think and behave across a variety of situations. Your personality tends to be stable throughout your life, and often it grows more pronounced over time.[3]

Research suggests that personality is formed in part by our genetic makeup.[4] For example, people who were judged shy as children still show a distinctive reaction in their brains as adults when they encounter new situations.[5] Some studies show that biology accounts for as much as half of communication-related personality traits such as extraversion,[6] shyness,[7] assertiveness,[8] verbal aggression,[9] and overall willingness to communicate.[10] In other words, to some degree, we come programmed to communicate in characteristic ways.

While you may have a disposition toward traits like shyness or aggressiveness, you can do a great deal to control how you actually communicate. More and more research suggests that personality is flexible, dynamic, and shaped by experiences.[11] Even shy people can learn how to reach out to others, and those with aggressive tendencies can learn to communicate in more-sociable ways. One author put it this way: "Experiences can silence genes or activate them. Even shyness is like Silly Putty once life gets hold of it."[12] Throughout this book you will learn about communication skills that, with practice, you can build into your repertoire.

Socialization and the Self-Concept How important are others in shaping our self-concept? Imagine growing up on a deserted island, with no one to talk to or share activities. How would you know how smart you are—or aren't? How would you gauge your attractiveness? How would you decide if you're short or tall, kind or mean, skinny or fat? Even if you could view your reflection in a mirror, you still wouldn't know how to evaluate your appearance without appraisals from others or people with whom to compare yourself. In fact, the messages we receive from the people in our lives play a central role in shaping how we regard ourselves. To gain an appreciation for this, try the exercise above.

Social scientists use the metaphor of a mirror to identify the process of **reflected appraisal**: the fact that each of us develops a self-concept that reflects the way we believe others see us. In other words, we are likely to feel less valuable, lovable, and capable to the degree that others have communicated ego-busting signals; and we will probably feel good about ourselves to the degree that others affirm our value.[13]

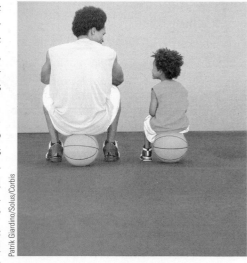

Patrik Giardino/Solus/Corbis

To illustrate this point further, let's start at the beginning. Children aren't born with any sense of identity. They learn to judge themselves only through the way others treat them. As children learn to speak and understand language, verbal messages contribute to a developing self-concept. Every day a child is bombarded with scores of appraisals about himself or herself. Some of these are positive: "You're so cute!" "I love you." "What a big girl." Other messages are negative: "What's the matter with you?" "Can't you do anything right?" "You're a bad boy." "Leave me alone. You're driving me crazy!" Evaluations like these are the mirror by which we know ourselves. Because children are trusting souls who have no other way of viewing themselves, they accept at face value both the positive and negative appraisals of the apparently all-knowing and all-powerful adults around them.

These same principles in the formation of the self-concept continue in later life, especially when messages come from what sociologists term **significant others**— people whose opinions we especially value. A look at the ego boosters and ego busters you described in the previous exercise will show that the evaluations of a few especially important people can be powerful. Family members are the most obvious type of significant other, and their ego busters can be particularly hurtful as a result.[14] Others, though, can also be significant others: a special friend, a teacher, someone you dated, or perhaps an acquaintance whose opinion you value can leave an imprint on how you view yourself—sometimes for better, sometimes for worse.[15] To see the importance of significant others, ask yourself how you arrived at your opinion of yourself as a student, as a person attractive to others, as a competent worker, and you'll see that these self-evaluations were probably influenced by the way others regarded you.

The impact of significant others remains strong during adolescence. Inclusion in (or exclusion from) peer groups is a crucial factor in self-concept development for teenagers.[16] The good news is that parents who are understanding of their children's self-concepts during the adolescent years typically have better communication with their teens and can help them create a strong self-concept.[17] The influence of significant others becomes less powerful as people grow older. After most people approach the age of thirty, their self-concepts don't change radically, at least without a conscious effort.[18]

So far we have looked at the way in which others' messages shape our self-concept. In addition to these messages, each of us forms our self-image by the process of **social comparison**: evaluating ourselves in terms of how we compare with others.

Two types of social comparison need highlighting. In the first, we decide whether we are *superior* or *inferior* by comparing ourselves to others. Are we attractive or ugly? A success or failure? Intelligent or stupid? It depends on those against whom we measure ourselves.[19] For instance, research shows that young women who regularly compare themselves with ultra-thin media models develop negative appraisals of their own bodies.[20] In one study, young women's perceptions of their bodies changed for the worse after watching just thirty minutes of televised images of the "ideal" female form.[21] Men, too, who compare themselves to media-idealized male physiques, evaluate their bodies negatively.[22] People also use others' online profiles as points of comparison, and they may feel less attractive after doing so.[23]

You'll probably never be as beautiful as a Hollywood star, as agile as a professional athlete, or as wealthy as a millionaire. When you consider the matter logically, these facts don't mean you're worthless. Nonetheless, many people judge themselves against unreasonable standards and suffer accordingly.[24] This is particularly true of people with perfectionistic tendencies, whose self-concepts have been shaped by demanding messages from significant others.[25] These distorted self-images can lead to serious behavioral disorders, such as depression, anorexia nervosa, and bulimia.[26] You'll read more about how to avoid placing perfectionistic demands on yourself in Chapter 4.

In addition to feelings of superiority and inferiority, social comparison provides a way to decide if we are the *same as* or *different from* others. A child who is interested in ballet and who lives in a setting where such preferences are regarded as weird will start to accept this label if there is no support from others. When at a dance camp, however, the child will likely flourish. Likewise, adults who want to improve the quality of their relationships but are surrounded by friends and family who don't recognize or acknowledge the importance of these matters may think of themselves as oddballs. Thus, it's easy to recognize that the **reference groups** against which we compare ourselves play an important role in shaping our view of ourselves.

You might argue that not every part of one's self-concept is shaped by others, insisting that certain objective facts are recognizable by self-observation. After all, nobody needs to tell a person that he is taller than others, speaks with an accent, has acne, and so on. These facts are obvious. Though it's true that some features of the self are immediately apparent, the *significance* we attach to them—the rank we assign them in the hierarchy of our list and the interpretation we give them—depends greatly on the opinions of others. After all, many of your features are readily observable, yet you don't find them important at all, because nobody has regarded them as significant.

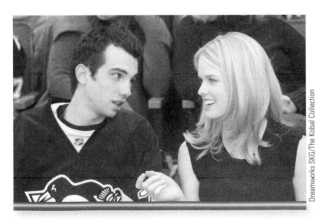

When average guy Kirk (Jay Baruchel) pursues a relationship with stunning Molly (Alice Eve), he worries that *She's Out of My League*. The film shows how reflected appraisals and social comparisons affect self-concepts and communication. (See the film summary at the end of this chapter.)

By now you might be thinking, "It's not my fault that I've always been shy or insecure. Because I developed a picture of myself as a result of the way others have treated me, I can't help being what I am." Though it's true that to a certain extent you are a product of your environment, to believe that you are forever doomed to a poor self-concept would be a big mistake. Having held a poor self-image in the past is no reason for continuing to do so in the future. You *can* change your attitudes and behaviors, as you'll soon read.

PAUSE AND REFLECT

"EGO BOOSTERS" AND "EGO BUSTERS"

1. Either by yourself or with a partner, recall someone you know or once knew who was an "ego booster"—who helped enhance your self-esteem by acting in a way that made you feel accepted, competent, worthwhile, important, appreciated, or loved. This person needn't have played a crucial role in your life as long as the role was positive. A family member with whom you've spent most of your life can be an "ego booster," but so can the stranger on the street who spontaneously offers you an unexpected compliment.

2. Now recall an "ego buster" from your life—someone who acted in a large or small way to reduce your self-esteem. As with ego-booster messages, ego-buster messages aren't always intentional. The acquaintance who forgets your name after you've been introduced or the friend who yawns while you're describing an important problem can diminish your feelings of self-worth.

3. Now that you've thought about how others shape your self-concept, recall a time when you were an ego booster to someone else—when you intentionally or unintentionally boosted another's self-esteem. Don't merely settle for an instance in which you were nice: Look for a time when your actions left another person feeling valued, loved, needed, and so on. You may have to ask the help of others to answer this question.

4. Finally, recall a recent instance in which you were an ego buster for someone else. What did you do to diminish another's self-esteem? Were you aware of the effect of your behavior at the time? Your answer might show that some events we intend as boosters have the effect of busters. For example, you might joke with a friend in what you mean as a friendly gesture, only to discover that your remarks are received as criticism.

After completing the exercise (you *did* complete it, didn't you?), you should begin to see that your self-concept is shaped by those around you. This process of shaping occurs in two ways: reflected appraisal and social comparison.

 You can complete this activity by visiting CengageBrain.com to access the Speech Communication CourseMate for *Looking Out/ Looking In*, and, if requested, email your responses to your instructor.

CHARACTERISTICS OF THE SELF-CONCEPT

Now that you have a better idea of how your self-concept developed, we can look closer at some of its characteristics.

The Self-Concept Is Subjective Although we tend to believe that our self-concept is accurate, in truth it may well be distorted. For example, researchers have found that there

Bloomimage/Collage/Corbis

is no relationship between the way college students rate their ability as interpersonal communicators, public speakers, or listeners and their true effectiveness.[27] In all cases, the self-reported communication skill is higher than actual performance. In another study, a random sample of men were asked to rank themselves on their ability to get along with others.[28] Defying mathematical laws, all subjects—every last one—put themselves in the top half of the population. Sixty percent rated themselves in the top 10 percent of the population, and an amazing 25 percent believed they were in the top 1 percent. Similarly, online daters often have a "foggy mirror"—that is, they see themselves more positively than others do.[29] This leads to inflated self-descriptions that don't always match what an objective third party might say about them.

Not all distortion of the self-concept is positive. Many people view themselves more harshly than the objective facts warrant. We have all experienced a temporary case of the "uglies," convinced that we look much worse than others assure us we do. Research confirms what common sense suggests: People are more critical of themselves when they are experiencing these negative moods than when they are feeling more positive.[30] Although we all suffer occasional bouts of self-doubt that affect our communication, some people suffer from long-term or even permanent states of excessive self-doubt and criticism.[31] It's easy to understand how this chronic condition can influence the way they approach and respond to others.

Distorted self-evaluations like these can occur for several reasons:

- *Obsolete information*. The effects of past failures in school or social relations can linger long after they have occurred, even though such events don't predict failure in the future. Likewise, your past successes don't guarantee future success.
- *Distorted feedback*. The remarks of overly critical parents, cruel friends, uncaring teachers, excessively demanding employers, or even memorable strangers can have a lasting effect. Other distorted messages are unrealistically positive. For instance, a child's inflated ego may be based on the praise of doting parents, and a boss's inflated ego may come from the praise of brownnosing subordinates.
- *Perfectionism*. From the time most of us learn to understand language, we are exposed to models who appear to be perfect. The implicit message is "A well-adjusted, successful person has no faults." Given this naive belief that everyone else is perfect and the knowledge that one isn't, it's easy to see how one's self-concept would suffer.
- *Social expectations*. Curiously, the perfectionist society to which we belong rewards those people who downplay the strengths we demand that they possess (or pretend to possess). We consider those who honestly appreciate their strengths to be "braggarts" or "egotists," confusing them with the people who boast about accomplishments they do not possess.[32] This convention leads most of us to talk freely about our shortcomings while downplaying our accomplishments.

After a while we begin to believe the types of statements we repeatedly make. The disparaging remarks are viewed as modesty and become part of our self-concept, and the strengths and accomplishments go unmentioned and are thus forgotten. And in the end we see ourselves as much worse than we are. One way to avoid falling into the trap of becoming overly critical is to recognize your strengths. The following exercise will give you a chance to suspend the ordinary rules of modesty and appreciate yourself publicly for a change.

PAUSE AND REFLECT

RECOGNIZING YOUR STRENGTHS

1. This exercise can be done either alone or with a group. If you are with others, sit in a circle so that everyone can see one another.

2. Each person should share three personal strengths or accomplishments. These needn't feature areas in which you are an expert, and they don't have to be concerned with momentous feats. On the contrary, it's perfectly acceptable to talk about some part of yourself that leaves you feeling pleased or proud. For instance, you might say that, instead of procrastinating, you completed a school assignment before the last minute, that you spoke up to a friend even though you were afraid of disapproval, or that you baked a fantastic chocolate cake.

3. If you're at a loss for items, ask yourself:
   a. What are some ways in which you've grown in the past year? How are you more skillful, wiser, or a better person than you previously were?
   b. Why do certain friends or family members care about you? What features do you possess that make them appreciate you?

4. After you've finished, consider the experience. Did you have a hard time thinking of things to share? Would it have been easier to list the things that are *wrong* with you? If so, is this because you are truly a wretched person, or is it because you are in the habit of stressing your defects and ignoring your strengths? Consider the impact of such a habit on your self-concept, and ask yourself whether it wouldn't be wiser to strike a better balance distinguishing between your strengths and weaknesses.

 You can complete this activity by visiting CengageBrain.com to access the Speech Communication CourseMate for *Looking Out/ Looking In*, and, if requested, email your responses to your instructor.

The Self-Concept Resists Change Although we all change, there is a tendency to cling to an existing self-concept, even when evidence shows that it is obsolete. This tendency to seek and attend to information that conforms to an existing self-concept has been labeled **cognitive conservatism**.

This tendency toward cognitive conservatism leads us to seek out people who support our self-concept. For example, both college students and married couples with high self-esteem seek out partners who view them favorably, whereas those with negative self-esteem are more inclined to interact with people who view them unfavorably.[33] It appears that we are less concerned with learning the "truth" about ourselves than with reinforcing a familiar self-concept.

It's understandable why we're reluctant to revise a previously favorable self-concept. A student who did well in earlier years but now has failed to study might be unwilling to admit that the label "good scholar" no longer applies. Likewise, a previously industrious worker might resent a supervisor's mentioning increased absences and low productivity. These people aren't *lying* when they insist that they're doing well despite the facts to the contrary; they honestly believe that the old truths still hold, precisely because their self-concepts are so resistant to change.

Curiously, the tendency to cling to an outmoded self-perception also holds when the new self-perception would be more favorable than the old one. We recall a former student whom almost anyone would have regarded as beautiful, with physical features attractive enough to appear in any glamour magazine. Despite her appearance, in a class exercise this woman characterized herself as "ordinary" and "unattractive." When questioned by her classmates, she described how as a child her teeth were extremely crooked and how she had worn braces for several years in her teens to correct this problem. During this time she was often teased by her friends, who never let her forget her "metal mouth," as she put it. Even though the braces had been off for two years, our student reported that she still saw herself as ugly and brushed aside our compliments by insisting that we were just saying these things to be nice—she knew how she *really* looked.

Communicators who are presented with information that contradicts their self-perception have two choices: They can either accept the new data and change their perception accordingly, or they can keep their original perception and in some way refute the new information. Because most communicators are reluctant to downgrade a favorable image of themselves, their tendency is to opt for refutation, either by discounting the information and rationalizing it away or by counterattacking the person who transmitted it. The problem of defensiveness is so great that we will examine it in detail in Chapter 10.

There are times when changing a distorted or obsolete self-concept can be a good thing. For example, you may view yourself as a less competent, desirable, skilled person than the facts would suggest. Here are a few suggestions for embracing a more positive self-image.

1. **Have a realistic perception of yourself.** While some people have inaccurately inflated egos, others are their own worst critic. A periodic session of recognizing your strengths, such as you tried earlier in this chapter, is often a good way to put your strengths and weaknesses into perspective. It's also wise to surround yourself with supportive people who will give you the positive feedback you need and deserve.

2. **Have realistic expectations.** If you demand that you handle every act of communication perfectly, you're bound to be disappointed. And if you constantly compare yourself with gifted people, you're going to come up short. Rather than feel miserable because you're not as talented as an expert, realize that you probably are a better, wiser, or more skillful person than you used to be, and that this is a legitimate source of satisfaction.

3. **Have the will to change.** Often we say we want to change, when in fact we're simply not willing to do what's required (we'll discuss the fallacy of helplessness and ridding yourself of "can't" statements in Chapter 4). You *can* change in many ways, if only you are motivated to do so.

4. **Have the skill to change.** Trying isn't always enough. In some instances you would change if you knew how to do so. Seek out advice from books such as this one, or ask for suggestions from instructors, counselors, and other experts. Observing models can also be a powerful way to master new ways of communicating. Watch what people you admire do and say, not so that you can copy them, but so that you can adapt their behavior to fit your own personal style.

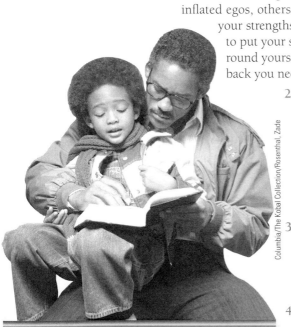

In *The Pursuit of Happyness*, Christopher Gardner (Will Smith) uses determination and persuasive communication to overcome poverty and build a better life for himself and his son. In so doing, he demonstrates both the will and the skill to change his self-concept. In Gardner's words, "If you want somethin', go get it. Period."

Columbia/The Kobal Collection/Rosenthal, Zade

CULTURE, GENDER, AND IDENTITY

We have already seen how experiences in the family, especially during childhood, shape our sense of who we are. Along with the messages we receive at home, many other forces mold our identity, and thus our communication, including age, physical ability/disability, sexual orientation, and socioeconomic status. Along with these forces, culture and gender are powerful forces that affect how we view ourselves and others and how we communicate. We will examine each of these forces now.

Culture Although we seldom recognize the fact, our sense of self is shaped, often in subtle ways, by the culture in which we have been reared.[34] Most Western cultures are highly individualistic, whereas other traditional cultures—most Asian ones, for example—are much more collectivist. When asked to identify themselves, individualists in the United States, Canada, Australia, and Europe would probably respond by giving their first name, surname, street, town, and country. Many Asians do it the other way around.[35] If you ask Hindus for their identity, they will give you their caste and village as well as their name. The Sanskrit formula for identifying one's self begins with lineage and goes on to state family, house, and ends with one's personal name.[36] When members of different cultures were asked to create an "I am" list similar to the one you completed earlier in this chapter, those from collectivist cultures made far more group references than those from individualistic cultures.[37]

These conventions for naming aren't just cultural curiosities: They reflect a very different way of viewing one's self and of what kinds of relationships are important. In collective cultures, a person gains identity by belonging to a group. This means that the perceived degree of interdependence among members of the society and its subgroups is high. Feelings of pride and self-worth are likely to be shaped not only by what the individual does but also by behavior of other members of the community. This linkage to others explains the traditional Asian denial of self-importance—a strong contrast to the self-promotion that is common in individualistic Western cultures.[38] In Chinese written language, for example, the pronoun *I* looks very similar to the word for selfish.[39]

The difference between individualism and collectivism shows up in everyday interaction. Communication researcher Stella Ting-Toomey has developed a theory that explains cultural differences in important norms, such as honesty and directness.[40] She suggests that in individualistic Western cultures where there is a strong "I" orientation, the norm of speaking directly is honored, whereas in collectivistic cultures, where the main desire is to build connections between the self and others, indirect approaches that maintain harmony are considered more desirable. "I gotta be me" could be the motto of a Westerner, but "If I hurt you, I hurt myself" is closer to the Asian way of thinking.

You don't need to travel overseas to appreciate the influence of culture on the self. Within societies, co-cultural identity plays an important role in how we see ourselves and others. For example, ethnicity can have a powerful effect on how people think of themselves and how they communicate. Recall how you described yourself in the "Who Am I?" list you created when you began this chapter. If you are a member of a nondominant ethnic group, it's likely that you included your ethnicity in the most important parts of who you are. There's no surprise here: If society keeps reminding you that your ethnicity is important, then you begin to think of yourself in those terms. If you are part of the dominant majority, you probably aren't as conscious of your ethnicity. Nonetheless, it plays an important part in your self-concept. Being part of the majority increases the chances that you have a sense of belonging to the society in which you live and of entitlement to being treated fairly. Members of less privileged ethnic groups often don't have these feelings.

Talking with Little Girls

Lisa Bloom is author of "Think: Straight Talk for Women to Stay Smart in a Dumbed Down World." Whether or not you agree with her position, note the important role she places on interpersonal messages in the development of a child's self-concept.

I went to a dinner party at a friend's home last weekend, and met her five-year-old daughter for the first time. Little Maya was all curly brown hair, doe-like dark eyes, and adorable in her shiny pink nightgown. I wanted to squeal, "Maya, you're so cute! Look at you! Turn around and model that pretty ruffled gown, you gorgeous thing!"

But I didn't. I always bite my tongue when I meet little girls, restraining myself from my first impulse, which is to tell them how darn cute/pretty/beautiful/well-dressed/well-manicured/well-coiffed they are.

What's wrong with that? It's our culture's standard talking-to-little-girls icebreaker, isn't it? And why not give them a sincere compliment to boost their self-esteem?

15 to 18 percent of girls under 12 now wear mascara, eyeliner and lipstick regularly; eating disorders are up and self-esteem is down; and 25 percent of young American women would rather win

Rocio Alba Gonzalez/Workbook Stock/Getty Images

America's Next Top Model than the Nobel Peace Prize. Even bright, successful college women say they'd rather be hot than smart.

Teaching girls that their appearance is the first thing you notice tells them that looks are more important than anything. It sets them up for dieting at age 5 and foundation at age 11 and boob jobs at 17 and Botox at 23. That's why I force myself to talk to little girls as follows:

"Maya," I said, crouching down at her level, looking into her eyes, "very nice to meet you. Hey, what are you reading?" I asked. Her eyes got bigger, and the practiced, polite facial expression gave way to genuine excitement over this topic.

"What's your favorite book?" I asked.

"I'll go get it! Can I read it to you?"

Purplicious was Maya's pick and a new one to me, as Maya snuggled next to me on the sofa and proudly read aloud every word. Not once did we discuss clothes or hair or bodies or who was pretty. It's surprising how hard it is to stay away from those topics with little girls.

So, one tiny bit of opposition to a culture that sends all the wrong messages to our girls. One tiny nudge towards valuing female brains. One brief moment of intentional role modeling.

Try this the next time you meet a little girl. Ask her what she's reading. What does she like and dislike, and why? There are no wrong answers. You're just generating an intelligent conversation that respects her brain. For older girls, ask her about current events issues: pollution, wars, school budgets slashed. What bothers her out there in the world? How would she fix it if she had a magic wand?

Here's to changing the world, one little girl at a time.

Lisa Bloom

Excerpted from "How to Talk to Little Girls" in Huffington Post. http://www.huffingtonpost.com/lisa-bloom/how-to-talk-to-little-gir_b_882510.html?ref=fb&src=sp

Sex and Gender One way to appreciate the tremendous importance of gender on your sense of self is to imagine how your identity would be different if you had been born as a member of the other sex. Would you express your emotions in the same way? Deal with conflict? Relate to friends and strangers? The answer is quite likely "no."

From the earliest months of life, being male or female shapes the way others communicate with us, and thus our sense of self. Think about the first questions most people ask when a child is born. One of them is almost always "Is it a boy or a girl?" After most people know what the baby "is," they often behave accordingly.[41] They use different pronouns and often choose gender-related nicknames. With boys, comments often focus on size, strength, and activity; comments about girls more often address beauty, sweetness, and facial responsiveness. It's not surprising that these messages shape a child's sense of identity and how he or she will communicate. The implicit message is that some ways of behaving are masculine and others feminine. Little girls, for example, are more likely to be reinforced for acting "sweet" than are little boys. The same principle operates in adulthood: A man who stands up for his beliefs might get approval for being "tough" or "persistent," whereas a woman who behaves in the same way could be described by critics as a "nag" or "bitch."[42] It's not hard to see how the gender roles and labels like these can have a profound effect on how men and women view themselves and on how they communicate.

Self-esteem is also influenced by gender. In a society that values competitiveness more in men than in women, it isn't surprising that the self-esteem of adolescent young men is closely related to having abilities that are superior in some way to those of their peers, whereas teenage women's self-worth is tied more closely to the success of their social relationships and verbal skills.[43] Research also suggests that young women struggle more with self-esteem issues than do young men. For example, the self-esteem of about two-thirds of the males in one study (ages 14 to 23) increased.[44] The same study revealed that about 57 percent of females in the same age group grew to feel *less* good about themselves.

Don't resign yourself to being a prisoner of expectations about your gender. Research demonstrates that our sense of self is shaped strongly by the people with whom we interact and by the contexts in which we communicate.[45] For example, a nonaggressive young man who might feel unwelcome and inept in a macho environment might gain new self-esteem by finding others who appreciate his style of communicating. A woman whose self-esteem is stifled by the limited expectations of bosses and coworkers can look for more hospitable places to work. Children usually can't choose the reference groups that shape their identities, but adults can.

THE SELF-FULFILLING PROPHECY AND COMMUNICATION

The self-concept is such a powerful force on the personality that it not only determines how you see yourself in the present but also can actually influence your future behavior and that of others. Such occurrences come about through a phenomenon called the self-fulfilling prophecy.

A **self-fulfilling prophecy** occurs when a person's expectations of an event, and his or her subsequent behavior based on those expectations, make the event more likely to occur than would otherwise have been true.[46] A self-fulfilling prophecy involves four stages:

1. Holding an expectation (for yourself or for others)
2. Behaving in accordance with that expectation
3. The expectation coming to pass
4. Reinforcing the original expectation

You can see how this process operates by considering an example. Imagine you're scheduled to interview for a job you really want. You are nervous about how you'll do, and not at all sure you are really qualified for the position. You share your concerns with a professor who knows you well and a friend who works for the company. Both assure you that you're perfect for the job and that the firm would be lucky to have you as an employee. Based on these comments, you come to the interview feeling good about yourself. As a result, you speak with authority and sell yourself with confidence. The employers are clearly impressed, and you receive the job offer. Your conclusion: "My friend and professor were right. I'm the kind of person an employer would want!"

This example illustrates the four stages of a self-fulfilling prophecy. Thanks to the assurances of your professor and friend, your expectations about the interview were upbeat (Stage 1). Because of your optimistic attitude, you communicated confidently in the interview (Stage 2). Your confident behavior—along with your other qualifications—led to a job offer (Stage 3). Finally, the positive results reinforced your positive self-assessment, and you'll probably approach future interviews with greater assurance (Stage 4).

It's important to recognize the tremendous influence that self-fulfilling prophecies play in our lives. To a great extent we become what we believe. In this sense, we and those around us constantly create and re-create our self-concepts.

Types of Self-Fulfilling Prophecies There are two types of self-fulfilling prophecies. *Self-imposed prophecies* occur when your own expectations influence your behavior. In sports you've probably psyched yourself into playing either better or worse than usual, so that the only explanation for your unusual performance was your attitude. Similarly, you've probably faced an audience at one time or another with a fearful attitude and forgotten your remarks, not because you were unprepared, but because you said to yourself, "I know I'll blow it."

Research has demonstrated the power of self-imposed prophecies.[47] In one study, communicators who believed they were incompetent proved less likely than others to pursue rewarding relationships and more likely to sabotage their existing relationships than did people who were less critical of themselves.[48] On the other hand, students who perceived themselves as capable achieved more academically.[49] In another study, subjects who were sensitive to social rejection tended to expect rejection, perceive it where it might not have existed, and overreact to their exaggerated perceptions in ways that jeopardized the quality of their relationships.[50] Research also suggests that communicators who feel anxious about giving speeches seem to create self-fulfilling prophecies about doing poorly that cause them to perform less effectively.[51]

A second category of self-fulfilling prophecies is imposed by one person on another. A classic example was demonstrated by Robert Rosenthal and Lenore Jacobson in a study described in their book *Pygmalion in the Classroom*.[52] The experimenters told teachers that 20 percent of the children in a certain elementary school showed unusual potential for intellectual growth. The names of these 20 percent were drawn randomly. Eight months later, these "gifted" children showed significantly greater gains in IQ than did the remaining children, who had not been singled out for the teachers' attention. The change in the teachers' behavior toward these allegedly special students led to changes in the intellectual performance of these randomly selected children. Among other things, the teachers gave the "smart" students more time to answer questions, more feedback, and more praise. In other words, the selected children did better—not because

"I don't sing because I am happy.
I am happy because I sing."

they were any more intelligent than their classmates, but because their teachers held higher expectations for them and treated them accordingly.

This type of self-fulfilling prophecy has been shown to be a powerful force for shaping the self-concept and thus the behavior of people in a wide range of settings outside of schools.[53] In one study, a group of welders with relatively equal aptitudes began training. Everyone, including the trainer, was told that five of the welders had higher scores on an aptitude test—even though they were chosen randomly. All five finished at the top of the class. They had fewer absences and significantly higher final test scores. Most impressively, they learned the skills of their trade twice as quickly as those who weren't identified as being so talented.[54] In another study, military personnel who were randomly labeled as having high potential performed up to the expectations of their superiors. They were also more likely to volunteer for dangerous special duty.[55]

It's important to note that an observer must do more than just *believe* to create a self-fulfilling prophecy for the person who is the target of the expectations. The observer also must *communicate* that belief in order for the prediction to have any effect. If parents have faith in their children, but the kids aren't aware of that confidence, they won't be affected by their parents' expectations. If a boss has concerns about an employee's ability to do a job but keeps those concerns to herself, the employee won't be influenced. In this sense, the self-fulfilling prophecies imposed by one person on another are as much a communication phenomenon as a psychological one.

Presenting the Self: Communication as Identity Management

So far we have described how communication shapes the way communicators view themselves. We will now turn the tables and focus on the topic of **identity management**—the communication strategies that people use to influence how others view them.[56] In the following pages, you will see that many of our messages aim at creating a desired identity.

PUBLIC AND PRIVATE SELVES

To understand how identity management operates, we have to discuss the notion of self in more detail. So far we have referred to the "self" as if each of us had only one identity. In truth, each of us has several selves, some private and others public. Often these selves are quite different.

The **perceived self** is a reflection of the self-concept. Your perceived self is the person you believe yourself to be in moments of honest self-examination. We can call the perceived self "private," because you are unlikely to reveal all of it to another person. You can verify the private nature of the perceived self by reviewing the self-concept list you developed at the beginning of this chapter. If you were completely forthright when compiling that list, you'll probably find some elements of yourself there that you would not disclose to many people and some that you would not share with anyone. You might, for example, be

"Hah! This is the Old King Cole nobody ever sees."

reluctant to share some feelings about your appearance ("I think I'm rather unattractive"), your intelligence ("I'm smarter than most of my friends"), your goals ("The most important thing to me is becoming rich"), or your motives ("I care more about myself than about others").

In contrast to the perceived self, the **presenting self** is a public image—the way we want others to view us. The presenting self is sometimes called one's **face**. In most cases the presenting self that we seek to create is a socially approved image: diligent student, loving partner, conscientious worker, loyal friend, and so on. Social norms often create a gap between the perceived and presenting selves. In one study of college students, both men and women said their perceived selves included being "friendly" and "responsible." When it came to their public selves, the men wanted to be seen as "wild" and "strong," while the women presented themselves as "active" and "able."[57]

You can recognize the difference between public and private behaviors by recalling a time when you observed a driver, alone in his or her car, acting in ways that would never be acceptable in public. All of us engage in backstage ways of acting that we would never do in public. Just recall how you behave in front of the bathroom mirror when the door is locked, and you will appreciate the difference between public and private behaviors. If you knew that someone was watching, would you act differently?

CHARACTERISTICS OF IDENTITY MANAGEMENT

Now that you have a sense of what identity management is, we can look at some characteristics of this process.

We Strive to Construct Multiple Identities It is an oversimplification to suggest that each of us uses identity management strategies to create just one identity. In the course of even a single day, most people perform a variety of roles: "respectful student," "joking friend," "friendly neighbor," and "helpful worker," to suggest just a few.

As you grew up you almost certainly changed characters as you interacted with your parents. In one context you acted as responsible adult ("You can trust me with the car!"), and in another context you were the helpless child ("I can't find my socks!"). At some times—perhaps on birthdays or holidays—you were a dedicated family member, and at other times you may have played the role of rebel. Likewise, in romantic relationships we switch among many ways of behaving, depending on the context: friend, lover, business partner, scolding critic, apologetic child, and so on. And as you read in Chapter 1, the ability to shift styles from setting to setting and culture to culture is a feature of communication competence.

Identity Management Is Collaborative Sociologist Erving Goffman used a dramatistic metaphor to describe identity management.[58] He suggested that each of us is a kind of playwright who creates roles that reflect how we want others to see us, as well as a performer who acts out those roles. But unlike the audience for most forms of acting, our audience is made up of other actors who are trying to create their own characters. Identity-related communication can be viewed as a kind of process theater in which we collaborate with other actors to improvise scenes in which our characters mesh.

You can appreciate the collaborative nature of identity management by thinking about how you might handle a gripe with a friend or family

PAUSE AND REFLECT

YOUR MANY IDENTITIES

You can get a sense of the many roles you try to create by keeping a record of the situations in which you communicate over a one- or two-day period. For each situation, identify a dramatic title to represent the image you try to create. A few examples might be "party animal," "helpful housekeeper," "wise older sibling," and "sophisticated film critic."

 You can complete this activity by visiting CengageBrain.com to access the Speech Communication CourseMate for *Looking Out/ Looking In*, and, if requested, email your responses to your instructor.

member who has not returned your repeated calls to coordinate important details for a party. Suppose that you decide to raise the issue tactfully in an effort to avoid seeming like a nag (desired role for yourself: "nice person") and also to save the other person from the embarrassment of being confronted (hoping to avoid suggesting that the other person's role is "screw-up"). If your tactful bid is accepted, the dialogue might sound like this:

You: By the way, I've left a couple of messages on your cell. I'm not sure whether you've gotten them. We need to talk about the invitations before they go out tomorrow.

Other: Oh, sorry. I've been meaning to get back with you. It's just that I've been really busy lately with school and work.

You: That's okay. Could we talk about it now?

Other: How about I call you back in an hour?

You: Sure, no problem.

In this upbeat conversation, both you and the other person accepted one another's bids for identity as thoughtful, responsible friends. As a result, the conversation ran smoothly. Imagine, though, how differently the outcome would be if the other person didn't accept your presenting self:

You: By the way, I've left two messages on your cell. I'm not sure whether you've gotten them . . .

Other: *(Defensively)* Okay, so I forgot. It's not that big a deal. You're not perfect yourself, you know!

At this point you have the choice of persisting in trying to play the original role of "nice person": "Hey, I'm not mad at you, and I know I'm not perfect!" Or, you might switch to the new role of "unjustly accused person," responding with aggravation, "I never said I was perfect. But we're not talking about me here . . ."

As this example illustrates, *collaboration* in identity management doesn't mean the same thing as *agreement*.[59] The small issue of the phone message might mushroom into a fight in which you and the other person both adopt the role of combatants. The point here is that virtually all conversations provide an arena in which communicators construct their identities in response to the behavior of others. As you read in Chapter 1, communication isn't made up of discrete events that can be separated from one another. Instead, what happens at one moment is influenced by what each party brings to the interaction and what happened in their relationship up to that point.

Identity Management Can Be Deliberate or Unconscious There's no doubt that sometimes we are highly aware of managing impressions. Most job interviews and first dates are clear examples of deliberate identity management. As noted in Chapter 1, high self-monitoring is usually helpful in these situations. But in other cases we unconsciously act in ways that are really small public performances.[60] For example, experimental subjects expressed facial disgust in reaction to eating sandwiches laced with a supersaturated saltwater solution only when there was another person present: When they were alone, they made no faces while eating the same sandwiches.[61]

Another study showed that communicators engage in facial mimicry (such as smiling or looking sympathetic in response to another's message) in face-to-face settings only when their expressions can be seen by the other person. When they are speaking over the phone, and their reactions cannot be seen, they do not make the same expressions.[62] Studies like these suggest that most of our behavior is aimed at sending messages to others—in other words, identity management.

The experimental subjects described in the preceding paragraphs didn't consciously think, "Somebody is watching me eat this salty sandwich, so I'll make a face" or "Because I'm in a face-to-face conversation, I'll show I'm sympathetic by mimicking the facial expressions of my conversational partner." Decisions like these are often instantaneous and outside of our conscious awareness. In the same way, many of our choices about how to act in the array of daily interactions aren't highly considered strategic decisions. Rather, they rely on "scripts" that we have developed over time.

Despite the pervasiveness of identity management, it seems like an exaggeration to suggest that *all* behavior is aimed at making impressions. Young children certainly aren't strategic communicators. A baby spontaneously laughs when pleased and cries when sad or uncomfortable without any notion of creating an impression in others. Likewise, there are times when we, as adults, act spontaneously. Despite these exceptions, most people consciously or unconsciously communicate in ways that help construct desired identities for themselves and others.

WHY MANAGE IDENTITIES?

Why bother trying to shape others' opinions of you? Social scientists have identified several overlapping reasons.[63]

To Start and Manage Relationships Think about times when you have consciously and carefully managed your approach when meeting someone you would like to know better. You may do your best to appear charming and witty—or perhaps cool and suave. You don't need to be a phony to act this way; you simply are trying to show your best side. Once relationships are up and running, we still manage our identities—perhaps not as much, but often.

To Gain Compliance of Others We often manage our identity to get others—both those we know and strangers—to act in ways we want. You might, for example, dress up for a visit to traffic court in the hope that your image (responsible citizen) will convince the judge to treat you sympathetically. You might chat sociably with neighbors you don't find especially interesting so that you can exchange favors or solve problems as they come up.

To Save Others' Face We often modify the way we present ourselves to support the way other people want to be seen. For example, able-bodied people often mask their discomfort upon encountering someone who is disabled by acting nonchalant or stressing similarities between themselves and the disabled person.[64] Young children who haven't learned about the importance of face-saving often embarrass their parents by

SELF-ASSESSMENT

Self-Monitoring Inventory
You can complete this activity by visiting CengageBrain.com to access the Speech Communication CourseMate for *Looking Out/ Looking In.*

behaving inappropriately ("Mommy, why is that man so fat?"); but by the time they enter school, behavior that might have been excusable or even amusing just isn't acceptable.

To Explore New Selves Sometimes we try on a new identity in the same way we try on a different style of clothing: to see if it changes the way others view us and how we think and feel about ourselves. Toward this end, trying on new selves can be a means to self-improvement. For example, one study found that teens—especially lonely ones—who experimented with new identities online wound up reaching out more to people of different ages and cultural backgrounds than they did in their face-to-face lives. As a result, they actually increased their social competence.[65]

MANAGING IDENTITIES IN PERSON AND ONLINE

How do we create a public face? In an age in which technology provides many options for communicating, the answer depends in part on the communication channel chosen.

Face-to-Face Identity Management In face-to-face interaction, communicators can manage their front in three ways: manner, appearance, and setting.[66] *Manner* consists of a communicator's words and nonverbal actions. Physicians, for example, display a wide variety of manners as they conduct physical examinations. Some are friendly and conversational, whereas others adopt a curt and impersonal approach. Much of a communicator's manner comes from what he or she says. A doctor who remembers details about your interests and hobbies is quite different from one who sticks to clinical questions. One who explains a medical procedure creates a different impression than another who reveals little information to the patient.

Along with the content of speech, nonverbal behaviors play a big role in creating impressions.[67] A doctor who greets you with a smile and a handshake comes across differently from one who gives nothing more than a curt nod. Manner varies widely in other professions and settings—professors, salespeople, hair stylists, and so on—and the impressions they create vary accordingly. The same principle holds in personal relationships. Your manner plays a major role in shaping how others view you. Chapters 5 and 6 will describe in detail how your words and nonverbal behaviors create impressions. Because you have to speak and act, the question isn't *whether* your manner sends a message, but rather *what* message it will send.

A second dimension of identity management is *appearance*—the personal items that people use to shape an image. Sometimes appearance is part of creating a professional image. A physician's white lab coat and a police officer's uniform both set the wearers apart as someone special. A tailored suit or a rumpled outfit creates very different impressions in the business world. Off the job, clothing is just as important. We choose clothing that sends a message about ourselves, sometimes trendy and sometimes traditional. Some people dress in ways that accent their sexuality, whereas others hide it. Clothing can say, "I'm an athlete," "I'm wealthy," or "I'm an environmentalist." Along with dress, other aspects of appearance play a strong role in identity management. Do you wear makeup? What is your hairstyle? Do you make an effort to look friendly and confident?

In the movie *Easy A*, Olive (Emma Stone) presents herself as fast and loose, which doesn't match her private self. This identity management allows her and her friends to achieve some of their personal and relational goals—but it comes with a host of ethical problems.

Tattoos offer an interesting example of how appearance can help create an identity. The very act of decorating one's skin makes a statement, and the design or words chosen say even more. One fascinating study explored the communicative function of tattoos worn by some people to announce their HIV-positive condition.[68] At the most obvious level, such tattoos convey important information about the health status of the wearer to medical workers. Beyond being a practical announcement, though, such tattoos can be a vehicle for identity management, intended for both the wearer and others. One tattoo wearer listed the messages that his visible label conveys: the refusal to internalize shame, a commitment to safer sex practices, a challenge to stereotypes about weak "AIDS victims," and an educational tool that generates discussion by making the condition visible.

A final way to manage identities is through the choice of *setting*—physical items that we use to influence how others view us. In modern Western society, the automobile is a major part of identity management. This explains why many people lust after cars that are far more expensive and powerful than they really need. A sporty convertible or fancy imported sedan doesn't just get drivers from one place to another; it also makes statements about the kind of people they are. The physical setting we choose and the way we arrange it are another important way to manage identities. What colors do you choose for the place you live? What artwork? What music do you play? Of course, we choose a setting that we enjoy, but in many cases we create an environment that will present the desired front to others.

"On the Internet, nobody knows you're a dog."

Online Impression Management The preceding examples involve face-to-face interaction, but impression management is just as common and important in other types of communication.

At first glance, the technology of mediated communication seems to limit the potential for impression management. Texting, emailing, and blogging, for example, appear to lack the richness of other channels. They don't convey the tone of your voice, postures, gestures, or facial expressions. However, communication scholars recognize that what is missing in online communication can actually be an *advantage* for communicators who want to manage the impressions they make.[69]

Communicating online generally gives us more control over managing impressions than we have in face-to-face communication. Asynchronous forms of mediated communication like email, blogs, and web pages allow you to edit your messages until your create just the desired impression.[70] With email (and, to a lesser degree, with text messaging), you can compose difficult messages without forcing the receiver to respond immediately, and ignore others' messages rather than give an unpleasant response. Perhaps most important, when communicating via text-based technology, you generally don't have to worry about stammering or blushing, apparel or appearance, or any other unseen factor that might detract from the impression you want to create. (Photos, video, and streaming may be involved in some mediated communication—but you have choices about those as well.)

Of course, communicating via social media also allows strangers to change their age, history, personality, appearance, and other matters that would be impossible to hide in person.[71] A survey of one online dating site's participants found that 86 percent felt others misrepresented their physical appearance in their posted descriptions.[72] Online daters acknowledge the delicate task of balancing an ideal online identity against the "real" self behind their profile. Many admit they sometimes fudge facts about themselves—using outdated photos or "forgetting" information about their age, for instance. But they are less tolerant when prospective dates post inaccurate identities. For example, one date seeker expressed resentment upon learning that a purported "hiker" hadn't hiked in years.[73] We'll talk about the ethics of such misrepresentations in the following section.

Blogs, personal web pages, and profiles on social networking sites all provide opportunities for communicators to construct an identity.[74] Even the simple choice of a screen name ("lovemyporsche"; "fun2bewith"; "footballdude") says something about you and is likely to lead others to create impressions of you.[75] And interestingly, research shows that regularly viewing your own Facebook page can enhance your self-esteem.[76] This makes sense: Assuming you're carefully managing your identity on that site, it can be an ego-booster to remind yourself what you look like "at your best."

Viewing your online presence from the perspective of a neutral third party can be a valuable identity management exercise. Enter your name in a search engine and see what pops up. You may decide it's time to engage in what researchers call *reputation management*. "Search engines and social media sites now play a central role in building one's identity online," says Pew Internet researcher Mary Madden. "Many users are changing privacy settings on profiles, customizing who can see certain updates and deleting unwanted information about them that appears online."[77]

IDENTITY MANAGEMENT AND HONESTY

After reading this far, you might think that identity management sounds like an academic label for manipulation or phoniness. There certainly are situations where identity management is dishonest. A manipulative date who pretends to be affectionate in order to gain sexual favors is clearly unethical and deceitful. So are job applicants who lie about academic records to get hired or salespeople who pretend to be dedicated to customer service when their real goal is to make a quick buck.

But managing impressions doesn't necessarily make you a liar. In fact, it is almost impossible to imagine how we could communicate effectively without making decisions about which front to present in one situation or another. It would be ludicrous to act the same way with strangers as you do with close friends, and nobody would show the same face to a two-year-old as he or she would to an adult.

Each of us has a repertoire of faces—a cast of characters—and part of being a competent communicator is choosing the best face for the situation. Consider a few examples:

- You offer to teach a friend a new skill: playing the guitar, operating a computer program, or sharpening up a tennis backhand. Your friend is making slow progress with the skill, and you find yourself growing impatient.
- You've been exchanging texts for several weeks with someone you met online, and the relationship is starting to turn romantic. You have a physical trait you haven't mentioned.
- At work you face a belligerent customer. You don't believe anyone has the right to treat you this way.
- A friend or family member makes a joke about your appearance that hurts your feelings. You aren't sure whether to make an issue of the joke or to pretend that it doesn't bother you.

In each of these situations—and in countless others every day—you have a choice about how to act. It is an oversimplification to say that there is only one honest way to behave in each circumstance and that every other response would be insincere and dishonest. Instead, identity management involves deciding which face—which part of yourself—to reveal. For example, when teaching a new skill, you choose to display the "patient" instead of the "impatient" side of yourself. In the same way, at work you have the option of acting defensive or nondefensive in difficult situations. With strangers, friends, or family you can choose whether to disclose your feelings. Which face to show to others is an important decision, but in any case you are sharing a real part of yourself. You may not be revealing everything, but as you will learn in the following section, complete self-disclosure is rarely appropriate.

 ## Self-Disclosure in Relationships

One way by which we judge the strength of our relationships is the amount of information we share with others. "We don't have any secrets," some people proudly claim. Opening up certainly is important. As you read in Chapter 1, disclosure is an ingredient in qualitatively interpersonal relationships. Given the obvious importance of self-disclosure, we need to look closer at the subject. Just what is it? When is it desirable? How can it best be done?

The best place to begin is with a definition. **Self-disclosure** is the process of deliberately revealing information about oneself that is significant and would not normally be known by others. Let's look closer at this definition. Self-disclosure must be *deliberate*. If you accidentally mention to a friend that you're thinking about quitting a job, or if your facial expression reveals irritation you wanted to hide, that doesn't qualify as self-disclosure. Besides being deliberate, the information must also be *significant*. Volunteering trivial facts, opinions, or feelings—that you like fudge, for example—hardly counts as disclosure. The third requirement is that the information being disclosed is *not known by others*. There's nothing noteworthy about telling others that you are depressed or elated if they already know that.

MODELS OF SELF-DISCLOSURE

Although our definition of self-disclosure is helpful, it doesn't reveal the important fact that not all self-disclosure is equally revealing—that some disclosing messages tell more about us than others.

Social psychologists Irwin Altman and Dalmas Taylor describe two ways in which communication can be more or less disclosing.[78] Their model of **social penetration** is pictured in Figure 2.2. The first dimension of self-disclosure in this model involves the **breadth** of information volunteered—the range of subjects being discussed. For example, the breadth of disclosure in your relationship with a co-worker will expand as you begin revealing information about your life away from the job as well as on-the-job information. The second dimension of self-disclosure is the **depth** of information volunteered, the shift from relatively impersonal messages to more personal ones.

Depending on the breadth and depth of information shared, a relationship can be casual or intimate. In a casual relationship the breadth may be great, but not the depth. A more intimate relationship is likely to have high depth in at least one area. The

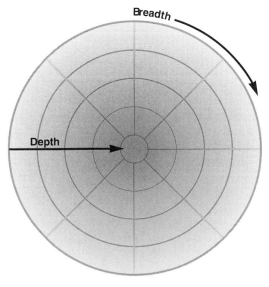

FIGURE 2.2 Social Penetration Model © Cengage Learning

LOOKING AT DIVERSITY

Lexie Lopez-Mayo: Culture, Gender, and Self-Disclosure

Photo courtesy of Lexie Lopez-Mayo

I was born in Mexico and have lived in the U.S. since I was ten. One of the things I've noticed about my Latin friends and family is that we tend to be more expressive and disclosing than many of my Euro-American friends. Of course there are exceptions to that rule, but overall I think people from my cultural background tend to reveal a lot. If we think it, we say it; if we feel it, we express it.

But culture isn't the only issue. Gender also plays a role. In my experience, Latin men easily express positive emotions, but they often hide negative feelings such as hurt and sadness. There's a strong cultural norm for Latinos to be tough, not admit failure, or show weakness—in other words, to be "macho."

I have other opportunities to see how culture and gender affect communication. My husband, who is African-American, is generally a laid-back, quiet kind of guy. However, when he's around his African-American buddies, he's much less reserved and much more disclosing. His language, volume, and mannerisms all change and he becomes a lot more expressive.

And of course, personality plays a role in communication. I know quiet Latinas and disclosing Latinos, so culture doesn't always dictate how people express themselves. In the end, I think the way people communicate is influenced by who they are, where they're from, and whom they're with. In my case, I'm a highly expressive Latina who will tell just about anybody what I think, feel, and want!

"Culture, Gender, and Self-Disclosure" by Lexie Lopez-Mayo. Used with permission of author.

most intimate relationships are those in which disclosure is great in both breadth and depth. Altman and Taylor see the development of a relationship as a progression from the periphery of their model to its center, a process that typically occurs over time. Each of your personal relationships probably has a different combination of breadth of subjects and depth of disclosure. Figure 2.3 pictures a student's self-disclosure in one relationship.

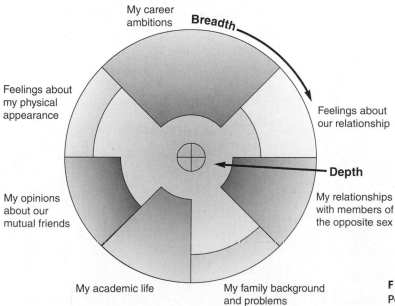

FIGURE 2.3 Sample Model of Social Penetration © Cengage Learning

What makes the disclosure in some messages deeper than others? One way to measure depth is by how far it goes on two of the dimensions that define self-disclosure. Some revelations are certainly more *significant* than others. Consider the difference between saying "I love my family" and "I love you." Other revelations qualify as deep disclosure because they are *private*. Sharing a secret that you've told to only a few close friends is certainly a revealing act of self-disclosure, but it's even more revealing to divulge information that you've never told anyone. In general, facts ("I'm new in town") are more disclosing than clichés; opinions ("I really like it here") more than facts; and feelings (". . . but I get a little lonely sometimes") more than opinions.

Another way to look at self-disclosure is by means of a device called the **Johari Window**.[79] (The window takes its name from the first names of its creators, Joseph Luft and Harry Ingham.) Imagine a frame like Figure 2.4 that contains everything there is to know about you: your likes and dislikes, your goals, your secrets, your needs—everything. This frame could be divided into information you know about yourself and things you don't know (Figure 2.5). It could also be split into things others know about you and things they don't know (Figure 2.6). Figure 2.7 reflects these divisions and has four parts.

Part 1 represents the information of which both you and the other person are aware. This part is your *open area*. Part 2 represents the *blind area*: information of which you are unaware but of which the other person is aware. You learn about information in the blind area primarily through feedback from others. Part 3 represents your *hidden area*: information that you know but aren't willing to reveal to others. Items in this hidden area become public primarily through self-disclosure, which is the focus of this section. Part 4 represents information that is *unknown* to both you and others. At first the unknown area seems impossible to verify. After all, if neither you nor others know what it contains, how can you be sure it exists? We can deduce its existence because we are constantly discovering new things about ourselves. It is not unusual to discover, for example, that you have an unrecognized talent, strength, or weakness.

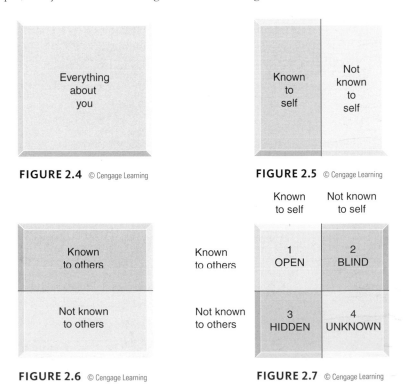

FIGURE 2.4 © Cengage Learning

FIGURE 2.5 © Cengage Learning

FIGURE 2.6 © Cengage Learning

FIGURE 2.7 © Cengage Learning

PAUSE AND REFLECT

BUILDING A JOHARI WINDOW

You can use the Johari Window model to examine the level of self-disclosure in your own relationships.

1. Use the format described in this section to draw two Johari Windows representing the relationship between you and one other person. Remember to reverse one of the windows so that your open area and that of the other person face each other.
2. Describe which parts of yourself you keep in the hidden area. Explain your reasons for doing so. Describe the advantages or disadvantages or both of not disclosing these parts of yourself.
3. Look at the blind area of your model. Is this area large or small because of the amount of feedback (much or little) that you get from your partner or because of your willingness to receive the feedback that is offered?
4. Explain whether you are satisfied with the results illustrated by your answers. If you are not satisfied, explain what you can do to remedy the problem.

 You can complete this activity by visiting CengageBrain.com to access the Speech Communication CourseMate for *Looking Out/ Looking In*, and, if requested, email your responses to your instructor.

BENEFITS AND RISKS OF SELF-DISCLOSURE

Occasionally we may blurt out a piece of revealing personal information, but most of the time our decision to self-disclose is conscious and deliberate. Communication researchers use the term **privacy management** to describe the choices people make to reveal or conceal information about themselves.[80] Those decisions are often made by weighing the pros and cons of self-disclosing. What are the risks and benefits of opening up?

Benefits of Self-Disclosure There are several reasons why people choose to share personal information. As you read about each of them, see which apply to you.

Catharsis Sometimes you might disclose information in an effort to "get it off your chest." In a moment of candor you might, for instance, reveal your regrets about having behaved badly in the past. Catharsis can provide mental and emotional relief—when handled properly.[81] Later in this chapter you'll read guidelines for disclosing that increase the odds that you can achieve catharsis in a way that helps, instead of harming relationships.

Reciprocity A well-documented conclusion from research is that one act of self-disclosure begets another.[82] There is no guarantee that your self-disclosures will trigger self-disclosures by others, but your own honesty can create a climate that makes others feel safer and perhaps even obligated to match your level of honesty. It's easy to imagine how telling a partner how you feel about the relationship ("I've been feeling bored lately . . .") would generate the same degree of candor ("You know, I've felt the same way!"). Reciprocity doesn't always

"Bob, as a token of my appreciation for this wonderful lunch I would like to disclose to you my income-tax returns for the past four years."

occur on a turn-by-turn basis. Telling a friend today about your job-related problems might help her feel comfortable opening up to you later about her family history, when the time is right for this sort of disclosure.

Self-Clarification Sometimes you can clarify your beliefs, opinions, thoughts, attitudes, and feelings by talking about them with another person. This sort of "talking the problem out" occurs with psychotherapists, but it also goes on with others, all the way from good friends to bartenders or hairdressers.

Self-Validation If you disclose information ("I think I did the right thing . . .") with the hope of obtaining the listener's agreement, you are seeking validation of your behavior—confirmation of a belief that you hold about yourself. On a deeper level, this sort of self-validating disclosure seeks confirmation of important parts of your self-concept. Self-validation through self-disclosure is an important part of the "coming out" process through which gay people recognize their sexual preference and choose to integrate this knowledge into their personal, family, and social lives.[83]

Building and Maintaining Relationships Getting a relationship started requires some self-disclosure. Consider the role it plays in everything from a first date to a job interview (although the types of disclosures will be very different in these two contexts). Self-disclosure also plays a role in ongoing relational success.[84] For example, there is a strong relationship between the quality of self-disclosure and marital satisfaction.[85] The same principle applies in other personal relationships.

Social Influence Revealing personal information may increase your control over the other person and sometimes over the situation in which you and the other person find yourselves. For example, an employee who tells the boss that another firm has made overtures probably will have an increased chance of getting raises and improvements in working conditions.

Risks of Self-Disclosure While the benefits of disclosing are certainly important, opening up can also involve risks that make the decision to disclose a difficult and sometimes painful one.[86] The risks of self-disclosure fall into several categories.[87]

Rejection John Powell summed up the risks of disclosing in answering the question that forms the title of his book, *Why Am I Afraid to Tell You Who I Am?*: "I am afraid to tell you who I am, because, if I tell you who I am, you may not like who I am, and that's all I have."[88] The fear of disapproval is powerful. Sometimes it is exaggerated and illogical, but there are real dangers in revealing personal information:

A: I'm starting to think of you as more than a friend. To tell the truth, I love you.

B: I think we should stop seeing one another.

Negative Impression Even if disclosure doesn't lead to total rejection, it can create a negative impression.

A: I've been thinking that we should get another dog.

B: To tell you the truth, I really don't like dogs. I haven't said so before because I know how much you love them.

A: Really? I can't imagine living with somebody who doesn't love dogs as much as I do.

Decrease in Relational Satisfaction Besides affecting others' opinions of you, disclosure can lead to a decrease in the satisfaction that comes from a relationship.

Self-Disclosure Test for Couples

If you are in a committed relationship, this test will help you explore the degree to which you share your thoughts and feelings with your partner. To take this test, visit CengageBrain.com to access the Speech Communication CourseMate for *Looking Out/ Looking In.*

"Since we're both being honest, I should tell you I have fleas."

he stripped

the dark circles

of mystery off

revealed his eyes

and thus

he waited

exposed

and I

did sing the song

around

until I found

the chorus

that speaks of
windows

looking out means
looking in

my friend

Ric Masten

A: I need to tell you something. I really don't like it when you want to cuddle so much.

B: But I want to be close to you. . . .

Loss of Influence Another risk of disclosure is a potential loss of influence in the relationship. Once you confess a secret weakness, your control over how the other person views you can be diminished.

A: (*Manager to employee*) I'd like to give you the weekend off, but to tell you the truth, I don't get to make any judgment calls around here. My boss makes all the decisions. In fact, he doesn't respect my opinions at all.

B: No kidding. I guess I know who to ask when I want to get anything done around here.

Hurting the Other Person Even if revealing hidden information leaves you feeling better, it might hurt others—cause them to be upset, for example. It's probably easy to imagine yourself in a situation like this:

A: I'm so ugly! I can't think of anything that will change the way I look.

B: Neither can I.

GUIDELINES FOR SELF-DISCLOSURE

By now it should be clear that deciding when and how much personal information to disclose is not a simple matter. The following guidelines can help you choose the level of self-disclosure that is appropriate in a given situation.

Is the Other Person Important to You? There are several ways in which someone might be important to you. Perhaps you have an ongoing relationship deep enough so that sharing significant parts of yourself justifies keeping your present level of togetherness intact. Or perhaps the person to whom you're considering disclosing is someone with whom you've previously related on a less personal level. But now you see a chance to grow closer, and disclosure may be the path toward developing that personal relationship.

Are the Amount and Type of Disclosure Appropriate? Some people have trouble with what's popularly known as "TMI"—sharing "too much information."[89] In general, it's wise not to divulge personal secrets with strangers, in classroom discussions, or on public Facebook postings, among other settings. Even students who appreciate self-disclosure from their teachers acknowledge that they don't want to hear too much, too often about

IN REAL LIFE

Appropriate and Inappropriate Self-Disclosure

Ramon has been working in an entry-level sales job for almost a year after graduating from the university. He likes the company, but he is growing frustrated at his lack of advancement. After much thought, he decides to share his concerns with his boss, Julie. Notice

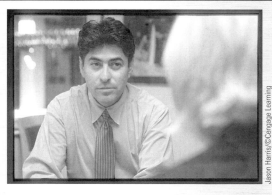

that Ramon's self-disclosure has the potential to enhance or jeopardize personal goals and relationships, depending on how well it follows the guidelines on pages 63–66.

Ramon: Do you have a few minutes to talk?

Julie: Sure, no problem. Come on in.

Ramon: Do you mind if we close the door?

Julie: *(Looking a bit surprised)* Sure.

Ramon: I'd like to talk to you about the future.

Julie: The future?

Ramon: Well, it's been over a year since I started to work here. One of the things you told me in the interview back then was that people move up fast here . . .

Julie: Well, . . .

Ramon: . . . and I'm confused because I've been doing pretty much the same work since I was hired.

Julie: Well, we do think a lot of your work.

Ramon: I'm glad to hear that. But I'm starting to wonder how much of a chance I'll have to grow with this company. *(Ramon is disclosing his concerns about career advancement— a very appropriate topic to raise with his boss. There is some risk in this sort of disclosure, but given Ramon's apparently good standing with his boss, it seems reasonable.)*

Julie: I can understand that you're anxious about taking on more responsibility. I can tell you that you've got a good shot at advancing, if you can just hang in there for a little while.

Ramon: *(Impatiently)* That sounds good, but I've been waiting—longer than I expected to. I'm starting to wonder if some of the things I've heard around here are true.

Julie: *(Suspiciously)* What kinds of things are you talking about, Ramon?

Ramon: Well, Bill and Latisha were telling me about some people who left here because they didn't get the promotions they were promised. *(Ramon discloses information that was told to him in confidence, jeopardizing the standing of two coworkers with Julie.)*

their instructors' personal lives.[90] Of course, it's also possible to *withhold* too much information—perhaps in a counseling session or at a doctor's appointment, or in intimate relationships where nondisclosure might be regarded as deceit. The key is to recognize that there's a time and a place for engaging in, and refraining from, self-disclosure.

Is the Risk of Disclosing Reasonable? Take a realistic look at the potential risks of self-disclosure. Even if the probable benefits are great, opening yourself up to almost certain rejection may be asking for trouble. On the other hand, knowing that your partner is trustworthy and supportive makes the prospect of disclosing more reasonable.

Revealing personal thoughts and feelings can be especially risky on the job.[91] The politics of the workplace sometimes requires communicators to keep feelings to themselves in order to accomplish both personal and organizational goals. You might,

Julie: *(Firmly)* Ramon, I'm sure you understand that I can't talk about personnel decisions involving former employees. I can tell you that we try to give people all the challenges and rewards they deserve, though it can take a while.

Ramon: A year seems like more than "a while." I'm starting to think this company is more interested in having somebody with a Hispanic name on the payroll than giving me a real shot at promotion. *(Ramon's concern may be legitimate, but the sarcastic tone of his disclosure isn't constructive.)*

Julie: Look: I probably shouldn't be saying this, but I'm as frustrated as you are that it's taking so long to get a promotion arranged for you. I can tell you that there will be some personnel changes soon that will give you a good chance to make the kinds of changes you want. I think you can expect to see some changes in the next six weeks. *(Julie offers two items of self-disclosure that encourage Ramon to reciprocate.)*

Ramon: That's really good to hear! I have to tell you that I've started to think about other career options. Not because I want to leave here, but because I just can't afford to stand still. I really need to start bringing home more money. I don't want to be one of those losers who still can't afford to buy his own house by the time he's forty. *(Ramon makes a big mistake disclosing his*

opinion about home ownership—a topic that has no relevance to the discussion at hand.)*

Julie: Gee, I'm still renting . . .

Ramon: Oh, I didn't mean that the way it sounded . . . *(But the damage from the inappropriate disclosure is already done.)*

Julie: Anyway, I'm glad you let me know about your concerns. I hope you can hang in there for just a little while longer.

Ramon: Sure. Six weeks, huh? I'll keep an eye on the calendar!

After the conversation, Julie still thinks Ramon is a candidate for promotion, but some of his inappropriate disclosures have left her with doubts about his maturity and good judgment, which she didn't have before they spoke. Julie makes a mental note to keep an eye on Ramon and to reconsider the amount of responsibility she gives him until he has demonstrated the ability to share his personal feelings and concerns more constructively.

Communication Scenarios

To watch and analyze a video related to this feature and this topic, visit CengageBrain.com to access the Speech Communication CourseMate for Looking Out/Looking In.

for example, find the opinions of a boss or customer personally offensive but decide to bite your tongue rather than risk losing your job or goodwill for the company.

In anticipating risks, be sure that you are realistic. It's sometimes easy to indulge in catastrophic expectations and imagine all sorts of disastrous consequences when in fact such horrors are unlikely to occur.

Will the Effect Be Constructive? Self-disclosure can be a vicious tool if it's not used carefully. Each person has a psychological "beltline." Below-the-belt jabs are a powerful way to disable another person, though usually at great cost to the relationship. It's important to consider the effects of your candor before opening up to others. Comments such as "I've always thought you were pretty unintelligent" or "Last year I made love to your best friend" can be devastating—to the listener, to the relationship, and to your self-esteem.

The characters in the 80s classic *The Breakfast Club* bared their souls during a Saturday detention session. Their self-disclosure helped forge new relationships, but we're left wondering whether all these confessions could come back to haunt them when they return to their cliques on Monday.

Is the Self-Disclosure Reciprocated? The amount of personal information you reveal will usually depend on how much the other person reveals. As a rule, disclosure is a two-way street. For example, couples are happiest when their levels of openness are roughly equal.[92]

There are a few times when one-way disclosure is acceptable. Most of them involve formal, therapeutic relationships in which a client approaches a trained professional with the goal of resolving a problem. For instance, you wouldn't necessarily expect to hear about your doctor's personal ailments during a physical checkup—although it's been known to happen, sometimes to the chagrin of the patient.[93]

Do You Have a Moral Obligation to Disclose? Sometimes we are morally obliged to disclose personal information. For example, surveys reveal that a majority of HIV-positive patients believe they have a duty to reveal their status to healthcare providers and partners, even when doing so risks their pride, dignity, and being stigmatized.[94] Despite this prevailing belief, two decades of research has shown that 40 percent of persons testing positive for HIV did not reveal this result to their sexual partners.[95]

SKILL BUILDER

APPROPRIATE SELF-DISCLOSURE

Use the guidelines on pages 63–66 to develop one scenario where you might reveal a self-disclosing message. Create a message of this type, and use the information in this chapter to discuss the advantages and disadvantages of sharing this message.

 Alternatives to Self-Disclosure

Although self-disclosure plays an important role in interpersonal relationships, it isn't the only type of communication available. To understand why complete honesty isn't always an easy or ideal choice, consider some familiar dilemmas:

A new acquaintance is much more interested in becoming friends than you are. She invites you to a party this weekend. You aren't busy, but you don't want to go. What would you say?

Your boss asks you what you think of his new wardrobe. You think it's cheap and flashy. Would you tell him?

You're attracted to your best friend's mate, who has confessed that s/he feels the same way about you. You both agreed that you won't act on your feelings and that even bringing up the subject would make your friend feel terribly insecure. Now your friend has asked whether you're attracted at all to the mate. Would you tell the truth?

You've just been given a large, extremely ugly painting as a gift by a relative who visits your home often. How would you respond to the question, "Where will you put it?"

Although total honesty is desirable in principle, it can have potentially unpleasant consequences. It's tempting to avoid situations where self-disclosure would be difficult, but examples like the preceding ones show that evasion isn't always possible. Research and personal experience show that communicators—even those with the best intentions—aren't always completely honest when they find themselves in situations in which honesty would be uncomfortable.[96] Four common alternatives to self-disclosure are silence, lying, equivocating, and hinting. We will look closer at each one.

SILENCE

One alternative to self-disclosure is to keep your thoughts and feelings to yourself. You can get a sense of how much you rely on silence instead of disclosing by keeping a record of when you do and don't express your opinions. You're likely to find that withholding thoughts and feelings is a common approach for you. Telling the whole truth may be honest, but it can jeopardize you, the other person, and your relationship. Most thoughtful communicators would keep quiet rather than blurt out unsolicited opinions like "You look awful" or "You talk too much." Social scientists have found that people often make distinctions between "lies of omission" and "lies of commission"—and that saying nothing (omission) is usually judged less harshly than telling an outright lie (commission).[97] One study showed that in the workplace, withholding information is often seen as a better alternative than lying or engaging in intentional deception.[98]

LYING

To most of us, lying appears as a breach of ethics. Although lying to gain unfair advantage over an unknowing victim seems clearly wrong, another kind of mistruth—the "benevolent lie"—isn't so easy to dismiss as completely unethical. A **benevolent lie** is defined (at least by the teller) as unmalicious, or even helpful, to the person to whom it is told.

Whether or not they are innocent, benevolent lies are quite common, both in face-to-face and online relationships.[99] In research spanning four decades, a significant majority of people acknowledged that even in their closest relationships, there are times when lying is justified.[100] In one study, 130 subjects were asked to keep track of the truthfulness of their everyday conversational statements.[101] Only 38.5 percent of these-statements—slightly more than one-third—proved to be totally honest. In another experiment, subjects recorded their conversations over a two-day period and later counted their own deceptions. The average lie rate: three fibs for every ten minutes of conversation.[102]

Most people think that benevolent lies are told for the benefit of the recipient. In the study cited earlier, the majority of subjects claimed that such lying is "the right thing to do." Other research paints a less flattering picture of who benefits most from lying. One study found that two out of every three lies are told for "selfish reasons."[103] Table 2.1 identifies many of the reasons that people choose to lie—some more self-serving than others.

Research has shown that lying does, in fact, threaten relationships.[104] Not all lies are equally devastating, however. One study suggests that a liar's motives make a significant difference in whether the deception is perceived as acceptable by others.[105] If a lie appears to be self-serving and exploitive, it will most likely be treated as a relational transgression. On the other hand, if a mistruth seems aimed at sparing another's feelings, the chances of being forgiven increase.

Feelings like dismay and betrayal are greatest when the relationship is most intense, when the importance of the subject is high, and when there is previous suspicion that the other person isn't being completely honest. Of these three factors, the importance of

IS MISLEADING YOUR SPOUSE FRAUD OR TACT?

When their marriage of more than a decade ended in divorce, Anaheim banker Ronald Askew sued his ex-wife for fraud because she admittedly concealed the fact that she had never felt sexually attracted to him. On Wednesday, an Orange County jury agreed, and ordered Bonnette Askew to pay her ex-husband $242,000 in damages.

"I'm astonished by this verdict and I've looked at divorce in 62 societies," said Helen Fisher, an American Museum of Natural History anthropologist who authored the recent book *Anatomy of Love: The Natural History of Monogamy, Adultery and Divorce.*

Bonnette Askew, 45, acknowledged in court that she had never been sexually attracted to her husband. But she said she always loved him and noted that their marriage was not sexless and that they had two children together.

She first admitted her lack of sexual desire for him during a joint therapy session in 1991. "I guess he confused sex with love," Bonnette Askew said, adding that she concealed her lack of desire because she "didn't want to hurt his male ego."

But Ronald Askew, 50, said his lawsuit had more to do with honesty and integrity than sex. He felt deceived, especially because he said he repeatedly asked her before their marriage to be honest with him and reveal any important secrets.

If Ronald Askew believes total honesty is the foundation of good marriages, Fisher has a message for him: "Grow up."

© Lou Brooks

"Since when is anyone truly honest with anyone?" Fisher said. "Did this man really want her to say: 'You're short, fat and you're terrible in bed'? Much of the world is amazed at what they see as brutal honesty in America. She was operating on an entirely different set of social values, which much of the world operates on—delicacy as opposed to brutal honesty."

Maria Cone

TABLE 2.1 SOME REASONS FOR LYING

REASON	EXAMPLE
Save face for others	"Don't worry—I'm sure nobody noticed that stain on your shirt."
Save face for self	"I wasn't looking at the files—I was accidentally in the wrong drawer."
Acquire resources	"Oh, *please* let me add this class. If I don't get in, I'll never graduate on time!"
Protect resources	"I'd like to lend you the money, but I'm short myself."
Initiate interaction	"Excuse me, I'm lost. Do you live around here?"
Be socially gracious	"No, I'm not bored—tell me more about your vacation."
Avoid conflict	"It's not a big deal. We can do it your way. Really."
Avoid interaction	"That sounds like fun, but I'm busy Saturday night."
Leave taking	"Oh, look what time it is! I've got to run!"

© Cengage Learning

the information lied about proved to be the key factor in provoking a relational crisis. We may be able to cope with "misdemeanor" lying, but "felonies" are a grave threat. In fact, the discovery of major deception can lead to the end of the relationship. More than two-thirds of the subjects in one study reported that their relationship had ended because they discovered a lie. Furthermore, they attributed the breakup directly to the lie.

The lesson here is clear: Lying about major parts of your relationship can have the gravest consequences. If preserving a relationship is important, honesty—at least about important matters—really does appear to be the best policy.

EQUIVOCATING

When faced with the dilemma of either lying or telling an unpleasant truth, communicators typically opt for a third approach—equivocation.[106] When a friend asks what you think of an awful outfit, you could say "It's really unusual—one of a kind!" Likewise, if you are too angry to accept a friend's apology but don't want to appear petty, you might say, "Don't worry about it." One humorous set of suggestions shows how equivocation can help a reluctant business contact provide ambiguous references for an incompetent job applicant:

> For a lazy worker: "You will be lucky to get this person to work for you."
>
> For someone with no talent: "I recommend this candidate with no qualifications."
>
> For a candidate who should not be hired under any circumstances: "Waste no time hiring this person."

The value of equivocation becomes clear when you consider the alternatives. Consider the dilemma of what to say when you've been given an unwanted present—an ugly painting, for example—and the giver asks what you think of it. How can you respond? On one hand, you need to choose between telling the truth and lying. On the other hand, you have a choice of whether to make your response clear or vague. Figure 2.8 displays these choices. Among the choices, it's clear that Option 1—an equivocal, true response—is preferable to the others in several respects.

As one team of researchers put it, "equivocation is neither a false message nor a clear truth, but rather an alternative used precisely when both of these are to be avoided."[107]

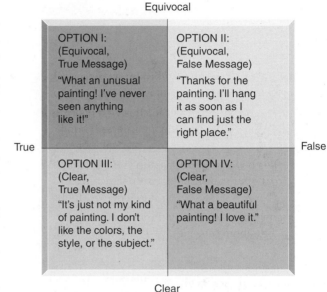

FIGURE 2.8 **Dimensions of Truthfulness and Equivocation**
© Cengage Learning 2013

Most people will usually choose to equivocate rather than tell a lie. In a series of experiments, subjects chose among telling a face-saving lie, telling the truth, and equivocating. Only 6 percent chose the lie, and only between 3 and 4 percent chose the hurtful truth. By contrast, more than 90 percent chose the equivocal response.[108] People *say* they prefer truth telling to equivocating, but given the choice, they prefer to finesse the truth.[109]

HINTING

Hints are more direct than equivocal statements. Whereas an equivocal statement isn't necessarily aimed at changing others' behavior, a hint does aim to get a desired response from others.[110]

Direct Statement	Face-Saving Hint
I'm too busy to continue with this conversation.	I know you're busy; I better let you go.
Please don't smoke in here because it's bothering me.	I'm pretty sure that smoking isn't permitted here.
I'd like to invite you out for lunch, but I don't want to risk a "no" answer.	Gee, it's almost lunchtime. Have you ever eaten at that new Italian restaurant around the corner?

Hinting can spare others discomfort that comes with the undiluted truth. The face-saving value of hints explains why communicators are more likely to be indirect than fully disclosing when they deliver a potentially embarrassing message.[111] The success of a hint depends on the other person's ability to pick up the unexpressed message. Your subtle remarks might go right over the head of an insensitive receiver—or one who chooses not to respond. If this happens, you may decide to be more direct. If the costs of a direct message seem too high, however, you can withdraw without risk.

THE ETHICS OF EVASION

It's easy to see why people choose hints, equivocations, and benevolent lies instead of complete self-disclosure. These strategies provide a way to manage difficult situations that is easier than the alternatives for both the speaker and the receiver of the message. In this sense, successful liars, equivocators, and hinters can be said to possess a certain kind of communicative competence. On the other hand, there are certainly times when honesty is the right approach, even if it's painful. At times like these, evaders could be viewed as lacking the competence or the integrity to handle a situation most effectively.

Are hints, benevolent lies, and equivocations ethical alternatives to self-disclosure? Some of the examples in these pages suggest that the answer is a qualified "yes." Many social scientists and philosophers agree. As the Ethical Challenge on page 71 shows, some argue that the morality of a speaker's *motives* for lying, not the lie itself, ought to be judged, and others ask whether the *effects* of a lie will be worth the deception.

Perhaps the right questions to ask are whether an indirect message is truly in the interests of the receiver and whether this sort of evasion is the only, or the best, way to behave in a given situation.

ETHICAL CHALLENGE

MUST WE ALWAYS TELL THE TRUTH?

"Is there really a Santa Claus?"
"Am I talking too much?"
"Isn't this the cutest baby you've ever seen?"
"Was it good for you?"

Questions like these often seem to invite answers that are less than totally honest. The research summarized on pages 66–70 reveals that, at one time or another, virtually everyone avoids telling the complete truth. We seem to be caught between the time-honored commandment "Thou shall not lie" and the fact that everybody does seem to bend the truth, if only for altruistic reasons. What, then, are the ethics of honesty?

Philosopher Immanuel Kant had a clear answer: We may be able to evade unpleasant situations by keeping quiet, but we must always tell the complete truth when there is no way to avoid speaking up. He said that "truthfulness in statements which cannot be avoided is the formal duty of an individual . . . however great may be the disadvantage accruing to himself or another."[a] Kant's unbending position didn't make any exception for lies or equivocations told in the best interests of the receiver. In his moral code, lying is wrong—period.

Not all ethicists have shared Kant's rigid standards of truth telling. Utilitarian philosophers claim that the way to determine the morality of a behavior is to explore whether it leads to the greatest happiness for the greatest number of people. While encouraging truth-telling whenever possible, philosopher Sissela Bok offers some circumstances in which deception may be justified: doing good, avoiding harm, and protecting a larger truth.[b]

Bok is realistic enough to recognize that liars are prone to self-deceptive justifications. For this reason, she tempers her utilitarian position with a *test of publicity*. She suggests that we ask how others would respond if they knew that we were being untruthful. If most disinterested observers with all the facts supported untruthful speech as the best course, then it passes the test of publicity.

Submit your case for avoiding the truth to a "court of self-disclosure":
1. Recall recent situations in which you have used each of the following evasive approaches: lying, equivocating, and hinting.
2. Write an anonymous description of each situation, including a justification for your behavior, on a separate sheet of paper. Submit the cases to a panel of "judges" (most likely fellow students), who will evaluate the morality of these decisions.

SUMMARY

The self-concept is a relatively stable set of perceptions that individuals hold about themselves. Self-esteem has to do with evaluations of self-worth. Some of the characteristics of the self are a result of inherited personality traits. In addition, the self-concept is created through messages from significant others—reflected appraisal—and through social comparison with reference groups. The self-concept is subjective and may vary from the way a person is perceived by others. Although the self evolves over time, the self-concept resists change. Other factors that affect the self-concept are culture, and sex/gender. One's self-concept, as well as the self-concepts of others, can be changed through self-fulfilling prophecies.

Identity management consists of strategic communication designed to influence others' perceptions of an individual. Identity management aims at presenting to others one or more faces, which may be different from private, spontaneous behavior that occurs outside of others' presence. Communicators engage in creating an identity by managing their manner, appearance, and the settings in which they interact with others. Identity management occurs both in face-to-face and mediated communication. Because each person has a variety of faces that he or she can reveal, choosing which one to present need not be dishonest.

An important issue in interpersonal relationships is self-disclosure: honest, revealing messages about the self that are intentionally directed toward others. The social penetration model and the Johari Window are tools for describing our self-disclosure with others. Communicators disclose personal information for a variety of reasons and benefits: catharsis, reciprocity, self-clarification, self-validation, identity management, relationship maintenance and enhancement, and social influence. The risks of self-disclosure include the possibility of rejection, making a negative impression, a decline in relational satisfaction, a loss of influence, and hurting the other person. Four alternatives to self-disclosure are silence, lying, equivocating, and hinting. These can be ethical alternatives to self-disclosure; however, whether they are depends on the speaker's motives and the effects of the deception.

KEY TERMS

benevolent lie (67)
breadth (58)
cognitive conservatism (45)
depth (58)
face (52)
identity management (51)
Johari Window (60)
perceived self (51)
personality (40)
presenting self (52)

privacy management (61)
reference groups (42)
reflected appraisal (41)
self-concept (38)
self-disclosure (58)
self-esteem (39)
self-fulfilling prophecy (49)
significant others (41)
social comparison (41)
social penetration (58)

ONLINE RESOURCES

Now that you have read this chapter, visit CengageBrain.com to access the Speech Communication CourseMate for *Looking Out/Looking In* for quick access to the electronic resources that accompany this text. Your CourseMate offers:

- **Study tools** that will help you assess your learning and prepare for exams (*digital glossary, key term flash cards, interactive quizzes*).
- **Activities and assignments** that will help you hone your knowledge, understand how theory and research applies to your own life (*Self-Assessment, Pause and Reflect*), consider ethical challenges in interpersonal communication (*Ethical Challenge*), and build your interpersonal communication skills throughout the course (*Skill Builder*). If requested, you can submit your answers to your instructor.
- **Media resources** that will allow you to watch and critique videos of interpersonal communication situations (*In Real Life, interpersonal video simulations, and interactive video activities*).
- In addition to interactive teaching and learning tools, CourseMate includes an **interactive eBook.** Take notes, highlight, search, and interact with embedded media specific to *Looking Out/Looking In*.

SEARCH TERMS

When searching online databases to research topics in this chapter, use the following terms (along with this chapter's key terms) to maximize the chances of finding useful information:

deception	self-evaluation
honesty	self-monitoring
identity management	self-perception
impression management	self-presentation
personal relationships	social networks
self-awareness	truthfulness
self-congruence	

FILM AND TELEVISION

You can see the communication principles described in this chapter portrayed in the following films.

INFLUENCES ON THE SELF-CONCEPT
She's Out Of My League (2010) Rated R

Kirk (Jay Baruchel) is just an average, ordinary guy, according to his own estimation and the appraisals of others. By chance, he meets and gets to know Molly (Alice Eve), who is regarded as a perfect "10" by all who behold her physical beauty. As Kirk considers pursuing a romantic relationship with Molly, he gets warned repeatedly that he's venturing out of his "league."

The movie illustrates many of the concepts discussed in this chapter. Reflected appraisals and social comparisons are in evidence in Kirk's conversations with his buddies. In one memorable scene, the guys rank each other's attractiveness on a 1–10 scale (they determine Kirk is a 5). And Kirk's relatively low self-esteem, especially when it comes to dating women, turns into a self-fulfilling prophecy. His lack of confidence leads him to engage in awkward behaviors that, while humorous for the audience, threaten to sabotage the goal he's pursuing.

The fact that our culture uses attractiveness rating scales and talks about "leagues" makes it clear that how we see ourselves is strongly influenced by the appraisals of, and comparisons with, significant others in our lives.

SELF-FULFILLING PROPHECIES
Pygmalion in the Movies

Brownhouse Prod./BOTNP INC./The Kobal Collection

This chapter describes a self-fulfilling prophecy experiment called "Pygmalion in the Classroom." *Pygmalion* is a fictional play about a professor who transforms a street ragamuffin into a refined socialite. It was the basis for the musical *My Fair Lady*, in which Henry Higgins radically changes the life of Eliza Doolittle.

A Pygmalion theme runs through many movie storylines, such as *The Princess Diaries* (pictured here). If you're familiar with *She's All That*, *Trading Places*, *Pretty Woman*, and *Miss Congeniality*, you know these films depict people who go through a significant conversion because of how others treat them—and how they then begin to think about themselves differently. These stories illustrate the power of communication to transform self-concepts and behaviors.

IDENTITY MANAGEMENT
Catfish (2010) Rated PG-13

Twentysomething New York photographer Nev Schulman is flattered and intrigued when a bright 8-year-old Michigan girl named Abby begins sending him fan mail and paintings based on his work. Nev and Abby strike up a long-distance friendship via email, Facebook, and phone. Soon the artist is also exchanging messages with Abby's family and friends.

Nev's brother Ariel and friend Henry are filmmakers, and they begin documenting Nev's adventures in cyberspace. The narrative becomes more intriguing when Nev falls into an online romance with Abby's older sister Megan, even though the two haven't met in person.

The most gripping parts of this documentary reveal what happens when the three New Yorkers take a road trip to Michigan to finally meet the family that has occupied a major part of their thoughts and time. Without spilling too many details, it's enough to say that the surprising ending to this story dramatizes ethical questions about identity management, self-disclosure, and relational development in mediated communication.

ALTERNATIVES TO SELF-DISCLOSURE

The Invention of Lying (2009) Rated PG-13

Liar, Liar (1997) Rated PG-13

Radar Pictures/The Kobal Collection

The Invention of Lying presents a reality exactly like ours, except that lying does not exist. Everyone tells the whole truth, all the time. Mark Bellison (Ricky Gervais) is a loser who accidentally discovers that lying is possible, easy, and apparently rewarding. In a gullible world, Mark's mistruths earn him fame, fortune, and the woman of his dreams. But soon enough, Mark learns the costs of deception.

In a similar but contrasting vein, *Liar, Liar* spins a fantasy in which lawyer Fletcher Reed (Jim Carrey) is unable to tell a single lie for a full day. The film provides an amusing look at why total self-disclosure is unrealistic in everyday situations. ("How are you today?" a judge asks attorney Fletcher in court. "I'm a little upset about a bad sexual episode last night," he replies.)

At the most simplistic level, these films argue that healthy relationships demand a measure of honesty and openness. But, for more sophisticated communication analysts, they show that both "the whole truth" and unethical deception have their pitfalls.

CHAPTER TWO

Communication and Identity: Creating and Presenting the Self

CHAPTER OUTLINE

Use this outline to take notes as you read the chapter in the text and/or as your instructor lectures in class.

I. **COMMUNICATION AND THE SELF**   _____

   A.   **Definitions**   _____

       1.   Self-concept   _____

       2.   Self-esteem

   B.   **Biological and Social Roots of the Self**   _____

       1.   Personality

       2.   Traits   _____

       3.   Socialization and the self-concept

          a.   Reflected appraisal   _____

          b.   Significant others

          c.   Social comparison   _____

              i.   Superior/inferior

              ii.   Same/different   _____

   C.   **Characteristics of the Self-Concept**

       1.   The self-concept is subjective

        a. Obsolete information

        b. Distorted feedback

        c. Emphasis on perfection

        d. Social expectations

  2. The self-concept resists change (cognitive conservatism)

        a. Have a realistic perception of yourself

        b. Have realistic expectations

        c. Have the will to change

        d. Have the skill to change

D. Culture, Gender, and Identity

  1. Culture

      a. Individualistic

      b. Collectivistic

  2. Sex and gender

E. The Self-Fulfilling Prophecy and Communication

  1. Self-fulfilling prophecy

      a. Holding an expectation

      b. Behaving within expectations

      c. The expectation coming to pass

      d. Reinforcing the original expectation

  2. Types

        a. Self-imposed

        b. Imposed by others

II. PRESENTING THE SELF: COMMUNICATION AS IDENTITY MANAGEMENT

A. Public and Private Selves

  1. Perceived self

  2. Presenting self (face)

B. Characteristics of Identity Management

  1. We construct multiple identities

  2. Identity management is collaborative

  3. Identity management can be deliberate or unconscious

C. Why Manage Identities?

1. To start and manage relationships
2. To gain the compliance of others
3. To save others' face
4. To explore new selves

D. **Managing Identities in Person and Online**
   1. Face-to-face identity management
      a. Manner
      b. Appearance
      c. Setting
   2. Online impression management
      a. Asynchronous mediated communication
      b. Ideal online identity versus "real" self
      c. Reputation management

E. **Identity Management and Honesty**
   1. Identity/impression management versus lying
   2. Situational behavior

III. **SELF-DISCLOSURE IN RELATIONSHIPS**
   A. **Definition**
   B. **Models of Self-Disclosure**
      1. Social penetration model
         a. Breadth
         b. Depth
      2. Johari Window
         a. Open
         b. Hidden
         c. Blind
         d. Unknown
   C. **Benefits and Risks of Self-Disclosure**
      1. Benefits of self-disclosure
         a. Catharsis
         b. Reciprocity
         c. Self-clarification
         d. Self-validation
         e. Building and maintaining

        relationships

    f. Social influence

2. Risks of self-disclosure

    a. Rejection

    b. Negative impression

    c. Decrease in relational satisfaction

    d. Loss of influence

    e. Hurting the other person

D. Guidelines for Self-Disclosure

    1.   Importance of the other to you

    2.   Appropriate amount and type

    3.   Reasonable risk

    4.   Constructive effects

    5.   Reciprocation

    6.   Moral obligation

IV.   ALTERNATIVES TO SELF-DISCLOSURE

  A. Silence

  B. Lying

    1.   Benevolent lies

    2.   Reasons for lying

    3.   Effects of lies—threats to the relationship

  C. Equivocating

  D. Hinting

    1.   May prevent receiver or sender embarrassment

    2.   Hints may not be perceived

  E. The Ethics of Evasion

    1.   Motives

    2.   Effects

KEY TERMS

benevolent lie	depth	Johari Window
breadth	face	perceived self
cognitive conservatism	identity management	personality

presenting self
privacy management
reference groups
reflected appraisal
self-concept
self-disclosure
self-esteem
self-fulfilling prophecy
significant others
social comparison
social penetration

ACTIVITIES

2.1 WHO DO YOU THINK YOU ARE?

LEARNING OBJECTIVES

- Describe the relationship between self-concept, self-esteem, and communication.

- Explain how self-fulfilling prophecies shape the self-concept and influence communication.

- Demonstrate how the principles in the chapter can be used to change the self-concept, and hence communication.

INSTRUCTIONS

1. First, if possible, take a The Jung Typology Test at http://www.humanmetrics.com/cgi-win/JTypes2.asp. This will get you thinking about the way you describe yourself.
2. For each category below, supply the words or phrases that describe you best.
3. After filling in the spaces within each category, organize your responses so that the most fundamental characteristic is listed first, with the rest of the items following in order of descending importance.

PART A: IDENTIFY THE ELEMENTS OF YOUR SELF-CONCEPT

1. How would you describe your social behaviors (friendly, shy, aloof, talkative, etc.)?

   a. _____   b. _____   c. _____

2. How would you describe your personality traits (stable, extraverted, introverted, etc.)?

   a. _____   b. _____   c. _____

3. What beliefs do you hold strongly (vegetarian, green, Christian, pacifist, etc.)?

   a. _____   b. _____   c. _____

4. What social roles are the most important in your life (brother, student, friend, bank teller, club president, etc.)?

   a. _____   b. _____   c. _____

5. How would you describe your intellectual capacity (curious, poor reader, good mathematician, etc.)?

   a. _____   b. _____   c. _____

6. How would you describe your physical condition and/or your appearance (fit, sedentary, tall, attractive, etc.)?

   a. _____   b. _____   c. _____

7. What talents do you possess or lack (good artist, lousy carpenter, competent swimmer, etc.)?

   a. _____   b. _____   c. _____

8. What other descriptors are important to describe you (cultural, ethnic, gender, sexual orientation, moods, feelings, others)?

   a. _____   b. _____   c. _____

PART B: ARRANGE YOUR SELF-CONCEPT ELEMENTS IN ORDER OF IMPORTANCE

1. _____   12. _____

2. _____   13. _____

3. _____   14. _____

4. _____   15. _____

5. _____   16. _____

6. _____   17. _____

7. _____   18. _____

8. _____   19. _____

9. _____   20. _____

10. _____

11. _____

Class _____   Name_____

Describe any factors that have contributed in a positive or negative way to the formation of your perceived self. Explain if some were due to obsolete information, social expectations, distorted feedback, or perfection beliefs. Include any other factors involved in the formation of your perceived self (for example, certain significant others, any strong reference groups).

_____

_____

_____

_____

What significant others or reference groups contributed to your self-concept? How?

_____

_____

_____

_____

NOTE: You will use these descriptors in Activity 2.2.

2.2 SELF-CONCEPT INVENTORY

LEARNING OBJECTIVES

- Describe the relationship between self-concept, self-esteem, and communication.

- Compare and contrast the perceived self and the presenting self as they relate to identity management.

INSTRUCTIONS

1. Transfer the list of up to 20 elements of your self-concept from the previous exercise (2.1) to index cards (or strips of paper).
2. Arrange your cards in a stack, with the one that *best* describes you at the top and the one that *least* describes you at the bottom.
3. Record the order in which you arranged the cards (1 is the most like you) in the Perceived Self column (Column 1). You may leave out some cards or add on to your list.
4. Without revealing your Perceived Self column, ask two other people (a friend, coworker, roommate, family member, classmate) to arrange the descriptors in an order in which they see you. Record these perceptions in Columns 2 and 3. Neither should see Column 1 or the other person's column. Record the name/relationship of your reviewers at the top of the appropriate column.
5. Compare the three tables, circling any descriptors that are exactly the same across the three columns. Highlight any that have similar ranks (no more than three numbers different).
6. Answer the questions at the end of this exercise.

Column 1 Perceived Self	Column 2 Presenting Self to _____ (relationship to you)	Column 3 Presenting Self to _____ (relationship to you)
1. _____	1. _____	1. _____
2. _____	2. _____	2. _____
3. _____	3. _____	3. _____
4. _____	4. _____	4. _____
5. _____	5. _____	5. _____
6. _____	6. _____	6. _____

Class _____   Name_____

7. _____	7. _____	7. _____
8. _____	8. _____	8. _____
9. _____	9. _____	9. _____
10. _____	10. _____	10. _____
11. _____	11. _____	11. _____
12. _____	12. _____	12. _____
13. _____	13. _____	13. _____
14. _____	14. _____	14. _____
15. _____	15. _____	15. _____
16. _____	16. _____	16. _____
17. _____	17. _____	17. _____
18. _____	18. _____	18. _____
19. _____	19. _____	19. _____
20. _____	20. _____	20. _____

Describe any differences between your perceived self and the ways your reviewers perceived you (your presenting selves). What factors contribute to the differences in perception? Whose view is the most accurate and why?

_____

_____

_____

_____

_____

Why might your reviewers in this exercise view you differently from the way you perceive yourself? Would other people in your life view you like either of the people in this exercise? Give some specific examples with reasons why they would or would not have a similar perception.

_____

_____

_____

_____

_____

2.3 EGO BOOSTERS AND BUSTERS

LEARNING OBJECTIVES

- Describe the relationship between self-concept, self-esteem, and communication.
- Demonstrate how the principles in Chapter 2 can be used to change the self-concept, and hence communication.
- Compare and contrast the perceived self and the presenting self as they relate to identity management.

INSTRUCTIONS

1. In the appropriate spaces below describe the actions of several "ego boosters": significant others who shaped your self-concept in a positive way. Also describe the behavior of "ego busters" who contributed to a more negative self-concept.
2. Next, recall several incidents in which you behaved as an ego booster or buster to others. Not all ego boosters and busters are obvious. Include in your description several incidents in which the messages were **subtle or nonverbal**.
3. Summarize the lessons you have learned from this experience by answering the questions at the end of this exercise.

EGO BOOSTER MESSAGES YOU HAVE RECEIVED

EXAMPLE

I perceive(d) _my communication lab partner_ (significant other) as telling me I am/was ___attractive___ (self-concept element) when he/she _kept sneaking glances at me and smiling during our taping project._

1. I perceived _____ (significant other) as telling me I am/was

    _____ (self-concept element) when he/she _____

    _____

    _____

Class _____   Name_____

2. I perceived _____ (significant other) as telling me I am/was

    _____ (self-concept element) when he/she _____

    _____

    _____

EGO BUSTER MESSAGES YOU HAVE RECEIVED

EXAMPLE

I perceive(d) _my neighbor_ (significant other) as telling me I am/was _not an important friend_ (self-concept element) when he/she _had a big party last weekend and didn't invite me._

1. I perceived _____ (significant other) as telling me I am/was

    _____(self-concept element) when he/she _____

    _____

    _____

2. I perceived _____ (significant other) as telling me I am/was

    _____(self-concept element) when he/she _____

    _____

    _____

EGO BOOSTER MESSAGES YOU HAVE SENT

EXAMPLE

I was a booster to _my instructor_ when I _told her I enjoyed last Tuesday's lecture._

1. I was a booster to _____ when I _____

    _____

    _____

Class _____   Name_____

2.   I was a booster to _____ when I _____

_____

_____

EGO BUSTER MESSAGES YOU HAVE SENT

EXAMPLE

I was a buster to _my sister_ when I _forgot to phone her or send even a card on her birthday._

1.   I was a buster to _____ when I _____

_____

2.   I was a buster to _____ when I _____

_____

CONCLUSIONS

Who are the people who have most influenced your self-concept in the past? What messages did each one send to influence you so strongly?

_____

_____

_____

What people are the greatest influences on your self-concept now? Is each person a positive or a negative influence? What messages does each one send to influence your self-concept?

_____

_____

_____

_____

Who are the people whom *you* have influenced greatly? What messages have you sent to each one about his or her self-concept? How have you sent these messages?

_____

_____

_____

_____

What ego booster or buster messages do you want to send to the important people in your life? How (with what channels) can you send each one?

_____

_____

_____

GROUP DISCUSSION

After completing the first part of this activity individually, share some of your answers with a small group of classmates. Then, as a group, answer the questions below.

1. What channels are most important for you to receive ego boosters? What booster or buster messages do you want to send to the important people in your life? How (with what channels) can you send each one?

_____

_____

_____

2. What channels are most often used for ego busters that are unintentional? What advice would you have in order to avoid inadvertently sending ego busters?

_____

_____

_____

3. After reviewing your experiences, what advice would you give to supervisors regarding ego boosters and ego busters?

_____

_____

_____

4. After reviewing your experiences, what advice would you give to parents regarding ego boosters and ego busters?

_____

_____

_____

2.4 REEVALUATING YOUR "CAN'TS"

LEARNING OBJECTIVES

- Explain how self-fulfilling prophecies shape the self-concept and influence communication.

INSTRUCTIONS

1. Complete the following lists by describing communication-related difficulties you have in the following areas.
2. After filling in each blank space, follow the starred instructions that follow the list (*).

DIFFICULTIES YOU HAVE COMMUNICATING WITH FAMILY MEMBERS

EXAMPLES

I can't *discuss politics with my dad without having an argument* because *he's so set in his ways.*
I can't *tell my brother how much I love him* because *I'll feel foolish.*

1. I can't _____

    because _____

2. I can't _____

    because _____

* Corrections (see instructions at end of exercise)

DIFFICULTIES YOU HAVE COMMUNICATING WITH PEOPLE AT SCHOOL OR AT WORK

EXAMPLES

I can't *say "no" when my boss asks me to work overtime* because *he'll fire me.*
I can't *participate in class discussions even when I know the answers or have a question* because *I just freeze up.*

1. I can't _____

    because _____

Class _____   Name_____

   2. I can't _____

       because _____

* Corrections (see instructions at end of exercise)

_____

_____

DIFFICULTIES YOU HAVE COMMUNICATING WITH STRANGERS
EXAMPLES

I can't *start a conversation with someone I've never met before* because *I'll look stupid.*
I can't *ask smokers to move or stop smoking* because *they'll get mad.*

   1. I can't _____

       because _____

   2. I can't _____

       because _____

* Corrections (see instructions at end of exercise)

_____

_____

DIFFICULTIES YOU HAVE COMMUNICATING WITH FRIENDS
EXAMPLES

I can't *find the courage to ask my friend to repay the money he owes me* because *I'm afraid he'll question our friendship.*
I can't *say no when friends ask me to do favors and I'm busy* because *I'm afraid they'll think I'm not their friend.*

   1. I can't _____

       because _____

   2. I can't _____

       because _____

Class _____   Name _____

_____

_____

DIFFICULTIES YOU HAVE COMMUNICATING WITH YOUR ROMANTIC PARTNER (PAST OR PRESENT)

EXAMPLES

I can't *tell Bill to wear a tie to the party* because *he'll laugh at me.*
I can't *bring up going to visit my parents* because *we'll fight.* _____

   1. I can't _____

       because _____

   2. I can't _____

       because _____

_____

PREDICTIONS MADE BY OTHERS

EXAMPLES

You'll never amount to anything.   You can't expect much with your background.
You're just like your father.   The James children never were too bright.

   1. _____

   2. _____

_____

*After you have completed the list, continue as follows:

   a. Read the list you have made. Actually say each item to yourself and note your feelings.

   b. Now read the list again, but with a slight difference. For each "can't," substitute the word "won't" or "until now I've chosen not to." For instance, "I can't say no to friends' requests" becomes "I won't say no" or "Until now I've chosen not to say no." Circle any statements that are actually "won'ts" or choices.

   c. Read the list for a third time. For this repetition substitute "I don't know how" or "I haven't yet learned to" for your original "can't." Instead of saying "I can't approach strangers," say, "I don't know how to approach strangers." *Correct* your original list to show which statements are truly "don't know how" or "haven't yet learned" statements.

   d. For the "Predictions Made by Others" section, substitute your strength(s) that make the prediction untrue. (Example: "I am my father's child, but I can choose not to repeat behaviors he has that I don't like.")

After completing this exercise, consider your greater awareness of the power that negative self-fulfilling prophecies have on your self-concept and thus on your communication behavior. Imagine how differently you would behave if you eliminated any incorrect uses of the word "can't" from your thinking.

2.5 MEDIATED MESSAGES — IDENTITY MANAGEMENT

LEARNING OBJECTIVES

- Compare and contrast the perceived self and the presenting self as they relate to identity management.
- Describe the role that identity management plays in both face-to-face and mediated relationships.

INSTRUCTIONS

Discuss each of the questions below in your group. For each question, take a minute of silence and let each person jot down some notes. Then go around and let each person share something. Then have a more extended discussion and, if directed by your instructor, prepare to report your group's conclusions back to the whole class.

1. Describe ways in which messages from the mass media (i.e., music, television, film, magazines, books) have contributed to your self concept or the self-concepts of people you know well.

_____

_____

2. Your text states that people often prefer mediated channels when their self-presentation is threatened (delivering bad news, declining invitations). Do your experiences refute or validate this conclusion? Give examples.

_____

_____

3. Identity management is important in mediated contexts. Describe how you manage identity in any mediated contexts you use (online dating services, written notes, email, instant messaging, blogging, personal ads, web pages).

_____

_____

4. Do you prefer to meet people online or face-to-face initially? Why? Is your answer the same or different for friendships than for work or career situations? Why?

_____

Class _____   Name_____

2.6 ASSESSING IDENTITY MANAGEMENT

LEARNING OBJECTIVES

- Compare and contrast the perceived self and the presenting self as they relate to identity management.

INSTRUCTIONS

Think of the many identities you have, such as friend, daughter, athlete, etc. Label and describe your presenting or public self in each situation. Describe how you manage them in the following situations. In the identity spaces below, list one of the identities you manage and describe the communication strategies you use to influence how others view you.

Identity #1 _____

At school:

_____

_____

_____

Identity #2 _____

With your family:

_____

_____

_____

Class _____   Name_____

Identity #3 _____

At work:

_____

_____

_____

Identity # 4 _____

Online:

_____

_____

_____

Class _____   Name_____

2.7 BREADTH AND DEPTH OF RELATIONSHIPS

LEARNING OBJECTIVES

- Identify the dimensions of intimacy that operate and how they are expressed in a specific relationship.
- Explain the need for both intimacy and distance in a given relationship.
- Use the social penetration and Johari Window models to identify the nature of self-disclosing communication in one of your relationships.
- Outline the potential benefits and risks of disclosing in a selected situation.

INSTRUCTIONS

1. Use the form below to make a social penetration model for a significant relationship you have, indicating the depth and breadth of various areas. See Figures 2.3 and 2.7 in Chapter 2 of *Looking Out/Looking In* for an example of the social penetration model.
2. Answer the questions at the end of the exercise.

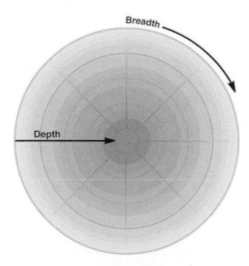

Social Penetration Model

Significant relationship described: _____

CONCLUSIONS

How deep or shallow is your relationship with this person?

_____

_____

Does the depth vary from one area (breadth) to another? In what way?

_____

_____

_____

Are you satisfied with the depth and breadth of this relationship? Why or why not?

_____

_____

_____

If you are not satisfied, what could you do to change the relationship? What would you predict the results would be?

_____

_____

_____

_____

_____

Class _____ Name_____

_____

_____

2.8 REASONS FOR NONDISCLOSURE

LEARNING OBJECTIVES

- Use the social penetration and Johari Window models to identify the nature of self-disclosing communication in one of your relationships.
- Outline the potential benefits and risks of disclosing in a selected situation.

INSTRUCTIONS

1. Choose a particular individual about whom you want to analyze your self-disclosing behavior.
2. In the column to the left of each item, indicate the extent to which you use each reason to avoid disclosing.

   5 = almost always   2 = rarely
   4 = often   1 = never
   3 = sometimes

3. In the column to the right of each item, indicate how reasonable and realistic the reason is.

   5 = totally realistic
   4 = mostly realistic
   3 = partly realistic, partly unrealistic
   2 = mostly unrealistic
   1 = totally unrealistic

How Frequently Do You Use the Reason?		How Realistic and Rational Is the Reason?
___ ___	1. I can't find the opportunity to self-disclose with this person.	_____
___ ___	2. If I disclose I might hurt the other person.	_____
___ ___	3. If I disclose I might be evaluating or judging the person.	_____
___ ___	4. I can't think of topics that I would disclose.	_____
___ ___	5. Self-disclosure would give information that might be used against me at some time.	_____
___ ___	6. If I disclose it might cause me to make personal changes.	_____
___ ___	7. Self-disclosure might threaten relationships I have with people other than the close acquaintance to whom I disclose.	_____

Class _____   Name_____

How Frequently Do You Use the Reason?			How Realistic and Rational Is the Reason?
___ ___	8.	Self-disclosure is a sign of weakness.	_____
___ ___	9.	If I disclose I might lose control over the other person.	_____
___ ___	10.	If I disclose I might discover I am less than I wish to be.	_____
___ ___	11.	If I disclose I might project an image I do not want to project.	_____
___ ___	12.	If I disclose the other person might not understand what I was saying.	_____
_____	13.	If I disclose the other person might evaluate me negatively.	_____
_____	14.	Self-disclosure is a sign of some emotional disturbance.	_____
_____	15.	Self-disclosure might hurt our relationship.	_____
_____	16.	I am afraid that self-disclosure might lead to an intimate relationship with the other person.	_____
_____	17.	Self-disclosure might threaten my physical safety.	_____
_____	18.	If I disclose I might give information that makes me appear inconsistent.	_____
_____	19.	Any other reasons: _____	_____

*Based on a survey developed by Lawrence B. Rosenfeld, "Self-Disclosure Avoidance: Why Am I Afraid to Tell You Who I Am?" *Communication Monographs* 46 (1979): 63–74.

What does this personal survey tell you about your thoughts and feelings about self-disclosure with this person?

_____

_____

_____

Do you think your level of self-disclosure is appropriate or inappropriate with this person? Why or why not?

_____

_____

Class _____   Name _____

How would you summarize and categorize the major reasons that you self-disclose using these categories: Catharsis, Reciprocity, Self-Clarification, Self-Validation, Identity Management, Relational Maintenance, Social Influence?

_____

_____

_____

How different would your survey look if you'd chosen a different relationship? Why?

_____

_____

2.9 DEGREES OF SELF-DISCLOSURE

LEARNING OBJECTIVES

- Use the social penetration and Johari Window models to identify the nature of self-disclosing communication in one of your relationships.
- Outline the potential benefits and risks of disclosing in a selected situation.

INSTRUCTIONS

For each of the following topics, write two statements for each level of self-disclosure. (See Chapter 2 of *Looking Out/Looking In* for descriptions of each level.)

EXAMPLE

TOPIC: SCHOOL

1. Clichés
    a. *Finals are no fun!*
    b. *Textbooks sure are expensive!*
2. Facts
    a. *I'm a psychology major at the university.*
    b. *I'm getting a teaching certificate so I'll be able to teach social studies.*
3. Opinions
    a. *I think people over 18 should be allowed to keep a driver's license if they don't vote.*
    b. *I don't think instructors should count attendance as part of a person's grade.*
4. Feelings
    a. *I feel scared when I think about the future. I'm almost finished with four years of college, and I'm still confused about what to do with my life.*
    b. *I get angry when Professor Autel doesn't prepare adequately for our class.*

TOPIC: MY FAMILY

1. Clichés

    a. _____

    b. _____

2. Facts

    a. _____

    b. _____

Class _____   Name_____

3. Opinions

    a. _____

    b. _____

4. Feelings

    a. _____

    b. _____

TOPIC: MY CAREER PLANS

1. Clichés

    a. _____

    b. _____

2. Facts

    a._____

    b. _____

3. Opinions

    a. _____

    b. _____

4. Feelings

    a. _____

    b. _____

TOPIC: POLITICS

1. Clichés

    a. _____

    b. _____

Class _____   Name_____

2. Facts

    a. _____

    b. _____

3. Opinions

    a. _____

    b. _____

4. Feelings

    a. _____

    b. _____

TOPIC: SPORTS

1. Clichés

    a. _____

    b. _____

2. Facts

    a. _____

    b. _____

3. Opinions

    a. _____

    b. _____

4. Feelings

    a. _____

    b. _____

2.10 DISCLOSURE AND ALTERNATIVES

LEARNING OBJECTIVES

- Use the social penetration and Johari Window models to identify the nature of self-disclosing communication in one of your relationships.
- Outline the potential benefits and risks of disclosing in a selected situation.
- Assess the most competent mixture of candor and equivocation in a given situation.

INSTRUCTIONS

1. For each situation described below, record responses for the types listed.
2. Evaluate the effectiveness and ethics of your responses.
3. Describe a disclosure situation of your own in the same manner.

EXAMPLE

Your friend asks you if you had a good time when you went out with his cousin last night.
Self-disclosure: *I didn't have a great time, but then we were just getting to know one another. I don't think that we had much in common.*
Silence: *If I don't answer or don't say anything, my friend might think it was worse than I do.*
Lying: *Your cousin was a lot of fun and the movie was great.*
Equivocating: *First dates are really times of discovery, aren't they?*
Hinting: *I don't think I have to have a great time every night.*
Which responses are most effective/which are the most ethical? *I think equivocating is effective. While I wasn't exactly self-disclosing with my friend, I just don't want to tell him how boring I think his cousin is. I haven't lied and both of them can save face, too.*

1. After your romantic partner has a bad week at work, his/her boss asks you how he/she is feeling about the company.

    Self-disclosure _____

    Silence _____

    Lying _____

    Equivocating _____

    Hinting _____

Which responses are most effective/which are the most ethical?_____

_____

_____

2. You are applying to rent an apartment that prohibits animals. You have a cat.

Self-disclosure _____

Silence _____

Lying _____

Equivocating _____

Hinting _____

Which responses are most effective/which are the most ethical?_____

_____

_____

3. Your siblings ask you about your financial status (which is much better than theirs).

Self-disclosure _____

Silence _____

Lying _____

Equivocating _____

Hinting _____

Which responses are most effective/which are the most ethical?_____

_____

_____

4. Your roommates ask what you think of the bright posters they've just put up around the living room.

Self-disclosure _____

Silence _____

Lying _____

Equivocating _____

Hinting _____

Which responses are most effective/which are the most ethical? _____

_____

_____

5. Your romantic partner asks how many other people you've really loved before you met him or her.

Self-disclosure _____

Silence _____

Lying _____

Equivocating _____

Hinting _____

Which responses are most effective/which are the most ethical? _____

_____

_____

6. Your very opinionated father, whose opinions differ from yours, asks what you think of the person running for governor.

Self-disclosure _____

Silence _____

Lying _____

Equivocating _____

Hinting _____

Which responses are most effective/which are the most ethical?_____

_____

_____

7. Your boss wants to know what your plans for the future are; you're looking around.

Self-disclosure _____

Silence _____

Lying _____

Equivocating _____

Hinting _____

Which responses are most effective/which are the most ethical?_____

_____

_____

8. Your mother asks you about what your brother has been up to lately. You know he is probably moving out of state in a few months but he doesn't want your mom to know yet.

Self-disclosure _____

Silence _____

Lying _____

Equivocating _____

Hinting _____

Which responses are most effective/which are the most ethical?_____

_____

_____

9. Your example: _____

Self-disclosure _____

Silence _____

Class _____ Name_____

Lying _____

Equivocating _____

Hinting _____

Which responses are most effective/which are the most ethical? _____

_____

_____

STUDY GUIDE

CHECK YOUR UNDERSTANDING

TRUE/FALSE

Mark the statements below as true or false. Correct statements that are false on the lines below to create a true statement.

_____   1. Collaboration in identity management means absolute agreement about each person's role.

_____

_____   2. Most researchers agree that we are born with a fully formed self-concept.

_____

_____   3. Some studies show that people strongly influenced by media body images develop more negative self-images.

_____

_____   4. Self-fulfilling prophecies can affect job performance.

_____

_____   5. Research has shown that people with high self-esteem seek out partners who view them unfavorably because they are strong enough to take the criticism.

_____

_____   6. Personality is flexible, dynamic, and shaped by experiences.

_____

_____   7. In individualistic societies, there is a higher degree of communication apprehension.

_____

_____   8. The self-concept is such a powerful force that it not only influences how you see yourself in the present but also can actually influence your future behavior and that of others.

_____

_____   9. Research shows that people who believe they are incompetent are more likely than others to pursue rewarding relationships in an attempt to ally themselves with competent people.

_____

_____ 10. High self-monitors feel less intimacy, satisfaction, and commitment in their romantic relationships because they do not hide what they really feel.
_____

_____ 11. Trying on a "new self" can be a means to self-improvement.
_____

_____ 12. Self-esteem has little to do with self-worth evaluations.
_____

COMPLETION

Fill in the blanks below with the correct terms chosen from the list below.

distorted feedback   obsolete information   self-delusion
ego booster   ego buster   realistic expectations
realistic perceptions   manner   self-fulfilling prophecy
appearance

1. _____ is someone who helps enhance your self-esteem by acting in ways that make you feel accepted, important, and loved.

2. _____ is someone who acts to reduce your self-esteem.

3. _____ are messages that others send to you that are unrealistically positive or negative.

4. _____ consists of a communicator's words and nonverbal actions that help create an impression.

5. _____ is information that was once true about you that is no longer true.

6. _____ are the personal items people use to shape an image.

7. _____ is the inability to see a real need for change in the self, due to holding an unrealistically favorable picture of yourself.

8. _____ are reasonable goals to set for self-growth.

9. _____ occurs when expectations of an event influences a person's behavior, which in turn influences the event's outcome.

10. _____ are relatively accurate views of the strengths and weaknesses of the self.

MULTIPLE CHOICE

Identify which principle influences the self-concept in each example.
   a. obsolete information
   b. distorted feedback
   c. emphasis on perfection
   d. social expectations

_____ 1. You always scored more points than anyone else on your team in high school. You still think you're the best even though your college teammates are scoring more than you.

_____ 2. You keep getting down on yourself because you can't cook as well as Megan, even though you are a great student and a fair athlete.

_____ 3. You believe people shouldn't brag or boast, so you tell others that you "blew" the chemistry test and got a "C–" but you never acknowledge your "A's" in math.

_____ 4. Your parents tell you, their friends, and all your relatives about all your wonderful accomplishments, even though you have only average achievements.

_____ 5. Janee says that you are insensitive to her perspective despite your many attempts to listen honestly to her and empathize.

_____ 6. You pay a lot of attention to the magazines showing perfectly dressed and groomed individuals and keep wishing you could look as good as they do.

_____ 7. You think of yourself as the shy fifth grader despite being at the social hub of at least three clubs on campus.

_____ 8. You feel uncomfortable accepting the compliments your friends honestly give you.

_____ 9. You're exhausted by trying to get all A's, work 30 hours a week, and be a loving romantic partner at the same time. You don't see how so many other people manage to get it all done.

_____ 10. "You're the perfect weight," your father tells you, despite your recent gain of 20 pounds over the normal weight for your height.

Choose the *best* answer for each statement below:

11. Deciding which part of your self-concept to reveal to others is termed
   a. prophecy.
   b. impression management.
   c. collectivism.
   d. two-faced syndrome.

12. The most significant part of a person's self-concept
    a. is the social roles the person plays.
    b. is his or her appearance.
    c. is his or her accomplishments.
    d. is different for different people.

13. Self-esteem has to do with evaluations of
    a. self-concept.
    b. self-image.
    c. self-worth.
    d. self-discovery.

14. Which of the following could be an example of a self-fulfilling prophecy?
    a. Sid was born with a very large nose.
    b. Margarita has a very large, extended family.
    c. Serge is a Russian immigrant.
    d. Joy has given up on trying to talk to her unreasonable father.

15. The fact that none of us can see ourselves completely accurately illustrates the _____ nature of the self-concept.
    a. subjective
    b. objective
    c. unrealistic
    d. verification

16. Which of the following statements about gender and self-concept is correct?
    a. Women struggle with self-esteem issues more than men.
    b. Men's sense of superiority tends to decrease over time.
    c. Men tend to have low appraisals of their leadership and athletic abilities.
    d. Women tend to have high appraisals of their leadership and athletic abilities.

17. The influence of significant others
    a. is the sole determinant of our self-concept.
    b. becomes less powerful as people grow older.
    c. is synonymous with the term reflected appraisal.
    d. only occurs in people with poor self-concepts.

18. Computer-mediated communication
    a. makes it impossible to manage identity.
    b. has only disadvantages for impression management.
    c. can be an effective tool for impression management.
    d. always lessens the amount of interpersonal communication.

19. Which is the fourth stage of a self-fulfilling prophecy?
    a. holding an expectation (for yourself or for others)
    b. behaving in accordance with that expectation
    c. the expectation coming to pass
    d. reinforcing the original expectation

20. Communicating ego busters to others would seem to violate which concept of moral rules theory?
    a. nonmaleficence
    b. self-improvement
    c. justice
    d. gratitude

CHAPTER TWO STUDY GUIDE ANSWERS

TRUE/FALSE

1.	F	5.	F	9.	F
2.	T	6.	T	10.	F
3.	T	7.	F	11.	T
4.	T	8.	T	12.	F

COMPLETION

1.	ego booster	5.	obsolete information	9.	self-fulfilling prophecy
2.	ego buster	6.	appearance	10.	realistic perceptions
3.	distorted feedback	7.	self-delusion		
4.	manner	8.	realistic expectations		

MULTIPLE CHOICE

1.	a	5.	b	9.	c	13.	c	17.	b
2.	c	6.	c	10.	b	14.	d	18.	c
3.	d	7.	a	11.	b	15.	a	19.	d
4	b	8.	d	12.	d	16.	a	20.	a

Perception:
What You See Is What You Get

After studying the topics in this chapter, you should be able to:

1. Describe how the processes of selection, organization, interpretation, and negotiation shape communication in a given situation.

2. Explain how the influences on perception listed on pages 86–93 affect communication in a specific situation.

3. Analyze how common perception tendencies described on pages 94–96 have distorted your appraisals of another person, and hence your communication. Use this information to present a more accurate alternative set of perceptions.

4. Demonstrate how you might use the skill of perception checking in a significant relationship.

5. Enhance your cognitive complexity by applying the "pillow method" in a significant disagreement. Explain how your expanded view of this situation might affect your communication with the other(s) involved.

Study M. C. Escher's drawing *Relativity* on this page. It pictures a strange universe in which the inhabitants of each world exist at right angles, disconnected from one another's experience. This surreal vision provides a useful metaphor for challenges we encounter every day. Each of us experiences a different reality, and failing to understand other people's point of view can lead to problems on both practical and relational levels. But perceptual differences can enhance as well as interfere with relationships. By seeing the world through others' eyes, you can gain insights that are different—and often more valuable—than those arising out of your own experiences.

This chapter will help you deal with the challenge of communicating in the face of perceptual differences. We will begin by looking at some of the reasons why the world appears different to each of us. In our survey we'll explore several areas: how our psychological makeup, personal needs, interests, and biases shape our perceptions; the physiological factors that influence our view of the world; the social roles that affect our image of events; and the role that culture plays in creating our ideas of what behavior is proper. After examining the perceptual factors that can drive us apart, we'll look at two useful skills for bridging the perceptual gap.

The Perception Process

Our perception of the world around us is affected by who we are. A simple walk in the park would probably be a different experience for companions with different interests. A botanist might notice the vegetation; a fashion designer might pay attention to the way people are dressed; and an artist might be aware of the colors and forms of the people and surroundings. It's simply impossible to be aware of everything, no matter how attentive we might be. There's just too much going on. Because this ability to organize our perceptions is such a critical factor in our ability to function, we need to begin our study of perception by taking a closer look at this process. We can do so by examining the four steps by which we attach meaning to our experiences: selection, organization, interpretation, and negotiation.

SELECTION

Since we're exposed to more input than we can possibly manage, the first step in perception is the **selection** of which impressions we will attend to. Several factors cause us to notice some things and ignore others.

Stimuli that are *intense* often attract our attention. Something that is louder, larger, or brighter stands out. This explains why—other things being equal—we're more likely to remember extremely tall or short people, and why someone who laughs or talks loudly at a party attracts more attention (not always favorable) than do quiet guests.

Repetitious stimuli, repetitious stimuli, repetitious stimuli, repetitious stimuli, repetitious stimuli, repetitious stimuli also attract attention.[1] Just as a quiet but steadily dripping faucet can come to dominate our awareness, people to whom we're frequently exposed become noticeable.

ATTENTION IS ALSO FREQUENTLY RELATED TO contrast OR change IN STIMULATION. Put differently, unchanging people or things become less noticeable. This principle gives an explanation (excuse?) for why we take wonderful people for granted when we interact with them frequently. It's only when they stop being so wonderful or go away that we appreciate them.

Motives also determine what information we select from our environment. If you're anxious about being late for a date, you'll notice whatever clocks may be around you; and if you're hungry, you'll become aware of any restaurants, markets, and billboards advertising food in your path. Motives also determine how we perceive people. For example, someone on the lookout for a romantic adventure will be especially aware of attractive potential partners, whereas the same person at a different time might be oblivious to anyone but police or medical personnel in an emergency.

Selection isn't just a matter of attending to some stimuli: It also involves ignoring other cues. If, for example, you decide that someone is a terrific person, you may overlook his or her flaws. If you are focused on examples of unfair male bosses, you might not recognize unfair female bosses. For an interesting example of how we select some stimuli and ignore others, enter "perception illusion" in your web browser and look for videos related to the work of researcher Daniel Simons.[2]

ORGANIZATION

Along with selecting information from the environment, we must arrange it in some meaningful way. You can see how the principle of **organization** works by looking at Figure 3.1. You can view the picture either as one of a vase or as one of two twins, depending on whether you focus on the light or the dark areas. In instances such as this, we make sense of stimuli by noticing some data that stand out as a *figure* against a less striking *ground*. The "vase-face" drawing is interesting, because it allows us to choose between two sets of figure-ground relationships.

This principle of figure-ground organization operates in communication, too. Recall, for instance, how certain speech can suddenly stand out from a

FIGURE 3.1 © Cengage Learning

babble of voices. Sometimes the words are noticeable because they include your name, whereas at other times they might be spoken by a familiar voice.

Each of us can organize our impressions of other communicators using a number of schemes (called *perceptual schema* by social scientists). Sometimes we classify people according to their *appearance*: male or female, beautiful or ugly, heavy or thin, young or old, and so on. At other times we classify people according to their *social roles*: student, attorney, wife, etc. Another way we classify people is by their *interaction style*: friendly, helpful, aloof, and sarcastic are examples. In other cases we classify people by their *psychological traits* such as curious, nervous, and insecure. Finally, we can use others' *membership*, classifying them according to the group to which they belong: Democrat, immigrant, Christian, and so on.

The perceptual schemas we use shape the way we think about and communicate with others. If you've classified a professor, for example, as "friendly," you'll handle questions or problems one way; if you've classified a professor as "mean," your behavior will probably be quite different. What constructs do you use to classify the people you encounter in your life? Consider how your relationship might change if you used different schemas.

PAUSE AND REFLECT

YOUR PERCEPTUAL SCHEMA

1. Identify the perceptual schema described in this section that you would use to classify people in each of the following contexts:
   a. Spending time with new acquaintances at a party
   b. Socializing with fellow workers on the job
   c. Choosing teammates for an important class project
   d. Offering help to a stranded motorist
   Describe both the general type of organizing scheme (e.g., "physical," "membership") and the specific category within each type (e.g., "attractive," "roughly the same age as me").

2. Consider:
   a. Other schema you might use in each context.
   b. The different consequences of using the schema you originally chose and the alternative you identified in the preceding step.
   c. How your relationships might change if you used different constructs.

 You can complete this activity by visiting CengageBrain.com to access the Speech Communication CourseMate for *Looking Out/ Looking In*, and, if requested, email your responses to your instructor.

Stereotyping After we've chosen an organizing scheme to classify people, we use that scheme to make generalizations and predictions about members of the groups who fit the categories we use. For example, if you're especially aware of gender, you might be alert to the differences between the way men and women behave or the way they are treated. If religion plays an important part in your life, you might think of members of your faith differently from others. If ethnicity is an important issue for you, you probably tune in to the differences between members of various ethnic groups. There's nothing wrong with generalizations as long as they are accurate. In fact, it would be impossible to get through life without them.

But when generalizations lose touch with reality, they lead to **stereotyping**—exaggerated generalizations associated with a categorizing system.[3] Stereotypes may be based on a kernel of truth, but they go beyond the facts at hand and make claims that usually have no valid basis.

You can begin to get a sense of your tendency to make generalizations and to stereotype by completing the following sentences:

1. Women are _____

2. Men are _____

3. Republicans are _____

4. Vegetarians are _____

5. Muslims are _____

6. Older people are _____

It's likely that you were able to complete each sentence without much hesitation. Does this mean you were stereotyping? You can answer this question by deciding whether your generalizations fit the three characteristics of stereotypes (we'll use "older people" as an example):

- *You often categorize people on the basis of an easily recognized characteristic.* Age is relatively simple to identify, so if you see someone who appears to be in her eighties, you might quickly categorize her as "elderly."
- *You ascribe a set of characteristics to most or all members of a category.* Based on your (limited) experiences with some elderly relatives, you conclude that older people have trouble hearing and are not mentally alert.

Characters in the TV series *Glee* seem to fit typical high school stereotypes. But fans of the show know that those characters can sometimes behave in ways that defy stereotypical categories. This reminds us that while generalizations may offer useful shortcuts, they can also limit our ability to perceive people accurately.

- *You apply the set of characteristics to any member of the group.* When you run into an elderly person at the store, you talk very loudly and slowly. Of course, that can be extremely annoying to energetic and sprightly older people who do not fit your stereotype.

Once we buy into stereotypes, we often seek out isolated behaviors that support our inaccurate beliefs. For example, men and women in conflict often remember only behaviors of the other sex that fit their gender stereotypes.[4] They then point to these behaviors—which might not be representative of how the other person typically behaves—as "evidence" to suit their stereotypical and inaccurate claims: "Look! There you go criticizing me again. Typical for a woman!"

Stereotypes can plague interracial communication.[5] Surveys of college student attitudes show that many blacks characterize whites as "demanding" and "manipulative," whereas many whites characterize blacks as "loud" and "ostentatious." Stereotypes like these can hamper professional relationships as well as personal ones. For example, doctor–patient communication in the United States—particularly between white physicians and minority patients—can suffer from stereotyping on both sides. Physicians may fail to provide important information because they think their patients

THE INVESTIGATION

HE WAS A REAL TALL GUY DRESSED NORMALLY, WITH LIGHT, DRY HAIR.

HE WAS A HEALTHY, GOOD LOOKING YOUNG KID... BUT DRESSED RATHER SHABBILY.

HE WAS REAL BIG AND REAL OLD.

HE WAS A WELL-DRESSED SORT, A LITTLE OVERWEIGHT AND WITH A LOT OF HAIR.

I REMEMBER HE HAD A LARGE HEAD AND HE SMELLED FUNNY.

HE WAS SURELY A WESTERNER.

HE WAS A SCRAWNY LITTLE SHORT-HAIRED TWERP FROM BACK EAST.

HE HAD DARK HAIR AND A CUTE NOSE. A REAL DOLL.

HE WAS A ROUGH, FURRY GUY WITH LITTLE BEADY EYES. PROBABLY INEDIBLE.

JONIK

John Jonik

SELF-ASSESSMENT

Exploring Your Biases

You can explore your hidden biases toward race, gender, age, disability, and other issues, by taking a series of self-tests online. You can find the link to these tests by visiting CengageBrain .com to access the Speech Communication CourseMate for *Looking Out/Looking In.*

won't understand, and patients may not ask important questions because they believe their doctors don't have time for them. These kinds of expectations lead to self-fulfilling spirals and poorer health care.[6]

Stereotyping doesn't always arise from bad intentions. In some cases, careless generalizations can grow from good intentions, and even from a little bit of knowledge. For example, knowing that people raised in collectivistic cultures (see page 47 in Chapter 2) tend to conform to group norms may lead you to mistakenly assume that anyone you meet from such a background is likely to be a selfless team player. But not all members of a group are equally collectivistic, or individualistic, for that matter. For example, a study of Americans of European and Latin descent showed differences within each group.[7] Some Latinos were more independent than some Euro Americans, and vice versa. Moreover, teens in Japan (a traditionally collectivist culture) say they often feel torn between individualism and collectivism, between time-honored traditions and contemporary trends.[8] As our world's "global village" becomes more connected by technology and media, generalizations about specific cultures are likely to become less accurate.

One way to avoid the kinds of communication problems that come from excessive stereotyping is to decategorize others, giving yourself a chance to treat them as individuals instead of assuming that they possess the same characteristics as every other member of the group to which you assign them. Consider how your communication with others might change if you moved some of their characteristics to the "background" and others to the "foreground" during your interactions.

Punctuation The process of organizing goes beyond our generalized perceptions of people. We also can sequence our interactions with others in different ways, and this can have a powerful effect on our relationships with others. Communication theorists use the term **punctuation** to describe the determination of causes and effects in a series of interactions.[9] You can begin to understand how punctuation operates by visualizing a running quarrel between a husband and wife. The husband accuses the wife of being too demanding, whereas she complains that he is withdrawing from her. Notice that the order in which each partner punctuates this cycle affects how the quarrel looks. The husband begins by blaming the wife: "I withdraw because you're so demanding." The wife organizes the situation differently, starting with the husband:

Punctuation #1

Demanding ⟶ Withdrawing ⟶ Demanding ⟶ Withdrawing

Punctuation #2

Withdrawing ⟶ Demanding ⟶ Withdrawing ⟶ Demanding

FIGURE 3.2 The Same Event Can Be Punctuated in More Than One Way © Cengage Learning

"I demand so much because you withdraw." These kinds of demand-withdraw arguments are frequent in intimate relationships.[10] After the cycle gets rolling, it is impossible to say which accusation is accurate. The answer depends on how the sentence is punctuated. Figure 3.2 illustrates how this process operates.

Differing punctuations can lead to a variety of communication problems. Notice how the following situations seem different depending on how they're punctuated:

"I don't like your friend because he never has anything to say."

"He doesn't talk to you because you act like you don't like him."

"I keep talking because you interrupt so much."

"I interrupt because you don't give me a chance to say what's on my mind."

The kind of finger-pointing that goes along with arguing over which punctuation scheme is correct will probably make matters worse. It's far more productive to recognize that a dispute can look different to each party and then move on to the more important question of "What can we do to make things better?"

SKILL BUILDER

PUNCTUATION PRACTICE

You can appreciate how different punctuation patterns can influence attitudes and behavior by following these directions.

1. Use the format pictured in Figure 3.2 to diagram the following situations:
   a. A father and daughter are growing more and more distant. The daughter withdraws because she interprets her father's coolness as rejection. The father views his daughter's aloofness as a rebuff and withdraws further.
   b. The relationship between two friends is becoming strained. One jokes to lighten up the tension, and the other becomes more tense.
   c. A dating couple is on the verge of breaking up. One partner frequently asks the other to show more affection. The other withdraws physical contact.
2. Identify two punctuating schemes for each of the situations described in step 1. Consider how the differing schemes would affect the way the two people in each situation respond to one another.

Now identify a difficult communication issue in your own life. Punctuate it in two ways: how you would punctuate it and how the other person might punctuate it. Discuss how seeing the issue from the other person's point of view might change the way you communicate as you discuss the issue.

 You can complete this activity by visiting CengageBrain.com to access the Speech Communication CourseMate for *Looking Out/ Looking In*, and, if requested, email your responses to your instructor.

INTERPRETATION

After we have selected and organized our perceptions, we interpret the information we've collected and sorted. **Interpretation**—attaching meaning to sense data—plays a role in virtually every interpersonal act. Is the person who smiles at you across a crowded room interested in romance or simply being polite? Is a friend's kidding a sign of affection or irritation? Should you take an invitation to "drop by any time" literally or not?

Several factors cause us to interpret an event in one way or another:

Degree of involvement with the other person. Two coworkers offer you the same excuse for why they were late to work. One is a close friend; the other is someone you barely know. Chances are good you'll interpret your friend's excuse far more charitably.

Personal experience. What meaning have similar events held? If, for example, you've been gouged by landlords in the past, you might be skeptical about an apartment manager's assurances that careful housekeeping will assure you the refund of your cleaning deposit.

Assumptions about human behavior. "People generally do as little work as possible to get by." "In spite of their mistakes, people are doing the best they can." Beliefs like these will shape the way we interpret another's actions.

Attitudes. The attitudes we hold shape the way we make sense of others' behaviors. For example, what would you think if you overheard one man say "I love you" to another? In one study, people with a high degree of homophobia (the fear of or discrimination against homosexuals) were likely to interpret this comment as an indication that the speaker was gay. Those with lower levels of homophobia were more likely to regard the affectionate statement as platonic rather than romantic.[11]

Expectations. Anticipation shapes interpretations.[12] As you read in Chapter 2, teachers who expect their students to do well will regard and treat those pupils differently. The same is true with our interpersonal interactions: Our expectations affect how we perceive and behave around others. We'll talk more about this common tendency later in the chapter.

Knowledge. If you know that a friend has just been jilted by a lover or been fired from a job, you'll interpret his aloof behavior differently than you would if you were unaware of what had happened. If you know that an instructor speaks sarcastically to all students, you won't be as likely to take her remarks personally.

Self-concept. When you're feeling insecure, the world is a very different place from the world you experience when you're feeling secure. For example, the recipient's self-concept is the most significant factor in determining whether people who are being teased interpret the teaser's motives as being friendly or hostile, and whether they respond with comfort or defensiveness.[13] The way we feel about ourselves strongly influences how we interpret others' behavior.

Relational satisfaction. The behavior that seems positive when you are happy with a partner might seem completely different when you are discontent with that person. For example, unsatisfied partners in a couple are more likely than satisfied partners to blame one another when things go wrong.[14] They are also more likely to believe that their partners are selfish and have negative intentions.

Although we have talked about selection, organization, and interpretation separately, the three phases of perception can occur in differing sequences. For example, a parent or babysitter's past interpretations (such as "Jason is a troublemaker") can influence future selections (his behavior becomes especially noticeable) and the organization of events (when there's a fight, the assumption is that Jason started it). As with all communication, perception is an ongoing process in which it is difficult to pin down beginnings and endings.

NEGOTIATION

So far our discussion has focused on the components of perception—selection, organization, and interpretation—that take place in each individual's mind. But perception isn't just a solitary activity: A big part of sense-making occurs between and among people as they influence one another's perceptions and try to achieve a shared perspective. This process is known as **negotiation**.

One way to understand how negotiation operates is to view interpersonal communication as an exchange of stories. Scholars call the stories we use to describe our personal world **narratives**.[15] Virtually every interpersonal situation can be described by more than one narrative. These narratives often differ. Ask two quarreling children why they're fighting, and they'll each describe how the other person is responsible for launching the conflict. Likewise, courtrooms are filled with opponents who tell very different narratives about who is the "villain" and who is the "hero." Even happy families have stories that place members in particular roles. (Think of the roles in some families you know: "scatterbrain," "the smart one," "athlete," and so on.) In best-case scenarios, family storytelling can actually enhance perspective-taking and lead to family satisfaction and functioning.[16]

When our narratives clash with those of others, we can either hang on to our own point of view and refuse to consider anyone else's (usually not productive), or we can try to negotiate a narrative that creates at least some common ground. Shared narratives provide the best chance for smooth communication. For example, romantic partners who celebrate their successful struggles against relational obstacles are happier than those who don't have this shared

Sidney Kimmel Entertainment/The Kobal Collection

The film *Lars and the Real Girl* offers a unique example of how shared narratives can bring people together. (See the film summary at the end of this chapter.)

appreciation.[17] Likewise, couples that agree about the important turning points in their relationships are more satisfied than those who have different views of what incidents were most important.[18]

Shared narratives don't have to be accurate to be powerful. Couples who report being happily married after fifty or more years seem to collude in a relational narrative that doesn't jibe with the facts.[19] They agree that they rarely have conflict, although objective analysis reveals that they have had their share of struggles. Without overtly agreeing to do so, they choose to blame outside forces or unusual circumstances for problems instead of blaming each other. They offer the most charitable interpretations of each other's behavior, believing that their spouse acts with good intentions when things don't go well. They seem willing to forgive, or even forget, transgressions. Communication researcher Judy Pearson evaluates these findings:

> Should we conclude that happy couples have a poor grip on reality? Perhaps they do, but is the reality of one's marriage better known by outside onlookers than by the players themselves? The conclusion is evident. One key to a long happy marriage is to tell yourself and others that you have one and then to behave as though you do!*

---

*Pearson, J. C. (1996). Positive distortion: "The most beautiful woman in the world." In K. M. Galvin & P. Cooper (Eds.), *Making connections: Readings in interpersonal communication* (p. 177). Beverly Hills, CA: Roxbury.

Influences on Perception

Now that we've explored the processes by which we perceive, it's time to look at some of the influences that cause us to select, organize, interpret, and negotiate information.

ACCESS TO INFORMATION

We can only make sense of what we know, and none of us knows everything about even the closest people in our lives. When new information becomes available, your perceptions of others change. If you see your instructor only when she's teaching in the classroom, your conclusions about her will be based solely on her behaviors in that role. You might change your perception if you observe her in the roles of rush-hour driver, concert-goer, or grocery shopper. (Many of us have memories of running into our grade school teachers at the store and being shocked that they had lives outside of school.)

We often gain access to new information about others when their roles overlap. Consider how that might occur at an office party. A person's "office" and "party" roles are usually quite different—so at an offsite work celebration, you may see behaviors you hadn't expected. Similarly, when your sweetheart takes you home to meet the family, you might get to watch your partner playing "spoiled son" or "princess daughter" roles. If you've ever said, "I saw a whole new side of you tonight," chances are good it's because you gained access to information you didn't have before.

Social media can provide new information that can affect perceptions. That's why job hunters are encouraged to clean up their Internet profiles, being careful to manage the impressions they might make. It's also why children and parents don't always want to be Facebook friends with each other (see the reading on the next page). Some roles are best kept private—or at least played to a select audience.

PHYSIOLOGICAL INFLUENCES

Another set of influences we need to examine involves our physical makeup. Within the wide range of human similarities, each of us perceives the world in a unique way because of physiological factors. In other words, although the same events exist "out there," each of us receives different images because of our unique perceptual hardware. Consider the long list of physiological factors that shapes our views of the world: the senses, age, health and fatigue, hunger, biological cycles, and psychological challenges.

The Senses The differences in how each of us sees, hears, tastes, touches, and smells stimuli can affect interpersonal relationships. Consider the following everyday situations:

> "Turn down that radio! It's going to make me go deaf."
> "It's not too loud. If I turn it down, it will be impossible to hear it."

> "It's freezing in here."
> "Are you kidding? We'll suffocate if you turn up the heat!"

> "Why don't you pass that truck? The highway is clear for a mile."
> "I can't see that far, and I'm not going to get us killed."

Parents as Facebook Friends: Too Much Information?

It's become an increasingly familiar cry among teens and young adults: "(NUTS)!—my parents are on Facebook!"

As the world's biggest social-networking site continues to grow, parents are joining—and invariably asking the kids to include them in their circle of online friends. Many young people are horrified at the idea of parents seeing their posts. "I don't want my mom asking me about everything I say on Facebook," said 15-year-old Evie Petersen, who is ignoring her mother's most recent friend request.

A survey by Kaplan Test Prep on social networking trends found that more than a third of teens whose parents are on Facebook have not agreed to friend them. Of this group, nearly 40 percent had simply ignored their parent's request, leaving them in Facebook limbo. The decision to friend a parent isn't always voluntary: Sixteen percent of those who did so reported that it was a condition of parental approval for starting a Facebook page.

When they tell parents their Facebook pages are off-limits, teens are drawing a line in the sand and asserting their independence, said Kristen Campbell, executive director of Kaplan's college prep programs. "They want to control their personal and private lives," she said. "It's something that parents should not take personally."

But that's not easy to do, said Gretta Petersen, mother of Evie, a high school sophomore who has friended her twice—only to unfriend her later. "I think at some level you can't help but take it personally," Petersen said. "It's kind of like, what don't you want me to know about you? You start making assumptions. But, on the other hand, they are at the point in their lives where they are starting to assert their independence."

Although her daughter has shut her out, Petersen has other options: she's been friended on Facebook by some of Evie's friends—including her best friend, Mary Taylor—which allows her an occasional glimpse into their lives. On Facebook, posts sometimes can be viewed second-hand.

Younger teens are more hesitant than older teens or young adults to friend parents, said Tamyra Pierce, associate professor of mass communication and journalism at California State University, Fresno. "Young people are in the stage of developing their identity and may not want their parents to see everything they do," she said. It's

Masterfile

a place where teens feel free to express themselves, Pierce said. Girls may be more sexually explicit than they otherwise would be, and boys might use foul language or talk about drinking, Pierce said, so "it's not cool if your parents are on there." As children mature, Pierce said, they become more accepting of their parents and less likely to see them as an embarrassment.

Experts say parents should be respectful of their child's personal space and resist the urge to comment or otherwise intrude on their Facebook page. Butting in on a teen's Facebook page, Pierce said, is "just like if they were talking on the phone to a friend and you got on the phone and said, 'Hey, I want to talk too.'"

Tracy Correa

Fresno Bee on January 25, 2011; http://www.fresnobee.com/2011/01/24/2245635/parents-facing-an-unfriendly-world.html. Reprinted with permission.

These disputes aren't just over matters of opinion. The sensory data we receive are different. Differences in vision and hearing are the easiest to recognize, but other differences exist as well. There is evidence that identical foods taste differently to different individuals.[20] Scents that please some people repel others. Likewise, temperature variations that leave some of us uncomfortable are inconsequential to others. Recognizing these differences won't eliminate them, but it will make it easier to remember that the other person's preferences aren't crazy, just different.

Psychological Challenges Some differences in perception are rooted in neurology. For instance, people with AD/HD (attention-deficit/hyperactivity disorder) are easily distracted from tasks and have difficulty delaying gratification. It's easy to imagine how those with AD/HD might find a long lecture boring and tedious, while other audience members are fascinated by the same lecture. People with bipolar disorder experience significant mood swings in which their perceptions of events, friends, and even family members shift dramatically. The National Institute of Mental Health estimates that between five and seven million Americans are affected by these two disorders alone—and many other psychological conditions influence people's perceptions.[21] It's important to remember that when others see and respond to the world differently than we do, there may be causes beyond what we immediately recognize.

Age We experience the world differently throughout our lifetimes. Besides the obvious physical changes, age also alters perspective. Consider, for instance, how you've viewed your parents through the years. When you were a child, you probably thought they were all-knowing and flawless. As a teen, you may have viewed them as old-fashioned and mean. In adulthood, most people begin to regard their parents as knowledgeable and perhaps even wise.

Health and Fatigue Recall the last time you came down with a cold, flu, or some other ailment. Do you remember how different you felt? You probably had much less energy. It's likely that you felt less sociable and that your thinking was slower than usual. These kinds of changes have a strong impact on how you relate to others. It's good to realize that someone else may be behaving differently because of illness. In the same way, it's important to let others know when you feel ill so that they can give you the understanding you need.

Just as being ill can affect your relationships, so can being overly tired. Trying to deal with important issues at such a time can get you into trouble. One study found that when married couples don't sleep well, they have more negative perceptions of each other the following day, leading to more interpersonal discord.[22]

Hunger People often get grumpy when they haven't eaten and get sleepy after stuffing themselves. Research confirms that lack of nutrition affects how we interact with others.

In one study, teenagers who reported that their family did not get enough food to eat were almost three times as likely to have been suspended from school, almost twice as likely to have difficulty getting along with others, and four times as likely to have no friends.[23]

Biological Cycles Are you a "morning person" or a "night person"? Most of us can answer this question easily, and there's a good physiological reason behind our response. Each of us is in a daily cycle in which all sorts of changes constantly occur, including body temperature, sexual drive, alertness, tolerance to stress, and mood.[24] Most of these changes are caused by hormonal cycles. For instance, adrenal hormones, which affect feelings of stress, are secreted at higher rates during some hours. In the same manner, the male and female sex hormones enter our systems at variable rates. We often aren't conscious of these changes, but they surely influence the way we relate to one another. After we're aware that our own daily cycles and those of others govern our feelings and behavior, it becomes possible to manage our lives so that we deal with important issues at the most effective times.

CULTURAL DIFFERENCES

So far you have seen how physical factors can make the world a different place for each of us. But there's another kind of perceptual gap that often blocks communication—the gap between people from different backgrounds. Every culture has its own worldview, its own way of looking at the world. At times it's easy to forget that people everywhere don't see things the way we do.

LOOKING AT DIVERSITY

Christa Kilvington: Socioeconomic Stereotyping

Courtesy of Christa Kilvington

What comes to mind when you hear the description "4.0 college student"? How about when you hear "welfare mom"? Most likely you get two very different mental pictures. Perhaps you imagine those kinds of people as complete opposites. And yet, I am both: A college student with straight-A grades who is also a single mother on public assistance. To some people, the combination doesn't fit. They figure that anyone smart enough to earn a 4.0 GPA shouldn't have ended up on welfare, or that anybody on welfare is probably too dumb and lazy to be in college and have straight-A grades.

The stereotypes people use to classify me shape the way they communicate. Most people who only know me from school and have no idea of my economic situation think of me as intelligent and ambitious—an academic standout. They speak to me formally and respectfully. Those who know me only by my income level—caseworkers, healthcare workers, grocery store clerks—tend to communicate with me in quite a different way. When I go to the welfare office, present my Medicaid card for a prescription, or pay for groceries with food stamps I am often treated as unintelligent, lazy, and dishonest. People speak to me in condescending and disrespectful tones.

Why do some people equate income level with intelligence? Why do they treat me and others differently based on our economic status? Why is it all right to treat people disrespectfully just because they are poor? Stereotypes exist for a reason, but it's important to go beyond them to find out each person's unique story. When you leave your mind open to the possibility that there is more to a person than meets the eye, that is when you grow as a person yourself.

"Socioeconomic Stereotyping" by Christa Kilvington. Used with permission of author.

The range of cultural differences is wide. In Middle Eastern countries, personal scents play an important role in interpersonal relationships. Arabs consistently breathe on people when they talk. As anthropologist Edward Hall explains:

> To smell one's friend is not only nice, but desirable, for to deny him your breath is to act ashamed. Americans, on the other hand, trained as they are not to breathe in people's faces, automatically communicate shame in trying to be polite. Who would expect that when our highest diplomats are putting on their best manners they are also communicating shame? Yet this is what occurs constantly, because diplomacy is not only "eyeball to eyeball" but breath to breath.*

Even beliefs about the very value of talk differ from one culture to another.[25] Western cultures view talk as desirable and use it for social purposes as well as for task performance. Silence has a negative value in these cultures. It is likely to be interpreted as lack of interest, unwillingness to communicate, hostility, anxiety, shyness, or a sign of interpersonal incompatibility. Westerners are uncomfortable with silence, which they find embarrassing and awkward.

On the other hand, Asian cultures perceive talk differently. For thousands of years, Asian cultures have discouraged the expression of thoughts and feelings. Silence is valued, as Taoist sayings indicate: "In much talk there is great weariness," or "One who speaks does not know; one who knows does not speak." Unlike most North Americans, who are uncomfortable with silence, Japanese and Chinese believe that remaining quiet is the proper state when there is nothing to be said. In Asian cultures, a talkative person is often considered a show-off or insincere.

It's easy to see how these different views of speech and silence can lead to communication problems when people from different cultures meet. Both the talkative American and the silent Asian are behaving in ways they believe are proper, yet each views the other with disapproval and mistrust. This may require them to recognize and deal with their **ethnocentrism**—the attitude that one's own culture is superior to others. An ethnocentric person thinks—either privately or openly—that anyone who does not belong to his or her in-group is somehow strange, wrong, or even inferior. Travel writer Rick Steves describes how an ethnocentric point of view can interfere with respect for other cultural practices:

> . . . we [Americans] consider ourselves very clean and commonly criticize other cultures as dirty. In the bathtub we soak, clean, and rinse, all in the same water. (We would never wash our dishes that way.) A Japanese visitor, who uses clean water for each step, might find our way of bathing strange or even disgusting. Many cultures spit in public and blow their nose right onto the street. They couldn't imagine doing that into a small cloth, called a hanky, and storing that in their pocket to be used again and again. Too often we think of the world in terms of a pyramid of "civilized" (us) on the top and "primitive" groups on the bottom. If we measured things differently (maybe according to stress, loneliness, heart attacks, hours spent in traffic jams, or family togetherness) things stack up differently.†

It isn't necessary to travel overseas to encounter differing cultural perspectives. Within this country there are many subcultures, and the members of each one have backgrounds that cause them to see things in different ways. Failure to recognize these differences can lead to unfortunate and unnecessary misunderstandings. For example, an uninformed Anglo teacher or police officer might interpret a lack of eye contact by a Latina as a sign of avoidance, or even dishonesty, when in fact this is the proper behavior in her culture for a female being addressed by an older man. To make direct eye contact in such a case would be considered undue brashness or even a sexual come-on.

---

*Hall, E. T. (1969). *The hidden dimension* (p. 160). New York, NY: Doubleday Anchor.
†Steves, R. (1996, May–September). Culture shock. Rick Steves (www.ricksteves.com).

It's encouraging to know that open-minded communicators can overcome preexisting stereotypes and learn to appreciate people from different backgrounds as individuals. In one study, college students who were introduced to strangers from different cultural backgrounds developed attitudes about their new conversational partners based more on their personal behavior than on preexisting expectations about how people from those backgrounds might behave.[26]

SOCIAL ROLES

From the time we're born, each of us is indirectly taught a whole set of roles that we'll be expected to play. In one sense this set of prescribed parts is necessary, because it enables a society to function smoothly and provides the security that comes from knowing what's expected of you. But in another sense, having roles defined in advance can lead to wide gaps in understanding. When roles become unquestioned and rigid, people tend to see the world from their own viewpoint, having no experiences that show them how other people see it. Let's look at how social roles affect our perception and communication.

Gender Roles Although people use the terms *sex* and *gender* as if they were identical, there is an important difference. *Sex* refers to biological characteristics of a male or female, whereas *gender* refers to the social and psychological dimensions of masculine and feminine behavior. A large body of research shows that males and females do perceive the world differently, for reasons ranging from genes to neurology to hormones.[27] However, even cognitive researchers who focus on biological differences between males and females acknowledge that societal gender roles and stereotypes affect perception dramatically.[28]

Gender roles are socially approved ways that men and women are expected to behave. Children learn the importance of gender roles by watching other people and by being exposed to media, as well as by receiving reinforcement.[29] After members of a society learn these customary roles, they tend to regard violations as unusual—or even undesirable.

Some theorists have suggested that stereotypical masculine and feminine behaviors are not opposite poles of a single continuum, but rather two separate sets of behavior.[30] With this view, an individual can act in a masculine manner or a feminine manner or exhibit both types of characteristics. The male–female dichotomy, then, is replaced with four psychological sex types: masculine, feminine, **androgynous** (combining masculine and feminine traits), and undifferentiated (neither masculine nor feminine). Combining the four psychological sex types with the traditional physiological sex types produces the eight categories listed in Table 3.1.

Each of these eight psychological sex types perceives interpersonal relationships differently. For example, masculine males may be likely to see their interpersonal relationships as opportunities for competitive interaction, as opportunities to win something.

TABLE 3.1 GENDER ROLES

	MALE	FEMALE
Masculine	Masculine males	Masculine females
Feminine	Feminine males	Feminine females
Androgynous	Androgynous males	Androgynous females
Undifferentiated	Undifferentiated males	Undifferentiated females

© Cengage Learning

Feminine females often see their interpersonal relationships as opportunities to be nurturing, to express their feelings and emotions. Androgynous males and females, on the other hand, differ little in their perceptions of their interpersonal relationships.

In the television show *Undercover Boss*, high-ranking company officials in disguise take on the duties of lower-level employees in their organizations. The bosses usually gain a new appreciation for the challenges faced by their employees, both on the job and in their personal lives. (See the TV summary at the end of this chapter.)

Occupational Roles The kind of work we do often influences our view of the world. Imagine five people taking a walk through the park. One, a botanist, is fascinated by the variety of trees and other plants. Another, a zoologist, is looking for interesting animals. The third, a meteorologist, keeps an eye on the sky, noticing changes in the weather. The fourth companion, a psychologist, is totally unaware of nature, instead concentrating on the interaction among the people in the park. The fifth person, being a pickpocket, quickly takes advantage of the others' absorption to make some money. There are two lessons in this little scenario. The first, of course, is to watch your wallet carefully. The second is that our occupational roles shape our perceptions.

Even within the same occupational setting, the different roles that participants have can affect their perceptions. Consider a typical college classroom, for example. The experiences of the instructor and students often are dissimilar. Having dedicated a large part of their lives to their work, most instructors see their subject matter—whether French literature, physics, or communication—as vitally important. Students who are taking the course to satisfy a general education requirement may view the subject differently: maybe as one of many obstacles that stand between them and a degree, or perhaps as a chance to meet new people. Another difference centers on the amount of knowledge possessed by the parties. To an instructor who has taught the course many times, the material probably seems extremely simple, but to students encountering it for the first time, it may seem strange and confusing. We don't need to spell out the interpersonal strains and stresses that come from such differing perceptions.

Relational Roles Think back to the "Who am I?" list you made in Chapter 2 (page 38). It's likely your list included roles you play in relation to others: daughter, roommate, husband, friend, and so on. Roles like these don't just define who you are—they also affect your perception.

Take, for example, the role of parent. As most new mothers and fathers will attest, having a child alters the way they see the world. They might perceive their crying baby as a helpless soul in need of comfort, while nearby strangers have a less charitable appraisal. As the child grows, parents often pay more attention to the messages in the child's environment. One father we know said he never noticed how much football fans curse and swear until he took his six-year-old to a game with him. In other words, his role as father affected what he heard and how he interpreted it.

The roles involved in romantic love can also dramatically affect perception. These roles have many labels: partner, spouse, boyfriend/girlfriend, sweetheart, and so on. There are times when your affinity biases the way you perceive the object of your affection. You may see your sweetheart as more attractive than other people do, and perhaps you overlook some faults that others notice.[31] Your romantic role can also change the way you view others. One study found that when people are in love, they view other romantic candidates as less attractive than they normally would.[32]

CBS/Photofest

PAUSE AND REFLECT

ROLE REVERSAL

Walk a mile in another person's shoes. Find a group that is foreign to you, and try to become a member of it for a while.

1. If you're down on the police, see if your local department has a ride-along program where you can spend several hours on patrol with one or two officers.
2. If you think the present state of education is a mess, become a teacher yourself. Maybe an instructor will give you the chance to plan one or more classes.
3. If you're a political conservative, try getting involved in a liberal organization; if you're a liberal, check out the conservatives.

Whatever group you join, try to become part of it as best you can. Don't just observe. Get into the philosophy of your new role and see how it feels. You may gain a new appreciation for people you didn't understand.

 You can complete this activity by visiting CengageBrain.com to access the Speech Communication CourseMate for *Looking Out/ Looking In*, and, if requested, email your responses to your instructor.

Perhaps the most telltale sign of the effect of "love goggles" is when they come off. Many people have experienced breaking up with a romantic partner and wondering later, "What did I ever see in that person?" The answer—at least in part—is that you saw what your relational role led you to see.

 # Common Tendencies in Perception

By now it's obvious that many factors affect the way we interpret the world. Social scientists use the term **attribution** to describe the process of explaining people's behavior.[33] We attribute meaning both to our own actions and to the actions of others, but we often use different yardsticks. Research has uncovered several perceptual tendencies that can lead to attribution errors.[34]

WE JUDGE OURSELVES MORE CHARITABLY THAN WE JUDGE OTHERS

In an attempt to convince ourselves and others that the positive face we show to the world is true, we tend to judge ourselves in the most generous terms possible. Social scientists have labeled this tendency the **self-serving bias**.[35] When others suffer, we often blame the problem on their personal qualities. On the other hand, when we suffer, we blame the problem on forces outside ourselves. Consider a few examples:

When *they* botch a job, we might think they weren't listening well or trying hard enough; when *we* botch a job, the problem was unclear directions or not enough time.

"Don't get me wrong, Ted. I like you, but you're not a special person. I'm a special person."

When *he* lashes out angrily, we say he's being moody or too sensitive; when *we* lash out angrily, it's because of the pressure we've been under.

When *she* gets caught speeding, we say she should have been more careful; when *we* get caught speeding, we deny that we were driving too fast or we say, "Everybody does it."

When *she* uses profanity, it's because of a flaw in her character; when *we* swear, it's because the situation called for it.[36]

One study of "honest but hurtful" messages shows how self-serving bias can operate in romantic relationships.[37] Partners who deliver these candid messages tend to perceive them as helpful and constructive. When on the receiving end, however, the same messages are seen as hurtful and mean. In other words, "I'm a good sweetheart when I tell you the painful truth, but you're a bad sweetheart when you do the same to me."

WE CLING TO FIRST IMPRESSIONS

Labeling people according to our first impressions is an inevitable part of the perception process. These labels are a way of making quick interpretations: "She seems cheerful"; "He appears sincere"; "They sound conceited." If such first impressions are accurate, they can be useful ways of deciding how to respond best to people in the future. Problems arise, however, when the labels we attach are inaccurate. After we form an opinion of someone, we tend to hang on to it and make any conflicting information fit our opinion.

Social scientists have coined the term **halo effect** to describe the tendency to form an overall positive impression of a person on the basis of one positive characteristic. One such characteristic is physical attractiveness, which can lead people to attribute all sorts of other virtues to the good-looking person.[38] For example, employment interviewers rate mediocre but attractive job applicants higher than their less attractive candidates.[39] And once employers form positive impressions, they often ask questions that confirm their image of the applicant.[40] For example, when an interviewer forms a positive impression, she might ask leading questions aimed at supporting her positive views ("What lessons did you learn from that setback?"), interpret answers in a positive light ("Ah, taking time away from school to travel was a good idea!"), encourage the applicant ("Good point!"), and sell the company's virtues ("I think you would like working here"). Likewise, applicants who create a negative first impression are operating under a cloud that may be impossible to dispel—a phenomenon sometimes referred to as "the devil effect."[41]

The power of first impressions is also important in personal relationships. A study of college roommates found that those who had positive initial impressions of each other were likely to have positive subsequent interactions, manage their conflicts constructively, and continue living together.[42] The converse was also true: Roommates who got off to a bad start tended to spiral negatively. This reinforces the wisdom and importance of the old adage, "You never get a second chance to make a first impression."

Given the almost unavoidable tendency to form first impressions, the best advice we can give is to keep an open mind and to be willing to change your opinion as events prove it mistaken.

WE ASSUME THAT OTHERS ARE SIMILAR TO US

In Chapter 2 you read one example of this principle: that people with low self-esteem imagine that others view them unfavorably, whereas people with high self-esteem

ON THE JOB

Sexual Harassment and Perception

Almost 50 years after the U.S. Civil Rights Act prohibited it, sexual harassment in the workplace remains a problem. Complaints of unwanted sexual advances and a hostile work environment have cost employers almost $50 million annually in recent years.[a]

Scholars have tried to understand why complaints of harassment persist when the law clearly prohibits behavior that creates a "hostile work environment." They have discovered that, while clear-cut examples of hostile sexism do exist, differing perceptions help explain many other incidents.

Not surprisingly, what constitutes harassment depends on gender: Women are more likely than men to rate a behavior as hostile and/or offensive.[b] Perhaps more surprisingly, younger people (both men and women) are less likely than older people to regard a scenario as sexual harassment.

Along with age and sex, cultural background helps shape perceptions of harassment.[c] People from cultures with high power distance are less likely to perceive harassment than those from places with low power distance.

Findings like these don't excuse harassment, but they do help explain it. The more members of an organization understand one another's perceptions, the better the odds that unpleasant and unfortunate feelings of harassment will arise.

imagine that others view them positively. The frequently mistaken assumption that others' views are similar to our own applies in a wide range of situations:

- You've heard a slightly raunchy joke that you think is pretty funny. You assume that it won't offend a somewhat straitlaced friend. It does.
- You've been bothered by an instructor's tendency to get off the subject during lectures. If you were an instructor, you'd want to know if anything you were doing was creating problems for your students, so you decide that your instructor will probably be grateful for some constructive criticism. Unfortunately, you're wrong.
- You lost your temper with a friend a week ago and said some things you regret. In fact, if someone said those things to you, you'd consider the relationship finished. Imagining that your friend feels the same way, you avoid making contact. In fact, your friend has avoided you because she thinks *you're* the one who wants to end things.

Examples like these show that others don't always think or feel the way we do and that assuming that similarities exist can lead to problems.[43] How can you find out the other person's real position? Sometimes by asking directly, sometimes by checking with others, and sometimes by making an educated guess after you've thought the matter out. All these alternatives are better than simply assuming that everyone would react as you do.

WE ARE INFLUENCED BY OUR EXPECTATIONS

Suppose you took a class and were told in advance that the instructor is terrific. Would this affect the way you perceive the teacher? Research shows that it almost certainly would. In one study, students who read positive comments about instructors on a

On *The Voice*, judges (such as Christina Aguilera, pictured here with her back to the contestant) use blind auditions in the opening rounds. On other performance shows, judges view contestants' appearance and sometimes even know their back stories before making an appraisal. Does that affect the judges' perceptions of the performer and the performance?

website viewed those teachers as more credible and attractive than did students who were not exposed to the same comments.[44]

Expectations don't always lead to more positive appraisals. There are times when we raise our expectations so high that we are disappointed with the events that occur. If you are told that someone you are about to meet is extremely attractive, you may create a picture in your mind of a professional model, only to be let down when the person doesn't live up to your unrealistic expectations. What if you had been told that the person isn't very good-looking? In that case, you might have been pleasantly surprised by the person's appearance, and perhaps you would rate the person's attractiveness more positively. The point is, our expectations influence the way we see others, both positively and negatively—and that may lead to self-fulfilling prophecies.[45]

WE ARE INFLUENCED BY THE OBVIOUS

The error of being influenced by what is most obvious is understandable. As you read at the beginning of this chapter, we select stimuli from our environment that are noticeable: intense, repetitious, unusual, or otherwise attention-grabbing. The problem is that the most obvious factor is not necessarily the only one—or the most significant one for an event. For example:

- When two children (or adults, for that matter) fight, it may be a mistake to blame the one who lashes out first. Perhaps the other one was at least equally responsible, teasing or refusing to cooperate.
- You might complain about an acquaintance whose malicious gossiping or arguing has become a bother, forgetting that by putting up with such behavior in the past you have been at least partially responsible.
- You might blame an unhappy working situation on the boss, overlooking other factors beyond her control, such as a change in the economy, the policy of higher management, or demands of customers or other workers.

 ## Perception Checking

Serious problems can arise when people treat interpretations as if they were matters of fact. Like most people, you probably resent others jumping to conclusions about the reasons for your behavior.

"Why are you mad at me?" (Who said you were?)

"What's the matter with you?" (Who said anything was the matter?)

"Come on now. Tell the truth." (Who said you were lying?)

As you'll learn in Chapter 10, even if your interpretation is correct, a dogmatic, mind-reading statement is likely to generate defensiveness. The skill of **perception checking** provides a better way to handle your interpretations.[46]

ELEMENTS OF PERCEPTION CHECKING

A complete perception check has three parts:

1. A description of the behavior you noticed
2. At least two possible interpretations of the behavior
3. A request for clarification about how to interpret the behavior

Perception checks for the preceding three examples would look like this:

"When you stomped out of the room and slammed the door," (*behavior*) "I wasn't sure whether you were mad at me" (*first interpretation*) "or just in a hurry." (*second interpretation*) "How *did* you feel?" (*request for clarification*)

"You haven't laughed much in the last couple of days." (*behavior*) "It makes me wonder whether something's bothering you" (*first interpretation*) "or whether you're just feeling quiet." (*second interpretation*) "What's up?" (*request for clarification*)

"You said you really liked the job I did." (*behavior*) "On the other hand, there was something about your voice that made me think you may not like it." (*first interpretation*) "Maybe it's just my imagination, though." (*second interpretation*) "How do you really feel?" (*request for clarification*)

Perception checking is a tool for helping you understand others accurately instead of assuming that your first interpretation is correct. Because its goal is mutual understanding, perception checking is a cooperative approach to communication. Besides leading to more accurate perceptions, it minimizes defensiveness by preserving the other person's face. Instead of saying, in effect, "I know what you're thinking . . . ," a perception check takes the more respectful approach that states or implies, "I know I'm not qualified to judge you without some help."

PERCEPTION CHECKING CONSIDERATIONS

Like every communication skill outlined in *Looking Out/Looking In*, perception checking isn't a mechanical formula that will work in every situation. As you develop the ability to check your perceptions, consider the following factors in deciding when and how to use this approach.

"Of course I care about how you imagined I thought you perceived I wanted you to feel."

Completeness Sometimes a perception check won't need all of the parts listed earlier to be effective:

"You haven't dropped by lately. Is anything the matter?" (*single interpretation combined with request for clarification*)

"I can't tell whether you're kidding me about being cheap or if you're serious." (*behavior combined with interpretations*) "Are you mad at me?"

"Are you sure you don't mind driving? I can use a ride if it's no trouble, but I don't want to take you out of your way." (*no need to describe behavior*)

Sometimes even the most skimpy perception check—a simple question like "What's going on?"—will do the job. You might also rely on other people to help you

IN REAL LIFE

Perception Checking in Everyday Life

Perception checking only works if it is sincere and fits your personal style. The following examples show how perception checking sounds in everyday life and may help you find ways to use it when you are faced with ambiguous messages.

My Texting Student

I'm a teacher who likes to have my class's complete attention when I'm talking. During a lecture last week, one of my students was typing away on her smartphone, fast and furiously. I assumed she was texting a friend, so I asked her to put the device away immediately. She looked a bit hurt, but she slipped it into her bookbag.

After class, the student approached me and said she wasn't using her PDA to talk with friends—she was using it to take notes. I found myself doubting the student until she pulled out the PDA and showed me several screens of information she had taken from my lecture.

I was really embarrassed and offered a sincere apology. A perception check sure would have helped in this case. I could have pulled her aside after class and said, "I noticed you were typing on your PDA a lot during my lecture. I assumed you were using it for personal reasons, but maybe you were just taking class notes. Could you please let me know, because your attention in class means a lot to me."

To be honest, I think a lot of students do use PDAs in class for personal reasons—but I want to be careful not to jump to that conclusion without checking the facts.

My Boss's Jokes

I get confused by my boss's sense of humor. Sometimes he jokes just to be funny, but other times he uses humor to make a point without coming right out and saying what's on his mind. Last week he was talking about the upcoming work schedule and he said with a laugh, "I own you all weekend!" I have a life besides work, so his comment left me worried.

I used a perception check to figure out what he meant: "Brad, when you told me 'I own you all weekend,' I wasn't sure whether you were kidding or whether you really expect me to work Saturday and Sunday. Were you serious?"

He kind of smiled and said, "No, I was just kidding. You only have to work Saturday and Sunday."

make sense of confusing behavior: "Rachelle has been awfully quiet lately. Do you know what's up?" A complete perception check is most necessary when the risk of sounding judgmental is highest.

Nonverbal Congruency A perception check can succeed only if your nonverbal behavior reflects the open-mindedness of your words. An accusing tone of voice or a hostile glare will contradict the sincerely worded request for clarification, suggesting that you have already made up your mind about the other person's intentions.

Cultural Rules The straightforward approach of perception checking has the best chance of working in what Chapter 5 identifies as *low-context cultures*: ones in which members use language as directly as possible. The dominant cultures of North America and Western Europe fit into this category, and members of these groups are most likely to appreciate perception checking. Members of *high-context cultures* (more common in Latin America and Asia), however, value social harmony over directness. High-context communicators are more likely to regard candid approaches like perception checking as potentially embarrassing, preferring instead less-direct ways of understanding one

I still couldn't be sure whether or not he was serious, so I checked again: "You're kidding, right?"

My boss replied, "Well, I do need you at least one day, and two would be better." Once I figured out what he really meant, we worked out a schedule that had me work Friday evening and Saturday morning, which gave me the time off I needed.

If I hadn't used the perception check, I would have wound up worrying about being tied up all weekend, and getting mad at my boss for no good reason. I'm glad I spoke up.

My Dad's Affection

My father and I have a great relationship. A while back I picked him up at the airport after a week-long business trip and a long cross-country flight. On the way home, he was quiet—not his usual self. He said he was exhausted, which I understood. When we got home, he brightened up and started joking and playing with my younger brother. This left me feeling unhappy. I thought to myself, "Why is he so happy to see my brother when he hardly said a word to me?" I didn't say anything at the time. The next day I found myself feeling resentful toward my dad, and it showed.

He said, "What's up with you?" But I was too embarrassed to say anything.

After learning this approach in class, I tried a perception check. I said, "Dad—when you were quiet on the way home after your business trip and then you perked up when you got home and saw Jaime, I wasn't sure what was up. I thought maybe you were happier to see him than me, or that maybe I'm imagining things. How come you said you were tired with me and then you perked up with Jaime?"

My dad felt awful. He said he was tired in the car, but once he got back to the house he was glad to be home and felt like a new man. I was too wrapped up in my mind to consider this alternative. Because I didn't use a perception check, I was unhappy and I started an unnecessary fight.

Communication Scenarios

 To watch and analyze a video related to this feature and this topic, visit CengageBrain .com to access the Speech Communication CourseMate for Looking Out/Looking In.

another. Thus, a "let's get this straight" perception check that might work well with a Euro American manager who was raised to value directness could be a serious mistake with a Mexican American or Asian American boss who has spent most of his or her life in a high-context culture.

Face Saving Along with clarifying meaning, perception checking can sometimes be a face-saving way to raise an issue without directly threatening or attacking the other person. Consider these examples:

"Are you planning on doing those dishes later, or did you forget that it's your turn?"

"Am I boring you, or do you have something else on your mind?"

In the first case, you might have been quite confident that the other person had no intention of doing the dishes, and in the second that the other person was bored. Even so, a perception check is a less threatening way of pointing out their behavior than direct confrontation. Remember: One element of competent communication is the ability to choose the best option from a large repertoire, and perception checking can be a useful strategy at times.

SKILL BUILDER

Practice your perception-checking ability by developing three-part verifications for the following situations:

1. You made what you thought was an excellent suggestion to an instructor. The instructor looked uninterested but said she would check on the matter right away. Three weeks have passed, and nothing has changed.
2. A neighbor and good friend has not responded to your "Good morning" for three days in a row. This person is usually friendly.
3. You haven't received the usual weekly phone call from the folks back home in over a month. The last time you spoke, you had an argument about where to spend the holidays.
4. An old friend with whom you have shared the problems of your love life for years has recently changed behavior when around you. The formerly casual hugs and kisses have become longer and stronger, and the occasions where you "accidentally" brush up against each other have become more frequent.

You can complete this activity by visiting CengageBrain.com to access the Speech Communication CourseMate for *Looking Out/ Looking In*, and, if requested, email your responses to your instructor.

Empathy, Cognitive Complexity, and Communication

Perception checking is a valuable tool for clarifying ambiguous messages, but ambiguity isn't the only cause of perceptual problems. Sometimes we understand what people mean without understanding why they believe as they do. At times like this, we are short on the vital ability to empathize.

EMPATHY

Empathy is the ability to re-create another person's perspective, to experience the world from the other's point of view. It may be impossible to ever experience another person's perspective completely, but with enough effort we can certainly gain a better idea of how the world appears to him or her.

As we'll use the term here, empathy involves three dimensions.[47] In one dimension, empathy involves *perspective taking*—an attempt to take on the viewpoint of another person. This requires a suspension of judgment so that for the moment you set aside your own opinions and try to understand the other person. Empathy also has an *emotional* dimension that helps us get closer to experiencing others' feelings: to gain a sense of their fear, joy, sadness, and so on. A third dimension of empathy is a genuine *concern* for the welfare of the other

"How would you feel if the mouse did that to you?"

LEARNING EMPATHY BY DOING

The banner on the side of the Capital University music conservatory has an outline of a sneaker and asks, "They walked a mile in someone else's shoes. How much did they learn?"

Inside the hall in Columbus, Ohio, a few hundred people wait to find out. They are here for the concluding event of the Empathy Experiment.

Board of Trustees member Ronald St. Pierre says the idea was for students to explore a social issue "not only by reading books and taking tests, but by immersing themselves in the realities of the situation." The eight-week program required, for example, that students undergo a temporary eviction, be processed and stay a night at a homeless shelter, and go a night without eating. "It was a good chance for students to, frankly, get out of their comfort zone," St. Pierre says. They were to move from sympathy to empathy.

University president Denny Bowman is introducing a series of videos and interviews concerning the students' experiences.

The video shows junior biology major Liz Delfing, partnered with Goodwill Columbus, as she tries to board a bus while spending a day in a wheelchair. Simple tasks become difficult: entering her apartment, reaching for items on a shelf, navigating her kitchen and bathroom. Delfing, back on her feet, believes empathy can be taught; but "the only way you

Fotosearch

can teach it is by doing things like this."

Diana Crandall, a first-year psychology major in a smart black jacket and tie, talks about the children she worked with through the Children's Hunger Alliance. "I know that I can't walk away from this and be the same person I was before."

Eric Leake

person. When we empathize, we go beyond just thinking and feeling as others do and genuinely care about their well-being.

Scores of recent studies show that humans are hardwired to empathize with others—it's built into our brains.[48] Best-selling author Daniel Goleman believes that cultivating this natural tendency toward empathy is the essence of "social intelligence."[49] The ability to empathize seems to exist in a rudimentary form in even the youngest children. Research sponsored by the National Institute of Mental Health revealed what many parents know from experience: Virtually from birth, infants become visibly upset when they hear another baby crying, and children who are a few months old cry when they observe another child in tears. Young children have trouble distinguishing others' distress from their own. If, for example, one child hurts its finger, another baby might put its own finger into her mouth as if she were feeling pain. Researchers report cases in which children who see their parents in tears wipe their own eyes, even though they are not crying.

Although children may have a basic capacity to empathize, studies with twins suggest that the degree to which we are born with the ability to sense how others are feeling seems to vary according to genetic factors.[50] Although some people may have an inborn edge, environmental experiences are the key to developing the ability to understand others. Specifically, the way in which parents communicate with their

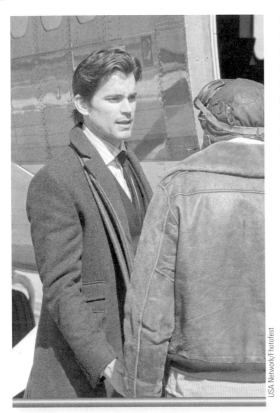

Con artist Neal Caffrey (Matt Bomer) is good at catching criminals in the television show *White Collar*. He is able to help the FBI because he identifies with the thieves he pursues and knows how they think. Similar experiences and backgrounds often help us empathize with and understand others. (See the TV summary at the end of this chapter.)

children seems to affect their ability to understand others' emotional states.[51] When parents point out to children the distress that others feel from their misbehavior ("Look how sad Jessica is because you took her toy. Wouldn't you be sad if someone took away your toys?"), those children gain a greater appreciation that their acts have emotional consequences than when parents simply label such behavior as inappropriate ("That was a mean thing to do!"). Studies also show that allowing children to experience and manage frustrating events can help increase their empathic concern for others later in life.[52]

Culture plays an important role in our ability to understand the perspectives of others. Research shows that people raised in individualist cultures (which value independence) are often less adept at perspective-taking than those from collectivist cultures (which value interdependence).[53] In one study, Chinese and American players were paired together in a communication game that required the participants to take on the perspective of their partners. In all measures, the collectivist Chinese had greater success in perspective-taking than did their American counterparts. This isn't to suggest that one cultural orientation is better than the other; it only shows that culture shapes the way we perceive, understand, and empathize with others.

It is easy to confuse empathy with **sympathy**, but the concepts are different. With sympathy, you view the other person's situation from *your* point of view. With empathy, you view it from *the other person's* perspective. Consider the difference between sympathizing and empathizing with an unwed mother or a homeless person. When you sympathize, it is the other person's confusion, joy, or pain. When you empathize, the experience becomes your own, at least for the moment. It's one thing to feel bad (or good) *for* someone; it's more profound to feel bad (or good) *with* someone. Nonetheless, empathy doesn't require you to *agree* with the other person. You can empathize with a difficult relative or a rude stranger without endorsing their behavior. Ultimately, all of us can profit from putting ourselves in others' shoes to better understand their worlds, as the reading on page 103 illustrates.

COGNITIVE COMPLEXITY

By now you can probably appreciate the value of empathy in boosting understanding and enhancing relationships. But how can we become more empathic? To answer that question, let's return to a feature of communication competence: cognitive complexity.

Cognitive Complexity and Communication As noted in Chapter 1, cognitive complexity is the ability to construct a variety of frameworks for viewing an issue. Researchers have found that cognitive complexity increases the chances of satisfying communication in a variety of contexts, including marriage,[54] helping others who are feeling distressed,[55] being persuasive,[56] and career advancement.[57]

It was six men of Indostan
To learning much inclined,
Who went to see the elephant
Though all of them were blind
That each by observation
Might satisfy his mind.

The first approached the elephant
And, happening to fall
Against the broad and sturdy side,
At once began to bawl:
"Why, bless me! But the elephant
Is very much like a wall!"

The second, feeling of the tusk,
Cried: "Ho! What have we here
So very round and smooth and sharp?
To me, 'tis very clear,
This wonder of an elephant
Is very like a spear!"

The third approached the animal,
And, happening to take
The squirming trunk within his hands
Thus boldly up he spake:
"I see," quoth he, "the elephant
Is very like a snake!"

The fourth reached out his eager hand
And felt about the knee:
"What most this wondrous beast is like
Is very plain," quoth he:
"'Tis clear enough the elephant
Is very like a tree!"

The fifth who chanced to touch the ear
Said: "E'en the blindest man
Can tell what this resembles most—
Deny the fact who can:
This marvel of an elephant
Is very like a fan!"

The sixth no sooner had begun
About the beast to grope
Than, seizing on the swinging tail
That fell within his scope,
"I see," quoth he, "the elephant
Is very like a rope!"

And so these men of Indostan
Disputed loud and long,
Each in his own opinion
Exceeding stiff and strong;
Though each was partly in the right,
And all were in the wrong.

John G. Saxe

Not surprisingly, studies show a connection between cognitive complexity and empathy.[58] The relationship makes sense: The more ways you have to understand others and interpret their behaviors, the greater is the likelihood that you can see the world from their perspective. Cognitive complexity can also help people describe situations more thoroughly and less simplistically.[59] Interestingly, one study showed that cognitive complex people are better able to identify and understand when others are using sarcasm—an abstract form of communication that is sometimes lost on those with less mental acumen.[60] The good news is that cognitive complexity can be enhanced through training.[61] With that in mind, let's look at a skill that can help you achieve that goal.

Increasing Your Cognitive Complexity: The Pillow Method The skill of perception checking discussed earlier in this chapter is a relatively quick, easy tool for clarifying potential misunderstandings, but some issues are too complex and serious to be handled with this approach. Writer Paul Reps describes a tool for boosting empathy when finding merit in another's position seems impossible.[62]

Developed by a group of Japanese schoolchildren, the **pillow method** gets its name from the fact that a problem has four sides and a middle, just like a pillow (Figure 3.3). As the examples in the following pages show, viewing an issue from each of these perspectives almost always leads to valuable insights—and in so doing enhances cognitive complexity.

Position 1: I'm Right, You're Wrong This is the perspective that we usually take when viewing an issue. We immediately see the virtues in our position and find fault with anyone who happens to disagree with us. Detailing this position takes little effort and provides little new information.

Position 2: You're Right, I'm Wrong At this point you switch perspectives and build the strongest possible arguments to explain how another person can view the issue differently from you. Besides identifying the strengths in the other's position, this is the time to play the devil's advocate and find flaws in your position. This requires discipline and a certain amount of courage, even though this is only an exercise, and you will soon be able to retreat to position 1 if you choose. But most people learn that switching perspectives reveals there is some merit to the other person's perspective.

FIGURE 3.3   The Pillow Method © Cengage Learning

ETHICAL CHALLENGE

EMPATHY AND THE GOLDEN RULE

Virtually everyone is familiar with the Golden Rule, which most of us learned in the form "Do unto others as you would have them do unto you." By obliging us to treat others as well as we would treat ourselves, this maxim seems to offer the foundation for a civil society in which everyone would behave with consideration.

Some ethicists have pointed out that the Golden Rule doesn't work well in situations where others don't want to be treated the same way you would. You may like to blast hip-hop music at top volume at 3 A.M., but appeals to the Golden Rule probably won't placate your neighbors who don't share your musical tastes or late-night hours. Likewise, just because you enjoy teasing banter, you aren't entitled to banter with others who might find this type of humor offensive or hurtful.

The Golden Rule presents special problems in cases of intercultural contacts, where norms for what is desirable vary dramatically. For example, most speakers from low-context cultures where English is the first language value honesty and explicit communication, but this level of candor would be offensive in the high-context cultures of Asia or the Middle East. A naive communicator following the Golden Rule might justify social blunders by claiming, "I was just communicating the way I'd like to be treated." This sort of ethnocentrism is a recipe for unsuccessful communication and perhaps for very unpleasant consequences.

In response to the challenge of differing wants, Milton Bennett proposed a "Platinum Rule": "Do unto others as they themselves would have done unto them." Unlike the Golden Rule, this rule requires us to understand how others think and what they want before we can determine how to act ethically.[a] Put differently, the Platinum Rule implies that empathy is a prerequisite for moral sensitivity.

Despite its initial appeal, the Platinum Rule poses its own problems. There are certainly cases where doing unto others what they want might compromise our own needs or even our ethical principles. It is easy to imagine cases in which the Platinum Rule would oblige us to cheat, steal, or lie on others' behalf.

Even if acting on the Platinum Rule is problematic, the benefit of thinking about it seems clear. An essential requirement for benign behavior is the ability to empathize, helping us recognize that what others want may be different than what we would want under the same circumstances.

Describe how applying the Golden Rule and the Platinum Rule would affect one of your important interpersonal relationships.
1. What communication is necessary before you could put each rule into practice?
2. Which rule seems to be preferable?

There are some issues where it seems impossible to call the other position "right." Criminal behavior, deceit, and disloyalty often seem beyond justification. At times like these, it is possible to arrive at position 2 by realizing that the other person's behavior is understandable. For example, without approving, you may be able to understand how someone would resort to violence, tell lies, or cheat. Whatever the particulars, the goal of position 2 is to find some way of comprehending how anyone could behave in a way that you originally found impossible to defend.

Position 3: Both Right, Both Wrong From this position, you acknowledge the strengths and weaknesses of each person's arguments. If you have done a good job with position 2, it should be clear that there is some merit in both points of view, and that each side has its demerits. Taking a more evenhanded look at the issue can lead you to be less critical and more understanding of another's point of view.

Position 3 can also help you find the commonalities between your position and others'. Perhaps you've both been right to care so much about the issue, but both wrong to fail to recognize the other person's concerns. Perhaps there are underlying values that you both share and similar mistakes that you've both made. In any case, the perspective of position 3 should help you see that the issue isn't as much a matter of complete right and wrong as it first appeared to be.

Position 4: The Issue Isn't as Important as It Seems Although it is difficult to consider some issues as unimportant, a little thought will show that most aren't as important as we make them out to be. The impact of even the most traumatic events—the death of a loved one or the breakup of a relationship, for example—usually lessens over time. The effects may not disappear, but we learn to accept them and get on with life. The importance of a dispute can also fade when you realize that you've let it overshadow other equally important parts of your relationship. It's easy to become so wrapped up in a dispute about one subject that you forget about the other ways in which you are close to the other person.

Position 5: There Is Truth in All Four Perspectives After completing the first four positions, a final step is to recognize that each of them has some merit. Although logic might suggest that it's impossible for a position to be both right and wrong, both important and unimportant, your own experience will show that there is some truth in each of the positions you have explored. After you have looked at an issue from these five perspectives, it is almost certain that you will gain new insights. These insights may not cause you to change your mind or even solve the problem at hand. Nonetheless, they can increase your understanding of the other person's position and thus improve the communication climate.

SKILL BUILDER

PILLOW TALK

Try using the pillow method in your life. It isn't easy, but after you begin to understand it, the payoff in increased understanding can be great.

1. Choose a person or viewpoint with whom or which you strongly disagree. If you've chosen a person, it's best to have him or her there with you, but if that's not possible, you can do it alone.

2. What disagreement should you choose? No doubt there are many in your life:

    Parent–child   Friend–friend
    Teacher–student   Nation–nation
    Employer–employee   Republican–Democrat
    Brother–sister

3. For each disagreement you choose, genuinely place yourself in each position on the pillow as you encounter it:

    a. Your position is correct, and your opponent's is wrong.

    b. Your opponent's position is correct, and yours is wrong.

    c. Both your positions are correct, and both are wrong.

    d. It isn't important which position is right or wrong.

    e. Finally, affirm the fact that there is truth in all four positions.

4. The more important the disagreement is to you, the harder it will be to accept positions 2 through 5 as valid, but the exercise will work only if you can suspend your present position and imagine how it would feel to hold the other ones.

5. How can you tell if you've been successful with the pillow method? The answer is simple: If, after going over all the steps, you can understand—not necessarily accept, but just understand—the other person's position, you've done it. After you've reached this *understanding*, do you notice any change in how you feel about the other person?

 You can complete this activity by visiting CengageBrain.com to access the Speech Communication CourseMate for *Looking Out/ Looking In*, and, if requested, email your responses to your instructor.

IN REAL LIFE

The Pillow Method in Action

My Father and Facebook

Background

My father recently opened a Facebook account and sent me an invitation to become his friend. I ignored this request for a couple of weeks until he finally asked why I hadn't responded. The talk turned into an argument. He couldn't understand why I didn't want him as a Facebook friend. I couldn't understand why he wanted to butt into my personal life.

Position 1: I'm Right, He's Wrong

Facebook was created for college students, not middle-aged parents. The fact that my dad wants access to my personal world feels like an invasion of privacy—like reading my diary or rummaging through my belongings. If he wants to keep up with his friends on Facebook, that's his business—but leave me out of it.

Position 2: He's Right, I'm Wrong

When I objected to my dad snooping, he said he would stop looking at my page if it makes him uncomfortable. So he's right in saying that I don't need to worry about his judgments. When I told him I'd be embarrassed to have him commenting on my life, he promised not to write on my Wall, tag embarrassing pictures of me, or do anything else visible.

Position 3: Both of Us Are Right, and Both Are Wrong

I'm justified to be concerned about my dad being freaked out by some things on my Facebook page.

He's justified in wanting to know more about my life and how my generation communicates. I'm probably overreacting when I worry about his reactions or demand that he keep his nose out of my business. He's wrong not to appreciate my desire for privacy.

Position 4: The Issue Isn't Important

I don't think anything I or my friends post on my Facebook page would change my relationship with my dad. Turning this into a major issue is probably not worth the hurt feelings that have resulted from this mini-crisis.

Position 5: There Is Truth In All Perspectives

Viewing this issue from several angles calmed me down and made it easier for my dad and me to have a good talk. We decided that I would friend him for a trial period. If I decide his looking at my page becomes a problem, he agreed to willingly remove himself from my friends list.

Planning a Wedding

Background

Who would have thought that planning a wedding would be such a nightmare? My fiancé and I are struggling to decide whether we should have a large, festive wedding or a small, intimate one. I'm in favor of having a big, expensive ceremony and party. He wants a smaller, more affordable one.

Position 1: I'm Right, He's Wrong

I have a big family, and I would feel guilty not inviting everyone. Also, we have lots of friends who would really miss not being present to celebrate our special day. If we invite one friend or relative, I say we have to invite them all to avoid hurting anybody's feelings. Otherwise, where do you draw the line? As far as money goes, I say that you get married only once, and this is no time to scrimp. My parents are willing to help pay the expenses, because they want our entire family to be there at the wedding.

Position 2: He's Right, I'm Wrong

My fiancé is right to say that we really don't have the funds to spend on a fancy wedding. Every dollar we spend on a lavish event will be one less dollar we have to buy a house, which we hope to do soon. My fiancé is right to say that a big wedding could postpone our house purchase for a year or two—maybe even longer, if real estate prices go up before we can buy. Even if my parents help pay for the event, our portion would still be more than we can afford. He's also right to say that no matter how many people we invite, someone is always going to be left out. It's just a case of where we draw the line. Finally, he's right to say that planning a big wedding will be a very stressful process.

Position 3: Both of Us Are Right, and Both Are Wrong

Both of us are right, and both are wrong. I'm right to want to include our extended families and friends on this joyous day, and I'm right to say that a special wedding would be a lifetime memory. He's right that doing so could still leave some hurt feelings and that it will postpone our house purchase. He also has a good point when he says that planning a big event could drive us crazy and distract us from the real importance of joining our lives.

Position 4: The Issue Isn't Important

After thinking about it, I've realized that getting married is different from being married. The decision about what kind of ceremony to have is important, but ultimately it won't affect the kind of marriage we have. How we behave after we're married will be much more important. And we are going to face a lot of decisions together—about children and jobs, for example—that will have much bigger consequences than this ceremony.

Position 5: There Is Truth In All Perspectives

Before using the pillow method to think through all sides of this issue, I was focused on getting my way. This attitude was creating some feelings between my fiancé and me that were not what we should be having as we faced this most important event. I've realized that if one or the other of us "wins" but the result is injured feelings, it won't be much of a victory. I don't know what kind of ceremony we will finally decide to have, but I'm determined to keep my focus on the really important goal of keeping our relationship positive and respectful.

Communication Scenarios

To watch and analyze a video related to this feature and this topic, visit CengageBrain .com to access the Speech Communication CourseMate for Looking Out/Looking In.

SUMMARY

There is more to the world "out there" than any person is capable of understanding. We make sense of our environment by the four-step process of selecting certain stimuli from the environment, organizing them into meaningful patterns, interpreting them in a manner that is shaped by a variety of factors, and negotiating them through narratives we share with others.

Many factors affect the way we select, organize, interpret, and negotiate information. Access to information plays an important role. So do physiological factors such as our senses, age, and health. Cultural background also influences the way we view the world, as do social roles. In addition to these factors, some common tendencies affect the way we assign meaning to others' behavior.

Perception checking can be a useful tool for verifying interpretations of others' behavior, instead of assuming that the first hunch is correct. A complete perception check includes a description of the other's behavior, at least two plausible interpretations of its meaning, and a request for clarification about what the behavior does mean.

Empathy is the ability to experience another person's point of view. Empathy differs from sympathy, because it involves seeing the situation from the other person's perspective rather than your own. Cognitive complexity is the ability to construct a variety of frameworks for understanding an issue. One means for boosting both empathy and cognitive complexity is the pillow method, which involves viewing an issue from five different perspectives.

KEY TERMS

androgynous (91)
attribution (93)
empathy (100)
ethnocentrism (90)
gender role (91)
halo effect (94)
interpretation (84)
narrative (85)
negotiation (85)

organization (79)
perception checking (96)
pillow method (104)
punctuation (82)
selection (79)
self-serving bias (93)
stereotyping (81)
sympathy (102)

ONLINE RESOURCES

Now that you have read this chapter, visit CengageBrain.com to access the Speech Communication CourseMate for *Looking Out/Looking In* for quick access to the electronic resources that accompany this text. Your CourseMate offers:

- **Study tools** that will help you assess your learning and prepare for exams (*digital glossary, key term flash cards, interactive quizzes*).
- **Activities and assignments** that will help you hone your knowledge, understand how theory and research applies to your own life (*Self-Assessment, Pause and Reflect*), consider ethical challenges in interpersonal communication (*Ethical Challenge*), and build your interpersonal communication skills throughout the course (*Skill Builder*). If requested, you can submit your answers to your instructor.
- **Media resources** that will allow you to watch and critique videos of interpersonal communication situations (*In Real Life, interpersonal video simulations, and interactive video activities*).
- In addition to interactive teaching and learning tools, CourseMate includes an **interactive eBook.** Take notes, highlight, search, and interact with embedded media specific to *Looking Out/Looking In*.

SEARCH TERMS

When searching online databases to research topics in this chapter, use the following terms (along with this chapter's key terms) to maximize the chances of finding useful information:

attribution error	intercultural communication
cognition	sense-making
cognitive complexity	social perception
emotional intelligence	

FILM AND TELEVISION

You can see the communication principles described in this chapter portrayed in the following films and television programs.

STEREOTYPING

Crash (2004) Rated R

Over the course of thirty-six hours in Los Angeles, the lives of several strangers collide. Because they come from such different backgrounds, this diverse group of people relies on stereotypes—usually relating to race—to form snap judgments of each other. Unfortunately, their judgments are almost always wrong.

Again and again, the characters' assumptions keep them from understanding the human beings they are encountering. Matt Dillon plays an angry cop who goes out of his way to humiliate a black citizen. An upper-class housewife (Sandra Bullock) believes a Mexican American locksmith (Michael Peña) is a gangbanger who plans to burgle her home, even though he is actually a gentle man struggling to build a safe life for his family. An Iranian businessman (Shaun Toub) keeps being misidentified as an Arab. Two clean-cut young black men (Larenz Tate and Ludacris) bemoan the fact that they are regarded with fear by whites in an upscale neighborhood.

Since childhood, most of us have been reminded not to judge a book by its cover. *Crash* provides a dramatic example of the problems that can result from ignoring this maxim.

NARRATIVES

Lars and the Real Girl (2007) Rated PG-13

Lars (Ryan Gosling) is a kind and decent but painfully shy 27-year-old. By choice, he lives alone in a garage and avoids conversation and contact with others as much as possible. Everyone in his small, close-knit town is stunned when Lars introduces his new girlfriend, Bianca—an anatomically correct silicone mannequin. Understandably worried about Lars's mental health, his brother and sister-in-law seek the help of their family doctor, who advises them to play along with his delusion and see what happens. Soon the entire town buys into the shared narrative that Bianca and Lars are a real couple. Bianca volunteers at the local hospital, "reads" stories to schoolchildren, and even wins a seat on the school board.

While this plot might seem far-fetched, critics and moviegoers have agreed that this tender drama-comedy showcases the power of a community to support one of its own. The obvious fiction they conspire to construct takes on its own reality, illustrating how communication can be a powerful tool for creating shared narratives.

INFLUENCES ON PERCEPTION
Temple Grandin (2010) Rated PG

Redin Van/HBO/The Kobal Collection

It's clear that something is different about teenaged Temple Grandin (played by Claire Danes in this HBO movie). As she steps off an airplane into Arizona's furnace-like summer heat, we perceive the world as she does. Sounds and images are chaotic and intensified to an almost unbearable level. Sudden movements are frightening. Grandin's awkward stature and too-loud voice soon make it clear that she occupies a place on the autism scale.

With the support of a devoted mother and caring teachers, Temple grows into a successful adult despite the prejudices and ignorance of the 1960s. Her love for large animals and her heightened sensitivity to their feelings leads to her life's work as a university professor and consultant, designing humane ways of managing livestock. She claims that her professional success is due in part to her hypersensitivity to the behavior and emotions of animals.

This true story reminds us that perceiving the world in unique ways can lead to triumphs as well as challenges. As Grandin's mother puts it, people with disabilities are "different, but not less."

For more information about Temple Grandin's life and work, see her website at www.templegrandin.com.

GAINING EMPATHY
White Collar (2009–) Rated TV-PG
Undercover Boss (2010–) Rated TV-PG

Neal Caffrey (Matt Bomer) is known as a "white collar criminal." He's an art and securities thief, counterfeiter, and racketeer. When cornered by the FBI, he strikes a deal: In exchange for not going to prison, he'll use his expertise to help the feds catch con artists like himself.

The premise of *White Collar* is a reminder that in order to understand the way others see the world, it helps to have similar backgrounds. Neal is good at catching criminals because he knows how they think. This shared understanding can be helpful in many professions. It's no surprise, for instance, that counselors and therapists often have had challenging lives of their own, and thus they have empathy for their patients' experiences.

Undercover Boss shows a way to gain empathy for those from different walks of life. In this TV series, high-ranking company officials don disguises and take on the roles of "blue collar" employees in their organizations. Some of them rediscover what it was like when they were working their way up the occupational ladder. Others gain new empathy for a world they've never known.

Regardless of the color of one's collar, these shows demonstrate that empathy is a valuable asset in communicating with others.

C H A P T E R   T H R E E

Perception: What You See Is What You Get

CHAPTER OUTLINE

Use this outline to take notes as you read the chapter in the text and/or as your instructor lectures in class.

I. **THE PERCEPTION PROCESS**
    A. **Selection** is influenced by
        1. Intense stimuli
        2. Repetitious stimuli
        3. Contrast or change in stimulation
        4. Motives
    B. **Organization**
        1. Figure–ground organization
        2. Perceptual schema
            a. Appearance
            b. Social roles
            c. Interaction style
            d. Psychological traits
            e. Membership
        3. Stereotyping
        4. Punctuation
    C. **Interpretation**
        1. Degree of involvement with the other person
        2. Personal experience
        3. Assumptions about human behavior
        4. Attitudes

        5. Expectations
        6. Knowledge
        7. Self-concept
        8. Relational satisfaction
    D. **Negotiation**
        1. Narratives tell our stories
        2. Narratives may clash
        3. Shared narratives

II. **INFLUENCES ON PERCEPTION**
    A. **Access to Information**
        1. Roles
        2. Social media
    B. **Physiological Influences**
        1. Senses
        2. Psychological challenges
        3. Age
        4. Health and fatigue
        5. Hunger
        6. Biological cycles
    C. **Cultural Differences**
        1. Worldview
        2. Value of talk and silence
        3. Ethnocentrism
        4. Subcultures
    D. **Social Roles**
        1. Gender roles (masculine, feminine, androgynous, undifferentiated)
        2. Occupational roles
        3. Relational roles

III. **COMMON TENDENCIES IN PERCEPTION**
    A. **We Judge Ourselves More Charitably Than We Judge Others**
    B. **We Cling to First Impressions**
    C. **We Assume that Others Are Similar to Us**

D. We Are Influenced by Our
    Expectations

E. We Are Influenced by the Obvious

IV. PERCEPTION CHECKING

A. Elements of Perception Checking

1. Describe behavior

2. Interpret behavior two ways

3. Request clarification

B. Perception Checking
    Considerations

1. Completeness

2. Nonverbal congruency

3. Cultural rules

    a. Low-context cultures

    b. High-context cultures

4. Face saving

V. EMPATHY, COGNITIVE
    COMPLEXITY, AND
    COMMUNICATION

A. Empathy

1. Definition

    a. Perspective taking

    b. Emotional dimension

    c. Genuine concern

2. Social intelligence

3. Cultural considerations

4. Sympathy

B. Cognitive Complexity

1. Communication

2. Increasing cognitive complexity:
    the pillow method

    a. Position One: I'm right, you're
        wrong

    b. Position Two: You're right, I'm
        wrong

| c. Position Three: Both right, both wrong
 d. Position Four: The issue isn't as important as it seems
 e. Position Five: There is truth in all four perspectives | _____
 _____
 |

KEY TERMS

androgynous

attribution

empathy

ethnocentrism

gender role

halo effect

interpretation

narrative

negotiation

organization

perception checking

pillow method

punctuation

selection

self-serving bias

stereotyping

sympathy

ACTIVITIES

3.1 GUARDING AGAINST PERCEPTUAL ERRORS

LEARNING OBJECTIVES

- Explain how the influences on perception listed in this chapter affect communication in a specific situation.
- Analyze how the tendencies described in this chapter have distorted your perceptions of another person, and hence your communication. Use this information to present a more accurate alternative set of perceptions.

INSTRUCTIONS

1. Identify two people about whom you've formed strong opinions. These opinions can be positive or negative. In either case, describe them.
2. Using the checklist provided, comment on the accuracy or inaccuracy of your perceptions of each person. See Chapter 3 of *Looking Out/Looking In* for a more detailed description of the checklist factors. NOTE: Not every factor may apply to each person.
3. Record your conclusions at the end of the exercise.
4. Compare your examples with those of other classmates.

	EXAMPLE	PERSON A	PERSON B
Identify each person. Describe your opinions.	Joni is my wife's good friend. I don't like her; I think she's boring. Her voice is shrill, and I find her annoying.		
1. We judge ourselves more charitably than we judge others.	When Joni lost her job, I thought it was Joni's fault because she's so annoying. Of course, when I got laid off a few months later, I blamed the economy and mentioned nothing about my performance or personality.		

	EXAMPLE	PERSON A	PERSON B
2. We pay more attention to other's negative characteristics.	Joni is attractive, intelligent, successful, and athletic. I tend to disregard all those positive qualities and focus on her shrill voice.		
3. We are influenced by the obvious.	Because she's my wife's friend, Joni is around a lot, so I probably notice her voice or her calls more than is usual.		
4. We cling to first impressions.	I haven't liked Joni from the beginning. She would call right at our dinner time. Even though she doesn't do this anymore, I still remember it and I'm sure it influences my opinion of her.		
5. We assume that others are similar to us.	I just assume that Joni will know when I don't want her around. I assume she'd be interested in things I'm interested in. Perhaps she finds the topics I talk about boring, too.		

CONCLUSIONS

Based on the observations above, how accurate or inaccurate are your perceptions of other people?

_____

_____

_____

Class _____   Name_____

What might you do in the future to guard against inaccurate perceptions of people?

_____

_____

_____

_____

Class _____   Name_____

3.2 SHIFTING PERSPECTIVES (PILLOW METHOD)

LEARNING OBJECTIVES

- Enhance your cognitive complexity by applying the "pillow method" in a significant disagreement. Explain how your expanded view of this situation might affect your communication with the other(s) involved.

INSTRUCTIONS

1. Select one disagreement or other issue that is now affecting an interpersonal relationship. This might be an issue such as "I think our children should go to public school; my spouse wants them to go to private school" or a more public disagreement such as "I think voting for a third party helps democracy in our country; my friend thinks it undermines democracy by drawing votes away from the two major parties."
2. Record enough background information for an outsider to understand your stance on the issue. Who is involved? How long has the disagreement been going on? What are the basic issues involved?
3. Describe the issue from each of the four positions listed below.
4. Record your conclusions at the end of this exercise.

OPTIONS

Create diverse groups of four; try to have gender, age, and ethnic diversity if possible. Let each person jot down a few notes about a disagreement and the four positions. Now, have one person at a time describe his/her situation and the first position. For each of the other positions, the other group members can help the speaker see even more ways to view the situation from other perspectives.

With a partner, role-play your situation orally for the class.

Brief Background Information

_____

_____

_____

_____

Class _____   Name_____

Position 1: "I'm right and you're wrong." Explain how you are right and the other person is wrong.

_____

_____

_____

_____

_____

_____

Position 2: "You're right and I'm wrong." Explain how the other person's position is correct, or at least understandable.

_____

_____

_____

_____

_____

_____

Position 3: "We're both right and we're both wrong." Show that there are both correct (or understandable) and mistaken (or unreasonable) parts of both positions.

_____

_____

_____

_____

_____

Position 4: "The issue may be less important than it seems; some other things may be more important." Describe at least two ways in which the elements developed in positions 1–3 might affect your relationship. Describe at least one way in which the issue might be seen as less important than it was originally and describe at least one way in which the issue might be seen as more important than it was originally.

_____

_____

_____

_____

_____

CONCLUSION

1. Explain how there is some truth in each of the preceding positions.

_____

_____

_____

_____

_____

2. Explain how viewing the issue from each of the preceding positions might change your perception of the issue and how it might change your behavior in the future.

_____

_____

_____

_____

_____

3. Explain how this issue and your understanding of it affect your relationship.

_____

_____

_____

_____

_____

_____

4. Explain the impact of hearing classmates explain how you might view the issue differently.

_____

_____

_____

_____

_____

_____

_____

3.3 PERCEPTION-CHECKING PRACTICE

LEARNING OBJECTIVES

- Describe how the processes of selection, organization, interpretation, and negotiation shape communication in a given situation.
- Explain how the influences on perception listed in this chapter affect communication in a specific situation.
- Demonstrate how you might use the skill of perception checking in a significant relationship.

INSTRUCTIONS

1. Alone or with a partner, write a perception check for each of the situations below or spontaneously create an oral perception check. If you write them first, practice delivering them aloud to each other.

EXAMPLE

Yesterday your friend Erin laughed at a joke about "dumb blonds." You found it offensive.

Perception-checking statement: *Erin, when Joey cracked the dumb blond joke last night, you laughed. I'm wondering if you disapproved of the joke but laughed just to make Joey feel comfortable, or if you really think that blonds are not as smart as the rest of the population. Can you clarify things for me?*

1. Last night you saw a recent date walking on the beach, holding hands with someone. You'd like to date again, but don't want to if a current relationship exists. You get a call from the recent date, asking you to a movie and dinner this weekend.

_____

_____

_____

_____

2. Ever since the school year began, your father has called weekly, asking how you are doing. He's just called and asked again.

_____

_____

_____

_____

3. Your friend was driving you home from a party last night when he began to weave the car between lanes on the highway. You were uncomfortable, but didn't say anything then. Now it is the next morning and he shows up to take you to a class. You have decided to bring up the incident.

_____

_____

_____

_____

4. For the last two weeks, when you are leaving your house, your roommate has asked for a ride somewhere. Your roommate has a car, but you haven't seen it lately. You are in a hurry now, and your roommate has just asked for another ride.

_____

_____

_____

_____

Class _____   Name_____

5. You return home at night to find your roommate reading on the couch. When you walk into the room and greet him, he grunts and turns his face away from you and keeps reading.

_____

_____

_____

_____

6. Last week your instructor returned your exam with a low grade and the comment, "This kind of work paints a bleak picture for the future." You have approached the instructor to discuss the remark.

_____

_____

_____

_____

7. In one of your regular long distance phone conversations you ask your favorite cousin about his romantic life. He sighs and says, "Oh, it's OK, I guess."

_____

_____

_____

_____

8. Your girlfriend, boyfriend, or spouse announces that she or he plans to spend next Friday night with friends from work. You usually spend Friday nights with each other.

_____

_____

_____

_____

9. Last week your supervisor at work, Ms. Black, gave you a big assignment. Three times since then she has asked you whether you're having any trouble with it.

_____

_____

_____

_____

10. Last weekend your next-door neighbor, Steve, raked a big pile of leaves near your property line, promising to clean them up after work on Monday. It's Wednesday, and the wind is blowing the leaves into your yard.

_____

_____

_____

_____

11. One of your classmates sits by you every day in class and you've done a lot of homework together; he's called you at home a few times a week. He suggests that you meet for dinner this weekend.

_____

_____

_____

_____

12. You've noticed one of your officemates looking over at you a number of times during the past few days. At first she looked away quickly, but now she smiles every time you look up and catch her looking at you. You've been under a lot of pressure at work lately and have been extremely busy. You can't understand why she keeps looking at you. You've decided to ask.

_____

_____

_____

_____

3.4 PERCEPTION CHECKING

LEARNING OBJECTIVES

- Explain how the influences on perception listed in this chapter affect communication in a specific situation.
- Demonstrate how you might use the skill of perception checking in a significant relationship.

INSTRUCTIONS

1. Identify a situation in your life in which a perception check might be appropriate. Describe the situation to the person who will be evaluating your skill. Possible topics: controversial issues, things that "bug" you, perceived injustices, personal dilemmas, and misperceptions.
2. Deliver a complete perception check to your evaluator, without using notes, following the criteria listed in Chapter 3 of *Looking Out/Looking In* and outlined in the checklist below.

CHECKLIST

_____   Describes background for a potential perception-checking situation.

_____   Delivers complete perception check.

    _____   Reports at least one behavior that describes, without evaluating or judging, what the person has said or done.

    _____   States two interpretations that are distinctly different, equally probable, and are based on the reported behavior.

    _____   Makes a sincere request for feedback clarifying how to interpret the reported behavior.

_____   Verbal and nonverbal behavior

    _____   Reflects sincere desire for clarification of the perception.

    _____   Sounds realistic and consistent with style of the speaker.

    _____   Uses nonthreatening, nondefensive voice and eye contact.

_____   Realistically and clearly assesses how perception checking and other alternatives can be used in everyday life.

    _____   In situation described here.

    _____   In other situations (be specific).

Class _____   Name_____

1. Describe how well perception checking might (or might not) work in the situation you have chosen. If you do not think a complete perception check is the best approach for this situation, explain why and describe a more promising alternative.

_____

_____

_____

_____

2. Describe various channels you can use for perception checking.

_____

_____

_____

_____

3. What is the impact on the person using a perception check of having to think of more than one possible interpretation?

_____

_____

_____

_____

4. What is the impact on the person hearing the perception check of hearing more than one possible interpretation?

_____

_____

_____

_____

5. What would you predict are some long- and short-term effects on relationships in which people use more perception checks? Consider employee/employer, parent/child, coworkers, friends, and partners.

_____

_____

_____

_____

Class _____   Name_____

3.5 MEDIATED MESSAGES—PERCEPTION

LEARNING OBJECTIVES

- Describe how the processes of selection, organization, interpretation, and negotiation shape communication in a given situation.
- Explain how the influences on perception affect communication in a specific situation.

INSTRUCTIONS

Discuss each of the questions below in your group. Prepare written answers for your instructor, or be prepared to contribute to a large group discussion, comparing your experiences with those of others in your class.

1. Think of ways in which messages sent through mediated messages may contribute to misperceptions. (Example: I called my grandmother and she thought my tone of voice sounded like I was irritated with her; she didn't say anything to me at the time, but complained to my mother about me.)

_____

_____

_____

_____

2. How do the influences on perception (physiological or cultural differences, social roles, self-concept) affect these mediated misperceptions? (Example: Physiological: I was tired when I called my grandmother and I know she has age-related hearing problems.)

_____

_____

_____

_____

3. Prepare a perception-checking statement that could be used in a mediated context. Specify the mediated channel and the likelihood of success of the perception-checking attempt. (Example: "When you said in your last email that you were busy on Saturday, I wondered if you had a previous commitment or if you were irritated with me for some reason I'm not aware of and so don't want to see me. What did you mean?" I think this perception-checking statement gives my partner a way to bring up anything that might be wrong, so it has a good likelihood of success.)

_____

_____

_____

_____

4. Are there times when using perception checks in mediated contexts might be preferable to using them face-to-face? Explain. Are there times when perception checks in mediated contexts might be less effective or appropriate? Explain.

_____

_____

_____

_____

3.6 PERCEPTION

LEARNING OBJECTIVES

- Explain how the influences on perception listed in this chapter affect communication in a specific situation.
- Analyze how the tendencies described in this chapter have distorted your perceptions of another person, and hence your communication. Use this information to present a more accurate alternative set of perceptions.
- Demonstrate how you might use the skill of perception checking in a significant relationship.

INSTRUCTIONS

Use the following case to explore the variety of communication issues involved in communication and perception.

CASE

Jorge is a registered nurse at a facility that cares for about 80 elderly patients. Jorge has been at the facility longer than any of the other nurses and has his choice of schedule; he believes he deserves this because of his service and seniority. There is now a shortage of nurses. Jorge's supervisor, Marisa, has been trying to hire new nurses, some of whom will only work if they can have Jorge's schedule. Marisa and Jorge are meeting to discuss the situation.

1. What factors are likely to influence the perceptions of Jorge and Marisa?

_____

_____

_____

_____

2. Prepare perception-checking statements for Jorge and Marisa to deliver to one another.

_____

_____

_____

_____

3. How can Marisa and Jorge communicate competently in order to come to a constructive conclusion to this situation?

_____

_____

_____

_____

4. What suggestions would you give Marisa and Jorge based on information in this chapter? Cite information from the text to back up your suggestions.

_____

_____

_____

_____

Class _____   Name_____

3.7 ASSESSING OUR PERCEPTION

LEARNING OBJECTIVES

- Explain how the influences on perception listed in this chapter affect communication in a specific situation.
- Analyze how the tendencies described in the text have distorted your perceptions of another person, and hence your communication. Use this information to present a more accurate alternative set of perceptions.

INSTRUCTIONS

Predict the feelings of a classmate on a current issue such as politics, economy, or pop culture. List the issue below and then list the reason for your prediction.

Classmate #1 Prediction:

_____

_____

_____

_____

Classmate #2 Prediction:

_____

_____

_____

_____

Class _____   Name_____

Classmate #3 Prediction:

_____

_____

_____

_____

Now that you have predicted what your classmates might feel on a certain issue, ask them how they feel on this issue and record their responses below.

Classmate #1 Response:

_____

_____

_____

_____

Classmate #2 Response:

_____

_____

_____

_____

Classmate #3 Response:

_____

_____

_____

_____

Class _____   Name_____

Now compare your classmates' responses with your predictions. Were your predictions accurate? What made you make your initial predication about each of your classmates and how has your perception on them changed since doing this exercise?

Classmate #1

_____

_____

_____

_____

Classmate #2

_____

_____

_____

_____

Classmate #3

_____

_____

_____

_____

STUDY GUIDE

CHECK YOUR UNDERSTANDING

TRUE/FALSE

Mark the statements below as true or false. Correct statements that are false on the lines below to create a true statement.

_____   1.   Androgynous males have a smaller repertoire of behaviors than masculine males.

           _____

_____   2.   Selection, organization, interpretation, and negotiation comprise the steps of the perception process.

           _____

_____   3.   The fact that we pay attention to some things and ignore others illustrates the fact that selection is an objective process.

           _____

_____   4.   Allowing children to experience and manage frustrating events can help increase their empathic concern for others in later life.

           _____

_____   5.   Generalizations and stereotypes of groups are generally accurate for everyone in the group.

           _____

_____   6.   The halo effect is the tendency to form an overall positive impression of a person on the basis of one positive characteristic.

_____   7.   Adrenal and sex hormones affect the way both men and women relate to others.

           _____

_____   8.   All cultures view talk as desirable, using it for social purposes as well as to perform tasks.

           _____

_____ 9. Societal gender roles and stereotypes do not dramatically affect perception.

_____

_____ 10. The way we perceive ourselves influences our opinions of ourselves, but not our opinions of others.

_____

_____ 11. Since we are able to perceive with our senses, our perceptions make us aware of all that is going on around us.

_____

_____ 12. Culture plays an important role in our ability to understand the perspectives of others.

_____

_____ 13. Recent studies show that humans are "hard-wired" to empathize with one another.

_____

_____ 14. Cognitive complexity is the ability to construct one framework for a variety of issues.

_____

COMPLETION

Fill in the blanks below with the correct terms chosen from the list below.

narrative   self-serving bias   sympathy
the pillow method   empathy   stereotypes
punctuation   ethnocentrism
androgynous   individualist culture

1. _____ is the belief that one's culture is superior to others.

2. _____ is the determination of causes and effects in a series of interactions.

3. _____ is a story created by shared perspectives to explain events and behavior.

4. _____ is the tendency to judge ourselves in the most generous terms possible.

5. _____ is the ability to re-create another person's perspective.

6. _____ is one means for boosting empathy and cognitive complexity.

7. _____ are exaggerated generalizations associated with a categorizing system.

8. _____ is an example of a psychological sex type that influences perception.

9. _____ is feeling compassion for another person.

10. _____ is generally less adept at perspective-taking.

MULTIPLE CHOICE

RECOGNIZING PERCEPTION-CHECKING ELEMENTS

For each of the following statements, identify which element of the perception-checking statement is missing. Place the letter of the most accurate evaluation of the statement on the line before the statement.

a. This statement doesn't describe behavior.
b. This statement doesn't give two distinctly different interpretations.
c. This statement doesn't request clarification of the behavior in an open-ended way.
d. There is nothing missing from this perception-checking statement.

_____ 1. "Why did you send me those flowers? Is this a special occasion or what?"

_____ 2. "When you went straight to bed when you came home, I thought you were sick. Are you all right?"

_____ 3. "You must be either really excited about your grades or anxious to talk about something important. What's going on?"

_____ 4. "When you ran out smiling, I figured you were glad to see me and ready to go, or maybe you were having such a good time here you wanted to stay longer."

_____ 5. "I thought you were angry with me when you didn't come over this afternoon like you'd said you would. But then I thought maybe something came up at work. What is it?"

_____ 6. "When you told me you expected to get an outline with my report, I thought you were trying to trick me into doing more work, or maybe you didn't realize that wasn't part of my job."

_____ 7. "When you told everyone my parents own the company, you must have been indicating I was hired here only because of them. Is that what you think?"

_____ 8. "When you passed the ball to me, I thought you wanted me to shoot. Did you?"

_____ 9. "Why is it that you're so pleased with yourself? Did you win the lottery or accomplish something great? What's up?"

_____ 10. "Dad, when you told my friend Art what a great athlete you think I am, I thought you were either really proud of me and wanted to brag a little, or maybe you wanted to see what Art and I had in common by the way he responded. What were your intentions?"

CHAPTER THREE STUDY GUIDE ANSWERS

TRUE/FALSE

1. F	4. T	7. T	10. F	13. T
2. T	5. F	8. F	11. F	14. F
3. F	6. T	9. F	12. T	

COMPLETION

1. ethnocentrism
2. punctuation
3. narrative
4. self-serving bias
5. empathy
6. the pillow method
7. stereotypes
8. androgynous
9. sympathy
10. individualist cultures

MULTIPLE CHOICE

1. b	3. a	5. d	7. b, c	9. a
2. b, c	4. c	6. c	8. b	10. d

Emotions:
Feeling, Thinking, and Communicating

After studying the topics in this chapter,
you should be able to:

1. Describe how the four components of emotions affect the way you feel, and hence your communication, in an important situation.

2. Describe how the influences on emotional expression listed on pages 121–125 have affected your communication in an important relationship.

3. Apply the guidelines for effectively communicating emotions (pages 126–134) in an important situation.

4. Identify and dispute the fallacies that are creating debilitative emotions in an important situation. Explain how more rational thinking can lead to more constructive communication.

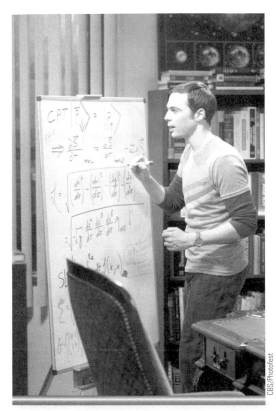

CBS/Photofest

In *The Big Bang Theory,* Sheldon Cooper (Jim Parsons) has a keen mind but lacks emotional intelligence. As a result, he often violates social rules and sometimes damages relationships. (See the TV summary at the end of this chapter.)

It's impossible to talk about communication without acknowledging the importance of emotions. Think about it: Feeling confident can assist you in everything from giving a speech to asking for a date, whereas feeling insecure can ruin your chances. Feeling angry or defensive can spoil your time with others, whereas feeling and acting calm will help prevent or solve problems. The way you share or withhold your feelings of affection can affect the future of your relationships. On and on goes the list of feelings that influence how we interact with others: appreciation, loneliness, joy, insecurity, curiosity, irritation. The point is clear: Communication shapes our feelings, and feelings shape our communication.

The role of emotions in human affairs is apparent to social scientists and laypeople alike. Researcher Daniel Goleman coined the term **emotional intelligence** to describe the ability to understand and manage one's own emotions and be sensitive to others' feelings.[1] Studies show that emotional intelligence is positively linked with self-esteem, life satisfaction, and self-acceptance,[2] as well as with healthy conflict management and relationships.[3] Emotional intelligence is unquestionably vital to both personal and interpersonal success.

Stop for a moment and try to identify someone you know who is emotionally intelligent. Perhaps it's a family member who is in touch with a wide range of feelings without being overwhelmed by them, or a boss who makes wise and rational choices even under stress. Now think of a person who might be lacking emotional intelligence. Maybe it's a colleague who is uptight and dismissive about honest human feelings, or a friend who blows up at the smallest inconvenience. And finally, assess your own emotional intelligence. How well do *you* understand and manage your emotions, and how sensitive are you to others' feelings?

Because emotions play such an important role in virtually all types of relationships, this chapter looks closer at analyzing and expressing them. The following pages will clarify what feelings are and how to recognize them. You'll read guidelines about when and how to best share your feelings with others. Finally, we will explore how to enhance emotions that make communication more rewarding and decrease ones that interfere with effective relationships. In later chapters we'll discuss how to interpret others' emotional states, but for now we'll focus on identifying and expressing your own emotions.

What Are Emotions?

Suppose that an extraterrestrial visitor asked you to explain emotions. How would you answer? You might start by saying that emotions are things that we feel. But this doesn't say much, because in turn you would probably describe feelings as synonymous with emotions. Social scientists generally agree that there are several components to the phenomena we label as feelings.[4]

PHYSIOLOGICAL FACTORS

When a person has strong emotions, many bodily changes occur.[5] For example, the physical components of fear include an increased heart rate, a rise in blood pressure, an increase in adrenaline secretions, an elevated blood sugar level, a slowing of digestion, and a dilation of the pupils. Marriage researcher John Gottman notes that symptoms like these also occur when couples are in intense conflicts.[6] He calls the condition "flooding" and has found that it impedes effective problem-solving. Some physiological changes are recognizable to the person having them: a churning stomach or tense jaw, for example. These cues can offer a significant clue to your emotions after you become aware of them.

NONVERBAL REACTIONS

Not all physical changes that accompany emotions are internal. Feelings are often apparent by observable changes. Some of these changes involve a person's appearance: blushing, sweating, and so on. Other changes involve behavior: a distinctive facial expression, posture, gestures, different vocal tone and rate, and so on. And research confirms what might be guessed: nonverbal expressions of emotions become more pronounced under the influence of alcohol.[7] Alcohol serves as an emotion enhancer—sometimes for better, sometimes for worse.

Although it's reasonably easy to tell when someone is feeling a strong emotion, it's more difficult to be certain exactly what that emotion might be. A slumped posture and sigh may be a sign of sadness, or they may be a sign of fatigue. Likewise, trembling hands might indicate excitement, or they may indicate fear. As you'll learn in Chapter 6, nonverbal behavior is usually ambiguous, and it's dangerous to assume that it can be read with much accuracy.

Although we usually think of nonverbal behavior as the reaction to an emotional state, there may be times when the reverse is true—when nonverbal behavior actually *causes* an emotional state. In one study, experimental subjects were able to create various emotional states by altering their facial expressions.[8] When subjects were coached to move their facial muscles in ways that appeared afraid, angry, disgusted, amused, sad, surprised, and contemptuous, the subjects' bodies responded as if they were having these feelings. In another experiment, subjects who were coached to smile actually reported feeling better, and when they altered their expressions to look unhappy, they felt worse than before.[9]

There's also a connection between verbalizing emotions and nonverbal reactions. One study showed that participants who generated words associated with pride and disappointment experienced a change in posture.[10] They unconsciously stood taller when talking about pride and slumped when using words for disappointment. The participants also experienced emotions associated with their words (e.g., feeling sad when speaking about disappointment). This reminds us that verbal and nonverbal expressions of emotion are often interconnected.

COGNITIVE INTERPRETATIONS

Although there may be situations in which physical behavior and emotional states are directly connected, in most situations the mind plays an important role in determining emotional states. As you read earlier, some physiological components of fear are a racing heart, perspiration, tense muscles, and elevated blood pressure. Interestingly enough, these symptoms are similar to the physical changes that accompany excitement, joy, and other positive emotions. In other words, if we were to measure the physical condition of someone having a strong emotion, we would have a hard time knowing whether that person was trembling with fear or quivering with excitement.

Introverts: Thoughtful, Not Shy

As a card-carrying introvert, I am one of the many people whose personality confers on them a preference for the inner world of their own mind rather than the outer world of sociability. Our psychic opposites, extraverts, prefer schmoozing and social life because such activities boost their mood. They get bored by too much solitude.

Often confused with shyness, introversion does not imply social reticence or discomfort. Rather than being averse to social engagement, introverts become overwhelmed by too much of it, which explains why the introvert is ready to leave a party after an hour and the extravert gains steam as the night goes on. Extraverts are comfortable thinking as they speak. Introverts prefer slow-paced interactions that allow room for thought. Brainstorming does not work for them. Email does.

Like individuals, cultures have different styles. America is a noisy culture, unlike, say, Finland, which values silence. Individualism, dominant in the U.S. and Germany, promotes the direct, fast-paced style of communication associated with extraversion. Collectivistic societies, such as those in East Asia, value privacy and restraint, qualities more characteristic of introverts.

Laurence Mouton/PhotoAlto/Corbis

"In verbal cultures, remaining silent presents a problem," report Anio Sallinen-Kuparinen, James McCroskey, and Virginia Richmond, who have studied communication styles in the U.S. and Finland. Perceptions of competence tend to be based on verbal behavior. An introvert who is silent in a group may actually be quite engaged—taking in what is said, thinking about it, waiting for a turn to speak—but will be seen in the U.S. as a poor communicator.

Introverts are not as mild-mannered as made out to be. They seethe and even will lash out at those who encroach upon or malign their personal comfort zones. Here are a few emotional buttons to avoid with your introverted companions.

- "'Why don't you like parties? Don't you like people?' is a common remark introverts hear," says Marti Laney, a psychologist and the author of *The Introvert Advantage*. "Usually we like people fine," she insists. "We just like them in small doses.

- "Don't demand immediate feedback from an introvert. "Extraverts think we have answers but just aren't giving them," Laney says. "They don't understand we need time to formulate them" and often won't talk until a thought is suitably polished.

- Don't interrupt if an introvert does get to talking. Listen closely. "Being overlooked is a really big issue for introverts," Laney says. Introverts are unlikely to repeat themselves; they will not risk making the same mistake twice.

- Above all, "we hate people telling us how we can be more extraverted, as if that's the desired state," says Beth Buelow, a life and leadership coach for introverts. Many introverts are happy with the way they are. And if you're not, that's your problem.

Laurie Helgoe

Excerpted from "Revenge of the Introvert" by Laurie Helgoe, *Psychology Today*, September 1, 2010; http://www.psychologytoday.com/articles/201008/revenge-the-introvert. Reprinted with permission.

The recognition that the bodily components of most emotions are similar led some psychologists to conclude that the experience of fright, joy, or anger comes primarily from the label we give to the same physical symptoms at a given time.[11] Psychologist Philip Zimbardo offers a good example of this principle:

> I notice I'm perspiring while lecturing. From that I infer I am nervous. If it occurs often, I might even label myself a "nervous person." Once I have the label, the next question I must answer is "Why am I nervous?" Then I start to search for an appropriate explanation. I might notice some students leaving the room, or being inattentive. I am nervous because I'm not giving a good lecture. That makes me nervous. How do I know it's not good? Because I'm boring my audience. I am nervous because I am a boring lecturer and I want to be a good lecturer. I feel inadequate. Maybe I should open a delicatessen instead. Just then a student says, "It's hot in here, I'm perspiring and it makes it tough to concentrate on your lecture." Instantly, I'm no longer "nervous" or "boring."*

Zimbardo found that changing his interpretation of the event affected the way he felt about it. Social scientists refer to this process as **reappraisal**—rethinking the meaning of emotionally charged events in ways that alter their emotional impact.[12] Research shows that reappraisal is vastly superior to suppressing one's feelings: It often leads to lower stress, higher self-esteem, and increased productivity.[13] Here are two examples:

- Your self-esteem has been shattered since you lost your job, particularly because some of your less-ambitious coworkers were not fired. You lack confidence as you look for new employment. You could reappraise the event as an opportunity to find a new position (or career) where your hard work and contributions will be better appreciated.
- A friend of yours says some malicious things about you behind your back. Although you are hurt, you decide her actions are a statement about *her* character, not yours—and that you'll demonstrate your character by not speaking poorly about her to others.

It's important to note that reappraisal is not about denying your feelings. Recognizing and acknowledging emotions such as anger, hurt, and grief (as well as happiness, love, and relief) are vital to psychological and relational health. However, when you're ready to move past difficult emotions, reappraisal can help. We'll take a closer look at using reappraisal to reduce debilitative emotions later in this chapter.

VERBAL EXPRESSION

As you will read in Chapter 6, nonverbal behavior is a powerful way of communicating emotion. In fact, nonverbal actions are better at conveying emotions than they are at conveying ideas. But sometimes words are necessary to express feelings. Saying "I'm really angry" is clearer and probably more helpful than stomping out of the room, and "I'm feeling nervous" might help explain a pained expression on your face.

Some researchers believe there are several basic or primary emotions.[14] However, there isn't much agreement among scholars about what those emotions are, or about what makes them basic.[15] Moreover, emotions that are primary in one culture may not be primary in others, and some emotions have no direct equivalent in other cultures.[16] For example, "shame" is a central emotion in the Chinese experience,[17] whereas it's much less familiar to most people from Western cultures. Despite this debate, most scholars acknowledge that *anger*, *joy*, *fear*, and *sadness* are common and typical human emotions.

---

*Zimbardo, P. (1977). *Shyness: What it is, what to do about it* (p. 53). Reading, MA: Addison-Wesley.

Annoyed	**Angry**	**Furious**
Pensive	**Sad**	**Grieving**
Content	**Happy**	**Ecstatic**
Anxious	**Afraid**	**Terrified**
Liking	**Loving**	**Adoring**

FIGURE 4.1 Intensity of Emotions
© Cengage Learning

We experience most emotions with different degrees of intensity, and it's important to use language that represents these differences. Figure 4.1 illustrates this point clearly. To say you're "annoyed" when a friend breaks an important promise, for example, would probably be an understatement. In other cases, people chronically overstate the strength of their feelings. To them, everything is "wonderful" or "terrible." The problem with this sort of exaggeration is that when a truly intense emotion comes along, they have no words left to describe it adequately. If chocolate chip cookies from the local bakery are "unbelievably fantastic," how does it feel to fall in love?

Researchers have identified a wide range of problems that arise for people who aren't able to talk about emotions constructively, including social isolation, unsatisfying relationships, feelings of anxiety and depression, and misdirected aggression.[18] Furthermore, the way parents talk to their children about emotions has a powerful effect on the children's development. Studies identify two distinct parenting styles: "emotion coaching" and "emotion dismissing."[19] The coaching approach gives children skills for communicating about feelings in later life that lead to much more satisfying relationships. Children who grow up in families where parents dismiss emotions are at higher risk for behavior problems than those who are raised in families that practice emotion coaching.[20] Later in this chapter you will find some guidelines for effectively communicating about emotions.

PAUSE AND REFLECT

RECOGNIZING YOUR EMOTIONS

Keep a three-day record of your feelings. You can do this by spending a few minutes each evening recalling what emotions you felt during the day, what other people were involved, and the circumstances in which the emotions occurred.

At the end of the three-day period, you can understand the role that emotions play in your communication by answering the following questions:

1. How did you recognize the emotions you felt: through physiological stimuli, nonverbal behaviors, or cognitive processes?
2. Did you have any difficulty deciding which emotions you were feeling?
3. What emotions do you have most often? Are they primary or mixed? Mild or intense?
4. In what circumstances do you or don't you show your feelings? What factors influence your decision to show or not show your feelings? The type of feeling? The person or persons involved? The situation (time, place)? The subject that the feeling involves (money, sex, and so on)?
5. What are the consequences of the type of communicating you just described in step 4? Are you satisfied with these consequences? If not, what can you do to become more satisfied?

 You can complete this activity by visiting CengageBrain.com to access the Speech Communication CourseMate for *Looking Out/ Looking In*, and, if requested, email your responses to your instructor.

Influences on Emotional Expression

Most people are reluctant to express their emotions, at least verbally. People are generally comfortable making statements of fact and often delight in expressing their opinion, but they balk at disclosing how they feel. Why do people hesitate to express their emotions? Let's look at several reasons.

PERSONALITY

There is an increasingly clear relationship between personality and the way we experience and communicate emotions.[21] For example, extraverted people—those with a tendency to be upbeat, optimistic, and to enjoy social contact—report more positive emotions in everyday life than less extraverted individuals.[22] Likewise, people with neurotic personalities (those with a tendency to worry, feel anxious, and be apprehensive) report more negative emotions in everyday life than less neurotic individuals. These personality traits are at least partially biological in nature.

Personality can be a powerful force, but it doesn't have to govern your communication satisfaction. For instance, people who are shy by nature can devise comfortable and effective strategies for reaching out. For example, the Internet has proven to be an effective way for reticent communicators to make contact, because it's been found to reduce social anxiety.[23] Email and computer dating services provide low-threat ways to approach others and get acquainted.[24]

"I'm not an emotional person myself. Fortunately, Georgine feels things for both of us."

CULTURE

People around the world generally experience the same emotions, but the same events can generate quite different feelings in different cultures.[25] The notion of eating snails might bring a smile of delight to some residents of France, whereas it would cause many North Americans to grimace in disgust. Culture also has an effect on how emotions are valued. One study found that Asian Americans and Hong Kong Chinese value "low arousal positive affect" (such as "calm") more than do European Americans, who tend to value "high arousal positive affect" (such as "excitement").[26] More specifically, the United States is known internationally as a "culture of cheerfulness." One author from Poland describes U.S. expressiveness this way: "Wow! Great! How nice! That's fantastic! I had a terrific time! It was wonderful! Have a nice day! Americans. So damned cheerful."[27]

There are also differences in the degree to which people in various cultures display their feelings. For example, social scientists have found support for the notion that people from warmer climates are more emotionally expressive than those who live in cooler climates.[28] Nearly 3,000 respondents representing 26 nationalities reported that people from the southern part of their countries were more emotionally expressive than were northerners.

One of the most significant factors that influences emotional expression is the position of a culture on the individualism-collectivism spectrum. Members of collectivistic cultures (such as Japan and India) prize harmony among members of their in-group and discourage expression of negative emotions that might upset relationships among people who belong to it. By contrast, members of highly individualistic cultures (such as the United States and Canada) feel comfortable revealing their emotions to people with whom they are close. It's easy to see how differences in display rules can lead to communication problems. For example, individualistic North Americans might view collectivistic Asians as less than candid, whereas Asians could easily regard North Americans as overly demonstrative.[29]

The phrase "I love you" offers an interesting case study of cultural differences in emotion expression. Researchers found that Americans say "I love you" more frequently (and to more people) than do members of most other cultures.[30] It's not that love isn't a universal experience; rather, there are significant cultural differences about when, where, how often, and with whom the phrase should be used. For instance, Middle Easterners in the study said that "I love you" should only be expressed between spouses, and they warned that American men who use the phrase cavalierly with Middle Eastern women might be misinterpreted as making a marriage proposal. They were not alone: Study participants from a variety of backgrounds (e.g., Eastern Europe, India, Korea) said they use the phrase quite sparingly, believing that its power and meaning would be lost if used too often. However, one factor was consistent across cultures: Women tend to say "I love you" more often than men. For more examples of the effect that gender has on emotion expression, read on.

GENDER

Even within a culture, biological sex and gender roles often shape the ways in which men and women experience and express their emotions.[31] In fact, biological sex is the best predictor of the ability to detect and interpret emotional expressions—better than academic background, amount of foreign travel, cultural similarity, or ethnicity.[32] For example, research suggests that women are more attuned to emotions than men,[33] both within and across cultures.[34] A team of psychologists tested men's and women's recall of emotional images and found that females were 10 to 15 percent more accurate in remembering them. Furthermore, women's reactions to these emotion-producing stimuli were significantly more intense than men's.

Research on emotional expression suggests that there is at least some truth to the cultural stereotype of the unexpressive male and the more expressive female.[35] In face-to-face communication, one study showed that fathers mask their emotions more than mothers do, which leads their children to have more difficulty reading their fathers' emotional expressions.[36] In online communication, similar differences between male and female emotional expressiveness apply. For example, women are more likely than men to use emoticons, such as the symbol :), to express their feelings.[37] Women also express more affection on Facebook than do men.[38]

The point is that while men and women generally experience the same emotions, there are some significant differences in the ways they express them.[39] These differences are due in large measure to social conventions, which we'll discuss now.

SOCIAL CONVENTIONS

In mainstream U.S. society, the unwritten rules of communication discourage the direct

In the television show *New Girl*, Jess (Zooey Deschanel) wears most of her emotions on her sleeve. Her male housemates are typically more circumspect about revealing their feelings. This matches patterns that are often seen in American culture.

LOOKING AT DIVERSITY

Todd Epaloose: A Native American Perspective on Emotional Expression

Todd Epaloose

Todd Epaloose was raised on the Zuñi pueblo in New Mexico. He spent part of his childhood on the reservation and part attending school in the city. He now lives in Albuquerque. As an urbanite who still spends time with his family on the reservation, Todd alternates between two worlds.

Zuñi and Anglo cultures are as different as night and day in the ways they treat communication about emotions. In mainstream U.S. culture, speaking up is accepted, or even approved. This is true from the time you are a child. Parents are proud when their child speaks up—whether that means showing affection, being curious, or even expressing unhappiness in a way that the parents approve. Being quiet gets a child labeled as "shy," and is considered a problem. Assertiveness is just as important in school, at work, and in adult relationships.

In Zuñi culture, emotions are much less public. We are a private people, who consider a public display of feelings embarrassing. Self-control is considered a virtue. I think a lot of our emotional reticence comes from a respect for privacy. Your feelings are your own, and showing them to others is just as wrong as taking off your clothes in public. It's not that traditional Zuñis have fewer or less intense feelings than people in the city: It's just that there is less value placed on showing them in obvious ways.

The way we express affection is a good example of Zuñi attitudes and rules for sharing emotions. Our families are full of love. But someone from the city might not recognize this love, since it isn't displayed very much. There isn't a lot of hugging and kissing, even between children and parents. Also, there isn't a lot of verbal expression: People don't say "I love you" to one another very much. We show our emotions by our actions: by helping one another, by caring for the people we love when they need us. That's enough to keep us happy.

Which approach is best? I think both cultures have strengths. Many Zuñis and other Native Americans who want to join the mainstream culture are at a disadvantage. They aren't very good at standing up for their rights, and so they get taken advantage of. Even at home, there are probably times when it's important to express feelings to prevent misunderstandings. On the other hand, I think some Native American emotional restraint might be helpful for people who are used to Anglo communication styles. Respecting others' privacy can be important: Some feelings are nobody else's business, and prying or demanding that they open up seems pushy and rude. Native American self-control can also add some civility to personal relationships. I'm not sure that "letting it all hang out" is always the best way.

One final word: I believe that in order to really understand the differences between emotional expression in Native American and Anglo cultures you have to live in both. If that isn't possible, at least realize that the familiar one isn't the only good approach. Try to respect what you don't understand.

expression of most emotions.[40] Count the number of genuine emotional expressions that you hear over a two- or three-day period ("I'm angry"; "I feel embarrassed") and you'll discover that emotional expressions are rare.

Not surprisingly, the emotions that people *do* share directly are usually positive ("I'm happy to say . . ."; "I really enjoyed . . ."). Communicators are reluctant to send messages that embarrass or threaten the "face" of others.[41] This is particularly true in the early stages

"It was a time when men regularly performed great feats of valor but were rarely in touch with their feelings."

of a new relationship, when a high ratio of positive-to-negative emotions is crucial to the relationship's development.[42] But even those in long-term relationships rarely express negative emotions directly. One study of married couples revealed that partners often share complimentary feelings ("I love you") or face-saving ones ("I'm sorry I yelled at you"). They also willingly disclose both positive and negative feelings about absent third parties ("I like Fred," "I'm uncomfortable around Gloria"). On the other hand, husbands and wives rarely verbalize face-threatening feelings ("I'm disappointed in you") or hostility ("I'm mad at you").[43]

Expression of emotions is also shaped by the requirements of many social roles. Researchers use the term **emotion labor** to describe situations in which managing and even suppressing emotions is both appropriate and necessary. Studies show that emotion labor is an important component of many if not most occupations (see the On the Job box on page 125 for specific examples).

FEAR OF SELF-DISCLOSURE

In a society that discourages the expression of emotions, revealing them can seem risky.[44] For a parent, boss, or teacher whose life has been built on the image of confidence and certainty, it may be frightening to say, "I'm scared about my future." A person who has made a life's work out of not relying on others has a hard time saying, "I'm lonesome. I want your friendship."

Moreover, someone who musters up the courage to share feelings such as these still risks unpleasant consequences. Others might misunderstand: An expression of affection might be construed as a romantic invitation,[45] and a confession of uncertainty might look like a sign of weakness. Another risk is that emotional honesty might make others feel uncomfortable. Finally, there's always a risk that emotional honesty could be used against you, either out of cruelty or thoughtlessness. As you recall, Chapter 2 discusses alternatives to complete disclosure and suggests circumstances when it can be both wise and ethical to keep your feelings to yourself.

"I'm not in one of my moods. I'm in one of your moods."

EMOTIONAL CONTAGION

Cultural rules and social roles aren't the only factors that affect our feelings. Our emotions are also influenced by the feelings of those around us through **emotional contagion**: the process by which emotions are transferred from one person to another.[46] As one commentator observed, "We catch feelings from one another as though they were some kind of social virus."[47] There is evidence that students catch the mood of their teachers,[48] customers are affected by the emotions of employees who serve them,[49] and husbands and wives directly influence each other's emotions.[50] In fact, studies show that our happiness (or unhappiness) can be affected by neighbors, friends of friends, or even total strangers.[51]

ON THE JOB

Emotion Labor in the Workplace

The rules for expressing emotions on the job are clearly different from those in personal life. In intimate relationships (at least in mainstream Western culture), it's often important to tell friends, family, and loved ones exactly how you feel. In the workplace, however, it can be just as important to *conceal* emotions for the sake of clients, customers, coworkers, and supervisors—and also to protect your job.

Emotion labor—the process of managing and sometimes suppressing emotions—has been studied in a variety of occupational contexts. A few examples:

- If firefighters don't mask their emotions of fear, disgust, and stress, it will impede their ability to help the people whose lives they are trying to save. Emotion-management training is therefore vital for new firefighters.[a]
- Correctional officers at two minimum-security prisons described the tension of needing to be "warm, nurturing, and respectful" to inmates while also being "suspicious, strong, and tough." The officers acknowledged that it's taxing to manage competing emotions and juggle conflicting demands.[b]

- Money is an emotion-laden topic, which means that financial planners often engage in emotion labor. Researchers concluded that "relationships and communication with clients may indeed be more central to the work of financial planners than portfolio performance reports and changes in estate tax laws."[c]

While some of these occupations deal with life-and-death situations, emotion management is equally important in less intensive jobs. For instance, most customer-service positions require working with people who may express their dissatisfaction in angry and inappropriate ways ("I hate this store—I'm never shopping here again!"). In situations like these, it's usually unwise to "fight fire with fire," even if that's your natural impulse. Instead, competent on-the-job communicators can use the listening, defense-reducing, and conflict-management skills described in Chapters 7, 10, and 11.

It's not always easy to manage emotions, especially when you're feeling fearful, stressed, angry, or defensive. Nevertheless, doing the work of emotion labor is often vital for success on the job.

Most of us recognize the degree to which emotions are infectious. You can almost certainly recall instances when being around a calm person leaves you feeling more at peace, or when your previously sunny mood was spoiled by contact with a grouch. Researchers have demonstrated that this process occurs quickly and doesn't require much, if any, verbal communication.[52] In one study, two volunteers completed a survey that identified their moods. Then they sat quietly, facing each other for a two-minute period, ostensibly waiting for the researcher to return to the room. At the end of that time, they completed another emotional survey. Time after time, the brief exposure resulted in the less expressive partner's moods coming to resemble the moods of the more expressive one. It's easy to understand how emotions can be even more infectious with prolonged contact. In just a few months, the emotional responses of both dating couples and college roommates become dramatically more similar.[53]

SELF-ASSESSMENT

Measuring Your EQ

You can get a clearer picture of your emotional intelligence by taking a simple online test. You can find the link to this site by visiting CengageBrain.com to access the Speech Communication CourseMate for *Looking Out/ Looking In.*

Guidelines for Expressing Emotions

As you just read, there aren't any universal rules for the best way to communicate emotions. Personality, culture, gender roles, and social conventions all govern what approach will feel right to the people involved and what is most likely to work in a given situation. It's easy to think of times when it's *not* smart to express emotions clearly and directly. You usually can't chew out authority figures like difficult bosses or professors, and it's probably not wise to confront dangerous looking strangers who are bothering you.

Despite all the qualifiers and limitations, there will be times when you can benefit from communicating your feelings clearly and directly—even if you aren't normally an expressive person. When those times come, the guidelines in the following pages can help you explain how you feel.

A wide range of research supports the value of expressing emotions appropriately. On one hand, underexpression of feelings can lead to serious ailments. Inexpressive people—those who value rationality and self-control, try to control their feelings and impulses, and deny distress—are more likely to get a host of ailments, including cancer, asthma, and heart disease.[54]

On the other hand, communicators who overexpress their negative feelings also suffer physiologically. When people lash out verbally, their blood pressure jumps an average of twenty points, and in some people it increases by as much as one hundred points.[55] The key to health, then, is to learn how to express emotions *constructively*.

Beyond the physiological benefits, another benefit of expressing emotions effectively is the chance of improving relationships.[56] As Chapter 2 explains, self-disclosure is one path (though not the only one) to intimacy. Even on the job, many managers and organizational researchers are contradicting generations of tradition by suggesting that constructively expressing emotions can lead to career success as well as help workers feel better.[57] Of course, the rules for expressing emotions in the workplace are usually more strict than those in personal relationships, so handle with care.[58]

Despite its benefits, expressing emotions effectively isn't a simple matter. It's obvious that showing every feeling of boredom, fear, anger, or frustration would get you into trouble. Even the indiscriminate sharing of positive feelings—love, affection, and so on—isn't always wise. But withholding emotions can be personally frustrating and can keep relationships from growing and prospering.

The following suggestions can help you decide when and how to express your emotions. Combined with the guidelines for self-disclosure in Chapter 2, they can improve the effectiveness of your emotional expression.

RECOGNIZE YOUR FEELINGS

Answering the question "How do you feel?" isn't as easy for some people as others. Some people (researchers call them "affectively oriented") are much more aware of their emotional states and use information about those emotional states when making important decisions.[59] By contrast, people with a low affective orientation usually aren't aware of their emotional states and tend to regard feelings as useless and unimportant information.

Beyond being *aware* of one's feelings, research shows that it's valuable to be able to *identify* one's emotions. Researchers have found that college students who can pinpoint the negative emotions they experience (such as "nervous," "angry," "sad," "ashamed," and "guilty") also have the best strategies for managing those emotions.[60] This explains why the ability to distinguish and label emotions is a vital component of emotional intelligence, both within and across cultures.[61]

My First Flame

To flame, according to *"Que's Computer User's Dictionary,"* is "to lose one's self-control and write a message that uses derogatory, obscene, or inappropriate language."

My flame arrived on a windy Friday morning. I got to work at nine, removed my coat, plugged in my PowerBook, and, as usual, could not resist *immediately* checking my email. I saw I had a message from a technology writer who does a column about personal computers for a major newspaper, and whom I knew by name only. I had recently published a piece about Bill Gates, the [former] chairman of Microsoft, and as I opened his email to me it was with the pleasant expectation of getting feedback from a colleague. Instead, I got:

> Crave this, a**hole: Listen, you toadying dips**t scumbag . . . remove your head from your rectum long enough to look around and notice that real reporters don't fawn over their subjects, pretend that their subjects are making some sort of special contact with them, or, worse, curry favor by telling their subjects how great the a**-licking profile is going to turn out and then brag in print about doing it.

I felt cold. People whose bodies have been badly burned begin to shiver, and the flame seemed to put a chill in the center of my chest which I could feel spreading slowly outward. The insults, being premeditated, were more forceful than insults spoken in the heat of the moment.

No one had ever said something like this to me before. In any other medium, these words would be, literally, unspeakable. The guy couldn't have said this to me on the phone, because I would have hung up and not answered if the phone rang again, and he couldn't have said it to my face, because I wouldn't have let him finish. If this had happened to me in the street, I could have used my status as a physically large male to threaten the person, but in the on-line world my size didn't matter. I suppose the guy could have written me a nasty letter: he probably wouldn't have used the word "rectum," though, and he probably wouldn't have mailed the letter; he would have thought twice while he was addressing the envelope. But the nature of email is that you don't think twice. You write and send.

What would Emily Post advise me to do? Flame the dips**t scumbag right back? I did spend most of that Friday in front of the screen composing the most vile insults I could dream up—words I have never spoken to another human being, and would never speak in any other medium, but which I found easy to type into the

David Plunkert/Spur Design

computer. I managed to restrain myself from sending my reply until I got home and asked my wife to look at it. She had the good sense to be horrified.

I asked [computer expert John Norstad] to look at it. He said, "My thirteen-year-old daughter is a Pearl Jam fan, and the other night she asked me if there might be some Pearl Jam stuff on the net. So we logged on and looked around, and we were able to download some Pearl Jam posters, some music, some song lyrics—really neat stuff. But then we came to the Pearl Jam newsgroup, and there was a really terrible flame war going on in there. People were saying really awful things to each other, things I was embarrassed to be sitting next to my daughter reading. . . . Terrible things. After a while, my daughter looked over at me and asked, 'Daddy, do these people have a life?' And I said, 'No, darling, most of them don't have a life.'"

John Seabrook

"My First Flame" by John Seabrook, *The New Yorker*, June 6, 1994. Originally published in *The New Yorker*. Reprinted by permission of the author.

As you read earlier in this chapter, feelings become recognizable in several ways. Physiological changes can be a clear sign of your feelings. Monitoring nonverbal behaviors is another excellent way to keep in touch with your emotions. You can also recognize your feelings by monitoring your thoughts as well as the verbal messages you send to others. It's not far from the verbal statement "I hate this!" to the realization that you're angry (or bored, nervous, or embarrassed).

RECOGNIZE THE DIFFERENCE BETWEEN FEELING, TALKING, AND ACTING

Just because you feel a certain way doesn't mean you must always talk about it, and talking about a feeling doesn't mean you must act on it. In fact, compelling evidence suggests that people who act out angry feelings—whether by lashing out, or even by hitting an inanimate punching bag—actually feel worse than those who experience anger without lashing out.[62]

Understanding the difference between having feelings and acting them out can help you express yourself constructively in tough situations. If, for instance, you recognize that you are upset with a friend, it becomes possible to explore exactly why you feel so upset. Sharing your feeling ("Sometimes I get so mad at you that I could scream") might open the door to resolving whatever is bothering you. Pretending that nothing is bothering you, or lashing out at the other person, is unlikely to diminish your resentful feelings, which can then go on to contaminate the relationship.

EXPAND YOUR EMOTIONAL VOCABULARY

Most people suffer from impoverished emotional vocabularies. Ask them how they're feeling, and the response will almost always include the same terms: *good* or *bad*, *terrible* or *great*, and so on. Take a moment now to see how many feelings you can write down. After you've done your best, look at Table 4.1 and see which ones you've missed.

Many communicators think they are expressing feelings when, in fact, their statements are emotionally counterfeit. For example, it sounds emotionally revealing to say, "I feel like going to a show" or "I feel we've been seeing too much of each other." But in fact, neither of these statements has any emotional content. In the first sentence the word *feel* really stands for an intention: "I *want* to go to a show." In the second sentence the "feeling" is really a thought: "I *think* we've been seeing too much of each other." You can recognize the absence of emotion in each case by adding a genuine word of feeling to it. For instance, "I'm *bored*, and I want to go to a show" or "I think we've been seeing too much of each other, and I feel *confined*."

Relying on a small vocabulary to describe feelings is as limiting as relying on a small vocabulary to describe colors. To say that the ocean in all its moods, the sky as it varies from day to day, and the color of your true love's eyes are all "blue" tells only a fraction of the story. Likewise, it's overly broad to use a term like *good* or *great* to describe how you feel in situations as different as earning a high grade, finishing a marathon, and hearing the words "I love you" from a special person.

There are several ways to express a feeling verbally:[63]

- By using *single words*: "I'm angry" (or "excited," "depressed," "curious," and so on).
- By describing what's happening *to you*: "My stomach is tied in knots," "I'm on top of the world."
- By describing what you'd like *to do*: "I want to run away," "I'd like to give you a hug," "I feel like giving up."

Sometimes communicators inaccurately minimize the strength of their feelings: "I'm a *little* unhappy" or "I'm *pretty* excited" or "I'm *sort of* confused." Of course, not all feelings are strong ones. We do feel degrees of sadness and joy, for example, but some people have a tendency to discount almost every feeling. Do you?

In other cases, communicators express feelings in a coded manner. This happens most often when the sender is uncomfortable about revealing the feeling in question. Some codes are verbal ones, as when the sender hints more or less subtly at the message.

For example, an indirect way to say "I'm lonesome" might be "I guess there's not much going on this weekend, so if you don't have any plans maybe you could text me and we could hang out." Such a message is so indirect that your real feeling may not be recognized. For this reason, people who send coded messages stand less of a chance of having their feelings understood—and their needs met.

If you do decide to express your feeling, you can be most clear by making sure that both you and your partner understand that your feeling is centered on a specific set of circumstances rather than being indicative of the whole relationship. Instead of saying "I resent you," say "I resent you when you don't keep your promises." Rather than saying "I'm bored with you," say "I'm bored when you talk about your money."

SHARE MULTIPLE FEELINGS

The feeling you express often isn't the only one you're experiencing. For example, you might often express your anger but overlook the confusion, disappointment, frustration, sadness, or embarrassment that preceded it. To understand why, consider the following examples. For each one, ask yourself two questions: "How would I feel? What feelings might I express?"

TABLE 4.1 COMMON HUMAN EMOTIONS

afraid	concerned	exhausted	hurried	nervous	sexy
aggravated	confident	fearful	hurt	numb	shaky
amazed	confused	fed	hysterical	optimistic	shocked
ambivalent	content	fidgety	impatient	paranoid	shy
angry	crazy	flattered	impressed	passionate	sorry
annoyed	defeated	foolish	inhibited	peaceful	strong
anxious	defensive	forlorn	insecure	pessimistic	subdued
apathetic	delighted	free	interested	playful	surprised
ashamed	depressed	friendly	intimidated	pleased	suspicious
bashful	detached	frustrated	irritable	possessive	tender
befuddled	devastated	furious	jealous	pressured	tense
bewildered	disappointed	glad	joyful	protective	terrified
bitter	disgusted	glum	lazy	puzzled	tired
bored	disturbed	grateful	lonely	refreshed	trapped
brave	ecstatic	happy	loving	regretful	ugly
calm	edgy	harassed	lukewarm	relieved	uneasy
cantankerous	elated	helpless	mad	resentful	up
carefree	embarrassed	high	mean	restless	vulnerable
cheerful	empty	hopeful	miserable	ridiculous	warm
cocky	enthusiastic	horrible	mixed	romantic	weak
cold	envious	hostile	mortified	sad	wonderful
comfortable	excited	humiliated	neglected	sentimental	worried

© Cengage Learning

PAUSE AND REFLECT

EXPANDING YOUR EMOTIONAL VOCABULARY

Use the online activity "Expressing Emotions by Expanding Your Feelings Vocabulary" to expand your emotional vocabulary. (For more suggestions, see Table 4.1 on page 129.) Using the guidelines for expressing emotions in this section, practice describing your feelings by writing statements for **each of the hypothetical situations listed at the website. You can find the link to this site by visiting CengageBrain.com to access the Speech Communication CourseMate for *Looking Out/Looking In*.**

An out-of-town friend has promised to arrive at your place at six o'clock. When he hasn't arrived by nine, you are convinced that a terrible accident has occurred. Just as you pick up the phone to call the police and local hospitals, your friend breezes in the door with an offhand remark about getting a late start.

A photo of you is posted by a friend on Facebook. On the one hand, you're flattered by your friend's display of affection for you. On the other hand, it's a picture that doesn't paint you in the best light. You wish the friend had asked first.

In situations like these, you would probably feel mixed emotions. Consider the case of the overdue friend. Your first reaction to his arrival would probably be relief: "Thank goodness, he's safe!" But you would also be likely to feel anger: "Why didn't he phone to tell me he'd be late?" The second example would probably leave you feeling pleased, embarrassed, and mad—all at the same time.

Despite the commonness of mixed emotions, we often communicate only one feeling—usually the most negative one. In both of the preceding examples, you might show only your anger, leaving the other person with little idea of the full range of your feelings. Consider the different reaction you would get by showing *all* of your emotions in these cases and in others.

Alan (Zach Galifianakis) tells his buddies how much they mean to him in *The Hangover*. It's an appropriate time and place for him to share these feelings. Of course, what happens in Vegas stays in Vegas.

Legendary Pictures/The Kobal Collection

CONSIDER WHEN AND WHERE TO EXPRESS YOUR FEELINGS

Often the first flush of a strong feeling is not the best time to speak out. If you're awakened by the racket caused by a noisy neighbor, storming over to complain might result in your saying things you'll regret later. In such a case, it's probably wiser to wait until you have thought out carefully how you might express your feelings in a way that would most likely be heard. Research shows that "imagined interactions" in advance of actual conversations can enhance relationships by allowing communicators to rehearse what they will say and to consider how others might respond.[64]

Even after you've waited for the first wave of strong feeling to subside, it's still important to choose the time that's best suited to the message.

Being rushed or tired or disturbed by some other matter is probably a good reason for postponing the expression of your feeling. In the same manner, you ought to be sure that the recipient of your message is ready to hear you out before you begin. Sometimes that means checking the other person's mood before you start sharing emotions. In other cases, it's about calculating whether that person is relationally ready to hear sentiments such as "I love you." And when making personal disclosures, it's often a good idea to ensure a measure of privacy. (YouTube is filled with examples of people being embarrassed by public declarations of affection.)

There are also cases where you may choose to never express your feelings. Even if you're dying to tell an instructor that her lectures leave you bored to a stupor, you might decide it's best to answer her question "How's class going?" with an innocuous "Okay." And even though you may be irritated by the arrogance of a police officer stopping you for speeding, the smartest approach might be to keep your feelings to yourself. In cases where you experience strong emotions but don't want to share them verbally (for whatever reason), writing out your feelings and thoughts has been shown to have mental, physical, and emotional benefits.[65] For instance, one study found that writing about feelings of affection can actually reduce the writer's cholesterol level.[66]

SKILL BUILDER

FEELINGS AND PHRASES

You can try this exercise alone or with a group:

1. Choose a situation from column A and a receiver from column B.
2. Develop an approach for communicating your feelings for this combination.
3. Now create approaches for the same situation with other receivers from column B. How are the statements different?
4. Repeat the process with various combinations, using other situations from column A.

Column A: Situations

a. You receive a terse text message cancelling a date or appointment. It's the third time the other person has cancelled at the last minute.
b. The other person posts an inappropriate comment on your Facebook Wall.
c. The other person compliments you on your appearance, then says, "I hope I haven't embarrassed you."
d. The other person gives you a hug and says, "It's good to see you."

Column B: Receivers

An instructor

A family member (you decide which one)

A classmate you don't know well

Your best friend

 You can complete this activity by visiting CengageBrain.com to access the Speech Communication CourseMate for *Looking Out/ Looking In*, and, if requested, email your responses to your instructor.

ACCEPT RESPONSIBILITY FOR YOUR FEELINGS

It's important to make sure that your language reflects the fact that you're responsible for your feelings.[67] Instead of saying "You're making me angry," say "I'm getting angry." Instead of saying "You hurt my feelings," say "I feel hurt when you do that." As you'll soon read, people don't make us like or dislike them, and believing that they do denies the responsibility that each of us has for our own emotions. Chapter 5 introduces "I" language, which offers a responsible way to express your feelings.

BE MINDFUL OF THE COMMUNICATION CHANNEL

As Chapter 1 explained, the channels we use to communicate make a difference in how others interpret our messages. This is particularly true when expressing emotions.

ETHICAL CHALLENGE

ARISTOTLE'S GOLDEN MEAN

Almost two and a half millennia ago, the philosopher Aristotle examined the question of "moral virtue": What constitutes good behavior, and what ways of acting enable us to function effectively in the world? One important part of his examination addresses the management and expression of emotion: what he defines as "passions and actions."

According to Aristotle, an important dimension of virtuous behavior is moderation, which he defines as "an intermediate between excess and deficit . . . equidistant from the extremes . . . neither too much nor too little." He acknowledges that it isn't realistic or desirable for a passionate person to strive for the same type of behavior as a dispassionate person. After all, a world in which everyone felt and acted identically would be boring.

Instead of a "one-size-fits-all" approach to emotional expression, Aristotle urges communicators to moderate their own style, to be "intermediate not in the object, but relative to us." Following Aristotle's injunction, a person with a hot temper would strive to cool down, whereas a person who rarely expresses his or her feelings ought to aim at becoming more expressive. The result would still be two people with different styles, but each of whom behaved better than before seeking the golden mean.

According to Aristotle, moderation also means that emotions should be suited to the occasion: We should feel (and express) them "at the right times, with reference to the right objects, towards the right people, with the right motive, and in the right way." We can imagine times when even a normally restrained person could reasonably act with anger and times when a normally voluble person could reasonably behave with restraint. Even then, too much emotion (rage, for example) or too little emotion falls outside the range of virtue. In Aristotle's words, when it comes to "passions and actions . . . excess is a form of failure and so is deficit."

How would your emotional expression be different if you strived for moderation? Answer this question by identifying which parts of your emotional expression are most extreme, either in their intensity or their absence.

1. How might your relationships change if you acted more moderately?
2. Are there any situations in your life when more extreme forms of emotional expression are both moral and effective?

Guidelines for Emotional Expression

After a long and frustrating search, Logan thinks he has found the ideal job that he wants and needs. The interview went well. As Logan was leaving, the interviewer said he was "very well qualified" and promised "You'll be hearing from us soon." That conversation took place almost two weeks ago, and Logan hasn't heard a word from the company.

The two transcripts below reflect very different ways of responding to this difficult situation. The first one ignores and the second one follows the Guidelines for Expressing Emotions described on pages 126–134. In each, Logan begins by ruminating (page 134) about the employer's failure to get in touch as promised.

Ignoring Guidelines for Expressing Emotions

Logan doesn't explicitly recognize a single emotion he is experiencing (pages 126–128), let alone any mixed emotions (pages 129–130). Rather than accepting responsibility for his own feelings, he blames the employer for "driving me crazy" (page 132).	"I can't believe those inconsiderate idiots! Who do they think they are, promising to call soon and then doing nothing? They're driving me crazy."
Logan jumps to the conclusion that a job offer isn't forthcoming, and lashes out without considering any alternatives.	"I give up. Since they aren't going to hire me, I'm going to call that interviewer and let her know what a screwed-up company they're running. I'll probably get her voice mail, but that's even better: That way I can say what's on my mind without getting nervous or being interrupted. They have no right to jerk me around like this, and I'm going to tell them just that." *(Angrily dials phone)*

Following Guidelines for Expressing Emotions

Logan identifies his mixture of feelings as a starting point for deciding what to do (pages 129–130).	"I'm mad at the company for not keeping in touch like they promised. I'm also confused about whether I'm as qualified as I thought I was, and I'm starting to worry that maybe I didn't do as well in the interview as I thought. I'm also sorry I didn't ask her for a more specific time than 'soon.' And I'm really unsure about whether to give up, wait for them to call me, or reach out to the company and ask what's going on."
He recognizes the difference between what he would like to do (chew out the interviewer) and what is more appropriate and effective (page 128).	"If I'm not going to get the job, I'd like to chew out that interviewer for promising to call. But that would probably be a bad idea—burning my bridges, as my family would say."
Logan uses a perception check (pages 96–100) and considers sharing his feelings with the employer in a nonblaming way. He deliberately considers when and how to express himself (pages 130–131), choosing email as the best channel to achieve his goals (pages 132–134).	"Maybe I'll call her and say something like 'I'm confused. You said at the interview that I'd hear from you soon, but it's been almost two weeks now with no word.' I could ask whether I misunderstood (although I doubt that), or whether they need some more information from me. Let me think about that overnight. If the idea still sounds good in the morning, I'll call them."
Having decided to email the employer, Logan could use the face-saving methods described in Chapter 10 (pages 326–331) to compose his message. He could begin by speaking positively about his continued interest in the company, then raise his concern about not having heard from them, and then close by saying that he's looking forward to hearing back from them.	"Actually, an email would be better: I could edit my words until they're just right, and an email wouldn't put the interviewer on the spot like a phone call would."

Communication Scenarios

To watch and analyze a video related to this feature and this topic, visit CengageBrain.com to access the Speech Communication CourseMate for Looking Out/Looking In.

Communicators today have many more channel choices than they did a few decades ago, and the decision about when to use mediated channels—such as email, instant messaging, cell phones, social media sites, and blogging—call for a level of analysis that wasn't required in the past.[68] For instance, is it appropriate to signal your desire to end a relationship in a voice mail message? When is it acceptable to use CAPITAL LETTERS in a blog post to express displeasure? If you're excited about some good news, should you first tell your family and friends in person before publishing it on Facebook?

Most people intuitively recognize that the selection of a channel depends in part on the kind of message they're sending. In one survey, students identified which channel they would find best for delivering a variety of messages.[69] Most respondents said they would have little trouble expressing positive messages in person, but preferred mediated channels for negative messages.

"Flaming" is an extreme example of how mediated channels lend themselves to expressing negative emotions. The kind of civility that most people honor in other communication channels seems to have less of a hold on the Internet—certainly among strangers, but even among people who belong to the same personal networks. Before saying something you may later regret, it's worth remembering the principle stated in Chapter 1 that communication is irreversible. Once you hit the "Send" button, you can't retract an emotional outburst.

Managing Difficult Emotions

Although feeling and expressing emotions usually adds to the quality of interpersonal relationships, not all feelings are beneficial. For instance, rage, depression, terror, and jealousy do little to help you feel better or improve your relationships. The following pages will give you tools to minimize these unproductive emotions.

FACILITATIVE AND DEBILITATIVE EMOTIONS

First, we need to make a distinction between **facilitative emotions**, which contribute to effective functioning, and **debilitative emotions**, which detract from effective functioning.

One difference between the two types is their *intensity*. For instance, a certain amount of anger or irritation can be constructive, because it often provides the stimulus that leads you to improve the unsatisfying conditions. Rage, however, usually makes matters worse—especially when driving, as illustrated by the problems associated with "road rage."[70] The same holds true for fear. A little bit of fear before an important athletic contest or job interview might give you the boost that will improve your performance.[71] (Mellow athletes or employees usually don't do well.) But total terror is something else.

Not surprisingly, debilitative emotions like communication apprehension can lead to a variety of problems in personal, business, educational, and even medical settings.[72] When people become anxious, they generally speak less, which means that their needs aren't met; and when they do manage to speak up, they are less effective at communicating than their more confident counterparts.[73]

A second characteristic that distinguishes debilitative feelings from facilitative ones is their extended *duration*. Feeling depressed for a while after the breakup of a relationship or the loss of a job is natural, but spending the rest of your life grieving over your loss would accomplish nothing. In the same way, staying angry at someone for a wrong inflicted long ago can be just as punishing to you as to the wrongdoer. Social scientists call this **rumination**—dwelling persistently on negative thoughts that, in turn, intensify negative feelings. A substantial body of research confirms that rumination increases feelings of sadness, anxiety, and depression.[74] Just as bad, people who ruminate are more likely to lash out with displaced aggression at innocent bystanders.[75]

Many debilitative emotions involve communication. Here are a few examples, offered by readers of *Looking Out/Looking In*:

> When I first came to college, I had to leave my boyfriend. I was living with three girls, and for most of the first semester I was so lonesome and unhappy that I was a pretty terrible roommate.

> I got so frustrated with my overly critical boss that I lost my temper and quit one day. I told him what a horrible manager he was and walked off the job right then and there. Now I'm afraid to list my former boss as a reference, and I'm afraid my temper tantrum will make it harder for me to get a new job.

> I've had ongoing problems with my family, and sometimes I get so upset that I can't concentrate on my work or school, or even sleep well at night.

In the following pages you will learn a method for dealing with debilitative feelings like these that can improve your effectiveness as a communicator. This method is based on the idea that one way to minimize debilitative feelings is to minimize unproductive thinking.

SOURCES OF DEBILITATIVE EMOTIONS

For most people, feelings seem to have a life of their own. You wish you could feel calm when approaching strangers, yet your voice quivers. You try to appear confident when asking for a raise, yet your eye twitches nervously. Where do feelings like these come from?

Physiology One answer lies in our genetic makeup. As you read in Chapter 2, temperament is, to a large degree, inherited. Communication traits like shyness, verbal aggressiveness, and assertiveness are rooted in biology. Fortunately, biology isn't destiny. As you'll soon read, it is possible to overcome debilitative feelings.

Beyond heredity, cognitive scientists tell us that the cause of some debilitative feelings—especially those involving fight-or-flight responses—lies deep inside the brain, in an almond-sized cluster of interconnected structures called the amygdala (pronounced uh-MIG-duh-luh). The amygdala acts as a kind of sentinel that scans every experience, looking for threats. In literally a split second, it can sound an alarm that triggers a flood of physiological reactions: speeding heart rate, elevating blood pressure, heightening the senses, and preparing the muscles to react.[76]

This defense system has obvious value when we are confronted with real physical dangers, but in social situations the amygdala can hijack the brain, triggering emotions like fear and anger when there is no real threat. You might find yourself feeling uncomfortable when somebody stands too close to you or angry when someone cuts in front of you in line. As you'll soon read, thinking clearly is the way to avoid overreacting to events like these.

Emotional Memory The source of some threats lies in what neuroscientists have termed our *emotional memory*. Seemingly harmless events can trigger debilitative feelings if they bear even a slight resemblance to troublesome experiences from the past. A few examples illustrate the point:

- Ever since being teased when he moved to a new elementary school, Darnell has been uncomfortable in unfamiliar situations.
- Alicia feels apprehensive around men, especially those with deep, booming voices. As a child, she was mistreated by a family member with a loud baritone voice.
- Miguel feels a wave of insecurity whenever he is around women who use the same perfume worn by a former lover who jilted him.

King Features © Zits Partnership

Self-Talk Beyond neurobiology, what we think can have a profound effect on how we feel. It's common to say that strangers or your boss make you feel nervous, just as you would say that a bee sting makes you feel pain. The apparent similarities between physical and emotional discomforts become clear if you look at them like this:

Event	Feeling
Bee sting	Physical pain
Meeting strangers	Nervous feelings

When looking at your emotions in this way, you seem to have little control over how you feel. However, this apparent similarity between physical pain and emotional discomfort (or pleasure) isn't as great as it seems to be. Cognitive psychologists argue that it is not *events* such as meeting strangers or being jilted by a lover that cause people to feel bad, but rather the *beliefs they hold* about these events. As discussed earlier in the chapter, *reappraisal* involves changing our thoughts to help manage our emotions.

Albert Ellis, who developed an approach to reappraisal called *rational-emotive therapy*, tells a story that makes this point clear. Imagine yourself walking by a friend's house and seeing your friend stick his head out of a window and call you a string of vile names. (You supply the friend and the names.) Under these circumstances it's likely that you would feel hurt and upset. Now imagine that instead of walking by a house, you are passing a mental institution. The same friend, who is obviously a patient there, shouts the same vile names at you. In this case, your feelings would probably be quite different—most likely sadness and pity. You can see that in this story the activating event of being called names was the same in both cases, yet the emotional consequences were very different. The reason for your different feelings has to do with your thinking in each case. In the first case, you would most likely think that your friend was very angry with you; further, you might imagine that you must have done something terrible to deserve such a response. In the second case, you would probably assume that your friend had some psychological difficulty, and most likely you would feel sympathetic.

From this example you can start to see that it's the *interpretations* that people make of an event, during the process of **self-talk**, that determine their feelings.[77] Thus, the model for emotions looks like this:

Event	Thought (Self-talk)	Feeling
Being called names	"I've done something wrong."	Hurt, upset
Being called names	"My friend must be sick."	Concern, sympathy

The same principle applies in more common situations. In job interviews, for example, people who become nervous are likely to use negative self-talk when they think about their performance: "I won't do well," "I don't know why I'm doing this."[78] In romantic relationships, thoughts shape satisfaction. The words "I love you" can be interpreted in a variety of ways. They could be taken at face value as a genuine expression of deep affection:

Event	Thought (Self-talk)	Feeling
Hearing "I love you"	"This is a genuine statement."	Delight (perhaps)

The same words might be decoded as a sincere but mistaken declaration uttered in a moment of passion, an attempt to make the recipient feel better, or an attempt at manipulation. For example,

Hearing "I love you"   "She's just saying this to manipulate me." Anger

One study revealed that women are more likely than men to regard expressions of love as genuine statements rather than attribute them to some other cause.[79] Other research shows the importance of self-talk in relationships. Members of couples who are unhappy with one another have more negative self-talk about their partner and fewer positive thoughts about their partner and the relationship.[80]

PAUSE AND REFLECT

TALKING TO YOURSELF

You can become better at understanding how your thoughts shape your feelings by completing the following steps:

1. Take a few minutes to listen to the inner voice you use when thinking. Close your eyes now and listen to it. Did you hear the voice? Perhaps it was saying, "What voice? I don't have any voice. . . ." Try again, and pay attention to what the voice is saying.

2. Now think about the following situations, and imagine how you would react in each. How would you interpret them with your inner voice? What feelings would follow from each interpretation?
   a. While sitting on a bus, in class, or on the street, you notice an attractive person sneaking glances at you.
   b. During a lecture your professor asks the class, "What do you think about this?" and looks toward you.
   c. You are telling friends about your vacation, and one yawns.
   d. You run into a friend on the street and ask how things are going. "Fine," she replies, and rushes off.

3. Now recall three recent times when you felt a strong emotion. For each one, recall the activating event and then the interpretation that led to your emotional reaction.

 You can complete this activity by visiting CengageBrain.com to access the Speech Communication CourseMate for *Looking Out/Looking In*, and, if requested, email your responses to your instructor.

IRRATIONAL THINKING AND DEBILITATIVE EMOTIONS

Many debilitative emotions come from accepting a number of irrational thoughts—we'll call them *fallacies* here—that lead to illogical conclusions and in turn to debilitative emotions. We usually aren't aware of these thoughts, which makes them especially powerful.[81]

1. The Fallacy of Perfection People who accept the **fallacy of perfection** believe that a worthwhile communicator should be able to handle every situation with complete confidence and skill.

If you accept the belief that it's desirable and possible to be a perfect communicator, you'll probably assume that people won't appreciate you if you are imperfect. Admitting your mistakes, saying "I don't know," and sharing feelings of uncertainty seem like social defects when viewed in this manner. Given the desire to be valued and appreciated, it's tempting to try to *appear* to be perfect, but the costs of such deception are high. If others ever find you out, they'll see you as a phony. Even when your act isn't uncovered, it uses up a great deal of psychological energy and thus makes the rewards of approval less enjoyable.

Subscribing to the myth of perfection not only can keep others from liking you, but also can act as a force to diminish your own self-esteem. How can you like yourself when you don't measure up to the way you ought to be? How liberated you become when you can comfortably accept the idea that you are not perfect.

Like everyone else, you sometimes have a hard time expressing yourself.

Like everyone else, you make mistakes from time to time, and there is no reason to hide this.

You are honestly doing the best you can to realize your potential, to become the best person you can be.

2. The Fallacy of Approval The **fallacy of approval** is based on the idea that it is not only desirable but also vital to get the approval of virtually every person. People who accept this idea go to incredible lengths to seek approval from others, even when they have to sacrifice their own principles and happiness to do so. Accepting this fallacy can lead to some ludicrous situations:

Feeling nervous because people you don't even like seem to disapprove of you

Feeling apologetic when others are at fault

Feeling embarrassed after behaving unnaturally to gain another's approval

The fallacy of approval is irrational because it implies that others will respect and like you more if you go out of your way to please them. Often this simply isn't true. Would *you* respect people who have compromised important values just to gain acceptance? Are you likely to think highly of people who repeatedly deny their own needs as a means of buying approval? Though others may find it tempting to use these individuals to suit their ends, these individuals hardly deserve genuine affection and respect.

Striving for universal approval is irrational because it's simply not possible. Sooner or later a conflict of expectations is bound to occur; one person will approve if you behave only in a certain way, but another will accept only the opposite behavior. What are you to do then?

Don't misunderstand: Abandoning the fallacy of approval doesn't mean living a life of selfishness. It's still important to consider the needs of others and to meet them whenever

CRITIC'S MATH

Larry David feels just like me and you when it comes to criticism.

You'd think he wouldn't. He co-created *Seinfeld*, the most successful sitcom of all time. His current show *Curb Your Enthusiasm* is a smash success. He's been on the cover of *Rolling Stone* Magazine. And yet, he still does the same math you and I do when it comes to critics.

What's critic's math? It's the mathematical formula most of us use when it comes to criticism. Here is an example of how it works:

1 insult + 1,000 compliments = 1 insult.

And we need look no further than a story about Larry David in that *Rolling Stone* article to see it in action. Here is an excerpt of the piece by Brian Hiatt:

One night during his stay (in New York), David went to Yankee Stadium to see a game. His image went up on the big screen as *Curb Your Enthusiasm's* theme song played over the big speakers. An entire stadium of fans stood and cheered for the hopeless case from Brooklyn. It should have been a life-defining moment, the redemptive final scene in the biopic. But as it turned out, not so much. As David left the stadium, a guy drove by and yelled, "Larry, you suck!" "That's

like, literally all he heard," Berg (David's friend) says.

David spent the ride back from the Bronx obsessing over that moment, running it over and over in his mind. It was as if the other 50,000 people, the ones who loved him, didn't exist. "Who's that guy? What was that?" He asked. "Who would do that? Why would you say something like that?"

That's critic's math. One insult was able to erase an entire stadium of adulation. More than 50,000 people disappeared at the hand of one point of bitterness. Critic's math might be the most powerful magic on the planet.

There are three things you need to know about it:

1. *It doesn't instantly go away with success.*
   If right now you're thinking "If I sell a certain number of books or get a job promotion, I won't worry so much about what critic's think," you're wrong. Larry David is incredibly successful. If you have a hard time with critic's math with 10 followers of Twitter, you'll still have a hard time with it with 1 million followers. Don't chase success as a way to beat critic's math.
2. *Every time you believe critic's math you make it more powerful.*

Stockbyte/Jupiter Images

Doubt and fear are like muscles. Every time you believe a lie it gets easier to believe the next time. It took Larry David a lifetime of critic's math to ignore a full stadium of fans.
3. *You're not the only one with a math problem.*
   You know which Amazon review for my book Quitter I think about the most? It's not the 95 5-star reviews the book got. It's the one 1-star review.

It's time you and me and maybe even Larry David let it go. Critic's math doesn't add up. In fact, it's all about subtraction. Subtracting compliments. Subtracting happiness. Subtracting joy.

Jon Acuff

http://www.jonacuff.com/blog/larry-david-the-3-problems-with-critics-math/. Reprinted with permission.

possible. It's also pleasant—we might say even necessary—to strive for the respect of those people you value. The point here is that when you must abandon your own needs and principles in order to seek these goals, the price is too high—as Jim Carrey's character learns in the movie *Yes Man* (see the film summary at the end of this chapter).

3. The Fallacy of Shoulds The **fallacy of shoulds** is the inability to distinguish between what is and what should be. You can see the difference by imagining a person who is full of complaints about the world:

"There should be no rain on weekends."

"People ought to live forever."

"Money should grow on trees."

"We should all be able to fly."

Complaints like these are obviously foolish. However pleasant wishing may be, insisting that the unchangeable should be changed won't affect reality one bit. And yet many people torture themselves by engaging in this sort of irrational thinking when they confuse preferences with shoulds. They say and think things like this:

"My friend should be more understanding."

"She shouldn't be so inconsiderate."

"They should be more friendly."

"You should work harder."

The message in each of these cases is that you would *prefer* people to behave differently. Wishing that things were better is perfectly legitimate, and trying to change them is, of course, a good idea; but it's unreasonable to *insist* that the world operate just as you want it to or to feel cheated when things aren't ideal.

Imposing the fallacy of shoulds on yourself can also lead to unnecessary unhappiness. Psychologist Aaron Beck points out some unrealistic self-imposed shoulds:[82]

"I should be able to find a quick solution to every problem."

"I should never feel hurt; I should always be happy and serene."

"I should always demonstrate the utmost generosity, considerateness, dignity, courage, unselfishness."

Becoming obsessed with shoulds like these has three troublesome consequences. First, it leads to unnecessary unhappiness, because people who are constantly dreaming about the ideal are seldom satisfied with what they have or who they are. Second, merely complaining without acting can keep you from doing anything to change unsatisfying conditions. Third, this sort of complaining can build a defensive climate with others, who will resent being nagged. It's much more effective to tell people about what you'd like than to preach. Say, "I wish you'd be more punctual" instead of "You should be on time." We'll discuss ways of avoiding defensive climates in Chapter 10.

4. The Fallacy of Overgeneralization The **fallacy of overgeneralization** comprises two types. The first occurs when we base a belief on a limited amount of evidence. For instance, how many times have you found yourself saying something like this:

"I'm so stupid! I can't even figure out how to download music on my iPod."

"Some friend I am! I forgot my best friend's birthday."

In cases like these, we focus on a limited type of shortcoming as if it represented everything about us. We forget that along with encountering our difficulties, we have solved tough problems; and that though we're sometimes forgetful, at other times we're caring and thoughtful.

A second type of overgeneralization occurs when we *exaggerate* shortcomings:

"You *never* listen to me."

"You're *always* late."

"I can't think of *anything*."

On closer examination, absolute statements like these are almost always false and usually lead to discouragement or anger. You'll feel far better when you replace over-generalizations with more accurate messages to yourself and others:

"You often don't listen to me."

"You've been late three times this week."

"I haven't had any ideas I like today."

5. The Fallacy of Causation The **fallacy of causation** is based on the irrational belief that emotions are caused by others rather than by one's own self-talk.

This fallacy causes trouble in two ways. The first plagues people who become overly cautious about communicating because they don't want to "cause" any pain or inconvenience for others. This attitude occurs in cases such as:

Visiting friends or family out of a sense of obligation rather than a genuine desire to see them

Keeping quiet when another person's behavior is bothering you

Pretending to be attentive to a speaker when you are already late for an appointment or feeling ill

Praising and reassuring others who ask for your opinion, even when your honest response would be negative

There's certainly no excuse for going out of your way to say things that will result in pain for others, and there will be times when you choose to inconvenience yourself to make life easier for those you care about. It's essential to realize, however, that it's an overstatement to say that you are the one who causes others' feelings. It's more accurate to say that they *respond* to your behavior with feelings of their own. For example, consider how strange it sounds to suggest that you make others fall in love with you. Such a statement simply doesn't make sense. It would be closer to the truth to say that you act in one way or another, and some people might fall in love with you as a result of these actions, whereas others wouldn't. In the same way, it's incorrect to say that you *make* others angry, upset, or happy, for that matter. It's more accurate to say that others respond to your behavior.

The fallacy of causation also operates when we believe that others cause *our* emotions. Sometimes it certainly seems as if they do, either raising or lowering our spirits by their actions. But think about it for a moment: The same actions that will cause you happiness or unhappiness one day have little effect at other times. The insult or compliment that affected your mood strongly yesterday leaves you unaffected today. Why? Because in the latter case you attached less importance to it. You certainly wouldn't feel some emotions without others' behavior, but your reaction, not their actions, determines how you feel.

6. The Fallacy of Helplessness The **fallacy of helplessness** suggests that satisfaction in life is determined by forces beyond your control. People who continuously see themselves as victims make such statements as:

"There's no way a woman can get ahead in this society. It's a man's world, and the best thing I can do is to accept it."

"I was born with a shy personality. I'd like to be more outgoing, but there's nothing I can do about that."

"I can't tell my boss that she is putting too many demands on me. If I do, I might lose my job."

The mistake in statements like these becomes apparent after you realize that you can do many things if you really want to. Most "can't" statements can be more correctly rephrased either as "won't" ("I can't tell him what I think" becomes "I won't be honest with him") or as "don't know how" ("I can't carry on an interesting conversation" becomes "I don't know what to say"). After you've rephrased these inaccurate "can'ts," it becomes clear that they're either a matter of choice or an area that calls for your action—both quite different from saying that you're helpless.

When viewed in this light, it's apparent that many "can'ts" are really rationalizations to justify not wanting to change. Lonely people, for example, tend to attribute their poor interpersonal relationships to uncontrollable causes. "It's beyond my control," they think. Also, they expect their relational partners to reject them. Notice the self-fulfilling prophecy in this attitude: Believing that your relational prospects are dim can lead you to act in ways that make you an unattractive prospect, whereas acknowledging that there is a way to change—even though it may be difficult—puts the responsibility for your predicament on your shoulders. You *can* become a better communicator—this book is one step in your movement toward that goal. Don't give up or sell yourself short.

7. The Fallacy of Catastrophic Expectations Fearful communicators who subscribe to the irrational **fallacy of catastrophic expectations** operate on the assumption that if something bad can possibly happen, it will. Typical catastrophic expectations include:

> "If I invite them to the party, they probably won't want to come."

> "If I speak up in order to try to resolve a conflict, things will probably get worse."

> "If I apply for the job I want, I probably won't be hired."

> "If I tell them how I really feel, they'll probably laugh at me."

After you start expecting catastrophic consequences, a self-fulfilling prophecy can begin to build. One study revealed that people who believed that their romantic partners would not change for the better were likely to behave in ways that contributed to the breakup of the relationship.[83]

PAUSE AND REFLECT

HOW IRRATIONAL ARE YOU?

1. Return to the situations described in the exercise "Talking to Yourself" on page 137. Examine each one to see whether your self-talk contains any irrational thoughts.
2. Keep a two- or three-day record of your debilitative emotions. Are any of them based on irrational thinking? Examine your conclusions, and see if you repeatedly use any of the fallacies described in the preceding section.
3. Take a class poll to see which fallacies are most popular. Also, discuss what subjects seem to stimulate most of this irrational thinking (e.g., schoolwork, dating, jobs, family).

 You can complete this activity by visiting CengageBrain.com to access the Speech Communication CourseMate for *Looking Out/Looking In*, and, if requested, email your responses to your instructor.

Although it's naive to assume that all of your interactions with others will meet with success, it's just as naive to assume that you'll fail. One way to escape from the fallacy of catastrophic expectations is to think about the consequences that would follow even if you don't communicate successfully. Keeping in mind the folly of trying to be perfect and of living only for the approval of others, realize that failing in a given instance usually isn't as bad as it might seem. What if people do laugh at you? Suppose you don't get the job? What if others do get angry at your remarks? Are these matters really *that* serious?

Before moving on, we need to add a few thoughts about thinking and feeling. First, you should realize that thinking rationally won't completely eliminate debilitative emotions. Some debilitative emotions, after all, are very rational: grief over the death of someone you love, euphoria over getting a new job, and apprehension about the future of an important relationship after a serious fight, for example. Thinking rationally can eliminate many debilitative emotions from your life, but not all of them.

MINIMIZING DEBILITATIVE EMOTIONS

How can you overcome irrational thinking? Social scientists and therapists have developed a simple yet effective approach.[84] When practiced conscientiously, it can help you cut down on the self-defeating thinking that leads to many debilitative emotions.

Monitor Your Emotional Reactions The first step is to recognize when you're feeling debilitative emotions. (Of course, it's also nice to recognize pleasant emotions when they occur.) As we suggested earlier, one way to recognize emotions is through monitoring physiological responses: butterflies in the stomach, racing heart, hot flashes, and so on. Although such stimuli might be symptoms of food poisoning, more often they are symptoms of a strong emotion. You can also recognize certain ways of behaving that suggest your feelings: stomping instead of walking normally, being unusually quiet, or speaking in a sarcastic tone of voice are some examples.

It may seem strange to suggest that it's necessary to look for emotions—they ought to be immediately apparent. The fact is, however, that we often suffer from debilitative emotions for some time without noticing them. For example, at the end of a trying day you've probably caught yourself frowning and realized that you've been wearing that mask for some time without noticing it.

Note the Activating Event After you're aware of how you're feeling, the next step is to figure out what activating event triggered your response. Sometimes it is obvious. For instance, a common source of anger is being accused unfairly (or fairly) of foolish behavior; a common source of hurt is being rejected by somebody important to you. In other cases, however, the activating event isn't so apparent.

Sometimes there isn't a single activating event but rather a series of small events that finally builds toward a critical mass and triggers a debilitative emotion. This happens when you're trying to work or sleep and are continually annoyed by a string of interruptions, or when you suffer a series of small disappointments.

The best way to begin tracking down activating events is to notice the circumstances in which you have debilitative emotions. Perhaps they occur when you're around *specific people*. In other cases, you might be bothered by certain

"So, when he says, 'What a good boy am I,' Jack is really reinforcing his self-esteem."

types of individuals because of their age, role, or background. Or perhaps certain *settings* stimulate unpleasant emotions: parties, work, school. Sometimes the *topic* of conversation is the factor that sets you off, whether it be politics, religion, or sex. Maybe even the *information source* is part of the problem. For instance, research suggests that regularly checking a romantic partner's Facebook site can feed feelings of jealousy.[85] That's because it offers access to ambiguous information that might not otherwise be available. Consider how easy it could be to misinterpret certain posts on your sweetheart's Wall.

Record Your Self-Talk This is the point at which you analyze the thoughts that are the link between the activating event and your feeling. If you're serious about getting rid of debilitative emotions, it's important to actually write down your self-talk when first learning to use this method. Putting your thoughts on paper will help you see whether they make any sense.

Monitoring your self-talk might be difficult at first. This is a new activity, and any new activity seems awkward. If you persevere, however, you'll find that you will be able to identify the thoughts that lead to your debilitative emotions. After you get in the habit of recognizing this internal monologue, you'll be able to identify your thoughts quickly and easily.

Reappraise Your Irrational Beliefs Reappraising your irrational beliefs is the key to success in the rational-emotive approach. Use the list of irrational fallacies on pages 138–143 to discover which of your internal statements are based on mistaken thinking.

You can do this most effectively by following three steps. First, decide whether each belief you've recorded is rational or irrational. Next, explain why the belief is rational or irrational. Finally, if the belief is irrational, you should write down an alternative way of thinking that is more rational and that can leave you feeling better when faced with the same activating event in the future.

Replacing self-defeating self-talk with more constructive thinking is an especially effective tool for improving self-confidence and relational communication.[86] Nonetheless, this approach triggers objections from some readers:

"The rational-emotive approach sounds like nothing more than trying to talk yourself out of feeling bad." This accusation is totally correct. After all, because we talk ourselves into feeling bad, what's wrong with talking ourselves out of feeling bad, especially when such feelings are based on irrational thoughts? Rationalizing may be an excuse and a self-deception, but there's nothing wrong with being rational.

King Features © Zits Partnership

"The kind of reappraising we just read sounds phony and unnatural. I don't talk to myself in sentences and paragraphs." There's no need to dispute your irrational beliefs in any special literary style. You can be just as colloquial as you want. The important thing is to clearly understand what thoughts led you into your debilitative emotions so that you can clearly reappraise them. While the approach is new to you, it's a good idea to write or talk out your thoughts in order to make them clear. After you've had some practice, you'll be able to do these steps in a quicker, less formal way.

"This approach is too cold and impersonal. It seems to aim at turning people into calculating, emotionless machines." This is simply not true. A rational thinker can still dream, hope, and love. There's nothing necessarily irrational about feelings like these. Basically rational people even indulge in a bit of irrational thinking once in a while, but they usually know what they're doing. Like healthy eaters who occasionally allow themselves a snack of junk food, rational thinkers occasionally indulge in irrational thoughts, knowing that they'll return to their healthy lifestyle soon with no real damage done.

"This technique promises too much. There's no chance I could rid myself of all unpleasant feelings, however nice that might be." We can answer this objection by agreeing that rational-emotive thinking probably won't totally solve your emotional problems. What it can do is to reduce their number, intensity, and duration. This method is not the answer to all your problems, but it can make a significant difference—which is not a bad accomplishment.

SKILL BUILDER

RATIONAL THINKING

1. Return to the diary of irrational thoughts you recorded on page 142. Dispute the self-talk in each case, and write a more rational interpretation of the event.

2. Now try out your ability to think rationally on the spot. You can do this by acting out the scenes listed in step 4. You'll need three players for each one: a subject, the subject's "little voice"—his or her thoughts—and a second party.

3. Play out each scene by having the subject and second party interact while the "little voice" stands just behind the subject and says what the subject is probably thinking. For example, in a scene where the subject is asking an instructor to reconsider a low grade, the little voice might say, "I hope I haven't made things worse by bringing this up. Maybe he'll lower the grade after rereading the test. I'm such an idiot! Why didn't I keep quiet?"

4. Whenever the little voice expresses an irrational thought, the observers who are watching the skit should call out, "Foul." At this point the action should stop while the group discusses the irrational thought and suggests a more rational line of self-talk. The players should then replay the scene with the little voice speaking in a more rational way.

Here are some scenes (of course, you can invent others as well):
   a. Two people are just beginning their first date.
   b. A potential employee has just begun a job interview.
   c. A teacher or boss is criticizing the subject for showing up late.
   d. A student and instructor run across each other in the supermarket.

 You can complete this activity by visiting CengageBrain.com to access the Speech Communication CourseMate for *Looking Out/ Looking In*, and, if requested, email your responses to your instructor.

IN REAL LIFE

Rational Thinking in Action

The following scenarios demonstrate how the rational thinking method described in this section applies in everyday challenges. Notice that thinking rationally doesn't eliminate debilitative emotions. Instead, it helps keep them in control, making effective communication more possible.

Situation 1: Dealing with Annoying Customers

Activating Event

I work in a shopping mall that swarms with tourists and locals. Our company's reputation is based on service, but lately I've been losing my patience with the customers. The store is busy from the second we open until we close. Many of the customers are rude, pushy, and demanding. Others expect me to be a tour guide, restaurant reviewer, medical consultant, and even a baby-sitter. I feel like I'm ready to explode.

Beliefs and Self-Talk

1. I'm sick of working with the public. People are really obnoxious!
2. The customers should be more patient and polite instead of treating me like a servant.
3. This work is driving me crazy! If I keep working here, I'm going to become as rude as the customers.
4. I can't quit: I could never find another job that pays this well.

Reappraising Irrational Beliefs

1. It's an overgeneralization to say that *all* people are obnoxious. Actually, most of the customers are fine. Some are even very nice. About 10 percent of them cause most of the trouble. Recognizing that most people are OK leaves me feeling less bitter.
2. It's true that obnoxious customers *should* be more polite, but it's unrealistic to expect that everybody will behave the way they ought to. After all, it's not a perfect world.
3. By saying that the customers are driving me crazy, I suggest that I have no control over the situation. I'm an adult, and I am able to keep a grip on myself. I may not like the way some people behave, but it's my choice how to respond to them.
4. I'm not helpless. If the job is too unpleasant, I can quit. I probably wouldn't find another

job that pays as well as this one, so I have to choose which is more important: money or peace of mind. It's my choice.

Situation 2: Meeting My Girlfriend's Family

Activating Event

Tracy and I are talking about marriage—maybe not soon, but eventually. Her family is very close, and they want to meet me. I'm sure I'll like them, but I am not sure what they will think about me. I was married once before, at a young age. It was a big mistake, and it didn't last. Furthermore, I was laid off two months ago, and I'm between jobs. The family is coming to town next week, and I am very nervous about what they will think of me.

Beliefs and Self-Talk

1. They've *got* to like me! This is a close family, and I'm doomed if they think I'm not right for Tracy.
2. No matter how sensibly I act, all they'll think of is my divorce and unemployment.
3. Maybe the family is right. Tracy deserves the best, and I'm certainly not that!

Reappraising Irrational Beliefs

1. The family's approval is definitely important. Still, my relationship with Tracy doesn't depend on it. She's already said that she's committed to me, no matter what they think. The sensible approach is to say I *want* their approval, but I don't *need* it.
2. I'm expecting the absolute worst if I think that I'm doomed no matter what happens when we meet. There is a chance that they will dislike me, but there's also a chance that things will work out fine. There's no point in dwelling on catastrophes.
3. Just because I've had an imperfect past doesn't mean I'm wrong for Tracy. I've learned from my past mistakes, and I am committed to living a good life. I know I can be the kind of husband she deserves, even though I'm not perfect.

Communication Scenarios

To watch and analyze a video related to this feature and this topic, visit CengageBrain.com to access the Speech Communication CourseMate for Looking Out/Looking In.

SUMMARY

Emotions have several dimensions. They are signaled by internal physiological changes, manifested by nonverbal reactions, and defined in most cases by cognitive interpretations. We can use this information to make choices about whether or not to verbalize our feelings.

There are several reasons why people do not verbalize many of the emotions they feel. Some people have personalities that are less prone toward emotional expression. Culture and gender also have an effect on the emotions we do and don't share with others. Social rules and roles discourage the expression of some feelings, particularly negative ones. Fear of consequences leads people to withhold expression of some emotions. Finally, contagion can lead us to experience emotions that we might not otherwise have had.

Because total expression of emotions is not appropriate, several guidelines help define when and how to express emotions effectively. Expanding your emotional vocabulary, becoming more self-aware, and expressing mixed feelings are important. Recognizing the difference between feeling, thinking, and acting, as well as accepting responsibility for feelings instead of blaming them on others, lead to better reactions. Choosing the proper time and place to share feelings is also important, as is choosing the best channel for expressing emotions.

Whereas some emotions are facilitative, others are debilitative and inhibit effective functioning. Many of these debilitative emotions are biological reactions rooted in the amygdala portion of the brain, but their negative impact can be altered through rational thinking. It is often possible to communicate more confidently and effectively by identifying troublesome emotions, identifying the activating event and self-talk that triggered them, and reappraising any irrational thoughts with a more logical analysis of the situation.

KEY TERMS

debilitative emotions (134)
emotional contagion (124)
emotional intelligence (116)
emotion labor (124)
facilitative emotions (134)
fallacy of approval (138)
fallacy of catastrophic expectations (142)
fallacy of causation (141)

fallacy of helplessness (141)
fallacy of overgeneralization (140)
fallacy of perfection (138)
fallacy of shoulds (140)
reappraisal (119)
rumination (134)
self-talk (136)

ONLINE RESOURCES

Now that you have read this chapter, visit CengageBrain.com to access the Speech Communication CourseMate for *Looking Out/Looking In* for quick access to the electronic resources that accompany this text. Your CourseMate offers:

- **Study tools** that will help you assess your learning and prepare for exams (*digital glossary, key term flash cards, interactive quizzes*).
- **Activities and assignments** that will help you hone your knowledge, understand how theory and research applies to your own life (*Self-Assessment, Pause and Reflect*), consider ethical challenges in interpersonal communication (*Ethical Challenge*), and build your interpersonal communication skills throughout the course (*Skill Builder*). If requested, you can submit your answers to your instructor.
- **Media resources** that will allow you to watch and critique videos of interpersonal communication situations (*In Real Life, interpersonal video simulations, and interactive video activities*).
- In addition to interactive teaching and learning tools, CourseMate includes an **interactive eBook.** Take notes, highlight, search, and interact with embedded media specific to *Looking Out/Looking In*.

SEARCH TERMS

When searching online databases to research topics in this chapter, use the following terms (along with this chapter's key terms) to maximize the chances of finding useful information:

affect	intrapersonal communication
communication apprehension	rational-emotive therapy
feelings	shyness

FILM AND TELEVISION

You can see the communication principles described in this chapter portrayed in the following films and television programs.

SOCIAL CONVENTIONS FOR EXPRESSING EMOTIONS
Mad Men (2007–) Rated TV-14

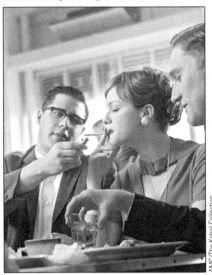

The business world of the 1960s was different than today. Many people smoked, even in elevators, and the two-martini lunch was commonplace. The executive suite was run by men. Casual sexual harassment, though no less distasteful than now, was often tolerated by the "girls" in the typing pool.

Relationships then evoked a wealth of emotions, but the rules for expressing those feelings were different. Women—whether at home or in the workplace—were expected to be deferential and positive. The ideal professional man was suave and unruffled. *Mad Men* makes it clear that social conventions masked a wealth of intense feelings about relationships. It also shows how important it seemed to avoid communicating about those feelings, and the costs of doing so.

It's easy to feel smug when looking back at what seems like such dated social conventions—until you wonder what people a half-century from now will think of us.

EMOTIONAL INTELLIGENCE
The Office (2005–) Rated TV-PG
The Big Bang Theory (2007–) Rated TV-PG

The Office's Dwight Schrute (Rainn Wilson) is no dummy. He has a computer-like memory for facts and trivia, and he knows all there is to know about the paper products he sells at Dunder Mifflin. Sheldon Cooper (Jim Parsons) on *The Big Bang Theory* might be even smarter than Dwight. He holds two doctorates and is a Caltech theoretical physicist.

While both characters may be book smart, they lack emotional intelligence. They're short on empathy, social skills, and the ability to express their emotions effectively. They can be blunt and sarcastic, with little regard for how that leaves others feeling. As a result, they regularly jeopardize their relationships with friends and coworkers.

This isn't to suggest that people with high IQs can't be emotionally savvy, or that emotionally intelligent people don't have personality quirks. Think of some of the other characters on these TV shows and you'll realize that emotional intelligence is best seen on a continuum—and some people have more of it than others. Unfortunately, Sheldon and Dwight are on the short end of that measuring stick.

DEBILITATIVE AND FACILITATIVE EMOTIONS
Yes Man (2008) Rated PG-13

Carl Allen (Jim Carrey) is a man of many emotions—most of them negative. He's been depressed and lonely since a recent divorce, and he regularly rejects his friends' attempts to get him out of the house. His pattern is to say "no" to every invitation that comes his way—until he attends a motivational seminar that convinces him he needs to say "yes." To everything.

Carl's new approach leads to a host of counterintuitive choices, many of which are risky and dangerous (and of course amusing). The adventures that follow help him experience happiness, contentment, and love that otherwise might have escaped him. But feeling obligated to say "yes" comes with a price. Carl wrestles with some of the debilitative emotions described in this chapter as he subscribes to the fallacies of approval, shoulds, and helplessness. Ultimately, he realizes there's a time for yes and a time for no. He also learns that sound choices based on rational thinking are the best route to happiness.

Class _____   Name_____

C H A P T E R   F O U R

Emotions: Feeling, Thinking, and Communicating

CHAPTER OUTLINE

Use this outline to take notes as you read the chapter in the text and/or as your instructor lectures in class.

I.   **WHAT ARE EMOTIONS?**
     A. **Physiological Factors**
     B. **Nonverbal Reactions**
     C. **Cognitive Interpretations**
     D. **Verbal Expression**

II. **INFLUENCES ON EMOTIONAL EXPRESSION**
     A. **Personality**
     B. **Culture**
     C. **Gender**
     D. **Social Conventions**
     E. **Fear of Self-Disclosure**
     F. **Emotional Contagion**

III. **GUIDELINES FOR EXPRESSING EMOTIONS**
     A. **Recognize Your Feelings**
     B. **Recognize the Difference between Feeling, Talking, and Acting**
     C. **Expand Your Emotional Vocabulary**

1. Avoid emotional counterfeits
   a. Express verbally
   b. Use single words
   c. Describe what's happening to you
   d. Describe what you'd like to do
2. Avoid minimizing feelings
3. Avoid coded feelings
4. Focus on a specific set of circumstances

D. **Share Multiple Feelings**
E. **Consider When and Where to Express Your Feelings**
F. **Accept Responsibility for Your Feelings**
G. **Be Mindful of the Communication Channel**

IV. **MANAGING DIFFICULT EMOTIONS**
A. **Facilitative and Debilitative Emotions**
   1. Intensity
   2. Duration
B. **Sources of Debilitative Emotions**
   1. Physiology
   2. Emotional memory
   3. Self-talk
C. **Irrational Thinking and Debilitative Emotions**
   1. Fallacy of perfection
   2. Fallacy of approval
   3. Fallacy of shoulds
   4. Fallacy of overgeneralization
      a. Limited amount of evidence
      b. Exaggerated shortcomings
   5. Fallacy of causation
      a. Belief: you cause emotions in others
      b. Belief: others cause your emotions
   6. Fallacy of helplessness

7. Fallacy of catastrophic expectations	_____
D. Minimizing Debilitative Emotions	_____
1. Monitor your emotional reactions	_____
2. Note the activating event	_____
3. Record your self-talk	
4. Reappraise your irrational beliefs	

KEY TERMS

debilitative emotions

emotional contagion

emotional intelligence

emotion labor

facilitative emotions

fallacy of approval

fallacy of catastrophic expectations

fallacy of causation

fallacy of helplessness

fallacy of overgeneralization

fallacy of perfection

fallacy of shoulds

reappraisal

rumination

self-talk

Class _____   Name_____

ACTIVITIES

4.1 THE COMPONENTS OF EMOTION

LEARNING OBJECTIVES

- Describe how the four components listed in this chapter affect your emotions, and hence your communication in an important situation.

INSTRUCTIONS

1. Read the situations below and describe how the emotions you would experience might manifest themselves in each of the components listed. If you are working in a group, after all have finished, compare the responses of group members.
2. Next record three examples of your own (include the incident, physiological changes, nonverbal reactions, cognitive interpretations, and verbal expressions). If you wish, share one example with the group.

EXAMPLES

1. Incident: Your romantic partner says, "I need to talk to you about something."

   Physiological changes: _____

   Nonverbal reactions: _____

   Cognitive interpretations: _____

   Verbal expression: _____

2. Incident: You run into an "ex" while out with a new partner.

   Physiological changes: _____

   Nonverbal reactions: _____

   Cognitive interpretations: _____

   Verbal expression: _____

3.   Incident: As you're telling a story, you notice your listener stifle a yawn.

Physiological changes: _____

Nonverbal reactions: _____

Cognitive interpretations: _____

Verbal expression: _____

4.   Incident: Your professor says, "I'd like to see you in my office after class."

Physiological changes: _____

Nonverbal reactions: _____

Cognitive interpretations: _____

Verbal expression: _____

YOUR EXAMPLES

1.   Incident: _____

Physiological changes: _____

Nonverbal reactions: _____

Cognitive interpretations: _____

Verbal expression: _____

2.   Incident: _____

Physiological changes: _____

Nonverbal reactions: _____

Cognitive interpretations: _____

Verbal expression: _____

Class _____   Name_____

3. Incident: _____

   Physiological changes: _____

   Nonverbal reactions: _____

   Cognitive interpretations: _____

   Verbal expression: _____

4.2 EXPRESS THE FEELINGS

LEARNING OBJECTIVES

• Apply the guidelines for effectively communicating emotions in an important situation.

INSTRUCTIONS

I. Analyze the statements below to determine which of the seven guidelines for expressing emotions are followed or ignored. There may be more than one.
   A. Recognize Your Feelings
   B. Recognize the Difference between Feeling, Talking, and Acting
   C. Expand Your Emotional Vocabulary
      1. Avoid emotional counterfeits
      2. Express verbally
         a. Use single words
         b. Describe what's happening to you
         c. Describe what you'd like to do
      3. Avoid minimizing feelings
      4. Avoid coded feelings
      5. Focus on a specific set of circumstances
   D. Share Multiple Feelings
   E. Consider When and Where to Express Your Feelings
   F. Accept Responsibility for Your Feelings
   G. Be Mindful of the Communication Channel
II. Rewrite statements that do not follow the above guidelines to clearly or accurately express the speaker's feelings.
III. Record examples of your own at the end of the exercise.

EXAMPLE

That's the most disgusting thing I've ever heard!

Analysis: *This isn't a satisfactory statement, since the speaker isn't clearly claiming that he or she is disgusted. The speaker doesn't seem to recognize feelings (A) and doesn't verbally express a feeling(C-2) and doesn't accept responsibility by using "I" language (F).*

Restatement: *I'm upset and angry that those parents left their young children alone overnight.*

1. You're being awfully sensitive about that.

   Analysis _____

   Restatement _____

   _____

2. I can't figure out how to approach him.

    Analysis _____

    Restatement _____

    _____

3. I'm confused about what you want from me.

    Analysis _____

    Restatement _____

    _____

4. I feel as if you're trying to hurt me.

    Analysis _____

    Restatement _____

    _____

5. You make me so mad when you're late.

    Analysis _____

    Restatement _____

    _____

6. I'm sort of upset with your behavior and a little bit annoyed that you don't apologize.

    Analysis _____

    Restatement _____

    _____

7. I see you're all in there enjoying the game while I clean up the kitchen.

    Analysis _____

    Restatement _____

    _____

8. I feel like the rug's been pulled out from under me.

Analysis _____

Restatement _____

_____

Now record three feeling statements of your own. Analyze and, if necessary, restate.

1. _____.

Analysis _____

Restatement _____

_____

2. _____.

Analysis _____

Restatement _____

_____

3. _____.

Analysis _____

Restatement _____

_____

FEEDBACK TO "4.2 EXPRESS THE FEELINGS"

1. The speaker here is labeling another's feelings, but saying nothing about his or her own feelings. Is the speaker concerned, irritated, or indifferent? We don't know. Possible restatement: "I worried that I teased you too much about your hair."
2. The emotion here is implied but not stated. The speaker might be frustrated, perplexed, or tired. Possible restatement: "I'm nervous about telling him why I was absent."
3. Here is a clear statement of the speaker's emotional state.
4. The statement is emotionally counterfeit. Just because we say "I feel" doesn't mean a feeling is being expressed. This is an interpretation statement because "I feel" can be replaced by "I think." The speaker is expressing that "I think you tried to hurt me" and could then go on to state "I'm anxious about trusting you after you lied to me last week."

5. The speaker doesn't accept responsibility but blames the other person. Possibly there are multiple feelings. Possible restatement: "I feel frustrated, hurt, and angry when you're late."

6. The use of minimizing words like "sort of" and "a bit." Possible restatement: "I'm upset with your behavior and annoyed that you don't apologize."

7. The statement is coded. Possible restatement: "I feel used and taken for granted and would like some help cleaning up so we can all watch the game."

8. Here's a metaphorical statement of feeling, strongly suggesting surprise or shock. This sort of message probably does an adequate job of expressing the emotion here, but it might be too vague for some people to understand. Possible restatement: "I feel insecure right now since I didn't get the job I was expecting."

4.3 STATING EMOTIONS EFFECTIVELY

LEARNING OBJECTIVES

- Describe how the four components listed in this chapter affect your emotions, and hence your communication in an important situation.
- Describe how the influences on emotional expression listed in this chapter have affected your communication in an important relationship.
- Apply the guidelines for effectively communicating emotions in an important situation.

INSTRUCTIONS

I. Identify what's ineffective or unclear about each of the following feeling statements.
II. Rewrite the feeling statements making them more effective using the guidelines from your text.
- A. Recognize Your Feelings
- B. Recognize the Difference between Feeling, Talking, and Acting
- C. Expand Your Emotional Vocabulary
  1. Avoid emotional counterfeits
  2. Express verbally
     - a. Use single words
     - b. Describe what's happening to you
     - c. Describe what you'd like to do
  3. Avoid minimizing feelings
  4. Avoid coded feelings
  5. Focus on a specific set of circumstances
- D. Share Multiple Feelings
- E. Consider When and Where to Express Your Feelings
- F. Accept Responsibility for Your Feelings
- G. Be Mindful of the Communication Channel

FEELING STATEMENT	IDENTIFY INEFFECTIVE, UNCLEAR ELEMENTS/REWRITE STATEMENT
EXAMPLE *When you complimented me in front of everyone at the party, I was really embarrassed.*	*I didn't express the mixed emotions I was feeling. I could have expressed this better by saying, "When you complimented me last night at the party, I was glad you were proud of me, but I was embarrassed that so many people heard it."*
1. You should be more sensitive.	

FEELING STATEMENT	IDENTIFY INEFFECTIVE, UNCLEAR ELEMENTS/REWRITE STATEMENT
2. I get kind of jealous when you have lunch with colleagues.	
3. I don't hear anyone offering to help with this project.	
4. Well, I guess you don't really care about this—or me.	
5. When you act like that, I don't want to be seen with you.	
6. You make me happy.	
7. Why should I help you now? You never show me any appreciation.	
8. I was a little ticked off when you didn't show up.	
9. You jerk—you forgot to put gas in the car!	
10. It's about time you paid up.	
11. I guess I'm a little attracted to him.	
12. With all that's happened, I feel like I'm in a time warp.	

4.4 EMOTIONAL LANGUAGE – SELF-TALK

LEARNING OBJECTIVES

- Identify and reappraise the fallacies that are creating debilitative emotions in an important situation. Explain how more rational thinking can lead to more constructive communication.

INSTRUCTIONS

1. In groups, analyze the statements below.
2. Expand the self-talk behind each statement by using details from your experience to help discover things people often say to themselves.
3. Identify any fallacies contained in the self-talk: approval, overgeneralization, perfection, helplessness, shoulds, catastrophic expectations, causation.
4. Reappraise any irrational self-talk.
5. As a group, record the most common examples of your own self-talk, the fallacies involved, and the reappraising you need to do to keep emotionally healthy.

STATEMENT	SELF-TALK	FALLACIES	REAPPRAISE ANY FALLACIES
EXAMPLE *She's so critical.*	*She never has anything good to say. She drives me crazy. I can't stand her. I'll never be able to make her happy.*	*Overgeneralization, causation, helplessness, approval*	*I need to focus on the good things she does say, not the criticisms. She doesn't make me crazy; I let her get to me. If I don't like what she is saying at the moment, I can leave. It would be nice to please her, but I don't need her approval to be happy.*
1. No one appreciates me around here.			
2. He's so moody.			

Class _____   Name_____

STATEMENT	SELF-TALK	FALLACIES	REAPPRAISE ANY FALLACIES
3. I don't know why I even bother to study for her stupid tests.			
4. Why can't he be more sensitive to my feelings?			
5. She is so embarrassing because she has no manners.			
6. He's a jerk just like his brother.			
7. She's the perfect boss. I'll be completely satisfied in this job.			
8. I'll never get out of here with all her talking.			

STATEMENT	SELF-TALK	FALLACIES	REAPPRAISE ANY FALLACIES
9. I can't believe you told me to buy this worthless car.			
10. It's no use talking to him; he's so unreasonable.			

Class _____   Name_____

STATEMENT	SELF-TALK	FALLACIES	REAPPRAISE ANY FALLACIES
1. (Your examples)			
2.			
3.			
4.			

4.5 REAPPRAISING IRRATIONAL THOUGHTS

LEARNING OBJECTIVES

- Identify and reappraise the fallacies that are creating debilitative emotions in an important situation. Explain how more rational thinking can lead to more constructive communication.

INSTRUCTIONS

1. Use the chart provided to record activating events in which you experience communication-related debilitative emotions. The events needn't involve overwhelming, intense, or intimate feelings; consider mildly debilitative emotions as well.
2. For each incident (activating event), record the self-talk that leads to the emotion you experienced.
3. If the self-talk you've identified is based on any of the irrational fallacies described in *Looking Out/Looking In*, identify them.
4. In each case where irrational thinking exists, reappraise the irrational fallacies and provide an alternative, more rational interpretation of the event.
5. After completing the examples, record your conclusions here (or put them on a separate page):

CONCLUSIONS

1. What are the situations in which you often experience debilitative emotions?

   _____

   _____

   _____

2. What irrational beliefs do you subscribe to most often? Label them and explain.

   _____

   _____

   _____

3.   How can you think more rationally to reduce the number and intensity of debilitative emotions? (Give specific examples related to other aspects of your life, as well as referring to the activating events you have described in this exercise.)

_____

_____

_____

ACTIVATING EVENT	SELF-TALK	IRRATIONAL FALLACIES	EMOTION(S)	REAPPRAISE FALLACIES AND PROVIDE ALTERNATE RATIONAL THINKING
EXAMPLE *Getting ready for a job interview*	*The employer will ask me questions I can't answer. I'll mess up for sure. I'll never get a good job – it's hopeless!*	*Catastrophic failure, overgeneralization, helplessness*	*Apprehension, despair*	*I've prepared for the questions and the interview, so if I'm asked something I don't know, I'll say I'll get back to them on that. I have interpersonal skills. I'll find a good job with time and effort.*
1.				
2.				
3.				

Class _____   Name_____

	ACTIVATING EVENT	SELF-TALK	IRRATIONAL FALLACIES	EMOTION(S)	REAPPRAISE FALLACIES AND PROVIDE ALTERNATE RATIONAL THINKING
4.					
5.					

SW-111

4.6 MESSAGES—EXPRESSING EMOTION

LEARNING OBJECTIVES

- Describe how the influences on emotional expression listed in this chapter have affected your communication in an important relationship.
- Apply the guidelines for effectively communicating emotions in this chapter in an important situation.

INSTRUCTIONS

Discuss each of the questions below in your group. Prepare written answers for your instructor, or be prepared to contribute to a large group discussion, comparing your experiences with those of others in your class.

1. Describe how to recognize emotions communicated in mediated channels such as sticky notes, email, and instant messaging.

   _____

   _____

   _____

   _____

2. Emotional expression may be more difficult in a mediated context (e.g., lack of touch or facial expression to communicate your empathy). On the other hand, mediated contexts may make emotional expression easier (e.g., write a note upon the death of someone rather than face them). Cite examples from your life where you used mediated contexts to express emotion.

   _____

   _____

   _____

   _____

3. In written communication, some stylistic devices (underlining, exclamation marks, capital letters, emoticons like the smiley, winking, or sad face) indicate emotion. How effective do you think these can be in expressing emotion? How easily and how often are they understood? Misunderstood?

_____

_____

_____

_____

4. Compare and contrast the effectiveness of voice messages and text messages for conveying emotion through words.

_____

_____

_____

_____

4.7 EMOTIONS—REAPPRAISAL

LEARNING OBJECTIVES

- Identify and reappraise the fallacies that are creating debilitative emotions in an important situation. Explain how more rational thinking can lead to more constructive communication.
- Describe how the influences on emotional expression listed in the text have affected your communication in an important relationship.
- Apply the guidelines for effectively communicating emotions in an important situation.

INSTRUCTIONS

We all have emotionally charged events in our lives. Think back on three emotionally charged events in your life. Briefly describe the event in the space below. Then describe the emotions this event brings to mind and how you can use reappraisal to change the emotional impact of this event.

Event 1 _____

Emotions Felt:

_____

_____

Reappraisal:

_____

_____

Event 2 _____

Emotions Felt:

_____

_____

Class _____   Name_____

Reappraisal:

_____

_____

Event 3 _____

Emotions Felt:

_____

_____

Reappraisal:

_____

_____

Class _____   Name_____

4.8 ASSESSING NONVERBAL REACTIONS

LEARNING OBJECTIVES

- Apply the guidelines for effectively communicating emotions in an important situation.

INSTRUCTIONS

Watch a television program or a scene from a movie with the mute button on. Observe four nonverbal reactions and predict the possible emotional meaning behind them without listening to the verbal communication. Describe what you observed below and predict the possible nonverbal meaning.

Observation 1

_____

_____

Possible Nonverbal Meaning

_____

_____

Observation 2

_____

_____

Possible Nonverbal Meaning

_____

_____

Observation 3

_____

_____

Possible Nonverbal Meaning

_____

_____

Class _____   Name_____

STUDY GUIDE

CHECK YOUR UNDERSTANDING

TRUE/FALSE

Mark the statements below as true or false. Correct statements that are false on the lines below to create a true statement.

_____ 1. Marriage researcher John Gottman found that when couples are in such intense conflict that bodily changes occur (increased heart rate, a rise in blood pressure, a dilation of pupils), effective problem solving is impeded.

_____

_____ 2. Emotion labor refers to situations where managing and suppressing emotions is appropriate and necessary.

_____

_____ 3. While expression of emotion varies with culture and gender, scholars find that around the world both men and women consistently and similarly speak the phrase "I love you."

_____

_____ 4. In mainstream North American society, the unwritten rules of communication encourage the direct expression of most emotion.

_____

_____ 5. "I feel confined" is an emotional counterfeit statement.

_____

_____ 6. Using many words to express a feeling is better than just summarizing feelings in a few words.

_____

_____ 7. When thoughts are irrational, unwelcome emotions can interfere with effective communication.

_____

SW-118

_____   8.   Reappraisal involves changing our thoughts to help manage our emotions.

_____

_____   9.   Subscribing to the myth of perfection usually enhances your own self-esteem, but it usually doesn't keep others from liking you.

_____

_____   10.   The fallacy of causation exists in two forms: you believe others cause your emotions or you believe you cause others' emotions.

_____

COMPLETION

Fill in the blanks below with the correct terms chosen from the list below.

catastrophic expectations   helplessness   causation
overgeneralization   shoulds   approval
perfection   activating event   reappraisal
rumination

1.   _____ is an irrational fallacy that operates on the assumption that if something bad can possibly happen, it will.

2.   _____ is an irrational fallacy that suggests that satisfaction in life is determined by forces beyond your control.

3.   _____ is an irrational fallacy based on the belief that emotions are the result of other people and things rather than one's own self-talk.

4.   _____ is an irrational fallacy that makes a broad claim based on a limited amount of evidence.

5.   _____ is an irrational fallacy based on the inability to distinguish between what is and what ought to be.

6.   _____ is an irrational fallacy in which people go to incredible lengths to seek acceptance from virtually everyone.

7.   _____ is an irrational fallacy in which people believe that worthwhile communicators should be able to handle every situation with complete confidence and skill.

8.   _____ is the single large incident or series of small incidents that lead to thoughts or beliefs about the incident.

9. _____ is the process of rethinking the meaning of emotionally charged events in a way that alter their emotional impact.

10. _____ is dwelling persistently on negative thoughts that, in turn, intensify negative feelings.

MULTIPLE CHOICE

Choose the letter of the irrational fallacy contained in the self-talk found below.

a. perfection
b. approval
c. shoulds
d. overgeneralization

e. causation
f. helplessness
g. catastrophic expectations

_____ 1. "If only I didn't put my foot in my mouth when I ask someone out."

_____ 2. "I just can't initiate conversations—that's all there is to it."

_____ 3. "He shouldn't be off with his friends on Friday night."

_____ 4. "If she doesn't like this shirt, I'll be so upset."

_____ 5. "There was a major fire the last time we left; there will probably be an earthquake this time."

_____ 6. "He's never romantic."

_____ 7. "She's always a cold fish; I'm lucky if I get a kiss."

_____ 8. "Other people ought to cut me some slack; they shouldn't be so critical."

_____ 9. "You're going to die or be seriously injured if you go to Mexico at spring break."

_____ 10. "I've had a class in interpersonal communication; I can't believe I insulted her just now."

_____ 11. "Shawn makes me so mad with all his great grades."

_____ 12. "She'll be devastated if I break up with her."

_____ 13. "It's not even worth trying to reach him."

_____ 14. "I hope they don't notice how much weight I've gained. They won't like it."

Choose the best answer for each of the statements below.

15. Which of the following statements about emotions and culture is true?
    a. The same events will generate the same emotions in all cultures.
    b. Some emotions seem to be experienced by people around the world.
    c. People from different cultures express happiness and sadness with different facial expressions.
    d. Fear of strangers is as strong in Japan as it is in the U.S.

16. Which of the following statements about rumination is not true?
    a. Rumination increases feelings of sadness.
    b. Rumination increases feelings of anxiety.
    c. Rumination increases feelings of depression.
    d. Rumination lessens aggression toward others.

17. Which of these represents coded emotions?
    a. I feel grateful when you bring soup to me when I'm sick.
    b. I'm upset because you borrowed my white-out.
    c. I feel like a door mat—just used by everyone.
    d. I don't hear any thank-you's. It sure would be nice to hear some appreciation.

18. Which of the following follows the text's guidelines for expressing feelings?
    a. "I feel like watching a movie."
    b. "I feel like you're lonely."
    c. "I'm irritated by the ticking clock."
    d. "I'm totally involved."

19. Which of the following *best* improves the expression of emotion in the statement "I feel like giving up"?
    a. "I'm frustrated after asking him to pay his telephone bill three times."
    b. "I'm going to kill him."
    c. "I am going to tell the landlord about this frustrating situation."
    d. "I feel he's been unreasonable."

20. In which job would emotion labor be needed the most?
    a. firefighter
    b. correctional officer
    c. judge
    d. emotion labor is equally important in all of these jobs

21.   Which of the following statements about culture is true?

    a.   All cultures are equal in every way.
    b.   Emotions are lacking in most collectivistic cultures.
    c.   People from different cultures express happiness and sadness with different facial expressions.
    d.   The easiest way to understand a culture is to live within it for a period of time.

22.   Which of the following statements about emotional intelligence is not true?

    a.   Emotional intelligence is helpful in the workplace.
    b.   Emotional intelligence is a sign of a competent communicator.
    c.   Emotional intelligence is as important as cognitive intelligence.
    d.   Emotional intelligence is a sign of an incompetent communicator.

CHAPTER FOUR STUDY GUIDE ANSWERS

TRUE/FALSE

1. T	3. F	5. F	7. T	9. F
2. T	4. F	6. F	8. T	10. T

COMPLETION

1. catastrophic expectations	5. shoulds	9. reappraisal
2. helplessness	6. approval	10. rumination
3. causation	7. perfection	
4. overgeneralization	8. activating event	

MULTIPLE CHOICE

1. a	5. g	9. g	13. f	17. d
2. f	6. d	10. a	14. b	18. c
3. c	7. d	11. e	15. b	19. a
4. b	8. c	12. e	16. d	20. d
				21. d
				22. d

Language: Barrier and Bridge

After studying the topics in this chapter, you should be able to:

1. Analyze a real or potential misunderstanding in terms of semantic or pragmatic rules.

2. Describe how principles presented in the section of this chapter titled "The Impact of Language" operate in your life.

3. Construct a message at the optimal level of specificity or vagueness for a given situation.

4. Recast "you" statements into "I" or "we" statements to reflect your responsibility for the content of messages.

5. Rephrase disruptive statements in less inflammatory terms.

6. In a given situation, analyze how gender or cultural differences (or both) may affect the quality of interaction.

Now the whole world had one language and a common speech.

As men moved eastward, they found a plain in Shinar and settled there.

They said to each other, "Come, let's make bricks and bake them thoroughly." They used brick instead of stone, and tar for mortar.

Then they said, "Come, let us build ourselves a city, with a tower that reaches to the heavens, so that we may make a name for ourselves and not be scattered over the face of the whole earth."

But the Lord came down to see the city and the tower that the men were building.

The Lord said, "If as one people speaking the same language they have begun to do this, then nothing they plan to do will be impossible for them.

Come, let us go down and confuse their language so they will not understand each other."

So the Lord scattered them from there over all the earth, and they stopped building the city.

That is why it was called Babel—because there the Lord confused the language of the whole world.

Genesis 11:1–9

The problems that began with Babel continue today. Sometimes it seems as if none of us speaks the same language. Yet despite its frustrations and challenges, language is clearly a marvelous tool. It is the gift that allows us to communicate in a way that no other animals appear to match. Without language, we would be more ignorant, ineffectual, and isolated.

In this chapter, we explore the nature of language, looking at how to take advantage of its strengths and minimize its weaknesses. After a quick explanation of the symbolic nature of language, we examine the sources of language-based misunderstandings. We then move beyond the challenges of simply understanding one another and explore how the language we use affects the climate of interpersonal relationships. Finally, we broaden our focus even more to look at how linguistic practices shape the attitudes of entire cultures.

Language Is Symbolic

In the natural world, signs have a direct connection with the things they represent. For example, smoke is a sign that something's burning, and a high fever is a sign of illness. There's nothing arbitrary about the relationship between natural signs and the things they represent. Nobody made them up, and they exist independently of human opinions.

In human language, the connection between signs and the things they represent isn't so direct. Instead, language is *symbolic*: There's only an arbitrary connection between words and the ideas or things to which they refer. For example, there is nothing particularly fivelike in the number five. The word represents the number of fingers on your hand only because English speakers agree that it does. To a speaker of French, the symbol *cinq* would convey the same meaning; to a computer programmer, the same value would be represented by the coded symbol 00110101.

Even sign language, as "spoken" by most hearing-impaired people, is symbolic in nature and not the pantomime it might seem. Because this form of communication is symbolic and not literal, hundreds of sign languages around the world have evolved independently whenever significant numbers of hearing-impaired people are in contact.[1] These distinct languages include American Sign Language, British Sign Language, French Sign Language, Danish Sign Language, Chinese Sign Language—even Australian Aboriginal and Mayan Sign Languages.

The symbolic nature of language is a blessing. It enables us to communicate in ways that wouldn't otherwise be possible about ideas, reasons, the past, the future, and things not present. Without symbolic language, none of this would be possible. However, the indirect relationship between symbols and the things they represent leads to communication problems only hinted about in the tower of Babel story.

If everyone used symbols in the same way, then language would be much easier to manage and understand—but your own experience shows that this isn't always the case. Messages that seem perfectly clear to you prove confusing or misleading to others. You tell the hairstylist to "take a little off the top" and are stunned to discover that her definition of "a little" was equivalent to your definition of "a lot." You have a heated argument about the merits of *feminism* without realizing that you and the other person have been using the word to represent entirely different ideas. Misunderstandings like these remind us that meanings are in people, not in words.

In Washington, D.C., an uproar developed when the city's ombudsman, David Howard, used the word *niggardly* to describe an approach to budgeting.[2] Howard, who is white, was accused by some African American critics of uttering an unforgivable racial slur. His defenders pointed out that the word, which means "miserly," is derived from Scandinavian languages and has no link to the racial slur it resembles. Even though the criticisms eventually died away, they illustrate that the meanings that people associate with words—correctly or not—have far more significance than do their dictionary definitions.

"What part of oil lamp next to double squiggle
over ox don't you understand?"

Understandings and Misunderstandings

Language is rather like plumbing: We pay the most attention to it when something goes wrong. But the problems that arise from misunderstandings aren't always immediately apparent, and they occur more often than we imagine. Most people vastly overestimate how well their explanations get through and how well they understand others.[3] Because misunderstandings are the greatest cause of concern for most people who study language, we'll begin our study by looking at sets of rules we use to understand—and sometimes misunderstand—one another's speech.

UNDERSTANDING WORDS: SEMANTIC RULES

Semantic rules reflect the ways in which users of a language assign meaning to a particular linguistic symbol, usually a word. Semantic rules make it possible for us to agree that "bikes" are for riding and "books" are for reading, and they help us know who we will and won't encounter when we use rooms marked "men" or "women." Without semantic rules, communication would be impossible because each of us would use symbols in unique ways, without sharing meaning. Semantic misunderstandings arise when people assign different meanings to the same words. In the next few pages, we will look at some of the most common ones.

Equivocation **Equivocal language** consists of statements that have more than one commonly accepted definition. Some equivocal misunderstandings are amusing, as the following newspaper headlines illustrate:

> Family Catches Fire Just in Time
>
> Man Stuck on Toilet; Stool Suspected
>
> 20-Year Friendship Ends at the Altar
>
> Trees Can Break Wind

Some equivocal misunderstandings can be embarrassing. As one woman recalls: "In the fourth grade the teacher asked the class what a period was. I raised my hand and shared everything I had learned about girls getting their period. But he was talking about the dot at the end of a sentence. Oops!"[4]

Other equivocal statements can be even more troubling. A nurse gave one of her patients a scare when she told him that he "wouldn't be needing" his robe, books, and shaving materials anymore. The patient became quiet and moody. When the nurse inquired about the odd behavior, she discovered that the poor man had interpreted her statement to mean he was going to die soon. In fact, the nurse meant he would be going home.

It's difficult to catch every equivocal statement and clarify it while speaking. For this reason, the responsibility for interpreting statements accurately rests in large part with the receiver. Feedback of one sort or another—for example, the kind of perception checking introduced in Chapter 3 and the paraphrasing described in Chapter 7—can help clear up misunderstandings.

Despite its obvious problems, equivocal language has its uses. As Chapter 2 describes in detail, there are times

"Be honest with me, Roger. By 'mid-course correction' you mean divorce, don't you."

when using language that is open to several interpretations can be useful. It helps people get along by avoiding the kind of honesty and clarity that can embarrass both the speaker and listener. For example, if a friend proudly shows you a newly completed painting and asks your opinion about it, you might respond equivocally by saying, "Gee, it's really unusual. I've never seen anything like it," instead of giving a less ambiguous but more hurtful response such as "This may be the ugliest thing I've ever seen!"

Relative Language **Relative words** gain their meaning by comparison. For example, do you attend a large or small school? This depends on what you compare it to. Alongside a huge state university, your school may not seem big, but compared with a small college, it may seem quite large. Relative words such as *fast* and *slow*, *smart* and *stupid*, *short* and *long* are clearly defined only through comparison.

Some relative terms are so common that we mistakenly assume they have a clear meaning. For instance, if a friend told you it's "likely" she'll show up at your party tonight, what are the chances she's going to come? In one study, students were asked to assign percentages to such terms as *doubtful*, *toss-up*, *likely*, *probable*, *good chance*, and *unlikely*.[5] There was a tremendous variation in the meaning of most of these terms. For example, the responses for *probable* ranged from 0 to 99 percent. *Good chance* fell between 35 percent and 90 percent, whereas *unlikely* fell between 0 and 40 percent.

One way to make words more measurable is to turn them into numbers. Healthcare practitioners have learned that patients often use vague descriptions when describing their pain: "It hurts a little"; "I'm pretty sore." The use of a numeric pain scale can give a more precise response—and lead to a better diagnosis.[6] When patients are asked to rank their pain from 1 to 10, with 10 being the most severe pain they've ever experienced, the number 7 is much more concrete and specific than "It aches a bit." The same technique can be used when asking people to rate anything from the movies they've seen to their job satisfaction.

Static Evaluation "Mark is a nervous guy." "Mia is short-tempered." "You can always count on Ming." Statements that contain or imply the word *is* lead to the mistaken assumption that people are consistent and unchanging—an incorrect belief known as **static evaluation**. Instead of labeling Mark as permanently and totally nervous, it would be more accurate to outline the particular situations in which he behaves nervously. The same goes for Mia, Ming, and the rest of us: We are more changeable than the way static, everyday language describes us.

Abstraction When it comes to describing problems, goals, appreciation, and requests, some language is more specific than others. **Abstract language** is vague in nature, whereas **behavioral language**—as its name implies—refers to specific things that people say or do. The "**abstraction ladder**" in Figure 5.1 illustrates how the same phenomenon can be described at various levels of specificity and abstraction. Notice how the ladder's bottom-rung description is more concrete and behavioral, and thus it is probably clearer than the top rung's abstract injunction to develop a "better attitude."

We use higher-level abstractions all the time. For instance, rather than saying, "Thanks for washing the dishes," "Thanks for vacuuming the rug," or "Thanks for making the bed," it's easier to say, "Thanks for cleaning up." In such everyday situations, abstractions are a useful kind of verbal shorthand.

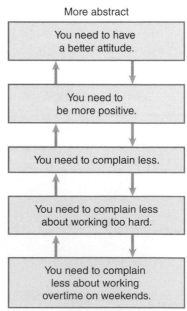

More abstract

You need to have a better attitude.

You need to be more positive.

You need to complain less.

You need to complain less about working too hard.

You need to complain less about working overtime on weekends.

More specific

FIGURE 5.1 Abstraction Ladder
© Cengage Learning

Although verbal shorthand like this can be useful, highly abstract language can lead to blanket judgments and stereotyping: "Marriage counselors are worthless," "Skateboarders are delinquents," or "Men are no good." Overly abstract expressions like these can cause people to *think* in generalities, ignoring uniqueness. As you learned in Chapter 3, stereotyping can injure interpersonal relationships, because it categorizes and evaluates people in ways that may not be accurate.

You can appreciate the value of behavioral descriptions by looking at the examples in Table 5.1. Notice how much more clearly they explain the speaker's thoughts than do the vaguer terms.

PAUSE AND REFLECT

AVOIDING TROUBLESOME LANGUAGE

For practice recognizing and overcoming the kinds of troublesome language and thinking described in a web-based introduction to general semantics, see the series of exercises at thisisnotthat.com. You can find the link to this site by visiting CengageBrain.com to access the Speech Communication CourseMate for *Looking Out/Looking In*.

SKILL BUILDER

DOWN-TO-EARTH LANGUAGE

You can appreciate the value of nonabstract language by translating the following into behavioral terms:

1. An abstract goal for improving your interpersonal communication (e.g., "be more assertive" or "stop being so sarcastic").
2. A complaint you have about another person (e.g., that he or she is "selfish" or "insensitive").
3. A request for someone to change (e.g., "I wish you'd be more punctual" or "Try to be more positive").
4. An appreciation you could share with another person (e.g., "Thanks for being so helpful" or "I appreciate your patience").

In each case, describe the person or persons involved, the circumstances in which the behavior occurs, and the precise behaviors involved. What differences can you expect when you use behavioral descriptions like the ones you have created here?

You can complete this activity by visiting CengageBrain.com to access the Speech Communication CourseMate for *Looking Out/Looking In*, and, if requested, email your responses to your instructor.

UNDERSTANDING STRUCTURE: SYNTACTIC RULES

Syntactic rules govern the grammar of a language. You can appreciate how syntax contributes to the meaning of a statement by considering two versions of a letter:

TABLE 5.1 ABSTRACT VERSUS BEHAVIORAL DESCRIPTIONS

	ABSTRACT DESCRIPTION	BEHAVIORAL DESCRIPTION			REMARKS
		WHO IS INVOLVED	IN WHAT CIRCUMSTANCES	SPECIFIC BEHAVIORS	
Problem	I talk too much.	People I find intimidating	When I want them to like me	I talk (mostly about myself) instead of giving them a chance to speak or asking about their lives.	Behavioral description more clearly identifies behaviors to change.
Goal	I want to be more constructive.	My roommate	When we talk about household duties	Instead of finding fault with her ideas, suggest alternatives that might work.	Behavioral description clearly outlines how to act, abstract description doesn't.
Appreciation	"You've really been helpful lately."	(Deliver to fellow worker)	"When I've had to take time off work because of personal problems . . ."	". . . you took my shifts without complaining."	Give both abstract and behavioral descriptions for best results.
Request	"Clean up your act!"	(Deliver to target person)	"When we're around my family . . ."	". . . please don't tell jokes that involve sex."	Behavioral description specifies behavior.

© Cengage Learning

Version 1

Dear John:

I want a man who knows what love is all about. You are generous, kind, thoughtful. People who are not like you admit to being useless and inferior. You have ruined me for other men. I yearn for you. I have no feelings whatsoever when we're apart. I can be forever happy—will you let me be yours?

Mary

Version 2

Dear John:

I want a man who knows what love is. All about you are generous, kind, thoughtful people, who are not like you. Admit to being useless and inferior. You have ruined me. For other men, I yearn. For you, I have no feelings whatsoever. When we're apart, I can be forever happy. Will you let me be?

Yours,
Mary

Semantic rules don't explain why these letters send virtually opposite messages. There's no ambiguity about the meaning of the words they contain: *love*, *kind*, *thoughtful*, and so on. The opposite meanings of the letters came from their different syntax.

Although most of us aren't able to describe the syntactic rules that govern our language, it's easy to recognize their existence when they are violated. A humorous example is the way the character Yoda speaks in the *Star Wars* movies. Phrases such as "The dark side are they" or "Your father he is" often elicit a chuckle because they bend syntactical norms. Sometimes, however, apparently ungrammatical speech is simply following a different set of syntactic rules, reflecting regional or co-cultural dialects. Linguists believe it is crucial to view such dialects as *different* rather than *deficient* forms of English.[7]

"I never said 'I love you.' I said 'I love ya.' Big difference!"

UNDERSTANDING CONTEXT: PRAGMATIC RULES

Semantic and syntactic problems don't account for all misunderstandings.[8] To appreciate a different type of communication challenge, imagine how a young female employee might struggle to make sense of her older male boss's statement, "You look very pretty today." She almost certainly would understand the meaning of the words, and the syntax is perfectly clear. Still, the boss's message could be interpreted in several ways. Was the remark a simple compliment? A come-on? Did it contain the suggestion that she didn't look nice on other days?

If the boss and employee share the same interpretation of the message, their communication would be smooth. But if they bring different perspectives to interpreting it, a problem exists. Table 5.2 shows several ways in which different perspectives of the boss and employee would lead to their attaching different meanings to the same words.

In situations like this one, we rely on **pragmatic rules** to decide how to interpret messages in a given context. Pragmatic rules govern the way speech operates in everyday

TABLE 5.2 PRAGMATIC RULES GOVERN THE USE AND MEANING OF A STATEMENT

	BOSS	EMPLOYEE
Statement	"You look very nice today."	
Self-Concept "Who am I?" "Who is s/he?"	Friendly guy	Woman determined to succeed on own merits
Episode "What's going on in this exchange?"	Casual conversation	Possible come-on by boss?
Relationship "Who are we to one another?"	Boss who treats employees like family members	Subordinate employee, dependent on boss's approval for advancement
Culture "What does my background say about the meaning here?"	Euro-American, raised in United States	Latina, raised in South America

Adapted from Pearce, W. B., & Cronen, V. (1980). *Communication, action, and meaning.* New York: Praeger; and Griffin, E. (2012). *A first look at communication theory* (8th ed.). New York: McGraw-Hill.

interaction. You can't look up pragmatic rules in any dictionary. They are almost always unstated, but they are just as important as semantic and syntactic rules in helping us make sense of one another's messages.

The best way to appreciate how pragmatic rules operate is to think of communication as a kind of cooperative game. Like all games, success depends on all of the players understanding and following the same set of rules. This is why communication scholars use the term *coordination* to describe the way conversation operates when everyone involved uses the same set of pragmatic rules.[9]

Some pragmatic rules are shared by most people in a culture. In North America, for instance, competent communicators understand that the question "How's it going?" usually isn't really a request for information. Anyone familiar with

In the movie *Gran Torino*, Walt Kowalski (Clint Eastwood) teaches Hmong immigrant Thao (Bee Vang) how to "talk like a man" in an American barbershop. Many of the terms he uses are considered vulgar and crude, but they are pragmatically appropriate for this exchange in this context.

the rules of conversation knows that the proper answer is something like "Pretty good. How's it going with you?" Likewise, most people understand the pragmatic rule that says that "Would you like a drink?" means "Would you like an alcoholic beverage?" whereas "Would you like something to drink?" is a more open-ended question.

Besides following cultural rules, people in individual relationships create their own sets of pragmatic rules. Consider the use of humor: The teasing and jokes you exchange with gusto with one friend might be considered tasteless or offensive in another relationship.[10] For instance, imagine an email message typed in CAPITAL LETTERS and filled with CURSE WORDS, INSULTS, NAME-CALLING, and EXCLAMATION MARKS!!! How would you interpret such a message? An outside observer may consider this an example of "flaming" and be appalled, when in fact the message might be a fun-loving case of "verbal jousting" between buddies.[11] If you have a good friend whom you call by a less-than-tasteful nickname as a term of endearment, then you understand the concept. Keep in mind, however, that those who aren't privy to your relationship's pragmatic rules are likely to misunderstand you, so you'll want to be wise about when and where to use these personal codes.

The Impact of Language

So far we have focused on language only as a medium for helping communicators understand one another. But along with this important function, language can shape our perceptions of the world around us and reflect the attitudes we hold toward one another.

NAMING AND IDENTITY

"What's in a name?" Juliet asked rhetorically. If Romeo had been a social scientist, he would have answered "A great deal."

PAUSE AND REFLECT

YOUR LINGUISTIC RULES

To what extent do linguistic rules affect your understanding of and relationships with others? Explore this question by following these steps:

1. Recall a time when you encountered someone whose speech violated the syntactic rules that you are used to. What was your impression of this person? To what degree was this impression influenced by her or his failure to follow familiar linguistic rules? Consider whether this impression was or was not valid.

2. Recall at least one misunderstanding that arose when you and another person followed different semantic rules. Use hindsight to consider whether this misunderstanding (and others like it) could be avoided. If semantic misunderstandings can be minimized, explain what approaches might be useful.

3. Identify at least two pragmatic rules that govern the use of language in one of your relationships. Share these rules with other students. Do they use language in the same way as you and your relational partner?

 You can complete this activity by visiting CengageBrain.com to access the Speech Communication CourseMate for *Looking Out/ Looking In*, and, if requested, email your responses to your instructor.

Research has demonstrated that names are more than just a simple means of identification: They shape the way others think of us, the way we view ourselves, and the way we act. For more than a century, researchers have studied the impact of rare and unique names on the people who bear them.[12] Early studies claimed that people with unusual names suffered everything from psychological and emotional disturbance to failure in college. More recent studies have shown that people often have negative appraisals not only of unusual names but also of unusual name spellings.[13] Of course, what makes a name (and its spelling) unusual changes with time. In 1900, the twenty most popular names for baby girls in the United States included Bertha, Mildred, and Ethel. By 2012, the top twenty names included Madison, Ava, and Chloe—names that would have been highly unusual a century earlier.[14]

Names are one way to shape and reinforce a child's personal identity. Naming a baby after a family member (e.g., "Junior" or "Trey") can create a connection between the youngster and his or her namesake. Name choice can also be a powerful way to make a statement about cultural identity. For example, in recent decades a large percentage of names given to African American babies have been distinctive to that co-culture.[15] In California, more than 40 percent of black girls born in a recent period had names that not a single white baby born in the entire state was given. Researchers suggest that distinctive names like these are a symbol of solidarity with the African American community. Conversely, choosing a less distinctive name can be a way of integrating the baby into the majority culture.

AFFILIATION

Besides shaping an individual's identity, speech can build and demonstrate solidarity with others. Research has demonstrated that communicators are attracted to others whose style of speaking is similar to theirs.[16] Likewise, communicators who want to show affiliation with one another adapt their speech in a variety of ways, including

Finding the Words to Talk About Disability

William came home from school a few weeks back and he said, "Mom." He said it as a sentence, the way he does when he has something important to tell me. And then again, "Mom. My friend Ashley is not good at listening. And she screams."

William is three. He attends a local public preschool, and he's in an "integrated" classroom, which is to say, a classroom where typically developing children learn and play alongside children with special needs. Three years ago, William's older sister Penny was in the same classroom. Penny has Trisomy 21, also known as Down syndrome, and that third chromosome impacts nearly every aspect of her development. She wears braces to support her flat feet and weak ankles. When she was in preschool, she relied on sign language in addition to spoken words to communicate.

But just because I have a daughter with a disability doesn't mean that I know how to talk about disabilities with my children. When Penny was first born, I found myself in a maze of words that had never mattered to me before— abnormality, disability, high-risk pregnancy, genetic counseling, special needs. It became easier with time. I started to use "people-first" language, calling her a baby with Down syndrome instead of a Down's baby. I substituted "normal" with "typical" when it came to describing other children. In my subsequent pregnancies, I talked about the "chance" of having another child with Down syndrome instead of the "risk."

And over time, the words became more than politically correct attempts to support my new identity as the mother of a child with a disability. Over time, the words became reality. I really did see Penny as a child first, with Down syndrome as a descriptive but secondary marker. I really did come to believe that individuals with disabilities were not people to be pitied or people in need of help but rather human beings who were just like me. Our particularities were different, but I came to understand that we all have limitations and places of vulnerability and need, and we all have possibilities for joy and relationships and self-giving.

I was delighted when William was accepted, via lottery, into the integrated preschool class. But I wondered if I would be able to put words to his experience. I wondered if I would be able to talk about disability in a way that was honest and positive, in a way that built bridges instead of creating categories or judgments. So when William told me that Ashley doesn't listen well and screams, I took a deep breath.

I said, "Maybe she hasn't learned how to listen yet." He nodded. And then I asked, "What is Ashley good at?"

He tilted his head. "Playin' games and runnin' around."

"What are you good at?"

"Listening."

kali9/the Agency Collection/Getty Images

"What's hard for you?"

"Coloring."

That was the end of our conversation. William has talked about Ashley since then, but only because he tells me things about his friend—that she takes the bus, that they pretend to do cooking together, that he wanted to have a sticker chart with prizes just like her. As far as William is concerned, Ashley is just another kid in his class. There are some things that are hard for her. There are some things she's good at. Just like him.

Eventually William will realize that many aspects of our culture—from language to legislation—erect walls between kids like him and kids like Ashley. But I hope that growing up with a sister with Down syndrome and going to school alongside boys and girls who have different challenges than he does will open his eyes, and his heart, to understanding our common humanity. I hope he will grow up with an ability to see beyond labels, to trust that he has something to offer to everyone he meets, but that he also has something to receive from them.

Amy Julia Becker

their choice of vocabulary, rate of talking, number and placement of pauses, and level of politeness—a process known as *speech accommodation*.[17] Adolescents who all adopt the same vocabulary of slang words and speech mannerisms illustrate the principle of linguistic solidarity. The same process works among members of other groups ranging from street gangs to military personnel. Communication researchers call the process of adapting one's speech style to match that of others **convergence**. One study even showed that adopting the swearing patterns of bosses and coworkers can help people feel connected on the job (see the On the Job sidebar on page 167 for more about swearing in the workplace).[18]

In one study, the likelihood of mutual romantic interest increased when conversational partners' use of pronouns, articles, conjunctions, prepositions, and negations matched.[19] The same study revealed that when couples used similar language styles while instant messaging, the chances of their relationship continuing increased by almost 50 percent. The researchers speculate that unconscious language-style matching relates to how much each is paying attention to what the other says. Another study found that members of online communities often develop a shared language and conversational style, and their affiliation with each other can be seen in increased uses of the pronoun *we*.[20]

Paramount/The Kobal Collection

When two or more people feel equally positive about one another, their linguistic convergence will be mutual. But when communicators want or need approval, they often adapt their speech to accommodate the other person's style, trying to say the "right thing" or speak in a way that will help them fit in. We see this process when immigrants who want to gain the rewards of material success in a new culture strive to master the host language. Likewise, employees who seek advancement tend to speak more like their bosses.

The principle of speech accommodation works in reverse, too. Communicators who want to set themselves apart from others adopt the strategy of **divergence**, speaking in a way that emphasizes their differences from others. For example, members of an ethnic group, even though fluent in the dominant language, might use their own dialect as a way of showing solidarity with one another—a sort of "us against them" strategy. The same behavior can occur across ethnic lines, such as teens who adopt the slang of particular subcultures to show divergence with adults and convergence with their peers.[21]

Of course, communicators need to be careful about when—and when not—to converge their language with others. Most of us can remember the embarrassment of hearing a parent using youthful slang and thinking, "You're too old to be saying that—quit trying to sound like us." On a more serious level, using ethnic or racial epithets when you're not a member of that in-group can be inappropriate and even offensive. One of the pragmatic goals of divergence is the creation of norms about who has the "right" to use certain words and who does not. (The film *The N Word*, described at the end of this chapter, offers a good discussion of this topic.)

The high school movie *Mean Girls* captures the role of linguistic convergence in defining and maintaining in-groups. (See the film summary at the end of this chapter.)

POWER

Communication researchers have identified several language patterns that add to or detract from a speaker's power to influence others. Notice the difference between these two statements from an employee to a manager:

> "Excuse me, sir. I hate to say this, but I . . . uh . . . I guess I won't be able to finish the project on time. I had a personal emergency, and . . . well . . . it was just impossible to finish it by today. I'll have it on your desk on Monday, OK?"

> "I won't be able to finish the project on time. I had a personal emergency, and it was impossible to finish it by today. I'll have it on your desk Monday."

Whether or not the boss finds the excuse acceptable, it's clear that the tone of the second one is more confident, whereas the tone of the first is apologetic and uncertain. Table 5.3 identifies several **powerless speech mannerisms** illustrated in the statements you just read. Some studies have shown that speakers whose talk is free of these mannerisms are rated as more competent, dynamic, and attractive than speakers who sound powerless.[22] Powerful speech can help candidates in job interviews. Employers rate applicants who use a powerful style as more competent and employable than candidates who speak less forcefully.[23] One study revealed that even a single type of powerless speech mannerism can make a person appear less authoritative or socially attractive.[24]

TABLE 5.3 EXAMPLES OF POWERLESS LANGUAGE

Hedges	"I'm *kinda* disappointed . . ." "I *think* we should . . ." "I *guess* I'd like to . . ."
Hesitations	"*Uh*, can I have a minute of your time?" "*Well*, we could try this idea . . ." "I wish you would—*er*—try to be on time."
Intensifiers	"I'm *really* glad to see you." "I'm not *very* hungry."
Polite forms	"Excuse me, *sir* . . ."
Tag questions	"It's about time we got started, *isn't it?*" "*Don't you think* we should give it another try?"
Disclaimers	"*I probably shouldn't say this, but* . . ." "*I'm not really sure, but* . . ."
Rising inflections	(See the reading on page 204 in Chapter 6.)

© Cengage Learning

A *disclaimer* is a type of powerless speech that attempts to distance a speaker from remarks that might be unwelcome. For example, you might preface a critical message by saying "I don't mean to sound judgmental, but . . ." and then go on to express your disapproval. One study showed that disclaimers actually *increase* negative judgments.[25] For instance, the phrase "I don't mean to sound arrogant . . ." followed by a high-handed comment led subjects to regard the speaker as *more* arrogant. Disclaimers involving other negative qualities such as laziness and selfishness produced similar results. It seems that disclaimers backfire because they sensitize listeners to look for—and find—precisely the qualities that the speaker is trying to disavow.

Powerful speech that gets the desired results in mainstream North American and European cultures doesn't succeed everywhere with everyone.[26] In Japan, saving face for others is an important goal, so communicators there tend to speak in ambiguous terms and use hedge words and qualifiers. Traditional Mexican culture, with its strong emphasis on cooperation, also uses hedging to smooth over interpersonal relationships. By not taking a firm stand with their speech language, Mexicans avoid making others feel ill at ease. The Korean culture represents yet another people who prefer "indirect" (e.g., "perhaps," "could be") over "direct" speech.

Even in cultures that value assertiveness, language that is *too* powerful may intimidate or annoy others. Consider these two different approaches to handling a common situation:

"Excuse me. My baby is having a little trouble getting to sleep. Would you mind turning down the music just a little?"

"My baby can't sleep because your music is too loud. You need to turn it down."

The more polite, if less powerful, approach would probably produce better results than the stronger statement. How can this fact be reconciled with the research on powerful language? As noted in Chapter 1, interpersonal competence is a balance between effectiveness and appropriateness. If you come across as too powerful, you may get what you're seeking in the short term but alienate the other person in ways that will make your relationship more difficult in the long term. Furthermore, a statement that is *too* powerful can convey relational messages of disrespect and superiority, which are just as likely to antagonize others as to gain their compliance.

In some situations, polite, less apparently powerful forms of speech can even enhance a speaker's effectiveness.[27] For example, a boss might say to a secretary, "Would you mind retyping this letter?" In truth, both the boss and secretary know that this is an order and not a request, but the questioning form is more considerate and leaves the secretary feeling better about the boss.[28] The importance of achieving both content and relational goals helps explain why a mixture of powerful speech and polite speech is usually most effective.[29]

DISRUPTIVE LANGUAGE

Not all linguistic problems come from misunderstandings. Sometimes people understand one another perfectly and still wind up in a conflict. Of course, not all disagreements can, or should be, avoided. But eliminating three linguistic habits from your communication repertoire can minimize the kind of disagreements that don't need to happen, allowing you to save your energy for the unavoidable and important disagreements.

Fact–Opinion Confusion Factual statements are claims that can be verified as true or false. By contrast, opinion statements are based on the speaker's beliefs. Unlike factual statements, they can never be proved or disproved. Consider a few examples of the difference between factual and opinion statements:

Fact	Opinion
You forgot my birthday.	You don't care about me.
You keep interrupting me.	You're a control freak.
You tell a lot of ethnic jokes.	You're a bigot.

When factual and opinion statements are set side by side like this, the difference is clear. In everyday conversation, however, we often present our opinions as if they were facts, and in doing so we invite an unnecessary argument. For example:

"That was a dumb thing to say!"

"Spending that much on a pair of shoes is a waste of money!"

"You can't get a fair shake in this country unless you're a white male."

ON THE JOB

Swearing in the Workplace

Swearing may offend some people, but it serves a variety of communication functions.[a] It's a way to express emotions and to let others know how strongly you feel. It can be a compliment ("that was #$&@ing terrific!") or a harsh insult. Swearing can even be a term of endearment.

Swearing on the job can be especially problematic.[b] Communication researchers Danette Johnson and Nicole Lewis investigated the effects of swearing in work settings. Not surprisingly, their research shows that the more formal the situation, the more negative the appraisal. The chosen swear word also makes a difference: "F-bombs" have been rated as more inappropriate than other less-volatile terms. Relational history also is important: Hearers who are surprised by a speaker's swearing are likely to deem the person as incompetent.

Despite its downside, swearing can have its place at work. Stanford University professor Robert Sutton notes that choosing *not* to swear can actually violate the norms of some organizations.[c] He maintains that swearing on rare occasions can be effective for the shock value. (The fact that Sutton authored a book called *The No Asshole Rule* suggests he practices what he preaches.)

But even Sutton adds a cautionary note about swearing on the job: "If you are not sure, don't do it." The rules of interpersonal competence apply: Analyze and adapt to your audience, and engage in self-monitoring. And when in doubt, err on the side of restraint.

Notice how much less antagonistic each statement would be if it were prefaced by a qualifier that takes responsibility for the opinion such as "I believe . . . ," "In my opinion . . . ," or "It seems to me. . . ." We'll discuss the importance of responsible "I" language later in this chapter.

Fact–Inference Confusion Problems also arise when we confuse factual statements with inferential statements—conclusions arrived at from an interpretation of evidence.

Arguments often result when we label our inferences as facts:

A: Why are you mad at me?
B: I'm not mad at you. Why have you been so insecure lately?
A: I'm not insecure. It's just that you've been so critical.
B: What do you mean, "critical"? I haven't been critical. . . .

Instead of trying to read the other person's mind, a far better course is to use the skill of perception checking that you learned in Chapter 3: Identify the observable behaviors (facts) that have caught your attention and describe one or more possible interpretations that you have drawn from them. After describing this train of thought, ask the other person to comment on the accuracy of your interpretation.

"When you didn't return my phone call (*fact*), I got the idea that you're mad at me (*interpretation*). Are you?" (*question*)

"You've been asking me whether I still love you a lot lately (*fact*), and that makes me think you're feeling insecure (*inference*). Or maybe I'm behaving differently. What's on your mind?" (*question*)

PAUSE AND REFLECT

CONJUGATING "IRREGULAR VERBS"

The technique is simple: Just take an action or personality trait and show how it can be viewed either favorably or unfavorably, according to the label it's given and the person who is engaging in the behavior. For example:

> I'm casual.
> You're a little careless.
> He's a slob.

Or try this one:

> I'm thrifty.
> You're money conscious.
> She's a tightwad.

Notice how these labels display the self-serving bias discussed in Chapter 3, as well as the principle that we're usually less charitable when describing others' behavior than our own.

1. Try a few conjugations yourself, using the following statements:
   a. I'm tactful.
   b. I'm conservative.
   c. I'm quiet.
   d. I'm relaxed.
   e. My child is high-spirited.
   f. I have high self-esteem.
2. Now recall at least two situations in which you used emotive language as if it was a description of fact and not an opinion. A good way to recall these situations is to think of a recent disagreement and imagine how the other people involved might have described it differently than you.

 You can complete this activity by visiting CengageBrain.com to access the Speech Communication CourseMate for *Looking Out/ Looking In*, and, if requested, email your responses to your instructor.

Emotive Language Emotive language seems to describe something but actually announces the speaker's attitude toward it. If you approve of a friend's roundabout approach to a difficult subject, you might call her "tactful"; if you don't approve of it, you might accuse her of "beating around the bush." Whether the approach is good or bad is more a matter of opinion than of fact, although this difference is obscured by emotive language.

You can appreciate how emotive words are really editorial statements when you consider these examples:

If you approve, say	If you disapprove, say
thrifty	cheap
traditional	old-fashioned
extravert	loudmouth
cautious	cowardly

progressive	radical
information	propaganda
military victory	massacre
eccentric	crazy

The best way to avoid arguments involving emotive words is to describe the person, thing, or idea you are discussing in neutral terms and to label your opinions as such. Instead of saying "Quit making sexist remarks," say "I really don't like it when you call us 'girls' instead of 'women.'" These behavioral statements not only are more accurate but also have a much better chance of being well received by others.

THE LANGUAGE OF RESPONSIBILITY

Besides providing a way to make the content of a message clear or obscure, language reflects the speakers' willingness to take responsibility for their beliefs and feelings. This acceptance or rejection of responsibility says a great deal about the speaker and can shape the tone of a relationship. To see how, read on.

"It" Statements Notice the difference between the sentences of each set:

> "It bothers me when you're late."
>
> "I'm worried when you're late."
>
> "It's nice to see you."
>
> "I'm glad to see you."
>
> "It's a boring class."
>
> "I'm bored in the class."

Dreamworks Pictures/The Kobal Collection

In *The Help*, white socialites use a positive-sounding title—"The Home Help Sanitation Initiative"—to try to enact a policy that reinforces their prejudices against black housekeepers (see the film summary at the end of this chapter). Abstract and ambiguous language can sometimes obscure the motives behind words.

As the name implies, **"it" statements** replace the personal pronoun *I* with the less immediate word *it*. By contrast, **"I" language** clearly identifies the speaker as the source of a message. Communicators who use "it" statements avoid responsibility for ownership of a message, attributing it instead to some unidentified source. This habit isn't just imprecise—more important, it is an unconscious way to avoid taking a position.

"But" Statements Statements that take the form "X-but-Y" can be confusing. A closer look at **"but" statements** explains why. In each sentence, the word *but* cancels the thought that precedes it:

> "You're really a great person, but I think we ought to stop seeing each other."

> "You've done good work for us, but we're going to have to let you go."

> "This paper has some good ideas, but I'm giving it a D grade because it's late."

These "buts" often are a strategy for wrapping the speaker's real but unpleasant message between more palatable ideas in a psychological sandwich. This approach can be a face-saving strategy worth using at times. When the goal is to be absolutely clear, however, the most responsible approach is to deliver the positive and negative messages separately so they both get heard.

"I" and "You" Language We've seen that "I" language is a way of accepting responsibility for a message. In contrast, **"you" language** expresses a judgment of the other person. Positive judgments ("You look great today!") rarely cause problems, but notice how each of the following critical "you" statements implies that the subject of the complaint is doing something wrong:

> "You left this place a mess!"

> "You didn't keep your promise!"

> "You're really crude sometimes!"

It's easy to see why "you" language can arouse defensiveness. A "you" statement implies that the speaker is qualified to judge the target—not an idea that most listeners are willing to accept, even when the judgment is correct.

Fortunately, "I" language provides a more accurate and less provocative way to express a complaint.[30] "I" language shows that the speaker takes responsibility for the complaint by describing his or her reaction to the other's behavior without making any judgments about its worth. Here are some "I" language alternatives for the examples offered above:

> "I don't want to be responsible for all of the cleaning in the apartment."

> "I'm angry that I was on time and you weren't."

> "I don't like when you tell off-color jokes in front of my parents."

The "In Real Life" sidebar in this section shows what "I" language sounds like as part of a conversation.

Despite its obvious advantages, even the best-constructed and delivered "I" message won't always succeed. As author and "I" language advocate Thomas Gordon acknowledges, "Nobody welcomes hearing that his behavior is causing someone a problem, no matter how the message is phrased."[31] Furthermore, "I" language in large doses can start to sound egotistical. Research shows that self-absorbed people, also known as "conversational narcissists," can be identified by their constant use of first-person singular pronouns.[32] For this reason, "I" language works best in moderation. Chapter 10 will discuss how to use "I" language effectively as a central component of the assertive message format.

"We" Language   One way to avoid overuse of "I" language is to consider the pronoun *we*. **"We" language** implies that the issue is the concern and responsibility of both the speaker and receiver of a message. Consider a few examples:

> "We need to figure out a budget that doesn't bankrupt us."

> "I think we have a problem. We can't seem to talk about your friends without fighting."

> "We aren't doing a very good job of keeping the place clean, are we?"

It's easy to see how "we" language can help build a constructive climate. It suggests a kind of "we're in this together" orientation that reflects the transactional nature of communication. People who use first-person plural pronouns signal their closeness, commonality, and cohesiveness with others.[33] For example, couples who use "we" language are more satisfied and manage conflict better than those who rely more heavily on "I" and "you" language.[34] Chapters 10 and 11 offer detailed advice on the value of achieving a "we" orientation.

On the other hand, "we" statements aren't always appropriate. Sometimes using this pronoun sounds presumptuous, because it suggests that you are speaking for the other person as well as yourself. It's easy to imagine someone responding to your statement "We have a problem . . ." by saying "Maybe you have a problem, but don't tell me I do!"

Given the pros and cons of both "I" language and "we" language, what advice can we give about the most effective pronouns to use in interpersonal communication? Researchers have found that "I" and "we" combinations (e.g., "I think that we . . ." or "I would like to see us . . .") have a good chance of being received favorably.[35] Because too much of any pronoun comes across as inappropriate, combining pronouns is generally a good idea. If your "I" language reflects your position without being overly self-absorbed, your "you" language shows concern for others without judging them, and your "we" language includes others without speaking for them, you will probably come as close as possible to the ideal use of pronouns. Table 5.4 summarizes the advantages and disadvantages of each type of language and offers suggestions for approaches that have a good chance of success.

TABLE 5.4 PRONOUN USE AND ITS EFFECTS

	ADVANTAGES	DISADVANTAGES	TIPS
"I" language	Takes responsibility for personal thoughts, feelings, and wants. Less defense-provoking than evaluative "you" language.	Can be perceived as egotistical, narcissistic, and self-absorbed.	Use "I" messages when other person doesn't perceive a problem. Combine "I" with "we" language.
"We" language	Signals inclusion, immediacy, cohesiveness, and commitment.	Can speak improperly for others.	Combine with "I" language. Use in group settings to enhance unity. Avoid when expressing personal thoughts, feelings, and wants.
"You" language	Signals other orientation, particularly when the topic is positive.	Can sound evaluative and judgmental, particularly during confrontations.	Use "I" language during confrontations. Use "you" language when praising or including others.

© Cengage Learning

IN REAL LIFE

"I" and "You" Language on the Job

For some time, Rebecca has been frustrated by her fellow worker Tom's frequent absences from the job. She hasn't spoken up because she likes Tom and also because she doesn't want to sound like a complainer. Lately, though, Tom's absences have become longer and more frequent. Today he extended his half-hour lunch an extra 45 minutes. When he returns to the office, Rebecca confronts him with her gripe using "you" language:

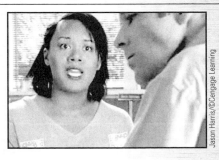
Jason Harris/©Cengage Learning

Rebecca: Where have you been? You were due back at 12:30, and it's almost 1:30 now.

Tom: *(Surprised by Rebecca's angry tone, which she has never used before with him)* I had a few errands to run. What's the problem?

Rebecca: We all have errands to run, Tom. But it's not fair for you to do yours on company time.

Tom: *(Feeling defensive after hearing Rebecca's accusation)* I don't see why you have to worry about how I do my job. Beth [their boss] hasn't complained, so why should you worry?

Rebecca: Beth hasn't complained because all of us have been covering for you. You should appreciate what a tight spot we're in, making excuses every time you come in late or leave early. *(Again, Rebecca uses "you" language to tell Tom how he should think and act.)*

Tom: *(Now too defensive to consider Rebecca's concerns)* Hey, I thought we all covered for one another here. What about the time last year when I worked late for a week so you could go to your cousin's wedding in San Antonio?

Rebecca: That's different! Nobody was lying then. When you take off, I have to make up stories about where you are. You're putting me in a very difficult spot, Tom, and it's not fair. You can't count on me to keep covering for you.

Tom: *(Feeling guilty but too angry from Rebecca's judgments and threat to acknowledge his mistakes)* Fine. I'll never ask you for a favor again. Sorry to put you out.

SKILL BUILDER

PRACTICING "I" LANGUAGE

You can develop your skill at delivering "I" messages by following these steps:

1. Visualize situations in your life when you might have sent each of the following messages:
   You're not telling me the truth!
   You think only of yourself!
   Don't be so touchy!
   Quit fooling around!
   You don't understand a word I'm saying!
2. Write alternatives to each statement using "I" language.
3. Think of three "you" statements you might make to people in your life. Transform each of these statements into "I" language and rehearse them with a classmate.

 You can complete this activity by visiting CengageBrain.com to access the Speech Communication CourseMate for *Looking Out/ Looking In*, and, if requested, email your responses to your instructor.

Rebecca may have succeeded in reducing Tom's lateness, but her choice of "you" language left him feeling defensive and angry. The climate in the office is likely to be more strained—hardly the outcome Rebecca was seeking.

Here's how she could have handled the same issue using "I" language to describe her problem instead of blaming Tom.

Rebecca: Tom, I need to talk to you about a problem. *(Notice how Rebecca identifies the problem as hers instead of attacking Tom.)*

Tom: What's up?

Rebecca: You know how you come in late to work sometimes or take long lunch hours?

Tom: *(Sensing trouble ahead and sounding wary)* Yeah?

Rebecca: Well, I need to tell you that it's putting me in a tight spot. *(Rebecca describes the problem in behavioral terms and then goes on to express her feeling.)* When Beth asks where you are, I don't want to say you're not here because that might get you in trouble. So sometimes I make excuses or even lie. But Beth is sounding suspicious of my excuses, and I'm worried about that.

Tom: *(Feeling defensive because he knows he's guilty but also sympathetic to Rebecca's position)* I don't want you to get in trouble. It's just that I've got to take care of a lot of personal business.

Rebecca: I know, Tom. I just want you to understand that it's getting impossible for me to cover for you.

Tom: Yeah, OK. Thanks for helping out.

Notice how "I" language made it possible for Rebecca to confront Tom honestly but without blaming or attacking him personally. Even if Tom doesn't change, Rebecca has gotten the problem off her chest, and she can feel proud that she did so in a way that didn't sound ugly or annoying.

Communication Scenarios

 To watch and analyze a video related to this feature and this topic, visit CengageBrain .com to access the Speech Communication CourseMate for Looking Out/Looking In.

Gender and Language

So far we have discussed language use as if it were identical for both sexes. Some popular writers and researchers believe that men and women speak in distinct ways, as if they are from different cultures.[36] Other scholars suggest that the differences are few and mostly not significant.[37] What are the similarities and differences between male and female language use?

CONTENT

The first research on conversational topics and gender was conducted more than two generations ago. Despite the changes in male and female roles since then, the results of several studies are remarkably similar.[38] In these studies, women and men ranging in age from 17 to 80 described the range of topics each discussed with friends of the same sex. Certain topics were common to both men and women: work, movies, and television. Both men and women tended to reserve discussions of sex and sexuality for members of the same sex.

The differences between the men and women in these studies were more striking than the similarities. Female friends spent much more time discussing personal

"Sometimes I think he can understand every word we're saying."

and domestic subjects, relationship problems, family, health and reproductive matters, weight, food and clothing, men, and other women. Men, on the other hand, were more likely to discuss music, current events, sports, business, and other men. Both men and women were equally likely to discuss personal appearance, sex, and dating in same-sex conversations. True to one common stereotype, women were more likely to gossip about close friends and family. By contrast, men spent more time gossiping about sports figures and media personalities. Women's gossip was no more derogatory than men's.

These differences can lead to frustration when men and women try to converse with one another. Researchers report that *trivial* is the word often used by both men and women to describe topics discussed by the opposite sex. "I want to talk about important things," a woman might say, "like how we're getting along. All he wants to do is talk about the news or what we'll do this weekend." Likewise, some men complain that women ask for and offer more details than necessary and focus too often on feelings and emotions.

REASONS FOR COMMUNICATING

Both men and women, at least in the dominant cultures of North America, use language to build and maintain social relationships. Regardless of the sex of the communicators, the goals of almost all ordinary conversations include making the conversation enjoyable by being friendly, showing interest in what the other person says, and talking about topics that interest the other person.[39] *How* men and women accomplish these goals is often different, though. Although most communicators try to make their interaction enjoyable, men are more likely than women to emphasize making conversation fun. Their discussions involve a greater amount of joking and good-natured teasing.

By contrast, women's discussions tend to involve feelings, relationships, and personal problems.[40] In fact, communication researcher Julia Wood flatly states that "for women, talk *is* the essence of relationships."[41] When members of a group of women were surveyed to find out what kinds of satisfaction they gained from talking with their friends, the most common theme mentioned was a feeling of empathy—"To know you're not alone," as some put it.[42] Whereas men commonly described same-sex conversations as something they *liked*, women described their same-sex conversations as a kind of contact they *needed*. The characteristically female orientation for relational communication is supported by studies of married couples showing that wives spend proportionately more time than husbands communicating in ways that help maintain their relationship.[43]

CONVERSATIONAL STYLE

Women tend to behave somewhat differently in conversations than do men, although the differences aren't as dramatic as you might imagine.[44] For instance, the popular myth that women are more talkative than men doesn't hold up under scientific scrutiny—researchers have found that men and women speak roughly the same number of words per day.[45]

SELF-ASSESSMENT

How Sexist Is Your Language?
To complete two quizzes related to this question, visit CengageBrain.com to access the Speech Communication CourseMate for *Looking Out/ Looking In.*

Women do ask more questions in mixed-sex conversations than do men—nearly three times as many, according to one study. Other research has revealed that in mixed-sex conversations, men interrupt women far more than the other way around. Men are also more likely than women to use judgmental adjectives ("Reading can be a drag"), directives ("Think of some more"), and "I" references ("I have a lot to do").[46] Women are more likely to use intensive adverbs ("He's *really* interested"), emotional references ("If he really cared about you . . ."), uncertainty verbs ("It seems to me . . ."), and contradictions ("It's cold, but that's okay"). Differences like these show that men's speech is characteristically more direct, succinct, and task-oriented. By contrast, women's speech is more typically indirect, elaborate, and focused on relationships.

Women typically use statements showing support for the other person, demonstrations of equality, and efforts to keep the conversation going.[47] With these goals, it's not surprising that traditionally female speech often contains statements of sympathy and empathy: "I've felt just like that myself," "The same thing happened to me!" Women are also inclined to ask questions that invite the other person to share information: "How did you feel about that?" "What did you do next?" The importance of nurturing a relationship also explains why female speech is often somewhat tentative. Saying, "This is just my opinion . . ." is less likely to put off a conversational partner than a more definite "Here's what I think. . . ."

An accommodating style isn't always a disadvantage. One study found that female authors often use less-powerful language when writing for a female audience and that this approach is particularly effective in health-focused magazines.[48] Another study revealed that women who spoke tentatively were actually more persuasive with men than those who used more powerful speech.[49]

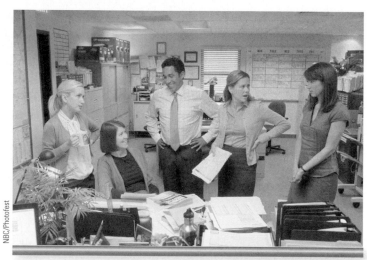

In comparison with other characters on *The Office*, Pam (Jenna Fischer) and Erin (Ellie Kemper) use a less-powerful speech style. This could be due to their occupational roles, gender, or personalities—or some combination. Their polite, other-oriented style helps them maintain relationships while (usually) achieving their goals.

NONGENDER VARIABLES

The link between gender and language use isn't as clear-cut as it might seem. Several research reviews have found that the ways women and men communicate are much more similar than different. For example, one analysis of more than 1,200 research studies found that only 1 percent of variance in communication behavior resulted from gender difference.[50] According to this research review, there is no significant difference between male speech and female speech in areas such as use of profanity, use of qualifiers ("I guess" or "This is just my opinion"), tag questions, and vocal fluency.[51]

Another study compared women's and men's use of "stance" words—the expression of attitude, emotion, certainty, doubt, and commitment—by analyzing 900,000 words of informal conversation in social and work settings.[52] There were no differences between the sexes in their use of many types of words—for example, opinion and attitude words (e.g., "amazing," "happy," "funny," and "interesting"), certainty, doubt, and factuality words (e.g., "of course," "right?," and "sure"), emphatic words (e.g., "absolutely" and "never"), and hedges (e.g., "almost" and "usually"). Only expletives (e.g., "cool," "damn," and "wow") had a significant difference between men and women. (Men use more of them.)

Some on-the-job research shows that male and female supervisors in similar positions behave the same way and are equally effective. In light of this research, which shows considerable similarities and relatively minor differences between the sexes, one communication scholar suggests that the "Men are from Mars, women are from Venus" metaphor should be replaced by the notion that "Men are from North Dakota, women are from South Dakota."[53]

A growing body of research explains some of the apparent contradictions between the similarities and differences between male speech and female speech. Research has revealed other factors that influence language use as much or more than does gender.[54] For example, social philosophy plays a role. Feminist wives talk longer than their partners, whereas nonfeminist wives speak less than their partners. In addition, cooperative or competitive orientations of speakers have more influence on how they interact than does their gender.[55] The speaker's occupation also influences speaking style. For example, male day-care teachers' speech to their students resembles the language of female teachers more closely than it resembles the language of fathers at home. And female farm operators working in a male-dominated profession often use more masculine language patterns by swearing and talking "tough as nails."[56]

Another powerful force that influences the way individual men and women speak is their gender role. Recall the gender roles described in Chapter 3 (pages 91–92): masculine, feminine, and androgynous. Remember that these gender roles don't necessarily line up neatly with biological sex. There are "masculine" females, "feminine" males, and androgynous communicators who combine traditionally masculine and feminine characteristics. These gender roles can influence a communicator's style more than his or her biological sex. For example, one study revealed that masculine subjects used significantly more dominance language than did either feminine or androgynous subjects.[57] Feminine subjects expressed slightly more submissive behaviors and more equivalence behaviors than did the androgynous subjects, and their submissiveness

PAUSE AND REFLECT

EXPLORING GENDER DIFFERENCES IN COMMUNICATION

Some pop-culture writers have claimed that the communication styles of men and women are so different that "men are from Mars, women are from Venus." Most researchers believe the differences aren't nearly so dramatic. One argues metaphorically that "men are from North Dakota, women are from South Dakota." Based on the research described in these pages and your personal experience, which approach seems more accurate to you? If your answer is "neither" or "both," create another geographical metaphor to describe your experience.

You can complete this activity by visiting CengageBrain.com to access the Speech Communication CourseMate for *Looking Out/ Looking In*, and, if requested, email your responses to your instructor.

and equivalence were much greater than those of the masculine subjects, regardless of their biological sex. And in gay and lesbian relationships, the conversational styles of partners reflect power differences in the relationship (e.g., who is earning more money) more than the biological sex of the communicators.[58]

While there are differences in male and female speech patterns, they may not be as great as some popular books suggest—and some of them may not result from biological sex at all. In practical terms, the best approach is to recognize that differences in communication style—whether they come from biological sex, gender, culture, or individual factors—present both challenges and opportunities. We need to take different styles into account but not exaggerate or use them to stigmatize one another.

 # Culture and Language

Anyone who has tried to translate ideas from one language to another knows that conveying the same meaning isn't always easy.[59] Sometimes the results of a bungled translation can be amusing. For example, the American manufacturers of Pet milk unknowingly introduced their product in French-speaking markets without realizing that the word *pet* in French means "to break wind."[60] Likewise, the English-speaking representative of a U.S. soft drink manufacturer naively drew laughs from Mexican customers when she offered free samples of Fresca soda pop. In Mexican slang, the word *fresca* means "lesbian."

Even choosing the right words during translation won't guarantee that non-native speakers will use an unfamiliar language correctly. For example, Japanese insurance companies warn their policyholders who are visiting the United States to avoid their cultural tendency to say "Excuse me" or "I'm sorry" if they are involved in a traffic accident.[61] In Japan, apologizing is a traditional way to express goodwill and maintain social harmony, even if the person offering the apology is not at fault. But in the United States an apology can be taken as an admission of fault and result in Japanese tourists being wrongly held responsible for accidents.

Difficult as it may be, translation is only a small part of the differences in communication between members of different cultures. Differences in the way language is used and the worldview that a language creates make communicating across cultures a challenging task.

VERBAL COMMUNICATION STYLES

Using language is more than just choosing a particular group of words to convey an idea. Each language has its own unique style that distinguishes it from others. Matters such as the amount of formality or informality, precision or vagueness, and brevity or detail are major ingredients in speaking competently. And when a communicator tries to use the verbal style from one culture in a different one, problems are likely to arise.[62]

One way in which verbal styles vary is in their *directness*. Anthropologist Edward Hall identified two distinct cultural ways of using language.[63] **Low-context cultures** generally value using language to express thoughts, feelings, and ideas as directly as possible. Low-context communicators look for the meaning of a statement in the words spoken. By contrast, **high-context cultures** value using language to maintain social harmony. Rather than upset others by speaking directly, high-context communicators

LOOKING AT DIVERSITY

Pilar Bernal de Pheils: Speaking the Patient's Language

Courtesy of Pilar Bernal de Pheils

A native of Colombia, Pilar Bernal de Pheils is a clinical professor in the School of Nursing at the University of California San Francisco. She supervises nurse practitioners in training at both San Francisco's Mission Neighborhood Health Center and Women's Community Clinic.

I work in a setting where linguistic and cultural barriers make communication especially challenging. At the Mission Neighborhood Health Center, almost all of our patients are monolingual Spanish speakers from underserved backgrounds. Most were born outside the USA, and very few have received anything beyond a basic education. Many seek help for medical and psychosocial issues that require linguistic and cultural sensitivity.

Everyone on our clinic staff is bilingual, which is important for the population we serve. Serious problems can occur when patients don't have the benefit of a healthcare provider or translator who can understand and speak their language fluently.

It can be especially dangerous to *think* you understand another language when you don't

know the nuances. For example, one common phrase Latino patients use to express the sensation of bloating is "Estoy inflamada." The literal translation is "I am inflamed," but that doesn't capture what the patient is trying to describe. A provider or trainee who lacks a good grasp of the language could misunderstand the patient and misdiagnose the problem.

I remind my trainees to keep humble, both because their linguistic skills may not as good as they may think, and because overconfidence can cause patients to feel intimidated. I also train my students to ask "Tell me more" as a way of increasing the odds that they will understand what our patients are trying to explain. And because the stakes are so high, it's important to provide a skilled professional translator when a staff member is not fluent in medical Spanish. It's expensive and time consuming, but in the end the results justify the costs.

It's hard enough for both patients and healthcare providers to communicate effectively under any circumstances, but the differences escalate when different languages are involved. Both attitude and skill are essential to bridge the gap.

"Speaking the Patient's Language" by Pilar Bernal de Pheils. Used with permission of author.

learn to discover meaning from the context in which a message is delivered: the non-verbal behaviors of the speaker, the history of the relationship, and the general social rules that govern interaction between people. Table 5.5 summarizes some key differences between the way low- and high-context cultures use language.

North American culture falls toward the low-context end of the scale. Residents of the United States and Canada value straight talk and grow impatient with "beating around the bush." By contrast, most Asian and Middle Eastern cultures fall toward the high-context end of the scale. In many Asian cultures, for example, maintaining harmony is important, so communicators will avoid speaking directly if that would threaten another person's face. For this reason, Japanese and Koreans are less likely than Americans to offer a clear "no" to an undesirable request. Instead they will probably use roundabout expressions such as "I agree with you in principle, but . . ." or "I sympathize with you. . . ."

TABLE 5.5 LOW- AND HIGH-CONTEXT COMMUNICATION STYLES

LOW CONTEXT	HIGH CONTEXT
Majority of information carried in explicit cues. High reliance on explicit verbal messages.	Important information not always expressed explicitly. Clues carried in the situational context (time, place, relationship).
Self-expression valued. Communicators state opinions and desires directly and strive to persuade others to accept their own viewpoint.	Relational harmony valued and maintained by indirect expression of opinions. Communicators abstain from saying "no" directly.
Clear, eloquent speech considered praiseworthy. Verbal fluency admired.	Communicators talk "around" the point, allowing the other to fill in the missing pieces. Ambiguity and use of silence admired.

© Cengage Learning

The same sort of clash between directness and indirectness can aggravate problems between straight-talking, low-context Israelis, who value speaking directly, and Arabs, whose high-context culture stresses smooth interaction. It's easy to imagine how the clash of cultural styles could lead to misunderstandings and conflicts between Israelis and their Palestinian neighbors. Israelis could view the Palestinians as evasive, whereas the Palestinians could view the Israelis as insensitive and blunt.

It's worth noting that even generally straight-talking residents of the United States raised in the low-context Euro-American tradition often rely on context to make their point. When you decline an unwanted invitation by saying, "I can't make it," it's likely that both you and the other person know that the choice of attending isn't really beyond your control. If your goal was to be perfectly clear, you might say, "I don't want to get together." As Chapter 2 explains in detail, we often equivocate precisely because we want to obscure our true thoughts and feelings.

Besides their degrees of clarity and vagueness, language styles can also vary across cultures in being *elaborate* or *succinct*. Speakers of Arabic, for instance, commonly use language that is much richer and more expressive than that of most communicators who use English. Strong assertions and exaggerations that would sound ridiculous in English are a common feature of Arabic. This contrast in linguistic styles can lead to misunderstandings between people from different backgrounds. As one observer put it:

> First, an Arab feels compelled to overassert in almost all types of communication because others expect him [or her] to. If an Arab says exactly what he [or she] means without the expected assertion, other Arabs may still think that he [or she] means the opposite. For example, a simple "no" by a guest to the host's requests to eat more or drink more will not suffice. To convey the meaning that he [or she] is actually full, the guest must keep repeating "no" several times, coupling it with an oath such as "By God" or "I swear to God." Second, an Arab often fails to realize that others, particularly foreigners, may mean exactly what they say even though their language is simple. To the Arabs, a simple "no" may mean the indirectly expressed consent and encouragement of a coquettish woman. On the other hand, a simple consent may mean the rejection of a hypocritical politician.*

Succinctness is most extreme in cultures where silence is valued. In many Native American cultures, for example, the favored way to handle ambiguous social situations is to remain quiet.[64] In contrasting this silent style to the talkativeness that is common in mainstream American cultures when people first meet, it's easy to imagine how the first encounter between an Apache or Navajo and an Anglo might feel uncomfortable to both people.

---

*Almaney, A., & Alwan, A. (1982). *Communicating with the Arabs*. Prospect Heights, IL: Waveland.

PAUSE AND REFLECT

HIGH- AND LOW-CONTEXT COMMUNICATION

Check your knowledge of high- and low-context communication styles with a self-test and sample dialogues available through CengageBrain .com, where you can access the Speech Communication CourseMate for *Looking Out/Looking In.* Click "next page" for further explanations, examples, and exercises that illustrate these direct and indirect communication styles.

A third way in which languages differ from one culture to another involves *formality* and *informality*. The informal approach that characterizes relationships in countries such as the United States, Canada, and Australia, as well as the Scandinavian countries, is quite different from the great concern for using proper speech in many parts of Asia and Africa. Formality isn't so much a matter of using correct grammar as of defining social position. In Korea, for example, the language reflects the Confucian system of relational hierarchies.[65] It has special vocabularies for different sexes, different levels of social status, different degrees of intimacy, and different types of social occasions. For example, there are different degrees of formality for speaking with old friends, nonacquaintances whose background one knows, and complete strangers. When you contrast these sorts of distinctions with the casual friendliness that many North Americans use even when talking with complete strangers, it's easy to see how a Korean might view communicators in the United States as boorish and how an American might view communicators in Korea as stiff and unfriendly.

"The Eskimos have eighty-seven words for snow and not one for malpractice."

LANGUAGE AND WORLDVIEW

Different linguistic styles are important, but there may be even more-important differences that separate speakers of various languages. For almost 150 years, theorists have put forth the notion of **linguistic relativism**: that the worldview of a culture is shaped and reflected by the language its members speak.[66] The best-known example of linguistic relativism is the notion that Eskimos have a large number of words (estimated at everything from seventeen to one hundred) for what we simply call *snow*. Different terms are used to describe conditions such as a driving blizzard, crusty ice, and light powder. This example suggests how linguistic relativism operates. The need to survive in an Arctic environment led Eskimos to make distinctions that would be unimportant to residents of warmer environments, and after the language makes these distinctions, speakers are more likely to see the world in ways that match the broader vocabulary.

Even though there is some doubt that Eskimos really have so many words for snow,[67] other examples do seem to support the principle of linguistic relativism.[68] For instance, bilingual speakers seem to think differently when they change languages. In one study, French American people were asked to interpret a series of pictures. When they described the pictures in French, their descriptions were far more romantic and emotional than when they described the pictures in English. Likewise, when students in Hong Kong were asked to complete a values test, they expressed more traditional Chinese values when they answered in Cantonese than when they answered in English. In Israel, both Arab and Jewish students saw greater distinctions between their group and "outsiders" when using their native language than when they used English, a neutral tongue for them. Examples like these show the power of language to shape cultural identity—sometimes for better and sometimes for worse.

The best-known declaration of linguistic relativism is the **Sapir-Whorf hypothesis**, formulated by Edward Sapir and Benjamin Whorf.[69] Following Sapir's theory, Whorf observed that the language spoken by Hopi Native Americans represents a view of reality that is dramatically different from that of more-familiar tongues. For example, the Hopi language makes no distinction between nouns and verbs. Therefore, the people who speak it describe the entire world as being constantly in process. Whereas in English we use nouns to characterize people or objects as being fixed or constant, Hopi view them more as verbs, constantly changing. In this sense, English represents much of the world rather like a snapshot camera, whereas Hopi language represents the world more like a motion picture.

Some languages contain terms that have no English equivalents.[70] For example, consider a few words in other languages:

nemawashi (Japanese): The process of informally feeling out all of the people involved with an issue before making a decision.

lagniappe (French/Creole): An extra gift given in a transaction that wasn't expected by the terms of a contract.

lao (Mandarin): A respectful term used for older people, showing their importance in the family and in society.

dharma (Sanskrit): Each person's unique, ideal path in life and knowledge of how to find it.

koyaanisqatsi (Hopi): Nature out of balance; a way of life so crazy it calls for a new way of living.

The effects of language on a speaker's thoughts and feelings can be seen in a study conducted at the University of Bristol.[71] Researchers asked participants to speak aloud three types of words: swear words, euphemisms for swear words (such as saying "the F-word" instead the actual term), and neutral words. When swearing, participants had much stronger physiological stress responses than when they used euphemistic or neutral terms. The researchers see this as an example of linguistic relativity: "Taboo words become directly associated with emotional centers in the brain. Accordingly, taboo words can evoke strong emotions even when they are uttered without any desire to offend." In other words, the language we use has an impact on our minds—sometimes in ways we don't even realize.

SUMMARY

Language is both a marvelous communication tool and the source of many interpersonal problems. Every language is a collection of symbols governed by a variety of rules: semantic, syntactic, and pragmatic.

Terms used to name people influence the way the people are regarded. The terms used to name speakers and the language they use reflect the level of affiliation of a speaker toward others. Language patterns also reflect and shape a speaker's perceived power.

Some language habits—such as confusing facts with opinions or inferences and using emotive terms—can lead to unnecessary disharmony in interpersonal relationships. Language also acknowledges or avoids the speaker's acceptance of responsibility for his or her thoughts and feelings.

There are some differences in the ways men and women speak. The content of their conversations varies, as do their reasons for communicating and their conversational styles. However, not all differences in language use can be accounted for by the speaker's biological sex. Gender roles, occupation, social philosophy, and orientation toward problem solving also influence people's use of language.

Different languages often shape and reflect the views of a culture. Some cultures value directness, brevity, and the succinct use of language, whereas others value indirect or elaborate forms of speech. In some societies, formality is important, whereas others value informality. Beyond these differences, there is evidence to support linguistic relativism—the notion that language exerts a strong influence on the worldview of the people who speak it.

KEY TERMS

abstraction ladder (157)
abstract language (157)
behavioral language (157)
"but" statements (170)
convergence (164)
divergence (164)
emotive language (168)
equivocal language (156)
high-context cultures (177)
"I" language (170)
"it" statements (170)

linguistic relativism (180)
low-context cultures (177)
powerless speech mannerisms (165)
pragmatic rules (160)
relative words (157)
Sapir-Whorf hypothesis (181)
semantic rules (156)
static evaluation (157)
syntactic rules (158)
"we" language (171)
"you" language (170)

ONLINE RESOURCES

Now that you have read this chapter, visit CengageBrain.com to access the Speech Communication CourseMate for *Looking Out/Looking In* for quick access to the electronic resources that accompany this text. Your CourseMate offers:

- **Study tools** that will help you assess your learning and prepare for exams (*digital glossary, key term flash cards, interactive quizzes*).
- **Activities and assignments** that will help you hone your knowledge, understand how theory and research applies to your own life (*Self-Assessment, Pause and Reflect*), consider ethical challenges in interpersonal communication (*Ethical Challenge*), and build your interpersonal communication skills throughout the course (*Skill Builder*). If requested, you can submit your answers to your instructor.
- **Media resources** that will allow you to watch and critique videos of interpersonal communication situations (*In Real Life, interpersonal video simulations, and interactive video activities*).
- In addition to interactive teaching and learning tools, CourseMate includes an **interactive eBook**. Take notes, highlight, search, and interact with embedded media specific to *Looking Out/Looking In*.

SEARCH TERMS

When searching online databases to research topics in this chapter, use the following terms (along with this chapter's key terms) to maximize the chances of finding useful information:

ambiguity

general semantics

language and languages

miscommunication

pragmatics

semantics

sociolinguistics

FILM AND TELEVISION

You can see the communication principles described in this chapter portrayed in the following films.

THE IMPORTANCE OF LANGUAGE

The Miracle Worker (1962) Not Rated

As a child, Helen Keller contracted scarlet fever. The disease left her deaf, blind, mute, and angry. Before consigning Helen to an institution, her parents hire a young tutor named Annie Sullivan in a long-shot hope of teaching their daughter to communicate. This true story captures the struggle and eventual triumph when Sullivan teaches Helen sign language, enabling Keller to live a rich and productive life as an author and political activist. The film offers profound insights into the potential and power of language in the human experience.

CULTURAL RULES FOR LANGUAGE

The N Word (2004) Not Rated

It is possibly the most inflammatory word in American culture—so much so that the letter "N" is substituted for the actual word in most public discussions of the term. But as this documentary shows, the "N word" has many and varied meanings, ranging from a degrading slur to a term of endearment. A host of scholars and celebrities (including Chris Rock, Whoopi Goldberg, George Carlin, Ice Cube, and Quincy Jones) discuss and debate when, where, how, by whom, and even whether the "N word" should be used.

The film offers a vivid illustration of how pragmatic rules and linguistic convergence and divergence operate in interpersonal and intercultural communication. It also shows how failing to know and abide by cultural meanings and rules can lead to significant misunderstandings and conflict.

LINGUISTIC CONVERGENCE

Mean Girls (2004) Rated PG-13

Cady Heron (Lindsay Lohan) was raised in African bush country by her zoologist parents. Back in the United States, Cady has her first experience in formal schooling when she enrolls at North Shore High. She soon learns that high school social life can be every bit as vicious as anything she witnessed among the primates. Her new school is rife with social cliques, including the high-status Plastics and the geeky Mathletes.

At the urging of her unpopular friends Janis (Lizzy Caplan) and Damian (Daniel Franzese), Cady infiltrates the Plastics to get information so they can demolish the prestige of the popular girls. For Cady, part of fitting in is to learn and use the vocabulary of the in-group Plastics. In an early conversation with these popular girls, their leader Regina (Rachel McAdams) exclaims to Cady, "Shut up!" Unfamiliar with the slang use of this term, Cady replies, "I didn't say anything." Soon Cady speaks Plastic fluently, tossing about words like "fetch" (cool), "word vomit" (babbling), and the self-explanatory "fugly."

In an interesting example of linguistic convergence, the more Cady "talks the talk" of being a Plastic, the more her values and behaviors become like theirs. By movie's end, she makes some important decisions about herself and her friends—including the decision not to talk or act like a "mean girl."

THE IMPACT OF LANGUAGE

Doubt (2008) Rated PG-13

Miramax/Schwartz Andrew/The Kobal Collection

Sister Aloysius (Meryl Streep) begins to have doubts about everyone's favorite priest, Father Flynn (Philip Seymour Hoffman), who seems to have become inappropriately close with one of his pupils. Father Flynn's only defense is accusing the Sister of fact–opinion confusion and pointing out that her use of accusatory language breaches the traditional power roles of the Church.

Throughout the movie, Flynn and other characters rely on evasive language in their attempts to refute the Sister's accusations. In the movie's most dramatic scene, the young boy's mother (Viola Davis) uses euphemisms and evasive language to explain to the Sister that she knows that Father Flynn is molesting her son. The film illustrates how linguistic hedging makes it possible to steer clear of lying without telling the truth.

The Help (2011) Rated PG-13

Eugenia "Skeeter" Phelen (Emma Stone) is determined to become a writer in 1960s Mississippi. She returns home from college to find that most of her friends in Jackson are married and busy having children and planning social events. They're also part of a Southern status quo in which blacks serve whites in low-paying, labor-intensive domestic jobs.

Ambiguous and equivocal language play a role in reinforcing the social order. Black maids are referred to as "the help," but they do far more than simply assist their employers. They are responsible for all the housekeeping and child rearing in the white homes. This frees up the socialites to play cards and create laws such as "The Home Help Sanitation Initiative." The white women try to pass off this act as a benefit for their hired hands, but it's just a means to sanction their unfounded prejudices about blacks being unclean and disease-ridden.

Skeeter isn't immune to using deceptive language. She writes a household advice column under the pseudonym "Miss Myrna," even though she doesn't know the first thing about cooking and cleaning. She gets her tips from Aibileen Clark (Viola Davis), her friend's maid. Over time, Skeeter decides she has far more important writing to do. She interviews Aibileen and a host of other maids and pens a book about their experiences in a segregated world. Skeeter's forthright depiction of events enacts a well-known phrase from the 1960s: telling it like it is.

C H A P T E R   F I V E

Language: Barrier and Bridge

CHAPTER OUTLINE

Use this outline to take notes as you read the chapter in the text and/or as your instructor lectures in class.

I. LANGUAGE IS SYMBOLIC
    A. Signs
    B. Symbols

II. UNDERSTANDINGS AND MISUNDERSTANDINGS
    A. **Understanding Words: Semantic Rules**
        1. Equivocation
        2. Relative language
        3. Static evaluation
        4. Abstraction versus behavioral language
            a. Advantages
            b. Problems
    B. **Understanding Structure: Syntactic Rules**
        1. Grammar
        2. Order
        3. Dialects
    C. **Understanding Context: Pragmatic**

Rules
1. Often unstated
2. Relies on coordination
3. Personal codes

III. **THE IMPACT OF LANGUAGE**

   A. **Naming and Identity**
     1. Personal identity
     2. Group identity

   B. **Affiliation**
     1. Convergence
     2. Divergence

   C. **Power**
     1. Powerless speech mannerism
     2. Culture and context

   D. **Disruptive Language**
     1. Fact-opinion confusion
     2. Fact-inference confusion
     3. Emotive language

   E. **The Language of Responsibility**
     1. "It" statements
     2. "But" statements
     3. "I" and "You" language
     4. "We" language
       a. "You" language judges
       b. "I" statements describe
         i. Other's behavior
         ii. Your interpretation
         iii. Your feelings
         iv. Consequences of the behavior
       c. Advantages of "I" language
         i. Accepts responsibility
         ii. Reduces defensiveness
         iii. Is more accurate
       d. Reservations about "I" language
         i. Anger impedes use
         ii. Defensiveness with

poor nonverbal

    iii. Sounds artificial without confidence

    iv. Too much sounds narcissistic

  e. "We" language

    i. May signal inclusion and commitment

    ii. May speak improperly for others

    iii. Consider combining "I" and "we"

IV. GENDER AND LANGUAGE

A. Content

1. Some common topics
2. Sex talk restricted to same gender
3. Many topics vary by gender

B. Reasons for Communicating

1. Build and maintain social relationships
   a. Men: more joking and good-natured teasing
   b. Women: more feelings and relationships
2. Women—nourish relationships, build harmony
3. Men—task-oriented, advice, status, independence

C. Conversational Style

1. Men: judge, direct, "I" language
2. Women: questions, intensifiers, emotion, uncertainty, support, maintain conversations

D. Nongender Variables

1. Occupation and social philosophy
2. Historical and gender roles

V. CULTURE AND LANGUAGE

A. Verbal Communication Styles

1. Direct/indirect (low-context and high-context cultures)
2. Elaborate/succinct
3. Formality/informality

B. Language and Worldview

1. Linguistic relativism
2. Sapir-Whorf hypothesis

_____
_____
_____
_____
_____

KEY TERMS

abstraction ladder
abstract language
behavioral language
"but" statements
convergence
divergence
emotive language
equivocal language
high-context cultures
"I" language
"it" statements

linguistic relativism
low-context cultures
powerless speech mannerisms
pragmatic rules
relative words
Sapir-Whorf hypothesis
semantic rules
static evaluation
syntactic rules
"we" language
"you" language

ACTIVITIES

5.1 MISUNDERSTOOD LANGUAGE

LEARNING OBJECTIVES

- Analyze a real or potential misunderstanding in terms of semantic or pragmatic rules.
- Construct a message at the optimal level of specificity or vagueness for a given situation.

INSTRUCTIONS

1. Label the language contained in each of the sentences below as relative language, static evaluation, or equivocal language.
2. Rewrite each sentence in more precise language.
3. Write your own examples of each variety of language in the spaces provided.

EXAMPLE 1

I'm trying to diet, so give me a **small** piece of cake.
Language: *Relative language*
Why you categorized it as you did and how can you best correct it: *It is relative because it can be compared to many other things; the best way to correct it is to use a number.*
Revised statement: *I'm trying to diet, so give me a piece of cake about 2 inches square.*

EXAMPLE 2

Helen **is** a troublemaker.
Language: *Static evaluation*
Why you categorized it as you did and how can you best correct it: *It is static because it uses the verb "to be," implying that "troublemaker" is a permanent condition of Helen. It can best be corrected with behavioral description.*
Revised statement: *Helen told my mother that I was out until 3 a.m. with Jim.*

EXAMPLE 3

There's a new book in the library; you should **check it out.**
Language: *Equivocal language*
Why you categorized it as you did and how can you best correct it: *It is equivocal because "check it out" can mean to appropriately remove it from the library in your name or to peruse it. Correct it by clarifying the meaning.*

Revised statement: *There's a new book in the library; you should peruse it and see if it is something you'd like to read.*

1. What do you want to know about our relationship?

   Language: _____

   Why you categorized it as you did and how can you best correct it: _____

   _____

   Revised statement: _____

   _____

2. They **are** real nerds.

   Language: _____

   Why you categorized it as you did and how can you best correct it: _____

   _____

   Revised statement: _____

   _____

3. She's very **conservative**.

   Language: _____

   Why you categorized it as you did and how can you best correct it: _____

   _____

   Revised statement: _____

   _____

4. I haven't done my laundry for a **long time**.

   Language: _____

   Why you categorized it as you did and how can you best correct it: _____

   _____

Revised statement: _____

_____

5. Your essay should be **brief**.

Language: _____

Why you categorized it as you did and how can you best correct it: _____

_____

Revised statement: _____

_____

6. My job isn't taking me **anywhere**.

Language: _____

Why you categorized it as you did and how can you best correct it: _____

_____

Revised statement: _____

_____

7. She **is** such a braggart.

Language: _____

Why you categorized it as you did and how can you best correct it: _____

_____

Revised statement: _____

_____

8. You've got especially poor attendance.

Language: _____

Why you categorized it as you did and how can you best correct it: _____

_____

Revised statement: _____

_____

Now write your own examples of each type of language and revise the statements to illustrate alternative language.

1. Equivocal language: _____

_____

Revised: _____

_____

2. Relative language: _____

_____

Revised: _____

_____

3. Static evaluation: _____

_____

Revised: _____

_____

5.2 BEHAVIORAL LANGUAGE

LEARNING OBJECTIVES

- Construct a message at the optimal level of specificity or vagueness for a given situation.

INSTRUCTIONS

In each of the situations below, change the language to describe behavior in specific terms. Remember to focus on the <u>behavior</u> (e.g., Bev <u>did</u> "x," rather than Bev <u>is</u> "x"). If you are giving instructions, be specific enough (low abstractions) to clearly get your idea across to someone else.

EXAMPLE 1

John's a live wire.
John ran a 5K in the morning, volunteered for two hours at the homeless shelter in the afternoon, and then danced at a party until dawn.

EXAMPLE 2

Go over that way.
Go across the footbridge, turn right, go up the five large steps to the third building on your left.

1. Will you just wash the car the right way this time?

   _____

   _____

2. Natasha needs to get real.

   _____

   _____

3. You can't rely on Randy.

   _____

   _____

4. That teacher is hard-headed.

   _____

   _____

5. Get organized.

_____

_____

6. Josh just blows me off when I have something important to say.

_____

_____

7. He acts weird.

_____

_____

9. Do the report correctly this time.

_____

_____

10. My parents are understanding.

_____

_____

11. Get a decent movie this time.

_____

_____

12. I like it that your family is emotional.

_____

_____

5.3 EFFECTIVE LANGUAGE

LEARNING OBJECTIVES

- Analyze a real or potential misunderstanding in terms of semantic or pragmatic rules.
- Describe how principles presented in the section of this chapter titled "The Impact of Language" operate in your life.

INSTRUCTIONS

1. For each of the situations below, record the type of language used by the speaker. Evaluate its effectiveness. If you cannot identify with the situation, substitute one of your own.
2. Record the language you would use in response. Again, record your own situation and language if you have a relevant one.
3. Label the type of language used and evaluate its effectiveness. Focus on high and low abstraction, powerful or powerless speech mannerisms, facts or opinions, inferences, high- and low-context language styles, and language and worldview.
4. Describe any alternative language you could use and its relative effectiveness.

EXAMPLE

Situation: Your supervisor at work has called you aside three times this week to correct work you have done. Each time she says, "You've messed up on this."
Type of language used with you/effectiveness: *My supervisor used "**you**" language and **high abstraction**. It wasn't very effective with me because I wasn't sure exactly what I'd messed up on, and I got very defensive, thinking she was about to fire me. She was very direct with me, however; she didn't keep silent about what was bothering her (this is consistent with the **low-context culture** in which I live).*
Language you'd use in response: *"You're on me all the time about something or other."*
Type of language and effectiveness: *"**You**" language and **high abstraction**. This is probably not very effective. My supervisor is likely to get defensive. Actually, my supervisor may think this is "helpful" and "caring" behavior and not realize that I am feeling hassled and threatened.*
Alternative language: *"Ms. Gomez, I'm worried that I'm not doing my job correctly because you've corrected me three times this week. Which part of the report do you want corrected?" This "I" language is more likely to let Ms. Gomez know what specifically is bothering me without raising a good deal of defensiveness. She's likely to appreciate my directness and specific request for help.*

1. Situation: Your romantic partner has been extremely busy with school and work the last two weeks, and you've been feeling left out. When you suggest going out to a party, your partner replies, "You need a personal circus to have fun."

   Type of language used with you/effectiveness:

   _____

   _____

Language you'd use in response:

_____

_____

Type of language and effectiveness:

_____

_____

Alternative language:

_____

_____

2. Situation: You have a hard time saying "no." Lately your roommate has been asking you to do chores that are not your responsibility. Tonight the roommate says, "You're such a great roommate. You won't mind doing the dishes for me tonight since I've got a date and you're just staying home anyway, will you?"

Type of language used with you/effectiveness:

_____

_____

Language you'd use in response:

_____

_____

Type of language and effectiveness:

_____

_____

Alternative language:

_____

_____

3. Situation: Cousins of yours are moving to town. They just called, addressing you by your old family nickname, and said, "You lucky person, you get to have the pleasure of our company for a while until we find a place to live. We thought you'd be glad to have us."

    Type of language used with you/effectiveness:

    _____

    _____

    Language you'd use in response:

    _____

    _____

    Type of language and effectiveness:

    _____

    _____

    Alternative language:

    _____

    _____

4. Situation: You're working on a project with a partner from class, and the partner says, "We'll never get this done. You're too meticulous about everything."

    Type of language used with you/effectiveness:

    _____

    _____

    Language you'd use in response:

    _____

    _____

Type of language and effectiveness:

_____

_____

Alternative language:

_____

_____

5. Situation: Your boss's five-year-old is visiting the workplace. The child has broken two items and is now running from door to door, laughing loudly. Two customers look your way. Your boss says, "Isn't he great? Really an energetic kid!"

Type of language used with you/effectiveness:

_____

_____

Language you'd use in response:

_____

_____

Type of language and effectiveness:

_____

_____

Alternative language:

_____

_____

Class _____   Name_____

Record a situation of your own here:

6. Situation:

_____

_____

Type of language used with you/effectiveness:

_____

_____

Language you'd use in response:

_____

_____

Type of language and effectiveness:

_____

_____

Alternative language:

_____

_____

5.4 MEDIATED MESSAGES – LANGUAGE

LEARNING OBJECTIVES

- Analyze a real or potential misunderstanding in terms of semantic or pragmatic rules.
- Describe how principles presented in the section of this chapter titled "The Impact of Language" operate in your life.
- In a given situation, analyze how gender and/or cultural differences may affect the quality of interaction.

INSTRUCTIONS

Discuss each of the questions below in your group. Prepare written answers for your instructor, or be prepared to contribute to a large group discussion, comparing your experiences with those of others in your class.

1. Our identity is tied to the names we use. Discuss your identity goals with the name(s) you use in mediated contexts (e.g., *your email address, web site identities, or your chat room identity*).

   _____

   _____

2. The language used in an answering machine, voice mail, or email can be very businesslike or very informal. Discuss the pros and cons of formal versus informal mediated messages.

   _____

   _____

3. Sometimes people fail to adapt their language style to the medium they are using (e.g., *they leave a 5-minute voice mail that should have been summarized in 30 seconds*). Should different mediated channels contain more language or less? Specify two different mediated channels and how much language is appropriate for each.

   _____

   _____

4. Describe the gender or social role differences you have noticed in the <u>language</u> of mediated communication. (Example: *My son is more comfortable "talking" about emotions in email, my daughter prefers the telephone.* Example: *My spouse's executive assistant uses very informal language to address me in an email that is never used with me face-to-face.*)

   _____

   _____

5.5 LANGUAGE

LEARNING OBJECTIVES

- In a given situation, analyze how gender and/or cultural differences may affect the quality of interaction.
- Construct a message at the optimal level of specificity or vagueness for a given situation.
- Recast "you" statements into "I" or "we" statements to reflect your responsibility for the content of messages.

INSTRUCTIONS

Use the case below and the discussion questions that follow to discuss the variety of communication issues involved in effective communication. Make notes on this page, add other pages on your own, or prepare a group report/analysis based on your discussion. Add your own experiences to individualize the analysis.

CASE

Professor Polle paired Matt and Magda as class project partners. After three weeks both Matt and Magda came to their professor to complain about the other. Matt called Magda a "flake" and said she didn't work hard enough and didn't take the project seriously. Magda said that Matt was "arrogant," wanted the project done only his way, and didn't care about all the commitments Magda had. It was too late in the semester for the professor to give them new partners.

1. Identify the language that Matt and Magda are using about one another. What effect does using this language have on their perception of each other? On the successful completion of their project?

_____

_____

2. Rewrite the high level abstractions that Matt and Magda use with specific, concrete language. How could this change their perceptions? Improve their situation?

_____

_____

3. Give an example of an "I" language statement from any of the three persons that could improve the situation.

_____

_____

4. Gender and culture may influence the way language is used. Identify differences mentioned in your text and describe how those differences might apply to this situation.

_____

_____

STUDY GUIDE

CHECK YOUR UNDERSTANDING

TRUE/FALSE

Mark the statements below as true or false. For statements that are false, correct them on the lines below to create a true statement.

_____   1. Words are not arbitrary symbols; they have meaning in and of themselves.

_____

_____   2. Language can both *shape* our perceptions of the world and *reflect* our attitudes toward others.

_____

_____   3. Since research shows that people are rated as more competent when their talk is free of powerless speech mannerisms, it is obvious that a consistently powerful style of speaking is always the best approach.

_____

_____   4. Even in low-context cultures there are times when indirect speech can help communicators achieve sound goals in ethically sound ways.

_____

_____   5. Linguists believe that we should view varying syntactic rules as deficient forms of English.

_____

_____   6. "How are we feeling today?" is an example of "we" language.

_____

_____   7. Naming children can be a way to express personal and ethnic identity.

_____

_____   8. Women's behavior in conversations varies dramatically from men's behavior.

_____

_____ 9. Swearing patterns of bosses and coworkers can help people feel connected on the job.

_____

_____ 10. Men are more likely to use language to accomplish a job, while women are more likely to use language to nourish relationships.

_____

COMPLETION

Fill in the blanks below with the correct terms chosen from the list below.

abstraction ladder	equivocation	convergence	divergence	polite forms
tag questions	elaborateness	hedges	disclaimers	succinctness
formality	informality			

1. _____ is the process of adapting one's speech style to match that of others with whom the communicator wants to identify.

2. _____ in language use involve denying direct responsibility for the statement, such as "I could be wrong, but . . . ."

3. _____ of language involve using respectful terms of address, such as "You're welcome, ma'am."

4. _____ involves speaking in a way that emphasizes a person's differences from the other persons with whom he or she is speaking .

5. _____ in language use involves using words that more than one commonly accepted definition, such as "They eat *healthy* food."

6. _____ in language use involve a negation statement, such as "*Didn't you think* that party was boring?"

7. _____ in language use make less of the feeling or intention statement, such as "I'm *rather* upset."

8. _____ is an illustration of how the same phenomenon can be described at various levels of specificity.

9. _____ involves speaking with few words, and it is usually most extreme in cultures where silence is valued.

10. _____ involves speaking with rich and expressive terms, sometimes involving strong assertions and exaggerations.

11. _____ is a way of using correct grammar as a way of defining social position in some cultures.

12. _____ is a way of using language that is casually friendly and does not reflect a series of relational hierarchies in a particular culture.

MULTIPLE CHOICE

Label the examples of language given below by writing the letter of the language type illustrated on the line in front of the example.

a. inference   b. relative word   c. abstract words
d. emotive word   e. equivocal language

_____ 1. John didn't call so he must be angry.

_____ 2. I have a stomach problem.

_____ 3. That place is expensive.

_____ 4. That guy is a real hunk.

_____ 5. My car is hot. (Temperature inside? Overheating? Good-looking? Stolen?)

_____ 6. She left the meeting early; she must have been irritated.

_____ 7. When I said I'd always help bail you out, I didn't mean from jail, just that I'd help you pay your bills.

_____ 8. As your governor, I'd improve education in the state.

_____ 9. He showed up, so he must agree with the protest.

_____ 10. He's a real tightwad.

_____ 11. All of the measures I've supported in Congress promote security.

_____ 12. Ian gave a long speech.

_____ 13. My grandfather is young.

_____ 14. My sister is a pill.

Choose the letter of the *least* abstract alternative to the high abstraction terms.

_____ 15. Jo's constantly complaining.

     a. Jo whines a lot.
     b. Jo complains often about the workload.
     c. Jo told me three times this week that she feels overworked.
     d. Every time we meet, Jo complains about all the work she does.

_____ 16. He can never do anything because he's always busy.

    a. He couldn't take me to dinner last night because he had to work.
    b. He can never do anything fun because he's always working.
    c. He didn't ever take time off to be with me.
    d. He works too much so we have a boring life.

_____ 17. There are a lot of problems associated with freedom.

    a. Freedom carries with it responsibility.
    b. Since I moved into my own apartment, I have to pay ten bills.
    c. I don't like all the responsibility of living on my own.
    d. My economic responsibilities limit my freedom.

_____ 18. Shannon is worthless as a roommate.

    a. Shannon is always gone, so she's really not part of our house.
    b. Shannon never does her part around here.
    c. Shannon's jobs seldom get done around here.
    d. Shannon has attended only one of our six house meetings.

_____ 19. Carlos is the most wonderful friend.

    a. Carlos has never told anyone about my fear of failing.
    b. Carlos listens to me about everything.
    c. Carlos is the best listener I've ever met.
    d. I can trust Carlos implicitly with all my secrets.

_____ 20. Keiko goes overboard in trying to make people like her.

    a. Keiko gave everyone on the team a valentine.
    b. Keiko is the biggest kiss-up you ever met.
    c. I think Keiko is trying to make my friends like her better than me.
    d. I want Keiko to stop trying to outdo everybody else.

Choose the best answer for each of the statements below:

_____ 21. Semantic misunderstandings arise when
    a. people assign the same meanings to the same words.
    b. people assign different meanings to different words.
    c. people assign different meanings to the same words.
    d. people assign the same meaning to different words.

_____　22. One way to make words more measurable is to
　　　　　a. use words such as "doubtful," "toss-up," "likely," "probable," "good chance," and "unlikely."
　　　　　b. use abstract concepts.
　　　　　c. use equivocal language.
　　　　　d. turn them into numbers.

_____　23. One way to make words more effective to the listener is to
　　　　　a. use words that offend but get your point across.
　　　　　b. use abstract concepts.
　　　　　c. use equivocal language.
　　　　　d. adapt to the listeners language patterns.

_____　24. Words are
　　　　　a. useless and should be avoided.
　　　　　b. arbitrary and their meaning is assigned by the receiver.
　　　　　c. the most important part of communication.
　　　　　d. helpful only if you chose the right ones.

CHAPTER FIVE STUDY GUIDE ANSWERS

TRUE/FALSE

1. F	3. F	5. F	7. T	9. T
2. T	4. T	6. F	8. F	10. T

COMPLETION

1. convergence	5. equivocation	9. succinctness
2. disclaimers	6. tag questions	10. elaborateness
3. polite forms	7. hedges	11. formality
4. divergence	8. abstraction ladder	12. informality

MULTIPLE CHOICE

1. a	5. e	9. a	13. b	17. b	21. c
2. c	6. a	10. d	14. d	18. d	22. d
3. b	7. e	11. c	15. c	19. a	23. d
4. d	8. c	12. b	16. a	20. a	24. b

Nonverbal Communication: Messages beyond Words

After studying the topics in this chapter,
you should be able to:

1. Explain the defining characteristics of nonverbal communication as described on pages
   188–195.

2. List and offer examples of each type of nonverbal message introduced in this chapter.

3. In a given situation, recognize your own
   nonverbal behavior and its relational
   significance.

4. Monitor and manage your nonverbal cues in
   ways that achieve your goals.

5. Share appropriately your interpretation
   of another's nonverbal behavior with that
   person.

Ocean/Corbis

What's going on in the photo to the left? You don't need to be a mind reader to recognize that unspoken messages are being expressed here. Some social scientists have argued that 93 percent of the emotional impact of a message comes from nonverbal cues. Others have reasoned more convincingly that the figure is closer to 65 percent.[1] Whatever the precise figure, the point remains: Nonverbal communication plays an important role in how we make sense of one another's behavior. In the following pages you'll become acquainted with the field of nonverbal communication: the way we express ourselves—not by what we say but rather by what we do.

We need to begin our study of nonverbal communication by defining that term. At first this might seem like a simple task: If *non* means "not" and *verbal* means "words," then *nonverbal communication* means "communicating without words." In fact, this literal definition isn't completely accurate. For instance, most communication scholars do not define American Sign Language as nonverbal even though the messages are unspoken. On the other hand, you'll soon read that certain aspects of the voice aren't really verbal, although they are vocal. (Can you think of any? Table 6.1 will help.)

For our purposes, we'll define **nonverbal communication** as "messages expressed by nonlinguistic means." This rules out sign languages and written words, but it includes messages transmitted by vocal means that don't involve language—such as sighs, laughs, throat clearing, and other assorted noises. In addition, our definition allows us to explore the nonlinguistic dimensions of the spoken word—volume, rate, pitch, and so on. It also encompasses more abstract factors such as physical appearance, the environment in which we communicate, how close or far we stand from each other, and the way we use time. And, of course, it includes the features most people think of when they consider nonverbal communication: body language, gestures, facial expression, and eye contact.

Characteristics of Nonverbal Communication

The definition in the preceding paragraph only hints at the richness of nonverbal communication. In the following pages, we'll look at characteristics that are true of all the many forms and functions of nonverbal communication.

NONVERBAL SKILLS ARE VITAL

It's hard to overemphasize the importance of effective nonverbal expression and the ability to read and respond to others' nonverbal behavior.[2] Nonverbal encoding and decoding skills are a strong predictor of popularity, attractiveness, and socioemotional

TABLE 6.1 TYPES OF COMMUNICATION

	VOCAL COMMUNICATION	NONVOCAL COMMUNICATION
Verbal Communication	Spoken words	Written words
Nonverbal Communication	Vocal tone, rate, pitch, volume, etc.	Gestures, movement, appearance, facial expression, touch, etc.

© Cengage Learning

well-being.[3] Good nonverbal communicators are more persuasive than people who are less skilled, and they have a greater chance of success in settings ranging from careers to poker games to romance. Nonverbal sensitivity is a major part of the "emotional intelligence" described in Chapter 4, and researchers have come to recognize that it is impossible to study spoken language without paying attention to its nonverbal dimensions.[4]

ALL BEHAVIOR HAS COMMUNICATIVE VALUE

Suppose you tried not to communicate any messages at all. What would you do? Stop talking? Close your eyes? Curl up into a ball? Leave the room? You can probably see that even these behaviors communicate messages—that you're avoiding contact. One study demonstrated this fact.[5] When communicators were told not to express nonverbal clues, others viewed them as dull, withdrawn, uneasy, aloof, and deceptive. This impossibility of not communicating is extremely important to understand because it means that each of us is a kind of transmitter that cannot be shut off. No matter what we do, we give off information about ourselves.[6]

The Artist won an Academy Award for Best Picture despite being a (mostly) silent film shot in black and white. It demonstrates the power of nonverbal communication to depict a broad range of human emotions.

Stop for a moment and examine yourself as you read this. If someone were observing you now, what nonverbal clues would that person get about how you're feeling? Are you sitting forward or reclining back? Is your posture tense or relaxed? Are your eyes wide open, or do they keep closing? What does your facial expression communicate? Can you make your face expressionless? Don't people with expressionless faces communicate something to you?

Of course, we don't always intend to send nonverbal messages. Unintentional nonverbal behaviors differ from intentional ones.[7] For example, we often stammer, blush, frown, and sweat without meaning to do so. Whether or not our nonverbal behavior is intentional, others recognize it and make interpretations about us based on their observations. Some theorists argue that unintentional behavior may provide information but that it shouldn't count as communication.[8] We draw the boundaries of nonverbal communication more broadly, suggesting that even unconscious and unintentional behavior conveys messages and thus is worth studying as communication.

NONVERBAL COMMUNICATION IS PRIMARILY RELATIONAL

Some nonverbal messages serve utilitarian functions. For example, a police officer directs the flow of traffic, and a team of street surveyors uses hand motions to coordinate its work. But nonverbal communication more commonly expresses the kinds of relational (rather than content) messages discussed in Chapter 1 and the kinds of identity messages that you read about in Chapter 2.[9]

Consider, for example, the role of nonverbal communication in *identity management*.[10] Chapter 2 discussed how we strive to create an image of ourselves as we want others to view us. Nonverbal communication plays an important role in this process—in many cases more important than verbal communication. For instance, think what happens when you attend a party where you are likely to meet strangers you would like to get to know better. Instead of projecting your image verbally ("Hi! I'm attractive, friendly, and easygoing"), you behave in ways that will present this identity. You might smile a lot and perhaps try to strike a relaxed pose. It's also likely that you dress carefully—even if the image involves looking as though you hadn't given a lot of attention to your appearance.

Along with identity management, nonverbal communication *reflects and shapes the kinds of relationships have with others*. Think about the wide range of ways you could behave when greeting another person. You could wave, shake hands, nod, smile, clap the other person on the back, give a hug, or avoid all contact. Each one of these decisions would send a message about the nature of your relationship with the other person. Within romantic relationships, nonverbal behaviors are especially important. For example, displays of affection such as sitting close, holding hands, and giving affectionate gazes are strongly connected to satisfaction and commitment in romantic relationships.[11]

Nonverbal communication performs a third valuable social function: *conveying emotions* that we may be unwilling or unable to express—or ones that we may not even be aware of. In fact, nonverbal communication is much better suited to expressing attitudes and feelings than ideas. You can prove this by imagining how you could express each item on the following list nonverbally:

a. You're tired.
b. You're in favor of capital punishment.
c. You're attracted to another person in the group.
d. You think prayer in the schools should be allowed.
e. You're angry at someone in the room.

This experiment shows that, short of charades, nonverbal messages are much better at expressing attitudes and emotions (a, c, and e) than other sorts of messages (b and d). Among other limitations, nonverbal messages can't convey:

> Simple matters of fact ("The book was written in 1997.")
>
> The past or future tenses ("I was happy yesterday"; "I'll be out of town next week.")
>
> An imaginary idea ("What would it be like if . . .")
>
> Conditional statements ("If I don't get a job, I'll have to move out.")

As technology develops, an increasing number of internet and phone messages will include both visual and vocal dimensions, making communication richer and enhancing understanding.[12] At present, most text, instant, and email messages offer fewer nonverbal cues about the speaker's feelings than do face-to-face encounters or even telephone voice conversations. Of course, this makes these messages ripe for misunderstandings. Probably the biggest problems arise from joking remarks being taken as serious statements. To solve this, electronic text correspondents have developed a series of symbols called *emoticons* that can be inserted to simulate nonverbal dimensions of a message.[13] Emoticons can clarify meanings that aren't obvious from words alone. Although they may be helpful, emoticons clearly aren't an adequate substitute for the rich mixture of nonverbal messages that flows in face-to-face exchanges.

NONVERBAL COMMUNICATION SERVES MANY FUNCTIONS

Just because this chapter focuses on nonverbal communication, don't get the idea that our words and our actions are unrelated. Quite the opposite is true: Verbal and nonverbal communication are interconnected elements in every act of communication. (See Table 6.2 for a comparison of verbal and nonverbal communication.) Nonverbal behaviors can operate in several relationships with verbal behaviors.

TABLE 6.2 SOME DIFFERENCES BETWEEN VERBAL AND NONVERBAL COMMUNICATION

	VERBAL COMMUNICATION	NONVERBAL COMMUNICATION
Complexity	One dimension (words only)	Multiple dimensions (voice, posture, gestures, distance, etc.)
Flow	Intermittent (speaking and silence alternate)	Continuous (it's impossible to not communicate nonverbally)
Clarity	Less subject to misinterpretation	More ambiguous
Impact	Has less impact when verbal and nonverbal cues are contradictory	Has stronger impact when verbal and nonverbal cues are contradictory
Intentionality	Usually deliberate	Often unintentional

© Cengage Learning

Repeating If someone asked you for directions to the nearest drugstore, you might say, "North of here about two blocks," **repeating** your instructions nonverbally by pointing north. This sort of repetition isn't just decorative: People remember comments accompanied by gestures more than those made with words alone.[14]

Complementing Even when it doesn't repeat language, nonverbal behavior can reinforce what's been said. **Complementing** nonverbal behaviors match the thoughts and emotions the communicator is expressing linguistically. You can appreciate the value of this function by imagining the difference between saying "Thank you" with a sincere facial expression and tone of voice and saying the same words in a deadpan manner.

Substituting When a friend asks "What's up?" you might shrug your shoulders instead of answering in words. Many facial expressions operate as substitutes for speech. It's easy to recognize expressions that function like verbal interjections and say "Gosh," "Really?," "Oh, please!," and so on.[15] Nonverbal **substituting** can be useful when communicators are reluctant to express their feelings in words. Faced with a message you find disagreeable, you might sigh, roll your eyes, or yawn when speaking out would not be appropriate. Likewise, a parent who wants a child to stop being disruptive at a party can flash a glare across the room without saying a word (and what child doesn't know the power of "the look" from Mom or Dad?).

Accenting Just as we use italics to emphasize an idea in print, we use nonverbal devices to emphasize oral messages. Pointing an accusing finger adds emphasis to criticism (as well as probably creating defensiveness in the receiver). **Accenting** certain words with the voice ("It was *your* idea!") is another way to add nonverbal emphasis.

Regulating Nonverbal behaviors can serve a **regulating** function by influencing the flow of verbal communication.[16] We can regulate conversations nonverbally by nodding (indicating "I understand" or "keep going"), looking away (signaling a lack of attention), or moving toward the door (communicating a desire to end the conversation). Of course, most of us have learned the hard way that nonverbal signals like these don't guarantee that the other party will pay attention to, interpret, or respond to them in the ways we had hoped.

Contradicting People often express **contradicting** messages in their verbal and nonverbal behaviors. A common example of this sort of **mixed message** is the experience

She dresses in flags

comes on

like a mack truck

she paints

her eyelids green

and her mouth

is a loud speaker rasping out

profanity

at cocktail parties

she is everywhere

like a sheep dog

working a flock

nipping at your sleeve

spilling your drink

bestowing

wet sloppy kisses

but i

have received

secret messages

carefully written

from the shy

quiet woman

who hides

in this

bizarre

gaudy castle

Ric Masten

© SuperStock/SuperStock

Poem "Flags" from *Even As We Speak* by Ric Masten. Copyright © Sunflower Ink, Palo Colorado Road, Carmel, CA 93923. Reprinted with permission.

we've all had of hearing someone with a red face and bulging veins yelling, "Angry? No, I'm not angry!" In situations like these, we tend to believe the nonverbal message instead of the words.[17] A humorous illustration of this concept can be seen in the Cingular cell phone commercial "Mother Love" (available on popular video sites). A mother and daughter appear to be having an argument with raised voices, flailing arms, and scowling faces. Careful listening to their words, however, reveals that they're slinging compliments and praise at each other, including the phrases "I really like it!" and "I love you!" What makes the commercial amusing is that their verbal and nonverbal messages don't match—and it's easy to believe they're angry rather than happy, no matter what their words say.

NONVERBAL COMMUNICATION OFFERS DECEPTION CLUES

When message senders are telling lies, their nonverbal behavior sometimes gives them away. Inadvertent signals of deception—often called **leakage**—can come through a variety of nonverbal channels. Some of these channels are more revealing than others. Facial expressions offer important information,[18] but deceivers also pay more attention to monitoring these cues in an attempt to maintain a "poker face." More reliable is pupil dilation, a physiological response that can't easily be controlled.[19] Speech patterns also offer a variety of leakage clues.[20] In one experiment, subjects who were encouraged to be deceitful made more speech errors, spoke for shorter periods of time, and had a lower rate of speech than did others who were encouraged to express themselves honestly. Another experiment revealed that the

TABLE 6.3 LEAKAGE OF NONVERBAL CUES TO DECEPTION

Deception cues are more likely when the deceiver

Wants to hide emotions being felt at the moment
Feels strongly about the information being hidden
Feels apprehensive or guilty about the deception
Gets little enjoyment from being deceptive
Has not had time to rehearse the lie in advance
Knows there are severe punishments for being caught

Based on Ekman, P. (2001). *Telling lies.* New York: Norton.

pitch of a liar's voice tends to be higher than that of a truth teller. Liars leak nonverbal cues of deception in some situations more than others. Table 6.3 outlines some conditions under which leakage is more likely.

A variety of self-help books and seminars claim that liars can be easily identified by monitoring their nonverbal cues, but scientific research doesn't support that notion. Communication scholars Judee Burgoon and Tim Levine have studied deception detection for years. In their review of decades of research on the subject, they came up with what they call "Deception Detection 101"—three findings that have been repeatedly supported in studies.[21] They are:

> We are accurate in detecting deception only slightly more than half the time—in other words, only a shade better than what we could achieve with a coin flip.

> We overestimate our abilities to detect other's lies—in other words, we're not as good at catching deception as we think we are.

> We have a strong tendency to judge others' messages as truthful—in other words, we want to believe people wouldn't lie to us (which biases our ability to detect deceit).

As one writer put it, "There is no unique telltale signal for a fib. Pinocchio's nose just doesn't exist, and that makes liars difficult to spot."[22] Moreover, some popular prescriptions about liars' nonverbal behaviors simply aren't accurate. For instance, conventional wisdom suggests that liars avert their gaze and fidget more than nonliars. Research, however, shows just the opposite: Liars often sustain *more* eye contact and fidget *less*, in part because they believe that to do otherwise might look deceitful.[23] While it's possible to make some generalizations about the nonverbal tendencies of liars, caution should be exercised in making evaluations of others' truth telling based on limited and ambiguous nonverbal cues.[24]

NONVERBAL COMMUNICATION IS AMBIGUOUS

You learned in Chapter 5 that verbal messages are open to multiple interpretations, but nonverbal messages are even more ambiguous. For example, consider the photo

"I knew the suspect was lying because of certain telltale discrepancies between his voice and nonverbal gestures. Also his pants were on fire."

Jupiterimages/Workbook Stock/Getty Images

on this page. What do you think is the relationship between the people in it? Can you be sure? Or consider the example of a wink: In one study, college students interpreted this nonverbal signal as meaning a variety of things, including an expression of thanks, a sign of friendliness, a measure of insecurity, a sexual come-on, and an eye problem.[25]

Even the most common nonverbal behavior can be ambiguous. A group of Safeway supermarket employees filed grievances over the company's "Superior Service" policy that required workers to smile and make eye contact with customers. The grocery clerks reported that some customers took the friendly greetings as come-ons.[26] Although nonverbal behavior can be very revealing, it can have so many possible meanings that it's impossible to be certain which interpretation is correct. Law-enforcement officials in California discouraged one motorist group from publicizing a set of hand signals drivers could use to signal one another with messages such as "Danger ahead" or "There's a problem with your car." They warned that hand signs could be misinterpreted as gang signs that would provoke violent reactions.[27]

The ambiguous nature of nonverbal behavior becomes clear in the area of courtship and sexuality. Does a kiss mean "I like you a lot" or "I want to have sex"? Does pulling away from a romantic partner mean "Stop now" or "Keep trying"? Communication researchers explored this question by surveying one hundred college students about sexual consent in twelve dating scenarios in order to discover under what conditions verbal approaches (for example, "Do you want to have sex with me?") were considered preferable to nonverbal indicators (such as kissing as an indicator of a desire to have sex).[28] In every scenario, verbal consent was seen as less ambiguous than nonverbal consent. This doesn't mean that romantic partners don't rely on nonverbal signals; many of the respondents indicated that they interpret nonverbal cues (such as kissing) as signs of sexual willingness. However, nonverbal cues were far less likely to be misunderstood when accompanied by verbal cues. The conclusions of this research seem obvious: Verbal messages are clearer than nonverbal messages in matters of sexual consent.

Some people have more difficulty decoding nonverbal signals than do others. For people with a syndrome called *nonverbal learning disorder* (NVLD), reading facial expressions, tone of voice, and other cues is dramatically more difficult.[29] Because of a processing deficit in the right hemisphere of the brain, people with NVLD have trouble making sense of many nonverbal cues. Humor or sarcasm can be especially difficult to understand for people—especially children—with NVLD. For example, if they learn the right way to introduce themselves to an unfamiliar adult (by shaking hands and saying "Pleased to meet you"), they may attempt the same response in a group of children where it might be viewed as odd or "nerdy." When peers do give them subtle feedback, such as raised eyebrows, they miss the information completely and therefore cannot modify their behavior next time.[30]

Even for those of us who don't suffer from NVLD, the ambiguity of nonverbal behavior can be frustrating. The perception-checking skill you learned in Chapter 3 can be a useful tool for figuring out what meanings you can accurately attach to confusing cues.

PAUSE AND REFLECT

BODY LANGUAGE

This exercise will both increase your skill in observing nonverbal behavior and show you the dangers of being too sure that you're a perfect reader of body language. You can try the exercise either in or out of class, and the period of time over which you do it is flexible—from a single class period to several days. In any case, begin by choosing a partner and then follow these directions:

1. For the first period of time (however long you decide to make it), observe the way your partner behaves. Notice movements, mannerisms, postures, style of dress, and so on. To remember your observations, jot them down. If you're doing this exercise out of class over an extended period of time, there's no need to let your observations interfere with whatever you'd normally be doing: Your only job here is to compile a list of your partner's behaviors. In this step, you should be careful *not to interpret* your partner's behaviors—just record what you see.

2. At the end of the time period, share what you've seen with your partner, who should do the same with you.

3. For the next period of time, your job not only is to observe your partner's behavior but also to *interpret* it. This time in your conference you should tell your partner what you thought his or her behaviors revealed. For example, does careless dressing suggest oversleeping, loss of interest in appearance, or the desire to feel more comfortable? If you noticed frequent yawning, did you think this meant boredom, fatigue after a late night, or sleepiness after a big meal? Don't feel bad if your guesses weren't all correct. Remember that nonverbal clues tend to be ambiguous. You may be surprised how checking out the nonverbal clues you observe can help build a relationship with another person.

 You can complete this activity by visiting CengageBrain.com to access the Speech Communication CourseMate for *Looking Out/ Looking In*, and, if requested, email your responses to your instructor.

Influences on Nonverbal Communication

The way we communicate nonverbally is influenced to a certain degree by biological sex and to a great degree by the way we are socialized. To learn more about these influences, read on.

GENDER

It's easy to identify stereotypical differences in male and female styles of nonverbal communication. Just think about exaggerated caricatures of macho men and delicate women that appear from time to time. Many jokes, as well as humorous films and plays, have been created around the results that arise when characters try to act like members of the opposite sex.

In the movie *Albert Nobbs*, actress Glenn Close plays a woman who disguises herself as a man to get and keep a job as a butler. Nobbs's nonverbal mannerisms, attire, and grooming are vital to maintaining a masculine image.

Although few of us behave like stereotypically masculine or feminine movie characters, there are recognizable differences in the way men and women look and act. Some of the most obvious differences are physiological: height, depth and volume of the voice, and so on. Other differences are rooted more in socialization. In general, females are usually more nonverbally expressive, and they are better at recognizing others' nonverbal behavior.[31] More specifically, research shows that, compared to men, women smile more; use more facial expression; use more head, hand, and arm gestures (but less expansive gestures); touch others more; stand closer to others; are more vocally expressive; and make more eye contact.[32]

After looking at differences like these, it might seem as if men and women communicate in radically different ways. In fact, men's and women's nonverbal communication is more similar than different in many respects.[33] Differences like the ones described in the preceding paragraph are noticeable, but they are outweighed by the similar rules we follow in areas such as making eye contact, posture, gestures, and so on. You can prove this by imagining what it would be like to use radically different nonverbal rules: standing only an inch away from others, sniffing strangers, or tapping the forehead of someone when you want his or her attention. Moreover, male–female nonverbal differences are less pronounced in conversations involving gay and lesbian participants.[34] Gender certainly has an influence on nonverbal style, but the differences are often a matter of degree rather than kind.

CULTURE

Cultures have different nonverbal languages as well as verbal ones.[35] Fiorello LaGuardia, legendary mayor of New York from 1933 to 1945, was fluent in English, Italian, and Yiddish. Researchers who watched films of his campaign speeches found that they could tell with the sound turned off which language he was speaking by noticing the changes in his nonverbal behavior.[36]

Some nonverbal behaviors have different meanings from culture to culture. The "OK" gesture made by joining the tips of thumb and forefinger to form a circle is a cheery affirmation to most Americans, but it has less positive meanings in other parts of the world.[37] In France and Belgium, it means "You're worth zero." In Greece and Turkey, it is a vulgar sexual invitation, usually meant as an insult. Given this sort of cross-cultural ambiguity, it's easy to imagine how an innocent tourist might wind up in serious trouble.

Even though we recognize that differences exist in the nonverbal rules of different cultures, subtle differences can damage relationships without the parties ever recognizing exactly what has gone wrong. Anthropologist Edward Hall points out that, whereas Americans are comfortable conducting business at a distance of roughly 4 feet, people from the Middle East stand much closer.[38] It is easy to visualize the awkward advance-and-retreat pattern that might occur when two diplomats or businesspeople from these cultures meet. The Middle Easterner would probably keep moving forward to close the gap, whereas the American would continually back away. Both would feel uncomfortable, probably without knowing why.

Like distance, patterns of eye contact vary around the world.[39] A direct gaze is considered appropriate, if not imperative, for speakers seeking power in Latin America, the Arab world, and southern Europe. However, Asians, Indians, Pakistanis, and northern Europeans gaze at a listener peripherally or not at all out of respect rather than a lack of interest.[40] In either case, deviations from the norm are likely to make a listener uncomfortable.

The use of time depends greatly on culture.[41] Some cultures (e.g., North American, German, and Swiss) tend to be **monochronic**, emphasizing punctuality, schedules, and completing one task at a time. Other cultures (e.g., South American, Mediterranean, and Arab) are more **polychronic**, with flexible schedules in which multiple tasks are pursued at the same time.[42] One psychologist discovered the difference between North and South American attitudes when teaching at a university in Brazil.[43] He found that some Brazilian students arrived halfway through a two-hour class and most of them stayed put and kept asking questions when the class was scheduled to end. A half-hour after the official end of the class, the psychologist finally closed off discussion because there was no indication that the students intended to leave. This flexibility of time is quite different from what is common in most North American colleges!

As Table 6.4 shows, differences in cultural rules can lead to misunderstandings. For example, observations have shown that black women in all-black groups are nonverbally more expressive and interrupt one another more than white women in all-white groups. This doesn't mean that black women always feel more intensely than their white counterparts. A more likely explanation is that the two groups follow different cultural rules. One study found that in racially mixed groups both black and white women moved closer to each others' style.[44] This nonverbal convergence shows that skilled communicators can adapt their behavior when interacting with members of other cultures or subcultures in order to make the exchange smoother and more effective.

TABLE 6.4 CULTURAL DIFFERENCES IN NONVERBAL COMMUNICATION CAN LEAD TO MISUNDERSTANDINGS

Behaviors that have one meaning for members of the same culture or co-culture can be interpreted differently by members of other groups.

BEHAVIOR	PROBABLE IN-GROUP PERCEPTION	POSSIBLE OUT-GROUP PERCEPTION
Avoidance of direct eye contact (Latino/Latina)	Used to communicate attentiveness or respect	A sign of inattentiveness; direct eye contact is preferred
Aggressively challenging a point with which one disagrees (African American)	Acceptable means of dialogue; not regarded as verbal abuse or a precursor to violence	Arguments are viewed as inappropriate and a sign of potential imminent violence
Use of finger gestures to beckon others (Asian)	Appropriate if used by adults for children, but highly offensive if directed at adults	Appropriate gesture to use with both children and adults
Silence (Native American)	Sign of respect, thoughtfulness, and/or uncertainty/ambiguity	Interpreted as boredom, disagreement, or refusal to participate
Touch (Latino/Latina)	Normal and appropriate for interpersonal interactions	Deemed appropriate for some intimate or friendly interactions; otherwise perceived as a violation of personal space
Public display of intense emotions (African American)	Accepted and valued as measure of expressiveness; appropriate in most settings	Violates expectations for self-controlled public behaviors; inappropriate in most public settings
Touching or holding hands of same-sex friends (Asian)	Acceptable in behavior that signifies closeness in platonic relationships	Perceived as inappropriate, especially for male friends

© Cengage Learning 2013

Despite the many cultural differences, some nonverbal behaviors have the same meanings around the world. Smiles and laughter are universal signals of positive emotions, for example, whereas sour expressions are universal signals of displeasure.[45] Charles Darwin believed that expressions like these are the result of evolution, functioning as survival mechanisms that allowed early humans to convey emotional states before the development of language. The innateness of some facial expressions becomes even clearer when we examine the behavior of children who are born with impaired hearing and sight.[46] Despite a lack of social learning, these children often display a broad range of expression. They smile, laugh, and cry in ways that are similar to those of seeing and hearing children. In other words, nonverbal behavior—like much of our communication—is influenced by both our genetic heritage and our culture.

 Types of Nonverbal Communication

Keeping the characteristics of nonverbal communication in mind, let's look at some of the ways we communicate in addition to words.

BODY MOVEMENT

The first area of nonverbal communication we'll discuss is the broad field of **kinesics**, or body position and motion. In this section, we'll explore the role that body orientation, posture, gestures, facial expressions, and eye contact play in our relationships with one another.

Body Orientation We'll start with **body orientation**—the degree to which we face toward or away from someone with our body, feet, and head. To understand how this kind of physical positioning communicates nonverbal messages, imagine that you and a friend are in the middle of a conversation when a third person approaches and wants to join you. You're not especially glad to see this person, but you don't want to sound rude by asking him to leave. By turning your body slightly away from the intruder, you can make your feelings very clear. The nonverbal message here is "We're interested in each other right now and don't want to include you in our conversation." The general rule is that facing someone directly signals your interest and facing away signals a desire to avoid involvement.

You can learn a good deal about how people feel by observing the way people position themselves. The next time you're in a crowded place where people can choose whom to face directly, try noticing who seems to be included in the action and who is being subtly shut out. And in the same way, pay attention to your own body orientation. You may be surprised to discover that you're avoiding a certain person without being conscious of it or that at times you're "turning your back" on people altogether. If this is the case, it may be helpful to figure out why.

Posture Another way we communicate nonverbally is through **posture**. To see if this is true, stop reading for a moment and notice how you're sitting. What does your position say nonverbally about how you feel? Are there any other people near you now? What messages do you get from their current posture? By paying attention to the postures of those around you, as well as your own, you'll find another channel of nonverbal communication that can furnish information about how people feel about themselves and one another.

An indication of how much posture communicates is shown by our language. It's full of expressions that link emotional states with body postures:

THE LOOK OF A VICTIM

Little Red Riding Hood set herself up to be mugged. Her first mistake was skipping through the forest to grandma's house. Her second mistake was stopping to pick flowers. At this point, as you might remember in the story, the mean heavy wolf comes along and begins to check her out. He observes, quite perceptively, that she is happy, outgoing, and basically unaware of any dangers in her surrounding environment. The big bad wolf catches these nonverbal clues and splits to grandma's house. He knows that Red is an easy mark. From this point we all know what happens.

Body movements and gestures reveal a lot of information about a person. Like Little Red Riding Hood, pedestrians may signal to criminals that they are easy targets for mugging by the way they walk. When was the last time you assessed your "muggability rating"? In a recent study two psychologists set out to identify those body movements that characterized easy victims. They assembled "muggability ratings"

of sixty New York pedestrians from the people who may have been the most qualified to judge—prison inmates who had been convicted of assault.

The researchers unobtrusively videotaped pedestrians on weekdays between 10:00 A.M. and 12:00 A.M. Each pedestrian was taped for 6 to 8 seconds, the approximate time it takes for a mugger to size up an approaching person. The judges (prison inmates) rated the "assault potential" of the sixty pedestrians on a 10-point scale. A rating of 1 indicated someone was "a very easy rip-off," of 2, "an easy dude to corner." Toward the other end of the scale, 9 meant a person "would be heavy; would give you a hard time," and 10 indicated that the mugger "would avoid it, too big a situation, too heavy." The results revealed several body movements that characterized easy victims: "Their strides were either very long or very short; they moved awkwardly, raising their left legs with their left arms (instead of alternating them); on each step

Jack Carey/Alamy

they tended to lift their whole foot up and then place it down (less muggable sorts took steps in which their feet rocked from heel to toe). Overall, the people rated most muggable walked as if they were in conflict with themselves; they seemed to make each move in the most difficult way possible."

Loretta Malandro and Larry Barker

From *Introduction to Nonverbal Communication* by L. Malandro and L. Baker, pp. 112–113. Copyright © 1982. Used by permission of The McGraw-Hill Companies.

I won't take this lying down! (Nor will I stand for it!)

I feel the weight of the world on my shoulders.

He's a real slouch in the office (but he's no slouch on the basketball court).

She's been sitting on that project for weeks.

Posture may be the least ambiguous type of nonverbal behavior. In one study, 176 computer-generated mannequin figures were created, and observers were asked to assign emotions to particular postural configurations. The raters had more than

90-percent agreement on postures that were connected with anger, sadness, and happiness.[47] Some postures seem easier to interpret than others. Disgust was the emotion that was hardest to identify from body posture, and some raters thought that surprise and happiness had similar postural configurations.

Tension and relaxation offer other postural keys to feelings. We take relaxed postures in nonthreatening situations and tighten up in threatening situations.[48] Based on this observation, we can tell a good deal about how others feel simply by watching how tense or loose they seem to be. For example, tenseness is a way of detecting status differences: The lower-status person is generally the more rigid and tense-appearing one, and the higher-status person appears more relaxed. Research shows that adopting a high-status pose—such as putting your feet up on a desk with hands clasped behind your head—can actually lead to increased feelings of power.[49]

Gestures Movements of the hands and arms—**gestures**—are an important type of nonverbal communication. Some social scientists claim that a language of gestures was the first form of human communication, preceding speech by tens of thousands of years.[50]

The most common forms of gestures are what social scientists call **illustrators**—movements that accompany speech but don't stand on their own.[51] For instance, if someone on a street corner asked you how to get to a restaurant across town, you might offer street names and addresses—but all the while you'd probably point with your fingers and gesture with your hands to illustrate how to get there. Remove the words from your directions and it's unlikely that the other person would ever find the restaurant. Think also of people who like to "talk with their hands," gesturing vigorously even when they're conversing on the phone and can't be seen by the other party. Research shows that North Americans use illustrators more often when they are emotionally aroused—trying to explain ideas that are difficult to put into words when they are furious, horrified, agitated, distressed, or excited.[52] Studies also show that it is easier to comprehend and learn a second language when it is accompanied by illustrators and other nonverbal cues.[53]

A second type of gestures is **emblems**—deliberate nonverbal behaviors that have a precise meaning and are known to virtually everyone within a cultural group. Unlike illustrators, emblems can stand on their own and often function as replacements for words. For example, all North Americans know that a head nod means "Yes," a head shake means "No," a wave means "Hello" or "Goodbye," and a hand to the ear means "I can't hear you." And almost every Westerner over the age of seven knows the meaning of a raised middle finger. It's important to remember, however, that the meanings of emblems like these are not universal. For instance, the "thumbs-up" sign means "good" in the United States but is an obscene gesture in Iraq and several other countries.[54]

A third type of gestures is **adaptors**—unconscious bodily movements in response to the environment. For instance, shivering when it's cold and folding your arms to get warmer are examples of adaptors. Of course, sometimes we cross our arms when we're feeling "cold" toward another person—and thus adaptors can reveal the climate of our relationships. In particular, self-touching behaviors—sometimes called **manipulators**—are often a sign of discomfort, such as fiddling with your hands or rubbing your arms during an interview.[55] But not *all* fidgeting signals uneasiness. People also are likely to engage in self-touching when relaxed. When they let down their guard (either alone or with friends), they will be more likely to fiddle with an earlobe, twirl a strand of hair, or clean their fingernails. Whether or not the fidgeter is hiding something, observers are likely to interpret these behaviors as a signal of dishonesty. Because not all fidgeters are dishonest, it's important not to jump to conclusions about the meaning of adaptors.

ON THE JOB

Nonverbal Communication in Job Interviews

The old adage "You never get a second chance to make a first impression" is never truer than in job interviews. The impression you make in the first few minutes of this crucial conversation can define the way a prospective employer views you—and thus the path of your career. Research highlights the vital role that nonverbal communication plays in shaping how interviewers regard job applicants.[a]

Here's a look at three specific behaviors that have been the subject of studies on employment interviewing:

- *Handshaking.* In American culture, most professional interactions begin with a handshake. As simple as this ritual might seem, research shows that the quality of a handshake is related to interviewer hiring recommendations. Handshakes should be firm and energetic without being overpowering—and this holds true for both men and women.[b]
- *Attire and Appearance.* Being well dressed and properly groomed is basic to interview success. A business-appropriate appearance enhances perceptions of a candidate's credibility and social skills. A rule of thumb is that

it's better to err on the side of formality than casualness, and conservative colors and fashion are preferable to being flashy.[c]
- *Smiling.* While it may seem obvious, one study found that "authentically smiling interviewees were judged to be more suitable and were more likely to be short-listed and selected for the job."[d] The word *authentically* is important—judges in the study made negative appraisals of plastered-on smiles that didn't seem genuine. The key is to smile naturally and regularly, exhibiting a friendly and pleasant demeanor.

It's easy to imagine how other nonverbal cues discussed in this chapter (e.g., eye contact, posture, tone of voice, etc.) are vital in making a good impression in a job interview. For more information, consult the myriad books and websites devoted to employment interviewing. You can also visit your school's career-development center or perhaps even take a course in interviewing. In every case, you'll be coached that what you do and how you look is as important as what you say in a job interview.

Actually, *too few* gestures may be just as significant an indicator of mixed messages as *too many*.[56] Limited gesturing may signal a lack of interest, sadness, boredom, or low enthusiasm. Illustrators also decrease whenever someone is cautious about speaking. For these reasons, a careful observer will look for either an increase or a decrease in the usual level of gestures.

Face and Eyes The face and eyes are probably the most noticed parts of the body, but this doesn't mean that their nonverbal messages are the easiest to read. The face is a tremendously complicated channel of expression for several reasons.

First, it's difficult to describe the number and kind of expressions we produce with our face and eyes. Researchers have found that there are at least eight distinguishable positions of the eyebrows and forehead, eight of the eyes and lids, and ten for the lower face.[57] When you multiply this complexity by the number of emotions we feel, you can see why it's almost impossible to compile a dictionary of facial expressions and their corresponding emotions.

Second, facial expressions are difficult to understand because of the speed with which they can change. For example, slow-motion films show **microexpressions** fleeting across a subject's face in as short a time as it takes to blink an eye.[58.] Researchers can use these filmed microexpressions to identify moments when people are telling lies. Also, it seems that different emotions show most clearly in different parts of the face: happiness and surprise in the eyes and lower face; anger in the lower face, brows, and forehead; fear and sadness in the eyes; and disgust in the lower face.

Despite the complex way in which the face shows emotions, you can still pick up clues by watching faces carefully. One of the easiest ways is to look for expressions that seem too exaggerated to be true. For instance, genuine facial expressions usually last no longer than five seconds—anything more and we start to doubt they are real (contestants in pageants with smiles plastered on their faces often come across as "fake" or "plastic").[59] Another way to detect feelings is to watch others' expressions when they aren't likely to be thinking about their appearance. We've all had the experience of glancing into another car while stopped in a traffic jam, or of looking around at a sporting event and seeing expressions that the wearer would probably never show in more guarded moments.

The eyes can send several kinds of messages. Meeting someone's glance with your eyes is usually a sign of involvement, whereas looking away is often a sign of a desire to avoid contact. This principle has a practical application in commerce: Customers leave larger tips when their servers (male and female) maintain eye contact with them.[60] Research also shows that communicators who make direct eye contact are far more likely to get others to comply with their requests than are those who make evasive glances.[61] We'll see later in this chapter how the same principle holds true with touching others—which is why the term *eye contact* is relevant. A sense of connection leads to compliance.

Another kind of message the eyes communicate is a positive or negative attitude.[62] When someone looks toward us with the proper facial expression, we get a clear message that the looker is interested in us—hence the expression "making eyes." At the same time, when our long glances toward someone else are avoided, we can be pretty sure that the other person isn't as interested in a relationship as we are. (Of course, there are all sorts of courtship games in which the receiver of a glance pretends not to notice any message by glancing away yet signals interest with some other part of the body.) The eyes can also communicate both dominance and submission.[63] We've all played the game of trying to stare down somebody, and there are times when downcast eyes are a sign of giving in.

VOICE

The voice is another channel of nonverbal communication. Social scientists use the term **paralanguage** to describe nonverbal, vocal messages. The way a message is spoken can give the same word or words many meanings. For example, note how many meanings come from a single sentence just by shifting the emphasis from one word to another:

This is a fantastic communication book. (Not just any book, but *this* one in particular.)

This is a *fantastic* communication book. (This book is superior, exciting.)

This is a fantastic *communication* book. (The book is good as far as communication goes; it may not be so great as literature or drama.)

This is a fantastic communication *book*. (It's not a play or album; it's a book.)

There are many other ways we communicate paralinguistically through tone, rate, pitch, volume—even through pauses. Consider two types of pauses that can lead to communication snags. The first is the *unintentional pause*—those times when people stop to collect their thoughts before deciding how best to continue their verbal message. It's no surprise that liars tend to have more unintentional pauses than truth tellers, as they often make up stories on the fly.[64] When people pause at length after being

LOOKING AT DIVERSITY

Annie Donnellon: Blindness and Nonverbal Cues

I have been blind since birth, so I've never had access to many of the nonverbal cues that sighted people use. In fact, I think that "sightlings" (a pet name for my friends who are sighted) take for granted how much of their meaning comes through nonverbal channels. When I recently took an interpersonal communication course, the material on nonverbal communication was in some ways a foreign language to me.

For instance, I felt a bit left out when the class discussed things like body movement, eye contact, and facial expressions. I understand how these cues work, but I haven't experienced many of them myself. I have never "stared someone down" or "shot a look" at anyone (at least not intentionally!). While I know that some people "talk with their hands," that's something I've never witnessed and rarely do.

When the subject turned to paralanguage, I was back on familiar territory. I listen very carefully to the way people speak to figure out what they're thinking and feeling. My family and friends tell me I'm more tuned in to these issues than most sightlings are. It's typical for me to ask "Are you okay today?" when friends send messages that seem mixed. They may say everything's fine, but their voice often tells a different story.

I'm a singer and performer, and some of my biggest frustrations have come from well-meaning teachers who coach me on my nonverbals. I remember one acting instructor asking me, "How do you think your character would express herself nonverbally in this scene?" and I thought to myself "I have no idea." People who are sighted may think that anger cues like clenched fists, rigid posture, or shrugged shoulders are "natural" expressions, but I believe that many of them are learned by watching others.

Let me pass along some keys that can help make communication smoother and more effective. It's important to mention your name when starting a conversation with people who are blind: Don't assume they can figure out who you are from your voice. At the end of a conversation, please say that you're leaving. I often feel embarrassed when I'm talking to someone, only to find out that they walked away mid-sentence.

Most important: Clue in visually-impaired people when something is going on that they can't see. Often at my sorority meetings, something will happen that everyone is laughing about, but I'm left out of the loop because I can't see the nonverbal cues. Over the years my friends and family have learned that whispering a quick description of the events helps me feel more a part of the interaction.

The interpersonal course I took was an enriching experience for me, my professor, and my classmates. I think we learned a lot from each other—especially about the vital and complex role of nonverbal communication in interpersonal relationships.

"Blindness and Nonverbal Cues" by Annie Donnellon. Used with permission of author.

asked a delicate question ("Did you like the gift I bought you?"), it might mean they're buying time to come up with a face-saving—and perhaps less-than-honest—response.

A second type of pause is the *vocalized pause*. These range from disfluencies such as "um," "er," and "uh" to filler words that are used habitually such as "like," "okay," and "ya know." Research shows that vocalized pauses reduce a person's perceived credibility[65] and negatively affect perceptions of candidates in job interviews.[66] When Caroline Kennedy was considering running for the Senate, her press tour interviews were filled with vocalized pauses. In one case she used "ya know" 142 times in a single interview with *The New York Times*. Although this wasn't the reason she decided not to run for office, many commentators noted that it certainly didn't help her professional image.[67]

THE WAY YOU TALK CAN HURT YOU?

Women have a distinctive style of speaking: "I was shopping last night? And I saw this wonderful dress? It was so black and slinky?" It's hard to convey intonation in print, but the question marks indicate a rise in pitch at the end of the sentence, as in a question. Many women, especially younger women, use this intonation in declarative sentences: "This is Sally Jones? I have an appointment with Dr. Smith? And I'd like to change it to another day?"

I cringe when I hear this. The rising intonation sounds timid and lacking in self-confidence; the speaker seems to be asking for approval or permission to speak when there's no need to. She should make her point straightforwardly, in an assertion that drops in pitch as it ends.

And I worry that rising intonation harms women. It gets them taken less seriously than they should be in public debates; it encourages salesmen and car mechanics to cheat them when they wouldn't try cheating a man.

A woman friend who studies languages says I've got it wrong. Unlike men, who use conversation to fight for status, she tells me, women see it as cooperative. And they use rising pitch to convey this to their audience. Their tone encourages the supportive interjections, such as "Uh-huh," "Exactly," and "I know what you mean," with which women far more than men interlard each other's speech. And it asks listeners to contribute their ideas on the speaker's topic.

At the very least, women's use of rising intonation involves an ambiguity. It uses a sound that in other contexts conveys timidity, for a very different purpose. Given this ambiguity, we shouldn't be surprised if female speakers who are trying to be cooperative are often heard as hesitant.

It's clearly idiotic to treat conversation as a contest, as so many men do. We'd all benefit from a more cooperative approach. But we need a new symbol to express this, one with no connotations of weakness.

If we find this symbol, we can all, men and women, speak in friendly but firm tones. We can tell anecdotes without lecturing but also without seeming to kowtow. When we call the doctor's, we can say: "This is Sally (or Sam) Jones." (No question about it.) "I have an appointment with Dr. Smith." (I'm reminding you of a fact.) "And I'd like to change it to another day." (Now: Can you help me?)

Thomas Hurka

Reprinted with permission from Thomas Hurka, *Principles: Short Essays on Ethics* (Toronto: Harcourt Brace, © 1994), pp. 201–233.

Researchers have identified the power of paralanguage through the use of content-free speech—ordinary speech that has been electronically manipulated so that the words are unintelligible but the paralanguage remains unaffected. (Hearing a foreign language that you don't understand has the same effect.) Subjects who hear content-free speech can consistently recognize the emotion being expressed as well as identify its strength.[68] Young children respond to the paralanguage of adults, warming up to those who speak warmly and shying away from those who speak in a less-friendly manner.[69]

Paralanguage can affect behavior in many ways, some of which are rather surprising. Researchers have discovered that communicators are most likely to comply with requests delivered by speakers whose rate was similar to their own: People who spoke rapidly responded most favorably to rapid talkers, whereas slow speakers preferred others whose rate was also slow.[70] Besides complying with same-rate speakers, listeners also feel more positively about people who speak at their own rate.

Sarcasm is one instance in which we use both emphasis and tone of voice to change a statement's meaning to the opposite of its verbal message. Experience this reversal yourself with the following three statements. First say them literally and then sarcastically.

"Thanks a lot!"

"I really had a wonderful time on my blind date."

"There's nothing I like better than lima beans."

As they do with other nonverbal messages, people often ignore or misinterpret the vocal nuances of sarcasm. Members of certain groups—children, people with weak intellectual skills, and poor listeners—are more likely to misunderstand sarcastic messages than others.[71] In one study, children younger than age ten lacked the linguistic sophistication to tell when a message was sarcastic.[72]

Some vocal factors are perceived more positively than others. For example, communicators who speak loudly and without hesitations are viewed as more confident than those who pause and speak quietly.[73] People with more-attractive voices are rated more highly than those with less-attractive voices.[74] Just what makes a voice attractive can vary. As Figure 6.1 shows, culture can make a difference. Surveys show that there are both similarities and differences between what Mexicans and Americans view as the ideal voice. Accent plays an important role in shaping perceptions. Generally speaking, accents that identify a speaker's membership in a group lead to more positive evaluations (if the group is high status) or to negative evaluations (if the group is low status).[75]

TOUCH

Shortly after her husband was elected U.S. president, First Lady Michelle Obama violated diplomatic protocol by returning the hug of Great Britain's Queen Elizabeth II. Some observers were appalled, and others delighted. Regardless of their reaction, everyone would have agreed that touch is a powerful way of communicating.

Social scientists use the word **haptics** to describe the study of touching. Touch can communicate many messages and signal a variety of relationships, such as the following:[76]

Functional and professional (dental exam, haircut)

Social and polite (handshake)

Friendship and warmth (clap on back, Spanish *abrazo*)

Sexual arousal (some kisses, strokes)

Aggression (shoves, slaps)

Some nonverbal behaviors occur in several types of relationships. A kiss, for example, can mean anything from a polite but superficial greeting to the most intense arousal. What makes a given touch more or less intense? Researchers have suggested several factors:

Which part of the body does the touching

Which part of the body is touched

How long the touch lasts

How much pressure is used

Whether there is movement after contact is made

Whether anyone else is present

The situation in which the touch occurs

The relationship between the people involved[77]

MEXICAN IDEAL SPEAKER'S VOICE

Medium in pitch
Medium in rate
Loud in volume

Clear enunciation
Well-modulated
Without regional accent
Cheerful

Firm
Low in pitch
Somewhat slow with pauses

U.S. IDEAL SPEAKER'S VOICE

FIGURE 6.1 A Comparison of the Ideal Speakers' Voice Types in Mexico and the United States
© Cengage Learning 2013

From this list you can see that there is, indeed, a complex language of touch. Because nonverbal messages are inherently ambiguous, it's no surprise that this language can often be misunderstood. Is a hug playful or suggestive of stronger feelings? Is a touch on the shoulder a friendly gesture or an attempt at domination? The ambiguity of nonverbal behavior often leads to serious problems.

Touch plays a powerful role in shaping how we respond to others. For instance, in a laboratory task, subjects evaluated partners more positively when they were touched (appropriately, of course) by them.[78] Besides increasing liking, touch also increases compliance. A restaurant server's fleeting touches on the hand and shoulder result in larger tips.[79] Touching customers in a store increases their shopping time, their evaluation of the store, and also the amount of shopping.[80] When an offer to try samples of a product is accompanied by a touch, customers are more likely to try the sample and buy the product.[81]

Some of the most pronounced benefits of touching occur in medicine and the health and helping professions. For example, patients are more likely to take their medicines when physicians give a slight touch while prescribing.[82] Massage can help premature children gain weight, help colicky children to sleep better, improve the mood of depressed adolescents, and boost the immune function of cancer and HIV patients.[83] Research shows that touch between therapists and clients has the potential to encourage a variety of beneficial changes: more self-disclosure, better client self-acceptance, and more positive client–therapist relationships.[84]

Touch also has an impact in school. Students are twice as likely to volunteer and speak up in class if they have received supportive touch on the back or arm from their teacher.[85] Even athletes benefit from touch. One National Basketball Association study revealed that the "touchiest" teams had the most successful records while the lowest-scoring teams had the least amount of touch among teammates.[86]

Of course, touch must be culturally appropriate. Furthermore, touching by itself is no guarantee of success, and too much contact can be bothersome, annoying, or even downright creepy. But research confirms that appropriate contact can enhance your success.

When his wife dumps him, Cal Weaver (Steve Carrell) turns to hunky Jacob Palmer (Ryan Gosling) for advice about how to act to attract women in *Crazy, Stupid Love*. Cal's efforts show that it isn't easy to fake nonverbal cues. (See the TV summary at the end of this chapter.)

Carousel Productions/The Kobal Collection

APPEARANCE

Whether or not we're aware of the fact, how we look sends messages to others. There are two dimensions to appearance: physical attractiveness and clothing.

Physical Attractiveness There is little dispute that people who are deemed physically attractive receive many social benefits.[87] For example, females who are perceived as attractive have more dates, receive higher grades in college, persuade males with greater ease, and receive lighter court sentences. Both men and women perceived by others as attractive are rated as being more sensitive, kind, strong, sociable, and interesting than their less-fortunate brothers and sisters. Physical attractiveness is also an asset in the professional world, affecting hiring, promotion, and performance evaluation decisions.[88] Occasionally, however, it has a negative effect: Interviewers may turn down highly attractive candidates because they're perceived as threats.[89]

PAUSE AND REFLECT

THE RULES OF TOUCH

Like most types of nonverbal behavior, touching is governed by cultural and social rules. Imagine that you are writing a guidebook for visitors from another culture. Describe the rules that govern touching in the following relationships. In each case, describe how the gender of the participants also affects the rules.

1. An adult and a five-year-old child
2. An adult and a twelve-year-old
3. Two good friends
4. Boss and employee

 You can complete this activity by visiting CengageBrain.com to access the Speech Communication CourseMate for *Looking Out/ Looking In*, and, if requested, email your responses to your instructor.

The influence of physical attractiveness begins early in life.[90] Preschoolers were shown photographs of children their own age and asked to choose potential friends and enemies. The researchers found that children as young as three agreed as to who was attractive and unattractive. Furthermore, the children valued their attractive counterparts—both of the same and the opposite sex—more highly. Teachers also are affected by students' attractiveness. Physically attractive students are usually judged more favorably—as being more intelligent, friendly, and popular—than their less-attractive counterparts.[91] Teacher-student assessments work in both directions—research shows that physically attractive professors receive higher evaluations from their students.[92]

Fortunately, attractiveness is something we can control without having to call a plastic surgeon. If you aren't totally gorgeous or handsome, don't despair: Evidence suggests that, as we get to know more about people and like them, we start to regard them as better looking.[93] Moreover, we view others as beautiful or ugly not just on the basis of their "original equipment" but also on the basis of how they use that equipment. Posture, gestures, facial expressions, and other behaviors can increase the physical attractiveness of an otherwise unremarkable person. Finally, the way we dress can make a significant difference in the way others perceive us, as you'll now see.

Clothing Besides being a means of protecting us from the elements, clothing is a means of communicating nonverbally. One writer has suggested that clothing conveys at least ten types of messages to others:[94]

Economic background

Economic level

Educational background

Educational level

Level of sophistication

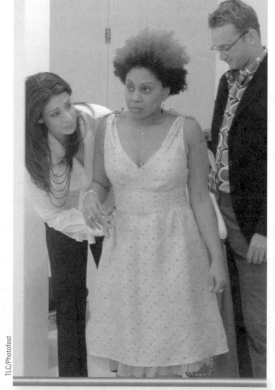

TLC/Photofest

Hosts of the TV show *What Not to Wear* offer apparel tips to people who are "fashion challenged." The show's participants not only look better after getting coached but also often feel better about themselves. (See the TV summary at the end of this chapter.)

"Tell me about yourself, Kugelman—your hopes, dreams, career path, and what that damn earring means."

Level of success

Moral character

Social background

Social position

Trustworthiness

Research shows that we do make assumptions about people based on their clothing.[95] For example, experimenters dressed in uniforms resembling police officers were more successful than those dressed in civilian clothing in requesting pedestrians to pick up litter and in persuading them to lend money to an overparked motorist. Likewise, solicitors wearing sheriff's and nurse's uniforms increased the level of contributions to law-enforcement and healthcare campaigns. We are also more likely to follow the lead of those in more formal attire when it comes to violating social rules. Eighty-three percent of the pedestrians in one study copied the action of a jaywalker dressed in higher-status clothing who violated a "wait" crossing signal, whereas only 48 percent followed a confederate dressed in lower-status clothing.

PHYSICAL SPACE

Proxemics is the study of the way people and animals use space. There are at least two dimensions of proxemics: distance and territoriality.

Distance Each of us carries around a sort of invisible bubble of personal space wherever we go. We think of the area inside this bubble as our private territory—almost as much a part of us as our own bodies. To appreciate this, take a moment to complete the "Distance Makes a Difference" exercise in this section. As you move closer to your partner, the distance between your bubbles narrows and at a certain point disappears altogether: Your space has been invaded, and this is the point at which you probably feel uncomfortable. As you move away again, your partner retreats out of your bubble, and you feel more relaxed.

Of course, if you were to try this experiment with someone very close to you—a romantic partner, for example—you might not have felt any discomfort at all, even while touching. The reason is that our willingness to get close to others—physically as well as emotionally—varies according to the person we're with and the situation we're in. And it's precisely the distance that we voluntarily put between ourselves and others that gives a nonverbal clue about our feelings and the nature of the relationship.

As you read earlier in this chapter, appropriate proxemic distances differ from culture to culture. Anthropologist Edward T. Hall has defined four distances that most North Americans use in their everyday lives.[96] He says we choose a particular distance depending on how we feel toward the other person at a given time, the context of the conversation, and our interpersonal goals.

- The first of Hall's four spatial zones begins with skin contact and ranges out to about 18 inches. We usually use **intimate distance** with people who are emotionally the closest to us and then mostly in private situations—making love, caressing, comforting, protecting.
- The second spatial zone, **personal distance**, ranges from 18 inches at its closest point to 4 feet at its farthest. Its closer range is the distance at which most couples stand in public. The far range runs from about 2½ to 4 feet. As Hall puts it, at this distance we can keep someone "at arm's length." This choice of words suggests the type of communication that goes on at this range: The contacts are still reasonably close, but they're much less personal than the ones that occur a foot or so closer.

PAUSE AND REFLECT

DISTANCE MAKES A DIFFERENCE

1. Choose a partner, and go to opposite sides of the room and face each other.
2. Very slowly begin walking toward each other while carrying on a conversation. You might simply talk about how you feel as you follow the exercise. As you move closer, try to be aware of any change in your feelings. Continue moving slowly toward each other until you are only an inch or so apart. Remember how you feel at this point.
3. Now, while still facing each other, back up until you're at a comfortable distance for carrying on your conversation.
4. Share your feelings with each other or the whole group.

 You can complete this activity by visiting CengageBrain.com to access the Speech Communication CourseMate for *Looking Out/ Looking In*, and, if requested, email your responses to your instructor.

- The third spatial zone, **social distance**, ranges from 4 to about 12 feet. Within it are the kinds of communication that usually occur in business. Its closer range, from 4 to 7 feet, is the distance at which conversations usually occur between salespeople and customers and between people who work together. We use the far range of social distance—7 to 12 feet—for more formal and impersonal situations. Sitting at this distance signals a far different and less-relaxed type of conversation than would pulling a chair around to the boss's side of the desk and sitting only three or so feet away.
- **Public distance** is Hall's term for the farthest zone, running outward from 12 feet. The closer range of public distance is the one that most teachers use in the classroom. In the farther ranges of public space—25 feet and beyond—two-way communication is almost impossible. In some cases, it's necessary for speakers to use public distance because of the size of their audience, but we can assume that anyone who voluntarily chooses to use it when he or she could be closer is not interested in having a dialogue.

Choosing the optimal distance can have a powerful effect on how we regard others and how we respond to them. For example, students are more satisfied with teachers who reduce the distance between themselves and their classes. They also are more satisfied with a course itself, and they are more likely to follow a teacher's instructions.[97] Likewise, medical patients are more satisfied with physicians who operate at the closer end of the social distance zone.[98]

Territoriality Whereas personal space is the invisible bubble we carry around as an extension of our physical being, **territory** remains stationary. Any geographical area such as a work area, room, house, or other physical space to which we assume some kind of "rights" is our territory. What's interesting about territoriality is that there is no real basis for the assumption of proprietary rights of "owning" many areas, but the feeling of ownership exists nonetheless. Your room at home probably feels like yours whether you're there or not, unlike personal space, which is carried around with you. In the same way, you may feel proprietary about the seat you always occupy in class, even though you have no illusions about owning that piece of furniture.

The way people use space can communicate a good deal about power and status.[99] Generally, we grant people with higher status more personal territory and greater privacy. We knock before entering the boss's office, whereas she can usually walk into our work area without hesitating. In traditional schools, professors have offices, dining rooms, and even toilets that are private, whereas students, who are presumably less important, have no such sanctuaries. Among the military, greater space and privacy usually come with rank: Privates sleep forty to a barrack, sergeants have their own private rooms, and generals have government-provided houses.

PHYSICAL ENVIRONMENT

Physical settings, architecture, and interior design affect our communication. The impressions that home designs communicate can be remarkably revealing. Researchers showed ninety-nine students slides of the insides or outsides of twelve upper-middle-class homes and then asked them to infer the personality of the owners from their impressions.[100] The students were especially accurate after glancing at interior photos. The decorating schemes communicated information about the homeowners' intellectualism, politeness, maturity, optimism, tenseness, willingness to take adventures, and family orientations. The home exteriors also gave viewers accurate perceptions of the owners' artistic interests, graciousness, privacy, and quietness.

Besides communicating information about the designer, an environment can shape the kind of interaction that takes place in it. In one experiment, subjects working in a "beautiful" room were more positive and energetic than those working in "average" or "ugly" spaces.[101] In another experiment, students perceived professors who occupied well-decorated offices as being more credible than those occupying less-attractive offices.[102] Doctors have shaped environments to improve the quality of interaction with their patients. Simply removing a doctor's desk makes patients feel almost five times more at ease during office visits.[103] In another study, redesigning a convalescent ward of a hospital greatly increased the interaction between patients. In the old design, seats were placed shoulder to shoulder around the edges of the ward. By grouping the seats around small tables so that patients faced each other at a comfortable distance, the amount of conversations doubled. And in office cubicles, occupants who face out (rather than in) send the message that they're open to communication—and it also allows them to better protect their work's confidentiality.[104]

TIME

Social scientists use the term **chronemics** to describe the study of how humans use and structure time. The way we handle time can express both intentional and unintentional messages.[105] For instance, sending a delayed response—or no response at all—to a work email can create the impression of untrustworthiness, especially from a subordinate or peer.[106]

In a culture that values time highly, waiting can be an indicator of status. "Important" people (whose time is supposedly more valuable than that of others) may be seen by appointment only, whereas it is acceptable to intrude without notice on lesser beings. A related rule is that low-status people must never make high-status people wait. It would be a serious mistake to show up late for a job interview, whereas the interviewer might keep you cooling your heels in the lobby. Important people are often whisked to the head of a restaurant or airport line, while presumably less-exalted masses are forced to wait their turn.

Time can be a marker not only of power and status but also of relationships. Research shows that the amount of time spent with a relational partner sends important messages about valuing that person.[107] In one study analyzing twenty nonverbal behaviors, "spending time together" was the most powerful predictor of both relational satisfaction and perceived interpersonal understanding.[108] Time is also measured and valued in mediated communication. Studies show that the length of time it takes for someone to respond to email messages or to postings in virtual groups has a strong correlation with perceptions of that person.[109] As you might guess, quick responses get positive appraisals, while tardy or neglected replies can have an adverse effect on trust and effectiveness in virtual groups.[110]

IN REAL LIFE

Recognizing Nonverbal Cues

You can appreciate how non-verbal cues reflect attitudes by reading the following transcript twice. The first time, imagine that Kim's non-verbal behavior signals that she is glad to meet Stacy and looking forward to getting to know Stacy better. For your second reading, imagine that Kim feels just the opposite: She is put off by Stacy and feels uncomfortable around her.

©Cengage Learning

Think about all the ways Kim's nonverbal behaviors might change, depending on her attitude toward Stacy. Even though she speaks the same words, imagine how her posture, gestures, facial expressions, voice, and use of distance might differ and how these nonverbal cues would reflect her feelings about her new neighbor.

Stacy: Hi. I'm new here. Just moved in to Unit 14 yesterday. My name's Stacy. (*Extends her hand, ready to shake*)

Kim: Hi! I'm Kim. I'm your next-door neighbor in number 12.

Stacy: Great! This looks like a nice place.

Kim: It is. Everybody's friendly, and we all get along really well.

Stacy: (*Glancing down at a magazine in Kim's mail*) Hmmm. *American Songwriter*. Are you a musician?

Kim: Yeah, I'm a singer-songwriter. Mostly acoustic. I play around town. Nothing too big yet, but I'm hoping . . .

Stacy: (*Excitedly*) Whoa! I'm a musician too!

Kim: Really!

Stacy: Yeah. I play rhythm guitar with The Festering Sores. Have you heard of us?

Kim: Yeah, I think so.

Stacy: Well, you'll have to come hear us some time. And maybe we could even jam together, since we're both guitarists.

Kim: That would be interesting!

Stacy: Wow! I can already tell I'm going to like it here. Hey . . . what's the attitude around here about pets?

Kim: They're pretty strict about the "No dogs or cats" policy.

Stacy: No problem! Jezebel isn't either.

Kim: Well, what is Jezebel?

Stacy: (*Proudly*) She's a green iguana. A real beauty.

Kim: You're kidding, right?

Stacy: Nope. You'll probably meet her one of these days. In fact, she's kind of a runaway, so you might find her in your place if you leave the door open. Especially when the weather cools down. (*Semi-kidding*) She really likes to snuggle up to a warm body.

Kim: Well, I'm more of a bird person, so . . .

Stacy: She makes friends with everybody. You'll love her!

Kim: Look, I've gotta run. I'm already late for a practice session.

Stacy: I'll see you around. Really glad we're gonna be neighbors!

Kim: Me too.

Communication Scenarios

To watch and analyze a video related to this feature and this topic, visit CengageBrain .com to access the Speech Communication CourseMate for Looking Out/Looking In.

SUMMARY

Nonverbal communication consists of messages expressed by nonlinguistic means such as body movement, vocal characteristics, touch, appearance, physical space, physical environment, and time.

Nonverbal skills are vital for competent communicators. Nonverbal communication is pervasive; in fact, it is impossible to not send nonverbal messages. Although many nonverbal behaviors are universal, their use is affected by both culture and gender. Most nonverbal communication reveals attitudes and feelings; in contrast, verbal communication is better suited to expressing ideas. Nonverbal communication serves many functions. It can repeat, complement, substitute for, accent, regulate, and contradict verbal communication. When presented with conflicting verbal and nonverbal messages, communicators are more likely to rely on the nonverbal ones. For this reason, nonverbal cues are important in detecting deception. It's necessary to exercise caution in interpreting such cues, however, because nonverbal communication is ambiguous.

KEY TERMS

accenting (191)
adaptors (200)
body orientation (198)
chronemics (210)
complementing (191)
contradicting (191)
emblems (200)
gestures (200)
haptics (205)
illustrators (200)
intimate distance (208)
kinesics (198)
leakage (192)
manipulators (200)
microexpression (202)

mixed message (191)
monochronic (197)
nonverbal communication (188)
paralanguage (202)
personal distance (208)
polychronic (197)
posture (198)
proxemics (208)
public distance (209)
regulating (191)
repeating (191)
social distance (209)
substituting (191)
territory (209)

ONLINE RESOURCES

Now that you have read this chapter, visit CengageBrain.com to access the Speech Communication CourseMate for *Looking Out/Looking In* for quick access to the electronic resources that accompany this text. Your CourseMate offers:

- **Study tools** that will help you assess your learning and prepare for exams (*digital glossary*, *key term flash cards*, *interactive quizzes*).
- **Activities and assignments** that will help you hone your knowledge, understand how theory and research applies to your own life (*Self-Assessment, Pause and Reflect*), consider ethical challenges in interpersonal communication (*Ethical Challenge*), and build your interpersonal communication skills throughout the course (*Skill Builder*). If requested, you can submit your answers to your instructor.
- **Media resources** that will allow you to watch and critique videos of interpersonal communication situations (*In Real Life, interpersonal video simulations, and interactive video activities*).
- In addition to interactive teaching and learning tools, CourseMate includes an **interactive eBook**. Take notes, highlight, search, and interact with embedded media specific to *Looking Out/Looking In*.

SEARCH TERMS

When searching online databases to research topics in this chapter, use the following terms (along with this chapter's key terms) to maximize the chances of finding useful information:

body language	personal space
eye contact	physical attractiveness
facial expression	vocalics
gaze	

FILM AND TELEVISION

You can see the communication principles described in this chapter portrayed in the following films and television programs.

READING NONVERBAL CUES
Downton Abbey (2011–) Rated TV-14

The television series *Downton Abbey* is set in early twentieth-century England. The show illustrates the historically British reservation at expressing emotions. As a result, viewers must watch closely for nonverbal cues—facial expressions, tone of voice, body language—to gauge how and what a character in the show is feeling.

Status differences in the show are easy to see. Members of the aristocratic Crawley family dress, sit, dine, and interact according to the rules of high society. The servants in the house are much less formal—unless they are in the presence of their employers. Immediately, their deportment changes. They are careful to stand at an appropriate distance, make limited eye contact, don serious faces, and act in deferential ways. It's likely that you could watch an episode of *Downton Abbey* with the audio off and know where each character stands in the household's social structure.

NONVERBAL IDENTITY MANAGEMENT
Hitch (2005) Rated PG
Crazy, Stupid Love (2011) Rated PG-13

Both films are about nonverbal makeovers. In *Hitch*, Alex "Hitch" Hitchens (Will Smith) is a New York "date doctor" who teaches men how to romance the women of their dreams. His latest client is Albert Brenneman (Kevin James), a nerdy accountant who needs to improve his style to win the affections of the wealthy and beautiful Allegra Cole (Amber Valletta). In *Crazy, Stupid Love*, Jacob Palmer (Ryan Gosling) offers similar advice to hapless Cal Weaver (Steve Carrell).

Both Hitchens and Palmer offer their protégés tips on nonverbal behaviors that will attract women, including how to walk, stand, and dance. Both of their own love lives demonstrate that romantic success depends on more than manipulating a few nonverbal cues.

DETECTING DECEPTION

Lie to Me (2009–2011) Rated TV-14

Dr. Cal Lightman (Tim Roth) is a deception-detection expert who studies facial expressions and involuntary body language to determine if someone is lying. His ability to spot and analyze deceivers is amazing—in fact, he seems to know more about the liars than they know about themselves.

Many of Lightman's conclusions are based on the studies of renowned social scientist Paul Ekman, who serves as a consultant for the show. Ekman's years of research offer compelling evidence that liars do indeed sometimes send unconscious nonverbal cues that "leak" how they really think and feel.

But some words of caution are in order for fans of the show. For starters, most of Lightman's conclusions come from analyzing slow-motion recordings—something few people have access to in their daily conversations. Second, many nonverbal cues have multiple meanings and are not necessarily indicators of deceit (just because liars often rub their eyes doesn't mean that an eye-rubber is telling a fib). Finally, Lightman (and Ekman) have far more training at analyzing nonverbal communication than the normal person. Their ability to detect deception is clearly the exception, not the norm.

Lie to Me should best be seen as an entertaining look at how social science gives experts some insights into detecting deceit. However, it would be unwise to use it as a layperson's guide for analyzing and judging the nonverbal behavior of friends and family. If you accuse someone of lying based on a few nonverbal cues, your chances of being right are only about 50 percent—and those aren't good odds when it could jeopardize a relationship.

Note: The website www.truthaboutdeception.com offers a thorough, current, scholarly, and easy-to-read review of issues related to deception and its detection.

APPEARANCE

What Not to Wear (2003–) Rated TV-PG

Does your style of dress affect how others perceive you? According to the television show *What Not to Wear*, the answer is a resounding yes. Hosts Stacy London and Clinton Kelly take poorly dressed "fashion victims" on a two-day shopping spree that is aimed at transforming the participants into well-dressed and groomed versions of their former selves. The show demonstrates how a change in appearance can make a difference both personally and professionally.

Besides illustrating the importance of nonverbal communication, most episodes demonstrate how attire is related to Chapter 3's discussion of identity and self-presentation. The participants often admit that they dress poorly because of a skewed self-concept or a lack of self-esteem. Adopting a new wardrobe typically changes how they think and feel about themselves, and the impression they make on others.

There's nothing academic about *What Not to Wear*, but the show offers a good example of how attire and grooming can play a key role in self-perception and relationships.

C H A P T E R   S I X

Nonverbal Communication: Messages beyond Words

CHAPTER OUTLINE

Use this outline to take notes as you read the chapter in the text and/or as your instructor lectures in class.

I. **CHARACTERISTICS OF NONVERBAL COMMUNICATION**

   A. **Nonverbal Skills Are Vital**

   B. **All Behavior Has Communicative Value**

     1. Deliberate

     2. Unintentional

   C. **Nonverbal Communication Is Primarily Relational**

     1. Managing identity

     2. Defining relationships

     3. Conveying emotion

   D. **Nonverbal Communication Serves Many Functions**

     1. Repeating

     2. Complementing

     3. Substituting

     4. Accenting

     5. Regulating

     6. Contradicting

   E. **Nonverbal Communication Offers**

Deception Clues

1. Leakage
2. Deception detection 101
   a. We are only accurate half the time
   b. We overestimate our ability to detect other's lies
   c. We have a strong tendency to judge other's messages as truthful

F. **Nonverbal Communication Is Ambiguous**

1. Silence
2. Sexual behavior
3. NVLD

II. **INFLUENCES ON NONVERBAL COMMUNICATION**

A. **Gender**
   1. Physical and social
   2. Cultural norms

B. **Culture**
   1. Sending nonverbal messages
   2. Interpreting nonverbal communication

III. **TYPES OF NONVERBAL COMMUNICATION**

A. **Body Movement**
   1. Body orientation
      a. Facing toward or away
      b. Signals interest or exclusion
   2. Posture
      a. Emotions
      b. Tension/relaxation
   3. Gestures
      a. Illustrators
      b. Emblems
      c. Adaptors (manipulators)

    4. Face and eyes

        a. Face: number, speed, microexpressions

        b. Eyes: involvement, attitude, dominance, interest

B. Voice (Paralanguage)

    1. Emphasis

    2. Tone, rate, pitch, volume, pauses (unintentional and vocalized)

    3. Sarcasm

    4. Credibility and liking

C. Touch (Haptics)

    1. Signals type of relationship

    2. Context matters: who, where, when

    3. Shapes responses: liking

    4. Essential to development and health

D. Appearance

    1. Physical attractiveness

    2. Clothing

E. Physical Space (Proxemics)

    1. Distance

        a. Intimate

        b. Personal

        c. Social

        d. Public

    2. Territoriality

F. Physical Environment

    1. Architecture and design

    2. Shaping interactions

G. Time (Chronemics)

    1. Status

    2. Culture: monochronic/polychronic

KEY TERMS

accenting

adaptors

body orientation

chronemics

complementing

contradicting

emblems

gestures

haptics

illustrators

intimate distance

kinesics

leakage

manipulators

microexpression

mixed message

monochronic

nonverbal communication

paralanguage

personal distance

polychronic

posture

proxemics

public distance

regulating

repeating

social distance

substituting

territory

ACTIVITIES

6.1 DESCRIBING NONVERBAL STATES

LEARNING OBJECTIVES

- Explain the defining characteristics of nonverbal communication as described in this chapter.
- List and offer examples of each type of nonverbal message introduced in this chapter.
- Share appropriately your interpretation of another's nonverbal behavior with that person.

INSTRUCTIONS

1. For each of the statements below, record the nonverbal behaviors that reflect the attitude or emotions described.
2. Compare your responses with those of others in the class and note the similarities and differences in your responses.
3. For each item, describe as many types of nonverbal behavior as you can: body movement (orientation, posture, gestures, face/eyes), voice, touch, appearance, physical space, physical environment, time.

EXAMPLE 1

He says I'm too eager to please.
I respond quickly after a request. I lean toward the person a lot. I smile and keep the smile on my face continuously. I gesture quickly. I stand a bit bowed over. I tilt my head to the side submissively.

EXAMPLE 2

She listens well.
Turns body toward me, leans forward, smiles once or twice, nods, maintains eye contact about 80 percent of the time.

1. My boss is mean.

_____

_____

2. My coworkers say I don't treat them well.

_____

_____

3. He's not into this project.

_____

_____

4. She can't stop flirting.

_____

_____

5. They tell me I'm too tense.

_____

_____

6. She acts like she's in charge.

_____

_____

7. He makes a big deal of everything.

_____

_____

8. You need to act more sure of yourself.

_____

_____

9. He seems friendly.

_____

_____

10. You're not exactly a ray of sunshine.

_____

_____

11. They tell me I'm too aggressive.

_____

_____

12. She's "hyper."

_____

_____

List how at least two of the preceding statements could be taken in both positive and negative ways (*e.g., number 6 could be positive if you are grateful that she's organizing things, but negative if you're resentful of her influence*).

_____

_____

_____

List the nonverbal behaviors that are associated with the alternate interpretation (the one you didn't record initially) and your reaction (*e.g., I can see the positive side of taking charge — assigning seating, standing erect, firm voice, keeping to a time schedule, nodding and making eye contact with those who should speak to you. There's often a small difference between the nonverbal behaviors I find positive and those I find annoying or bossy*).

_____

_____

_____

6.2 DESCRIBING NONVERBAL BEHAVIORS

LEARNING OBJECTIVES

- Explain the defining characteristics of nonverbal communication as described in the text.
- In a given situation, recognize your own nonverbal behavior and its relational significance.
- Monitor and manage your nonverbal cues in ways that achieve your goals.

INSTRUCTIONS

1. For each of the social situations below, list the nonverbal behaviors you believe will achieve the stated goal.
2. Compare your answers with those of others in your class.
3. Reflect on the behavior of yourself and others important to you. How might you change some of the nonverbal cues you display to communicate what you desire more effectively?
4. Use as many categories of nonverbal behavior as you can: body movement (orientation, posture, gestures, face/eyes), voice, touch, appearance, physical space, physical environment, time.

EXAMPLE

Initiate conversation with a stranger at a party.

Make eye contact, offer hand in greeting, smile, come within 4 feet of other person, turn body toward other person, nod occasionally when other is talking.

1. Take control or exercise leadership in a class group.

_____

_____

2. Come across well in a job interview.

_____

_____

3. Tell an interesting joke or story.

_____

_____

4. Appear friendly and warm without "coming on too strong."

_____

_____

5. Signal your desire to leave a conversation when the other person keeps on talking.

_____

_____

6. Appear confident when asking boss for a raise.

_____

_____

7. Appear interested in class lecture.

_____

_____

8. Avoid talking with a person on a plane or bus.

_____

_____

9. Show kindness toward an elderly relative.

_____

_____

10. Appear concerned about a friend's dilemma.

_____

_____

Class _____   Name_____

11. Describe two of your usual nonverbal behaviors in a particular context that you might want to change.

_____

_____

_____

_____

_____

12. Why might you want to change them?

_____

_____

_____

_____

_____

6.3 AMBIGUITY, CONTRADICTION, AND CONGRUENCE

LEARNING OBJECTIVES

- In a given situation, recognize your own nonverbal behavior and its relational significance.
- Monitor and manage your nonverbal cues in ways that achieve your goals.

INSTRUCTIONS

1. In each of the following situations, describe verbal and nonverbal behaviors likely to occur: body movement (orientation, posture, gestures, face/eyes), voice, touch, appearance, physical space, physical environment, time. Nonverbal behaviors seldom occur alone, so describe clusters of at least three nonverbal behaviors for each situation. Note whether the verbal and nonverbal behaviors are ambiguous, contradictory, or congruent. Finally, evaluate the possible consequences of the ambiguity, contradictions, or congruency.
2. Next, describe situations from your own life and how you would send verbal and nonverbal messages. Include the possible consequences of your congruent or ambiguous behaviors.
3. After you've completed the examples, answer the questions about congruency/ambiguity.

SITUATION	YOUR VERBAL BEHAVIOR	YOUR NONVERBAL BEHAVIOR (USE A CLUSTER OF BEHAVIORS HERE)	ARE BEHAVIORS CONTRADICTORY, AMBIGUOUS, OR CONGRUENT?	POSSIBLE CONSEQUENCES
EXAMPLE Person I like a lot takes me out to dinner and I have a good time and enjoy the food.	"I'm really enjoying this; the food is terrific and so is the company."	I look at my partner when I talk, smiling and tilting my head, and leaning slightly forward. I touch my partner lightly on the arm and hand.	My verbal and nonverbal behaviors are congruent, not ambiguous.	I hope my partner will understand how much I care and enjoy our time together. I run the risk of being hurt if my partner's feelings don't match mine, but I'm willing to take that risk.

Class _____   Name_____

SITUATION	YOUR VERBAL BEHAVIOR	YOUR NONVERBAL BEHAVIOR (USE A <u>CLUSTER</u> OF BEHAVIORS HERE)	ARE BEHAVIORS CONTRADICTORY, AMBIGUOUS, OR CONGRUENT?	POSSIBLE CONSEQUENCES
1. My boss asks me to work late when I've made other plans.				
2. My roommate asks, while I'm doing homework, if I can make dinner.				
3. My relative drops in to visit me when other people are over for the evening.				
4. My romantic partner says I act like I'm indifferent when we discuss our future.				
5. Our waiter starts to take my plate and asks if I'm finished while food is still on my plate.				

Class _____   Name_____

SITUATION	YOUR VERBAL BEHAVIOR	YOUR NONVERBAL BEHAVIOR (USE A CLUSTER OF BEHAVIORS HERE)	ARE BEHAVIORS CONTRADICTORY, AMBIGUOUS, OR CONGRUENT?	POSSIBLE CONSEQUENCES
6. (Your example)				
7. (Your example)				
8. (Your example)				

REFLECTIONS

1. Are there situations in which it is advantageous to express yourself ambiguously? Explain how sending one message verbally and another one nonverbally could be beneficial or explain why you believe it never is advantageous.

_____

_____

_____

_____

2. Describe situations in which ambiguity clearly is not desirable. Describe how you could best match your verbal and nonverbal behaviors in these situations.

_____

_____

_____

_____

_____

3. What are the ethical considerations of nonverbal ambiguity or contradiction? Is it ever ethical to intentionally be ambiguous or contradictory? Why or why not? Can you think of situations in which it is never or ever ethical to intentionally send ambiguous or contradictory nonverbal messages?

_____

_____

_____

_____

4. Are there situations in which nonverbal ambiguity or contradiction is unintentional and unavoidable? Explain your answer

_____

_____

_____

_____

6.4 NONVERBAL ANALYSIS

LEARNING OBJECTIVES

- Explain the defining characteristics of nonverbal communication as described in the text.

- Share appropriately your interpretation of another's nonverbal behavior with that person.

INSTRUCTIONS

Use the case below and the discussion questions that follow to discuss the variety of communication issues involved in effective communication. Make notes on this page, add other pages on your own, or prepare a group report/analysis based on your discussion. Add your own experiences to individualize the analysis.

CASE

Malena and Dolly are coworkers in different departments in a large company. Over coffee one day Malena tells Dolly that she's been feeling very uneasy lately about her boss's behavior. "I'm not exactly sure how to describe it," Malena says, "but I think he's coming on to me, and I don't know what to do."

1. Malena would do well to be able to describe her boss's behavior. Imagine a situation like this and describe the possible behavior of Malena's boss.

   _____

   _____

2. Which of the behaviors listed in question 1 might be intentional and which might be unintentional? Why?

   _____

   _____

3. Describe possible intentional or unintentional nonverbal behaviors of Malena that might be misunderstood.

   _____

   _____

4.   Using ideas from this and the previous chapters in the text, what could Malena do verbally and nonverbally to handle this issue?

_____

_____

_____

_____

Class _____   Name_____

6.5 ASSESSING NONVERBAL BEHAVIOR

LEARNING OBJECTIVES

- List and offer examples of each type of nonverbal message introduced in this chapter.

INSTRUCTIONS

Watch a scene in a movie or TV show on mute. Evaluate how the actor/actress uses nonverbal behavior to convey an emotion. Record your descriptions in the spaces below.

Scene 1 _____

Emotion being conveyed _____

Body movement _____

Posture _____

Gestures _____

Face and eyes _____

Appearance _____

Scene 2 _____

Emotion being conveyed _____

Body movement _____

Posture _____

Class _____   Name_____

Gestures _____

Face and eyes _____

Appearance _____

STUDY GUIDE

CHECK YOUR UNDERSTANDING

TRUE/FALSE

Mark the statements below as true or false. Correct statements that are false on the lines below to create a true statement.

_____   1. Nonverbal behaviors are, by their nature, intentional.

_____

_____   2. Nonverbal communication encompasses abstract factors such as physical appearance, the environment in which we communicate, and the way we use time.

_____

_____   3. The concept of nonverbal convergence illustrates that skilled communicators can adapt their behavior when interacting with members of other cultures or co-cultures in order to make the exchange more effective.

_____

_____   4. Nonverbal communication is much better suited to expressing attitudes and feelings than it is to expressing concrete ideas.

_____

_____   5. Research on nonverbal communication and lying shows that individuals who are trying to deceive others are less likely to show nonverbal evidence of lying if they haven't had a chance to rehearse their lying and when they feel strongly about the information being hidden.

_____

_____   6. In studies of detecting lying, men are consistently more accurate than women at detecting the lies and discovering the underlying truth.

_____

_____   7. Pupil dilation is less reliable than facial expressions in picking up on deception clues.

_____

_____   8. Unlike verbal communication that is intermittent (starts and stops), nonverbal communication is continuous and never ending.

_____

_____   9. The nonverbal impact of messages is more powerful than the verbal impact.
            _____

_____   10. Nonverbal communication is clearer than verbal communication.
            _____

_____   11. The concept of leakage is most often associated with deception.
            _____

_____   12. We are accurate in detecting deception only slightly more than half the time.
            _____

_____   13. Behaviors that have one meaning for members of the same culture or co-culture
               can be interpreted differently by members of another group.
            _____

_____   14. Women are more likely to believe the deception of an intimate partner than are
               men.
            _____

_____   15. When you use nonverbal behavior to regulate other's behavior, it guarantees that
               the other will pay attention to, interpret, or respond as you intended.
            _____

COMPLETION

Fill in the blanks below with the correct terms chosen from the list below.

illustrator	intimate	personal	social	body orientation
relaxation	paralanguage	emblem	adaptor	touch
public	text-based messages			

1. _____ is the distance zone identified by Hall that ranges from 4 to about
    12 feet; within it are the kinds of communication that usually occur in business.

2. _____ is a postural cue such as leaning back or lowering shoulders that a
    higher status person usually exhibits when not feeling threatened.

3. _____ is a deliberate, nonverbal behavior that has a very precise
    meaning known to virtually everyone within a cultural group.

4. _____ is the distance zone identified by Hall that ranges from 18 inches
    to 4 feet and includes behavior found in most social conversations.

5. _____ is a gesture that accompanies speech but doesn't stand on its own.

6. _____ is the degree to which we face toward or away from someone with our body, feet, and head.

7. _____ is the distance zone identified by Hall that ranges from skin contact to about 18 inches; we usually use this distance with people in private who are emotionally very close to us.

8. _____ is the distance zone identified by Hall that ranges from 12 feet outward and includes communication such as that found in a typical classroom.

9. _____ is nonverbal behavior that includes having a foreign accent.

10. _____ is nonverbal behavior that includes brushing up against someone.

11. _____ is an unconscious body movement that helps us adjust to the environment.

12. _____ can use linguistic shortcuts and acronyms to indicate nonverbal messages.

MULTIPLE CHOICE

Choose the letter of the type of nonverbal communication that is illustrated below.

a. environnent   b. paralinguistics   c. proxemics   d. territoriality

_____   1. No one dared to sit in Ralph's chair.

_____   2. Jeremy put a "NO ENTRANCE" sign on his door.

_____   3. The students rearranged the chairs in the classroom.

_____   4. Manuela stepped back 3 feet from her friend.

_____   5. The lovers were sitting only inches apart.

_____   6. Rob's voice softened when he spoke to her.

_____   7. There was a long pause after the decision was made.

_____   8. Mitchell sighed audibly.

_____   9. Gretchen took the third seat down from Yayoi.

_____   10. Kevin was annoyed that someone was leaning on his car.

a. body orientation   b. gesture   c. touch   d. face and eyes

_____   11.   The children playfully kicked one another.

_____   12.   Professor Jimenez illustrated her lecture with many arm movements.

_____   13.   Leland shifted his shoulders toward the speaker.

_____   14.   Ernie avoided looking at her.

_____   15.   The executive stared at her employee.

_____   16.   Martin turned his body away from his brother.

_____   17.   The officer pointed in the correct direction.

_____   18.   Letoya didn't appreciate the slap on the back.

_____   19.   Blake set his jaw in disgust.

_____   20.   Francesca signaled "OK" across the room.

Choose the best answer for each of the statements below:

_____   21.   Paralanguage describes
           a. nonverbal, silent messages.
           b. vocal messages.
           c. verbal messages.
           d. nonverbal, vocal messages.

_____   22.   According to researchers women tend to
           a. smile less than men.
           b. use more facial expressions.
           c. use less facial expressions.
           d. are less vocally expressive than men.

_____   23.   Deceivers try to maintain a
           a. poker face when communicating.
           b. blank face when communicating.
           c. plain face when communicating.
           d. pleasant face when communicating.

_____   24.   Touch can
           a. increase liking.
           b. increase compliance.
           c. both a and b
           d. none of the above

CHAPTER SIX STUDY GUIDE ANSWERS

TRUE/FALSE

1. F	4. T	7. F	10. F	13. T
2. T	5. F	8. T	11. T	14. T
3. T	6. F	9. T	12. T	15. F

COMPLETION

1. social	5. illustrator	9. paralanguage
2. relaxation	6. body orientation	10. touch
3. emblem	7. intimate	11. adaptor
4. personal	8. public	12. text-based messages

MULTIPLE CHOICE

1. d	5. c	9. c	13. a	17. b	21. d
2. d	6. b	10. d	14. d	18. c	22. b
3. a	7. b	11. c	15. d	19. d	23. a
4. c	8. b	12. b	16. a	20. b	24. c

Listening: More Than Meets the Ear

After studying the topics in this chapter, you should be able to:

1. Identify the situations in which you listen mindfully and those when you listen mindlessly and then evaluate the appropriateness of each style in a given situation.

2. Identify the circumstances in which you listen ineffectively and the poor listening habits you use in these circumstances.

3. Identify the response styles you commonly use when listening to others.

4. Demonstrate a combination of listening styles you could use to respond effectively in a given situation.

I have just

wandered back

into our conversation

and find

that you

are still

rattling on

about something

or other

i think i must

have been gone

at least

twenty minutes

and you

never missed me

now this might say

something

about my acting ability

or it might say

something about

your sensitivity

one thing

troubles me tho

when it

is my turn

to rattle on

for twenty minutes

which I

have been known to do

have you

been missing too.

Ric Masten

Nancy Louie/iStockphoto

Ric Masten's poem on this page shows there's more to listening than gazing politely at a speaker and nodding your head. As you will soon learn, listening is a demanding and complex activity—and just as important as speaking in the communication process.

If we use frequency as a measure, then listening easily qualifies as the most important kind of communication. We spend more time listening to others than in any other type of communication. One study (summarized in Figure 7.1) revealed that college students spend about 11 percent of their communicating time writing, 16 percent speaking, and 17 percent reading—but more than 55 percent listening.[1] On the job, listening is just as important. Studies show that most employees of major corporations in North America spend about 60 percent of each workday listening to others.[2]

Besides being the most frequent form of communication, listening is at least as important as speaking in terms of making relationships work. In committed relationships, listening to personal information in everyday conversations is considered a vital ingredient of satisfaction.[3] In one survey, marital counselors identified "failing to take the other's

11.4% Writing

16.1% Speaking

17.1% Reading

27.9% Media listening

27.5% Interpersonal listening

FIGURE 7.1 **Time Devoted to Communication Activities**
© Cengage Learning

perspective when listening" as one of the most frequent communication problems in the couples with whom they worked.[4] When a group of adults was asked what communication skills were most important in family and social settings, listening was ranked first.[5]

The *International Journal of Listening* devoted an entire issue to exploring various contexts in which listening skills are crucial, including education,[6] healthcare,[7] religion,[8] and the business world.[9] The On the Job box on page 220 explores in detail the vital role listening plays in the workplace.

This chapter will explore the nature of listening. After defining listening, we will examine the elements that make up the listening process and look at challenges that come with becoming a better listener. Finally, you will read about a variety of listening response styles that you can use to better understand and even help others.

Listening Defined

So far we've used the term *listening* as if it needs no explanation. Actually, there's more to this concept than you might think. We will define **listening**—at least the interpersonal type—as the process of making sense of others' spoken messages. Because listening is a response to speech, there's obviously a nonverbal dimension as well. As you read in Chapter 6, the way a statement is expressed can affect its meaning. So a good listener pays attention to paralanguage, facial expression, and a host of other nonverbal cues. We'll focus now on explaining what is—and isn't—involved in receiving and responding to others' messages.

HEARING VERSUS LISTENING

People often think of hearing and listening as the same thing, but they are quite different. *Hearing* is the process in which sound waves strike the eardrum and cause vibrations that are transmitted to the brain. (You'll read more about hearing in the following section.) *Listening* occurs when the brain reconstructs these electrochemical impulses into a representation of the original sound and then gives them meaning. Barring illness, injury, or cotton plugs, you can't stop hearing.[10] Your ears will pick up sound waves and transmit them to your brain whether you want them to or not.

Listening, however, isn't automatic. As the cartoon on page 221 shows, people hear all the time without listening. Sometimes we automatically and unconsciously block out irritating sounds, such as a neighbor's lawnmower or the roar of nearby traffic. We also stop listening when we find a subject unimportant or uninteresting. Boring stories, TV commercials, and nagging complaints are common examples of messages we may hear but tune out.

MINDLESS LISTENING

When we move beyond hearing and start to listen, researchers note that we process information in two very different ways—sometimes referred to as the *dual-process theory*.[11] Social scientists use the terms *mindless* and *mindful* to describe these different ways of listening.[12] **Mindless listening** occurs when we react to others' messages automatically and routinely, without much mental investment. Words such as *superficial* and *cursory* describe mindless listening better than terms like *ponder* and *contemplate*.

While the term *mindless* may sound negative, this sort of low-level information processing is a potentially valuable type of communication because it frees us to focus our minds on messages that require our careful attention.[13] Given the number of messages to which we're exposed, it's impractical to listen carefully and thoughtfully 100 percent of the time. It's also unrealistic to devote your attention to long-winded stories, idle

ON THE JOB

Listening in the Workplace

Being an effective speaker is important in career success, but good listening skills are just as vital. A study examining the link between listening and career success revealed that better listeners rose to higher levels in their organizations.[a] When human resource executives across the country were asked to identify skills of the ideal manager, the ability to listen effectively ranked at the top of the list.[b] In problem-solving groups, effective listeners are judged as having the most leadership skills.[c]

Listening is just as important in careers that involve cold facts as in ones that involve lots of one-on-one interaction. For example, a survey of more than 90,000 accountants identified effective listening as the most important communication skill for professionals entering that field.[d] When a diverse group of senior executives was asked what skills are most important on the job, listening was identified more often than any other skill, including technical competence, computer knowledge, creativity, and administrative talent.[e]

Just because businesspeople believe listening is important doesn't mean they do it well. A survey in which 144 managers were asked to rate their listening skills illustrates this point. Astonishingly, not one of the managers described himself or herself as a "poor" or "very poor" listener, whereas 94 percent rated themselves as "good" or "very good."[f] The favorable self-ratings contrasted sharply with the perceptions of the managers' subordinates, many of whom said their bosses' listening skills were weak. Of course, managers aren't the only people whose listening needs work—all of us could stand to improve our skills.

chatter, or remarks you've heard many times before. The only realistic way to manage the onslaught of messages is to be "lazy" toward many of them. In situations like these, we forgo careful analysis and fall back on the schemas—and sometimes the stereotypes—described in Chapter 3 to make sense of a message. If you stop right now and recall the messages you have heard today, it's likely that you processed most of them mindlessly.

MINDFUL LISTENING

By contrast, **mindful listening** involves giving careful and thoughtful attention and responses to the messages we receive. You tend to listen mindfully when a message is important to you and also when someone you care about is speaking about a matter that is important to him or her. Think of how your ears perk up when someone starts talking about your money ("The repairs will cost me how much?") or how you tune in carefully when a close friend tells you about the loss of a loved one. In situations like these, you want to give the message sender your complete and undivided attention.

Sometimes we respond mindlessly to information that deserves—and even demands—our mindful attention. Ellen Langer's determination to study mindfulness began when her grandmother complained about headaches coming from a "snake crawling around" beneath her skull. The doctors quickly diagnosed the problem as senility—after all, they reasoned, senility comes with old age and makes people talk nonsense. In fact, the grandmother had a brain tumor that eventually took her life. The event made a deep impression on Langer:

> For years afterward I kept thinking about the doctors' reactions to my grandmother's complaints, and about our reactions to the doctors. They went through the motions of diagnosis, but were not open to what they were hearing. Mindsets about senility interfered. We did not question the doctors; mindsets about experts interfered.[14]

Most of our daily decisions about whether to listen mindfully don't have life-and-death consequences, but the point should be clear: There are times when we need to consciously and carefully listen to what others are telling us. That kind of mindful listening will be the focus of the remainder of this chapter.

Elements in the Listening Process

By now, you can begin to see that there is more to listening than sitting quietly while another person speaks. In truth, listening is a process that consists of five elements: hearing, attending, understanding, responding, and remembering.[15]

HEARING

As we have already discussed, **hearing** is the physiological dimension of listening. It occurs when sound waves strike the ear at a certain frequency and loudness. Hearing is influenced by a variety of factors, including background noise. If there are other loud noises, especially at the same frequency as the message we are trying to hear, we find it difficult to sort out the important signals from the background. Hearing is also affected by auditory fatigue, a temporary loss of hearing caused by continuous exposure to the same tone or loudness. If you spend an evening at a loud party, you may have trouble hearing well, even after getting away from the crowd. If you are exposed to loud noise often enough, permanent hearing loss can result—as many rock musicians and fans can attest.

For many communicators, the challenge of hearing is even more difficult as a result of physiological problems. In the United States alone, more than 31 million people communicate with some degree of hearing loss.[16] One study revealed that, on any given day, one-fourth to one-third of the children in a typical classroom do not hear normally.[17] As a competent communicator, you need to recognize when you may be speaking to someone with a hearing loss and adjust your approach accordingly.

ATTENDING

Whereas hearing is a physiological process, **attending** is a psychological one and is part of the process of selection described in Chapter 3. We would go crazy if we attended to every sound we hear, so we filter out some messages and focus on others. Needs, wants, desires, and interests determine what is attended to. It is not surprising that research shows we attend most carefully to messages when there's a payoff for doing so.[18] If you're planning to see a movie, you'll listen to a friend's description more carefully than you would have otherwise. And when you want to get better acquainted with others, you'll pay careful attention to almost anything they say in hopes of improving the relationship.

It is surprising, though, that attending helps more than the listener: It also helps the message sender. Participants in one study viewed brief movie segments and then described them to listeners who varied in their degree of attentiveness to the speakers. Later on, the researchers tested the speakers' long-term recall of details from the movie segments. Those who had recounted the movie to attentive listeners remembered more details of the film.[19]

Masterfile

UNDERSTANDING

Understanding occurs when we make sense of a message. It is possible to hear and attend to a message without understanding it at all. And, of course, it's possible to misunderstand a message. Communication researchers use the term **listening fidelity** to describe the degree of congruence between what a listener understands and what the message sender was attempting to communicate.[20] This chapter describes the many reasons why we misunderstand others—and why they misunderstand us. It also outlines skills that will help you improve your understanding of others.

RESPONDING

Responding to a message consists of giving observable feedback to the speaker. Although listeners don't always respond visibly to a speaker, research suggests they should do so more often. One study of 195 critical incidents in banking and medical settings showed that a major difference between effective and ineffective listening was the kind of feedback offered.[21] Good listeners show they are attentive by nonverbal behaviors such as keeping eye contact and reacting with appropriate facial expressions—which was of particular importance to children in one study who were asked to evaluate "good" versus "bad" listeners.[22] Verbal behavior—answering questions and exchanging ideas, for example—also demonstrates attention. It's easy to imagine how other responses would signal less-effective listening. A slumped posture, bored expression, and yawning send a clear message that you are not tuned in to the speaker.

Adding responsiveness to our listening model demonstrates a fact that we discussed in Chapter 1: Communication is *transactional* in nature. Listening isn't just a passive activity. As listeners, we are active participants in a communication transaction. At the same time that we receive messages, we also send them. Responding is such an integral part of good listening that we'll devote an entire section to listening responses in the second half of this chapter.

REMEMBERING

Remembering is the ability to recall information. If we don't remember a message, listening is hardly worth the effort. Research suggests that most people remember only about 50 percent of what they hear immediately after hearing it.[23] Within 8 hours, the 50 percent remembered drops to about 35 percent. After two months, the average recall is only about 25 percent of the original message. Given the amount of information we process every day—from teachers, friends, the radio, TV, cell phones, and other sources—the residual message (what we remember) is a small fraction of what we hear. You can begin to get a sense of how tough it is to listen effectively by trying the exercise on the next page.

LOOKING AT DIVERSITY

Austin Lee: Culture and Listening Responses

Seungcheol Austin Lee

As a researcher who also teaches courses in intercultural communication, I pay close attention to the impact of culture on interpersonal interaction. It's easy to see how culture affects factors such as nonverbal cues and language style. It's not quite as simple to see the role culture plays in people's listening styles. Over the years, however, I've made a few observations.

I was born and raised in South Korea, where power distance is an important ingredient in communication patterns. People in roles of authority—parents, teachers, employers—are treated with great respect and deference. This affects listening styles—and more particularly, listening responses. A person with low power will usually listen silently to a person in authority. To ask questions or offer suggestions might be perceived as an inappropriate challenge. On the other hand, people in high power positions are likely to offer listening responses such as analyzing, advising, and judging. In fact, they would probably view such responses as their obligation.

When I came to the United States as a graduate student, I learned that remaining silent during conversations can create the wrong impression. Some of my professors thought I was passive and uninterested because I was listening silently when I was trying to show respect. They expected me to offer suggestions and feedback. This wasn't easy as it contradicted deep-rooted norms of my culture.

Another cultural difference I have noticed is about interruptions. When I stumble with words, Americans are less likely to help me out by suggesting the word or phrase that I'm searching for, while Koreans are willing to jump in and fill in the blanks, and even complete the sentence for me. In American culture, interruptions may be perceived as an attempt to take over the floor. But in a collectivistic society like Korea, people show their connectedness with good-natured interruptions to help the conversation flow. But again, this only happens when talking to peers or subordinates. Most Koreans wouldn't dare interrupt when a higher-up is talking.

"Culture and Listening Responses" by Austin Lee. Used with permission of author.

PAUSE AND REFLECT

LISTENING BREAKDOWNS

You can overcome believing in some common myths about listening by recalling specific instances when:

1. You heard another person's message but did not attend to it.
2. You attended to a message but forgot it almost immediately.
3. You attended to and remembered a message but did not understand it accurately.
4. You understood a message but did not respond sufficiently to convey your understanding to the sender.
5. You failed to remember some or all of an important message.

 You can complete this activity by visiting CengageBrain.com to access the Speech Communication CourseMate for *Looking Out/ Looking In*, and, if requested, email your responses to your instructor.

The Challenge of Listening

It's easy to acknowledge that listening is important and to describe the steps in the listening process. What's difficult is to actually become a better listener. This section will describe the challenges that listeners must face and overcome to become more effective communicators. We'll look at various types of ineffective listening, then we'll explore the many reasons we don't listen better. As you read this material, think to yourself, "How many of these describe *me*?" The first step to becoming a better listener is to recognize areas that need improvement.

TYPES OF INEFFECTIVE LISTENING

Your own experience will probably confirm the fact that poor listening is all too common. Although a certain amount of ineffective listening is inescapable and sometimes even understandable, it's important to be aware of these types of problems so you can avoid them when listening well really counts.

Pseudolistening Whereas mindless listening may be a private matter, **pseudolistening** is an imitation of the real thing—an act put on to fool the speaker. Pseudolisteners give the appearance of being attentive: They look you in the eye; they may even nod and smile. But the show of attention is a polite façade because their minds are somewhere else. Paradoxically, pseudolistening can take more effort than simply tuning out the other person.

Stage-Hogging Stage-hogs (sometimes called *conversational narcissists*) try to turn the topic of conversations to themselves instead of showing interest in the speaker.[24] One **stage-hogging** strategy is a *shift-response*—changing the focus of the conversation from the speaker to the narcissist: "You think your math class is tough? You ought to try my physics class!" Interruptions are another hallmark of stage-hogging. Besides preventing the listener from learning potentially valuable information, they can damage the relationship between the interrupter and the speaker. For example, applicants who interrupt the questions of employment interviewers are likely to be rated less favorably than applicants who wait until the interviewer has finished speaking before they respond.[25]

Selective Listening Selective listeners respond only to the parts of your remarks that interest them, rejecting everything else. Sometimes **selective listening** is legitimate, as when we screen out radio commercials and music and keep an ear cocked for a weather report or an announcement of the time. Selective listening is less appropriate in personal settings when obvious inattention can be a slap in the face to the other person. Consider how you feel when listeners perk up only when the topic relates to them.

Insulated Listening Insulated listeners are almost the opposite of their selective cousins just described. Instead of looking for specific information, these people avoid it. Whenever a topic arises that they'd rather not deal with, those who use **insulated listening** simply fail to hear or acknowledge it. You remind them about a problem, and they'll nod or answer you—and then promptly ignore or forget what you've just said.

Defensive Listening Defensive listeners take others' remarks as personal attacks. The teenager who perceives her parents' questions about her friends and activities as distrustful snooping uses **defensive listening**, as do touchy parents who view any questioning by their children as a threat to their authority and parental wisdom.

Ambushing Ambushers listen carefully to you, but only because they're collecting information that they'll use to attack what you say. The technique of a cross-examining prosecution attorney is a good example of **ambushing**. Needless to say, using this kind of strategy will justifiably initiate defensiveness in the other person.

Insensitive Listening Those who use **insensitive listening** respond to the superficial content in a message but miss the more important emotional information that may not be expressed directly. "How's it going?" an insensitive listener might ask. When you reply by saying "Oh, okay I guess" in a dejected tone, he or she responds "Well, great!" Insensitive listeners tend to ignore the nonverbal cues described in Chapter 6 and lack the empathy described in Chapter 3.

WHY WE DON'T LISTEN BETTER

After thinking about the styles of ineffective listening described previously, most people begin to see that they listen carefully only a small percentage of the time. Sad as it may be, it's impossible to listen well *all* of the time for several reasons that we'll outline here.

Message Overload It's especially difficult to focus on messages—even important ones—when you are bombarded by information. Face-to-face messages come from friends, family, work, and school. Personal media—text messages, phone calls, emails, and instant messages—demand your attention. Along with these personal channels, we are awash in messages from mass media. This deluge of communication has made the challenge of attending tougher than at any time in human history.[26]

Preoccupation Another reason we don't always listen carefully is that we're often wrapped up in personal concerns that seem more important than the messages that others are sending. It's difficult to pay attention to someone else when you're worrying about an upcoming exam or thinking about the great time you plan to have over the next weekend.

Rapid Thought Listening carefully is also difficult for a physiological reason. Although we're capable of understanding speech at rates of 600 words per minute, the average person only speaks between 100 and 150 words per minute.[27] Thus, we have mental "spare time" while someone is talking. The temptation is to use this time in ways that don't relate to the speaker's ideas: thinking about personal interests, daydreaming, planning a rebuttal, and so on. The trick is to use this spare time to understand the speaker's ideas better rather than to let your attention wander.

Effort Listening effectively is hard work. The physical changes that occur during careful listening show the effort it takes: The heart rate quickens, respiration increases, and body temperature rises.[28] Notice that these changes are similar to the body's reaction to physical

In *The Devil Wears Prada*, the domineering boss Miranda Priestly (Meryl Streep) is a model of ineffective listening. (See the film summary at the end of this chapter.)

20TH CENTURY FOX/THE KOBAL COLLECTION/LACOMBE, BRIGITTE

Christina Kennedy/Pixland/Jupiter Images

effort. This is no coincidence: Listening carefully to a speaker can be just as taxing as a workout—which is why some people choose not to make the effort.[29] If you've come home exhausted after an evening of listening intently to a friend in need, you know how draining the process can be.

External Noise The physical world in which we live often presents distractions that make it difficult to pay attention to others. Consider, for example, how the efficiency of your listening decreases when you are seated in a crowded, hot, stuffy room surrounded by others talking next to you and traffic noises outside. It's not surprising that noisy classrooms often make learning difficult for students.[30] In such circumstances, even the best intentions aren't enough to ensure clear understanding.

Faulty Assumptions We often make faulty assumptions that lead us to believe we're listening attentively when quite the opposite is true. When the subject is a familiar one, it's easy to tune out because you think you've heard it all before. A related problem arises when you assume that a speaker's thoughts are too simple or too obvious to deserve careful attention when, in fact, they do. At other times just the opposite occurs: You think that another's comments are too complex to be understood (as in some lectures), so you give up trying to make sense of them.

Lack of Apparent Advantages It often seems that there's more to gain by speaking than by listening. When business consultant Nancy Kline asked some of her clients why they interrupted their colleagues, these are the reasons she heard:

> My idea is better than theirs.
>
> If I don't interrupt them, I'll never get to say my idea.
>
> I know what they are about to say.
>
> They don't need to finish their thoughts since mine are better.
>
> Nothing about their idea will improve with further development.
>
> It is more important for me to get recognized than it is to hear their idea.
>
> I am more important than they are.[31]

Even if some of these thoughts are true, the egotism behind them is stunning. Furthermore, nonlisteners are likely to find that the people they cut off are less likely to treat their ideas with respect. Like defensiveness, listening is often reciprocal. You get what you give.

Lack of Training Even if we want to listen well, we're often hampered by a lack of training. A common but mistaken belief is that listening is like breathing—an activity that people do well naturally. "After all," the common belief goes, "I've been listening since I was a child. I don't need to study the subject in school." The truth is that listening is a skill much like speaking: Virtually everybody does it, though few people do it well. Unfortunately, there is no connection between how competently most communicators *think* they listen and how competent they really are in their ability to understand others.[32] The good news is that listening can be improved through instruction and training.[33] Despite this fact, the amount of time spent teaching listening is far less than that spent on other types of communication. Table 7.1 reflects this upside-down arrangement.

TABLE 7.1 COMPARISON OF COMMUNICATION ACTIVITIES

	LISTENING	SPEAKING	READING	WRITING
Learned	First	Second	Third	Fourth
Used	Most	Next to most	Next to least	Least
Taught	Least	Next to least	Next to most	Most

© Cengage Learning

Hearing Problems Sometimes a person's listening ability suffers from a physiological hearing problem. In such cases, both the person with the problem and others can become frustrated at the ineffective communication that results. One survey explored the feelings of adults who have spouses with hearing loss. Nearly two-thirds of the respondents said they feel annoyed when their partner can't hear them clearly. Almost one-quarter said that beyond just being annoyed, they felt ignored, hurt, or sad. Many of the respondents believe their spouses are in denial about their condition, which makes the problem even more frustrating.[34] If you suspect that you or someone you know suffers from a hearing loss, then it's wise to have a physician or audiologist perform an examination.

MEETING THE CHALLENGE OF LISTENING BETTER

After reading the last few pages, you might decide that listening well is next to impossible. Fortunately, with the right combination of attitude and skill, you can indeed listen better. The following guidelines will show you how.

Talk Less Zeno of Citium put it most succinctly: "We have been given two ears and but a single mouth, in order that we may hear more and talk less." If your true goal is to understand the speaker, avoid the tendency to hog the stage and shift the conversation to your ideas. Talking less doesn't mean you must remain completely silent. As you'll soon read, giving feedback that clarifies your understanding and seeks new information is an important way to understand a speaker. Nonetheless, most of us talk too much when we're claiming to understand others. Other cultures, including many Native American ones, value listening at least as much as talking.[35] You can appreciate the value of this approach by trying the "Talking Stick" Pause and Reflect on page 228.

Get Rid of Distractions Some distractions are external: ringing telephones, radio or television programs, friends dropping in, and so on. Other distractions are internal: preoccupation with your own problems, an empty stomach, and so on. If the information you're seeking is really important, do everything possible to eliminate the internal and external distractions that interfere with careful listening. This might mean turning off the TV, shutting off your cell phone, or moving to a quiet room where you won't be bothered by the lure of the computer, the work on your desk, or the food on the counter. (See the reading on page 229 for an example of removing distractions from business meetings.)

Seymour Hewitt/The Image Bank/Getty Images

PAUSE AND REFLECT

SPEAKING AND LISTENING WITH A "TALKING STICK"

Explore the benefits of talking less and listening more by using a "talking stick." This exercise is based on the Native American tradition of "council." Gather a group of people in a circle, and designate a particular object as the talking stick. (Almost any manageable object will do.) Participants then pass the object around the circle. Each person may speak:

1. When holding the stick
2. For as long as he or she holds the stick
3. Without interruption from anyone else in the circle

When a member is through speaking, the stick passes to the left, and the speaker surrendering the stick must wait until it has made its way around the circle before speaking again.

After each member of the group has had the chance to speak, discuss how this experience differed from more common approaches to listening. Decide how the desirable parts of this method could be introduced into everyday conversations.

You can complete this activity by visiting CengageBrain.com to access the Speech Communication CourseMate for *Looking Out/ Looking In*, and, if requested, email your responses to your instructor.

Don't Judge Prematurely Most people would agree that it's essential to understand a speaker's ideas before judging them. However, all of us are guilty of forming snap judgments, evaluating others before hearing them out. This tendency is greatest when the speaker's ideas conflict with our own. Conversations that ought to be exchanges of ideas turn into verbal battles, with the "opponents" trying to ambush one another in order to win a victory. It's also tempting to judge prematurely when others criticize you, even when those criticisms may contain valuable truths and when understanding them may lead to a change for the better. Even if there is no criticism or disagreement, we tend to evaluate others based on sketchy first impressions, forming snap judgments that aren't at all valid. The lesson contained in these negative examples is clear: Listen first. Make sure you understand. *Then* evaluate.

Look for Key Ideas It's easy to lose patience with long-winded speakers who never seem to get to the point—or *have* a point, for that matter. Nonetheless, most people do have a central idea. By using your ability to think more quickly than the speaker can talk, you may be able to extract the central idea from the surrounding mass of words you're hearing. If you can't figure out what the speaker is driving at, you can always use a variety of response skills, which we'll examine now.

 ## Types of Listening Responses

Of the five components of listening (hearing, attending, understanding, responding, and remembering), *responding* lets us know how well others are tuned in to what we're

MEETINGS GOING "TOPLESS"

As the capital of information technology, Silicon Valley may have more gadgets per capita than any other place on the planet. Yet, even here, "always on" can be a real turnoff.

Frustrated by workers so plugged in that they tuned out in the middle of business meetings, a growing number of companies are going "topless," as in no laptops allowed. Also banned from some conference rooms: BlackBerrys, iPhones, and other devices on which so many people have come to depend.

Over the years, companies have come up with innovative ways to keep meetings from sucking up time. Some remove chairs and force people to stand. Others get everyone to drink a glass of water beforehand.

Comstock Images/Getty Images

But as laptops got lighter and smartphones even smarter, people discovered a handy diversion—making more eye contact with their screens than one another. The practice became so pervasive that Todd Wilkens, who runs a San Francisco design firm, waged a "personal war against CrackBerry."

"In this age of wireless Internet and mobile e-mail devices, having an effective meeting or working session is becoming more

and more difficult," he wrote on his company blog in November. "Laptops, Blackberries, Sidekicks, iPhones, and the like keep people from being fully present. Aside from just being rude, partial attention generally leads to partial results."

Wilkens's firm, Adaptive Path, now encourages everyone to leave their laptops at their desks. His colleague, Dan Saffer, coined the term "topless" as in laptop-less. Mobile and smartphones must be stowed on a counter or in a box during meetings.

"All of our meetings got a lot more productive," Wilkens said.

Jessica Guynn, Los Angeles Times

From "Silicon Valley Meetings Go 'Topless,'" Copyright © Jessica Guynn, 2008, Los Angeles Times. Reprinted by permission. http://articles.latimes.com/2008/mar/31/business/fi-nolaptops31

saying. Think for a moment of someone you consider a good listener. Why did you choose that person? It's probably because of the way she or he responds while you are speaking: making eye contact and nodding when you're talking, staying attentive while you're telling an important story, reacting with an exclamation when you say something startling, expressing empathy and support when you're hurting, and offering another perspective or advice when you ask for it.[36]

The rest of this chapter will describe a variety of response styles. We'll begin by describing responses that are focused on gathering more information to better understand the speaker. By chapter's end, our focus will be on listening responses that offer a speaker our assessment and direction.

PROMPTING

In some cases, the best response a listener can give is a small nudge to keep the speaker talking. **Prompting** involves using silences and brief statements of encouragement to draw others out. Besides helping you better understand the speaker, prompting can also help others clarify their thoughts and feelings. Consider this example:

Pablo: Julie's dad is selling a complete computer system for only $600, but if I want it, I have to buy it now. He's got another interested buyer. It's a great deal, but buying it would wipe out my savings. At the rate I spend money, it would take me a year to save up this much again.

Tim: Uh-huh.

Pablo: I wouldn't be able to take that ski trip over winter break . . . but I sure could save time with my schoolwork . . . and do a better job, too.

Tim: That's for sure.

Pablo: Do you think I should buy it?

Tim: I don't know. What do you think?

Pablo: I just can't decide.

Tim: *(Silence)*

Pablo: I'm going to do it. I'll never get a deal like this again.

In cases like this, your prompting can be a catalyst to help others find their own answers. Prompting will work best when it's done sincerely. Your nonverbal behaviors—eye contact, posture, facial expression, tone of voice—have to show that you are concerned with the other person's problem. Mechanical prompting is likely to irritate instead of help.

QUESTIONING

It's easy to understand why **questioning** has been called "the most popular piece of language."[37] Asking for information can help both the person doing the asking and the one providing answers.

Questioning can help you, the asker, in at least three ways. Most obviously, the answers you get can fill in facts and details that will sharpen your understanding ("Did he give you any reasons for doing that?" "What happened next?"). Also, by asking questions you can learn what others are thinking and feeling ("What's on your mind?" "Are you mad at me?"), as well as what they might want ("Are you asking me to apologize?").

Besides being useful to the person doing the asking, questions can also be a tool for the one who answers. As people in the helping professions know, questions can encourage self-discovery. You can use questions to encourage others to explore their thoughts and feelings. "So, what do you see as your options?" may prompt an employee to come up with creative problem-solving alternatives. "What would be your ideal solution?" might help a friend get in touch with various wants and needs. Most important is that encouraging discovery rather than dispensing advice indicates you have faith in others' ability to think for themselves. This may be the best message that you can communicate as an effective listener.

Despite their apparent benefits, not all questions are equally helpful. Whereas **sincere questions** are aimed at understanding others, **counterfeit questions** are aimed at sending a message, not receiving one. Counterfeit questions come in several varieties:

- *Questions that trap the speaker.* When your friend says, "You didn't like that movie, did you?", you're being backed into a corner. It's clear that your friend disapproves, so the question leaves you with two choices: You can disagree and defend your position, or you can devalue your reaction by lying or equivocating—"I guess it wasn't perfect." Consider how much easier it would be to respond to the sincere question, "What did you think of the movie?"

- *A tag question.* Phrases like "did you?" or "isn't that right?" at the end of a question can be a tip-off that the asker is looking for agreement, not information. Although some tag questions are genuine requests for confirmation, counterfeit ones are used to coerce agreement: "You said you'd call at 5 o'clock, but you forgot, didn't you?" Similarly, leading questions that begin with "Don't you" (such as "Don't you think he would make a good boss?") direct others toward a desired response. As a simple solution, changing "Don't you?" to "Do you?" makes the question less leading.

- *Questions that make statements.* "Are you *finally* off the phone?" is more of a statement than a question—a fact unlikely to be lost on the targeted person. Emphasizing certain words can also turn a question into a statement: "You lent money to *Tony*?" We also use questions to offer advice. The person who asks "Are you going to stand up to him and give him what he deserves?" clearly has stated an opinion about what should be done.

- *Questions that carry hidden agendas.* "Are you busy Friday night?" is a dangerous question to answer. If you say "No," thinking the person has something fun in mind, you won't like hearing, "Good, because I need help moving my piano." Obviously, such questions are not designed to enhance understanding: They are setups for the proposal that follows. Other examples include, "Will you do me a favor?" and "If I tell you what happened, will you promise not to get mad?" Wise communicators answer questions that mask hidden agendas cautiously, with responses like "It depends" or "Let me hear what you have in mind before I answer."

- *Questions that seek "correct" answers.* Most of us have been victims of questioners who want to hear only a particular response. "Which shoes do you think I should wear?" can be a sincere question—unless the asker has a predetermined preference. When this happens, the asker isn't interested in listening to contrary opinions, and "incorrect" responses get shot down. Some of these questions may venture into delicate territory. "Honey, do you think I look fat?" can be a request for a "correct" answer.

- *Questions based on unchecked assumptions.* "Why aren't you listening to me?" assumes that the other person isn't paying attention. "What's the matter?" assumes that something is wrong. As Chapter 3 explains, perception checking is a much better way of checking out assumptions. As you recall, a perception check offers a description and interpretations followed by a sincere request for clarification: "When you kept looking over at the TV, I thought you weren't listening to me, but maybe I was wrong. Were you paying attention?"

PARAPHRASING

For all its value, questioning won't always help you understand or help others. For example, consider what might happen when you ask for directions to a friend's home. Suppose that you've received these instructions: "Drive about a mile and then turn left at the traffic signal." Now imagine that a few common problems exist in this simple message. First, suppose that your friend's idea of "about a mile" differs from yours: Your mental picture of the distance is actually closer to 2 miles, whereas your friend's is closer to 300 yards. Next, consider that "traffic signal" really means "stop sign"; after all, it's common for us to think one thing and say another. Keeping these problems in mind, suppose that you tried to verify your understanding of the directions by asking,

IN REAL LIFE

Paraphrasing on the Job

This conversation between two coworkers shows how paraphrasing can help people solve their own problems. Notice how Jill comes to a conclusion without Mark's advice. Notice also how the paraphrasing sounds natural when combined with sincere questions and other helping styles.

Jill: I've had the strangest feeling about John *(their boss)* lately.

Mark: What's that? *(A simple question invites Jill to go on)*

Jill: I'm starting to think maybe he has this thing about women—or maybe it's just about me.

Mark: You mean he's coming on to you? *(Mark paraphrases what he thinks Jill has said)*

Jill: Oh, no, not at all! But it seems like he doesn't take women—or at least me—seriously. *(Jill corrects Mark's misunderstanding and explains herself)*

Mark: What do you mean? *(Mark asks another simple question to get more information)*

Jill: Well, whenever we're in a meeting or just talking around the office and he asks for ideas, he always seems to pick men. He gives orders to women—men, too—but he never asks the women to say what they think.

Mark: So you think maybe he doesn't take women seriously, is that it? *(Mark paraphrases Jill's last statement)*

Jill: He sure doesn't seem interested in their ideas. But that doesn't mean he's a total woman hater. I know he counts on some women in the office. Teresa has been here forever, and he's always saying he couldn't live without her. And when Brenda got the new computer system up and running last month, I know he appreciated that. He gave her a day off and told everybody how she saved our lives.

Mark: Now you sound confused. *(Reflects her apparent feeling)*

Jill: I am confused. I don't think it's just my imagination. I mean I'm a good producer, but he has never—not once—asked me for my ideas about how to improve sales or anything. And I can't remember a time when he's asked any other women. But maybe I'm overreacting.

Mark: You're not positive whether you're right, but I can tell that this has you concerned. *(Mark*

"After I turn at the signal, how far should I go?" to which your friend replies that the house is the third from the corner. Clearly, if you parted after this exchange, you would encounter a lot of frustration before finding the elusive residence.

Because questioning doesn't always provide the information you need, consider another kind of listening response—one that would tell you whether you understood what had already been said before you asked additional questions. This type of feedback involves restating in your own words the message you thought the speaker just sent, without adding anything new. Statements that reword the listener's interpretation of a message are commonly termed **paraphrasing**. If the listener in the preceding scenario had offered this paraphrase—"You're telling me to drive down to the traffic light by the high school and turn toward the mountains, is that it?"—it probably would have led the speaker to clarify the message.

The key to success in paraphrasing is to restate the other person's comments in your own words as a way of cross-checking the information. If you simply repeat the other person's comments verbatim, you will sound foolish—and you still might well be misunderstanding what has been said. Notice the difference between simply parroting a statement and true paraphrasing:

paraphrases both Jill's central theme and her feeling)

Jill: Yes. But I don't know what to do about it.

Mark: Maybe you should . . . *(Starts to offer advice but catches himself and decides to ask a question instead)* So what are your choices?

Jill: Well, I could just ask him if he's aware that he never asks women's opinions. But that might sound too aggressive and angry.

Mark: And you're not angry? *(Tries to clarify how Jill is feeling)*

Jill: Not really. I don't know whether I should be angry because he's not taking ideas seriously, or whether he just doesn't take my ideas seriously, or whether it's nothing at all.

Mark: So you're mostly confused. *(Reflects Jill's apparent feeling again)*

Jill: Yes! I don't know where I stand with John, and not being sure is starting to get to me. I wish I knew what he thinks of me. Maybe I could just tell him I'm confused about what is going on here and ask him to clear it up. But what if it's nothing? Then I'll look insecure.

Mark: *(Mark thinks Jill should confront the boss, but he isn't positive that this is the best approach, so he paraphrases what Jill seems to be saying)* And that would make you look bad.

Jill: I'm afraid maybe it would. I wonder if I could talk it over with anybody else in the office and get their ideas . . .

Mark: . . . see what they think . . .

Jill: Yeah. Maybe I could ask Brenda. She's easy to talk to, and I do respect her judgment. Maybe she could give me some ideas about how to handle this.

Mark: Sounds like you're comfortable with talking to Brenda first. *(Paraphrases)*

Jill: *(Warming to the idea)* Yes! Then if it's nothing, I can calm down. But if I do need to talk to John, I'll know I'm doing the right thing.

Mark: Great. Let me know how it goes.

Communication Scenarios

 To watch and analyze a video related to this feature and this topic, visit CengageBrain .com to access the Speech Communication CourseMate for Looking Out/Looking In.

Speaker: I'd like to go, but I can't afford it.
Parroting: You'd like to go, but you can't afford it.
Paraphrasing: So if we could find a way to pay for you, you'd be willing to come. Is that right?

Speaker: You look awful!
Parroting: You think I look terrible.
Paraphrasing: Sounds like you think I've put on too much weight.

There are two levels at which you can paraphrase messages. The first involves paraphrasing *factual information* that will help you understand the other person's ideas more clearly. At the most basic level, this sort of reflecting can prevent frustrating mix-ups: "So you want to meet *this* Tuesday, not next week, right?"

You can also paraphrase *personal information*: "So my joking makes you think I don't care about your problem." This sort of nondefensive response may be difficult when you are under attack, but it can short-circuit defensive arguments. Chapter 10 will explain in more detail how to use paraphrasing when you're being criticized.

Paraphrasing personal information can also be a tool for helping others, as the In Real Life transcript on pages 232–233 shows.[38] Reflecting the speaker's thoughts and feelings (instead of judging or analyzing, for example) shows your involvement and concern. The nonevaluative nature of paraphrasing encourages the problem holder to discuss the matter further. Reflecting thoughts and feelings allows the problem holder to unload more of the concerns he or she has been carrying around, often leading to the relief that comes from catharsis. Finally, paraphrasing helps the problem holder to sort out the problem. The clarity that comes from this sort of perspective can make it possible to find solutions that weren't apparent before. These features make paraphrasing a vital skill in the human services professions, leadership training, and even hostage negotiation.[39]

Effective paraphrasing is a skill that takes time to develop. You can make your paraphrasing sound more natural by taking any of three approaches, depending on the situation:

1. **Change the speaker's wording:**

    Speaker: Bilingual education is just another failed idea of bleeding-heart liberals.
    Paraphrase: Let me see if I've got this right. You're mad because you think bilingual ed sounds good, but it doesn't work?

2. **Offer an example of what you think the speaker is talking about:**

    Speaker: Lee is such a jerk. I can't believe the way he acted last night.
    Paraphrase: You think those jokes were pretty offensive, huh?

3. **Reflect the underlying theme of the speaker's remarks:**

    Paraphrase: You keep reminding me to be careful. Sounds like you're worried that something might happen to me. Am I right?

Paraphrasing won't always be accurate. But expressing your restatement tentatively gives the other person a chance to make a correction. (Note how the examples end with questions in an attempt to confirm if the paraphrase was accurate.)

Because it's an unfamiliar way of responding, paraphrasing may feel awkward at first; but if you start by paraphrasing occasionally and then gradually increase the frequency of such responses, you can begin to learn the benefits. You can begin practicing paraphrasing by trying the Skill Builder on page 235.

There are several factors to consider before you decide to paraphrase:

1. **Is the issue complex enough?** If you're fixing dinner, and someone wants to know when it will be ready, it would be exasperating to hear, "You're interested in knowing when we'll be eating."

2. **Do you have the necessary time and concern?** Paraphrasing can take a good deal of time. Therefore, if you're in a hurry, it's wise to avoid starting a conversation you won't be able to finish. Even more important than time is concern. Paraphrasing that comes across as mechanical or insincere reflecting can do more harm than good.[40]

3. **Can you withhold judgment?** Use paraphrasing only if you are willing to focus on the speaker's message without injecting your own judgments. It can be tempting to rephrase others' comments in a way that leads them toward the position you think is best without ever clearly stating your intentions.

4. **Is your paraphrasing in proportion to other responses?** Paraphrasing can become annoying when it's overused. This is especially true if you suddenly add this approach to your style. A far better way to use paraphrasing is to gradually introduce it into your repertoire.

SKILL BUILDER

PARAPHRASING PRACTICE

This exercise will help you see that it is possible to understand someone who disagrees with you without arguing or sacrificing your point of view.

1. Find a partner. Designate one person as *A* and the other as *B*.
2. Find a subject on which you and your partner apparently disagree—a current events topic, a philosophical or moral issue, or perhaps simply a matter of personal taste.
3. Person *A* begins by making a statement on the subject. Person *B*'s job is then to paraphrase the statement. *B*'s job is simply to understand here, and doing so in no way should signify agreement or disagreement with *A*'s remarks.
4. *A* then responds by telling *B* whether her response was accurate. If there was some misunderstanding, *A* should make the correction, and *B* should feed back his or her new understanding of the statement. Continue this process until you're both sure that *B* understands *A*'s statement.
5. Now it's *B*'s turn to respond to *A*'s statement and for *A* to help the process of understanding by correcting *B*.
6. Continue this process until each partner is satisfied that they have explained themselves fully and have been understood by the other person.
7. Now discuss the following questions:
   a. How did your understanding of the speaker's statement change after you used active listening?
   b. Did you find that the gap between your position and that of your partner narrowed as a result of active listening?
   c. How did you feel at the end of your conversation? How does this feeling compare to your usual feeling after discussing controversial issues?
   d. How might your life change if you used paraphrasing at home? At work? With friends?

 You can complete this activity by visiting CengageBrain.com to access the Speech Communication CourseMate for *Looking Out/ Looking In*, and, if requested, email your responses to your instructor.

SUPPORTING

There are times when other people want to hear more than a reflection of how *they* feel: They would like to know how *you* feel for and about them. **Supporting** reveals a listener's solidarity with the speaker's situation. One scholar describes supporting as "expressions of care, concern, affection, and interest, especially during times of stress or upset."[41]

There are several types of listening responses that can provide support:

Empathizing	"I can understand why you'd be upset about this." "Yeah, that class was tough for me, too."
Agreement	"You're right—the landlord is being unfair." "Sounds like the job is a perfect match for you."
Offers to help	"I'm here if you need me." "I'd be happy to study with you for the next test if you'd like."
Praise	"Wow—you did a fantastic job!" "You're a terrific person, and if she doesn't recognize it, that's her problem!"

Adam (Joseph Gordon-Levitt) receives a variety of listening responses—some more helpful than others—from friends, family, and professionals as he battles cancer in the movie *50/50*. (See the film summary at the end of this chapter.)

Reassurance   "The worst part seems to be over. It will probably get easier from here."

"I'm sure you'll do a great job."

It's easy to identify what effective support *doesn't* sound like. Some scholars have called these messages "cold comfort."[42] As the following examples suggest, you're probably *not* being supportive if you:

- *Deny others the right to their feelings.* Consider the stock remark "Don't worry about it." Although it may be intended as a reassuring comment, the underlying message is that the speaker wants the person to feel differently. The irony is that the suggestion probably won't work—after all, it's unlikely that people can or will stop worrying just because you tell them to do so. Research about such responses is clear: "Messages that explicitly acknowledge, elaborate, and legitimize the feelings and perspective of a distressed person are perceived as more helpful messages than those which only implicitly recognize or deny the feelings and perspective of the other."[43]

- *Minimize the significance of the situation.* Consider the times you've been told, "Hey, it's only ___." You can probably fill in the blank in a variety of ways: "a job," "her opinion," "a test," "puppy love," "a party." To someone who has been the victim of verbal abuse, the hurtful message isn't "just words"; to a child who didn't get an invitation, it isn't "just a party"; to a worker who has been chewed out by the boss, it isn't "just a job."

- *Focus on "then and there" rather than "here and now."* Although it is sometimes true that "you'll feel better tomorrow," it sometimes isn't. Even if the prediction that "ten years from now you won't remember her name" proves correct, it provides little comfort to someone experiencing heartbreak today.

- *Cast judgment.* It usually isn't encouraging to hear "You know, it's your own fault—you really shouldn't have done that" after you've confessed to making a poor decision. As you'll learn in Chapter 10, evaluative and condescending statements are more likely to engender defensiveness than to help people change for the better.

- *Focus on yourself.* It can be tempting to talk at length about a similar experience you've encountered ("I know exactly how you feel. Something like that happened to me. . . ."). While your intent might be to show empathy, research shows that such messages aren't perceived as helpful because they draw attention away from the distressed person.[44]

- *Defend yourself.* When your response to others' concerns is to defend yourself ("Don't blame me; I've done my part"), it's clear that you are more concerned with yourself than with supporting the other person.

How often do people fail to provide appropriate supportive responses? One survey of mourners who had recently suffered from the death of a loved one reported that 80 percent of the statements made to them were unhelpful.[45] Nearly half of the "helpful" statements were advice: "You've got to get out more." "Don't question God's will." Despite their frequency, these suggestions were helpful only 3 percent of the time. Far more helpful were expressions that acknowledged the mourner's feelings, such as

"This must be so hard—I know how much she meant to you." (See the reading on this page for further discussion on allowing people to grieve.) Chapter 9 will describe other ways to supply social support to family and friends.

When handled correctly, supporting responses *can* be helpful. Guidelines for effective support include:

1. **Recognize that you can support another person's struggles without approving of his or her decisions.** Suppose, for instance, that a friend has decided to quit a job that you think she should keep. You could still be supportive by saying, "I know you've given this a lot of thought and that you're doing what you think is best." Responses like this can provide face-saving support without compromising your principles.[46]

2. **Monitor the other person's reaction to your support.** If it doesn't seem to help, consider other types of responses that let him or her explore the issue.

3. **Realize that support may not always be welcome.** In one survey, some people reported occasions when social support wasn't necessary because they felt capable of handling the problem themselves.[47] Many regarded uninvited support as an intrusion, and some said it left them feeling more nervous than before. The majority of respondents expressed a preference for being in control of whether their distressing situation should be discussed with even the most helpful friend.

4. **Make sure you're ready for the consequences.** Talking about a difficult event may reduce distress for the speaker but increase distress for the listener.[48] Recognize that supporting another person is a worthwhile but potentially taxing venture.

WHY WON'T ANYONE LET ME FEEL SAD?

The number one offense grievers must confront is being told that they shouldn't feel sad or bad. The tragedy is that they are told this at the precise time when it makes the most sense to feel sad or bad—when someone important to them has died. If you can't feel sad in reaction to a death, then when can you ever feel sad?

A typical lament from a broken-hearted griever is, "Everyone keeps telling me not to feel bad or sad and giving me all kinds of reasons that don't make sense to me. They say, 'Don't feel bad, she's in a better place.' But *I'm* not in a better place! I'm sad, I miss her terribly, and I'm confused when people tell me not to feel bad. Is there something wrong with me?"

There's nothing wrong with you.

Being told not to feel bad is always followed by a reason that makes no sense relative to how the griever feels—things like "she's in a better place" or "at least her suffering is over." Those explanations are about the person who died, not about the grieving person. Even if the griever agrees with those ideas and sentiments, the comments don't address what the griever is feeling.

As a griever, the healthiest thing you can do is tell the truth about how you feel in any given moment. As a person who is talking to a griever, the healthiest thing you can do is listen without judgment or criticism of feelings,

Laurence Mouton/PhotoAlto/Getty Images

and never give the illogical advice that your friend shouldn't feel sad or bad.

Russell Friedman and John W. James

Excerpted from http://www.tributes.com/grief_recovery_center/article/3; © 2012 Russell P. Friedman, John W. James and The Grief Recovery Institute®. www.griefrecoverymethod.com. All rights reserved.

ANALYZING

When **analyzing**, the listener offers an interpretation of a speaker's message. Analyses like these are probably familiar to you:

"I think what's really bothering you is . . ."

"She's doing it because . . ."

"I don't think you really meant that."

"Maybe the problem started when he . . ."

Interpretations are often effective ways to help people with problems to consider alternative meanings—meanings they would have never thought of without your help. Sometimes an analysis will make a confusing problem suddenly clear, either suggesting a solution or at least providing an understanding of what is occurring.

In other cases, an analysis can create more problems than it solves. There are two potential problems with analyzing. First, your interpretation may not be correct, in which case the speaker may become even more confused by accepting it. Second, even if your analysis is correct, telling it to the problem holder might not be useful. There's a chance that it will arouse defensiveness (because analysis implies superiority). Even if it doesn't, the person may not be able to understand your view of the problem without working it out personally.

How can you know when it's helpful to offer an analysis? There are several guidelines to follow:

- *Offer your interpretation as tentative rather than as absolute fact.* There's a big difference between saying "Maybe the reason is . . ." or "The way it looks to me . . ." and insisting, "This is the truth."
- *You ought to be sure that the other person will be receptive to your analysis.* Even if you're completely accurate, your thoughts won't help if the problem holder isn't ready to consider them.
- *Be sure that your motive for offering an analysis is truly to help the other person.* It can be tempting to offer an analysis to show how brilliant you are or even to make the other person feel bad for not having thought of the right answer in the first place. Needless to say, an analysis offered under such conditions isn't helpful.

ADVISING

When we are approached with another's problem, a common tendency is to respond with **advising**: to help by offering a solution.[49] Advice can sometimes be helpful, as long as it's given in a respectful, caring way.[50]

Despite its apparent value, advice has its limits. Research has shown that it is actually *unhelpful* at least as often as it's helpful.[51] Studies on advice giving offer the following important considerations when trying to help others:[52]

- *Is the advice needed?* If the person has already taken a course of action, giving advice after the fact ("I can't believe you got back together with him") is rarely appreciated.
- *Is the advice wanted?* People generally don't value unsolicited advice. It's usually best to ask if the speaker is interested in hearing your counsel. Remember that sometimes people just want a listening ear, not solutions to their problems.
- *Is the advice given in the right sequence?* Advice is more likely to be received after the listener first offers supporting, paraphrasing, and questioning responses to better understand the speaker and the situation.

- *Is the advice coming from an expert?* If you want to offer advice about anything from car purchasing to relationship managing, it's important to have experience and success in those matters. If you *don't* have expertise, it's a good idea to offer the speaker supportive responses, then encourage that person to seek out expert counsel.
- *Is the advisor a close and trusted person?* Although sometimes we seek out advice from people we don't know well (perhaps because they have expertise), in most cases we value advice given within the context of a close and ongoing interpersonal relationship.
- *Is the advice offered in a sensitive, face-saving manner?* No one likes to feel bossed or belittled, even if the advice is good. Remember that messages have both content and relational dimensions, and sometimes the unstated relational messages when giving advice ("I'm smarter than you"; "You're not bright enough to figure this out yourself") will keep people from hearing counsel.[53]

PAUSE AND REFLECT

WHEN ADVISING DOES AND DOESN'T WORK

To see why advising can be tricky business, follow these steps:

1. Recall an instance when someone gave you advice that proved helpful. See how closely that advising communication followed the guidelines in the bulleted list on pages 238–239.
2. Now recall an instance when someone gave you advice that *wasn't* helpful. See whether that person violated any of the guidelines in the bulleted list on pages 238–239.
3. Based on your insights here, describe how you can advise (or not advise) others in a way that is truly helpful.

You can complete this activity by visiting CengageBrain.com to access the Speech Communication CourseMate for *Looking Out/Looking In*, and, if requested, email your responses to your instructor.

Zits Partnership/King Features

JUDGING

A **judging** response evaluates the sender's thoughts or behaviors in some way. The judgment may be favorable—"That's a good idea" or "You're on the right track now"—or unfavorable—"An attitude like that won't get you anywhere." But in either case it implies that the person doing the judging is in some way qualified to pass judgment on the speaker's thoughts or actions.

Sometimes negative judgments are purely critical. How many times have you heard such responses as "Well, you asked for it!" or "I *told* you so!" or "You're just feeling sorry for yourself"? Although responses like these can sometimes serve as a verbal slap that brings problem holders to their senses, they usually make matters worse.

In other cases, negative judgments are less critical. These involve what we usually call *constructive criticism*, which is intended to help the problem holder improve in the future. This is the sort of response given by friends about everything from the choice of clothing to jobs to friends. Another common setting for constructive criticism occurs in school, where instructors evaluate students' work to help them master concepts and skills. But whether it's justified or not, even constructive criticism runs the risk of arousing defensiveness because it may threaten the self-concept of the person at whom it is directed (we'll discuss this further in Chapter 10).

Judgments have the best chance of being received when two conditions exist:

1. **The person with the problem should have requested an evaluation from you.** Occasionally an unsolicited evaluation may bring someone to his or her senses, but more often an unsolicited evaluation will trigger a defensive response.

2. **The intent of your judgment should be genuinely constructive and not designed as a put-down.** If you are tempted to use judgments as a weapon, don't fool yourself into thinking that you are being helpful. Often the statement "I'm telling you this for your own good . . ." simply isn't true.

Now that you're aware of all the possible listening responses, try the exercise on page 241 to see how you might use them in everyday situations.

Modern Family's Phil Dunphy (Ty Burrell) gets a lesson on listening during a day at the spa. The women there tell him that his wife would value his empathy and support more than his evaluation and advice.

CHOOSING THE BEST LISTENING RESPONSE

By now you can see that there are many ways to respond as a listener. Research shows that, in the right circumstances, *all* response styles can help others accept their situation, feel better, and have a sense of control over their problems.[54] But there is enormous variability in which style will work with a given person.[55] This fact explains why communicators who use a wide variety of response styles are usually more effective than those who use just one or two styles.[56] However, there are other factors to consider when choosing how to respond to a speaker.

Gender Research shows that men and women differ in the ways they listen and respond to others.[57] Women are more likely than men to give supportive responses when presented with another person's problem,[58] are more skillful at composing such messages,[59] and are more likely to seek out such responses from

ABC/Photofest

PAUSE AND REFLECT

WHAT WOULD YOU SAY?

1. In each of the following situations, describe what you would say in response to the problem being shared:

   a. My family doesn't understand me. Everything I like seems to go against their values, and they just won't accept my feelings as being right for me. It's not that they don't love me—they do. But they don't accept me.

   b. I've been pretty discouraged lately. I just can't get a good relationship going with any guys. I've got plenty of male friends, but that's always as far as it goes. I'm tired of being just a pal . . . I want to be more than that.

   c. *(Child to parents)* I hate you guys! You always go out and leave me with some stupid sitter. Why don't you like me?

   d. I don't know what I want to do with my life. I'm tired of school, but there aren't any good jobs around. I could just drop out for a while, but that doesn't really sound very good, either.

   e. Things really seem to be kind of lousy in my marriage lately. It's not that we fight much, but all the excitement seems to be gone. We're in a rut, and it keeps getting worse. . . .

   f. I keep getting the idea that my boss is angry at me. It seems as if lately he hasn't been joking around very much, and he hasn't said anything at all about my work for about three weeks now. I wonder what I should do.

2. After you've written your response to each of these messages, imagine the probable outcome of the conversation that would have followed. If you've tried this exercise in class, you might have two group members role-play each response. Based on your idea of how the conversation might have gone, decide which responses were productive and which were unproductive.

 You can complete this activity by visiting CengageBrain.com to access the Speech Communication CourseMate for *Looking Out/ Looking In*, and, if requested, email your responses to your instructor.

listeners.[60] By contrast, men are less skillful at providing emotional support to those who are distressed,[61] and they're more likely to respond to others' problems by offering advice or by diverting the topic. In a study of helping styles in sororities and fraternities, researchers found that sorority women frequently respond with emotional support when asked to help; also, they rated their sisters as being better at listening nonjudgmentally and on comforting and showing concern for them. Fraternity men, on the other hand, fit the stereotypical pattern of offering help by challenging their brothers to evaluate their attitudes and values.[62]

The temptation when hearing these facts is to conclude that in times of distress, women want support and men want advice—but research doesn't bear that out. Numerous studies show that both men and women prefer and want supportive, endorsing messages in difficult situations.[63] The fact that women are more adept at creating and delivering such messages explains why both males and females tend to seek out women listeners when they want emotional support. When it comes to gender, it's important to remember that while men and women sometimes use different response styles, they all need a listening ear.

The Situation Sometimes people need your advice. At other times, people need encouragement and support, and in still other cases your analysis or judgment will be most helpful. And, as you have seen, sometimes your probes and paraphrasing can help people find their own answers. In other words, a competent communicator needs to analyze the situation and develop an appropriate response.[64] As a rule of thumb, it's often wise to begin with responses that seek understanding and offer a minimum of direction, such as prompting, questioning, paraphrasing, and supporting. Once you've gathered the facts and demonstrated your interest and concern, it's likely that the speaker will be more receptive to (and perhaps even ask for) your analyzing, advising, and evaluating responses.[65]

The Other Person Besides considering the situation, you should also consider the other person when deciding which style to use. Some people are able to consider advice thoughtfully, whereas others use advice to avoid making their own decisions. Many communicators are extremely defensive and aren't capable of receiving analysis or judgments without lashing out. Still others aren't equipped to think through problems clearly enough to profit from paraphrasing and probing. One study found that highly rational people tend to respond more positively to advice than do more emotional people.[66]

Sophisticated listeners choose a style that fits the person. One way to determine the most appropriate response is to ask the speaker what she or he wants from you. A simple question such as "Are you looking for my advice, or do you just want a listening ear right now?" can help you give others the kinds of responses they're looking for.

Your Personal Style Finally, consider yourself when deciding how to respond. Most of us reflexively use one or two response styles. You may be best at listening quietly, offering a prompt from time to time. Or perhaps you are especially insightful and can offer a truly useful analysis of the problem. Of course, it's also possible to rely on a response style that is unhelpful You may be overly judgmental or too eager to advise, even when your suggestions aren't invited or productive. As you think about how to respond to another's messages, consider both your strengths and weaknesses and adapt accordingly.

ETHICAL CHALLENGE

UNCONDITIONAL POSITIVE REGARD

Carl Rogers was the best-known advocate of paraphrasing as a helping tool. As a psychotherapist, Rogers focused on how professionals can help others, but he and his followers were convinced that the same approach can work in all interpersonal relationships.

Rogers used several terms to describe his approach. Sometimes he labeled it *nondirective*, sometimes *client-centered*, and at other times *person-centered*.[a] All of these terms reflect his belief that the best way to help another is to offer a supportive climate in which the people seeking help can find their own answers. Rogers believed that advising, judging, analyzing, and questioning are not the best ways to help others solve their problems. Instead, Rogers and his followers were convinced that people are basically good and that they can improve without receiving any guidance from others, after they accept and respect themselves.

An essential ingredient for person-centered helping is what Rogers called *unconditional positive regard*. This attitude requires the helper to treat the speaker's ideas respectfully and nonjudgmentally. Unconditional positive regard means accepting others for who they are, even when you don't approve of their posture toward life. Treating a help seeker with unconditional positive regard doesn't oblige you to agree with everything the help seeker thinks, feels, or does, but it does oblige you to suspend judgment about the rightness or wrongness of the help seeker's thoughts and actions.

A person-centered approach to helping places heavy demands on the listener. At the skill level, it demands an ability to reflect the speaker's thoughts and feelings perceptively and accurately. Even more difficult, though, is the challenge of listening and responding without passing judgment on the speaker's ideas or behavior.[b]

Unconditional positive regard is especially hard when we are faced with the challenge of listening and responding to someone whose beliefs, attitudes, and values differ profoundly from our own. This approach requires the helper to follow the familiar prescription of loving the sinner while hating the sin.

SUMMARY

Listening is the most common—and perhaps the most overlooked—form of communication. There is a difference between hearing and listening, and there is also a difference between mindless and mindful listening. Listening, defined as the process of making sense of others' spoken messages, consists of five elements: hearing, attending, understanding, responding, and remembering.

Several responding styles masquerade as listening but actually are only poor imitations of the real thing. We listen poorly for a variety of reasons. Some reasons have to do with the tremendous number of messages that bombard us daily and with the personal preoccupations, noise, and rapid thoughts that distract us from focusing on the information we are exposed to. Another set of reasons has to do with the considerable effort involved in listening carefully and the mistaken belief that there are more rewards in speaking than in listening. A few listeners fail to receive messages because of physical hearing defects; others listen poorly because of lack of training. Some keys to better listening are to talk less, reduce distractions, avoid making premature judgments, and seek the speaker's key ideas.

Listening responses are the primary way we evaluate whether and how others are paying attention to us. Some listening responses put a premium on gathering information and providing support; these include prompting, questioning, paraphrasing, and supporting. Other listening responses focus more on providing direction and evaluation: analyzing, advising, and judging. The most effective communicators use a variety of these styles, taking into consideration factors such as gender, the situation at hand, the person with the problem, and their own personal style.

KEY TERMS

advising (238)
ambushing (225)
analyzing (238)
attending (221)
counterfeit questions (230)
defensive listening (225)
hearing (221)
insensitive listening (225)
insulated listening (225)
judging (240)
listening (219)
listening fidelity (222)
mindful listening (220)

mindless listening (219)
paraphrasing (232)
prompting (229)
pseudolistening (224)
questioning (230)
remembering (222)
responding (222)
selective listening (224)
sincere questions (230)
stage-hogging (224)
supporting (235)
understanding (222)

ONLINE RESOURCES

Now that you have read this chapter, visit CengageBrain.com to access the Speech Communication CourseMate for *Looking Out/Looking In* for quick access to the electronic resources that accompany this text. Your CourseMate offers:

- **Study tools** that will help you assess your learning and prepare for exams (*digital glossary, key term flash cards, interactive quizzes*).
- **Activities and assignments** that will help you hone your knowledge, understand how theory and research applies to your own life (*Self-Assessment, Pause and Reflect*), consider ethical challenges in interpersonal communication (*Ethical Challenge*), and build your interpersonal communication skills throughout the course (*Skill Builder*). If requested, you can submit your answers to your instructor.
- **Media resources** that will allow you to watch and critique videos of interpersonal communication situations (*In Real Life, interpersonal video simulations, and interactive video activities*).
- In addition to interactive teaching and learning tools, CourseMate includes an **interactive eBook.** Take notes, highlight, search, and interact with embedded media specific to *Looking Out/Looking In*.

SEARCH TERMS

When searching online databases to research topics in this chapter, use the following terms (along with this chapter's key terms) to maximize the chances of finding useful information:

attention	conversation
communication fidelity	empathy
compassion	memory
comprehension	

FILM AND TELEVISION

You can see the communication principles described in this chapter portrayed in the following films and television programs.

THE IMPORTANCE OF LISTENING

CSI (2000–) Rated TV-14

Law & Order (1990–2010) Rated TV-14

The crime shows *CSI* and *Law & Order* have become a fixture of television programming. In their many forms, these franchises have one thing in common: Their main characters must engage in active listening to do their jobs effectively. Sometimes a lawyer uses prompting and support to draw out a difficult confession. Other times a private investigator asks probing questions and offers analyzing responses to arrive at important conclusions. In still other instances, a police officer carefully attends to and remembers specific details during a testimony, which later helps solve a case. And in a variety of situations, the characters offer advising and judging responses to their clients, colleagues, and coworkers. Watch an episode of one of these programs and see how many of the listening responses from this chapter you can observe. Chances are, you'll find quite a few.

INEFFECTIVE LISTENING

The Devil Wears Prada (2006) Rated PG-13

Miranda Priestly (Meryl Streep) is every employee's nightmare. She's a self-centered, domineering, hard-driven boss who treats the people who work for her like slaves. Priestly offers a tour de force of every poor listening habit. She attends only to things that matter to her ("The details of your incompetence do not interest me") and does so insensitively ("Bore someone else with your questions"). Pseudolistening, defensive listening, and stage-hogging? She does them all. She also interrupts, rolls her eyes when she doesn't like what she's hearing, and walks out on her subordinates in mid-conversation. Priestly may be a successful businesswoman, but she fails on many other counts—especially as a listener.

SUPPORTIVE LISTENING
50/50 (2011) Rated R

Adam (Joseph Gordon-Levitt) is in his twenties and leading a good life in Seattle—until he is diagnosed with cancer. Once they learn he has a 50/50 chance of living, Adam's mother (Anjelica Huston), girlfriend (Bryce Dallas Howard), best buddy (Seth Rogen), therapist (Anna Kendrick), and a support group try to help him deal with the challenge. Sometimes they laugh; sometimes they cry; sometimes they offer unhelpful advice; sometimes they just hear him out. Their various ways of trying to help offer an instructive catalog of supportive response styles.

Class _____   Name_____

C H A P T E R   S E V E N

Listening: More Than Meets the Ear

CHAPTER OUTLINE

Use this outline to take notes as you read the chapter in the text and/or as your instructor lectures in class.

I.   **LISTENING DEFINED**
    A. **Hearing versus Listening** _____
    B. **Mindless Listening**
    C. **Mindful Listening** _____

II. **ELEMENTS IN THE LISTENING PROCESS** _____
    A. **Hearing**
    B. **Attending** _____
    C. **Understanding**
    D. **Responding** _____
    E. **Remembering**

III. **THE CHALLENGE OF LISTENING** _____
    A. **Types of Ineffective Listening**
      1. Pseudolistening _____
      2. Stage-hogging
      3. Selective listening _____
      4. Insulated listening
      5. Defensive listening _____
      6. Ambushing
      7. Insensitive listening _____
    B. **Why We Don't Listen Better**
      1. Message overload

2. Preoccupation
3. Rapid thought
4. Effort
5. External noise
6. Faulty assumptions
7. Lack of apparent advantages
8. Lack of training
9. Hearing problems

C. **Meeting the Challenge of Listening Better**

1. Talk less
2. Get rid of distractions
3. Don't judge prematurely
4. Look for key ideas

IV. **TYPES OF LISTENING RESPONSES**

A. **Prompting**

B. **Questioning**

1. Ask sincere questions
2. Avoid counterfeit questions that:
    a. Trap the speaker
    b. Tag questions
    c. Make statements
    d. Carry hidden agendas
    e. Seek "correct" answers
    f. Are based on unchecked assumptions

C. **Paraphrasing**

1. Factual information
2. Personal information
    a. Change the speaker's wording
    b. Offer an example
    c. Reflect the underlying theme
3. When to paraphrase
    a. If the problem is complex enough
    b. If you have necessary time

and concern

    c.   Withhold judgment

    d.   If it is proportional

D. Supporting

  1.   Types

    a.   Empathizing agreement

    b.   Offers to help

    c.   Praise

    d.   Reassurance

  2.   Cold comfort

    a.   Denying others the right to their feelings

    b.   Minimizing the significance of the situation

    c.   Focusing on "then and there," not "here and now"

    d.   Casting judgment

    e.   Defending yourself

  3.   Guidelines

    a.   Approval not necessary

    b.   Monitor reactions

    c.   Support may not always be welcome

    d.   Be ready for the consequences

E. Analyzing

  1.   Be tentative

  2.   Have a receptive other

  3.   Be sure your motives are to help

F. Advising

  1.   Is the advice needed?

  2.   Is the advice wanted?

  3.   Is the advice given in the right sequence?

  4.   Is the advice coming from an expert?

  5.   Is the advisor a close and trusted person?

  6.   Is the advice offered in a sensitive, face-saving manner?

G. Judging
    1. Negative judgments
    2. Constructive criticism
       a. The person should have requested an evaluation
       b. The intent of your judgment should be genuinely constructive
H. Choosing the Best Listening Response
    1. Gender
    2. The situation
    3. The other person
    4. Your personal style
	_____
	
	_____
	
	_____
	
	_____
	
	_____
	
	_____
	
	_____

KEY TERMS

advising
ambushing
analyzing
attending
counterfeit questions
defensive listening
hearing
insensitive listening
insulated listening
judging
listening
listening fidelity
mindful listening
mindless listening
paraphrasing

prompting
pseudolistening
questioning
remembering
responding
selective listening
sincere questions
stage-hogging
supporting
understanding

Class _____   Name_____

ACTIVITIES

7.1 LISTENING DIARY

LEARNING OBJECTIVES

- Identify the situations in which you listen mindfully and those when you listen mindlessly, and evaluate the appropriateness of each style in a given situation.
- Identify the circumstances in which you listen ineffectively, and the poor listening habits you use in these circumstances.

BACKGROUND

Looking Out/Looking In identifies several styles of effective and ineffective listening that you can use when listening to others:

pseudolistening	insensitive listening	supporting
stage-hogging	ambushing	analyzing
selective listening	prompting	advising
insulated listening	questioning	judging
defensive listening	paraphrasing	

INSTRUCTIONS

1. Use the following form to record the listening styles you use in various situations.
2. After completing your diary, record your conclusions.

TIME AND PLACE	PEOPLE	SUBJECT	LISTENING STYLE(S)	CONSEQUENCES
EXAMPLE *Saturday night party*	*My date and several new acquaintances*	*Good backpacking trips*	*Stage-hogging: I steered everybody's remarks around to my own experiences*	*I guess I was trying to get everyone to like me, but my egotistical attitude probably accomplished the opposite.*
1.				

Class _____   Name_____

	TIME AND PLACE	PEOPLE	SUBJECT	LISTENING STYLE(S)	CONSEQUENCES
2.					
3.					
4.					

Based on your observations, what styles of effective and ineffective listening do you use most often? In what situations do you use each of these styles? (Consider the people involved, the time, subject, and your personal mood when determining situational variables.)

_____

_____

_____

Class _____   Name_____

What are the consequences of using the listening styles you have just described?

_____

_____

_____

What other listening styles might increase your effectiveness? Why?

_____

_____

_____

7.2 EFFECTIVE QUESTIONING

LEARNING OBJECTIVES

- Identify the response styles that you commonly use when listening to others.
- Demonstrate a combination of listening styles you could use to respond effectively in a given situation.

INSTRUCTIONS

1. For each of the following statements, write two questions to get more information. Avoid counterfeit questions that trap the speaker, carry hidden agendas, seek "correct" answers, or are based on unchecked assumptions.
2. Enter statement examples of your own and two questions each to solicit information.

EXAMPLE

"It's not fair that I have to work so much. Other students can get better grades because they have the time to study."
How do you feel when others score higher than you?
How many hours a week do you work?

1. "I guess it's OK for you to use my computer, but you have to understand that I've put a lot of time and money into it."

_____

_____

2. "You'll have the best chance at getting a loan for the new car you want if you give us a complete financial statement and credit history."

_____

_____

3. (Instructor to student) "This paper shows a lot of promise. It could probably earn you an A grade if you just develop the idea about the problems that arise from poor listening a bit more."

_____

_____

4. "I do like the communication course, but it's not at all what I expected. It's much more *personal,* if you know what I mean."

_____

_____

5. "We just got started on your car's transmission. I'm pretty sure we can have it ready tonight."

_____

_____

6. "I do think it's wrong to take any lives, but sometimes I think certain criminals deserve capital punishment."

_____

_____

7. "My son never tells me what's going on in his life. And now he's moving away."

_____

_____

8. "My family is so controlling. They make it impossible for me to escape."

_____

_____

9. "It was a great game, I guess. I played a lot, but only scored once. The coach put Ryan in ahead of me."

_____

_____

10. "We had a great evening last night. The dinner was fantastic; so was the party. We saw lots of people. Erin loves that sort of thing."

_____

_____

Class _____   Name_____

11. Your example: _____

     _____

     _____

12. Your example: _____

     _____

     _____

7.3 PARAPHRASING

LEARNING OBJECTIVES

- Demonstrate a combination of listening styles you could use to respond effectively in a given situation.

BACKGROUND

The most helpful paraphrasing responses reflect both the speaker's thoughts and feelings. In order for this style of helping to be effective, you also have to sound like yourself, and not another person or a robot. There are many ways to reflect another's thoughts and feelings:

"It sounds like you're . . ."   "And so . . ."
"I hear you saying . . ."   "Is it that . . ."
"Let me see if I've got it. You're saying . . ."   "Are you . . ."
"So you're telling me . . ."   "Could you mean . . ."

Leave your paraphrase open (tentative) by using words that invite the speaker to clarify or correct your paraphrase (e.g., "Is that right?").

INSTRUCTIONS

Write a paraphrasing response for each of the statements that follow. Be sure that the response fits your style of speaking, while at the same time it reflects the speaker's *thoughts* and *feelings*.

EXAMPLE

"Stan always wants to tell me about the woman he's currently going out with or the project he's currently working on. He gives me details that take hours, but he rarely asks about who I'm going out with or what I'm interested in."
"It seems like you might be tired (feeling) of hearing about Stan's love life (thoughts) and maybe a little put out (feeling) that he doesn't solicit information from you about whom you're dating (thoughts) — is that it?"

1. "I hate this instructor. First she told me my paper was too short, so I gave her more information. Now she tells me it's too wordy."

   _____

   _____

   _____

2. "I worked up that whole study—did all the surveying, the compiling, the writing. It was my idea in the first place. But he turned it in to the head office with his name on it, and he got the credit."

_____

_____

_____

3. "We can't decide whether to put Grandmother in a nursing home. She hates the idea, but she can't take care of herself anymore, and it's just too much for us."

_____

_____

_____

4. "She believed everything he said about me. She wouldn't even listen to my side—just started yelling at me. I thought we were better friends than that."

_____

_____

_____

5. "I'm really starting to hate my job. Every day I do the same boring, mindless work. But if I quit, I might not find any better work."

_____

_____

_____

6. "My girlfriend hasn't called me in forever. I think she must be mad at me."

_____

_____

_____

7. "How can I tell him how I really feel? He might get mad, and then we'd start arguing. He'll think I don't love him if I tell him my real feelings. I'm at a loss."

_____

_____

_____

8. "Why don't you try to be a little less messy around here? This place looks like a dump to all our friends."

_____

_____

_____

9. "There's no reasoning with him. All he cares about is his image—not all the work I have to do to cover for him."

_____

_____

_____

10. "You'd think someone who loves you would take off to be with you now and then, wouldn't you?"

_____

_____

_____

11. "This new software program is supposed to save time? That's a joke."

_____

_____

_____

12. "He acts as if staying home with two children all day is easy. I'm more tired now than when I worked full-time — and I got paid then and had weekends and evenings off!"

_____

_____

_____

13. "My father is so needy since my mother died. I have no life of my own."

_____

_____

_____

14. "Group projects are a nightmare. There should be a warning sign for classes that require them."

_____

_____

_____

7.4 LISTENING CHOICES

LEARNING OBJECTIVES

- Demonstrate a combination of listening styles you could use to respond effectively in a given situation.
- Identify the response styles that you commonly use when listening to others.

INSTRUCTIONS

For each of the problem statements below, write a response in each style of helping discussed in *Looking Out/Looking In*. Make your response as realistic as possible. Then record a situation of your own and write listening responses for it.

EXAMPLE

"I don't know what to do. I tried to explain to my professor why the assignment was late, but he wouldn't even listen to me."

Prompting: *(Short silence) And so . . . ? (Look expectantly at partner)*

Questioning: *What did he say? Can you make up the assignment? How do you feel about this?*

Paraphrasing: *You sound really discouraged, since he didn't even seem to care about your reasons — is that it?*

Supporting: *All of your work has been so good that I'm sure this one assignment won't matter. Don't worry!*

Analyzing: *I think the reason he wasn't sympathetic is because he hears lots of excuses this time of year.*

Advising: *You ought to write him a note. He might be more open if he has time to read it and think about it.*

Judging: *You have to accept these things. Moping won't do any good, so quit feeling sorry for yourself.*

---

1. My girlfriend says she wants to date other guys this summer while I'm away, working construction. She claims it's just to keep busy and that it won't make any difference with us, but I think she wants to break off permanently, and she's trying to do it gently.

   Prompting _____

   _____

   Questioning _____

   _____

   Paraphrasing _____

   _____

Supporting _____
_____

Analyzing _____
_____

Advising _____
_____

Judging _____
_____

Which listening styles do you think are most appropriate in this situation? Why?
_____
_____

Which listening styles do you think are most inappropriate in this situation? Why?
_____
_____

2. My roommate and I can't seem to get along. She's always having her boyfriend over, and he doesn't know when to go home. I don't want to move out, but I can't put up with this much longer. If I bring it up I know my roommate will get defensive, though.

Prompting _____
_____

Questioning _____
_____

Paraphrasing _____
_____

Supporting _____
_____

Analyzing _____

_____

Advising _____

_____

Judging _____

_____

Which listening styles do you think are most appropriate in this situation? Why?

_____

_____

Which listening styles do you think are most inappropriate in this situation? Why?

_____

_____

3. The pressure of going to school and doing all the other things in my life is really getting to me. I can't go on like this, but I don't know where I can cut back.

What would be your long- and short-term goals in this situation?

_____

_____

Circle the type of response you think will help you meet your goals (prompting, questioning, paraphrasing, supporting, analyzing, advising, judging). Why do you think this is the best type of listening response? _____

_____

Now write this type of response. _____

_____

4.   You'd think that by the time you become an adult your parents would stop treating you like a child, but not mine! If I wanted their advice about how to live my life, I'd ask.

What would be your long- and short-term goals in this situation?

_____

_____

Circle the type of response you think will help you meet your goals (prompting, questioning, paraphrasing, supporting, analyzing, advising, judging). Why do you think this is the best type of listening response? _____

_____

Now write this type of response. _____

_____

5. (Record a situation of your own here) _____

_____

What would be your long- and short-term goals in this situation?

_____

_____

Circle the type of response you think will help you meet your goals (prompting, questioning, paraphrasing, supporting, analyzing, advising, judging). Why do you think this is the best type of listening response? _____

_____

Now write this type of response. _____

_____

REFLECTIONS

1. Are there types of listening responses that you are familiar with that are not mentioned here?

_____

_____

_____

2. Are there listening responses that you have trouble categorizing? Which ones? Why are they difficult to categorize?

_____

_____

_____

3. Is there value to learning these categories? Why or why not?

_____

_____

_____

7.5 LISTENING ANALYSIS

LEARNING OBJECTIVES

- Identify the response styles that you commonly use when listening to others.
- Demonstrate a combination of listening styles you could use to respond effectively in a given situation.

INSTRUCTIONS

Use the case below and the discussion questions that follow to discuss the variety of communication issues involved in effective communication. Make notes on this page, add other pages on your own, or prepare a group report/analysis based on your discussion. Add your own experiences to individualize the analysis.

CASE

Larry and Sam have been friends since elementary school and are now in their thirties. Larry has been happily married for ten years. Sam has been engaged four times, and each time has broken it off as the marriage date approaches. Sam has just announced another engagement.

1. What are the likely barriers that would prevent Larry from listening effectively?

   _____

   _____

2. What types of ineffective listening are likely to occur if Larry doesn't carefully consider his listening options?

   _____

   _____

3. What listening style(s) could Larry use that would be most helpful to Sam? Why? Construct a response for Larry using that style.

   _____

   _____

4. Suppose that the two friends described here are both women. How would your responses to the preceding questions change?

_____

_____

7.6 ASSESSING LISTENING SITUATIONS

LEARNING OBJECTIVES

- Demonstrate a combination of listening styles you could use to respond effectively in a given situation.

INSTRUCTIONS

We all face challenges in listening to others. Read the following scenarios and describe what strategy you would use to maintain effective listening.

1. You are trying to talk to your friend about problems with her parents while you are at a bar with loud music in the background.

Strategy:

_____

_____

_____

2. Your friend needs to talk to you about her new relationship but you have a difficult time listening because you have an early morning history test to study for and have a trip to plan. With all this on your mind, how can you maintain effective listening?

Strategy:

_____

_____

_____

3. You are talking on your cell phone and the reception is bad.

Strategy:

_____

_____

_____

STUDY GUIDE

CHECK YOUR UNDERSTANDING

TRUE/FALSE

Mark the statements below as true or false. Correct false statements on the lines below to create a true statement.

_____   1.   We spend more time listening to others than in any other type of communication.

_____

_____   2.   Speaking is active; listening is passive.

_____

_____   3.   All interruptions are attempts at stage-hogging.

_____

_____   4.   Both men and women want supportive, endorsing messages in difficult situations.

_____

_____   5.   Listening skills are just as vital as speaking skills for career success.

_____

_____   6.   People speak at about the same rate as others are capable of understanding their speech.

_____

_____   7.   The advantages of listening are more obvious to people than the advantages of speaking.

_____

_____ 8. Responding to a message rarely involves giving observable feedback to the speaker.

     _____

_____ 9. Judging as a listening response may be favorable or negative.

     _____

_____ 10. A good listener pays attention to paralanguage.

     _____

COMPLETION

Fill in the blanks below with the correct terms chosen from the list below.

residual message	attending	conversational narcissist
sincere question	counterfeit question	constructive criticism
agreement	understanding	remembering
hearing	selective	insulated

1. _____ is a name given to a nonlistening stage hog.

2. _____ is a genuine request for new information aimed at understanding others.

3. _____ is the information we store (remember) after processing information from teachers, friends, radio, TV, and other sources.

4. _____ is the psychological process of listening.

5. _____ is a query that is a disguised attempt to send a message, not receive one.

6. _____ is a lesser form of negative judgment that is intended to help the problem holder improve in the future.

7. _____ is the physiological process of listening.

8. _____ is the process of making sense of a message.

9. _____ is the ability to recall information.

10. _____ is a listening response designed to show solidarity with speakers by telling them how right they are.

11. _____ is a nonlistening style that responds only to what the listener cares about.

12. _____ is a nonlistening style that ignores information the listener doesn't want to deal with.

MULTIPLE CHOICE

Match the letter of the listening type with its example found below.

a. advising   c. analyzing   e. supporting   g. paraphrasing
b. judging   d. questioning   f. prompting

_____ 1. "So what do you mean by that?"

_____ 2. "You're mad at me for postponing the meeting?"

_____ 3. "You're probably just more upset than usual because of the stress of exams."

_____ 4. "What reason did she give for not attending?"

_____ 5. "Well, that was good of him not to complain."

_____ 6. "Have you tried praising her?"

_____ 7. "Have you tried talking to him about it?"

_____ 8. "Are you as excited as you sound about this big meet?"

_____ 9. "Jim should not have said that to Amy after you asked him not to."

_____ 10. "And then what happened?"

_____ 11. "So why did you go to Ellie's in the first place?"

_____ 12. "You really are good; they'll recognize that."

_____ 13. "It's not fair for you to have to work nights."

_____ 14. "Maybe you should give her a taste of her own medicine."

_____ 15. "And so you feel like retaliating because you're hurt?"

_____ 16. "Maybe you're a little insecure because of the divorce?"

_____ 17. "Like what?"

_____ 18. "What makes you think that he's cheating?"

_____ 19. "You've always pulled out those grades before—I know you can do it again."

_____ 20. "She's probably jealous so that's why she's doing that."

Choose the best listening response to each statement below.

21. Boss to employee: "Draft a letter that denies this request for a refund, but make it tactful." Identify the best paraphrasing of content response.

    a. "What do you want me to say?"
    b. "How can I say no tactfully?"
    c. "So I should explain nicely why we can't give a refund, right?"
    d. "In other words, you want me to give this customer the brush-off?"

22. Friend says, "How do they expect us to satisfy the course requirements when there aren't enough spaces in the classes we're supposed to take?" Identify the best questioning response.

    a. "What class do you need that you can't get into?"
    b. "You think that some of the courses are worthless—is that it?"
    c. "Sounds like you're sorry you chose this major."
    d. "Why don't you write a letter to the chairperson of the department?"

23. Friend says, "Why don't I meet you after class at the student union?" Identify the best questioning response.

    a. "So you want me to pick you up at the student union?"
    b. "You want me to pick you up *again*?"
    c. "What time do you think you'll be there?"
    d. "Why can't you drive yourself? Is your car broken again?"

24. Coworker advises, "When you go in for a job interview, be sure and talk about the internship, your coursework, and your extracurricular activities. Don't expect them to ask you." Identify the best paraphrasing response.

    a. "You think they won't ask about those things?"
    b. "Won't that sound like bragging?"
    c. "Why should I talk about the internship?"
    d. "So you're saying not to be bashful about stressing my experience?"

25. Friend says, "I don't think it's right that they go out and recruit women when there are plenty of good men around." Identify the best supporting response.

    a. "I think you're job hunting well in spite of the challenges."
    b. "You shouldn't let that bother you."
    c. "That's just the way life is."
    d. "I can see that you're angry. What makes you think women are being given an unfair advantage?"

For each of the statements below, identify which response is the most complete and accurate paraphrasing of the speaker's thoughts and feelings.

26. "Sometimes I think I'd like to drop out of school, but then I start to feel like a quitter."

    a. "Maybe it would be helpful to take a break. You can always come back, you know."
    b. "You're afraid that you might fail if you stay in school now, is that it?"
    c. "I can really relate to what you're saying. I feel awkward here myself sometimes."
    d. "So you'd feel ashamed of yourself if you quit now, even though you'd like to?"

27. "I don't want to go to the party. I won't know anyone there, and I'll wind up sitting by myself all night."

    a. "You're anxious about introducing yourself to people who don't know you."
    b. "You never know; you could have a great time."
    c. "So you really don't want to go, eh?"
    d. "What makes you think it will be that way?"

28. "I get really nervous talking to my professor. I keep thinking that I sound stupid."

    a. "Talking to her is really a frightening experience."
    b. "You're saying that you'd rather not approach her."
    c. "You get the idea that she's evaluating you, so you feel inadequate.
    d. "You think that talking to her might affect your grade for the worse."

29. "I don't know what to do about my kids. Their whining is driving me crazy."

    a. "Even though whining is natural, it's getting to you."
    b. "Sometimes you lose patience and feel irritated when they complain."
    c. "You're getting angry at them."
    d. "Even the best parents get irritated sometimes."

30. "I just blew another test in that class. Why can't I do better?"

    a. "You probably need to study harder. You'll get it!"
    b. "You're feeling sorry for yourself because you can't pull a better grade."
    c. "Where do you think the problem is?"
    d. "You're discouraged and frustrated because you don't know what you're doing wrong."

Choose the best answer for each of the statements below:

_____ 31.   A good listener pays attention to
a. paralanguage.
b. facial expression.
c. nonverbal cues.
d. all of the above

_____ 32.   When we move beyond hearing and start to listen and process information in two different ways, we are engaging in
a. dual process theory.
b. process theory.
c. critical listening.
d. careful listening.

_____ 33.   In a survey that questioned adults who had spouses with hearing loss,
a. many respondents were unfazed when their partner couldn't hear them correctly.
b. many respondents felt that their spouses are open and upfront about their hearing obstacles.
c. many respondents believed their spouses were in denial about their condition.
d. less than a quarter of respondents felt annoyed when their partner couldn't hear them correctly.

_____ 34.   When paraphrasing, it is a good idea to

a. assume your paraphrase is correct.
b. end with a question to confirm the paraphrase was accurate.
c. paraphrase in a variety of ways to ensure accuracy.
d. avoid paraphrasing if it feels awkward.

CHAPTER SEVEN STUDY GUIDE ANSWERS

TRUE/FALSE

1.	T	3.	F	5.	T	7.	F	9.	T
2.	F	4.	T	6.	F	8.	F	10.	T

COMPLETION

1.	conversational narcissist	5.	counterfeit question	9.	remembering
2.	sincere question	6.	constructive criticism	10.	agreement
3.	residual message	7.	hearing	11.	selective
4.	attending	8.	understanding	12.	insulated

MULTIPLE CHOICE

1.	f	7.	a	13.	b	19.	e	25.	a	31.	d
2.	g	8.	g	14.	a	20.	c	26.	d	32.	a
3.	c	9.	b	15.	g	21.	c	27.	a	33.	c
4.	d	10.	f	16.	c	22.	a	28.	c	34.	b
5.	b	11.	d	17.	f	23.	c	29.	b		
6.	a	12.	e	18.	d	24.	d	30.	d		

Communication and Relational Dynamics

After studying the topics in this chapter, you should be able to:

1. Identify factors that have influenced your choice of relational partners.

2. Use Knapp's model to describe the nature of communication in the various stages of a relationship.

3. Describe the dialectical tensions in a given relationship, how they influence communication, and the most effective strategies for managing them.

4. Explain how change and culture affect communication in interpersonal relationships.

5. Identify the content and relational dimensions of communication in a given transaction.

6. Describe how metacommunication can be used to improve the quality of a given relationship.

"We have a terrific relationship."

"I'm looking for a better relationship."

"Our relationship has changed a lot."

"We need to talk about our relationship."

Relationship is one of those words that people use all the time but have trouble defining. Take a moment to see if you can explain the term in your own words. It isn't as easy as it might seem. For instance, most would agree that it's important to form relationships with clients and customers—but, of course, those relationships are quite different from those with sweethearts or close friends. You have a relationship with your family members (after all, they're *related* to you)—but those relationships might be strained or even broken. And social media users know that it's a big deal to declare online that they're "in a relationship."

Rather than define (and therefore limit) the concept of "relationship," this chapter will look at relational dynamics and how communication operates as people form, manage, and sometimes end their relationships. You will see that relationships aren't static like a painting or photograph: They change over time like an ongoing dance or drama. Even the most stable and satisfying relationships wax and wane in a variety of ways as communication patterns change. By the time you finish reading the following pages, you will have a better sense of how communication both defines and reflects our interpersonal world.

Why We Form Relationships

What makes us seek relationships with some people and not with others? Sometimes we don't have a choice. Children can't select their parents, and most workers aren't able to choose their bosses or colleagues. In many other cases, however, we seek out some people and actively avoid others. Social scientists have collected an impressive body of research on interpersonal attraction.[1] The following are some of the factors they have identified that influence our choice of relational partners.

APPEARANCE

Most people claim that we should judge others on the basis of how they act, not how they look. However, as Chapter 6 explained (see pages 206–208), the reality is quite the opposite.[2] Appearance is especially important in the early stages of a relationship. In one study, a group of more than seven hundred men and women were matched as blind dates for a social event. After the party was over, they were asked whether they would like to date their partners again. The result? The more physically attractive the person (as judged in advance by independent raters), the more likely he or she was seen as desirable. Other factors—social skills and intelligence, for example—didn't seem to affect the decision.[3]

In a more contemporary example, physical appearance is the primary basis of attraction for speed daters.[4] Perhaps this is why online daters routinely enhance their photographs and information about their height and weight to appear more attractive to potential suitors.[5] (See the reading on page 252.) Online profile owners are also rated more positively when they have pictures of physically attractive friends on their sites, suggesting that they're known—and found attractive—by the company they keep.[6]

Even if your appearance isn't beautiful by societal standards, consider these encouraging facts: First, after initial impressions have passed, ordinary-looking people with pleasing personalities are likely to be judged as attractive.[7] Second, physical factors become less important as a relationship progresses.[8] In fact, as romantic relationships develop, partners create "positive illusions," viewing one another as more attractive over time.[9] As one social scientist put it, "Attractive features may open doors, but apparently it takes more than physical beauty to keep them open."[10]

SIMILARITY

A large body of research confirms the fact that we like people who are similar to us, at least in most cases.[11] For example, the more similar a married couple's personalities are, the more likely they are to report being happy and satisfied in their marriage.[12] Friends in middle and high school report being similar to one another in many ways, including having mutual friends, enjoying the same sports, liking the same social activities, and using (or not using) alcohol and cigarettes to the same degree.[13] Friendships seem most likely to last decades when the friends are similar to one another.[14] For adults,

Fancy Collection/Superstock

similarity is more important to relational happiness than even communication ability: Friends who have equally low levels of communication skills are just as satisfied with their relationships as are friends who have high levels of communication skills.[15]

One theory for why we are attracted to similar others is that it provides a measure of ego support. If we judge those who are like us to be attractive, then we must be attractive, too (or so goes the theory). One study described the lengths to which this *implicit egotism* can affect perceptions of attractiveness.[16] Results showed that people are disproportionately likely to marry others whose first or last names resemble their own, and they are also attracted to those with similar birthdays or even sports jersey numbers. We're also attracted to those whose language style matches our own.[17] On a more substantive level, similar values about politics and religion were found in one study to be the best predictors of mate choice—significantly more than attraction to physical appearance or personality traits.[18]

Attraction is greatest when we are similar to others in a high percentage of important areas. For example, two people who support each other's career goals, enjoy the same friends, and have similar beliefs about human rights can tolerate trivial disagreements about the merits of sushi or rap music. With enough similarity in key areas, they can even survive disputes about more important subjects such as how much time to spend with their families or whether separate vacations are acceptable. But if the number and content of disagreements become too great, then the relationship may be threatened.

Similarity turns from attraction to dislike when we encounter people who are like us in many ways but who behave in a strange or socially offensive manner.[19] For instance, you have probably disliked people others have said were "just like you" but who talked too much, were complainers, or had some other unappealing characteristic. In fact, there is a tendency to have stronger dislike for similar but offensive people than for those who are offensive but different. One likely reason is that such people threaten our self-esteem, causing us to fear that we may be as unappealing as they are. In such circumstances, the reaction is often to put as much distance as possible between ourselves and this threat to our ideal self-image.

ONLINE LIARS LEAVE LEADS

Online daters intent on fudging their personal information have a big advantage: most people are terrible at identifying a liar. But new research is turning the tables on deceivers using their own words.

"Generally, people don't want to admit they've lied," says Catalina Toma, communication science professor at the University of Wisconsin-Madison. "But we don't have to rely on the liars to tell us about their lies. We can read their handiwork."

Using personal descriptions written for Internet dating profiles, Toma and Jeffrey Hancock, communication professor at Cornell University, have identified clues as to whether the author was being deceptive.

A linguistic analysis of the group's written self-descriptions published in the *Journal of Communication* revealed patterns in the liars' writing. The more deceptive a dater's profile, the less likely they were to use the first-person pronoun "I."

The liars often employed negation, a flip of the language that would restate "happy" as "not sad" or "exciting" as "not boring." And the fabricators tended to write shorter self-descriptions in their profiles—a hedge, Toma expects, against weaving a more tangled web of deception. "They don't want to say too much," Toma says. "Liars experience a lot of cognitive load. They have a lot to think about. The less they write, the fewer untrue things they may have to remember and support later."

Liars were also careful to skirt their own deception. Daters who had lied about their age, height or weight or had included a photo the researchers found to be less than representative of reality, were likely to avoid discussing their appearance in their written descriptions, choosing instead to talk about work or life achievements.

About 80 percent of the 78 profiles in the study strayed from the truth on some level. "Almost everybody lied about something, but the magnitude was often small," Toma says. Weight was the most frequent transgression, with women off by an average of 8.5 pounds and men missing by 1.5 pounds on average. Half lied

John Lund/Sam Diephuis/Blend Images/Corbis

about their height, and nearly 20 percent changed their age.

Studying lying through online communication such as dating profiles opens a door on a medium in which the liar has more room to maneuver. "You have all the time in the world to say whatever you want. You're not expected to be spontaneous. You can write and rewrite as many times as you want before you post, and then in many cases return and edit yourself."

Chris Barncard

COMPLEMENTARITY

The familiar saying that "opposites attract" seems to contradict the principle of similarity we just described. In truth, though, both are valid. Differences strengthen a relationship when they are *complementary*—when each partner's characteristics satisfy the other's needs.

Research suggests that attraction to partners who have complementary temperaments might be rooted in biology.[20] Individuals, for instance, are often likely to be attracted to each other when one partner is dominant and the other passive.[21]

Relationships also work well when the partners agree that one will exercise control in certain areas ("You make the final decisions about money") and the other will exercise control in different areas ("I'll decide how we ought to decorate the place"). Strains occur when control issues are disputed. One study shows that "spendthrifts and tightwads" are often attracted to each other, but their differences in financial management often lead to significant conflict over the course of a relationship.[22]

When successful and unsuccessful couples are compared over a twenty-year period, it becomes clear that partners in successful marriages are similar enough to satisfy each other physically and mentally but different enough to meet each other's needs and keep the relationship interesting. Successful couples find ways to keep a balance between their similarities and differences, adjusting to the changes that occur over the years. We'll have more to say about balancing similarities and differences later in this chapter.

RECIPROCAL ATTRACTION

We like people who like us—usually.[23] The power of reciprocal attraction is especially strong in the early stages of a relationship. At that time we are attracted to people who we believe are attracted to us. Conversely, we will probably not care for people who either attack or seem indifferent toward us.

It's no mystery why reciprocal liking builds attractiveness: People who approve of us bolster our feelings of self-esteem. This approval is rewarding in its own right, and it can also confirm a presenting self-concept that says, "I'm a likable person."

You can probably think of cases where you haven't liked people who seemed to like you. For example, you might think the other person's supposed liking is counterfeit—an insincere device to get something from you. At other times the liking may not fit with your own self-concept. When someone says you're good-looking, intelligent, and kind, but you believe you're ugly, stupid, and mean, you may choose to disregard the flattering information and remain in your familiar state of unhappiness. Groucho Marx summarized this attitude when he said he would never join any club that would consider having him as a member.

COMPETENCE

We like to be around talented people, probably because we hope their skills and abilities will rub off on us. We are uncomfortable around those who are *too* competent, however, probably because we look bad by comparison. Given these contrasting attitudes, it's no surprise that people are generally attracted to those who are talented but who have visible flaws that show that they are human, just like us.[24] Moreover, we're attracted to people whose competence is paired with interpersonal warmth. "Competent but cool" is generally not seen as an attractive mix.[25]

DISCLOSURE

As noted in Chapter 2, revealing important information about yourself can help build liking.[26] Sometimes the basis of this liking comes from learning about how we are similar, either in experiences ("I broke off an engagement myself") or in attitudes ("I feel nervous with strangers, too"). Self-disclosure also builds liking because it is a sign of regard. When people share private information with you, it suggests that they respect and trust you—a kind of liking that we've already seen increases attractiveness. Disclosure plays an even more important role as relationships develop beyond their earliest stages. This is the case in both online and face-to-face communication and relationships.[27] Remember, of course, that online disclosures can sometimes stretch the truth, as the reading on page 252 explains.

Not all disclosure leads to liking. Research shows that the key to satisfying self-disclosure is *reciprocity*: getting back an amount and kind of information equivalent to that which you reveal.[28] A second important ingredient in successful self-disclosure is *timing*. It's probably unwise to talk about your sexual insecurities with a new acquaintance or express your pet peeves to a friend at your birthday party. Finally, for the sake of self-protection, it's important to reveal personal information only when you are sure the other person is trustworthy.[29]

PROXIMITY

As common sense suggests, we are likely to develop relationships with people we interact with frequently.[30] In many cases, proximity leads to liking. For instance, we're more likely to develop friendships with close neighbors than with distant ones, and chances are good that we'll choose a mate with whom we cross paths often. Facts like these are understandable when we consider that proximity allows us to get more information about other people and benefit from a relationship with them. Also, people in close proximity may be more similar to us than those who are not close; for example, if we live in the same neighborhood, odds are we share the same socioeconomic status. The Internet provides a new means for creating closeness, as users are able to experience "virtual proximity" in cyberspace.[31]

REWARDS

Some social scientists believe that all relationships—both impersonal and personal are based on a semi-economic model called *social exchange theory*.[32] This model suggests that we often seek out people who can give us rewards that are greater than or equal to the costs we encounter in dealing with them. According to social exchange theory, relationships suffer when one partner feels "underbenefited."[33]

LOOKING AT DIVERSITY

Kevin Schomaker: Forging Relationships with Social Media

Kevin Schomaker

Building new relationships is tough for me because I have cerebral palsy. I can't move my arms and legs, and I have difficulty speaking. When I'm in face-to-face situations I usually talk by typing words that get spoken in a computerized voice. This works okay with people who know me, but it isn't an ideal way to start a relationship. People often are so preoccupied with my physical condition that it's hard for them to get beyond that first impression and learn who I am.

Online communication has been great for me because it makes my physical condition almost irrelevant. I met one of my best friends through Facebook. We chatted online for a couple of months before we ever met in person, and later we became suitemates in college because of the relationship we started online. Similarly, I got an email from a student who said she was going to be my Residential Assistant in the fall. I looked her up on Facebook, friended her, and found out we had a lot in common by reading her information page. By the time I arrived at my dorm that year, she and I were already good friends.

For some people, online communication is a nice convenience—but for me, it's been a life-changer. It has increased and enhanced my interpersonal relationships, and for that I'm grateful.

"Forging Relationships with Social Media" by Kevin Schomaker. Used with permission of author.

Rewards may be tangible (a nice place to live, a high-paying job) or intangible (prestige, emotional support, companionship). Costs are undesirable outcomes: unpleasant work, emotional pain, and so on. A simple formula captures the social exchange theory of why we form and maintain relationships:

Rewards – Costs = Outcome

According to social exchange theorists, we use this formula (often unconsciously) to decide whether dealing with another person is a "good deal" or "not worth the effort," based on whether the outcome is positive or negative.

At its most blatant level, an exchange approach seems cold and calculating, but in some types of relationships it seems quite appropriate. A healthy business relationship is based on how well the parties help one another, and some friendships are based on an informal kind of barter: "I don't mind listening to the ups and downs of your love life, because you rescue me when the house needs repairs." Even close relationships have an element of exchange. Friends and lovers often tolerate each other's quirks because the comfort and enjoyment they get make the less-than-pleasant times worth accepting. In more serious cases, social exchange explains why some people stay in abusive relationships. Sadly, these people often report that they would rather be in a bad relationship than have no relationship at all.

"I'd like to buy everyone a drink. All I ask in return is that you listen patiently to my shallow and simplistic views on a broad range of social and political issues."

At first glance, the social exchange approach seems to present a view of relationships that is very different from one based on the need to seek intimacy. In fact, the two approaches aren't incompatible. Seeking intimacy of any type—whether emotional, physical, or even intellectual—has its costs, and our decision about whether to "pay" those costs is, in great measure, made by considering the likely rewards. If the costs of seeking and maintaining an intimate relationship are too great or the payoffs are not worth the effort, we may decide to withdraw.

Models of Relational Dynamics

Your own experience demonstrates that relational beginnings are a unique time. How does communication change as we spend time with others and get to know them? Communication scholars have different perspectives on this question. We'll look at two approaches—developmental and dialectical—in this section.

A DEVELOPMENTAL PERSPECTIVE

One of the best-known models of relational stages was developed by communication researcher Mark Knapp. It breaks the rise and fall of relationships into ten stages, contained in the two broad phases of "coming together" and "coming apart."[34] Other researchers have suggested that any model of relational communication ought to contain a third phase of **relational maintenance**—communication aimed at keeping

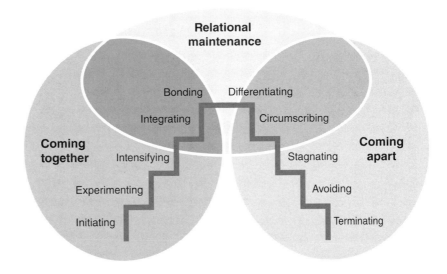

FIGURE 8.1 Stages of Relational Development © Cengage Learning

relationships operating smoothly and satisfactorily.[35] (We'll discuss relational maintenance in detail in Chapter 9.) Figure 8.1 shows how Knapp's ten stages fit into this three-phase view of relational communication.

This model seems most appropriate for describing communication between romantic partners, but in many respects it works well for other types of close relationships.[36] As you read the following section, consider how the stages could describe a long-term friendship, a couple in love, or even business partners.

Initiating The goals in the first stage of a relationship are to show that you are interested in making contact and that you are the kind of person worth talking to. Communication during this **initiating** stage is usually brief, and it generally follows conventional formulas: handshakes, remarks about innocuous subjects like the weather, and friendly expressions. These kinds of behavior may seem superficial and meaningless, but they are a way of signaling that we're interested in building some kind of relationship with the other person. They allow us to say without saying, "I'm a friendly person, and I'd like to get to know you."

Initiating relationships—especially romantic ones—can be particularly difficult for people who are shy. Making contact via the Internet can be helpful in cases like this. One study of an online dating service found that participants who identified themselves as shy expressed a greater appreciation for the system's anonymous, nonthreatening environment than did more outgoing users.[37] The researchers found that many shy users employed the online service specifically to help overcome their inhibitions about initiating relationships in face-to-face settings. This helps explain why many young adults—shy or not—use social media sites such as Facebook to initiate relationships.[38]

Experimenting After we have made contact with a new person, the next stage is to decide whether we are interested in pursuing the relationship further. This involves *uncertainty reduction*—the process of getting to know others by gaining more information about them.[39] A usual part of uncertainty reduction is the search for common ground, and it involves the conversational basics such as "Where are you from?" or "What's your major?" From there we look for other similarities: "You're a runner, too? How many miles do you do a week?"

ON THE JOB

Memorable Messages: Initiating Company Newcomers

Getting off to a good start is just as important on the job as it is in romances or friendships. Scholars use the terms *assimilation* and *socialization* to describe how employees are integrated into their organizations. Not surprisingly, communication plays a major role in the socialization process. When helpful information is plentiful, new employees grow more satisfied with and committed to their jobs in the long run.[a]

In one study, researchers explored the nature of socialization messages.[b] While orientation sessions, handbooks, emails, and memos were useful, new employees reported that the most valuable messages often come via informal conversations—over 90 percent of which took place in face-to-face settings.

Many of the helpful messages were about professional behavior and office rules ("It's crucial to be punctual"; "Be careful when you challenge the boss"). Office politics also came into play ("Always be nice to the secretary, Nadine, because she's the gateway to the supervisor"). Not all of the messages were warnings; some were warm and welcoming ("It's one big family here"; "We're glad they hired you"). Regardless of the specific content, virtually all of the messages were perceived as positive, supportive, and designed to help the recipient, the company, or both.

It's important to remember the importance of messages—both large and small, deliberate and offhand—in building a happy, effective work team. As a newcomer, it's wise to seek the counsel and support of your colleagues. As a veteran, it's important to help rookies get off to a good start.

The hallmark of the **experimenting** stage is small talk. Even though we may dislike it, we tolerate the ordeal of small talk because it serves several functions. First, it is a useful way to find out what interests we share with the other person. It also provides a way to audition the other person—to help us decide whether a relationship is worth pursuing. In addition, small talk is a safe way to ease into a relationship. You haven't risked much as you decide whether to proceed further.

For communicators who are interested in one another, the move from initiating to experimenting seems to occur even more rapidly in cyberspace than in person. One study found that people who develop relationships via email begin asking questions about attitudes, opinions, and preferences more quickly than those engaged in face-to-face contact.[40] It probably helps that emailers can't see each other's nonverbal reactions; they don't have to worry about blushing, stammering, or looking away if they realize that they asked for too much information too quickly.

Social media, such as Facebook, may change the nature of this stage of relational development. As one communication scholar points out, information gathering that used to occur over a gradual period of self-disclosure can now be done much more quickly:

By perusing someone's social networking profile, I can, more often than not, learn many of the same things I'd learn from them during the first couple of dates without the other person being present. From what they disclose on the general information page, I can learn their relationship statuses, political preferences, favorite hobbies, music, books, and movies. By looking through their pictures and their wall, I can get a pretty good sense of the kinds of people they like to hang out with, what they like to do on weekends, their personal styles.[*]

[*]Shonbeck, K. (2011). Communicating in a connected world. In K. M. Galvin (Ed.), *Making connections: Readings in relational communication* (5th ed., pp. 393–400). New York: Oxford.

Intensifying In the **intensifying** stage, the kind of truly interpersonal relationship defined in Chapter 1 begins to develop. Several changes in communication patterns occur during intensifying. The expression of feelings toward the other becomes more common. Dating couples use a wide range of communication strategies to describe their feelings of attraction.[41] About one-quarter of the time they express their feelings directly, openly discussing the state of the relationship. More often they use less direct methods of communication: spending an increasing amount of time together, asking for support from one another, doing favors for the partner, giving tokens of affection, hinting and flirting, expressing feelings nonverbally, getting to know the partner's friends and family, and trying to look more physically attractive. In developing friendships, intensifying can include participating in shared activities, hanging out with mutual friends, or taking trips together.[42]

In the movie *(500) Days of Summer*, Tom (Joseph Gordon-Levitt) and Summer (Zooey Deschanel) don't always agree on the relational stage they're in. (See the film summary at the end of this chapter.)

The intensifying stage is usually a time of relational excitement and even euphoria. For romantic partners, it's often filled with star-struck gazes, goosebumps, and daydreaming. As a result, it's a stage that's regularly depicted in movies and romance novels—after all, we love to watch lovers in love.[43] The problem, of course, is that the stage doesn't last forever. Sometimes romantic partners who stop feeling goosebumps begin to question whether they're still in love. Although it's possible that they're not, it's also possible that they've simply moved on to a different, less emotional stage in their relationship—integrating.

Integrating As a relationship strengthens, the parties begin to take on an identity as a social unit. In romantic relationships, invitations begin to come addressed to the couple. Social circles merge. The partners begin to take on each other's commitments: "Sure, we'll spend Thanksgiving with your family." Common property may begin to be designated—our apartment, our car, our song.[44] Partners develop unique, ritualistic ways of behaving.[45] Close friends may even begin to speak alike, using personal idioms and sentence patterns.[46] In this sense, the **integrating** stage is a time when individuals give up some characteristics of their old selves and develop shared identities.

In contemporary relationships, integrating may include going "Facebook Official" by declaring publically that the couple is "in a relationship." Of course, problems can arise when one partner wants to be "FBO" and the other partner doesn't.[47] This may occur because the status is seen as requiring some of the commitment (and restrictions) of bonding, a stage we'll look at now.

Bonding During the **bonding** stage, the parties make symbolic public gestures to show the world that their relationship exists. What constitutes a bonded, committed relationship isn't always easy to define.[48] Terms such as *common-law*, *cohabitation*, and *life partners* have been used to describe relationships that don't have the full support of custom and law but still involve an implicit or explicit bond. Nonetheless, given the importance of bonding in validating relationships and taking them to another level, it's not surprising that the gay and lesbian communities are striving to have legally sanctioned and recognized marriages.

For our purposes here, we'll define bonded relationships as those involving a significant measure of public commitment. These can include engagement or marriage, sharing a residence, a public ceremony, or a written or verbal pledge. The key is that bonding is the culmination of a developed relationship—the "officializing" of a couple's integration. We'll talk more about the role of commitment in relationships in Chapter 9.

Bonding marks a turning point in a relationship. Up until now the relationship may have developed at a steady pace. Experimenting gradually moved into intensifying and then into integrating. Now, however, there is a spurt of commitment. The public display and declaration of exclusivity make this a distinct stage in the relationship.

Relationships don't have to be romantic to achieve bonding. Consider, for example, the contracts that formalize a business partnership or the initiation ceremony in a fraternity or sorority. As one author notes, even friendships can achieve bonding with acts that "officialize" the relationship:

> Some Western cultures have rituals to mark the progress of a friendship and to give it public legitimacy and form. In Germany, for example, there's a small ceremony called *Duzen*, the name itself signifying the transformation in the relationship. The ritual calls for the two friends, each holding a glass of wine or beer, to entwine arms, thus bringing each other physically close, and to drink up after making a promise of eternal brotherhood with the word *Bruderschaft*. When it's over, the friends will have passed from a relationship that requires the formal *Sie* mode of address to the familiar *du*.*

Differentiating Bonding is the peak of what Knapp calls the "coming together" phase of relational development, but people in even the most committed relationships need to assert their individual identities. This **differentiating** stage is the point where the "we" orientation that has developed shifts, and more "me" messages begin to occur. Instead of talking about "our" weekend plans, differentiating conversations focus on what "I" want to do. Relational issues that were once agreed upon (such as "You'll be the breadwinner and I'll manage the home") may now become points of contention: "Why am *I* stuck at home when I have better career potential than *you*?" The root of the term *differentiating* is the word *different*, suggesting that change plays an important role in this stage.

Differentiating is likely to occur when a relationship begins to experience the first, inevitable feelings of stress. This need for autonomy and change needn't be a negative experience, however. People need to be individuals as well as parts of a relationship, and differentiation is a necessary step toward autonomy. Think, for instance, of young adults who want to forge their own unique lives and identity, even while maintaining their relationships with their parents.[49] As the model on page 256 illustrates, differentiating is often a part of normal relational maintenance, in which partners manage the inevitable changes that come their way. The key to successful differentiating is maintaining a commitment to the relationship while creating the space for being an individual as well. (This is a challenge that we will discuss in more detail later in this chapter when we discuss dialectical tensions in relationships.)

Circumscribing In the **circumscribing** stage, communication between members decreases in quantity and quality. Restrictions and restraints characterize this stage. Rather than discuss a disagreement (which requires energy on both sides), members opt for withdrawal—either mental (silence or daydreaming and fantasizing) or

*Rubin, L. (1985). *Just friends: The role of friendship in our lives*. New York: Harper & Row.

physical (where people spend less time together). Circumscribing doesn't involve total avoidance, which may come later. Rather, it involves a shrinking of interest and commitment—the opposite of what occurred in the integrating stage.

The word *circumscribe* comes from the Latin meaning "to draw circles around." Distinctions that emerged in the differentiating stage become more clearly marked and labeled: "my friends" and "your friends"; "my bank account" and "your bank account"; "my room" and "your room." As you'll soon read, such distinctions can be markers of a healthy balance between individual and relational identity—between autonomy and connection. They become a problem when there are clearly more areas of separation than integration in a relationship, or when the areas of separation seriously limit interaction, such as "my vacation" and "your vacation."

Gary (Vince Vaughn) and Brooke (Jennifer Aniston) go through all the stages of relational deterioration in *The Break-Up*. (See the film summary at the end of this chapter.)

Stagnating If circumscribing continues, the relationship enters the **stagnating** stage. The excitement of the intensifying stage is long gone, and the partners behave toward each other in old, familiar ways without much feeling. No growth occurs. The relationship is a hollow shell of its former self. We see stagnation in many workers who have lost enthusiasm for their job, yet continue to go through the motions for years. The same sad event occurs for some couples who unenthusiastically have the same conversations, see the same people, and follow the same routines without any sense of joy or novelty.

Avoiding When stagnation becomes too unpleasant, parties in a relationship begin to create physical distance between each other. This is the **avoiding** stage. Sometimes they do it indirectly under the guise of excuses ("I've been sick lately and can't see you"); sometimes they do it directly ("Please don't call me; I don't want to see you now"). In either case, by this point the relationship's future is in doubt.

The deterioration of a relationship from bonding through circumscribing, stagnating, and avoiding isn't inevitable. One of the key differences between marriages that end in separation and those that are restored to their former intimacy is the communication that occurs when the partners are unsatisfied.[50] Unsuccessful couples deal with their problems by avoidance, indirectness, and less involvement with each other. By contrast, couples who repair their relationship communicate much more directly. They confront each other with their concerns (sometimes with the assistance of a counselor) and spend time and effort negotiating solutions to their problems.

Terminating Not all relationships end. Many career partnerships, friendships, and marriages last for a lifetime once they've been established. But many do deteriorate and reach the final stage of **terminating**. Characteristics of this stage include summary dialogues of where the relationship has gone and the desire to dissociate. The relationship may end with a cordial dinner, a note left on the kitchen table, a phone call, or a legal document. Depending on each person's feelings, this stage can be quite short, or it may be drawn out over time.

Relationships don't always move toward termination in a straight line. Rather, they take a back-and-forth pattern, where the trend is toward dissolution.[51] Regardless of how long it takes, termination doesn't have to be totally negative. Understanding each other's investments in the relationship and needs for personal growth may dilute the hard feelings. In fact, many relationships aren't so much terminated as redefined. A divorced couple, for example, may find new, less intimate ways to relate to each other.

In romantic relationships, the best predictor of whether the parties will be friends after reaching the terminating stage is whether they were friends before their emotional involvement.[52] The way the couple splits up also makes a difference. It's no surprise to find that friendships are most possible when communication during the breakup is positive (expressions that there are no regrets for time spent together, other attempts to minimize hard feelings). When communication during termination is negative (being manipulative, complaining to third parties), friendships are less likely.

After termination, couples often engage in "grave-dressing"—retrospective attempts to explain why the relationship failed.[53] The narrative each partner creates about "what went wrong" has an impact on how the couple will get along after their breakup (imagine the difference between saying and hearing "We just weren't right for each other" versus "He was too selfish and immature for a committed relationship").[54]

While Knapp's model offers insights into relational stages, it doesn't describe the ebb and flow of communication in every relationship. For instance, Knapp suggests that movement among stages is generally sequential, so that relationships typically progress from one stage to another in a predictable manner as they develop and deteriorate. One study found that many terminated friendships did follow a pattern similar to the one described by Knapp.[55] However, several other patterns of development and deterioration were also identified. In other words, not all relationships begin, progress, decline, and end in the same linear fashion.

Finally, Knapp's model suggests that a relationship exhibits only the most dominant traits of just one of the ten stages at any given time, but elements of other stages are usually present. For example, two lovers deep in the throes of integrating may still do their share of experimenting ("Wow, I never knew that about you!") and have differentiating disagreements ("Nothing personal, but I need a weekend to myself"). Likewise, family members who spend most of their energy avoiding each other may have an occasional good spell in which their former closeness briefly intensifies. The notion that relationships can experience features of both "coming together" and "coming apart" at the same time is explored in the following section on relational dialectics.

PEARLS BEFORE SWINE © 2011 Stephan Pastis. Reprinted by permission of Universal Uclick for UFS. All rights reserved.

PAUSE AND REFLECT

YOUR RELATIONAL STAGE

You can gain a clearer appreciation of the accuracy and value of relational stages by answering the following questions:

1. If you are in a relationship, describe its present stage and the behaviors that characterize your communication in this stage. Give specific examples to support your assessment.
2. Discuss the trend of the communication in terms of the stages described on pages 256–261. Are you likely to remain in the present stage, or do you anticipate movement to another stage? Which one? Explain your answer.
3. Describe your level of satisfaction with the answer to question 2. If you are satisfied, describe what you can do to increase the likelihood that the relationship will operate at the stage you described. If you are not satisfied, discuss what you can do to move the relationship toward a more satisfying stage.
4. Because both parties define a relationship, define your partner's perspective. Would she or he say that the relationship is in the same stage as you described? If not, explain how your partner would describe it. What does your partner do to determine the stage at which your relationship operates? (Give specific examples.) How would you like your partner to behave in order to move the relationship to or maintain it at the stage you desire? What can you do to encourage your partner to behave in the way you desire?
5. Now consider a relationship (friendship or romance) you have been in that has terminated. How well does the Knapp model describe the development and decline of that relationship? If the model doesn't match, develop a new model to illustrate your relationship's pattern.

 You can complete this activity by visiting CengageBrain.com to access the Speech Communication CourseMate for *Looking Out/ Looking In*, and, if requested, email your responses to your instructor.

A DIALECTICAL PERSPECTIVE

Not all theorists agree that stage-related models like the one described in the preceding pages are the best way to explain interaction in relationships. Some suggest that communicators grapple with the same kinds of challenges whether a relationship is brand new or decades old. They argue that communicators seek important but inherently incompatible goals throughout virtually all of their relationships. The struggle to achieve these goals creates **dialectical tensions**: conflicts that arise when two opposing or incompatible forces exist simultaneously. Communication scholars have identified several dialectical forces that make successful communication challenging.[56] They suggest that the struggle to manage these dialectical tensions creates the most powerful dynamics in relational communication. In the following pages, we will discuss three powerful dialectical tensions.

Connection versus Autonomy No one is an island. Recognizing this fact, we seek out involvement with others. But, at the same time, we are unwilling to sacrifice our entire identity to even the most satisfying relationship. The conflicting desires for both dependence and independence are embodied in the **connection-autonomy dialectic**.

Research on relational breakups demonstrates the consequences for relational partners who can't find a way to manage this dialectical tension.[57] Some of the most common reasons for relational breakups involve failure of partners to satisfy each other's needs for connection: "We barely spent any time together," "She wasn't committed to the relationship," "We had different needs." But other relational complaints involve excessive demands for connection: "I was feeling trapped," "I needed freedom."[58] Perhaps not surprisingly, some research suggests that men value autonomy in relationships more than women do, whereas women tend to value connection and commitment.[59]

The levels of connection and autonomy that we seek can change over time. In his book *Intimate Behavior*, Desmond Morris suggests that each of us repeatedly goes through three stages: "Hold me tight," "Put me down," and "Leave me alone."[60] This cycle becomes apparent in the first years of life, when children move from the "hold-me-tight" stage that characterizes infancy into a new "put-me-down" stage of exploring the world by crawling, walking, touching, and tasting. The same three-year-old who insists "I can do it myself" in August may cling to parents on the first day of preschool in September. As children grow into adolescents, the "leave-me-alone" orientation becomes apparent. Teenagers who used to happily spend time with their parents now may groan at the thought of a family vacation or even the notion of sitting down at the dinner table each evening. As adolescents move into adulthood, they typically grow closer to their families again.[61]

In adult relationships, the same cycle of intimacy and distance repeats itself. In marriages, for example, the "hold-me-tight" bonds of the first year are often followed by a desire for autonomy. This desire can manifest itself in several ways, such as wanting to make friends or engage in activities that don't include the spouse or the need to make a career move that might disrupt the relationship. As the discussion of relational stages earlier in this chapter explained, this movement from connection to autonomy may lead to the breakup of relationships, but it can also be part of a cycle that redefines the relationship in a new form that can recapture or even surpass the intimacy that existed in the past.

Both men and women in heterosexual romantic pairs cite the connection-autonomy dialectic as one of the most significant factors affecting their relationship.[62] This dialectical tension is crucial in negotiating turning points related to commitment, conflict, disengagement, and reconciliation. On a smaller level, studies have found that satisfied couples negotiate and adhere to rules about cell phone usage as a means to balance connection-autonomy needs.[63] Cell phones allow people to stay connected, but rules help manage expectations about how often couples will (or won't) talk to and text each other. This can help establish a measure of autonomy for partners who want and need it.

Managing the tension between connection and autonomy is also important at the end of a relationship, as partners seek ways to salvage the positive parts of their relationship (if only the good memories) and take steps toward their new independence.[64] Even at the end of life, the connection-autonomy dialectic comes into play. When a loved one is in an extended period of declining health, the partner often feels torn between the desire to stay close and the need to let go. This tension is especially poignant when one partner suffers from a condition like Alzheimer's disease and becomes mentally absent while physically present.[65]

Cyrus (Jonah Hill) and his mom Molly (Marisa Tomei) really love one another. Molly's suitor John (John C. Reilly) discovers that their connection makes a romantic relationship difficult. (See the film summary at the end of this chapter.)

Openness versus Privacy As Chapter 1 explained, disclosure is one characteristic of interpersonal relationships. Yet, along with the need to disclose, we have an equally important drive to maintain some space between ourselves and others. These conflicting needs create the **openness-privacy dialectic**.

Even the strongest interpersonal relationships require some distance. Lovers may go through periods of much sharing and periods of relative withdrawal. Likewise, they experience periods of passion and then periods of little physical contact. Friends have times of high disclosure when they share almost every feeling and idea and then disengage for days, months, or even longer.

What do you do in an intimate relationship when a person you care about asks an important question that you don't want to answer? As Chapter 2 notes, questions such as "Do you think I'm attractive?" and "Are you having a good time?" can pose self-disclosure dilemmas. Your commitment to honesty may compel you toward a candid response, but your concern for the other person's feelings and a desire for privacy may lead you to be less than completely honest. Partners use a variety of strategies to gain privacy from each other.[66] For example, they may confront the other person directly and explain that they don't want to continue a discussion, or they may be less direct and offer nonverbal cues, change the topic, or leave the room.

Communication via social media adds challenges to privacy management. Facebook, Twitter, blogs, and other mediated outlets make it easy to broadcast personal information. Just because it's easy, however, doesn't mean it's always wise. This is particularly true when the information you're revealing involves someone else. It's important to know how to use privacy controls on social media tools, and also to negotiate what you will and won't share about your relationships with others.[67]

Predictability versus Novelty Stability is an important need in relationships, but too much of it can lead to feelings of staleness. The **predictability-novelty dialectic** reflects this tension. Humorist Dave Barry exaggerates only slightly when he talks about the boredom that can come when husbands and wives know each other too well:

"And do you, Rebecca, promise to make love only to Richard, month after month, year after year, and decade after decade, until one of you is dead?"

After a decade or so of marriage, you know *everything* about your spouse, every habit and opinion and twitch and tic and minor skin growth. You could write a seventeen-pound book solely about the way your spouse *eats*. This kind of intimate knowledge can be very handy in certain situations—such as when you're on a TV quiz show where the object is to identify your spouse from the sound of his or her chewing—but it tends to lower the passion level of a relationship.[*]

Although too much familiarity can lead to the risk of boredom and stagnation, nobody wants a completely unpredictable relational partner. Too many surprises can threaten the foundations upon which the relationship is based ("You're not the person I married!").

The challenge for communicators is to juggle the desire for predictability with the desire for novelty that keeps the relationship fresh and interesting.

People differ in their desire for predictability and novelty, so there is no optimal mixture of the two. As you will read shortly, people can use several strategies to manage these contradictory drives.

[*]Barry, D. (1990). *Dave Barry turns 40* (p. 47). New York: Fawcett.

Managing Dialectical Tensions Although all of the dialectical tensions play an important role in managing relationships, some occur more frequently than others. In one study, young married couples reported that connection-autonomy was the most frequent tension (30.8 percent of all reported contradictions).[68] Predictability-novelty was second (21.7 percent). Least common was openness-privacy (12.7 percent).

Managing the dialectical tensions outlined in these pages presents communication challenges. There are many ways to meet these challenges, and some work better than others.[69]

- *Denial.* In the strategy of denial, communicators respond to one end of the dialectical spectrum and ignore the other. For example, a couple caught between the conflicting desires for predictability and novelty might find their struggle for change too difficult to manage and choose to follow predictable, if unexciting, patterns of relating to each other.
- *Disorientation.* In this strategy, communicators feel so overwhelmed and helpless that they are unable to confront their problems. In the face of dialectical tensions, they might fight, freeze, or even leave the relationship. Two people who discover soon after the honeymoon that a "happily ever after," conflict-free life isn't realistic might become so terrified that they would come to view their marriage as a mistake.
- *Alternation.* Communicators who use this strategy choose one end of the dialectical spectrum at some times and the other end at other times. Friends, for example, might manage the connection-autonomy dialectic by alternating between times when they spend a large amount of time together and other times when they live independent lives.
- *Segmentation.* Partners who use this tactic compartmentalize different areas of their relationship. For example, a couple might manage the openness-privacy dialectic by sharing almost all their feelings about mutual friends with each other, but keeping certain parts of their past romantic histories private. Segmentation is the most frequently used method for stepchildren to manage openness-privacy tensions with their nonresident parents.[70] In the "Zits" cartoon on this page, Jeremy realizes he has forgotten to use his usual approach of segmentation to manage the openness-privacy dialectic with his inquisitive parents.
- *Balance.* Communicators who try to balance dialectical tensions recognize that both forces are legitimate and try to manage them through compromise. As Chapter 11 points out, compromise is inherently a situation in which everybody loses at least a little of what he or she wants. A couple caught between the conflicting desires for predictability and novelty might seek balance by compromising with a lifestyle that is neither as predictable as one wants nor as surprise-filled as the other wants—not an ideal outcome.

Zits Partnership/King Features

- *Integration.* With this strategy, communicators simultaneously accept opposing forces without trying to diminish them. Communication researcher Barbara Montgomery describes a couple that accepts the needs for both predictability and novelty by devising a "predictably novel" approach: Once a week they would do something together that they had never done before.[71] In a similar way, some step-families manage the tension between the "old family" and the "new family" by adapting and blending their family rituals.[72]
- *Recalibration.* Communicators can respond to dialectical challenges by reframing them so that the apparent contradiction disappears. For example, a change in thinking can transform your attitude from loving someone *despite* your differences to loving him or her *because* of those differences.[73] Or consider how two people who each felt hurt by each other's unwillingness to share parts of his or her past might redefine the secrets to create an attractive aura of mystery, instead of seeing them as a problem to be solved. The desire for privacy would still remain, but it would no longer compete with a need for openness about every aspect of the past.
- *Reaffirmation.* This strategy acknowledges that dialectical tensions will never disappear. Instead of trying to make them go away, reaffirming communicators accept—or even embrace—the challenges that the tensions present. The metaphorical view of relational life as a kind of roller coaster reflects this strategy, and communicators who use reaffirmation view dialectical tensions as part of the ride.

Which of these strategies do you use to manage the dialectical tensions in your life? How successful is each one? Which strategies might serve your communication better? Generally speaking, the last three options above are seen as the most productive, and researchers suggest it's wise to make use of multiple strategies.[74] For example, broken-up couples report having used denial, alternation, and segmentation less than successfully, and they tended to rely on only one strategy rather than using the variety at their disposal.[75] Since dialectical tensions are a part of life, choosing how to communicate about them can make a tremendous difference in the quality of your relationships.

PAUSE AND REFLECT

YOUR DIALECTICAL TENSIONS

Describe how each of the dialectical tensions described in these pages operate in one of your important relationships. What incompatible goals do you and your relational partner(s) seek? Which of the strategies described on pages 265–266 do you use to manage these tensions? Are you satisfied with this strategy, or can you suggest better strategies?

 You can complete this activity by visiting CengageBrain.com to access the Speech Communication CourseMate for *Looking Out/ Looking In*, and, if requested, email your responses to your instructor.

Characteristics of Relationships

Whether you analyze a relationship in terms of developmental stages or dialectical tensions, two characteristics are true of every interpersonal relationship. As you read about each, consider how it applies to your own experience.

RELATIONSHIPS ARE CONSTANTLY CHANGING

Relationships are certainly not doomed to deteriorate, but even the strongest ones are rarely stable for long periods. In fairy tales a couple may live "happily ever after," but in real life this sort of equilibrium is less common. Consider a couple that has been married for some time. Although they have formally bonded, their relationship will probably shift from one dimension of a relational dialectic to another, and forward or backward along the spectrum of stages. Sometimes the partners will feel the need to differentiate from each other, and at other times they will need to seek intimacy. Sometimes they will feel secure in the predictable patterns they have established, and at other times one or both will feel hungry for novelty. The relationship may become circumscribed or even stagnant. From this point the marriage may fail, but this fate isn't certain. With effort, the partners may move from the stage of stagnating to experimenting, or from circumscribing to intensifying.

Communication theorist Richard Conville describes the constantly changing, evolving nature of relationships as a cycle in which partners move through a series of stages, returning to ones they previously encountered, although at a new level[76] (see Figure 8.2). In this cycle, partners move from security (integration, in Knapp's terminology) to disintegration (differentiating) to alienation (circumscribing) to resynthesis (intensifying, integrating) to a new level of security. This process is constantly repeating.

RELATIONSHIPS ARE AFFECTED BY CULTURE

Many of the qualities that shape personal relationships are universal.[77] For example, social scientists have found that communication in all cultures has both the content and relational dimensions described later in this chapter, that the same facial expressions signal the same emotions in all cultures, and that the distribution of power is a factor in every human society. Males in all cultures (in fact, in all species of mammals) are likely to invest less emotionally in sexual relationships, and they are typically more competitive.

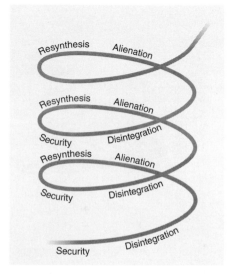

FIGURE 8.2 **A Helical Model of Relational Cycles** © Cengage Learning

Although the general elements of relationships are universal, the particulars often differ from one culture to another. Consider, for example, how the Western notion of romance and marriage is reflected in the model of relational stages described earlier. The notion that bonding only follows after experimenting, intensifying, and integrating doesn't apply everywhere.[78] Indeed, in some cultures, the bride and groom may meet only weeks, days, or even minutes before they become husband and wife. Research shows that these relationships can be both successful and satisfying.[79]

A variety of differences—profound, but not always apparent—can make relationships between people from different cultures challenging.[80] For example, deciding how much (or how little) to share what's on your mind is a challenge in any relationship. As noted in Chapter 2, this decision can be especially tricky when the cultural rules about self-disclosure vary. Low-context cultures such as the United States value directness, whereas high-context ones like Japan consider tact far more important. The titles of two self-help books offer a revealing peek at the mindset of these approaches. One American self-help book is titled *How to Say No Without Feeling Guilty*,[81] while the Japanese counterpart is titled *16 Ways to Avoid Saying No*.[82] It's easy to see how differing notions of appropriateness could lead to challenges in intercultural relationships.

When challenges arise out of cultural differences, the kinds of intercultural competence described in Chapter 1 become especially important. Motivation, tolerance for ambiguity, open-mindedness, knowledge of others' practices, and skill at adapting to others' communication styles are likely to make communication more smooth and relationships more satisfying.

Communicating about Relationships

By now you understand that relationships are complex, dynamic, and important. But what kinds of messages do we exchange as we communicate in those relationships?

"You say 'off with her head,' but what I'm hearing is, 'I feel neglected.'"

CONTENT AND RELATIONAL MESSAGES

In Chapter 1, you read that every message has a *content* and a *relational* dimension. The most obvious component of most messages is their content—the subject being discussed. The content of such statements as "It's your turn to do the dishes" or "I'm busy Saturday night" is obvious.

Content messages aren't the only thing being exchanged when two people communicate. In addition, almost every message—both verbal and nonverbal—has a second, relational dimension, which makes statements about how the parties feel toward one another.[83] As you'll read in the following section, these relational messages deal with one or more social needs, most commonly affinity, immediacy, respect, and control. Consider the two examples we just mentioned:

- Imagine two ways of saying "It's your turn to do the dishes": one that is demanding and another that is matter-of-fact. Notice how the different nonverbal messages make statements about how the sender views control in this part of the relationship. The demanding tone says, in effect, "I have a right to tell you what to do around the house," whereas the matter-of-fact tone suggests, "I'm just reminding you of something you might have overlooked."
- You can easily visualize two ways to deliver the statement "I'm busy Saturday night": one with little affinity and the other with warmth and immediacy (in which you sound disappointed and hope for a rescheduling).

Notice that in each of these examples the relational dimension of the message was never discussed. In fact, most of the time we aren't conscious of the many relational messages that bombard us every day. Sometimes we are unaware of relational messages because they match our belief about the amount of respect, control, and affection that is appropriate. For example, you probably wouldn't be offended if your boss told you to do a certain job, because you agree that supervisors have the right to direct employees. In other cases, however, conflicts arise over relational messages, even though content is not disputed. If your boss delivered the order in a condescending, sarcastic, or abusive tone of voice, you probably would be offended. Your complaint wouldn't be with the order itself, but rather with the way it was delivered. "I may work for this company," you might think, "but I'm not a slave or an idiot. I deserve to be treated like a human being."

How are relational messages communicated? As the boss–employee example suggests, they are usually communicated nonverbally (which includes tone of voice). To test this fact for yourself, imagine how you could act while saying "Can you help me for a minute?" in a way that communicates each of the following relationships:

Superiority	Friendliness	Sexual desire
Helplessness	Aloofness	Irritation

Although nonverbal behaviors are a good source of relational messages, they are ambiguous. The sharp tone that you receive as a personal insult might be a result of fatigue, and the interruption that you assume is an attempt to ignore your ideas might be a sign of pressure that has nothing to do with you. Before you jump to conclusions about relational clues, it's a good idea to check them out verbally, using the perception-checking skills described in Chapter 3.

TYPES OF RELATIONAL MESSAGES

The number and variety of content messages are almost infinite, ranging from black holes to doughnut holes, from rock and roll to *Rock of Ages*. But unlike the range of content messages, there is a surprisingly narrow range of relational messages. Virtually all of them fit into one of four categories: affinity, immediacy, respect, or control.

Affinity An important kind of relational communication involves **affinity**—the degree to which people like or appreciate one another.[84] Not surprisingly, affection is the most important ingredient in romantic relationships.[85] Not all affinity messages are positive, though: A glare or an angry word shows the level of (dis)liking just as clearly as a smile or profession of love.

Immediacy Immediacy refers to the degree of interest and attention that we feel toward and communicate to others. Not surprisingly, immediacy is an important element of relationships.[86] A great deal of immediacy comes from nonverbal behavior, such as eye contact, facial expression, tone of voice, and the distance we put between ourselves and others.[87] Immediacy can also come from our language. For example, saying "we have a problem" is more immediate than saying "you have a problem." Chapters 5 and 6 discuss nonverbal and verbal immediacy in more detail.

Immediacy isn't the same thing as affinity: It's possible to like someone without being immediate with them. For instance, you can

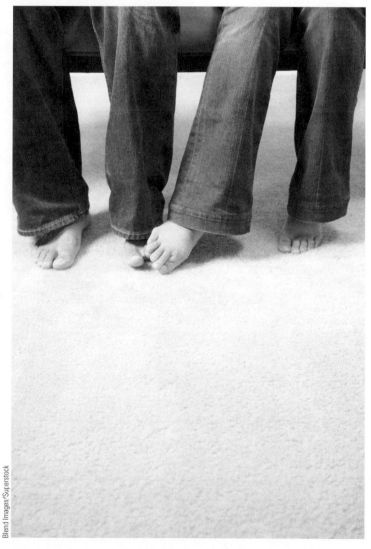

Blend Images/Superstock

convey liking with a high degree of immediacy, such as with a big hug and kiss or by shouting "I really like you!" You can also imagine situations where you like someone but operate with a low degree of immediacy. (Picture a quiet, pleasant evening at home where you and another person each read or work comfortably but independently.) You can also imagine communicating dislike in high- and low-immediacy ways.

The most obvious types of immediacy involve positive feelings, but it's possible to express disapproval and disliking with either high or low intensity. Imagine, for instance, the difference between mild and extreme ways—both verbal and nonverbal—of letting a friend know that you are unhappy about something he or she has done.

Highly immediate communication certainly has its value, but there are also times when a low degree of intensity is desirable. It would be exhausting to interact with full intensity all the time. It would also be inappropriate to communicate with high immediacy in cultures that frown upon such behaviors, particularly in public settings. In most cases, the key to relational satisfaction is to create a level of immediacy that works for you and the other person.

Respect At first glance, respect might seem identical to affinity, but the two attitudes are different.[88] Whereas affinity involves liking, **respect** involves esteem. It's possible to like others without respecting them. For instance, you might like—or even probably love—your two-year-old cousin without respecting her. In the same way, you might have a great deal of affection for some friends, yet not respect the way they behave. The reverse is also true: It's possible to respect people you don't like. You might hold an acquaintance in high esteem for being a hard worker, honest, talented, or clever, yet not particularly enjoy that person's company.

Respect is an extremely important ingredient in good relationships. In fact, it is a better predictor of relational satisfaction than liking, or even loving.[89] Your own experience will show that being respected is sometimes more important than being liked. Think about occasions in school when you were offended because an instructor or fellow students didn't seem to take your comments or questions seriously. The same principle holds on the job, where having your opinions count often means more than being popular. Even in more personal relationships, conflicts often focus on the issue of respect. Being taken seriously is a vital ingredient of self-esteem.

Control A final dimension of relational communication involves **control**—the degree to which the parties in a relationship have the power to influence one another. Some types of control involve *conversation*—who talks the most, who interrupts whom, and who changes the topic most often.[90] Another dimension of control involves *decisions*: Who has the power to determine what will happen in the relationship? What will we do Saturday night? Shall we use our savings to fix up the house or to take a vacation? How much time should we spend together and how much should we spend apart?

Relational problems arise when the people involved don't have similar ideas about the distribution of control. If you and a friend each push for your own idea, problems are likely to arise. (It can also be difficult when neither person wants to make a decision: "What do you want to do tonight?" "I don't know . . . why don't you decide?" "No, *you* decide.")

Most healthy relationships handle the distribution of control in a flexible way. Rather than clinging to the lopsidedness of one-up/one-down relationships or the unrealistic equality of complete shared responsibility, partners shift between one-up, one-down, and straight-across roles. John may handle the decisions about car repairs and menu planning, as well as taking the spotlight at parties with their friends. Mary may manage the finances and make most of the decisions about childcare, as well as controlling the conversation when she and John are alone. When a decision is very important to one partner, the other willingly gives in, knowing that the favor will be returned later. When issues are important to both partners, they try to share power equally. But when an impasse occurs, each will make concessions in a way that keeps the overall balance of power equal.

METACOMMUNICATION

Not all relational messages are nonverbal. Social scientists use the term **metacommunication** to describe messages that people exchange, verbally or nonverbally, about their relationship.[91] In other words, metacommunication is communication about communication. Whenever we discuss a relationship with others, we are metacommunicating: "I hate it when you use that tone of voice," or "I appreciate how honest you've been with me." Verbal metacommunication is an essential ingredient in successful relationships. Sooner or later it becomes necessary to talk about what is going on between you and the other person. The ability to focus on the kinds of issues described in this chapter can keep the relationship on track.

Metacommunication isn't just a tool for handling problems. It is also a way to reinforce the satisfying aspects of a relationship: "I really appreciate it when you compliment me about my work in front of the boss." Comments like this serve two functions. First, they let others know that you value their behavior; second, they boost the odds that others will continue the behavior in the future.

Despite the benefits of metacommunication, bringing relational issues out in the open does have its risks. Your desire to focus on the relationship might look like a bad omen—"Our relationship isn't working if we have to keep talking it over."[92] Furthermore, metacommunication does involve a certain degree of analysis ("It seems like you're angry with me"), and some people resent being analyzed. These cautions don't mean that verbal metacommunication is a bad idea. They do suggest, though, that this tool needs to be used carefully.

SUMMARY

People form interpersonal relationships for a variety of reasons. Attraction can come from physical appearance, perceived similarity, complementarity, reciprocal attraction, perceived competence, disclosure of personal information, proximity, and rewards.

Two models offer somewhat different perspectives on the dynamics of interpersonal relationships. A stage-related model characterizes communication as exhibiting different characteristics as people come together and draw apart. A dialectical model characterizes communicators in every stage as being driven by the need to manage a variety of mutually incompatible needs.

Communication occurs on two levels: content and relational. Relational communication can be both verbal and nonverbal. Relational messages usually refer to one of four dimensions of a relationship: affinity, immediacy, respect, or control. Metacommunication consists of messages that refer to the relationship between the communicators.

KEY TERMS

affinity (269)
avoiding (260)
bonding (258)
circumscribing (259)
connection-autonomy dialectic (262)
control (270)
dialectical tensions (262)
differentiating (259)
experimenting (257)
immediacy (269)

initiating (256)
integrating (258)
intensifying (258)
metacommunication (271)
openness-privacy dialectic (264)
predictability-novelty dialectic (264)
relational maintenance (255)
respect (270)
stagnating (260)
terminating (260)

ONLINE RESOURCES

Now that you have read this chapter, visit CengageBrain.com to access the Speech Communication CourseMate for *Looking Out/Looking In* for quick access to the electronic resources that accompany this text. Your CourseMate offers:

- **Study tools** that will help you assess your learning and prepare for exams (*digital glossary*, *key term flash cards*, *interactive quizzes*).
- **Activities and assignments** that will help you hone your knowledge, understand how theory and research applies to your own life (*Self-Assessment, Pause and Reflect*), consider ethical challenges in interpersonal communication (*Ethical Challenge*), and build your interpersonal communication skills throughout the course (*Skill Builder*). If requested, you can submit your answers to your instructor.
- **Media resources** that will allow you to watch and critique videos of interpersonal communication situations (*In Real Life, interpersonal video simulations, and interactive video activities*).
- In addition to interactive teaching and learning tools, CourseMate includes an **interactive eBook.** Take notes, highlight, search, and interact with embedded media specific to *Looking Out/Looking In*.

SEARCH TERMS

When searching online databases to research topics in this chapter, use the following terms (along with this chapter's key terms) to maximize the chances of finding useful information:

apologizing	interpersonal communication
attractiveness	interpersonal relations
forgiveness	relational dialectics theory
interpersonal attraction	relational satisfaction

FILM AND TELEVISION

You can see the communication principles described in this chapter portrayed in the following films and television programs.

RELATIONAL ATTRACTION

TV Reality Shows

Beginning with *The Real World* in the 1990s, many so-called reality shows have allowed viewers to watch people create, maintain, and end interpersonal relationships in televised episodes. Some of these programs (such as *The Bachelor/Bachelorette*) are matchmaking contests in which participants select relational partners. Physical attractiveness plays an important role in initial attraction in these shows, but increased proximity and disclosure allow participants to assess the costs and rewards of an ongoing relationship with their selected partners.

Other reality shows (such as the long-running *Survivor* and *Big Brother*) pit participants against each other, with each person vying not to be voted off the show by fellow contestants. In many cases, alliances form based on similarities (women versus men; older participants versus younger ones) and proximity (allied teammates spend more time with each other and often—but not always—grow to like each other). Competence is also a factor in that participants are attracted to those who perform well in the shows' survival contests. And complementarity plays a role when participants' differing talents create "odd bedfellow" partnerships.

Although reality shows don't always match most people's real worlds, the interpersonal relationships that develop on these programs often mirror what happens in everyday life.

RELATIONAL STAGES

(500) Days of Summer (2009) Rated PG-13

"You should know upfront, this is not a love story" intones the narrator ominously at the outset of *(500) Days of Summer.* Indeed, this is not a typical romantic comedy. The story of Tom (Joseph Gordon-Levitt) and Summer (Zooey Deschanel) is told by reviewing various days, non-chronologically, in their tumultuous relationship.

Relational stages play an important role for this couple. Tom believes their romance has long-term potential, and he wants them to move toward what Knapp would label as integrating and bonding. Summer, on the other hand, seems content to stay at the stages of experimenting and intensifying. When Tom pushes for more commitment, Summer engages in behaviors typical of stages of relational deterioration.

The movie illustrates that relational stages are often a matter of perception, and that the parties involved might not agree on the stage they are—or want to be—in.

The Break-Up (2006) Rated PG-13

This tragicomedy chronicles the disintegration of the relationship between Brooke Meyers (Jennifer Aniston) and Gary Grobowski (Vince Vaughn) in ways that closely match the "coming apart" stages of Knapp's developmental model. We watch their communication pass through the stages of circumscribing (quite literally, as they cordon off their own spaces in the apartment), stagnating, avoiding, and eventually terminating. The movie also illustrates the dialectical tension between connection and autonomy, with Brooke wanting more of the former and Gary wanting more of the latter. *The Break-Up* dramatizes the message in the old song lyric: Breaking up is hard to do.

RELATIONAL DIALECTICS

Cyrus (2010) Rated R

John (John C. Reilly) knows he's a lucky man when he strikes up a relationship with Molly (Marisa Tomei) after seven desperate years of singleness. There's just one problem—Molly's 21-year-old, live-at-home son Cyrus (Jonah Hill).

Cyrus has never outgrown his connection to his mom. Like John, we become increasingly creeped out by his jealous possessiveness. It soon becomes clear that Cyrus is out to destroy the bond between Molly and John so he won't have to share her affection.

Until the final moments of this serio-comedy, we don't know whether John will succeed in persuading mother and son to bring their autonomy-connection dialectic into better balance. What we do see clearly is how, in relationships, too much of a good thing can become a bad thing.

RELATIONAL MESSAGES

Parenthood (2010–) Rated TV-PG

The television show *Parenthood* follows the joys and heartaches of the large and colorful Braverman family. The clan's patriarch Zeek (Craig T. Nelson) and matriarch Camille (Bonnie Bedelia) do their best to impart their love and wisdom to their children and grandchildren.

One of the struggles that parents face is managing relational messages as their youngsters become adolescents and then adults. Across several generations, the mothers and fathers in this show do their best to communicate affinity and immediacy with their children, while trying to maintain a level of respect and control. It's a delicate balance that sometimes works better than others—just like in real life.

C H A P T E R   E I G H T

Communication and Relational Dynamics

CHAPTER OUTLINE

Use this outline to take notes as you read the chapter in the text and/or as your instructor lectures in class.

I. **WHY WE FORM RELATIONSHIPS**
    A. **Appearance**
    B. **Similarity**
    C. **Complementarity**
    D. **Reciprocal Attraction**
    E. **Competence**
    F. **Disclosure**
    G. **Proximity**
    H. **Rewards**

II. **MODELS OF RELATIONAL DYNAMICS**
    A. **A Developmental Perspective**
       1. Initiating
       2. Experimenting
       3. Intensifying
       4. Integrating
       5. Bonding
       6. Differentiating
       7. Circumscribing
       8. Stagnating

9. Avoiding
10. Terminating
B. **A Dialectical Perspective**
    1. Connection versus autonomy
    2. Openness versus privacy
    3. Predictability versus novelty
    4. Managing dialectical tensions
      a. Denial
      b. Disorientation
      c. Alternation
      d. Segmentation
      e. Balance
      f. Integration
      g. Recalibration
      h. Reaffirmation

III. **CHARACTERISTICS OF RELATIONSHIPS**
A. **Relationships Are Constantly Changing**
    1. Security
    2. Disintegration
    3. Alienation
    4. Resynthesis
    5. New level of security
B. **Relationships Are Affected by Culture**

IV. **COMMUNICATING ABOUT RELATIONSHIPS**
A. **Content and Relational Messages**
    1. Content: subject
    2. Relational: feelings
B. **Types of Relational Messages**
    1. Affinity
    2. Immediacy
    3. Respect
    4. Control

a. Decisional	
b. Conversational	
C. Metacommunication	

KEY TERMS

affinity

avoiding

bonding

circumscribing

connection-autonomy dialectic

control

dialectical tensions

differentiating

experimenting

immediacy

initiating

integrating

intensifying

metacommunication

openness-privacy dialectic

predictability-novelty dialectic

respect

stagnating

terminating

ACTIVITIES

8.1 DISCOVERING DIALECTICS

LEARNING OBJECTIVES

- Describe the dialectical tensions in a given relationship, how they influence communication, and the most effective strategies for managing them.

INSTRUCTIONS

1. Identify the dialectical tensions operating in the situations below, taking time to explain the conflicting feelings and thoughts in each: *connection versus autonomy, openness versus privacy, predictability versus novelty.*
2. Identify one or more of the eight strategies for managing dialectical tensions (*denial, disorientation, alternation, segmentation, balance, integration, recalibration, and reaffirmation*) that you believe would be most beneficial to the relationship, and explain how the relationship would deal with the dialectical tension under these circumstances.
3. Describe dialectical tensions at work in your own relationships and label and explain the strategies that you use to deal with them.

SITUATION	DIALECTICAL TENSION	STRATEGY FOR MANAGING
EXAMPLE *Sandra, nineteen, and her mother, Tracy, have become good friends over the past few years. Sandra now has a serious boyfriend and spends less time talking to her mother.*	*The openness-privacy dialectic is probably at work here. Sandra and Tracy continue to share the intimacy of their mother-daughter relationship, but privacy needs about the boyfriend probably keep them at more of a distance.*	*Sandra and Tracy are likely to use the segmentation strategy, in which they maintain openness about many areas but keep certain areas of the boyfriend relationship "off limits."*
1. Daryl is new to the software firm where Steve has been for five years. Daryl has asked Steve to play golf this weekend. Steve is uncomfortable about mixing business and pleasure, but still wants to have a good working relationship with Daryl.		

SITUATION	DIALECTICAL TENSION	STRATEGY FOR MANAGING
2. Nesto and Gina have been dating for six months. They continue to enjoy one another's company, but each has begun to notice annoying little habits that the other one has.		
3. Jenner and A. J. are siblings who have always relied on one another completely. Jenner appreciates A. J.'s dependability, but wishes their times together weren't so boring.		
4. Eugenia and Shane have worked at the same business for twenty years. They have collaborated on a number of projects. They've tried to get together socially, but their spouses don't seem to get along.		
5. Christina and Nicole are roommates. Christina wants them to share everything, but Nicole is not proud of a few things she's done and doesn't want to face her friend's judgment.		
6. (Your example)		
7. (Your example)		

8.2 RELATIONAL STAGES

LEARNING OBJECTIVES

- Identify factors that have influenced your choice of relational partners.
- Use Knapp's model to describe the nature of communication in the various stages of a relationship.
- Describe the dialectical tensions in a given relationship, how they influence communication, and the most effective strategies for managing them.

INSTRUCTIONS

1. Discuss the various situations listed below.
2. Identify the relational stage(s) that many of these behaviors illustrate (e.g., initiating, experimenting, intensifying, integrating, bonding, differentiating, circumscribing, avoiding, stagnating, terminating).
3. Cite a brief passage from Chapter 8 of *Looking Out/Looking In* that verifies the stage of the relationship.
4. Record relational situations of your own in the same manner.

EXAMPLE

Two friends are discussing the effects of divorce in their families.
Relational stage illustrated: *This type of self-disclosure would most likely occur in an intensifying stage of a relationship, where the friends have gone beyond the small talk of experimenting and are beginning to develop more trust, more depth rather than breadth of self-disclosure, and where secrets are told and favors given.*

1. Two friends are telling one another about using/refusing drugs.

   Relational stage illustrated: _____

   Cite a brief passage to verify the stage of the relationship

   _____

   _____

2. Two classmates are comparing the results of their first exam.

   Relational stage illustrated: _____

Cite a brief passage to verify the stage of the relationship

_____

_____

3. Two people seated next to each other on an overseas flight begin telling one another about their past romantic involvements.

   Relational stage illustrated: _____

   Cite a brief passage to verify the stage of the relationship

   _____

   _____

4. Two long-term friends are discussing their worries and feelings of responsibility regarding their parents' advancing age.

   Relational stage illustrated: _____

   Cite a brief passage to verify the stage of the relationship

   _____

   _____

5. Cousins who practically lived at each other's homes as teenagers five years ago now seem to have nothing to talk about.

   Relational stage illustrated: _____

   Cite a brief passage to verify the stage of the relationship

   _____

   _____

6. A divorced couple meets briefly to discuss education and vacation plans for their children.

   Relational stage illustrated: _____

   Cite a brief passage to verify the stage of the relationship

   _____

   _____

7. A man and woman who dated for six months during college ten years ago now find themselves working for the same company.

   Relational stage illustrated: _____

   Cite a brief passage to verify the stage of the relationship

   _____

   _____

8. A manager and employee have agreed to sit down and talk about the problems they are experiencing with each other.

   Relational stage illustrated: _____

   Cite a brief passage to verify the stage of the relationship

   _____

   _____

9. Your example: _____

   Relational stage illustrated: _____

   Cite a brief passage to verify the stage of the relationship

   _____

   _____

10. Your example: _____

    Relational stage illustrated: _____

    Cite a brief passage to verify the stage of the relationship

    _____

    _____

8.3 RECOGNIZING RELATIONAL MESSAGES

LEARNING OBJECTIVES

- Identify the content and relational dimensions of communication in a given transaction.

INSTRUCTIONS

1. Read each message below. Picture in your mind the nonverbal behaviors that accompany each of the statements.
2. Describe the relational issues that seem to be involved in each of the situations. Use your text to *label and explain* the relational dimensions of **affinity, immediacy, respect, and control** shown by the speaker in each example.

MESSAGE CONTENT	RELATIONAL DIMENSION (affinity, immediacy, respect, control)
EXAMPLE *You tell your romantic partner, ". . . Anyhow, that's what I think. What do you think?"*	*High in immediacy because I invite involvement and show interest by my tone.* *High in affinity as I show liking by my eye contact and touch.*
EXAMPLE *Your instructor invites the class to "Tell me what's working and what isn't."*	*Low in control as the instructor invites influence over how the course is run.* *High in respect by valuing the opinions of students.*
1. You ask a friend to come over and the reply is, "I'm sorry, but I have to work."	
2. Someone you live with complains, "You don't help out enough around the house."	
3. Your roommate says, "You're no fun. I think I'm going to bed."	
4. Your boss asks, "Are your hours working out?"	

MESSAGE CONTENT	RELATIONAL DIMENSION (affinity, immediacy, respect, control)
5. Your boss says, "You'll need a doctor's note to verify your illness."	
6. Your friend teases, "You can't seem to remember the important stuff."	
7. Your parent says, "I know you'll make the right decision."	
8. Your romantic partner says, "I need you to let me know where you are."	
9. Someone reminds you, "Drive carefully."	
10. A family member says you should spend more time at home and you reply, "I'll do what I please."	
11. The doctor's receptionist says, "Can you hold, please?" when you call to make an appointment.	
12. You are getting ready to leave and your partner says, "You're going to wear *that*?"	
13. A friend says "Fine" and hangs up the phone.	
14. When you ask if you can take time off, your boss rolls her eyes and sighs, "Again?"	
15. You tell your friend you don't feel well, and the response is, "Had too good a time last night?"	

8.4 FORMING RELATIONSHIPS

LEARNING OBJECTIVES

- Identify factors that have influenced your choice of relational partners.

INSTRUCTIONS

Identify three relationships. First, list the type of relationship (friend, significant relationship, family member, etc). Then identify three relationship-forming factors (appearance, similarity, complementarity, disclosure, etc). Finally, describe how these three factors helped you form that relationship.

Relationship type 1: _____

Relationship forming factors: _____

Description:

_____

_____

_____

Relationship type 2: _____

Relationship forming factors: _____

Description:

_____

_____

_____

Relationship type 3: _____

Relationship forming factors: _____

Description:

_____

_____

_____

8.5 APPLYING KNAPP'S MODEL

LEARNING OBJECTIVES

- • Use Knapp's model to describe the nature of communication in the various stages of a relationship.

INSTRUCTIONS

Think of a romantic or close relationship that you had that ended in termination. Describe in the spaces below how your relationship fulfilled Knapp's model of communication.

Initiating:

_____

_____

_____

Experimenting:

_____

_____

_____

Intensifying:

_____

_____

_____

Integrating:

_____

_____

_____

Class _____   Name_____

Bonding:

_____

_____

_____

Differentiating:

_____

_____

_____

Circumscribing:

_____

_____

_____

Stagnating:

_____

_____

_____

Avoiding:

_____

_____

_____

Terminating:

_____

_____

_____

STUDY GUIDE

CHECK YOUR UNDERSTANDING

TRUE/FALSE

Mark the statements below as true or false. Correct false statements on the lines below to create a true statement.

_____   1. Romantic partners create positive illusions of one another and view each other as more attractive over time.

_____

_____   2. The stage-related model advocates maintenance in relationships, whereas the dialectical model emphasizes commitment.

_____

_____   3. Forgiveness usually increases emotional distress and aggression.

_____

_____   4. Lack of eye contact and increased distance from someone are ways to communicate immediacy.

_____

_____   5. Email is not helpful in maintaining interpersonal relationships.

_____

_____   6. The struggle to achieve important, but seemingly incompatible, goals in relationships results in the creation of dialectical tension.

_____

_____   7. The struggle between independence and dependence in a relationship is called the openness-privacy dialectic.

_____

_____   8. "I like the way we don't discuss our political differences in public" is an example of metacommunication.

_____

_____   9. The best chance for righting a wrong is taking responsibility for your
              transgression.

              _____

_____   10. Relational partners often go through evolving cycles in which they can repeat a
              relational stage at a new level.

              _____

_____   11. Research suggests that even when forgiven, transgressors are as likely to repeat
              their offenses as those who have not received forgiveness.

              _____

_____   12. Relational commitment involves a promise to remain in a relationship, sometimes
              explicitly, sometimes implied.

              _____

COMPLETION

Fill in the blanks below with the correct terms chosen from the list below.

dialectical	positivity	relational transgression
openness	attraction variable	metacommunication
forgiveness	immediacy	appearance
complementarity		

1. _____ are the messages people exchange about their communication;
    communication about communication.

2. _____ is a relational maintenance strategy of keeping the relational
    climate upbeat and avoiding disapproval or unconstructive remarks.

3. _____ is a strategy to maintain a relationship that involves talking
    directly about the relationship and disclosing needs and concerns.

4. _____ is an explanation for what makes us want to develop personal
    relationships with some people and not with others.

5. _____ is a violation of the explicit or implicit terms of the relationship.

6. _____ is a method of relational repair that promotes physical and
    emotional health.

7. _____ is an attraction variable that is most important at the beginning of
    relationships and less important over time.

8. _____ is an attraction variable in which people are different in ways that meet each of their needs.

9. _____ is a relational message that conveys involvement and interest.

10. _____ is a tension that arises when two incompatible goals exist in a relationship.

MULTIPLE CHOICE

Place the letter of the developmental stage of the relationship on the line before its example below.

a. initiating
b. experimenting
c. intensifying
d. integrating
e. bonding

f. differentiating
g. circumscribing
h. stagnating
i. avoiding
j. terminating

_____ 1. A public ritual marks this stage.

_____ 2. First glances and "sizing up" each other typifies this stage.

_____ 3. Called the "we" stage, this stage involves increasing self-disclosure.

_____ 4. Lots of "small talk" typifies this stage.

_____ 5. This stage involves much focus on individual rather than dyadic interests.

_____ 6. There's very little growth or experimentation in this stage.

_____ 7. This stage involves much behavior that talks around the relational issues because the partners expect bad feelings.

_____ 8. The partners' social circles merge at this stage and they make purchases or commitments together.

_____ 9. No attempts are made to contact the other at this stage.

_____ 10. The relationship is redefined or dissolved at this stage.

_____ 11. A marriage ceremony would be typical here.

_____ 12. Roommates who make sure they are never in the same room and who are tolerating one another only until the lease is up might be at this stage.

_____ 13. A couple who avoids talking about future commitment because they are afraid of how the discussion will go is probably at this stage.

Choose the best answer for each of the statements below:

_____ 14. Research suggests that attraction to partners who have complementary temperament is rooted in

    a. family history.
    b. socialization.
    c. biology.
    d. communication styles.

_____ 15. Revealing personal information only when you are sure the other person is trustworthy is a practice in

    a. self-protection.
    b. self-privacy.
    c. self-defense.
    d. self-disclosure.

_____ 16. In the early stages of a relationship, _____ is especially important.

    a. metacommunication
    b. a positive illusion
    c. behavior
    d. appearance

CHAPTER EIGHT STUDY GUIDE ANSWERS

TRUE/FALSE

1. T	4. F	7. F	10. T
2. F	5. F	8. T	11. F
3. F	6. T	9. T	12. T

COMPLETION

1. metacommunication	5. relational transgression	9. immediacy
2. positivity	6. forgiveness	10. dialectical
3. openness	7. appearance	
4. attraction variable	8. complementarity	

MULTIPLE CHOICE

1. e	4. b	7. g	10. j	13. g	16. d
2. a	5. f	8. d	11. e	14. c
3. c	6. h	9. i	12. i	15. a

Interpersonal Communication in Close Relationships

After studying the topics in this chapter, you should be able to:

1. Identify the level and types of intimacy in a specific relationship and describe ways in which the quality and extent of intimacy could be improved.

2. For a specific family, explain how family roles are created and perpetuated through communication.

3. Describe the systemic properties of a particular family unit and also describe that family's communication patterns.

4. Identify the various types of friendships in your life and evaluate how effectively they are sustained through communication.

5. Identify the turning points and conflict styles in a specific romantic relationship.

6. Evaluate how effectively the partners in a specific romantic relationship adapt to one another's love languages.

7. Choose and use communication strategies to help maintain and support a close, committed relationship.

8. Describe the possible strategies for repairing a given relational transgression.

How important are close, intimate relationships? Empirical studies offer some answers. Researchers asked people who were dying in hospices and hospitals what mattered most in life. Fully 90 percent of these terminally ill patients put intimate relationships at the top of the list. As a fifty-year-old mother of three children who was dying of cancer put it, "You need not wait until you are in my condition to know nothing in life is as important as loving relationships."[1] Another researcher concludes that close relationships "may be the *single most important* source of life satisfaction and emotional well-being, across different ages and cultures."[2]

This chapter will take a close look at close relationships. We'll begin by investigating the role of intimacy in making some relationships more personal and meaningful than others. We'll then look at three contexts—family, friends, and romantic partners—where most of our intimate relationships occur. Finally, we'll provide some tips for improving communication in close relationships.

Intimacy in Close Relationships

Webster's *New Collegiate Dictionary* defines **intimacy** as a state of "close union, contact, association, or acquaintance." Intimacy can occur in a variety of relationships. When researchers asked several hundred college students to identify their "closest, deepest, most involved, and most intimate relationship," the answers were varied.[3] Roughly half (47 percent) identified a romantic partner. About one-third (36 percent) chose a friendship. Most of the rest (14 percent) cited a family member. Let's look at how intimacy operates in these contexts.

Masterfile

DIMENSIONS OF INTIMACY

What *kinds* of behavior make a relationship intimate? In fact, intimacy has several dimensions. The first dimension is *physical*. Even before birth, the fetus experiences a physical closeness with its mother that will never happen again, "floating in a warm fluid, curling inside a total embrace, swaying to the undulations of the moving body and hearing the beat of the pulsing heart."[4] As they grow up, fortunate children are continually nourished by physical intimacy: being rocked, fed, hugged, and held. As we grow older, the opportunities for physical intimacy are less regular but still possible and important. Some, but by no means all, physical intimacy is sexual—and it's not always connected with a close relationship. One study revealed that more than half of sexually active teens had partners that they weren't dating, and the majority of the respondents expressed no desire to establish a dating relationship.[5]

A second dimension of intimacy comes from *intellectual* sharing. Not every exchange of ideas counts as intimacy, of course. Talking about next week's midterm with your professor or classmates isn't likely to forge strong relational bonds. But when you engage another person in an exchange of important ideas, a kind of closeness develops that can be powerful and exciting.

A third dimension of intimacy is *emotional*: exchanging important feelings. Sharing personal information can both reflect and create feelings of closeness. Chapter 2 describes the role of self-disclosure in relational development, and Chapter 5 explains how emotions affect interpersonal communication. When you share your feelings with others or tell them personal things about you, a measure of bonding occurs.

If we define intimacy as being close to another person, then *shared activities* is a fourth dimension that can achieve intimacy. Shared activities can include everything from working side by side at a job to meeting regularly for exercise workouts. When partners spend time together, they can develop unique ways of relating that transform the relationship from an impersonal one to an interpersonal one. For example, both friendships and romantic relationships are often characterized by several forms of play. Partners invent private codes, fool around by acting like other people, tease one another, and play games—everything from having punning contests to arm wrestling.[6] Not all shared activities create and express intimacy, but the bond that comes from experiencing significant events with another person is too frequent and significant to ignore. Companions who have endured physical challenges together—in athletics or emergencies, for example—form a bond that can last a lifetime.

Some intimate relationships exhibit all four dimensions: physical, intellectual, emotional, and shared activities. Other intimate relationships exhibit only one or two. Some relationships aren't intimate in any way. Acquaintances, roommates, and coworkers may never become intimate. In some cases, even family members develop smooth but relatively impersonal relationships.

Not even the closest relationships always operate at the highest level of intimacy. At times you might share all of your thoughts or feelings with a friend, family member, or lover; at other times, you might withdraw. You might freely share your feelings about one topic and stay more aloof about another one. The same principle holds for physical intimacy, which waxes and wanes in most relationships.

Although no relationship is *always* intimate, living without *any* sort of intimacy is hardly desirable. For example, people who fear intimacy in dating relationships anticipate less satisfaction in a long-term relationship and report feeling more distant from even longtime dating partners. A great deal of evidence supports the conclusion that fear of intimacy can cause major problems in both creating relationships and sustaining them.[7]

MASCULINE AND FEMININE INTIMACY STYLES

Until recently, most social scientists believed that women are better than men at developing and maintaining intimate relationships.[8] This view grew from the assumption that the disclosure of personal information is the most important ingredient of intimacy. Most research *does* show that women (taken as a group) are somewhat more willing than men to share their thoughts and feelings, although the differences aren't as dramatic as some people might think.[9] In terms of the amount and depth of information exchanged, female–female relationships are at the top of the disclosure list. Male–female relationships come in second, whereas male–male relationships involve less disclosure than any other type. At every age, women disclose more than men, and the information they disclose is more personal and more likely to involve feelings.

A few decades ago, social scientists interpreted the relative lack of male self-disclosure as a sign that men are unwilling or even unable to develop close relationships. Some argued that the female trait of disclosing personal information

The main characters in the movie *I Love You, Man* forge a close relationship based on several dimensions of intimacy. (See the film summary at the end of this chapter.)

DEBBIE, I HAVE A PROBLEM WITH INTIMACY — TONY

and feelings makes women more "emotionally mature" and "interpersonally competent" than men. The title of one book captured this attitude of female superiority and male deficiency: *The Inexpressive Male: A Tragedy of American Society*.[10] Personal-growth programs and self-help books urged men to achieve closeness by learning to open up and share their feelings.

More recent scholarship, however, has shown that emotional expression isn't the *only* way to develop close relationships. As you'll read later in this chapter, men often experience and express intimacy through shared activities and by doing things for and with others. The same pattern holds in communication between fathers and their sons. Whereas mothers typically express their love toward sons directly through words and nonverbal behaviors such as hugs and kisses, fathers are less likely to be so direct with their young adult sons.[11] Instead, they often show their sons affection by doing favors and helping the sons with tasks and challenges.

Actually, biological sex isn't most significant in shaping how men express intimacy. Rather, it's the *gender role* that a particular man adopts. Recall that Chapter 3 explained how both men and women can adopt a gender role—masculine, feminine, or androgynous—that may or may not match their biological sex. Applying this range of styles to intimacy reveals that masculine men are most likely to express caring via helping behaviors and shared activities.[12] Men whose communication style includes some stereotypically feminine elements are more likely to express affection more directly, especially to other men.

The difference between male and female measures of intimacy helps explain some of the stresses and misunderstandings that can arise between the sexes. For example, a woman who looks for emotional disclosure as a measure of affection may overlook an "inexpressive" man's efforts to show he cares by doing favors or spending time together. Fixing a leaky faucet or taking a hike may look like ways to avoid getting close, but to the man who proposes them, they may be measures of affection and bids for intimacy. Likewise, differing ideas about the timing and meaning of sex can lead to misunderstandings. Whereas many women think of sex as a way to express intimacy that has already developed, men are more likely to see it as a way to *create* that intimacy.[13] In this sense, the man who encourages sex early in a relationship or after a fight may not be just a testosterone-crazed lecher: He may view the shared activity as a way to build closeness. By contrast, the woman who views personal talk as the pathway to intimacy may resist the idea of physical closeness before the emotional side of the relationship has been discussed.

As always, it's important to realize that generalizations don't apply to every person. Also, notions of what constitutes appropriate male behavior are changing.[14] For example, one analysis of prime-time television sitcoms revealed that male characters who disclose personal information generally receive favorable responses from other characters.[15] Researchers also note that a cultural shift is occurring in North America in which fathers are becoming more affectionate with their sons than they were in previous generations—although some of that affection is still expressed through shared activities.[16]

PAUSE AND REFLECT

YOUR IQ (INTIMACY QUOTIENT)

What is the level of intimacy in your important relationships? Find out by following these directions.

1. Identify the point on each scale below that best describes one of your important relationships.

   a. Your level of physical intimacy

1	2	3	4	5

   low ————————————————————————————high

   b. Your amount of emotional intimacy

1	2	3	4	5

   low ————————————————————————————high

   c. The extent of your intellectual intimacy

1	2	3	4	5

   low ————————————————————————————high

   d. The degree of shared activities in your relationship

1	2	3	4	5

   low ————————————————————————————high

2. Now answer the following questions:

   a. What responses to each dimension of intimacy seem most significant to you?

   b. Are you satisfied with the intimacy profile outlined by your responses?

   c. If you are not satisfied, what steps can you take to change your degree of intimacy?

 You can complete this activity by visiting CengageBrain.com to access the Speech Communication CourseMate for *Looking Out/ Looking In*, and, if requested, email your responses to your instructor.

CULTURAL INFLUENCES ON INTIMACY

Historically, the notions of public and private behavior have changed dramatically.[17] What would be considered private behavior in modern terms was quite public at times in the past. For example, in sixteenth-century Germany, a new husband and wife were expected to consummate their marriage upon a bed carried among witnesses who would validate the marriage![18] Conversely, at the same time in England as well as in colonial America, the customary level of communication between spouses was rather formal—not much different from the way acquaintances or neighbors spoke to one another.

Even today, the notion of intimacy varies from one culture to another. In one study, researchers asked residents of Britain, Japan, Hong Kong, and Italy to describe their use of thirty-three rules that governed interaction in social relationships.[19] These included a wide range of communication behaviors: everything from using humor to shaking hands to managing money. The results showed that the greatest differences between Asian and European cultures focused on the rules for dealing with intimacy: showing emotions, expressing affection in public, conducting sexual activity, respecting privacy, and so on.

In some collectivist cultures such as Taiwan and Japan, there is an especially great difference in the way people communicate with members of their in-groups (such as family and close friends) and with their out-groups.[20] They generally do not reach out to outsiders, often waiting until they are properly introduced before entering into a conversation. After they are introduced, they address outsiders with a degree of formality. They go to extremes to hide unfavorable information about in-group members from outsiders on the principle that one doesn't air dirty laundry in public.

By contrast, members of more individualistic cultures such as the United States and Australia make fewer distinctions between personal relationships and casual ones. They act more familiar with strangers and disclose more personal information, making them excellent "cocktail party conversationalists." Social psychologist Kurt Lewin captured the difference nicely when he noted that Americans are easy to meet but difficult to get to know, whereas Germans are difficult to meet but easy to get to know.[21]

Cultural differences in intimacy are becoming less prominent as the world becomes more connected through the media, travel, and technology. For instance, romance and passionate love were once seen as particularly American concepts of intimacy. Recent evidence shows, however, that men and women in a variety of cultures—individualist and collectivist, urban and rural, rich and poverty-stricken—may be every bit as romantic as Americans.[22] These studies suggest that the large differences that once existed between Western and Eastern cultures may be fast disappearing.

Masterfile

INTIMACY IN MEDIATED COMMUNICATION

A few decades ago, it would have been difficult to conceive that the words *computer* and *intimacy* could be positively linked. Electronic devices were viewed as impersonal machines that couldn't transmit important features of human communication such as facial expression, tone of voice, and touch. However, as Chapters 1 and 2 described, researchers now know that mediated communication can be just as personal as face-to-face interaction. In fact, studies show that relational intimacy may develop *more* quickly through mediated channels than in face-to-face communication[23] and that texting, blogging, Facebooking, and so on enhance verbal, emotional, and social intimacy in interpersonal relationships.[24]

Your own experience probably supports these claims. The relative anonymity of chat rooms, blogs, and online dating services provides a freedom of expression that might not occur in face-to-face meetings,[25] giving relationships a chance to get started. In addition, emailing, text messaging, videoconferencing, and social networking offer more constant contact with friends, family, and partners than might otherwise be possible.[26] The potential for developing and maintaining intimate relationships via computer is captured well by one user's comment (which has a fun double meaning): "I've never clicked this much with anyone in my life."[27]

Of course, intimate connections in cyberspace can also be problematic. In the digital age, some people are "virtually unfaithful," carrying on romantic relationships online while being in a committed face-to-face relationship. Two different studies found that people regard online infidelity as much as or even more of a betrayal as cheating in person.[28] Although it's tempting to think that a lack of physical intimacy keeps a cyber-relationship "above board," the truth is that most people perceive emotional intimacy—the kind that can be created easily online—as just as important to relational fidelity.

This doesn't mean that all cyber-relationships are (or will become) intimate. Just as in face-to-face relationships, communicators choose varying levels of self-disclosure with their cyberpartners, including the way they manage their privacy settings on social-network sites.[29] Some online relationships are relatively impersonal; others are highly interpersonal. In any case, mediated communication is an important component in creating and maintaining intimacy in contemporary relationships.

THE LIMITS OF INTIMACY

It's impossible to have a close relationship with everyone you know—nor is that necessarily desirable. Social psychologist Roy Baumeister makes a compelling case that, on average, most people want four to six close, important relationships in their lives at any given time.[30] Although fewer than four such relationships can lead to a sense of social deprivation, he argues that more than six leads to diminishing returns: "It is possible that people simply do not have the time or energy to pursue emotional closeness with more than a half dozen people."

Even if we could seek intimacy with everyone we encountered, few of us would want that much closeness. Consider the range of everyday contacts that don't require any sort of intimacy. Some are based on economic transactions (the people at work or the shopkeeper you visit several times a week), some on group membership (church or school), some on physical proximity (neighbors, carpooling), and some grow out

ON THE JOB

Romance in the Workplace

Mixing work with pleasure can be risky business, especially when it comes to romance. As you read on page 254, proximity often leads to attraction. When coworkers spend many hours interacting with one another, it's no surprise that workplace romances are relatively common. Research on the topic has produced these findings:[a]

- 40 percent of employees in one survey said they had had an office romance at some point in their careers.
- 76 percent of employees in another study said that workplace romances are far more frequent than they were ten years ago.
- 70 percent of human resource professionals said their company had no official verbal or written policy on workplace romance.

Companies that do have policies about office romances discourage them. "Dating on the job is like eating at your desk: Invariably, it's going to get messy," said one researcher. "Workplace romances can seem terrific up front, but if they explode—and they usually do—that shrapnel can land in the workplace and be very distracting."[b]

On a more positive note, 34 percent of people who said they dated a coworker ended up marrying that person. Human resource professionals suggest that if you're going to have a romantic relationship with a coworker, you should know and follow company policies. It's also important to be subtle and discrete about your romance—especially in the office and on company time.

of third-party connections (mutual friends, child care). Simply engaging in conversational give-and-take with both strangers and acquaintances can be enjoyable.

Some scholars have pointed out that an obsession with intimacy can actually lead to *less* satisfying relationships.[31] People who consider intimate communication as the only kind worth pursuing place little value on relationships that don't meet this standard. This can lead them to regard interaction with strangers and casual acquaintances as superficial or, at best, as the groundwork for deeper relationships. When you consider the pleasure that can come from polite but distant communication, the limitations of this view become clear. Intimacy is definitely rewarding, but it isn't the only way of relating to others.

Communication in Families

When you think of the word *family*, images from your own history may come to mind. Some of your memories probably trigger positive feelings. Others may evoke less-pleasant ones. Popular author Erma Bombeck captured the mixture of struggles and joys that are present in even the happiest families:

> We were a strange little band of characters trudging through life sharing diseases and toothpaste, coveting one another's desserts, hiding shampoo, borrowing money, locking each other out of our rooms, inflicting pain and kissing to heal it in the same instant, loving, laughing, defending, and trying to figure out the common thread that bound us all together.*

Today, the meaning of *family* has expanded beyond the traditional set of relationships bound by genetics, legalities, and long-standing customs. You may be from a blended family that includes stepparents and half-siblings. You probably know people in families without biological connections (such as adoptions) or who operate as a family without legal bonds (such as cohabitating couples or foster parents). We'll consider all of these arrangements as we look at the distinctive properties that characterize family communication.

"Here's to family . . ."

Adam Zygus, Buffalo News

CHARACTERISTICS OF FAMILY COMMUNICATION

Whatever form families take, their communication has the same fundamental characteristics.

Family Communication Is Formative Messages from family members are the earliest (and among the most important) ones we will ever receive.[32] For example, messages from mothers shape the way daughters view romantic relationships.[33] It's easy to imagine the impact of maternal messages such as "Marriage is the best thing that ever happened to me" or "All men are jerks." Along with attitudes about romance, parental communication shapes attitudes on other subjects. For instance, the messages children hear about academics while growing up influence whether or not they persist or drop out of high school.[34]

---

*Bombeck, E. (1987). *Family—The ties that bind . . . and gag!* (p. 11). New York: Random House.

Communication in the family of origin can have lifelong effects. *Attachment theory* argues that children develop bonds—either secure or insecure—with family members. Insecure attachment in childhood often leads to adults who are anxious about new relationships, uncomfortable with intimacy, and worried about losing relationships.[35] Romantic partners who fear rejection and abandonment are likely to act in ways that increase the odds of their fears coming to pass.[36] In other words, their dismal expectations create dysfunctional self-fulfilling prophecies.

Fortunately the opposite is also true: When attachment is secure, children grow up to communicate more confidently, develop greater intimacy, and maintain effective relationships with teachers, peers, and others.[37] When both partners in a romantic relationship have secure attachment styles, they tend to communicate constructively, even during conflicts.[38]

Findings like this are likely to help you appreciate the importance of raising secure children. But even if you haven't had the good luck to be nurtured in a positive environment, it's possible to learn ways of communicating that can lead to happier relationships as an adult. This book is loaded with many such skills.

Along with nurturing (and non-nurturing) messages, birth order also plays an important role in shaping how we communicate.[39] For example, first-born siblings are often more extraverted than their younger brothers or sisters. They also are more concerned with control. Middle-borns tend to be closer with their friends but are likely to have more difficult relationships with their family. "Caboose" children who are born last are often more committed and closer to their family members than their older siblings.

Family Communication Is Role-Driven A **role** is a set of expectations about how to communicate. Some roles grow from kinship position. You can probably make a mental list of traditional role norms for a dad, mom, son, and daughter. (Take a moment and do that.) Of course, many of those norms are changing in modern society—and that requires negotiating. When family members communicate according to role expectations, communication is likely to run smoothly. But problems can arise when roles are challenged. (Think about the reaction to a talkative, assertive son or daughter in a family where the rule is "Children should be seen but not heard.")

As children grow, they are labeled (overtly or more subtly) by other family members.[40] Terms such as "the good one," "the black sheep," "the smart kid," and "the screwup" may sound familiar. Once these labels exist, they tend to create the kind of self-fulfilling prophecies described in Chapter 2.[41] If roles are positive, then the expectations can shape good outcomes. But when predictions are negative ("Can't you do *anything* right?") or perhaps even more damaging ("Why can't you be more like your brother?"), the results may include decreased closeness and increased conflict.[42] The effects of this labeling can plague families for decades.[43]

Although labels may persist, family roles can change as both parents and children grow older. During the years of emerging adulthood (typically between ages eighteen and twenty-five), children who once required close supervision from their parents assert their independence.[44] Communication often changes during this period, reflecting transitions in the relationship. In many families, adult children and parents treat one another more as equals. Conflicts arise when children expect to be regarded as adults and parents insist on sticking with roles from earlier years. As parents age, children may take on a caregiving role for parents who are ill or elderly—and thus complete the family circle of life.

Sibling relationships and roles also change over time.[45] During childhood, brothers and sisters consider one another important sources of companionship—and sometimes competition. In adulthood, siblings can often develop a stronger bond as they

SELF-ASSESSMENT

Your Attachment Style

What is your attachment style? How does it affect your communication in close relationships? To help answer these questions, visit CengageBrain.com to access the Speech Communication CourseMate for *Looking Out/ Looking In* and complete the survey.

Lantana Prods/The Kobal Collection

In the movie *Irreconcilable Differences*, daughter Casey (young Drew Barrymore) decides to "divorce" her parents because she doesn't like how they treat her or each other. Although the idea of divorcing difficult parents may be amusing (or even appealing), in real life most family members are "stuck" with one another, for better or worse.

focus again on communication and companionship with one another, perhaps with less rivalry.[46]

Family Communication Is Involuntary You have the freedom to choose friends and dating partners, but you can't choose your parents, siblings, or other relatives. Even if you take the drastic step of cutting off communication with some relatives, their influence is likely to persist like the phantom pain from a missing limb. Family members may be estranged, but they will always be family.

The web of involuntary family connections grows even more complex in adulthood. The relational partners we choose as adults also come with their own set of relatives. Whether or not they like it, a committed couple is tied to three families: the one they create and the family of origin for each partner.[47] Once children arrive, they are eternally connected to a greater or lesser degree with their kin.[48]

FAMILIES AS SYSTEMS

Before reading on, imagine a family—perhaps *your* family— represented in a mobile. Visualize a photo of each member suspended on its own thread, connected by bars to the hanging images of other members. This family mobile is a simplistic but useful model of a **family system**—a group of interdependent individuals that interact and adapt together as a whole.[49] As you read about the characteristics of family systems, thinking about this mobile will help you understand some important concepts.

Family Systems Are Interdependent Touch one piece of a mobile and all the other pieces will move. In the same way, one family member's behavior is likely to influence everyone else. If someone in your family is unhappy, your life is likely to be affected. If a member is happy, the atmosphere of the entire family is likely to be more positive. Because of this interdependence, family therapists usually recognize that it's a mistake to give treatment to a single member. It's far more realistic and effective to look at how members affect one another and to treat the entire group.[50]

Family Systems Are Manifested Through Communication Just as threads and bars connect the pieces of a mobile, communication connects the members of a family system. Words and symbolic actions jiggle the equilibrium of family life, sometimes for better and sometimes for worse. As you read on in this chapter, you'll see how communication is a potent force that shapes the welfare of families.

Family Systems Are Nested Within every family system, *subsystems* operate. In a traditional family, the mother and father have their own unique relationship. Siblings form their own systems, and every child's interaction with each parent forms a subsystem (e.g., mother–daughter, father–daughter). The larger the family, the larger number of subsystems.

Families are also members of larger *suprasystems*. You could illustrate this by expanding your imaginary mobile to include the extended family—grandparents, uncles and aunts, cousins, stepsiblings, in-laws, and so on.

Beyond kinship, families are also part of the society in which they operate. For example, children who grow up in violent environments tend to be more anxious and have weaker social skills in adulthood.[51] They also are more likely to act aggressively themselves.[52] The school environment can also shape the way children communicate, for better or worse.[53]

Families Are More Than the Sum of Their Parts Just as the mobile you've been visualizing is more than a collection of photos, a family is more than a collection of individuals. Even if you knew each of the members independently, you wouldn't understand the family until you saw them all interact. When those members are together, new ways of communicating emerge.[54] For instance, you may have known friends who turned into very different people when they became a couple. Maybe they became better as individuals—more confident, clever, and happy. Or perhaps they became more aggressive and defensive. Likewise, the nature of a couple's relationship is likely to change when a child arrives, and that family's interaction will change again with the arrival of each subsequent baby.

The characters in the TV hit *Modern Family* all belong to the same suprasystem, but they also form many subsystems. (See the TV summary at the end of this chapter.)

COMMUNICATION PATTERNS WITHIN FAMILIES

What families talk about is common and unsurprising: reports on activities, logistics, shared events, and so on. But *how* families communicate can vary significantly in two ways: modes of conversation and levels of conformity.[55]

Conversation orientation relates to how open families are to discussing a range of topics. Families with a high conversation orientation interact freely, often, and spontaneously. That's quite different from families with a low conversation orientation, where many topics are taboo and others can only be broached in a restricted way. You can get a sense of the conversation orientation in your family of origin by recalling the rules (probably unstated) about topics including religion, sex, politics, and the personal histories and feelings of each family member.

Families with a high conversation orientation view communicating as a way to express affection and pleasure, and to relax.[56] When conflicts arise, they try to find solutions that work for all members.[57] By contrast, members of families with a low conversation orientation interact less, and there are fewer exchanges of private thoughts. It's no surprise that families with a strong conversation orientation regard communication as rewarding[58] and that children who grow up in these families have a greater number of interpersonal skills in their later relationships.[59]

After reading this far, you might find it easy to conclude that open family communication is good and closed communication is not. But even in families with a high conversation orientation, it's important to recognize that some topical boundaries are necessary and useful.[60] None of us is comfortable or willing to share every bit of our personal history, thoughts, or feelings—even with the people we love the most. And even the most open families have boundaries that protect personal information from the outside world. For example, one study found that adult children who knew about a parent's infidelity kept this information secret from those outside the family as a way

LOOKING AT DIVERSITY

Scott Johnson: Multicultural Families and Communication Challenges

In the decade since adopting our Haitian children and becoming a bi-racial family, we've found the learning curve continues to point steeply upward. At first we didn't understand how simple things like taking photos would change—as our earliest family images show perfectly exposed white parents with their underexposed black children. We didn't understand the importance of hair in the black community—but shopping brought frequent reminders, as black women would politely ask, "Are these your kids? Do you need help with her hair?" We didn't understand how uncertain our whole culture can be when trying to bridge racial differences.

One hot afternoon at a community pool, our then 4-year-old son picked up a younger white admirer who followed him around, playing and chattering happily. As they sat for a time on the edge of the kiddie pool, the younger boy leaned over and licked my son on the shoulder. My wife asked the boy what he was doing, and as if reading from a bad sitcom script, he said, "I wanted to see if he tasted like chocolate."

A friend and professor of African American Studies once told me my children were growing up without what he called the "warm blanket of acceptance" of the black community that stands against the world's racism. I don't know if he's right about that, and I don't know what other versions (innocent or ill-willed) of "tasting like chocolate" they'll face. I just know our kids have a life they couldn't have dreamed of in their native Haiti. I know they're being raised by white people who are learning a lot about the role of race in our lives. And I know they're feeling the warmest blanket of acceptance we can provide in our home, where we've made family the centerpiece of life. We talk frankly about race and difference and prejudice, and our son and daughter have learned we will face together the challenges of difference that lie ahead.

"Multicultural Families and Communication Challenges" by Scott Johnson. Used with permission of author.

to protect the family member, demonstrate loyalty, and keep the family cohesive.[61] This tension between what families share and what they keep private is part of the openness-privacy dialectic discussed in Chapter 8 (page 264).

Conformity orientation refers to how strongly a family enforces the uniformity of attitudes, values, and beliefs. High-conformity families manage communication in order to seek harmony, avoid conflict, foster interdependence, and gain obedience. They are often hierarchical, with a clear sense that some members have more authority than others. It's not surprising that conflict in these families is characterized by avoiding and obliging strategies.[62] By contrast, communication in families with a low conformity orientation is characterized by individuality, independence, and equality. The belief in such families is that individual growth should be encouraged and that the interests of each individual member are more important than those of the family as a whole.

Conversation and conformity orientations can combine in four ways, as shown in Figure 9.1. Each of these modes reflects a different **family communication pattern**: consensual, pluralistic, protective, or laissez-faire.

To understand these combinations, imagine four different families. In each, a fifteen-year-old daughter wants to get a very visible and irreverent tattoo that

CONFORMITY ORIENTATION

		HIGH	LOW
CONVERSATION ORIENTATION	**HIGH**	Consensual families	Pluralistic families
	LOW	Protective families	Laissez-faire families

FIGURE 9.1 **Conversation and Conformity Shape Family Communication** © Cengage Learning 2013

concerns the parents. Now imagine how communication surrounding this issue would differ depending on the various combinations of conversation and conformity orientations.

A family high in both conversation orientation and conformity orientation is *consensual.* Communication reflects the tension between the pressure to agree and preserve the hierarchy of authority and an interest in open communication and exploration. In a consensual family, the daughter would feel comfortable making her case for the tattoo, and the parents would be willing to hear the daughter out. Ultimately, the decision would rest with the mother and father.

Families high in conversation orientation and low in conformity orientation are *pluralistic.* Communication in these families is open and unrestrained, with all family members' contributions evaluated on their own merits. It's easy to visualize an ongoing family discussion about whether the tattoo is a good idea. Older and younger siblings—and maybe even other relatives—would weigh in with their perspectives. In the best of worlds, a consensus would emerge from these discussions.

Families low in conversation orientation and high in conformity orientation are *protective.* Communication in these families emphasizes obedience to authority and the reluctance to share thoughts and feelings. In a protective family, there would be little if any discussion about the tattoo. The parents would decide, and their word would be final.

Families low in both conversation orientation and conformity orientation are *laissez-faire.* Laissez-faire roughly translates from French as "hands off." Communication in these families reflects family members' lack of involvement with each other, and decision making is individual. In this type of family, the daughter might not even bring the tattoo up for discussion before making a decision. If she did, the parents would have little to say about whether their daughter did or didn't decorate her body with permanent art. With the tattoo—and most other matters—their response would be an indifferent "Whatever."

A growing body of research suggests that some communication patterns are more productive and satisfying than others.[63] For example, young adults from consensual and pluralistic families are more confident listeners and more intellectually flexible than those from protective and laissez-faire backgrounds.[64] Offspring from pluralistic families are less verbally aggressive than those from any other type.[65] By contrast, a protective approach by parents leads to more secrecy by children and lower satisfaction for all members of a family.[66] In other words, open communication and shared decision making produces better results than do power plays and refusal to have open dialogue.

PAUSE AND REFLECT

YOUR FAMILY'S COMMUNICATION PATTERNS

Use the categories introduced in the text and pictured in Figure 9.1 to describe which communication pattern best describes your family of origin, the family in which you now live, or both. How productive and satisfying is this pattern? Would a different pattern be better?

 You can complete this activity by visiting CengageBrain.com to access the Speech Communication CourseMate for *Looking Out/ Looking In,* **and, if requested, email your responses to your instructor.**

 # Communication in Friendships

You can't choose the family into which you are born, and you have little say about your neighbors or the people you work with. But friendships are voluntary: We can end them much more easily than we can escape the relational orbit of family, the bonds of marriage, or even the relationships that come with a career. The ease of cutting friendship ties—as well as the hard work of keeping the relationship positive—helps explain why friendships are more likely to end than any other relationship.[67]

Chapter 8 (pages 250–255) describes some of the ways we form relationships. Whatever the reasons, friendships are created and maintained through communication. In the coming pages, we'll look at the nature of friendships and examine how communication operates in this important context.

TYPES OF FRIENDSHIPS

The word *friend* covers a wide variety of relationships—everything from preschoolers who play make-believe games with each other, to teens whose alliances shift in the social currents of high school, to couples who socialize together, to the best friend forever (BFF) for whom you would do anything. As you'll now see, different types of friendships involve different kinds of communication.

Youthful versus Mature Some elements of friendship hold true across the life span. For instance, self-disclosure is typical in close relationships from childhood to old age.[68] But in other ways, the nature of friendships varies as the participants mature.[69]

Preschool children rarely have enduring friendships. Instead, they enjoy time with temporary playmates. As they grow older, children usually form more stable friendships, but primarily to meet their own needs and with little sense of empathy. During adolescence, friendships become a central feature of social life—often more important than family. In these teen years, friends begin to be valued for their personal qualities, not just as playmates or activity companions.

As they move away from familiar environments, young adults expand their circle of friends in ways that often prove highly satisfying.[70] By this point in life, the qualities that are important in a friend become stable and mature: helpfulness, support, trust, commitment, and self-disclosure. As the responsibilities of marriage and family grow, the desire to have strong friendships may stay the same, but the time available to support them can decline.[71] But in older adulthood, friendships become especially valuable as a means of social support. Having strong relationships contributes to both satisfaction and health.[72]

Long Term versus Short Term Some friendships last for years or even a lifetime, while others fade or end because of life changes (such as finishing high school, moving to a new location, or switching jobs). Although modern technologies decrease the likelihood that a friendship will end because of a long-distance move,[73] some falter or fail without face-to-face contact. Another reason some friendships may be short term is due to a change in values.[74] Perhaps you once had a group of friends with whom you enjoyed parties and nightlife, but as you grew out of that phase of your life, the mutual attraction waned.

Relationship Oriented versus Task Oriented Sometimes we choose friends because of shared activities: teammates in a softball league, coworkers, or fellow movie buffs. These types of friendships are considered task oriented if they primarily revolve around certain activities. On the other hand, relationship-oriented friendships are grounded in mutual liking and social support independently of shared activities. Of course, these categories overlap: Some friendships are based in both joint activities and emotional support.

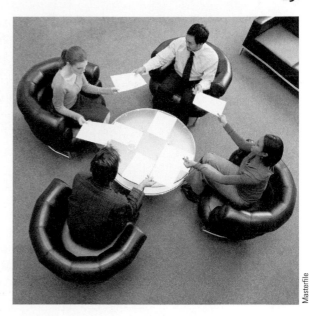

High-Disclosure versus Low Disclosure How much do you tell your friends about yourself? No doubt your level of disclosure differs from friend to friend. Some only know general information about you, whereas others are privy to your most personal secrets. The social penetration model in Chapter 2 (pages 58–60) can help you explore the breadth and depth of your disclosure with your various friends.

High Obligation versus Low Obligation There are some friends for whom we would do just about anything—no request is too big. We feel a lower sense of obligation to other friends, both in terms of what we would do for them and how quickly we would do it. Our closest friends usually get fast responses when they ask for a favor, give us a call, on even post on our Facebook Wall.

Frequent Contact versus Occasional Contact You probably keep in close touch with some friends. Perhaps you work out, travel, socialize, or Skype daily. Other friendships have less frequent contact—maybe an occasional phone call or e-message. Of course, infrequent contact doesn't always correlate with levels of disclosure or obligation. Many close friends may see each other only once a year, but they pick right back up in terms of the breadth and depth of their shared information.

After reading this far, you can begin to see that the nature of communication can vary from one friendship to another. Furthermore, communication *within* a friendship can also change over time. Impersonal friendships can have sudden bursts of disclosure. The amount of communication can swing from more to less frequent. Low-obligation friendships can evolve into stronger commitments and vice versa. In a few pages, you'll read about types of communication that are common in virtually all good friendships. But for now it's important to recognize that variety is a good thing.

SEX, GENDER, AND FRIENDSHIP

Not all friendships are created equal. Along with the differences described in the preceding pages, gender plays a role in how we communicate with friends.

Same-Sex Friendships Communication within same-sex friendships typically differs for men and women. Most women place a somewhat higher value on talking about personal matters as a measure of closeness, whereas men are more likely to create and express closeness through shared activities—what one scholar called "closeness in the doing."[75] In one study, more than 75 percent of the men surveyed said that their most meaningful experiences with friends came from shared activities.[76] They reported that by doing things together they "grew on one another," developed feelings of interdependence, showed appreciation for one another, and demonstrated mutual liking. Likewise, men regarded practical help as a measure of caring. Findings like these show that, for many men, closeness grows from activities that don't always depend heavily on disclosure: A friend is a person who does things *for* you and *with* you.

By contrast, women tend to disclose more personal information than men, both in face-to-face relationships[77] and online.[78] Although both men and women value friends who provide emotional support, women are generally more skilled at doing so and are more likely to seek out female friends when they need this type of support.[79] Of course, findings like these are generalizations that may not apply to specific friendships. The Pause and Reflect questions on page 293 will help you see how closely they apply to you.

Cross-Sex Friendships Cross-sex friendships offer benefits that same-sex relationships can't provide.[80] They provide a chance to see things from a different perspective, which can be a welcome contrast to the kinds of interaction that characterize communication with friends of the same sex.[81] For men, this often means a greater chance to share emotions and focus on relationships. For women, it can be a chance to lighten up and enjoy banter and activities without emotional baggage.

Cross-sex friendships—at least for heterosexuals—present some challenges that don't exist among all-male or all-female companionships. The most obvious is the reality or potential for sexual attraction.[82] As Billy Crystal said to Meg Ryan in the classic film *When Harry Met Sally*, "[M]en and women can't be friends because the sex part always gets in the way."

Research suggests that Harry was at least partly right. In one survey of 150 working professionals, more than 60 percent noted that sexual tension was a factor in their cross-sex relationships.[83] Although it's possible to have romance-free friendships with people of the other sex, defining that sort of relationship takes work. Some evidence suggests that communicating more online (rather than in person) can help to keep a cross-sex relationship platonic.[84]

When it comes to the potential for romance, heterosexual cross-sex friendships fit into one of four categories.[85] (We can assume the same holds true for same-sex friendships among gay men and lesbians.) Some carry the promise of *mutual romance*: Both partners want the friendship to turn romantic. These relationships often await a relational turning point, as we'll discuss later in this chapter. Others are *strictly platonic*: Neither partner wants the friendship to turn romantic. In a third category, *one partner desires romance*, while believing that the friend does not. In the fourth condition, one partner *rejects romance* but thinks the friend is interested in moving the friendship to a more intimate level. It is not surprising that the last two types of relationships are the most complicated. In these situations, the less-interested partner often uses strategies to communicate "no-go" messages: less routine contact and activity, less flirtation, and more talk about outside romances.

Friends with Benefits **Friends with benefits (FWB)** is a popular term for nonromantic heterosexual friendships that include sexual activity. One study claims that nearly 60 percent of university students report having been involved in at least one FWB relationship.[86]

Men and women are equally likely to be in FWB relationships. Some surveys suggest that both appreciate the chance to take care of physical needs without the challenges of emotional commitment.[87] Despite this similarity, there are gender differences in the way FWB relationships turn out. Although the majority of men describe their relationships as primarily sexual, women are much more likely to become emotionally involved. From findings like these, some observers have commented that women are typically more focused on being "friends" while men are more likely to be interested in the "benefits."[88]

Given the chance that sexual activity might lead to unreciprocated desires for romantic commitment, it would seem logical that FWB partners would regularly discuss the status of their relationship—

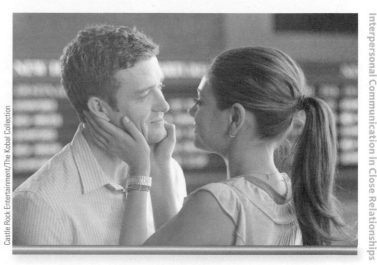

Ever since Harry met Sally, films have explored the question of whether friends can become physically intimate without damaging the relationship. In *Friends with Benefits*, the answer is "It's not easy."

but researchers have found that FWBs routinely avoid explicit communication about this important topic. The researchers concluded that "FWB relationships are often problematic for the same reasons that they are attractive."[89]

Gender Considerations Biological sex isn't the only factor to consider when we examine different sorts of friendships. Another important consideration is gender role (see Chapter 3, pages 91–92). For instance, a friendship between a masculine male and a feminine female might have very different properties than a friendship between a masculine female and a feminine male—even though these are both technically cross-sex relationships.

Sexual orientation is another factor that can shape friendships. Most obviously, for gay men and lesbians the potential for sexual attraction shifts from opposite- to same-sex relationships. But physical attraction aside, sexual orientation can still play a significant role in friendships. For example, many heterosexual women report that they value their friendships with gay men because (1) they often share interests, (2) the potential for romantic complications is small or nonexistent,[90] and (3) the women feel more attractive.[91]

PAUSE AND REFLECT

GENDER AND FRIENDSHIP

Analyze how gender affects communication in your friendships by keeping logs of communication in two relationships: same-sex and cross-sex. For each incident in your log, record both the subject being discussed (e.g., school, finances) and the nature of the interaction (e.g., emotional expression, personal information, shared activities). Based on your findings, do you see a different pattern in communication with same- and opposite-sex friendships?

You can complete this activity by visiting CengageBrain.com to access the Speech Communication CourseMate for *Looking Out/ Looking In*, and, if requested, email your responses to your instructor.

Castle Rock Entertainment/The Kobal Collection

FRIENDSHIP AND SOCIAL MEDIA

IRL (in real life) it's not hard to tell who counts as a friend. The Internet has made friendship more complicated. Consider Facebook, where a "friend" could be someone you met once at a party or on vacation, a former classmate or neighbor whom you haven't seen in years, someone you met online but have never known in person, or even a "publicity whore" who only sought you out to boost the size of his or her friends list.

Despite all the possibilities, research shows that social-networking sites are used primarily to maintain current friendships or to revive old ones rather than to build new relationships.[92] For example, the highest proportion of Facebook connections is between high school classmates. Even when strangers have met online, it's likely that they will attempt a face-to-face meeting if the relationship becomes close.[93] Findings like these show that social media typically isn't a *replacement* for face-to-face communication, but is a means to support and rekindle friendships that were developed in person.[94]

Perhaps the most intriguing scholarship about friendship and social media has to do with the number of friends one has on social-networking sites. A survey by the Pew Research Center found that the average Facebook user has 245 friends.[95] Research shows that the principle "the more friends the better" is only true up to a point. There is a curvilinear relationship between the number of Facebook friends and the perception of those friendships by others.[96] If you have too few Facebook friends, others may regard you (perhaps unfairly) as not very social or friendly. On the other hand, if you have too many online friends, people might perceive those relationships as less than genuine.

He had over 2,000 Facebook friends. I was expecting a bigger turnout.

BIZARROCOMICS.COM   Dist. by King Features 2012   1·26·12

Bizarro Blog! Dan Piraro/King Features Syndicate

One evolutionary anthropologist suggests that the maximum number of relationships the human brain can handle is 150.[97] The precise numbers may change in the years to come, but the point remains: Calling a large number of people "friends" stretches the definition most would use for a meaningful relationship. Facebook users would likely acknowledge that many of their "friends" on that site could more accurately be labeled as "acquaintances."

Of course, social-networking sites aren't the only media for communicating with friends. Phoning, texting, emailing, and even blogging are means for keeping up friendships. Later in this chapter, we'll talk about the important role of social media in maintaining and supporting all our close relationships.

 ## Communication in Romantic Relationships

The ancient Greeks knew that love comes in many forms. Their terminology can help us understand the different styles of love.[98] *Storge* and *philia* are about friendly love—the kind that a couple might enjoy during shared activities or a friend may express in the phrase "I love ya, bro." *Pragma* is a practical, logical affinity—the type of affection that long-term couples might feel or working partners could develop over time. *Agape* characterizes selfless, altruistic compassion—the kind that leads someone to care for a sick partner or for a parent to comfort a child in distress. When it comes to romantic relationships, the Greek words often associated are *mania* (a starstruck, tumultuous experience) and *eros* (from which we get the word *erotic*). Clearly, this is love of a different variety.

The following pages will focus on communication in romantic relationships: longer-term, loving connections between partners. Typically (but not always), romantic relationships have unique displays of physical affection and some measure of commitment. For our purposes, they can include couples who are dating exclusively, partners who live together, and spouses who have been married for years. The crucial issue is whether the people involved identify themselves as being romantically connected. We'll look at turning points for romantic couples, the communication styles they use in conflict, and the ways they can express their affection to each other. At the end of the chapter, we'll talk about maintaining and improving not only romantic relationships, but all of our close relationships.

ROMANTIC TURNING POINTS

If you ask couples when their romantic relationship began, chances are good they can identify a particular marker. Maybe it was a specific date, a special embrace, or the first time a partner uttered the words "I love you." Communication researchers call these **relational turning points**—transformative events that alter the relationship in a fundamental way.[99]

Angelo Cavalli/SuperStock

Although other close relationships can have turning points,[100] these events are especially important in romantic relationships. Consider a couple on the verge of moving from "just friends" to "something more." It's easy to imagine a transitional moment ("and then we kissed") when the relationship becomes romantic.[101]

Relational turning points often mark movement among the stages discussed in Chapter 8 (pages 255–262). They can involve everything from Facebook declarations[102] to physical intimacy[103] to the "first big fight"[104] to breakups and makeups.[105] From this list it's easy to see that not all turning points are positive. It is not surprising that couples who can identify more negative turning points than positive ones have lower levels of relational satisfaction.[106]

Turning points can provide clues about the status of the relationship: "I think you've been avoiding me since we visited your family" or "I feel much more connected after our big talk last week." Toward that end, they are useful tools for communicating—and metacommunicating—about the status of a romantic relationship.

COUPLES' CONFLICT STYLES

The fact that "the first big fight" is a common romantic turning point suggests that conflict is a normal part of couples' communication. And for most partners, the first disagreement is rarely the last. John Gottman has spent years studying romantic relationships and finds that couples tend to fall into one of the three following conflict styles.[107]

PAUSE AND REFLECT

RELATIONAL TURNING POINTS

Identify the turning points in a romantic relationship, either past or present. If you prefer not to analyze a personal relationship, then use one from a film or book. Describe if and how the turning points you identified mark the transition from one relational stage to another, using the stages described in pages 255–262 of Chapter 8.

 You can complete this activity by visiting CengageBrain.com to access the Speech Communication CourseMate for *Looking Out/ Looking In*, and, if requested, email your responses to your instructor.

1. **Volatile:** These couples have intense, heated arguments—sometimes over small issues. They raise their voices, compete to hold the floor, and make their cases passionately. Conflicts for these couples are often seen as contests to be won.

2. **Avoidant:** Couples who use this style prefer to ignore issues rather than confront them. They minimize disagreements and steer clear of sensitive topics. The partners acknowledge that they have conflicts, but they handle them quickly and dispassionately.

3. **Validating:** These couples openly and cooperatively manage conflicts. When they have differences of opinion, they talk them through in civil ways without denying their feelings. They listen carefully to each other and look for collaborative solutions to their problems.

The validating style matches the approach advocated in this book, and it appears to be the ideal way of communicating.[108] Nonetheless, Gottman has come to acknowledge that the other two styles can be successful in some cases. Here's what he learned about happily married volatile couples:

> It turns out that these couples' volcanic arguments are just a small part of an otherwise warm and loving marriage. The passion and relish with which they fight seems to fuel their positive interactions even more. Not only do they express more anger but they laugh and are more affectionate than the average validating couple.*

And this is what Gottman discovered about satisfied couples who use an avoidant style:

> Rather than resolve conflicts, avoidant couples appeal to their basic shared philosophy of marriage. They reaffirm what they love and value in the marriage, accentuate the positive, and accept the rest. In this way, they often end an unresolved discussion still feeling good about one another.*

So if conflict style isn't the crucial factor in successful romantic relationships, then what is? Gottman maintains it's the number of positive to negative communicative acts. He calls 5:1 "the magic ratio" and says that as long as couples have five times as many positive interactions—touching, smiling, paying compliments, laughing, kind words, and so on—as negative ones, they are likely to have happy and successful relationships. It's easy for avoidant couples to keep the negative number low, as it is for volatile couples to keep the positive number high. The key for all couples, including validating partners, is to maintain the appropriate ratio.

*Gottman, J. (1994). *Why marriages succeed or fail* (pp. 41, 45). New York: Simon & Schuster.

LANGUAGES OF LOVE

"If you love me, please listen."

"If you love me, say so."

"If you love me, show me."

The underlying message in statements like these is, "Here is what love means to me." Author Gary Chapman argues that each of us has our own notion of what counts as love. He calls these notions **love languages** and suggests that we get into trouble when we fail to recognize that our way of expressing love may not match our partner's.[109]

Chapman identifies the following five love languages in romantic relationships, and research offers support for these categories.[110]

1. **Words of affirmation:** These include compliments, words of praise, verbal support, written notes or letters, or other ways of saying that a person is valued and appreciated. People who use this love language are easily hurt by insults or ridicule or when their efforts aren't verbally acknowledged.

2. **Quality time:** This is about being present and available for your partner and giving that person your complete, undivided attention for a significant period of time. Being inattentive or distracted takes the "quality" out of time spent together.

3. **Gifts:** People who measure love in terms of gifts believe "it's the thought that counts." A gift needn't be expensive to be meaningful. The best ones are the type that the recipient will appreciate. To gift-oriented partners, neglecting to honor an important event is a transgression.

4. **Acts of service:** Taking out the trash, filling the car with gas, doing laundry—the list of chores that can be acts of service is endless. Similar to gifts, the key to service is knowing which acts would be most appreciated by your partner. (Hint: It's probably the chore that your partner hates most.)

5. **Physical touch:** Although this might include sexual activity, meaningful touch can also include other expressions of affection: an arm around the shoulder, a held hand, a brush of the cheek, or a neck rub.

Partners understandably but mistakenly can assume that the love language they prefer is also the one that their mate will appreciate. For example, if your primary love language is "gifts," then you probably expect presents from loved ones on special occasions—and perhaps even on ordinary ones. You're also likely to give gifts regularly and assume that they'll be received appreciatively.

As you can imagine, the assumption that your partner speaks the same love language as you can be a setup for disappointment. Chapman says this is often the case in marriages:

> We tend to speak our primary love language, and we become confused when our spouse does not understand what we are communicating. We are expressing our love, but the message does not come through because we are speaking what, to them, is a foreign language.*

Most people learn love languages in their family of origin. To a degree then, we're imprinted with ways to give and receive affection from an early age. The good news is that we can learn to communicate love in different ways—especially with help from our romantic partners. Take a look at the types of love languages in the list above and see if you can identify your primary style. You can then ask your partner to do the same and compare notes. The Self-Assessment on this page provides a link to a more formal diagnostic tool. The reading on the following page offers a narrative from someone who engaged in such a self-appraisal.

---

*Chapman, G. (2010). *The 5 love languages* (p. 15). Chicago: Northfield.

SELF-ASSESSMENT

Your Love Languages

What are your preferred love languages? What languages best reach your partner? To find out, use the assessment tools available at CengageBrain .com, where you can access the Speech Communication CourseMate for *Looking Out/ Looking In.*

LEARNING THE LANGUAGES OF LOVE

I used to be in a relationship in which my significant other liked to lavish me with gifts on special occasions. He also never hesitated to help solve any problem I, or any member of my family, had.

I, on the other hand, was physically affectionate. I also liked doing activities together. We were together for a long time, but our relationship eventually fell apart because we each felt unloved by the other. Had we'd known each other's love language, we might still be together.

I recently read *The 5 Love Languages* by Dr. Gary Chapman. According to him, if we don't learn our partner's love language, we might as well be speaking in Russian to them.

In my past relationship, I would accuse my partner of not loving me because he didn't spend quality time with me or show enough affection. He'd point at the beautiful jewelry around my neck and ask, "How do you like your necklace?"

That would infuriate me. I always thought he was just trying to be a jerk and avoid the conversation. What he was doing was showing me a physical symbol of how much he did love me. Apparently, his love language was "gifting," but mine was not.

He, in turn, would accuse me of not caring for him, because I didn't help him by taking his clothes to the cleaners when he was busy at work. Apparently, his other love language was "acts of service." So, round and round we went, accusing each other of withholding love.

After reading Chapman's book, I've learned that my love languages are physical touch and quality time. I had been loving my partner the way I wanted to be loved, and he had been expressing his love in the ways he wanted to be loved.

My favorite passage in the book is this one: "People tend to criticize their spouse most loudly in the area where they themselves have the deepest emotional need. Their criticism is an ineffective way of pleading for love. If we understand that, it may help us process their criticism in a more productive manner."

Corbis Cusp/Alamy

Chapman says the beginning of a relationship is the "in-love" stage. During this period of euphoria, your partner can do no wrong, has no flaws, and everything is possible. Once that phase is over, long-lasting emotional love becomes a choice. We have to choose to love our partners for who they are, and love them in the way they need to be loved—in their own love language.

Edie Vaughan

 ## Improving Close Relationships

Good relationships don't just happen. They need good communication skills to remain alive and vital. In this section, we'll look at ways to keep your important relationships close—and perhaps even help them become closer.

RELATIONSHIPS REQUIRE COMMITMENT

Some common statements suggest the central role commitment plays in our ongoing interactions with others: "I'm looking for a committed relationship." "Our relationship didn't work because my partner wasn't committed." "I'm just not ready for commitment."

Relational commitment involves a promise—sometimes implied, and sometimes explicit—to remain in a relationship and to make that relationship successful. Commitment is important in every type of interpersonal relationship, whether it's a friendship ("Friends for life!"), family ("We're always here for you"), a close-knit working team ("I've got you covered"), or a romantic relationship ("Till death do us part").

Dragan Trifunovic/iStockphoto

As these examples suggest, commitment is both formed and reinforced through communication. Table 9.1 spells out commitment indicators in romantic relationships. Research shows that frequent use of these indicators enhances relationships and reduces uncertainty about them.[111] You can probably imagine how similar indicators of commitment would operate in other sorts of close relationships.

As Table 9.1 suggests, words alone aren't a surefire measure of true commitment. Deeds are also important. Simply saying "You can count on me" doesn't guarantee loyalty. But without language, commitment may not be clear. For this reason, the kinds of bonding ceremonies described on page 259 are an important way to recognize and cement loyalty.

There is a strong and clear connection between relational commitment and relational maintenance.[112] If you're invested in a relationship, you'll want to communicate in ways that make it grow and thrive, as we'll now explore.

TABLE 9.1 MAJOR INDICATORS OF A COMMITTED ROMANTIC RELATIONSHIP

Providing affection
Providing support
Maintaining integrity
Sharing companionship
Making an effort to communicate regularly
Showing respect
Creating a relational future
Creating a positive relational atmosphere
Working on relationship problems together
Reassuring one's commitment

© Cengage Learning 2013

RELATIONSHIPS REQUIRE MAINTENANCE AND SUPPORT

Just as gardens need tending, cars need tune-ups, and bodies need exercise, close relationships need ongoing maintenance to keep them successful and satisfying. And when the chips are down, we want to count on friends, lovers, and family members to offer support.

Relational Maintenance As noted in Chapter 8, **relational maintenance** can be broadly defined as communication that keeps relationships running smoothly and satisfactorily. To keep a family afloat, a friendship alive, or a romance ablaze requires some measure of maintenance. What kinds of communication help maintain relationships? Researchers have identified five strategies that couples use to keep their interaction satisfying.[113]

1. **Positivity:** Keeping the relational climate polite and upbeat, and also avoiding criticism. (Chapter 10 addresses this topic in detail.)

2. **Openness:** Talking directly about the nature of the relationship and disclosing your personal needs and concerns. (Chapter 2 describes the challenges of finding the optimal amount of self-disclosure.)

3. **Assurances:** Letting the other person know—both verbally and nonverbally—that he or she matters to you and that you are committed to the relationship.

4. **Social networks:** Being invested in each other's friends, family, and loved ones.

5. **Sharing tasks:** Helping one another take care of life's chores and obligations.

You can probably see how sharing tasks and offering assurances are related to the love languages of "acts of service" and "words of affirmation" described earlier in the chapter. In fact, one study found a strong correlation between love languages and relational maintenance.[114] However, these maintenance strategies aren't only for romantic relationships. One study analyzed college students' email to see which maintenance approaches they used.[115] With family and friends, two strategies were used most: openness ("Things have been a little crazy for me lately") and social networks ("How are you and Sam? Hopefully good"). With romantic partners, however, assurances ("This is just a little email to say I love you") were the most-used maintenance device.

The preceding example shows that social media can play an important role in maintaining close relationships.[116] For instance, tools such as Facebook give loved ones the chance to keep up with each other through status updates and posting comments on each other's Walls.[117] Phone calls and emails can help too, with phoning being particularly valuable for more intimate topics.[118] One study found that women use social media for relational maintenance more often than do men, regardless of the type of relationship maintained.[119] This is consistent with research showing that women expect and receive more maintenance communication with their female friends than men do with other males.[120]

Social media are especially useful for meeting the challenges of long-distance relationships. These relationships are increasingly common; contrary to popular assumptions, they can be as stable or more so than geographically close relationships.[121] This is true not only for romantic and family relationships but also for friendships.[122] The key is a commitment to relational maintenance. In one study, female college students said that openness and mutual problem solving are vital maintenance strategies in long-distance dating relationships.[123] In another study, both men and women reported that openness (self-disclosure) was the most important factor for maintaining closeness with their long-distance friends. (They conceded that sharing tasks and practical help are less viable options in long-distance relationships.)[124]

Social Support Although relational maintenance is about keeping a relationship thriving, **social support** is about helping loved ones during challenging times by providing emotional, informational, or instrumental resources.[125] Communication plays a central role in giving this aid to those we love. Here's a closer look at those three support resources:

Andrea Sperling Productions/The Kobal Collection

Forced to live in separate countries, Anna (Felicity Jones) and Jacob (Anton Yelchin) struggle to maintain a long-distance relationship. They discover that, despite their love and communication technology, distance creates an emotional gap as well as a physical one. (See the "Like Crazy" film summary at the end of this chapter.)

1. **Emotional support:** Few things are more helpful during times of stress, hurt, or grief than a loved one who listens with empathy and responds in caring ways. Chapter 7 (pages 235–237) describes what supporting does and doesn't sound like when responding to others' emotional needs. It's important to keep your message *person-centered*—that is, focused on the emotions of the speaker ("This must be difficult for you") rather than minimizing those feelings ("It's not the end of the world") or diverting attention ("The sun will come up tomorrow").[126]

2. **Informational support:** The closest people in our lives can often be our best information sources. They can give us recommendations for shopping, advice about relationships, or observations about our blind spots. You can probably recall times when you've said to a loved one with gratitude, "Thanks for letting me know." Of course, it's important to remember the tips about advice giving on pages 238–239. Information is most likely to be regarded as supportive when it's wanted and requested by the person in need.

3. **Instrumental support:** Sometimes support is best given by rolling up your sleeves and doing a task or favor for a person you love. This can be as simple as a ride to the airport or as involved as caregiving during an illness. We count on romantic partners and family members to offer assistance in times of need, and instrumental support is a primary marker of a close friendship ("A friend in need is a friend indeed").[127]

It's worth noting that social support can also come from people we may never meet in person. Because online support groups and blogs are relatively anonymous and the participants are similar, they can offer help in ways that make strangers seem like close friends.[128] For instance, approximately 20 percent of Internet users have gone online to find others with similar health problems.[129] When asked why, a common response is that they feel more comfortable talking with like-minded people with whom they have few formal ties—particularly when the health issues are embarrassing or stigma laden. For example, one study looked at how blogs offer social support for people who are morbidly obese.[130] These sites become interactive communities, where people with similar conditions share their struggles and offer each other affirming feedback. One blogger in the study put it this way: "When I have a bad week on the scale or a problem I don't know how to handle, all I have to do is write up an entry and post it on the blog. My readers are always full of good advice, comments and support."

PAUSE AND REFLECT

MAINTAINING YOUR RELATIONSHIPS

How well are you maintaining your important relationships through constructive communication? Choose one relationship that matters to you: with family members, friends, or a romantic partner. Analyze the degree to which you and the others involved use the maintenance strategies listed above to keep the relationship strong and satisfying. What steps could you take to improve matters?

 You can complete this activity by visiting CengageBrain.com to access the Speech Communication CourseMate for *Looking Out/ Looking In*, and, if requested, email your responses to your instructor.

REPAIRING DAMAGED RELATIONSHIPS

Sooner or later, even the strongest relationships hit a bumpy patch. Some problems arise from outside forces: work, finances, competing relationships, and so on. At other times, problems arise from differences and disagreements within your relationship. Chapter 11 offers guidelines for dealing with these sorts of challenges.

A third type of relational problem comes from **relational transgressions**: when one partner violates the explicit or implicit terms of the relationship, letting the other one down in some important way.[131]

Types of Relational Transgressions Table 9.2 lists some types of relational transgressions. Violations like these fall into different categories.[132]

TABLE 9.2 SOME TYPES OF RELATIONAL TRANSGRESSIONS

Lack of Commitment	Failure to honor important obligations (e.g., financial, emotional, task-related) Self-serving dishonesty Unfaithfulness
Distance	Physical separation (beyond what is necessary) Psychological separation (avoidance, ignoring)
Disrespect	Criticism (especially in front of third parties)
Problematic Emotions	Jealousy Unjustified suspicion Rage
Aggression	Verbal hostility Physical violence

© Cengage Learning

Minor versus Significant Some of the items listed in Table 9.2 aren't inherently transgressions, and in small doses they can actually aid relationships. For instance, a *little* distance can make the heart grow fonder, a *little* jealousy can be a sign of affection, and a *little* anger can start the process of resolving a gripe. In large and regular doses, however, these acts become serious transgressions that can damage personal relationships.

Social versus Relational Some transgressions violate *social rules* shared by society at large. For example, almost everyone would agree that ridiculing or humiliating a friend or family member in public is a violation of a fundamental social rule regarding saving others' face. Other rules are *relational* in nature—unique norms constructed by the parties involved. For instance, some families have a rule stating "If I'm going to be more than a little bit late, I'll let you know so you don't worry." Once such a rule exists, failure to honor it feels like a violation, even though outsiders might not view it as such.

Deliberate versus Unintentional Some transgressions are unintentional. You might reveal something about a friend's past without realizing that this disclosure would be embarrassing. Other violations, though, are intentional. In a fit of anger, you might purposely lash out with a cruel comment, knowing that it will hurt the other person's feelings.

One-Time versus Incremental The most obvious transgressions occur in a single episode: an act of betrayal, a verbal assault, or stalking out in anger. But more subtle transgressions can occur over time. Consider emotional withdrawal: Everybody has times when they need isolation, and we usually give one another the space to do just that. But if the withdrawal slowly becomes pervasive, it becomes a violation of the fundamental rule in most relationships that partners should be available to one another.

Strategies for Relational Repair

Research confirms the common-sense notion that a first step toward repairing a transgression is to talk about the violation.[133] Chapter 10 offers tips for sending clear, assertive messages when you believe you've been wronged: "I was really embarrassed when you yelled at me in front of everybody last night." In other cases, you might be responsible for the transgression and want to raise it for discussion: "What did I do that you found so hurtful?" "Why was my behavior a problem for you?" Asking questions like these—and listening nondefensively to the answers—can be an enormous challenge. Chapter 7 offers guidelines for listening, and Chapter 10 provides tips about how to manage criticism.

ABC-TV/The Kobal Collection

Relational transgressions are a regular occurrence in the television series *Desperate Housewives*. Some of the transgressions are easily reparable; others are not.

The best chance for righting a wrong is taking responsibility for your transgression.[134] It isn't easy to apologize, especially in Western cultures, where saving one's own face is a strong concern.[135] But not expressing regret can be worse than saying "I'm sorry." Participants in one study reported that they had more remorse over apologies they didn't offer than about those they did.[136] There's another benefit of seeking forgiveness: Research shows that transgressors who have been forgiven are less likely to repeat their offenses than those who have not received forgiveness.[137]

Love language author Gary Chapman maintains that the language of apologies is important and that certain apology components matter more to some than others.[138] Page 304 lists the five components he identifies. Consider which is the most important for you to hear when someone apologizes to you.

PAUSE AND REFLECT

YOUR RELATIONAL TRANSGRESSIONS

1. Identify transgressions you have made in one important relationship. Describe whether these transgressions were minor or significant, social or relational, deliberate or unintentional, and one-time or incremental. (If you think the relationship can handle it, consider asking the "victim" of your transgression to describe your behavior and its effects.)
2. Consider (or ask the other person) whether it's necessary to repair your transgression. Examine the strategies described in this section and then decide how you could put them into action.
3. Which of the five components identified by Chapman mean the most to you when someone apologizes? Which are the hardest for you to say?

 You can complete this activity by visiting CengageBrain.com to access the Speech Communication CourseMate for *Looking Out/ Looking In*, and, if requested, email your responses to your instructor.

1. **Expressing regret:** "I'm sorry." "I feel bad about what I did."
2. **Accepting responsibility:** "I was wrong." "It was my fault."
3. **Making restitution:** "What can I do to make it right?"
4. **Genuinely repenting:** "I'll try not to do that again."
5. **Requesting forgiveness:** "Will you please forgive me?"

An apology will only be convincing if the speaker's nonverbal behaviors match his or her words. Even then, it may be unrealistic to expect immediate forgiveness. Sometimes, especially with severe transgressions, expressions of regret and promises of new behavior need to be demonstrated over time before the aggrieved party accepts them as genuine.[139]

Forgiving Transgressions Many people think of forgiveness as a topic for theologians and philosophers. However, social scientists have found that forgiving others has both personal and relational benefits. On a personal level, forgiveness has been shown to reduce emotional distress and aggression[140] as well as improve cardiovascular functioning.[141] Interpersonally, extending forgiveness to lovers, friends, and family can help restore damaged relationships.[142]

"I said I'm sorry."

Research suggests that the most effective conversations about forgiveness contain two elements from the offended person:

1. **An explicit statement:** "I can't forget what you did, but I believe your apology and I accept it."

2. **A discussion of the implications of the transgression and the future of the relationship:** "I have to be honest. It's going to take time before I can trust you again—but I'm willing to try."[143]

Not surprisingly, some transgressions are harder to forgive than others.[144] One study of dating partners found that sexual infidelity and breaking up with the partner were the two least forgivable offenses.[145] And, as noted earlier, being emotionally unfaithful—as occurs in some online affairs—can be as distressing as sexual infidelity.[146]

Even when a sincere apology is offered, forgiving others can be difficult. Research shows that one way to improve your ability to forgive is to recall times when you have mistreated or hurt others in the past—in other words, to remember that you, too, have wronged others and needed their forgiveness.[147] Knowing that it's in our own best interest to be forgiving, communication researcher Douglas Kelley encourages us to remember these words: "When we have been hurt we have two alternatives: be destroyed by resentment, or forgive. Resentment is death; forgiving leads to healing and life."[148]

SUMMARY

Intimacy in interpersonal relationships has four dimensions: physical, intellectual, emotional, and shared activities. Both gender and culture affect the way intimacy is expressed. Intimacy can occur through mediated communication as well as in face-to-face interaction. Not all relationships are intimate; communicators must make choices about when, where, and with whom they will be intimate.

Family relationships are formative, role driven, and generally involuntary. Families operate as systems and develop communication patterns that involve the merging of particular conversation and conformity orientations.

Communication in friendships often varies according to the age of the participants, relational history and frequency of contact, level of obligation, task or relational foundations, level of disclosure and obligation, and gender of the friends. Social media play an important role in contemporary relationships.

Romantic partnerships often begin, continue, and end based on relational turning points. Couples typically use one of three conflict styles: volatile, avoidant, or validating. Each partner in a romantic relationship favors one of five love languages, and it's helpful for both to become fluent in the other's language.

Close relationships require commitment and maintenance. They also need emotional, informational, and instrumental support. When relationships become damaged by transgressions, repair strategies and forgiveness become important skills for both parties.

KEY TERMS

conformity orientation (288)
conversation orientation (287)
family communication pattern (288)
family system (286)
friends with benefits (FWB) (292)
intimacy (278)
love languages (297)

relational commitment (299)
relational maintenance (299)
relational transgression (302)
relational turning point (295)
role (285)
social support (300)

ONLINE RESOURCES

Now that you have read this chapter, visit CengageBrain.com to access the Speech Communication CourseMate for *Looking Out/Looking In* for quick access to the electronic resources that accompany this text. Your CourseMate offers:

- **Study tools** that will help you assess your learning and prepare for exams (*digital glossary, key term flash cards, interactive quizzes*).
- **Activities and assignments** that will help you hone your knowledge, understand how theory and research applies to your own life (*Self-Assessment, Pause and Reflect*), consider ethical challenges in interpersonal communication (*Ethical Challenge*), and build your interpersonal communication skills throughout the course (*Skill Builder*). If requested, you can submit your answers to your instructor.
- **Media resources** that will allow you to watch and critique videos of interpersonal communication situations (*In Real Life, interpersonal video simulations, and interactive video activities*).
- In addition to interactive teaching and learning tools, CourseMate includes an **interactive eBook**. Take notes, highlight, search, and interact with embedded media specific to *Looking Out/Looking In*.

SEARCH TERMS

When searching online databases to research topics in this chapter, use the following terms (along with this chapter's key terms) to maximize the chances of finding useful information:

family communication	marriage
fidelity	parent–child relationships
forgiveness	relational satisfaction
friendships	siblings
intimate communication	systems theory
love	

FILM AND TELEVISION

You can see the communication principles described in this chapter portrayed in the following films and television programs.

INTIMACY AND GENDER

I Love You, Man (2009) Rated R

Terms such as *bromance* and *man crush* suggest that people are looking for new ways to describe close friendships between heterosexual men. *I Love You, Man* explores this theme.

Peter Claven (Paul Rudd) doesn't have a close friend to serve as best man at his upcoming wedding. So he goes on a series of "man dates" to find a BFF. Peter bumps into Sidney Fife (Jason Segel) at a house showing, and they quickly develop a strong bond.

Peter and Sidney experience intimacy on a variety of levels. They have emotional and intellectual connections, with plenty of open conversations and personal disclosures. They also enjoy shared activities, especially rock-and-roll jam sessions. And on a physical level, there are lots of arms around shoulders and several bear hugs.

An interesting subplot involves what happens when Peter's newfound friendship with Sidney infringes on his relationship with his fiancée. This dynamic highlights the challenge of managing the demands of multiple close relationships.

COMMITMENT AND SUPPORT

Intervention (2005–) Rated TV-14

A&E Television Networks/Photofest

This award-winning reality series takes an inside look at people in close relationships as they confront their loved ones about chronic problems. The interventions address issues such as substance abuse, eating disorders, gambling addictions, and mental and physical health challenges. Although the confrontations sometimes require "tough love," the interveners clearly demonstrate and embody relational commitment and support—and, in some cases, forgiveness.

FAMILY SYSTEMS

Modern Family (2009–) Rated TV-PG

This critically acclaimed TV sitcom chronicles the misadventures of three households who are all part of the same extended clan.

As the title suggests, the diverse range of relationships in *Modern Family* would have been improbable in previous generations. The most traditional household includes cheerfully uncool dad Phil (Ty Burrell), overstressed mom Claire (Julie Bowen), and their three very different children. Claire's father, Jay (Ed O'Neill), is in a second marriage with Colombian wife Gloria (Sofia Vergara), who is half his age. They live with Manny (Rico Rodriguez), Gloria's son from a previous relationship. Claire's brother Mitchell (Jesse Tyler Ferguson) is in a committed relationship with his gay partner Cameron (Eric Stonestreet), and they have an adopted Vietnamese daughter.

Each episode of *Modern Family* illustrates the principles of family systems described in this chapter. This series captures the rich, complicated, interdependent nature of relationships among partners, parents, children, grandparents, siblings, in-laws, stepcousins, and more.

LONG-DISTANCE RELATIONSHIPS

Like Crazy (2011) Rated PG-13

Like many couples, Anna (Felicity Jones) and Jacob (Anton Yelchin) fall in love after meeting in college. But life gets complicated when an expired student visa forces Anna to return to her native England. Email, texting, and phoning make keeping in touch easy enough. But the young lovers discover that mediated communication can only go so far in keeping the relationship intact.

The film offers a realistic picture of the challenges of a long-distance relationship, and it helps explore the question of whether love and technology are enough to keep a couple together in the absence of personal contact. As in real life, the answer for Jacob and Anna is ambiguous.

REPAIRING DAMAGED RELATIONSHIPS

Atonement (2007) Rated R

On an English estate, thirteen-year-old Briony Tallis (Saoirse Ronan) spies two encounters between her older sister Cecilia (Keira Knightley) and Robbie Turner (James McAvoy), the son of the family's housekeeper. Driven by her overactive imagination and a jealous crush on Robbie, Briony jumps to mistaken conclusions and accuses Robbie of a crime he didn't commit.

Briony's indictment destroys three lives, including her own. She spends the rest of her days atoning for her impetuous accusations. By illustrating the principle that communication is irreversible, this story illustrates the immense challenges of trying to repair severely damaged relationships.

Focus Features/The Kobal Collection

C H A P T E R   N I N E

Interpersonal Communication in Close Relationships

CHAPTER OUTLINE

Use this outline to take notes as you read the chapter in the text and/or as your instructor lectures in class.

I. **INTIMACY IN CLOSE RELATIONSHIPS**	_____
A. **Dimensions of Intimacy**	_____
1. Physical	_____
2. Intellectual	_____
3. Emotional	_____
4. Shared activities	_____
B. **Masculine and Feminine Intimacy Styles**	_____
1. Women tend to value talk to develop intimacy	_____
2. Men tend to value activities to develop intimacy	_____
3. Gender role, not biological sex, influences intimacy styles	_____
C. **Cultural Influences on Intimacy**	_____
1. Historical	_____
2. Regional cultures	_____
a. Individualist	
b. Collectivist	_____
3. Co-cultures and class	
D. **Intimacy in Mediated**	

Communication

1. Speed of intimacy development through mediated communication

2. Importance of mediated communication in contemporary relationships

E. **The Limits of Intimacy**

1. Diminishing returns

2. Necessity of nonintimate relationships

II. **COMMUNICATION IN FAMILIES**

A. **Characteristics of Family Communication**

1. Family communication is formative

    a. Attachment theory
    b. Birth order

2. Family communication is role-driven

3. Family communication is involuntary

B. **Families as Systems**

1. Family systems are interdependent

2. Family systems are manifested through communication

3. Family systems are nested

4. Families are more than the sum of their parts

C. **Communication Patterns Within Families**

1. Conversation orientation

    a. High conversation orientation
    b. Low conversation orientation

2. Conformity orientation

3. Family communication pattern

    a. Consensual

b. Pluralistic

c. Protective

d. Laissez-faire

III. COMMUNICATION IN FRIENDSHIPS

A. Types of Friendships

1. Youthful versus mature

2. Long term versus short term

3. Relationship oriented versus task oriented

4. High disclosure versus low disclosure

5. High obligation versus low obligation

6. Frequent contact versus occasional contact

B. Sex, Gender, and Friendship

1. Same-sex friendships

2. Cross-sex friendships

3. Friends with benefits

4. Gender considerations

C. Friendship and Social Media

IV. COMMUNICATION IN ROMANTIC RELATIONSHIPS

A. Romantic Turning Points

B. Couples' Conflict Styles

1. Volatile

2. Avoidant

3. Validating

C. Languages of Love

1. Words of affirmation

2. Quality time

3. Gifts

4. Acts of service

5. Physical touch

V. IMPROVING CLOSE RELATIONSHIPS

A. Relationships Require Commitment

B. Relationships Require Maintenance and Support

1. Relational maintenance
   a. Positivity
   b. Openness
   c. Assurances
   d. Social networks
   e. Sharing tasks
2. Social support
   a. Emotional support
   b. Informational support
   c. Instrumental support

C. Repairing Damaged Relationships
   1. Types of relational transgressions
      a. Minor versus significant
      b. Social versus relational
      c. Deliberate versus unintentional
      d. One-time versus incremental
   2. Strategies for relational repair
      a. Acknowledgment
      b. Apology
      c. Compensation
   3. Forgiving transgressions

KEY TERMS

conformity orientation

conversation orientation

family communication pattern

family system

friends with benefits (FWB)

intimacy

love languages

relational commitment

relational maintenance

relational transgression

relational turning point

role

social support

ACTIVITIES

9.1 ASSESSING SELF-CONCEPT AND FAMILY COMMUNICATION

LEARNING OBJECTIVES

- Describe the relationship between self-concept, self-esteem, and communication.
- Compare and contrast the perceived self and the presenting self as they relate to identity management.

INSTRUCTIONS

Family plays an important role in developing our self-concepts and self-esteem. Answer the following questions about your family below. Indicate how the information about your family has contributed to your self-concept.

1. What are some of your family values?

_____

_____

_____

2. How does your family communicate with each other?

_____

_____

_____

3. What physical traits does your family have?

_____

_____

4. How has your family contributed to your self-esteem?

_____

_____

Class _____   Name_____

Now that you have assessed how your family has influenced your self-concept, interview a friend and ask them the same questions about their family. Record their answers and compare and contrast the similarities and differences between your families on the next page.

1. What are some of your family values?

_____

_____

_____

2. How does your family communicate with each other?

_____

_____

_____

3. What physical traits does your family have?

_____

_____

4. How has your family influenced your self-esteem?

_____

_____

Now list the similarities and differences between you and your friend.

SIMILARITIES   **DIFFERENCES**

9.2 RELATIONAL DYNAMICS

LEARNING OBJECTIVES

- Outline the potential benefits and risks of disclosing in a selected situation.

INSTRUCTIONS

Use the case below and the discussion questions that follow to discuss the variety of communication issues involved in effective communication. Make notes on this page, add other pages on your own, or prepare a group report/analysis based on your discussion. Add your own experiences to individualize the analysis.

CASE

Alora and Malcolm dated one another exclusively for three years. They broke up for six months, and now are back together and talking about getting married. While they were broken up, Alora became intimate with a casual friend of Malcolm's for a brief time before she realized that she really loved only Malcolm. During this same time period, Malcolm dated around; but he did not get serious about anyone. Malcolm has now told Alora that he believes they should tell one another everything about the time they were apart.

1. Do you think full self-disclosure is important in this relationship? Why or why not?

   _____

   _____

2. Use other relationships (your own and others) to evaluate how important full self-disclosure is to committed relationships. Cite times when full disclosure may be more harmful than helpful.

   _____

   _____

3. Evaluate the alternatives to self-disclosure in this situation. Explain how lies, benevolent lies, partial disclosure, equivocation, or hinting might be more effective than full disclosure?

   _____

   _____

4. Using quotations from the text, evaluate how much Alora and Malcolm should disclose to each other about the six months they were apart.

    _____

    _____

Class _____   Name_____

9.3 ASSESSING CULTURAL AND GENDER INFLUENCES ON INTIMACY IN INTERPERSONAL RELATIONSHIPS

LEARNING OBJECTIVES

- Identify the dimensions of intimacy that operate and how they are expressed in a specific relationship.
- Explain the need for both intimacy and distance in a given relationship.

INSTRUCTIONS

Interview a classmate who is a different gender or is from another culture; ask the following questions about how the dimensions of intimacy influence their relationships. Record their answers to the following questions below. Ask yourself the same questions, and record your own answers.

QUESTIONS FOR CLASSMATE

Relationship description: (boyfriend/girlfriend, parent/child, etc.) _____

What role does physical intimacy play in your relationship?

_____

_____

What role does intellectual intimacy play in your relationship?

_____

_____

What role does emotional intimacy play in your relationship?

_____

_____

Class _____   Name_____

What role do shared activities play in your relationship?

_____

_____

Why is intimacy needed in your relationship?   _

_____

_____

Why is there a need for distance in your relationship?

_____

_____

QUESTIONS FOR YOU

Relationship description: (boyfriend/girlfriend, parent/child, etc.) _____

What role does physical intimacy play in your relationship?

_____

_____

What role does intellectual intimacy play in your relationship?

_____

_____

What role does emotional intimacy play in your relationship?

_____

_____

Class _____   Name_____

What role do shared activities play in your relationship?

_____

_____

Why is intimacy needed in your relationship?   _

_____

_____

Why is there a need for distance in your relationship?

_____

_____

Now that you have interviewed your classmate on the dimensions of intimacy in their relationship, compare your answers to theirs on the worksheet below and on the next page. Indicate how culture or gender may have contributed to any differences.

SIMILARITIES	DIFFERENCES	HOW CULTURE OR GENDER MIGHT CONTRIBUTE
Physical:	Physical:	
Intellectual:	Intellectual:	
Emotional:	Emotional:	

Class _____   Name_____

SIMILARITIES	DIFFERENCES	HOW CULTURE OR GENDER MIGHT CONTRIBUTE
Shared activities:	Shared activities:	
Need for intimacy:	Need for intimacy:	
Need for distance:	Need for distance:	

STUDY GUIDE

CHECK YOUR UNDERSTANDING

TRUE/FALSE

Mark the statements below as true or false. Correct statements that are false on the lines below to create a true statement.

_____ 1. Intimacy is definitely rewarding, so maximizing intimacy is the best way of relating to others.

_____

_____ 2. Catharsis can provide mental and emotional relief.

_____

_____ 3. Research shows that male-male relationships involve less disclosure than male-female or female-female relationships.

_____

_____ 4. Using IM or Facebook, or writing in a blog, is a way to enhance intimacy in interpersonal relationships.

_____

_____ 5. Relational intimacy may develop more quickly through mediated channels than face-to-face communication.

_____

_____ 6. Less than truthful communication is uncommon in the closest of relationships.

_____

_____ 7. In a casual relationship, the depth of self-disclosure may be great, but not the breadth.

_____

_____ 8. Self-disclosure usually leads to reciprocity.

_____

_____ 9. Physical intimacy is sexual and is always connected with a close interpersonal relationship.

_____

_____ 10. People justify over half of their lies as ways to avoid embarrassment for themselves or others.

_____

_____ 11. Sexual intimacy is always associated with a close relationship.

_____

COMPLETION

Fill in the blanks below with the correct terms chosen from the list below.

suprasystem	role	attachment theory	intellectual
physical	emotional	hinting	personal preference

1. _____ is the type of intimacy that comes from an exchange of important ideas.

2. _____ is the type of intimacy that comes from touching, struggling, or sex.

3. _____ is the type of intimacy that comes from exchanging important feelings.

4. _____ is an explanation for what makes us want to develop personal relationships with some people and not with others.

5. _____ argues that children develop bonds (either secure or insecure) with family members.

6. A_____ is a set of expectations about how to communicate.

7. Families are also members of larger _____.

8. _____ is an alternative to self-disclosure in which the person gives only a clue to the direct meaning of the response.

MULTIPLE CHOICE

1. Which of these is *not* a dimension of intimacy in interpersonal relationships?
   a. physical
   b. shared activities
   c. chronological
   d. emotional

2. Researchers have found that in a "friends with benefits" situation people
    a. always form romantic relationships.
    b. never form romantic relationships.
    c. are afraid to develop feelings for the other person because they might be unreciprocated.
    d. have no feelings for the other person.

3. Self-disclosure, by definition, is all of these except
    a. intentional.
    b. significant.
    c. not known by others.
    d. accidental.

4. Self-disclosure can be all of these except
    a. impossible.
    b. insignificant.
    c. significant.
    d. accidental.

5. "Friends with benefits" deals specifically with friends who also
    a. engage in physical intimacy.
    b. dislike one another without saying.
    c. are part of a family dynamic.
    d. engage in significant emotional and intellectual intimacy.

6. Which of these is a dimension of intimacy in interpersonal relationships?
    a. ignoring the other person
    b. shared activities
    c. shutting down when your partner begins to self-disclose
    d. using the word "feel" as much as possible

7. Fear of intimacy can cause major problems in
    a. creating relationships.
    b. sustaining relationships.
    c. a and b
    d. none of the above

8. Self-validation, identity management, and relationship maintenance have been identified as reasons why people
    a. self-disclose.
    b. reject intimacy.
    c. create relationships.
    d. create relational tensions.

9. According to the text, people want
    a. ten to twelve close relationships in their lives.
    b. one to two close relationships in their lives.
    c. four to six close relationships in their lives.
    d. two to three close relationships in their lives.

10. Self-disclosure
    a. usually occurs in large groups.
    b. usually occurs incrementally.
    c. is generally coerced, not voluntary.
    d. is the only ethical response in most situations.

CHAPTER NINE STUDY GUIDE ANSWERS

TRUE/FALSE

1. F	4. T	7. F	10. T
2. T	5. T	8. T	11. F
3. T	6. F	9. F	

COMPLETION

1. intellectual	5. attachment theory
2. physical	6. role
3. emotional	7. suprasystem
4. personal preference	8. hinting

MULTIPLE CHOICE

1. c	4. a	7. c	10. b
2. c	5. a	8. a	
3. d	6. b	9. c	

Improving Communication Climates

After studying the topics in this chapter, you should be able to:

1. Identify confirming, disagreeing, and disconfirming messages and patterns in your own important relationships and describe their consequences.

2. Describe how the messages you identified in the previous objective either threaten or honor the self (face) of the communicators involved.

3. Use Gibb's categories and the assertive message format to create messages that are likely to build supportive rather than defensive communication climates.

4. Create appropriate nondefensive responses to real or hypothetical criticisms.

Personal relationships are a lot like the weather. Some are fair and warm, whereas others are stormy and cold; some are polluted and others healthy. Some relationships have stable climates, whereas others change dramatically—calm one moment and turbulent the next. You can't measure the interpersonal climate by looking at a thermometer or glancing at the sky, but it's there nonetheless. Every relationship has a feeling, a pervasive mood that colors the interactions of the participants.

Although we can't change the external weather, we *can* change an interpersonal climate. This chapter will explain the forces that make some relationships pleasant and others unpleasant. You will learn what kinds of behavior contribute to defensiveness and hostility and what kinds lead to more positive feelings. After reading these pages, you will have a better idea of the climate in each of your important relationships and—even more important—how to improve it.

Communication Climate and Confirming Messages

The term **communication climate** refers to the emotional tone of a relationship. A climate doesn't involve specific activities as much as the way people feel about and treat each other as they carry out those activities. Consider two interpersonal communication classes, for example. Both meet for the same length of time and follow the same syllabus. It's easy to imagine how one of these classes might be a friendly, comfortable place to learn, whereas the other could be cold and tense—even hostile.

The same principle holds in other contexts. For example, the communication climate that parents create for their children affects the way they interact.[1] Children who lack confirmation suffer a broad range of emotional and behavioral problems, whereas those who feel confirmed have more open communication with their parents, higher self-esteem, and lower levels of stress.[2] The satisfaction that siblings feel with one another drops sharply as aggressive, disconfirming messages increase.[3] And communication climate plays a vital role in workplace relationships, as the On the Job sidebar on page 316 describes.

Like their meteorological counterparts, communication climates are shared by everyone involved. It's rare to find one person describing a relationship as open and positive while another describes it as cold and hostile. Also, just like the weather, communication climates can change. A relationship can be overcast at one time and sunny at another. Carrying the analogy to its conclusion, we need to acknowledge that communication climate forecasting is not a perfect science. Unlike the weather, however, people can change the communication climates in their relationships.

Despite some quirky characters and eccentric personalities, the office climate for the employees of *Parks and Recreation* is generally sunny and warm.

NBC/Photofest

LEVELS OF MESSAGE CONFIRMATION

What makes a communication climate positive or negative? In large part, the answer is surprisingly simple. The climate of a relationship is shaped by the degree to which the people believe themselves to be *valued* by one another.

Social scientists use the term **confirming communication** to describe messages that convey valuing and **disconfirming communication** to describe those that show a lack of regard. In one form or another, confirming messages say "You exist," "You matter," "You're important." By contrast, disconfirming communication signals a lack of value. In one form or another, disconfirming messages say "I don't care about you," "I don't like you," "You're not important to me."

Like beauty, the decision about whether a message is confirming or disconfirming is determined by the beholder.[4] Consider, for example, times when you took a comment that might have sounded unsupportive to an outsider ("You turkey!") as a sign of affection within the context of your personal relationship. Likewise, a comment that the sender might have meant to be helpful ("I'm telling you this for your own good . . .") could easily be regarded as a disconfirming attack.

What makes some messages more confirming than others? Table 10.1 outlines the levels of message confirmation that are described in the following pages.

TABLE 10.1 LEVELS OF MESSAGE CONFIRMATION AND DISCONFIRMATION

DISCONFIRMING	DISAGREEING		CONFIRMING
Impervious	Aggressiveness		
Interrupting	Complaining		
Irrelevant		Argumentativeness	
Tangential		Recognition	
Impersonal			Acknowledgment
Ambiguous			Endorsement
Incongruous			
LEAST VALUING			**MOST VALUING**

© Cengage Learning

Disconfirming Messages Disconfirming communication shows a lack of value for the other person, either by disregarding or ignoring some important part of that person's message.[5] Communication researchers have identified seven types of disconfirming messages.[6]

Impervious Responses An **impervious response** doesn't acknowledge the other person's message. Whether it's accidental or intentional, few things are more disconcerting than getting no reaction from the person with whom you're attempting to communicate.

As you read in the opening pages of Chapter 1, being ignored can be more disconfirming than being dismissed or attacked. In the working world, research shows that employees sometimes nudge unwanted coworkers to quit their jobs by avoiding interaction with them, creating a chilling communication climate.[7] In marriage, ignoring a partner (sometimes called *stonewalling*) has been identified as a strong predictor of divorce.[8] On a less-deliberate level, people who tune out others while texting may communicate imperviousness.

Interrupting Beginning to speak before the other person has finished talking can show a lack of concern about what the other person has to say. The occasional **interrupting**

response is not likely to be taken as a disconfirmation, but repeatedly interrupting a speaker can be both discouraging and irritating.

Irrelevant Responses A comment unrelated to what the other person has just said is an **irrelevant response**.

A: What a day! I thought it would never end. First the car overheated, and I had to call a tow truck, and then the computer broke down at work.

B: Listen, we have to talk about a present for Ann's birthday. The party is on Saturday, and I have only tomorrow to shop for it.

A: I'm really beat. Could we talk about it in a few minutes? I've never seen a day like this one.

B: I just can't figure out what would suit Ann. She's got everything. . . .

Tangential Responses Conversational "takeaways" are called **tangential responses**. Instead of ignoring the speaker's remarks completely, the other party uses them as a starting point for a shift to a different topic.

A: I'd like to know for sure whether you want to go skiing during vacation. If we don't decide whether to go soon, it'll be impossible to get reservations anywhere.

B: Yeah, and if I don't pass my botany class, I won't be in the mood to go anywhere. Could you give me some help with this homework?

Impersonal Responses **Impersonal responses** are loaded with clichés and other statements that never truly respond to the speaker.

A: I've been having some personal problems lately, and I'd like to take off work early a couple of afternoons to clear them up.

B: Ah, yes. We all have personal problems. It seems to be a sign of the times.

Ambiguous Responses **Ambiguous responses** contain messages with more than one meaning, leaving the other party unsure of the responder's position.

A: I'd like to get together with you soon. How about Tuesday?

B: Uh, maybe so.

A: Well, how about it? Can we talk Tuesday?

B: Oh, probably. See you later.

Incongruous Responses An **incongruous response** contains two messages that seem to deny or contradict each other. Often at least one of these messages is nonverbal.

A: Darling, I love you.

B: I love you, too. (*said in a monotone while watching TV*)

Disagreeing Messages Between disconfirming and confirming communication lie disagreeing messages. As their name implies, **disagreeing messages** say "You're wrong" in one way or another. As you'll read here, some disagreements are quite hostile. But others aren't so disconfirming as they might first seem. Because there are better and worse ways to disagree with others, disagreeing messages need to be put on a negative-to-positive scale. We will do just that in this section as we discuss three types of disagreement: aggressiveness, complaining, and argumentativeness.

Aggressiveness The most destructive way to disagree with another person is through **aggressiveness**. Researchers define verbal aggressiveness as the tendency to attack the self-concepts of other people in order to inflict psychological pain.[9] Unlike argumentativeness (described later), aggressiveness demeans the worth of others. Name-calling, put-downs, sarcasm, taunting, yelling, badgering—all are methods of "winning" disagreements at others' expense.

Aggressiveness isn't limited to face-to-face encounters. Cyberbullying is disturbingly common: About 15 percent of students report abusing someone else online, and twice as many report having been victims.[10] The consequences of cyberbullying can be devastating. Online abuse leaves victims feeling angry, frustrated, sad, frightened, and embarrassed. Targets often respond with apathy and cheating in school, substance abuse, violence, and self-destructive behaviors—and suicide in the most severe cases.

It's no surprise that aggressiveness has such serious consequences. Chapter 11 describes how win–win approaches to conflict are healthier and more productive than the win–lose tactics of aggression.

Complaining When communicators aren't prepared to argue but still want to register dissatisfaction, they often complain. As is true of all disagreeing messages, some ways of **complaining** are better than others. Satisfied couples tend to offer behavioral complaints ("You always throw your socks on the floor"), whereas unsatisfied couples make more complaints aimed at personal characteristics ("You're a slob").[11] Personal complaints are more likely to result in an escalated conflict episode.[12] The reason should be obvious: Complaints about personal characteristics attack a more fundamental part of the presenting self. Talking about socks deals with a habit that can be changed; calling someone a slob is a character assault that is unlikely to be forgotten when the conflict is over. Marriage researcher John Gottman has found that complaining isn't necessarily a sign of a troubled relationship. In fact, it's usually healthy for spouses to get their concerns out in the open as long as the complaint is a behavioral description rather than a personal criticism.[13]

Argumentativeness Normally, when we call a person *argumentative*, we're making an unfavorable evaluation. However, the ability to create and deliver a sound argument is something we admire in lawyers, talk-show participants, letters to the editor, and political debates. Taking a positive approach to the term, communication researchers define **argumentativeness** as presenting and defending positions on issues while attacking positions taken by others.[14] Rather than being a negative trait, argumentativeness is associated with several positive attributes such as enhanced self-concept, communicative competence, and positive climate in the workplace.

The key for maintaining a positive climate while arguing a point is the *way* you present your ideas. It is crucial to attack issues, not people. In addition, a sound argument is better received when it's delivered in an affirming manner.[15] The supportive kinds of messages outlined later in this chapter show how it is possible to argue in a respectful, constructive way.

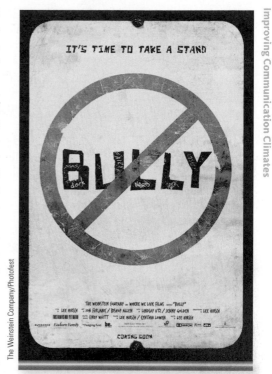

The documentary *Bully* shows the devastating impact of child-to-child aggressiveness. It provides a disturbing look at the damage that can be done with abusive words and deeds. (See the film summary at the end of this chapter.)

ON THE JOB

Communication Climate and Job Satisfaction

During your career, you are likely to spend more waking hours on the job than in any other setting. This means the emotional climate of the workplace can be just as important as salary or working conditions in shaping the quality of your life.

Research confirms that positive communication climates lead to increased job satisfaction.[a] Two factors are consistently connected to supportive workplace environments.[b] The first is praise and encouragement: Employees feel valued when their work is recognized. Acknowledgment doesn't require promotions, raises, or awards, although those are always welcome. As researcher Daniel Goleman notes, "Small exchanges—a compliment on work well done, a word of support after a setback—add up to how we feel on the job."[c] The second climate-boosting practice is open communication. Employees appreciate managers and coworkers with open-door policies, allowing them opportunities to get and give feedback, make suggestions, and voice concerns.

Climate is just as important in virtual organizations as in face-to-face communication.[d] When most contact is text based, taking time to treat coworkers cordially can make a real difference. One study revealed that morale and trust were higher in companies where email correspondence opened with friendly greetings (even a simple "Hi") and closed with a friendly farewell ("Thanks," "Have a nice day") than in those where messages lacked these elements.[e]

When you're on a job search, it can be smart to explore the kind of climate you might be entering. Take a tour around your potential workplace. Look for cues about how you might feel spending a major part of your life in this environment. Ask current employees for their opinions about the organization's climate.

In challenging times, any job may seem to be better than none; but you can save yourself much grief by including organizational climate on your list of employment criteria.

Confirming Messages Research shows that three increasingly positive types of messages have the best chance of being confirming: recognition, acknowledgement, and endorsement.[16]

Recognition The most fundamental act of confirmation is to recognize the other person. Recognition seems easy and obvious, and yet there are many times when we don't respond to others on this basic level. Failure to return an email or phone message are common examples. So is a sales clerk who fails to signal awareness that you're waiting for service. Of course, this lack of recognition may simply be an oversight. Nonetheless, if the other person *perceives* you as avoiding contact, then the message has the effect of being disconfirming.

Acknowledgment Acknowledging the ideas and feelings of others is a stronger form of confirmation. Listening is probably the most common form of acknowledgment. Of course, counterfeit listening—ambushing, stage hogging, pseudolistening, and so on—has the opposite effect of acknowledgment. More active acknowledgment includes asking questions, paraphrasing, and reflecting. It is not surprising that employees highly rate managers who solicit their opinions—even when the managers don't accept every opinion.[17] As you read in Chapter 7, reflecting the speaker's thoughts and feelings can be a powerful way to offer support when others have problems.

Endorsement Whereas acknowledgment means that you are interested in another's ideas, endorsement means that you agree with them or otherwise find them important. It's easy to see why endorsement is the strongest type of confirming message: It communicates the highest form of valuing. The most obvious form of endorsement is agreeing. Fortunately, it isn't necessary to agree completely with another person in order to endorse her or his message. You can probably find something in the message that you endorse. "I can see why you were so angry," you might reply to a friend, even if you don't approve of his outburst. Of course, outright praise is a strong form of endorsement and one that you can use surprisingly often after you look for opportunities to compliment others.

HOW COMMUNICATION CLIMATES DEVELOP

As soon as two people start to communicate, a relational climate begins to develop. If their messages are confirming, then the climate is likely to be a positive one. If their messages are disconfirming, then the relationship is likely to be hostile, cold, or defensive.

Verbal messages certainly contribute to the climate of a relationship, but many climate-shaping messages are nonverbal.[18] The very act of approaching others is confirming—and avoiding them can be disconfirming. Smiles or frowns, the presence or absence of eye contact, tone of voice, the use of personal space—all these and other cues send messages about how the parties feel toward one another.

After a climate is formed, it can take on a life of its own and grow in a self-perpetuating **spiral**: a reciprocating communication pattern in which each person's message reinforces the other's.[19] In positive spirals, one partner's confirming message leads to a similar message from the other person. This positive reaction leads the first person to be even more confirming. Negative spirals are just as powerful, although they leave the partners feeling worse about themselves and each other.

Research shows how spirals operate in relationships to reinforce the principle that "what goes around comes around." In one study of married couples, each spouse's response in conflict situations was similar to the other's statement.[20] Conciliatory statements (e.g., supporting, accepting responsibilities, agreeing) were likely to be followed by conciliatory responses. Confrontational acts (such as criticism, hostile questions, and fault finding) were likely to trigger equally confrontational responses. The same pattern held for other kinds of messages: Avoidance begets avoidance, analysis begets analysis, and so on. Table 10.2 illustrates reciprocal communication patterns that have the potential to create positive and negative spirals.

	1	2	3	4	5	6	7	8	9	10	11	12	13	14	15	16	17	18	19	20	21	22	23	24	25	26	27	28	29	30	31	R	H	E
TAT	3	0	0	1	0	0	0	0	0	0	0	6	0	0	0	1	0	0	0	0	0	8	0	0	3	9	7	1	1	2	6	48	63	6
TIT	3	0	0	1	0	0	0	0	0	0	6	0	0	1	0	0	0	0	0	8	0	0	3	9	7	1	1	2	6	48	63	6		

Game called on account of infinity.

TABLE 10.2 POSITIVE AND NEGATIVE RECIPROCAL COMMUNICATION PATTERNS

NEGATIVE RECIPROCAL PATTERN	
PATTERN	EXAMPLE
Complaint–countercomplaint	A: I wish you weren't so self-centered. B: Well, I wish you weren't so critical.
Disagreement–disagreement	A: Why are you so hard on Marta? She's a great boss. B: Are you kidding? She's the biggest phony I've ever seen. A: You wouldn't know a good boss if you saw one. B: Neither would you.
Mutual indifference	A: I don't care if you want to stay. I'm exhausted, and I'm getting out of here. B: Go ahead if you want, but find your own way home.
Arguments involving punctuation	A: How can I talk when you won't listen? B: How can I listen when you won't talk?
POSITIVE RECIPROCAL PATTERNS	
PATTERN	EXAMPLE
Validation of other's perspective	A: This assignment is really confusing. Nobody can figure out what we're supposed to do. B: I can understand how it might be unclear. Let me try to explain . . .
Recognizing similarities	A: I can't believe you want to take an expensive vacation! We should be saving money, not spending more! B: I agree we should be saving. But I think we can take this trip and still save some money. Let me show you what I've figured out . . .
Supportiveness	A: I'm going crazy with this job. It was supposed to be temporary. I have to do something different, and soon. B: I can see how much you hate it. Let's figure out how we can get the project finished soon, so you can get back to your regular work.

Adapted from *Competence and Interpersonal Conflict*, by W. Cupach and D. Canary. Reproduced by permission of William Cupach and Daniel Canary.

Escalatory conflict spirals are the most visible way that disconfirming messages reinforce one another.[21] One attack leads to another until a skirmish escalates into a full-fledged battle:

A: (*Mildly irritated*) Where were you? I thought we agreed to meet here a half-hour ago.

B: (*Defensively*) I'm sorry. I got hung up at the library. I don't have as much free time as you do, you know.

A: I wasn't blaming you, so don't get so touchy. I do resent what you just said, though. I'm plenty busy. And I've got lots of better things to do than wait around for you!

B: Who's getting touchy? I just made a simple comment. You've sure been defensive lately. What's the matter with you?

Although they are less obvious, **de-escalatory conflict spirals** can also be destructive.[22] Rather than fighting, the parties slowly lessen their dependence on each other, withdraw, and become less invested in the relationship. The good news is that spirals can also be positive. A word of praise can lead to a *returned compliment* that can lead to an act of kindness, which can result in an improved relational climate.

Spirals—whether positive or negative—rarely go on indefinitely. Most relationships pass through cycles of progression and regression. If the spiral is negative, partners may find the exchange growing so unpleasant that they switch from negative to positive messages without discussing the matter. In other cases, they may engage in *metacommunication*. "Hold on," one might say. "This is getting us nowhere." This ability to rebound from negative spirals and turn them in a positive direction is a hallmark of successful relationships.[23] However, if the partners pass the "point of no return" and continue spiraling downward, their relationship may end.

Positive spirals also have their limit. Even the best relationships go through periods of conflict and withdrawal, although a combination of time and communication skills can eventually bring the partners back into greater harmony.

PAUSE AND REFLECT

EVALUATING COMMUNICATION CLIMATES

You can probably recognize the communication climate in each of your relationships without much analysis. But taking the following steps will help explain why these climates exist. Taking these steps may also suggest ways in which to improve negative climates:

1. Identify the communication climate of an important interpersonal relationship. Using weather metaphors (sunny, gloomy, calm) may help.
2. List the confirming or disconfirming communications that created and now maintain this climate. Be sure to list both verbal and nonverbal messages.
3. Describe what you can do either to maintain the existing climate (if positive) or to change it (if negative). Again, list both verbal and nonverbal messages.

 You can complete this activity by visiting CengageBrain.com to access the Speech Communication CourseMate for *Looking Out/ Looking In*, and, if requested, email your responses to your instructor.

Defensiveness: Causes and Remedies

The word ***defensiveness*** suggests guarding oneself from attack, but what kind of attack? Surely, few if any of the times you become defensive involve a physical threat. If you're not threatened by bodily injury, then *what* are you guarding against? To answer this question, we need to talk more about the notions of the *presenting self* and *face* introduced in Chapter 2. Next, we'll look at ways to reduce defensiveness in others.

FACE-THREATENING ACTS

Recall that a person's face consists of the physical traits, personality characteristics, attitudes, aptitudes, and all the other parts of the image that he or she wants to present to the world. Actually, it is a mistake to talk about a single face: We try to project different faces to different people. You might, for instance, try to impress a potential employer with your seriousness but want your friends to see you as a joker.

When others are willing to accept and acknowledge important parts of our presenting image, there is no need to feel defensive. On the other hand, when others confront us with **face-threatening acts**—messages that seem to challenge the image we want to project—we are likely to resist their messages.[24] Defensiveness, then, is the process of protecting our presenting self, our face.

You can understand how defensiveness operates by imagining what might happen if an important part of your presenting self were attacked. Suppose, for instance, that your boss criticized you for making a stupid mistake. Or consider how you would feel if a friend called you self-centered or your sweetheart called you lazy. You would probably feel threatened if these attacks were unjustified. But notice that you might very well react defensively even if you knew deep inside that the attacks were justified. For instance, you have probably responded defensively at times when you *did* make a mistake, acted selfishly, or cut corners on your work. In fact, we often feel most defensive when criticism is right on target.[25] The drive to defend a presenting image—even when it is false—leads some people to act in destructive ways such as being sarcastic or verbally abusive.[26]

So far, we have talked about defensiveness as if it is the responsibility of only the person who feels threatened. If this were the case, then the prescription would be simple: Grow a thick skin, admit your flaws, and stop trying to manage impressions. This prescription isn't just unrealistic; it also ignores the role played by those who send face-threatening messages. In fact, competent communicators protect others' face needs as well as their own.[27] For instance, skilled instructors try to support their students' presenting faces, especially when offering constructive criticism. This facework leads to less-defensive responses from their students.[28] Likewise, effective supervisors use face-saving statements such as "You're on the right track and your work has potential" to buffer corrections.[29] We'll talk more about the importance of sending face-saving messages later in this chapter.

PREVENTING DEFENSIVENESS IN OTHERS

The influential work of researcher Jack Gibb offers some useful tools for reducing defensiveness.[30] After observing groups for several years, Gibb was able to isolate six types of defense-arousing communication and six contrasting behaviors that lessen the level of threat and defensiveness by conveying face-honoring relational messages of respect. The **Gibb categories** are listed in Table 10.3 and summarized in the following pages.

TABLE 10.3 THE GIBB CATEGORIES OF DEFENSIVE AND SUPPORTIVE BEHAVIORS

DEFENSIVE BEHAVIORS	SUPPORTIVE BEHAVIORS
1. Evaluation	1. Description
2. Control	2. Problem Orientation
3. Strategy	3. Spontaneity
4. Neutrality	4. Empathy
5. Superiority	5. Equality
6. Certainty	6. Provisionalism

Source: Jack Gibb

Evaluation versus Description The first type of defense-arousing behavior that Gibb noted is **evaluation**. Most people become irritated at judgmental statements, which they are likely to interpret as indicating a lack of regard. One form of evaluation is "you" language, which is described in Chapter 5.

Unlike evaluative "you" language, **description** focuses on the *speaker's* thoughts and feelings instead of judging the other person. Descriptive messages often are expressed in "I" language, which tends to provoke less defensiveness than "you" language.[31] Contrast the following evaluative "you" claims with their descriptive "I" counterparts:

Evaluation: "You don't know what you're talking about!"

Description: "I don't understand how you came up with that idea."

Evaluation: "This place is a mess!"

Description: "When you don't clean up, I have to either do it or live with your mess. That's why I'm mad!"

Evaluation: "Those jokes are disgusting!"

Description: "When you tell those off-color jokes, I get really embarrassed."

Note how each of the descriptive statements focuses on the speaker's thoughts and feelings without judging the other person. Despite its value, descriptive language isn't the only element necessary for success. Its effectiveness depends in part on when, where, and how the language is used. You can imagine how each of the preceding descriptive statements would go over if said in front of a room full of bystanders or in a whining tone of voice. Even the best timing and delivery of a descriptive message won't guarantee success. Some people will react defensively to anything you say or do. Nonetheless, it's easy to see that describing how the other person's behavior affects you is likely to produce better results than judgmentally attacking the other person.

Control versus Problem Orientation A second defense-provoking message involves some attempt to control another. **Controlling communication** occurs when a sender seems to be imposing a solution on the receiver with little regard for the receiver's needs or interests. The object of control can involve almost anything: where to eat dinner, what TV program to watch, whether to remain in a relationship, or how to spend a large sum of money. Whatever the situation, people who act in controlling ways create a defensive climate. Whether it is done through words, gestures, tone of voice, or some other channel, the controller generates hostility wherever he or she goes. The unspoken message that such behavior communicates is "I know what's best for you, and if you do as I say, we'll get along."

By contrast, communicators with a **problem orientation** focus on finding a solution that satisfies both their needs and those of the others involved. The goal here isn't to win at the expense of your partner, but rather to work out some arrangement in which everybody feels like a winner. Problem orientation is often typified by "we" language (see Chapter 5), which suggests the speaker is making decisions *with* rather than *for* other people.[32] University chairpersons found to be most effective by members of their departments were best characterized as using few control communications and adopting a problem orientation.[33] Chapter 11 has a great deal to say about win–win problem-solving as a way to find problem-oriented solutions.

SELF-ASSESSMENT

How Critical Are You?

You can get a sense of how critical you are by taking a short online test at RateYourself .com. Besides receiving your own score, you can compare your results with the average ratings of other quiz takers. You can find the link to this site by visiting CengageBrain.com to access the Speech Communication CourseMate for *Looking Out/ Looking In*.

Here are some examples of how some controlling and problem-orientation messages might sound.

Controlling: "You need to stick around for the next two hours."

Problem orientation: "I'm expecting an important package to arrive soon. Can you cover the office while I go on a sales call?"

Controlling: "There's only one way to handle this problem . . ."

Problem orientation: "Looks like we have a problem. Let's work out a solution we can both live with."

Strategy versus Spontaneity Gibb uses the word *strategy* to characterize defense-arousing messages in which speakers hide their ulterior motives. The words *dishonesty* and *manipulation* capture the essence of strategy. Even if the motives of strategic communication are honorable, the victim of such deception who discovers the attempt to deceive is likely to feel offended at being played for a naïve sucker.

Spontaneity is the behavior that contrasts with strategy. Spontaneity simply means being honest with others rather than manipulating them. What it doesn't mean is blurting out what you're thinking as soon as an idea comes to you. As we discussed in Chapter 2, there are appropriate (and inappropriate) times for self-disclosure. You would undoubtedly threaten others' presenting selves if you were "spontaneous" about every opinion that crossed your mind. Gibb's notion of spontaneity involves setting aside hidden agendas that others both sense and resist. These examples illustrate the difference.

Strategy: "What are you doing Friday after work?"

Spontaneity: "I have a piano I need to move Friday after work. Can you give me a hand?"

Strategy: "Jermaine and Brianna go out to dinner every week."

Spontaneity: "I'd like to go out to dinner more often."

This is a good place to talk about larger issues regarding the Gibb model. First, Gibb's emphasis on being direct is better suited for a low-context culture such as the United States, which values self-assertion, than for high-context cultures. Second, there are ways in which each communication approach Gibb labels as "supportive" can be used to exploit others and, therefore, violate the spirit of positive climate building. For instance, consider spontaneity. Although it sounds paradoxical at first, spontaneity can be a strategy, too. Sometimes you'll see people using honesty in a calculating way, being just frank enough to win someone's trust or sympathy. This "leveling" is probably the most defense-arousing strategy of all, because once you have learned someone is using frankness as a manipulation, you are less likely to trust that person in the future.

Neutrality versus Empathy Gibb uses the term *neutrality* to describe a fourth behavior that arouses defensiveness. Probably a better descriptive word would be *indifference*. A neutral attitude is disconfirming because it communicates a lack of concern and implies that the welfare of the other person isn't very important to you. This perceived indifference is likely to promote defensiveness, because people do not like to think of themselves as worthless, and they'll protect a self-concept that regards them as worthwhile.

Notice the following differences between neutral and empathic statements.

Neutral: "That's what happens when you don't plan properly."

Empathic: "Ouch—looks like this didn't turn out the way you expected."

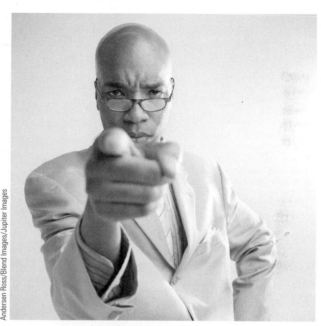

Neutral: "Sometimes things just don't work out. That's the way it goes."

Empathic: "I know you put a lot of time and effort into this project."

The negative effects of neutrality become apparent when you consider the hostility that most people have for the large, impersonal organizations with which they have to deal: "They think of me as a number instead of a person"; "I felt as if I were being handled by computers and not human beings." These two common statements reflect reactions to being handled in an indifferent way. Gibb found that empathy helps rid communication of the quality of indifference. **Empathy** means accepting another's feelings and putting yourself in another's place. This doesn't mean that you need to agree with that person. By simply letting that person know of your care and respect, you'll be acting in a supportive way.

Superiority versus Equality A fifth behavior that arouses defensiveness is **superiority**. Any message that suggests "I'm better than you" is likely to arouse feelings of defensiveness in the recipients. A body of research confirms that patronizing messages irritate recipients ranging from young students to senior citizens, at least in Western cultures.[34] Some superiority comes from the content of messages. In other cases, the *way* we deliver messages suggests a one-up approach. Consider, for example, how using simplified grammar and vocabulary, talking loudly and slowly, not listening, and varying speaking pitch convey a patronizing attitude.

Here are two examples of the difference between superiority and equality.

Superior: "You don't know what you're talking about."

Equal: "I see it a different way."

Superior: "No, that's not the right way to do it!"

Equal: "If you want, I can show you a way that has worked for me."

There are certainly times when we communicate with others who possess talents or knowledge lesser than ours, but even then it isn't necessary to communicate an attitude of superiority. Gibb found ample evidence that many people who have superior skills and talents are capable of projecting feelings of **equality** rather than superiority. Such people convey the attitude that, although they may have greater talent in certain areas, they see others as having just as much worth as human beings.

Certainty versus Provisionalism Have you ever run into people who are positive they're right, who know that theirs is the only or proper way of doing something, who insist that they have all the facts and need no additional information? If you have, then you've met individuals who project the defense-arousing behavior that Gibb calls **certainty**. Communicators who regard their own opinions with certainty while disregarding the ideas of others demonstrate a lack of regard and respect. It's likely that the receiver will take the certainty as a personal affront and react defensively.

Andersen Ross/Blend Images/Jupiter Images

RANKISM: THE POISON THAT DESTROYS RELATIONSHIPS

Rankism is a degrading assertion of rank. It's what's happening when a person, a group, or nation acts as if it outranks another and attempts to demean, humiliate, or exploit it.

I got a close look at the poison of rankism in second grade when my classmate Arlene was sent into the hall for the whole day. Arlene lived on a farm and wore the same dress to school every day. One day Miss Belcher told Arlene to go to the hall and stay there until her fingernails were clean. If there was no remedy in the hall, then the reason for sending Arlene there must be to embarrass her and scare the rest of us. Later, filing out to the playground, we snuck glances at her. She must have heard the snickering as we passed. Arlene felt like a nobody.

Other kids whom my classmates regarded as nobodies, and so as legitimate targets of abuse, included Frank, who was shamed with the F-word; Jimmy, who had Down syndrome and was ridiculed with the R-word; and Tommie and Trudy who were teased for their weight. The N-word was used warily, typically from the safety of the bus carrying our all-white basketball team home in the wake of a loss to a school fielding black players.

Not belonging to any of the groups targeted for abuse, I was spared till I got to college. There I realized that higher education was less about the pursuit of truth than about establishing a pecking order. I found myself playing games of one-upmanship, and was reminded of my classmate Arlene.

The toxic relationships mentioned above are all based on a trait that marks people for abuse: class (Arlene), sexuality (Frank), disability (Jimmy), body shape (Tommie and Trudy), color, and academic standing. There are no valid justifications for treating anyone as a nobody—that is, for rankism—any more than there ever was a justification for racism, sexism, ageism, ableism, or homophobia.

By now, you're probably thinking, "But wait. Some people do have higher status than others; some people are more talented." Yes, some people do outrank other people in the sense that they're higher in a hierarchy. And some people outrank others in the sense that they're better at something,

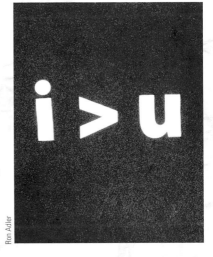

Ron Adler

i.e., basketball, geometry, violin, etc. But we do not feel kindly toward people who abuse their rank. Therein lies the poison: not in the fact of rank itself (when it's legitimate), but rather in the abuse of rank (legitimate or not).

The task confronting us today is to put rankism in the doghouse alongside the other disreputable "isms." Make it uncool. This means ceasing to put individuals, groups, or other countries down. Going forward, the only thing as important as how we treat the Earth is how we treat each other.

Robert Fuller

Excerpted from *Huffington Post* June 12, 2012. "Rankism: The Poison that Destroys Relationships." Robert Fuller. http://www.huffingtonpost.com/robert-fuller/rankism-the-poison-that-d_h_1587815.htm

In contrast to certainty is **provisionalism**, in which people may have strong opinions but are willing to acknowledge that they don't have a corner on the truth and will change their stance if another position seems more reasonable. Consider these examples that contrast certain and provisional approaches.

Certain: "That will never work!"

Provisional: "I think you'll run into problems with that approach."

Certain: "You don't know what you're talking about!"

Provisional: "I've never heard anything like that before. Where did you hear it?"

There is no guarantee that using Gibb's supportive, confirming approach to communication will build a positive climate. The other person may simply not be receptive. But the chances for a constructive relationship will be greatest when communication consists of the supportive approach described here. Besides boosting the odds of getting a positive response from others, supportive communication can leave you feeling better in a variety of ways: more in control of your relationships, more comfortable, and more positive toward others.

"I understand completely. I like good movies, and you like bad movies."

PAUSE AND REFLECT

DEFENSIVENESS FEEDBACK

1. Approach an important person in your life and request some help in learning more about yourself. Inform the other person that your discussion will probably take at least an hour, so make sure that both of you are prepared to invest the necessary amount of time.

2. Begin by explaining all twelve of the Gibb behaviors to your partner. Be sure to give enough examples so that each category is clearly understood.

3. When your explanation is complete and you've answered all of your partner's questions, ask him or her to tell you which of the Gibb categories you use. Seek specific examples so that you are certain to understand the feedback fully. (Because you are requesting an evaluation, be prepared for a little defensiveness on your own part at this point.) Inform your partner that you are interested in discovering both the defense-arousing and supportive behaviors you use and that you are sincerely interested in receiving a candid answer. (*Note:* If you don't want to hear the truth from your partner, don't try this exercise.)

4. As your partner speaks, record the categories that he or she lists in sufficient detail for both of you to be sure that you have understood the comments.

5. When you have finished your list, show it to your partner. Listen to your partner's reactions and make any corrections that are necessary to reflect an accurate understanding of the comments. When your list is accurate, have your partner sign it to indicate that you have understood it clearly.

6. In a concluding statement note:
   a. how you felt as your partner was describing you,
   b. whether you agree with the evaluation, and
   c. what effect your use of the Gibb categories has on your relationship with your partner.

 You can complete this activity by visiting CengageBrain.com to access the Speech Communication CourseMate for *Looking Out/ Looking In*, and, if requested, email your responses to your instructor.

LOOKING AT DIVERSITY

Abdel Jalil Elayyadi: Promoting Understanding

Photo courtesy of Abdel Jalil Elayyadi

I grew up in Morocco and moved to the United States when I was 19. I love the U.S. and have many wonderful friends here—but communicating with strangers is often tense because I'm an Arab Muslim. Many Americans equate Arabs and Muslims with terrorism, and that creates a defensive communication climate.

I feel as if I'm easily stereotyped and misunderstood by people who prejudge me because of my religion and nationality. When I encounter people who think that all Muslims are terrorists who hate Americans, I try to do three things to change the defensive climate.

First, I quickly explain that Muslims are peace-loving people who abhor the taking of innocent life. I want them to know that I completely agree with their disdain for the terrorists. That builds a bridge of trust that allows us to keep talking.

Second, I try to use examples to help them understand how terrorists don't represent most Muslims or Arabs. I ask them how they would feel if Arabs judged Americans by the acts of Oklahoma City bomber Timothy McVeigh, or Christians by the acts of the Ku Klux Klan. This usually helps them view Muslims in a different and more accurate light.

Finally, the more we talk, the more we focus on things we have in common and beliefs we share. The goal is to discover that we are not enemies simply because we have different religions or nationalities—and in fact, there is no reason we can't be friends.

What do these conversations accomplish? In some cases, not a lot—because there are a few people who prefer to keep their prejudices rather than change them. But in other cases, I think I've made a difference, however small, in promoting peace and understanding in the world.

"Promoting Understanding after 9/11" by Abdel Jalil Elayyadi. Used with permission of author.

Saving Face

Gibb's categories of supportive communication offer useful guidelines for reducing defensiveness. In the following pages, you will learn some specific ways to use these approaches when you need to deliver challenging messages.

THE ASSERTIVE MESSAGE FORMAT

As you've already seen, an essential ingredient in building a supportive climate is to avoid attacking others—to preserve their face. At the same time, you need to share your legitimate concerns when problems arise in a relationship.

The next few pages will describe a method for speaking your mind in a clear, direct, yet nonthreatening assertive way that expresses your needs, thoughts, and feelings clearly and directly without judging or dictating to others. This **assertive message format** builds on the perception-checking skill you learned in Chapter 3 and the "I" language approach you learned in Chapter 5. This new skill works for a variety of messages: your hopes, problems, complaints, and appreciations.[35] We'll examine each part one by one and then discuss how to combine them in your everyday communication.

Behavior As you read in Chapter 5, a behavioral description describes the raw material to which you react. A behavioral description should be *objective*, describing an event without interpreting it. Two examples of behavioral descriptions might look like this:

Example 1

"One week ago John promised me that he would ask my permission before smoking in the same room with me. Just a moment ago he lit up a cigarette without asking for my OK."

Example 2

"Chris has acted differently over the last week. I can't remember her laughing once since the holiday weekend. She hasn't dropped by my place like she usually does, hasn't suggested we play tennis, and hasn't returned my phone calls."

Notice that both statements describe only facts. The observer hasn't attached any meaning.

Interpretation An **interpretation statement** describes the meaning you've attached to the other person's behavior. The important thing to realize about interpretations is that they are *subjective*. As you learned via the skill of perception checking (see Chapter 3), we can attach more than one interpretation to any behavior. For example, look at these two different interpretations of each of the preceding descriptions:

Example 1

Interpretation A: "John must have forgotten about our agreement that he wouldn't smoke without asking me first. I'm sure he's too considerate to go back on his word on something he knows I feel strongly about."

Interpretation B: "John is a rude, inconsiderate person. After promising not to smoke around me without asking, he's just deliberately done so. This shows that he cares only about himself. In fact, I bet he's deliberately doing this to drive me crazy!"

Example 2

Interpretation A: "Something must be bothering Chris. It's probably her family. She'll probably just feel worse if I keep pestering her."

Interpretation B: "Chris is probably mad at me. It's probably because I kidded her about losing so often at tennis. I'd better leave her alone until she cools off."

After you become aware of the difference between observable behavior and interpretation, some of the reasons for communication difficulties become clear. Many problems occur when a sender fails to describe the behavior on which an interpretation is based. For instance, imagine the difference between hearing a friend say

"You are a tightwad!" (*No behavioral description*)

versus explaining

"When you never offer to pay me back for the coffee and snacks I often buy you, I think you're a tightwad." (*Behavior plus interpretation*)

SKILL BUILDER

BEHAVIORS AND INTERPRETATIONS

1. Tell two other group members several interpretations that you have recently made about other people in your life. For each interpretation, describe the behavior on which you based your interpretations.
2. With your partners' help, consider some alternate interpretations of the behavior that might be as plausible as your original one.
3. After considering the alternate interpretations, decide
   a. which one was most reasonable and
   b. how you might share that interpretation (along with the behavior) with the other person involved in a tentative, provisional way.

 You can complete this activity by visiting CengageBrain.com to access the Speech Communication CourseMate for *Looking Out/ Looking In*, and, if requested, email your responses to your instructor.

Feeling Reporting behavior and sharing your interpretations are important, but **feeling statements** add a new dimension to a message. For example, consider the difference between saying

> "When you laugh at me *(behavior)*, I think you find my comments foolish *(interpretation)*, and *I feel embarrassed.*"

and

> "When you laugh at me, I think you find my comments foolish, and *I feel angry.*"

It's important to recognize that some statements *seem* as if they're expressing feelings but are actually interpretations or statements of intention. For instance, it's not accurate to say "I feel like leaving" (really an intention) or "I feel you're wrong" (an interpretation). Statements like these obscure the true expression of feelings.

SKILL BUILDER

NAME THE FEELING

Add a feeling that you would be likely to have to each of the following messages:
1. I felt _____ when I found out you didn't invite me on the camping trip. You said you thought I wouldn't want to go, but I have a hard time accepting that.
2. I felt _____ when you offered to help me move. I know how busy you are.
3. When you tell me you still want to be a friend but you want to "lighten up a little," I get the idea you're tired of me, and I feel _____.
4. You told me you wanted my honest opinion about your paintings, and then when I tell you what I think, you say I don't understand them. I'm _____.

How would the impact of each message be different if it didn't include a feeling statement?

 You can complete this activity by visiting CengageBrain.com to access the Speech Communication CourseMate for *Looking Out/ Looking In*, and, if requested, email your responses to your instructor.

Consequence A **consequence statement** explains what happens as a result of the situation you've described so far. There are three types of consequences:

- What happens to you, the speaker
  - "When you didn't tell me that the landlord came by to ask about last month's rent *(behavior)*, I didn't know that my check had bounced *(consequences)*. It seems to me that you don't care about my credit record or appreciate what it takes for me to handle our rent for the apartment *(interpretation)*, and that's why I'm so mad *(feeling)*."
- What happens to the person you're addressing
  - "When you have four or five drinks at a party after I've warned you to slow down *(behavior)*, you start to act strange: You make crude jokes that offend everybody, and on the way home you drive poorly *(consequences)*. For instance, last night you almost hit a telephone pole while you were backing out of the driveway *(more behavior)*. I don't think you realize how differently you act *(interpretation)*, and I'm worried *(feeling)* about what will happen if you don't drink less."
- What happens to others
  - "You probably don't know because you couldn't hear her cry *(interpretation)*, but when you rehearse your lines for the play without closing the doors *(behavior)*, the baby can't sleep *(consequence)*. I'm especially concerned *(feeling)* about her because she's had a cold lately."

Consequence statements are valuable for two reasons. First, they help you understand more clearly why you are bothered or pleased by another's behavior. Just as important, telling others about the consequences of their actions can clarify for them the results of their behavior. As with interpretations, we often think that others should be aware of consequences without being told, but the fact is that they often aren't. By explicitly stating consequences, you can be sure that you or your message leaves nothing to the listener's imagination.

Intention **Intention statements** are the final element of the assertive message format. They can communicate three kinds of messages:

- Where you stand on an issue
  - "When you call us 'girls' after I've told you we want to be called 'women' *(behavior)*, I get the idea you don't appreciate how important the difference is to us *(interpretation)* and how demeaning it feels *(feeling)*. Now I'm in an awkward spot: Either I have to keep bringing the subject up or else drop it and feel bad *(consequence)*. I want you to know how much this bothers me *(intention)*."
- Requests of others
  - "When I didn't hear from you last night *(behavior)*, I thought you were mad at me *(interpretation)*. I've been thinking about it ever since *(consequence)*, and I'm still worried *(feeling)*. I'd like to know whether you are angry *(intention)*."
- Descriptions of how you plan to act in the future
  - "I've asked you to repay the twenty-five dollars I lent you three times now *(behavior)*. I'm getting the idea that you've been avoiding me *(interpretation)*, and I'm pretty angry about it *(feeling)*. I want you to know that unless we clear this up now, you shouldn't expect me ever to lend you anything again *(intention)*."

As in the preceding cases, we are often motivated by one single intention. Sometimes, however, we act from a combination of intentions, which may even be in conflict with each other. When this happens, our conflicting intentions often make it difficult for us to reach decisions:

"I want to be truthful with you, but I don't want to violate my friend's privacy."

"I want to continue to enjoy your friendship and company, but I don't want to get too attached right now."

"I want to have time to study and get good grades, but I also want to have a job with some money coming in."

IN REAL LIFE

The Assertive Message Format

While the elements of the assertive message format don't vary, the way they sound will depend on the situation and your personal style. Here are a few examples to show how this approach can operate in real life.

You can appreciate the value of the assertive approach by imagining how different the likely outcome would be if each message had been delivered in a blaming, aggressive way . . . or not at all.

To a Neighbor

I had an awful scare just now *(feeling)*. I was backing out of the driveway, and Angela *(neighbor's toddler)* wandered right behind my car *(behavior)*. Thank God I saw her, but she is so small, and it would have been easy to miss her. I can't bear to think what might have happened if I hadn't seen her *(consequences for others)*. I know how hard it is to keep an eye on little kids *(interpretation)*, but I really hope you can keep her inside unless you're watching her *(intention)*.

To a Friend

I just checked my Facebook account and saw that you tagged me in your photos from the party last weekend *(behavior)*. I told you before that I'm trying to get a good job, and I'm afraid those kinds of pictures could blow my chance *(consequence for you)*. I know you like to post lots of pictures, and you probably think I'm overreacting *(interpretations)*. Anyway, this is a big deal for me. So I need you to remember not to post any pictures that

you think would embarrass me. If you aren't sure about a photo, just ask me *(intention)*.

To a Boss

I've got a favor to ask *(intention)*. Last month I told you I wanted to work extra hours, and I know you're doing me a favor by giving me more shifts *(interpretation)*. But it would really help if you could give me a couple of days' advance notice instead of telling me the night before you want me to work *(clarifies intention)*. That way I can say "yes" to the extra shifts *(consequence for boss)*. It would also cause a lot less stress for me *(feeling)*.

To an Auto Mechanic

I need to tell you that I'm pretty unhappy *(feeling)*. When I dropped the car off yesterday, you told me it would definitely be ready today by noon. Now it's 12:30 and it isn't done *(behavior)*. I'm going to be late for an important meeting *(consequence for you)*. I know you aim to please *(interpretation)*, but you have to understand that I can't bring my car to you unless I can count on it being ready when you promise *(consequence for others)*.

Communication Scenarios

To watch and analyze a video related to this feature and this topic, visit CengageBrain.com to access the Speech Communication CourseMate for Looking Out/ Looking In.

Using the Assertive Message Format Before you try to deliver messages by using the clear message format, there are a few points to remember.

1. **The elements may be delivered in mixed order.** As the examples on the preceding pages show, it's sometimes best to begin by stating your feelings. At other times you can start by sharing your intentions or interpretations or by describing consequences.

2. **Word the message to suit your personal style.** Instead of saying, "I interpret your behavior to mean . . ." you might choose to say "I think . . ." or "It seems to me . . ." or perhaps "I get the idea. . . ."

    In the same way, you can express your intentions by saying, "I hope you'll understand (or do) . . ." or perhaps, "I wish you would. . . ." The words that you choose should sound authentic in order to reinforce the genuineness of your statement.

3. **When appropriate, combine two elements in a single phrase.** The statement ". . . and ever since then I've been wanting to talk to you" expresses both a consequence and an intention. In the same way, saying, ". . . and after you said that, I felt confused" expresses a consequence and a feeling. Whether you combine elements or state them separately, the important point is to be sure that each one is present in your statement.

4. **Take your time delivering the message.** It isn't always possible to deliver messages such as the ones here all at one time, wrapped up in neat paragraphs. It will often be necessary to repeat or restate one part before the other person understands what you're saying. As you've already read, there are many types of psychological and physical noise that make it difficult for us to understand each other. In communication, as in many other activities, patience and persistence are essential.

    Now try your hand at combining all these elements in the Skill Builder exercise on this page.

SKILL BUILDER

PUTTING YOUR MESSAGE TOGETHER

1. Join with two other class members. Each person in turn should share a message that he or she might want to send to another person, being sure to include behavior, interpretation, feeling, consequence, and intention statements in the message.

2. The others in the group should help the speaker by offering feedback about how the message could be made clearer if there is any question about the meaning.

3. After the speaker has composed a satisfactory message, he or she should practice actually delivering it by having another group member play the role of the intended receiver. Continue this practice until the speaker is confident that he or she can deliver the message effectively.

4. Repeat this process until each group member has had a chance to practice delivering a message.

 You can complete this activity by visiting CengageBrain.com to access the Speech Communication CourseMate for *Looking Out/ Looking In*, and, if requested, email your responses to your instructor.

RESPONDING NONDEFENSIVELY TO CRITICISM

The world would be a happier place if everyone communicated supportively and assertively. But how can you respond nondefensively when others send aggressive messages that don't match the prescriptions outlined in this chapter? Despite your best intentions, it's difficult to be reasonable when you're being attacked. Being attacked is hard enough when the criticism is clearly unfair, but it's often even harder when the criticism is on target. Despite the accuracy of your critic, the tendency is either to counterattack aggressively with a barrage of verbal aggression or to withdraw nonassertively.

Because neither of these counterattacks is likely to resolve a dispute, we need alternative ways of behaving. There are two such ways. Despite their apparent simplicity, they have proven to be among the most valuable skills many communicators have learned.[36]

Seek More Information The response of seeking more information makes good sense when you realize that it's foolish to respond to a critical attack until you understand what the other person has said. Even attacks that on first consideration appear to be totally unjustified or foolish often prove to contain at least a grain of truth and sometimes much more.

Many readers object to the idea of asking for details when they are criticized. Their resistance stems from confusing the act of *listening open-mindedly* to a speaker's comments with *accepting* the comments. After you realize that you can listen to, understand, and even acknowledge the most hostile comments without necessarily accepting them, it becomes much easier to hear another person out. If you disagree with a person's criticism, you will be in a much better position to explain yourself after you understand the criticism. On the other hand, after carefully listening to the person's criticism, you might just see that it is valid, in which case you have learned some valuable information about yourself. In either case, you have everything to gain and nothing to lose by paying attention to the critic.

Of course, after one has spent years instinctively resisting criticism, learning to listen to the other person will take some practice. To make matters clearer, here are several ways in which you can seek additional information from your critics.

Ask for Specifics Often the vague attack of a critic is virtually useless even if you sincerely want to change. Abstract attacks such as "You're being unfair" or "You never help out" can be difficult to understand. In such cases it is a good idea to request more specific information from the sender. "What do I *do* that's unfair?" is an important question to ask before you can judge whether the attack is correct. "When haven't I helped out?" you might ask before agreeing with or disagreeing with the attack.

If you have already asked for specifics and are still accused of reacting defensively, the problem may be in the *way* you ask. Your tone of voice and facial expression, posture, and other nonverbal clues can give the same words radically different connotations. For example, think of how you could use the words "Exactly what are you talking about?" to communicate either a genuine desire to know or your belief that the speaker is crazy. It's important to request specific information only when you genuinely want to learn more from the speaker because asking under any other circumstances will make matters only worse.

Guess about Specifics On some occasions even your sincere and well-phrased requests for specific information won't meet with success. Sometimes your critics won't be able to define precisely the behavior they find offensive. At these times, you'll hear such comments as "I can't tell you exactly what's wrong with your sense of humor—all I can say is that I don't like it." At other times, your critics may know the exact behaviors they don't like, but for some reason seem to get a perverse satisfaction out of making you struggle to figure it out. At times like this, you hear such comments as, "Well, if you don't know what you did to hurt my feelings, I'm certainly not going to tell you!"

Needless to say, failing to learn the specifics of another's criticism when you genuinely want to know can be frustrating. In instances like these, you can often learn more clearly what is bothering your critic by *guessing* at the specifics of a criticism. In a sense you become both detective and suspect, the goal being to figure out exactly what "crime" you have committed. Like the technique of asking for specifics, guessing must be done with goodwill if it's to produce satisfying results. You need to convey to the critic that for both your sakes you're truly interested in finding out what is the matter. After you have communicated this intention, the emotional climate generally becomes more comfortable because, in effect, both you and the critic are seeking the same goal.

Here are some typical questions you might hear from someone guessing about the specifics of another's criticism:

"So you object to the language I used in writing the paper. Was my language too formal?"

"Okay, I understand that you think the outfit looks funny. What's so bad? Is it the color? Does it have something to do with the fit? The fabric?"

"When you say that I'm not doing my share around the house, do you mean that I haven't been helping enough with the cleaning?"

Paraphrase the Speaker's Ideas Another strategy is to draw out confused or reluctant speakers by paraphrasing their thoughts and feelings and using the active listening skills described in Chapter 7. Paraphrasing is especially good in helping others solve their problems. Because people generally criticize you because your behavior creates some problem for them, the strategy is especially appropriate at such times.

One advantage of paraphrasing is that you don't have to guess about the specifics of your behavior that might be offensive. By clarifying or amplifying what you understand critics to be saying, you'll learn more about their objections. A brief dialogue between a disgruntled customer and an especially talented store manager using paraphrasing might sound like the following.

Customer: The way you people run this store is disgusting! I just want to tell you that I'll never shop here again.

Manager: (*Reflecting the customer's feeling*) It seems that you're quite upset. Can you tell me your problem?

Customer: It isn't my problem; it's the problem your salespeople have. They seem to think it's a great inconvenience to help a customer find anything around here.

Manager: So you didn't get enough help locating the items you were looking for, is that it?

"When will he be able to sit up and take criticism?"

Customer: Help? I spent twenty minutes looking around in here before I even talked to a clerk. All I can say is that it's a hell of a way to run a store.

Manager: So what you're saying is that the clerks seemed to be ignoring the customers?

Customer: No. They were all busy with other people. It just seems to me that you ought to have enough help around to handle the crowds that come in at this hour.

Manager: I understand now. What frustrated you most was the fact that we didn't have enough staff to serve you promptly.

Customer: That's right. I have no complaint with the service I get after I'm waited on, and I've always thought you had a good selection here. It's just that I'm too busy to wait so long for help.

Manager: Well, I'm glad you brought this to my attention. We certainly don't want loyal customers going away mad. I'll try to see that it doesn't happen again.

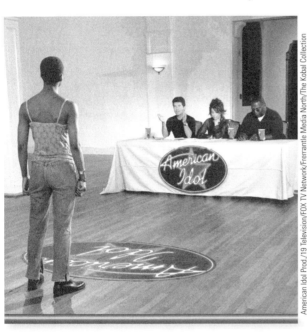

On TV shows such as *American Idol*, performers have the opportunity to receive and profit from criticism by judges. Some do so better than others. (See the TV summary at the end of this chapter.)

This conversation illustrates two advantages of paraphrasing. First, the critic often reduces the intensity of the attack after he or she realizes that the complaint is being heard. As soon as the manager genuinely demonstrated interest in the customer's plight, the customer began to feel better and was able to leave the store relatively calm. Of course, this sort of reflective listening won't always mollify your critic, but even when it doesn't, there's still another benefit that makes the strategy worthwhile. In the sample conversation, for instance, the manager learned some valuable information by taking time to understand the customer. The manager discovered that there were certain times when the number of employees was insufficient to help the crowd of shoppers and also that the delays at these times seriously annoyed at least some shoppers, thus threatening a loss in business. This knowledge is certainly important, and by reacting defensively to the customer's complaint, the manager would not have learned from it.

Ask What the Critic Wants Sometimes your critic's demand will be obvious:

"Turn down that music!"

"I wish you'd remember to tell me about phone messages."

"Would you clean up your dirty dishes now?"

At other times, however, you'll need to do some investigating to find out what the critic wants from you:

Alex: I can't believe you invited all those people over without asking me first!

Barb: Are you saying you want me to cancel the party?

Alex: No, I just wish you'd ask me before you make plans.

Cynthia: You're so critical! It sounds like you don't like anything about this paper.

Donna: But you asked for my opinion. What do you expect me to do when you ask?

Cynthia: I want to know what's wrong, but I don't just want to hear criticisms. If you think there's anything good about my work, I wish you'd tell me that, too.

This last example illustrates the importance of accompanying your questions with the right nonverbal behavior. It's easy to imagine two ways in which Donna could have nonverbally supported her response, "What do you expect me to do when you ask?"

One would show a genuine desire to clarify what Cynthia wanted, whereas the other would have been clearly hostile and defensive. As with all the styles in this section, your responses to criticism have to be sincere to work.

Ask about the Consequences of Your Behavior As a rule, people criticize your behavior only when some need of theirs is not being met. One way to respond to this kind of criticism is to find out exactly what troublesome consequences your behavior has for them. You'll often find that behaviors that seem perfectly legitimate to you cause some difficulty for your critic; after you have understood this, criticisms that previously sounded foolish take on a new meaning.

Neighbor A: You say that I ought to have my cat neutered. Why is that important to you?

Neighbor B: Because at night he picks fights with my cat, and I'm tired of paying the vet's bills.

Worker A: Why do you care whether I'm late to work?

Worker B: Because when the boss asks, I feel obligated to make up some story so you won't get in trouble, and I don't like to lie.

Husband: Why does it bother you when I lose money at poker? You know I never gamble more than I can afford.

Wife: It's not the cash itself. It's that when you lose, you're in a grumpy mood for two or three days, and that's no fun for me.

Ask What Else Is Wrong It might seem crazy to invite more criticism, but sometimes asking about other complaints can uncover the real problem:

Raul: Are you mad at me?

Tina: No. Why are you asking?

Raul: Because the whole time we were at the picnic you hardly spent any time talking to me. In fact, it seemed like whenever I came over to where you were, you went off somewhere else.

Tina: Is anything else wrong?

Raul: Well, I've been wondering lately if you're tired of me.

This example shows that asking if anything else bothers your critic isn't just an exercise in masochism. If you can keep your defensiveness in check, probing further can lead the conversation to issues that are the source of the critic's real dissatisfaction.

Sometimes soliciting more information from a critic isn't enough. What do you do, for instance, when you fully understand the other person's criticism and still feel a defensive response on the tip of your tongue? You know that if you try to defend yourself, you'll wind up in an argument; on the other hand, you simply can't accept what the other person is saying about you. The solution to such a dilemma is outrageously simple and is discussed in the following section.

Agree with the Critic But, you protest, how can you honestly agree with criticisms that you don't believe are true? The following pages will answer this question by showing that in virtually every situation you can honestly accept the other person's point of view while still maintaining your own position. To see how this can be so, you need to realize that there are two different types of agreement you can use in almost any situation.

Agree with the Facts This is the easiest type of agreement to understand, though not always to practice. Research suggests that it is also highly effective in restoring a damaged reputation with a critic.[37] You agree with your critic when the accusation is factually correct:

ETHICAL CHALLENGE

NONVIOLENCE: A LEGACY OF PRINCIPLED EFFECTIVENESS

Among the most familiar and challenging biblical injunctions is Christ's mandate, "If someone strikes you on one cheek, turn to him the other. . . ."

The notion of meeting aggression with nonviolence is an ancient one. The Taoist doctrine of *wu-wei*, promulgated more than 2,400 years ago in China, advocates nonaction in the face of an attack. In ancient India, the principle of *ahimsa*—nonharming—was shared by Buddhists, Jains, and many Hindus. In the West, some Greek stoics advocated nonaction in the face of threats.

Pacifism has a moral foundation, but by the nineteenth century it was used as a potent strategy for achieving political goals. In the United States, abolitionist William Lloyd Garrison advocated the use of nonviolence to protest slavery. On both sides of the Atlantic, the suffragette movement used nonviolent resistance as a tool to secure rights for women. In czarist Russia, Count Leo Tolstoy led a pacifist movement rejecting war and advocating civil disobedience as a tool for inhibiting violence.

In the twentieth century, nonviolence proved to be a powerful tool for political change. Mahatma Gandhi was demonstrably the most successful practitioner of this tool, first in South Africa and later in India, where his approach of *satyagraha* (truth-force) played a decisive role in the 1947 withdrawal of imperial Britain from India. In the 1950s and 1960s, Martin Luther King, Jr., and his followers used nonviolence to demonstrate against the evils of racial segregation, contributing to the passage of groundbreaking civil rights laws.

The effectiveness of nonviolence in achieving social change can also be effective in interpersonal situations. Nonconfrontational strategies provide communicators with an approach that is both principled and pragmatic.

"You're right, I am angry."

"I suppose I *was* being defensive."

"Now that you mention it, I did get pretty sarcastic."

Agreeing with the facts seems sensible when you realize that certain facts are indisputable. If you agree to be somewhere at four o'clock and don't show up until five o'clock, you are tardy, no matter how good your explanation for tardiness. If you've broken a borrowed object, run out of gas, or failed to finish a job you started, there's no point in denying it. In the same way, if you're honest, you may have to agree with many interpretations of your behavior even when they're not flattering. You do get angry, act foolishly, fail to listen, and behave inconsiderately. After you rid yourself of the myth of perfection, it's much easier to acknowledge these truths.

If many criticisms aimed at you are accurate, why is it so difficult to accept them without being defensive? The answer to this question lies in a confusion between agreeing with the *facts* and accepting the *judgment* that so often accompanies them. Most critics don't merely describe the action that offends them; they also evaluate it, and it's this evaluation that we resist:

"It's silly to be angry."

"You have no reason for being defensive."

"You were wrong to be so sarcastic."

SKILL BUILDER

COPING WITH CRITICISM

Take turns practicing nondefensive responses with a partner:

1. Choose one of the following criticisms and brief your partner on how it might be directed at you:
   a. You're so selfish sometimes. You think only of yourself.
   b. Don't be so touchy!
   c. You say you understand me, but you don't really.
   d. I wish you'd do your share around here.
   e. You're so critical!
2. As your partner criticizes you, answer with the appropriate response from the preceding pages. As you do so, try to adopt an attitude of genuinely wanting to understand the criticism and finding parts that you can sincerely agree with.
3. Ask your partner to evaluate your response. Does it follow the forms described in the previous pages? Does it sound sincere?
4. Replay the same scene, trying to improve your response.

 You can complete this activity by visiting CengageBrain.com to access the Speech Communication CourseMate for *Looking Out/ Looking In*, and, if requested, email your responses to your instructor.

It's evaluations like these that we resent. By realizing that you can agree with—and even learn from—the descriptive part of many criticisms and still not accept the accompanying evaluations, you'll often have a response that is both honest and nondefensive.

Of course, to reduce defensiveness, your agreements with the facts must be honest ones admitted without malice. It's humiliating to accept descriptions that aren't accurate, and maliciously manipulatively pretending to accept these leads only to trouble. You can imagine how unproductive the conversation given earlier would have been if the store manager had spoken the same words in a sarcastic tone. Agree with the facts only when you can do so sincerely. Though this won't always be possible, you'll be surprised at how often you can use this simple response.

Agree with the Critic's Perception Agreeing with your critics may be fine when you acknowledge that the criticisms are justified, but how can you agree when they seem to be completely unjustified? You've listened carefully and asked questions to make sure you understand the criticisms, but the more you listen, the more positive you are that the critics are totally out of line. Even in these cases there is a way of agreeing—this time not with the critics' conclusions but with their right to see things their way.

A: I don't believe that you've been all the places you were just describing. You're probably just making all this up to impress us.

B: Well, I can see how you might think that. I've known people who lie to get approval.

C: I want to let you know right from the start that I was against hiring you for the job. I think you got it because you're a woman.

D: I can understand why you'd believe that with all the antidiscrimination laws on the books. I hope that after I've been here for awhile, you'll change your mind.

E: I don't think you're being totally honest about your reason for wanting to stay home. You say it's because you have a headache, but I think you're avoiding Mary.

F: I can see why that would make sense to you because Mary and I got into an argument the last time we were together. All I can say is that I do have a headache.

IN REAL LIFE

Responding Nondefensively to Criticism

Defending yourself— even when you're right— isn't always the best approach. This dialogue shows the importance of using self-control and thinking before responding when you are being criticized. The employee realizes that arguing won't change her boss's mind, so she decides to reply as honestly as she can without becoming defensive.

Jason Harris/© Cengage Learning

Boss: How'd things go while I was out?

Employee: Pretty well, except for one thing. Mr. Macintosh—he said you knew him—came in and wanted to buy about $200 worth of stuff. He wanted me to charge him wholesale, and I asked him for his tax resale number, just like you told me. He said he didn't have it, so I told him he'd have to pay retail. He got pretty mad.

Boss: He's a good customer. I hope you gave him the discount.

Employee: *(Beginning to sound defensive)* Well, I didn't. You told me last week that the law said we had to charge full price and sales tax unless the customer had a resale number.

Boss: Oh, my gosh! Didn't Macintosh tell you he had a number?

Employee: *(Becoming more defensive)* He did, but he didn't have it with him. I didn't want to get you mad at me for breaking the law.

Boss: *(Barely concealing her exasperation)* Well, customers don't always have their resale numbers memorized. Macintosh has been coming here for years, and we just fill in his number on the records later.

Employee: *(Deciding to respond nondefensively instead of getting into an argument that she knows she can't win)* I can see why it looks like I gave Mr. Macintosh a hard time. You don't ask him for the number, and I insisted on having it. *(Agrees with the boss's perception)*

Boss: Yes! There's a lot of competition in this business, and we have to keep our customers happy— especially the good ones—or we'll lose them. Macintosh drives across town to do business with us. There are places right near him. If we jerk him around he'll go there, and we'll lose a good customer.

Employee: That's true. *(Agrees with the fact that it is important to keep customers happy)* And I want to know how to treat customers right. But I'm confused about how to handle people who want a discount and don't have resale numbers. What should I do? *(Asks what the boss wants)*

One key to feeling comfortable with acknowledging accurate criticism is to understand that *agreeing* with a critic doesn't necessarily oblige you to *apologize*. Sometimes you aren't responsible for the behavior that your critic finds objectionable, in which case an explanation might be more appropriate than an apology:

"I know I'm late. There was an accident downtown, and the streets are jammed." *(Spoken in an explanatory, nondefensive tone)*

In other cases, your behavior might be understandable, if not perfect. When this happens, you can acknowledge the validity of the criticism without apologizing:

"You're right. I *did* lose my temper. I've had to remind you three or four times, and I guess I finally used up all my patience." *(Again, delivered as an explanation, not a defense or counterattack)*

Boss: Well, you need to be a little flexible with good customers.

Employee: How should I do that? *(Asks for specifics)*

Boss: Well, it's OK to trust people who are regulars.

Employee: So I don't need to ask regular customers for their resale numbers. I should look them up later? *(Paraphrases to clarify boss's ambiguous directions to "trust" regular customers)*

Boss: That's right. You've got to use your head in business!

Employee: *(Ignores the indirect accusation about not "using her head," recognizing that there's no point in defending herself)* OK, so when regular customers come in, I won't even ask them for their resale numbers . . . right? *(Paraphrases again to be sure she has the message correct; the employee has no desire to get criticized again about this matter)*

Boss: No, go ahead and ask for the number. If they have it, we won't have to look it up later. But if they don't have the number, just say OK and give them the discount.

Employee: Got it. I only have one question: How can I know who the regular customers are? Should I take their word for it? *(Asks for specifics)*

Boss: Well, you'll get to know most of them after you've been here awhile. But it's OK to trust them until then. If they say they're regulars, just take their word for it. You've got to trust people sometimes, you know!

Employee: *(Ignores the fact that the boss originally told her not to trust people but rather to insist on getting their number; decides instead to agree with the boss)* I can see how important it is to trust good customers.

Boss: Right.

Employee: Thanks for clearing up how to handle the resale numbers. Is there anything else I ought to know so things will run smoothly when you're not in the store? *(Asks if anything else is wrong)*

Boss: I don't think so. *(Patronizingly)* Don't get discouraged; you'll catch on. It took me twenty years to build this business. Stick with it, and some day you could be running a place like this.

Employee: *(Trying to agree with her boss without sounding sarcastic)* That would be great.

The employee's refusal to act defensively turned what might have been a scolding into a discussion about how to handle a business challenge in the future. The employee might not like the boss's patronizing attitude and contradictory directions, but her communication skill kept the communication climate positive—probably the best possible outcome for this situation.

Communication Scenarios

 To watch and analyze a video related to this feature and this topic, visit CengageBrain .com to access the Speech Communication CourseMate for Looking Out/Looking In.

In still other cases, you can acknowledge your critic's right to see things differently than you without backing off from your position.

> "I can understand why you think I'm overreacting. I know this doesn't seem as important to you as it does to me. I hope you can understand why I think this is such a big deal."

Apologizing is fine if you can do so sincerely; but you will be able to agree with critics more often if you understand that doing so doesn't require you to grovel.

Some critics don't seem to deserve the kinds of respectful responses outlined here. They seem more interested in attacking you than explaining themselves. Before you counterattack these hostile critics, ask yourself whether a defensive response will be worth the consequences.

SUMMARY

Every relationship has a communication climate. Positive climates are characterized by confirming messages, which make it clear that the parties value one another. Negative climates are usually disconfirming. In one way or another, messages in disconfirming relationships convey indifference or hostility. Disagreeing messages have some combination of confirmation and disconfirmation. Communication climates develop early in a relationship from both verbal and nonverbal messages. After they are created, reciprocal messages create either positive or negative spirals in which the frequency and intensity of either positive or negative messages are likely to grow.

Defensiveness hinders effective communication. Most defensiveness occurs when people try to protect key parts of a presenting self-image that they believe is under attack. Using the supportive behaviors defined by Jack Gibb when expressing potentially threatening messages can reduce the likelihood of triggering defensive reactions in others. In addition, we can share our thoughts and feelings with others in face-saving ways by using the assertive message format. A complete, clear message describes the behavior in question, at least one interpretation, the speaker's feelings, the consequences of the situation, and the speaker's intentions in making the statement.

When faced with criticism by others, it is possible to respond nondefensively by attempting to understand the criticism and by agreeing with either the facts or the critic's perception.

KEY TERMS

aggressiveness (314)

ambiguous response (314)

argumentativeness (315)

assertive message format (326)

certainty (323)

communication climate (312)

complaining (315)

confirming communication (312)

consequence statement (329)

controlling communication (321)

de-escalatory conflict spiral (318)

defensiveness (319)

description (321)

disagreeing messages (314)

disconfirming communication (312)

empathy (323)

equality (323)

escalatory conflict spiral (318)

evaluation (321)

face-threatening act (319)

feeling statement (328)

Gibb categories (320)

impersonal response (314)

impervious response (313)

incongruous response (314)

intention statement (329)

interpretation statement (327)

interrupting response (313)

irrelevant response (314)

neutrality (322)

problem orientation (321)

provisionalism (324)

No spiral (317)

spontaneity (322)

strategy (322)

superiority (323)

tangential response (314)

ONLINE RESOURCES

Now that you have read this chapter, visit CengageBrain.com to access the Speech Communication CourseMate for *Looking Out/Looking In* for quick access to the electronic resources that accompany this text. Your CourseMate offers:

- **Study tools** that will help you assess your learning and prepare for exams (*digital glossary, key term flash cards, interactive quizzes*).
- **Activities and assignments** that will help you hone your knowledge, understand how theory and research applies to your own life (*Self-Assessment, Pause and Reflect*), consider ethical challenges in interpersonal communication (*Ethical Challenge*), and build your interpersonal communication skills throughout the course (*Skill Builder*). If requested, you can submit your answers to your instructor.
- **Media resources** that will allow you to watch and critique videos of interpersonal communication situations (*In Real Life, interpersonal video simulations, and interactive video activities*).
- In addition to interactive teaching and learning tools, CourseMate includes an **interactive eBook**. Take notes, highlight, search, and interact with embedded media specific to *Looking Out/Looking In*.

SEARCH TERMS

When searching online databases to research topics in this chapter, use the following terms (along with this chapter's key terms) to maximize the chances of finding useful information:

assertiveness	criticism
cognitive dissonance	defense mechanisms
communication patterns	supportive communication

FILM AND TELEVISION

You can see the communication principles described in this chapter portrayed in the following films and television programs.

CONFIRMING AND DISCONFIRMING COMMUNICATION

Everybody Loves Raymond (1996–2005) Rated TV-G

The title character of this situation comedy is sportswriter Raymond Barone (Ray Romano), but fans of the show know that the central character in the family's communication patterns is his mother, Marie (Doris Roberts). The messages she sends, both verbally and nonverbally, clearly communicate how she feels about each family member.

In Marie's eyes, Ray can do no wrong, so she lavishes him with acknowledgment and endorsement. On the other hand, her husband, Frank (Peter Boyle), and daughter-in-law, Debra (Patricia Heaton), often can do no right in Marie's eyes, so she sends them messages filled with arguing, complaining, and even aggression. Her other son, Robert (Brad Garrett), who lives in Raymond's shadow, gets heavy doses of impervious, irrelevant, and impersonal communication—almost as if he doesn't exist.

What keeps the family relatively sane is that they call each other on the carpet when these patterns get out of hand. They repair the communication climate just in time to start back in on each other the following episode.

Bully (2011) Rated PG-13

The lives of bullied children are tragic, but their stories often go untold. The documentary *Bully* takes a closeup look at five families whose worlds are rocked by aggression and abuse at the hands of childhood peers. Sadly, two of the film's subjects committed suicide, and their heartbreaking stories are told retrospectively by loved ones who wish they could have done more to protect the victims.

Some of the adults depicted in this documentary take naïve approaches to bullying, believing that aggressive behavior is simply a matter of "kids being kids." But others clearly understand that vicious words, taunts, and threats are more than just "sticks and stones"—and that bullying hurts everyone involved, not just the victimized child.

SUPPORTIVE AND DEFENSIVE CLIMATES

The King's Speech (2010) Rated R

See-Saw Films/The Kobal Collection

On the eve of World War II, Prince Albert Frederick Arthur George (Colin Firth) reluctantly ascends to the throne of England. The new King George VI is paralyzed by a humiliating stutter that undermines his ability to rally the British Empire to resist the Nazi juggernaut.

After a series of prestigious but ineffective professionals fail to help, the king travels incognito to the basement flat of Australian speech coach Lionel Logue (Geoffrey Rush). Logue's approach is unconventional. He insists on addressing his royal client by his family nickname of "Bertie," saying that in therapy "it's better that we're equals."

At first, the king—a shy, aloof, but proud man—bridles at Logue's approach. But as the two men work together, two minor miracles happen. The king's speech becomes more fluent, and a lifelong friendship grows between commoner and monarch.

The King's Speech is a touching reminder that, in close relationships, mutual affection and respect are far more important than social roles.

GIVING AND RECEIVING CRITICISM

TV Performance Contests

Televised performance shows such as *American Idol*, *The Voice*, and *The X Factor* require contestants to perform not only in front of millions of TV viewers and a live audience but also before a panel of judges who publicly critique the performers and their talents (or lack thereof). Receiving criticism is always a face-threatening process, but particularly so when a huge audience is listening in.

It's interesting to watch how the contest judges offer their criticisms and how the singers respond. When the verdict is negative, some judges are curt and evaluative ("That was awful!") or broad and vague ("That didn't work"). The most helpful criticisms focus on specific behaviors and suggestions for change ("I think you need a song in a lower range—you seemed to be straining for the high notes").

Of course, performers don't always respond well to suggestions. Many quickly defend themselves ("I thought I did just fine") or shift the blame ("I didn't choose the song"). Others follow principles described in this chapter such as seeking more information or agreeing with the critic in hopes of improving their next performance.

Shows like these are designed for entertainment, not education—but from a communication perspective, they offer valuable lessons about giving and receiving criticism.

C H A P T E R   T E N

Improving Communication Climates

CHAPTER OUTLINE

Use this outline to take notes as you read the chapter in the text and/or as your instructor lectures in class.

I. COMMUNICATION CLIMATE AND CONFIRMING MESSAGES	
A. Levels of Message Confirmation	
1. Confirming communication	
a. Recognition	
b. Acknowledgment	
c. Endorsement	
2. Disconfirming communication	
a. Impervious responses	
b. Interrupting	
c. Irrelevant responses	
d. Tangential responses	
e. Impersonal responses	
f. Ambiguous responses	
g. Incongruous responses	
3. Disagreeing messages	
a. Aggressiveness	
b. Complaining	
c. Argumentativeness	
4. Confirming messages	
a. Recognition	
b. Acknowledgment	
c. Endorsement	
B. How Communication Climates Develop	

      1.   Escalatory conflict spirals

      2.   De-escalatory conflict spirals

II.   **DEFENSIVENESS: CAUSES AND REMEDIES**

    A. **Face-Threatening Acts**

    B. **Preventing Defensiveness in Others**

      1.   Evaluation versus description

      2.   Control versus problem orientation

      3.   Strategy versus spontaneity

      4.   Neutrality versus empathy

      5.   Superiority versus equality

      6.   Certainty versus provisionalism

III. **SAVING FACE: THE ASSERTIVE MESSAGE FORMAT**

    A. **Behavior**

    B. **Interpretation**

      1.   Based on experience, assumptions

      2.   Subjective

    C. **Feeling**

    D. **Consequence**

      1.   What happens to you, the speaker

      2.   What happens to the person you're addressing

      3.   What happens to others

    E. **Intention**

      1.   Where you stand on an issue

      2.   Requests of others

      3.   How you plan to act in the future

    F. **Using the Assertive Message Format**

      1.   Order may vary

2. Use personal style
3. Combine elements
4. Take your time
G. Responding Nondefensively to Criticism
  1. Seek more information
  2. Ask for specifics
  3. Guess about specifics
  4. Paraphrase the speaker's ideas
  5. Ask what the critic wants
  6. Ask about the consequences
  7. Ask if anything else is wrong
H. Agree with the Critic
  1. Agree with the facts
  2. Agree with the critic's perception
  3. Agreeing versus apologizing
	_____
	_____
	_____
	_____
	_____
	_____
	_____
	_____
	_____
	_____

KEY TERMS

aggressiveness

ambiguous response

argumentativeness

assertive message format

certainty

communication climate

complaining

confirming communication

consequence statement

controlling communication

de-escalatory conflict spiral

defensiveness

description

disagreeing messages

disconfirming communication

empathy

equality

escalatory conflict spiral

evaluation

face-threatening act

feeling statement

Gibb categories

impersonal response

impervious response

incongruous response

intention statement

interpretation statement

interrupting response

irrelevant response

neutrality

problem orientation

provisionalism

spiral

spontaneity

strategy

superiority

tangential response

ACTIVITIES

10.1 UNDERSTANDING DEFENSIVE RESPONSES

LEARNING OBJECTIVES

- Identify confirming, disagreeing, and disconfirming messages and patterns in your own important relationships, and describe their consequences.

- Describe how the messages you identified in the previous objective either threaten or honor the self (face) of the communicators involved.

- Use Gibb's categories and the assertive message format to create messages that are likely to build supportive rather than defensive communication climates.

- Use the guidelines in this chapter to present critical messages in a constructive manner.

- Create appropriate nondefensive responses to real or hypothetical criticisms.

INSTRUCTIONS

1. Identify the person or people who would be most likely to deliver each of the following critical messages to you. If you are unlikely to hear one or more of the following messages, substitute a defensiveness-arousing topic of your own.
2. For each situation, describe
   a. the person likely to deliver the message.
   b. the typical content of the message.
   c. the general type of response(s) you make: attacking, distorting, or avoiding.
   d. your typical verbal response(s).
   e. your typical nonverbal response(s).
   f. the part of your presenting self being defended.
   g. the probable consequences of these response(s).

EXAMPLE

A negative comment about your use of time.
Person likely to deliver this message: *my parents*
Typical content of the message: *wasting my time watching TV instead of studying*
General type(s) of response: *attacking, distorting*
Your typical verbal response(s): *"Get off my back! I work hard! I need time to relax." "I'll study later; I've got plenty of time."*
Your typical nonverbal response(s): *harsh tone of voice, sullen silence for an hour or two*
Part(s) of presenting self being defended: *good student, not lazy*
Probable consequences of your response(s): *uncomfortable silence, more criticism from parents in the future*

Class _____ Name_____

1. Negative comment about your managing money.

   Person likely to deliver this message _____

   Typical content of the message _____

   _____

   General type(s) of response _____

   Your typical verbal response(s) _____

   _____

   Your typical nonverbal response(s) _____

   _____

   Part(s) of presenting self being defended _____

   Probable consequences of your response(s) _____

   _____

   _____

2. Criticism about your choice of friends.

   Person likely to deliver this message _____

   Typical content of the message _____

   _____

   General type(s) of response _____

   Your typical verbal response(s) _____

   _____

   Your typical nonverbal response(s) _____

   _____

Part(s) of presenting self being defended _____

Probable consequences of your response(s) _____

_____

_____

3. Criticism of a job you've just completed.

Person likely to deliver this message _____

Typical content of the message _____

_____

General type(s) of response _____

Your typical verbal response(s) _____

_____

Your typical nonverbal response(s) _____

_____

Part(s) of presenting self being defended _____

Probable consequences of your response(s) _____

_____

_____

4. Criticism of your schoolwork.

Person likely to deliver this message _____

Typical content of the message _____

_____

General type(s) of response _____

Your typical verbal response(s) _____

_____

Your typical nonverbal response(s) _____

_____

Part(s) of presenting self being defended _____

Probable consequences of your response(s) _____

_____

_____

5. Criticism of your politics, political action, or lack of political involvement.

Person likely to deliver this message _____

Typical content of the message _____

_____

General type(s) of response _____

Your typical verbal response(s) _____

_____

Your typical nonverbal response(s) _____

_____

Part(s) of presenting self being defended _____

Probable consequences of your response(s) _____

_____

_____

6. A negative comment about your exercise (or lack of it).

Person likely to deliver this message _____

Class _____   Name_____

Typical content of the message _____

_____

General type(s) of response _____

Your typical verbal response(s) _____

_____

Your typical nonverbal response(s) _____

_____

Part(s) of presenting self being defended _____

Probable consequences of your response(s) _____

_____

_____

10.2 DEFENSIVE AND SUPPORTIVE LANGUAGE

LEARNING OBJECTIVES

- Use Gibb's categories and the assertive message format to create messages that are likely to build supportive rather than defensive communication climates.
- Use the guidelines in the text to present critical messages in a constructive manner.
- Create appropriate nondefensive responses to real or hypothetical criticisms.

INSTRUCTIONS

1. For each of the situations below, write one statement likely to arouse defensiveness and one statement likely to promote a support climate.
2. Label the Gibb category of language that each statement represents (evaluation, description, control, problem-orientation, strategy, spontaneity, neutrality, empathy, superiority, equality, certainty, or provisionalism).

EXAMPLE

A neighbor's late-night stereo music playing is disrupting your sleep.
Defense-arousing statement: *Why don't you show a little consideration and turn that damn thing down? If I hear any more noise I'm going to call the police!*
Type(s) of defensive language: *evaluation, control*
Supportive statement: *When I hear your stereo music late at night I can't sleep, which leaves me more and more tired. I'd like to figure out some way you can listen and I can sleep.*
Type(s) of supportive language: *description, problem orientation*

1. You're an adult child who moves back in with your parents. They say they expect you to follow the "rules of the house."

   Defense-arousing statement _____

   _____

   Type(s) of defensive language _____

   Supportive statement _____

   _____

   Type(s) of supportive language _____

2. Your roommate tells you you're trying to be "somebody you're not."

Defense-arousing statement _____

_____

Type(s) of defensive language _____

Supportive statement _____

_____

Type(s) of supportive language _____

3. A friend asks you what you see in your new romantic partner.

Defense-arousing statement _____

_____

Type(s) of defensive language _____

Supportive statement _____

_____

Type(s) of supportive language _____

4. Your boss says, "You call that finished?"

Defense-arousing statement _____

_____

Type(s) of defensive language _____

Supportive statement _____

_____

Type(s) of supportive language _____

5. Your friend buys the same thing you did after you bragged about the deal you got.

   Defense-arousing statement _____

   _____

   Type(s) of defensive language _____

   Supportive statement _____

   _____

   Type(s) of supportive language _____

6. On many occasions a friend drops by your place without calling first. Since you often have other plans, this behavior puts you in an uncomfortable position.

   Defense-arousing statement _____

   _____

   Type(s) of defensive language _____

   Supportive statement _____

   _____

   Type(s) of supportive language _____

7. Your roommate says, "You left the lights on *again*."

   Defense-arousing statement _____

   _____

   Type(s) of defensive language _____

   Supportive statement _____

   _____

   Type(s) of supportive language _____

8. Your parent praises your sibling for something without mentioning you.

Defense-arousing statement _____

_____

Type(s) of defensive language _____

Supportive statement _____

_____

Type(s) of supportive language _____

9. Your situation: _____

Defense-arousing statement _____

_____

Type(s) of defensive language _____

Supportive statement _____

_____

Type(s) of supportive language _____

10.3 WRITING ASSERTIVE MESSAGES

LEARNING OBJECTIVES

- Use the guidelines in the text to present critical messages in a constructive manner.

INSTRUCTIONS

Imagine a situation in which you might have said each of the statements below. Rewrite the messages in the assertive message format, being sure to include each of the five elements described in your text.

EXAMPLE

Unclear message: "It's awful when you can't trust a friend."

Assertive message:

Lena, when I gave you the keys to my house so you could borrow those clothes, I

came back and found the house unlocked.   (behavior)

I figured you'd know to lock up again when you left.   (interpretation)

I was worried and scared.   (feeling)

I thought there was a break-in and was nervous about going in. (consequence)

I want to know if you left the house unlocked and let you know how upset I am. (intention)

1. "Just get off my case; you're not my warden."

_____ (behavior)

_____ (interpretation)

_____ (feeling)

_____ (consequence)

_____ (intention)

2. "I wish you'd pay more attention to me."

_____ (behavior)

_____ (interpretation)

_____ (feeling)

_____ (consequence)

_____ (intention)

3.   "You've sure been thoughtful lately."

_____ (behavior)

_____ (interpretation)

_____ (feeling)

_____ (consequence)

_____ (intention)

4.   "You're the greatest!"

_____ (behavior)

_____ (interpretation)

_____ (feeling)

_____ (consequence)

_____ (intention)

5.   "Matt, you're such a slob!"

_____ (behavior)

_____ (interpretation)

_____ (feeling)

_____ (consequence)

_____ (intention)

6. "Let's just forget it; forget I ever asked for a favor."

_____   (behavior)

_____   (interpretation)

_____   (feeling)

_____   (consequence)

_____   (intention)

Now list three significant messages that you could send to important people in your life: one complaint, one request, and one expression of appreciation. Write them in the assertive message format.

8. _____   (behavior)

_____   (interpretation)

_____   (feeling)

_____   (consequence)

_____   (intention)

9. _____   (behavior)

_____   (interpretation)

_____   (feeling)

_____   (consequence)

_____   (intention)

10. _____   (behavior)

_____   (interpretation)

_____   (feeling)

Class _____   Name_____

_____ (consequence)

_____ (intention)

CRITICAL THINKING

1. Compare and contrast the perception checking process with the assertive message format.

2. You are faced with a coworker's difficult behavior: taking credit for work that you did. Would you use a perception check? An assertive message ? Both? In what order? Why?

10.4 MEDIATED MESSAGES—CLIMATE

LEARNING OBJECTIVES

- Identify confirming, disagreeing, and disconfirming messages and patterns in your own important relationships, and describe their consequences.
- Describe how the messages you identified in the previous objective either threaten or honor the self (face) of the communicators involved.

INSTRUCTIONS

Discuss each of the questions below in your group. Prepare written answers for your instructor, or be prepared to contribute to a large group discussion, comparing your experiences with those of others in your class.

1. Describe how the use of mediated forms of communication channels (e.g., telephone, email) contributes to the communication climate (emotional tone) of your relationships.

   _____

   _____

2. Compile a list of the ways we can use mediated messages to recognize, acknowledge, and endorse others.

   _____

   _____

3. Give examples of how mediated messages have contributed to or helped minimize defensive spirals (negative, ineffective patterns of communication) in your relationships.

   _____

   _____

   _____

4. Your text describes ways we can respond nondefensively to criticism. In which mediated contexts can this skill be used most effectively?

   _____

   _____

10.5 CLIMATE ANALYSIS

LEARNING OBJECTIVES

- Identify confirming, disagreeing, and disconfirming messages and patterns in your own important relationships, and describe their consequences.

INSTRUCTIONS

Use the case below and the discussion questions that follow to discuss the variety of communication issues involved in effective communication. Make notes on this page, add other pages on your own, or prepare a group report/analysis based on your discussion. Add your own experiences to individualize the analysis.

CASE

Gil and Lydia are brother and sister. They love one another and feel close. Their mother often tells Gil how wonderful Lydia is to call her so often, how smart Lydia is, what a good athlete she is, and how much she enjoys Lydia bringing home her friends to visit. Mom tells Lydia how generous Gil is, how hard he works, how many interesting things he does, and how well he manages money. The overall climate of the relationship between Gil and Lydia and their mother is good, but both Gil and Lydia find themselves getting defensive when their mom spends so much time praising the other.

1. Use aspects of Gibb's theory to explain why Gil and Lydia get defensive about these positive statements about the other.

   _____

   _____

   _____

   _____

2. Discuss situations similar to the one above in which people get defensive about statements that, on the surface, are positive and supportive.

   _____

   _____

   _____

3. Write coping with criticism responses for Gil or Lydia to use the next time their mother praises their sibling.

_____

_____

_____

4. How could Gil and Lydia's mother change the comments she makes about each sibling to reduce defensive reactions?

_____

_____

_____

10.6 APPLYING THE "SANDWICH METHOD"

LEARNING OBJECTIVES

- Use Gibb's categories and the assertive message format to create messages that are likely to build supportive rather than defensive communication climates.
- Use the guidelines in the text to present critical messages in a constructive manner.
- Create appropriate nondefensive responses to real or hypothetical criticisms.

INSTRUCTIONS

Read the first three scenarios below and apply the "sandwich method" to turn a possible defensive situation into a nondefensive one. Then describe two situations where you can apply the sandwich method in your own life and describe how you will apply this method.

1. You are working on a project for one of your classes with a partner. While your partner is friendly and contributes good ideas to the project, she always arrives late to your project meetings and spends the first 30 minutes of your work time talking about her new boyfriend. You wish the two of you could get to work sooner so you could complete the project and have more free time. Use the sandwich method to offer constructive criticism to your partner.

Positive Comment:

_____

_____

Concern:

_____

_____

Positive Comment:

_____

_____

2.   Your new college roommate constantly returns to your dorm late at night and makes a lot of noise when saying good night to her friends. This noise wakes you up at night and you start to struggle to get up for your 7:30 a.m. class. Use the sandwich method to offer constructive criticism to your roommate.

Positive Comment:

_____

_____

  Concern:

_____

_____

Positive Comment:

_____

_____

3.   One of your coworkers has a tendency to tell inappropriate jokes that you find offensive. Use the sandwich method to offer your coworker some constructive criticism.

Positive Comment:

_____

_____

Concern:

_____

_____

Positive Comment:

_____

_____

Class _____   Name_____

Now apply the sandwich method to a situation in your own life.

Situation 1 Description _____

Positive Comment:

_____

_____

Concern:

_____

_____

Positive Comment:

_____

_____

Situation 2 Description _____

Positive Comment:

_____

_____

Concern:

_____

_____

Class _____   Name_____

Positive Comment:

_____

_____

STUDY GUIDE

CHECK YOUR UNDERSTANDING

TRUE/FALSE

Mark the statements below as true or false. Correct false statements on the lines below to create true statements.

_____   1.   The tone or climate of a relationship is shaped by the degree to which the people believe themselves to be valued by one another.

_____

_____   2.   Between confirming and disconfirming communication lie disagreeing messages.

_____

_____   3.   Most experts agree that it is psychologically healthier to have someone ignore you than disagree with you.

_____

_____   4.   Both positive and negative communication spirals have their limits; they rarely go on indefinitely.

_____

_____   5.   In a marriage, ignoring or "stonewalling" a partner is a strong predictor of divorce.

_____

_____   6.   Communicators strive to resolve inconsistencies or conflicting pieces of information because this "dissonant" condition is uncomfortable.

_____

_____   7.   Using Jack Gibb's supportive behaviors will eliminate defensiveness in your receivers.

_____

_____   8.   Constructive criticism can increase odds of successful confrontation, and rarely requires future acknowledgment.

_____

_____   9.   The assertive message format works for a variety of messages: hopes, problems, complaints, and appreciations.

_____

_____ 10. When you truly understand hostile comments, you just naturally accept them.
_____

_____ 11. Verbal aggressiveness is the tendency to support the concepts of others and to relieve psychological pain of another.
_____

_____ 12. Failure to return an email is one example of lack of recognition.
_____

COMPLETION

The Gibb categories of defensive and supportive behavior are six sets of contrasting styles of verbal and nonverbal behavior. Each set describes a communication style that is likely to arouse defensiveness and a contrasting style that is likely to prevent or reduce it. Fill in the blanks with the Gibb behavior described chosen from the list below.

evaluation	description	control	problem orientation	strategy
spontaneity	neutrality	empathy	superiority	equality
certainty	provisionalism			

1. _____ is the attitude behind messages that dogmatically imply that the speaker's position is correct and that the other person's ideas are not worth considering.

2. _____ is communication behavior involving messages that describe the speaker's position without evaluating others.

3. _____ is a supportive style of communication in which the communicators focus on working together to solve their problems instead of trying to impose their own solutions on one another.

4. _____ is a defense-arousing style of communication in which the sender tries to manipulate or deceive a receiver.

5. _____ is a supportive style of communication in which the sender expresses a willingness to consider the other person's position.

6. _____ is a defense-arousing style of communication in which the sender states or implies that the receiver is not worthy of respect.

7. _____ is a supportive communication behavior in which the sender expresses a message openly and honestly without any attempt to manipulate the receiver.

8. _____ is a defense-arousing behavior in which the sender expresses indifference toward a receiver.

9. _____ is a defense-arousing message in which the sender tries to impose some sort of outcome on the receiver.

10. _____ is a type of supportive communication that suggests that the sender regards the receiver as worthy of respect.

11. _____ is a defense-arousing message in which the sender passes some type of judgment on the receiver.

12. _____ is a type of supportive communication in which the sender accepts the other's feelings as valid and avoids sounding indifferent.

MULTIPLE CHOICE

Choose the letter of the defensive or supportive category that is best illustrated by each of the situations below.

a. evaluation
b. control
c. strategy
d. neutrality
e. superiority
f. certainty

g. description
h. problem orientation
i. spontaneity
j. empathy
k. equality
l. provisionalism

_____ 1. Gerry insists he has all the facts and needs to hear no more information.

_____ 2. Richard has a strong opinion but will listen to another position.

_____ 3. Lina kept looking at the clock as she was listening to Nan, so Nan thought Lina didn't consider her comments very important.

_____ 4. "I know Janice doesn't agree with me," Mary said, "but she knows how strongly I feel about this, and I think she understands my position."

_____ 5. "Even though my professor has a Ph.D.," Rosa pointed out, "she doesn't act like she's the only one who knows something; she is really interested in me as a person."

_____ 6. "When I found out that Bob had tricked me into thinking his proposal was my idea so I'd support it, I was really angry."

_____ 7. "Even though we *all* wait tables here, Evanne thinks she's better than any of us— just look at the way she prances around!"

_____ 8. Clara sincerely and honestly told Georgia about her reservations concerning Georgia's planned party.

_____ 9. The coworkers attempted to find a solution to the scheduling issue that would satisfy both of their needs.

_____ 10. "It seems as though my father's favorite phrase is `I know what's best for you' and that really gripes me."

_____ 11. "You drink too much."

_____ 12. "I was embarrassed when you slurred your speech in front of my boss."

_____ 13. "The flowers and presents are just an attempt to get me to go to bed with him."

_____ 14. "She looked down her nose at me when I told her I didn't exercise regularly."

_____ 15. "Well, if you need more money and I need more help around here, what could we do to make us both happy?"

Choose the letter of the type of coping with criticism that is best illustrated by each of the situations below.

  a. ask for specific details of criticism
  b. guess about specific details
  c. paraphrase to clarify criticism
  d. ask what the critic wants
  e. ask what else is wrong
  f. agree with true facts
  g. agree with critic's right to perceive differently
  h. ask about the consequences

Criticism: "You never seem to care about much."

_____ 16. "Are you referring to my not going to the office party?"

_____ 17. "You're right that I didn't call you back within 24 hours."

_____ 18. "What do you want me to care more about?"

_____ 19. "I can see why you'd be upset with me for not coming to the party because you've told me you want me to be more involved with your work's social events."

_____ 20. "When I didn't come to the party, were you embarrassed or something?"

_____ 21. "So not calling you back right away was a problem. Have I upset you any other way?"

_____ 22. "So you're upset that I'm not visiting you every week, and you think that shows a lack of affection on my part—is that it?"

_____ 23. "What do you mean?"

_____ 24. "You're correct in that I couldn't visit this week because of finals."

_____ 25. "Because I wasn't at the party, it reflected badly on you."

Identify which element of an assertive message is being used in each statement according to the following key:

a. behavioral description
b. interpretation
c. feeling
d. consequence
e. intention

_____ 26. That's a good idea.

_____ 27. I'm worried about this course.

_____ 28. Jim looked angry today.

_____ 29. I want to talk to you about the $20 you borrowed.

_____ 30. I notice that you haven't been smiling much lately.

_____ 31. I don't know whether you're serious or not.

_____ 32. I'm glad you invited me.

_____ 33. Ever since then I've found myself avoiding you.

_____ 34. I'm sorry you didn't like my work.

_____ 35. I want you to know how important this is to me.

_____ 36. It looks to me like you meant to embarrass me.

_____ 37. After the party at Art's, you seemed to withdraw.

_____ 38. I see you're wearing my ring again.

_____ 39. From now on you can count on me.

_____ 40. I've never heard you say a curse word before.

_____ 41. . . . and since then I've been sleeping at my dad's house.

_____ 42. Because that occurred, they won't work overtime.

_____ 43. Dave sighed and looked out the window.

_____ 44. I'm excited about the possibility.

_____ 45. I'll get another place to live.

CHAPTER TEN STUDY GUIDE ANSWERS

TRUE/FALSE

1.	T	3.	F	5.	T	7.	F	9.	T	11. F
2.	T	4.	T	6.	T	8.	F	10.	F	12. T

COMPLETION

1. certainty
2. description
3. problem orientation
4. strategy

5. provisionalism
6. superiority
7. spontaneity
8. neutrality

9. control
10. equality
11. evaluation
12. empathy

MULTIPLE CHOICE

1.	f	10.	b	19.	g	28.	b	37.	b
2.	l	11.	a	20.	b	29.	e	38.	a
3.	d	12.	g	21.	e	30.	a	39.	e
4.	j	13.	c	22.	c	31.	b	40.	a
5.	k	14.	e	23.	a	32.	c	41.	d
6.	c	15.	h	24.	f	33.	d	42.	d
7.	e	16.	b	25.	b	34.	c	43.	a
8.	l	17.	f	26.	b	35.	e	44.	c
9.	h	18.	d	27.	c	36.	b	45.	e

Managing Interpersonal Conflicts

After studying the topics in this chapter, you should be able to:

1. Identify the conflicts in your important relationships and how satisfied you are with the way they have been handled.

2. Describe your personal conflict styles, evaluate their effectiveness, and suggest alternatives as appropriate.

3. Identify the relational conflict styles, patterns of behavior, and conflict rituals that define a given relationship.

4. Demonstrate how you could use the win–win approach in a given conflict.

For most people, conflict has about the same appeal as a trip to the dentist. A quick look at a thesaurus offers a clue about the distasteful nature of conflict. Synonyms for the term include *battle*, *brawl*, *clash*, *competition*, *discord*, *disharmony*, *duel*, *fight*, *strife*, *struggle*, *trouble*, and *violence*.

Even the metaphors we use to describe our conflicts show that we view conflict as something to be avoided.[1] We often talk about conflict as a kind of war: "He shot down my arguments." "Okay, fire away." "Don't try to defend yourself!" Other metaphors suggest that conflict is explosive: "Don't blow up!" "I needed to let off steam." "You've got a short fuse." Sometimes conflict seems like a kind of trial in which one party accuses another: "Come on, admit you're guilty." "Stop accusing me!" "Just listen to my case." Language suggesting that conflict is a mess is also common: "Let's not open this can of worms." "That's a sticky situation." "Don't make such a stink!" Even the metaphor of a game implies that one side has to defeat the other: "That was out of bounds." "You're not playing fair." "I give up; you win!"

Despite images like these, the truth is that conflict *can* be constructive. With the right set of communication skills, conflict can be less like a struggle and more like a kind of dance in which partners work together to create something that would be impossible without their cooperation. You may have to persuade the other person to become your partner rather than your adversary, and you may be clumsy at first, but with enough practice and goodwill, you can work together instead of at cross-purposes.

The attitude you bring to your conflicts can make a tremendous difference between success and failure. One study revealed that college students in close romantic relationships who believed that conflicts are destructive were most likely to neglect or quit the relationship and less likely to seek a solution than couples who had less-negative attitudes.[2] Of course, attitudes alone won't always guarantee satisfying solutions to conflicts—but the kinds of skills you will learn in this chapter can help well-intentioned partners handle their disagreements constructively.

The Nature of Conflict

Before focusing on how to solve interpersonal problems constructively, we need to look briefly at the nature of conflict. What is it? Why is it an inevitable part of life? How can it be beneficial?

CONFLICT DEFINED

Before reading further, make a list of the interpersonal conflicts in your life. They probably involve many different people, revolve around very different subjects, and take many different forms. Some become loud, angry arguments. Others may be expressed in calm, rational discussions. Still others might simmer along most of the time with brief but bitter flare-ups.

Whatever form they may take, all interpersonal conflicts share certain characteristics. William Wilmot and Joyce Hocker provide a thorough definition when they define **conflict** as "an expressed struggle between at least two interdependent parties who perceive incompatible goals, scarce resources, and interference from the other party in achieving their goals."[3] A closer look at the key parts of this definition will help you recognize how conflict operates in your life.

Expressed Struggle A conflict can exist only when both parties are aware of a disagreement. For instance, you may be upset for months because a neighbor's loud stereo keeps you awake at night, but no conflict exists between the two of you until the neighbor learns of your problem. Of course, the expressed struggle doesn't have to be verbal. A dirty look, the silent treatment, and avoiding the other person are all ways of expressing yourself. One way or another, both parties must know that a problem exists before they're in conflict.

Perceived Incompatible Goals All conflicts look as if one party's gain would be another's loss. For instance, consider the neighbor whose stereo keeps you awake at night. Doesn't somebody have to lose? If the neighbor turns down the noise, she loses the enjoyment of hearing the music at full volume, but if the neighbor keeps the volume up, you're still awake and unhappy.

The goals in this situation really aren't completely incompatible; there are solutions that allow both parties to get what they want. For instance, you could achieve peace and quiet by closing your windows or getting the neighbor to close hers. You might use a pair of earplugs, or perhaps the neighbor could get a set of earphones, allowing the music to be played at full volume without bothering anyone. If any of these solutions prove workable, then the conflict disappears. Unfortunately, people often fail to see mutually satisfying solutions to their problems. As long as they *perceive* their goals to be mutually exclusive, a conflict exists.

Perceived Scarce Resources Conflicts also exist when people believe there isn't enough of something to go around. The most obvious example of a scarce resource is money—a cause of many conflicts. If a worker asks for a raise in pay and the boss would rather keep the money or use it to expand the business, then the two parties are in conflict.

Time is another scarce commodity. Many people struggle to meet the competing demands of school, work, family, and friends. "If there were only more hours in a day" is a common refrain, and making time for the people in your life—and for yourself—is a constant source of conflict.

Interdependence However antagonistic they might feel, the parties in conflict are usually dependent on each other. The welfare and satisfaction of one depend on the actions of another. If not, then even in the face of scarce resources and incompatible goals, there would be no need for conflict. Interdependence exists between conflicting nations, social groups, organizations, friends, and lovers. In each case, if the two parties didn't need each other to solve the problem, they would go their separate ways. One of the first steps toward resolving a conflict is to take the attitude that "we're all in this together."

Interference from the Other Party No matter how much one person's position may differ from another's, a full-fledged conflict won't occur until the participants act in ways that prevent one another from reaching their goals. For example, you might let some friends know that you object to their driving after drinking alcohol, but the conflict won't escalate until you act in ways that prevent them from getting behind the wheel. Likewise, a parent–child dispute about what clothing and music are appropriate will blossom into a conflict when the parents try to impose their position on the child.

Lionsgate/The Kobal Collection

In *The Hunger Games*, Katniss Everdeen (Jennifer Lawrence) faces conflicts with life-or-death consequences. Even when rewards are scarce and goals seem incompatible, she learns that interdependence and collaboration are keys to survival. (See the film summary at the end of this chapter.)

CONFLICT IS NATURAL

Every relationship of any depth at all has conflict.[4] No matter how close, how understanding, how compatible you and other people are, there will be times when your ideas or actions or needs or goals won't match. You like rap music, but your companion likes classical; you want to date other people, but your partner wants to keep the relationship exclusive; you think a paper that you've written is fine, but your instructor wants it changed; you like to sleep late on Sunday mornings, but your housemate likes to get up early and exercise loudly. There's no end to the number and kinds of disagreements possible.

College students who have kept diaries of their relationships report that they take part in about seven arguments per week. Most have argued with the other person before, often about the same topic.[5] In another survey, 81 percent of the respondents acknowledged that they had conflicts with friends.[6] Even the 19 percent who claimed that their friendships were conflict free used phrases such as "push and pull" and "little disagreements" to describe the tensions that inevitably occurred. Among families, conflict can be even more frequent. Researchers recorded dinner conversations for fifty-two families and found an average of 3.3 "conflict episodes" per meal.[7]

At first this might seem depressing. If problems are inevitable in even the best relationships, does this mean that you're doomed to relive the same arguments, the same hurt feelings, over and over? Fortunately, the answer to this question is a definite "no." Even though conflict is part of a meaningful relationship, you can change the way you deal with it.

CONFLICT CAN BE BENEFICIAL

Because it is impossible to avoid conflicts, the challenge is to handle them well when they do arise. Effective communication during conflicts can actually keep good relationships strong. People who use the constructive skills described in this chapter are more satisfied with their relationships[8] and with the outcomes of their conflicts.[9]

Perhaps the best evidence of how constructive conflict skills can benefit a relationship focuses on communication between husbands and wives. More than twenty years of research shows that couples in both happy and unhappy marriages have conflicts, but that they manage conflict in very different ways.[10] One nine-year study revealed that unhappy couples argue in ways that we have catalogued in this book as destructive.[11] They are more concerned with defending themselves than with being problem oriented; they fail to listen carefully to each other, have little or no empathy for their partners, use evaluative "you" language, and ignore each other's nonverbal relational messages.

Many satisfied couples think and communicate differently when they disagree. They view disagreements as healthy and recognize that conflicts need to be faced.[12] Although they may argue vigorously, they use skills such as perception checking to find out what the other person is thinking, and they let each other know that they understand the other side of the argument.[13] They are willing to admit their mistakes, which contributes not only to a harmonious relationship but also to solving the problem at hand.

In the following pages, we'll review communication skills that can make conflicts constructive and introduce still more skills that you can use to resolve the inevitable conflicts you face. Before doing so, however, we need to examine how individuals behave when faced with a dispute.

 # Conflict Styles

Most people have default styles of handling conflict. (See Figure 11.1.) These habitual styles work sometimes, but they may not be effective in all situations. What styles do you typically use to deal with conflict? Find out by thinking about how two hypothetical characters—Paul and Lucia—manage a problem.

Paul and Lucia have been running partners for more than a year. Three times every week, they spend an hour or more together working out. The two runners are equally matched, and they enjoy challenging one another to cover longer distances at a quicker pace. During their time on the road, the friends have grown quite close. Now they often talk about personal matters that they don't share with anyone else.

Recently, Lucia has started to invite some of her friends along on the runs. Paul likes Lucia's friends, but they aren't strong athletes, so the outings become a much less-satisfying workout. Also, Paul fears losing the special one-on-one time that he and Lucia have had. Paul shared his concerns with Lucia, but she dismissed them. "I don't see what the problem is," she replied. "We still get plenty of time on the road, and you said you like my friends." "But it isn't the same," replied Paul.

This situation has all the elements of a conflict: expressed struggle (their differences are in the open and they still disagree), seemingly incompatible goals and interference (Lucia wants to run with her friends; Paul wants to run with just Lucia), apparently scarce resources (they only have so much time for running), and interdependence (they enjoy one another's company and run better together than separately).

FIGURE 11.1 Conflict Styles Adapted from Wilmot, W., & Hocker, J. L. (2010). *Interpersonal conflict* (8th ed.). New York: McGraw-Hill.

Here are five ways Paul and Lucia could handle the matter. Each represents a particular approach to managing conflict:

- They could say "Let's just forget it" and stop running together.
- Paul could give in, sacrificing his desire for one-on-one conversations and challenging runs. Or Lucia could give in, sacrificing her other friendships to maintain her friendship with Paul.
- One or the other could issue an ultimatum: "Either we do it my way, or we stop running together."
- They could compromise, inviting friends along on some runs but excluding them on other days.
- Lucia and Paul could brainstorm ways they could run with her friends and still get their workouts and one-on-one time with each other.

These approaches represent the five styles depicted in Figure 11.1, each of which is described in the following paragraphs.

AVOIDING (LOSE–LOSE)

Avoiding occurs when people nonassertively ignore or stay away from conflict. Avoidance can be physical (steering clear of a friend after having an argument) or conversational (changing the topic, joking, or denying that a problem exists). It can be tempting to avoid conflict, but research suggests that this approach has its costs: Partners of *self-silencers* report more frustration and discomfort when dealing with the avoiding partner than with those who face conflict more constructively.[14]

Avoidance reflects a pessimistic attitude about conflict under the belief that there is no good way to resolve the issue at hand. Some avoiders believe it's easier to put up with the status quo than to face the problem head-on and try to solve it. Other avoiders believe it's better to quit (on either the topic or the relationship) than to keep facing the same issues without hope of solution. In either case, avoiding often results in *lose–lose* outcomes in which no party gets what it wants.

In the case of Paul and Lucia, avoiding means that, rather than struggling with their disagreement, they just stop running together. Although it means they'll no longer be fighting, it also means they'll both lose a running partner and an important component of their friendship (and maybe their friendship altogether). This solution illustrates how avoiding can produce lose–lose results.

Although avoiding may keep the peace temporarily, it typically leads to unsatisfying relationships.[15] Chronic misunderstandings, resentments, and disappointments pile up and contaminate the emotional climate. For this reason, we can say that avoiders have a low concern both for their own needs and for the interests of the other person, who is also likely to suffer from unaddressed issues (see Figure 11.1).

Despite its obvious shortcomings, avoiding isn't always a bad idea.[16] You might choose to avoid certain topics or situations if the risk of speaking up is too great, such as triggering an embarrassing fight in public or even risking physical harm. You might also avoid a conflict if the relationship it involves isn't worth the effort. Even in close relationships, though, avoidance has its logic. If the issue is temporary or minor, then you might let it pass. These reasons help explain why the communication of many happily married couples is characterized by "selectively ignoring" the other person's minor flaws.[17] This doesn't mean that a key to successful relationships is avoiding *all* conflicts. Instead, it suggests that it's smart to save energy for the truly important ones.

ACCOMMODATING (LOSE–WIN)

Accommodating occurs when you allow others to have their way rather than asserting your own point of view. Figure 11.1 depicts accommodators as having low concern for themselves and high concern for others, which results in *lose–win*, "we'll do it your way" outcomes. In our hypothetical scenario, Paul could accommodate Lucia by letting her friends join in on their runs, even though it means less of a physical challenge and quality time with Lucia—or Lucia could accommodate Paul by running with just him.

The motivation of an accommodator plays a significant role in this style's effectiveness. If accommodation is a genuine act of kindness, generosity, or love, then chances are good that it will enhance the relationship. Most people appreciate those who "take one for the team," "treat others as they want to be treated," or "lose the battle to win the war." However, people are far less appreciative of those who habitually use this style to play the role of "martyr, bitter complainer, whiner, or saboteur."[18]

We should pause here to mention the important role that culture plays in perceptions of conflict styles. People from high-context, collectivist backgrounds (such as many Asian cultures) are likely to regard avoidance and accommodation as face-saving and noble ways to handle conflict.[19] In low-context, individualist cultures (such as the United States), avoidance and accommodation are often viewed less positively. For instance, think of the many unflattering terms that Americans use for people who give up or give in during conflicts ("pushover," "yes man," "doormat," "spineless"). As you will read later in this chapter, collectivist cultures have virtuous words and phrases to describe these same traits. The point here is that all conflict styles have value in certain situations and that culture plays a significant role in determining how each style is valued.

The Harry Potter tales are filled with conflict. Some contests are good-spirited competition between the school's houses; others are larger battles of good versus evil. What approaches to conflict does each character use, and what are the consequences of their choices?

Warner Bros. Pictures/Photofest

ON THE JOB

Workplace Bullying

Every job has its interpersonal conflicts, but workplace bullying is more intense, malicious, ongoing, and damaging than anything employees have a right to expect.[a] The most obvious form of bullying is *direct aggression*: abusive language, threats, and even physical displays of anger. Less obvious but equally damaging bullying comes in the form of *criticism*—nitpicking, unreasonable demands for work, impossible deadlines, and expectations of perfection. An even more insidious form of bullying involves *sabotage*, in which the bully criticizes the victim behind his or her back. Bosses can also bully by unfair *gatekeeping*: controlling resources such as money, staffing, and time in order to keep employees from being successful.[b]

Victims of bullying may feel helpless, but they do have choices. Based on more than a decade of research, management professors Christine Pearson and Christine Porath provide several options.[c]

- *Reframe your thinking.* When you're the target of demeaning communication, it's easy to start imagining that you somehow deserve the abuse. But there's no justification for bullying. Despite this fact, you may feel less victimized if you recognize that you may have contributed to the painful communication pattern by letting uncivil behavior slide or even contributed to that pattern in an effort to get along. Or perhaps you accepted a job working with or for a bully when your gut feeling or other people warned you against doing so.
- *Negotiate with the offender.* If you decide it's worth the discomfort and risks to approach the offender, consider whether you want to

do so one on one, or whether a mediator might be able to help manage the meeting. Choose a neutral meeting place—perhaps a semipublic spot such as a restaurant where the presence of bystanders might moderate the behavior of the other person.

- *Appeal to a third party.* This might be a coworker who can command the attention and respect of the offender, or perhaps your boss. If your boss *is* the offender, then your situation might be bad enough for you to take the unconventional step of going up the chain of command. Realize this approach has its risks. Your boss almost certainly won't appreciate the move, and it's possible that the authority to whom you appeal might support the offender. Despite the risks, this "nuclear option" may be worth considering.
- *Back off.* You may decide that retreating from the offender is the best approach. Some strategic options include communicating via phone or email whenever possible rather than in person, working at different times and places (perhaps from home if the job permits), and working with the offender's assistants or associates. It may even be necessary to back off from your workplace physically and emotionally until you can find a better situation: avoiding company social events, taking the sick days and vacation time you've earned, and not serving on committees that put you in uncomfortable settings. This isn't a recommendation to do less than your best job. Rather, it's a strategy for protecting yourself.

COMPETING (WIN–LOSE)

The flip side of accommodating is **competing**. This *win–lose* approach to conflict involves high concern for self and low concern for others. As Figure 11.1 shows, competition seeks to resolve conflicts "my way." If Lucia and Paul each tried to force the other to concede, one of them might prevail, but at the other's expense.

People resort to competing when they perceive a situation as being an either–or one: Either I get what I want or you get what you want. The most clear-cut examples of win–lose situations are certain games such as baseball or poker in which the rules require a winner and a loser. Some interpersonal issues seem to fit into this win–lose framework: two coworkers seeking a promotion to the same job, or a couple who disagree on how to spend their limited money.

There are cases when competing can enhance a relationship. One study revealed that some men and women in satisfying dating relationships use competition to enrich their interaction.[20] For example, some found satisfaction by competing in play (who's the better racquetball player?), in achievement (who gets the better job offer?), and in altruism (who's more romantic?). These satisfied couples developed a shared narrative (see Chapter 3) that defined competition as a measure of regard, quite different from conflict that signaled a lack of appreciation and respect. Of course, it's easy to see how these arrangements could backfire if one partner became a gloating winner or a sore loser. Feeling like you've been defeated can leave you wanting to get even, creating a downward competitive spiral that degrades to a *lose–lose* relationship.[21]

Power is the distinguishing characteristic in win–lose problem solving because it is necessary to defeat an opponent to get what one wants. The most obvious kind of power is physical. Some parents threaten their children with warnings such as "Stop misbehaving or I'll send you to your room." Adults who use physical power to deal with each other usually aren't so blunt, but the legal system is the implied threat. "Follow the rules or we'll lock you up."

Real or implied force isn't the only kind of power used in conflicts. People who rely on authority of many types engage in win–lose methods without ever threatening physical coercion. In most jobs, supervisors have the authority to assign working hours, job promotions, and desirable or undesirable tasks—and, of course, to fire an unsatisfactory employee. Teachers can use the power of grades to coerce students to act in desired ways. Even the usually admired democratic system of majority rule is a win–lose method of resolving conflicts. However fair it may seem, with this system one group is satisfied and the other is defeated.

The dark side of competition is that it often breeds aggression.[22] Sometimes aggression is obvious, but at other times it can be more subtle. To understand how, read on.

Direct Aggression **Direct aggression** occurs when a communicator expresses a criticism or demand that threatens the face of the person at whom it is directed. Communication researcher Dominic Infante identified several types of direct aggression: character attacks, competence attacks, physical appearance attacks, maledictions (wishing the other ill fortune), teasing, ridicule, threats, swearing, and nonverbal emblems.[23]

Direct aggression can severely affect the target. Recipients can feel embarrassed, inadequate, humiliated, hopeless, desperate, or depressed.[24] These results can lead to decreased effectiveness in personal relationships, on the job, and in families.[25] There is a significant connection between verbal aggression and physical aggression,[26] but even if the attacks never lead to blows, the psychological effects can be devastating. For example, siblings who were teased by a brother or sister report less satisfaction and trust than those whose relationships were relatively free of this sort of aggression,[27] and high school teams with aggressive coaches lose more games than those whose coaches are less aggressive.[28]

Passive Aggression **Passive aggression** occurs when a communicator expresses hostility in an obscure or manipulative way. As the Ethical Challenge below explains, this behavior has been termed **crazymaking**. It occurs when people have feelings of resentment, anger, or rage that they are unable or unwilling to express directly. Instead of keeping these feelings to themselves, a crazymaker sends aggressive messages in subtle, indirect ways, thus maintaining the front of kindness. This amiable façade eventually crumbles, leaving the crazymaker's victim confused and angry at having been fooled. The targets of the crazymaker can either react with aggressive behavior of their own or retreat to nurse their hurt feelings. In either case, passive aggression seldom has anything but harmful effects on a relationship.[29] In our scenario, Lucia could take a passive-aggressive approach to Paul's desire to keep their workouts exclusive by showing up late to run just to annoy him. Paul could become passive aggressive by agreeing to include Lucia's friends, then pouring on the speed and leaving them behind.

ETHICAL CHALLENGE

DIRTY FIGHTING WITH CRAZYMAKERS

Psychologist George Bach uses the term *crazymakers* to describe passive-aggressive behavior. His term reflects the insidious nature of indirect aggression, which can confuse and anger a victim who may not even be aware of being victimized. Although a case can be made for using all of the other approaches to conflict described in this chapter, it is difficult to find a justification for passive-aggressive crazymaking.

The following categories represent a nonexhaustive list of crazymaking. They are presented here as a warning for potential victims, who might choose to use perception checking, "I" language, assertion, or other communication strategies to explore whether the user has a complaint that can be addressed in a more constructive manner.

The Avoider. Avoiders refuse to fight. When a conflict arises, they leave, fall asleep, pretend to be busy at work, or keep from facing the problem in some other way. Because avoiders won't fight back, this strategy can frustrate the person who wants to address an issue.

The Pseudoaccommodator. Pseudoaccommodators pretend to give in and then continue to act in the same way.

The Guiltmaker. Instead of expressing dissatisfaction directly, guiltmakers try to make others feel responsible for causing pain. A guiltmaker's favorite line is "It's okay; don't worry about me . . ." accompanied by a big sigh.

The Mind Reader. Instead of allowing their partners to express feelings honestly, mind readers go into character analysis, explaining what the partner really means or what's wrong with the partner. By behaving this way, mind readers refuse to handle their own feelings and leave no room for their partners to express themselves.

The Trapper. Trappers play an especially dirty trick by setting up a desired behavior for their partners and then, when it's met, attacking the very behavior they requested. An example of this technique is for the trapper to say, "Let's be totally honest with each other" and then attack the partner's self-disclosure.

ETHICAL CHALLENGE (*Continued*)

The Crisis Tickler. Crisis ticklers almost bring what's bothering them to the surface but never quite come out and express themselves. Instead of admitting concern about the finances, they innocently ask, "Gee, how much did that cost?", dropping a rather obvious hint but never really dealing with the crisis.

The Gunnysacker. These people don't share complaints as they arise. Instead, they put their resentments into a psychological gunnysack, which bulges after awhile with both large and small gripes. Then, when the sack is about to burst, the gunnysacker pours out all the pent-up aggressions on the overwhelmed and unsuspecting victim.

The Trivial Tyrannizer. Instead of honestly sharing their resentments, trivial tyrannizers do things they know will get their partners' goat—leaving dirty dishes in the sink, clipping fingernails in bed, belching out loud, turning up the television too loud, and so on.

The Beltliner. Everyone has a psychological "beltline," and below it are subjects too sensitive to be approached without damaging the relationship. Beltlines may have to do with physical characteristics, intelligence, past behavior, or deeply ingrained personality traits that a person is trying to overcome. In an attempt to "get even" or hurt their partners, beltliners will use intimate knowledge to hit below the belt, knowing it will hurt.

The Joker. Because they are afraid to face conflicts squarely, jokers kid around when their partners want to be serious, thus blocking the expression of important feelings.

The Withholder. Instead of expressing their anger honestly and directly, withholders punish their partners by keeping back something—courtesy, affection, good cooking, humor, sex. As you can imagine, this is likely to build up even greater resentments in the relationship.

The Benedict Arnold. These characters get back at their partners by sabotage, by failing to defend them from attackers, and even by encouraging ridicule or disregard from outside the relationship.

COMPROMISING (PARTIAL LOSE–LOSE)

Compromising gives both people at least some of what they want, although both sacrifice part of their goals. People usually settle for a compromise when it seems that partial satisfaction is the best they can hope for. In the case of Paul and Lucia, they could strike a halfway deal by alternating workouts with and without her friends. Unlike avoidance, where both parties lose because they don't address their problem, compromisers actually negotiate a solution that gives them some of what they want, but it also leaves everybody losing something.

Compromise may be better than losing everything, but there are times when this approach hardly seems ideal. One observer has asked why it is that if someone says, "I will compromise my values," we view the action unfavorably, yet we have favorable views of parties in a conflict who compromise to reach a solution.[30] Although compromises may be the best obtainable result in some conflicts, it's important to realize that both people in a conflict can often work together to find much better solutions. In such cases, *compromise* is a negative word.

Most of us are surrounded by the results of bad compromises. Consider a common example: the conflict between one person's desire to smoke cigarettes and another's need for clean air. The win–lose outcomes of this issue are obvious: Either the smoker abstains or the nonsmoker gets polluted lungs—neither option is very satisfying. But a compromise in which the smoker gets to enjoy only a rare cigarette or must retreat outdoors and in which the nonsmoker still must inhale some fumes or feel like an ogre is hardly better. Both sides have lost a considerable amount of both comfort and goodwill. Of course, the costs involved in other compromises are even greater. For example, if a divorced couple compromises on child care by haggling over custody and then grudgingly agrees to split the time with their children, it's hard to say that anybody has won.

Some compromises do leave both parties satisfied. You and the seller might settle on a price for a used car that is between what the seller was asking and what you wanted to pay. Although neither of you got everything you wanted, the outcome would still leave both of you satisfied. Likewise, you and your companion might agree to see a film that is the second choice for both of you in order to spend an evening together. As long as everyone is satisfied with an outcome, compromise can be an effective way to resolve conflicts. When compromises are satisfying and successful, it might be more accurate to categorize them as the final style we'll discuss: collaborating.

PAYING IT FORWARD PAYS BACK

What makes a leader effective? Sound decision making, knowing how to manage people, taking charge, and inspiring others to achieve goals are a few of the qualities.

But helping others develop their full potential is also an integral part of successful leadership. According to one study, it pays off not only for emerging talent but for those who invest time in cultivating them. High-potential talent who were themselves mentored, coached, or sponsored to advance in their careers are more likely to "pay it forward" by developing the next generation of leaders, according to a report by the business research firm Catalyst.

Paying it forward pays back: It benefits not only protégés but leads to career advancement and compensation growth for those providing the assistance—$25,075 in additional compensation over one three-year period, according to the report. Why? It may be that developing other talent creates more visibility and a following within the organization for the high-potentials who are doing the developing, which leads to greater reward and recognition for the extra effort.

Women, the report finds, are even more likely than men to develop other talent. Sixty-five percent of women who received career development support are now developing new talent, compared to 56 percent of men, and 73 percent of the women developing new talent are developing women, compared to only 30 percent of men. This

finding helps bust the oft-cited "Queen Bee" myth that women are reluctant to provide career support to other women and may even actively undermine each other.

"Paying it forward is an essential element of being an outstanding leader," said Ilene Lang, president and CEO of the research firm. "It benefits everyone involved—it's a virtuous circle that leads to more of the same."

Catalyst

Javier Pierini/Jupiter Images

http://www.catalyst.org/press-release/207/paying-it-forward-pays-back-for-business-leaders

COLLABORATING (WIN–WIN)

Collaborating seeks *win–win* solutions to conflict. Collaborators show a high degree of concern for both themselves and others. Rather than trying to solve problems "my way" or "your way," their focus is on "our way." In the best case, collaborating can lead to a win–win outcome: Everybody gets what they want.

If Lucia and Paul were to collaborate, they might determine that the best way for both of them to get what they want is to continue their one-on-one workouts but invite Lucia's friends to join in for a few miles at the end of each run. They might schedule other, less-challenging workouts that include the friends. Or they might find other ways to get together with Lucia's friends that are fun for both of them.

The goal of collaboration is to find a solution that satisfies the needs of everyone involved. Not only do the partners avoid trying to win at the other's expense, but they also believe that by working together it is possible to find a solution that goes beyond a mere compromise and allows all parties to reach their goals. Consider a few examples.

- A newly married husband and wife find themselves arguing frequently over their budget. The husband enjoys buying impractical and enjoyable items for himself and for the house, whereas the wife fears that such purchases will ruin their carefully constructed budget. Their solution is to set aside a small amount of money each month for "fun purchases." The amount is small enough to be affordable yet gives the husband a chance to escape from their spartan lifestyle. The wife is satisfied with the arrangement because the luxury money is now a budget category by itself, which gets rid of the out-of-control feeling that comes when her husband makes unexpected purchases. The plan works so well that the couple continues to use it even after their income rises, increasing the amount devoted to luxuries.
- Marta, a store manager, hates the task of rescheduling employee work shifts to accommodate their social and family needs. She and her staff develop an arrangement in which employees arrange schedule swaps on their own and notify her in writing after they are made.
- Wendy and Kathy are roommates who have different study habits. Wendy likes to do her work in the evenings, which leaves her days free for other things, but Kathy feels that nighttime is party time. The solution they worked out is that Monday through Wednesday evenings Wendy studies at her boyfriend's place while Kathy does anything she wants; Thursday and Sunday, Kathy agrees to keep things quiet around the house.

The point here isn't that these solutions are the correct ones for everybody with similar problems. The win–win method doesn't work that way. Different people might have found other solutions that suit them better. Collaboration gives you a way of creatively finding just the right answer for your unique problem—and that answer might be one that neither party thought of or expected before collaborating. By generating win–win solutions, you can create a way of resolving your conflicts that everyone can live with comfortably. Later in this chapter, you'll learn a specific process for arriving at collaborative solutions to problems.

WHICH STYLE TO USE?

Collaborating might seem like the ideal approach to solving problems, but it's an oversimplification to imagine that there is a single "best" way.[31] Generally speaking, win–win approaches are preferable to win–lose and lose–lose solutions. But we've already seen that there are times when avoiding, accommodating, competing, and compromising are appropriate. Table 11.1 lists some of the issues to consider when deciding which style to use when facing a conflict. As you decide which approach to use, consider the following factors.

1. **The relationship.** When someone else clearly has more power than you, accommodating may be the best approach. If the boss tells you to fill that order "Now!", it may be smart to do so without comment. A more assertive response ("I'm still tied up with the job you gave me yesterday") might be reasonable, but it could also cost you your job.

2. **The situation.** Different situations call for different conflict styles. After haggling over the price of a car for hours, it might be best to compromise by simply splitting the difference. In other cases, though, it may be a matter of principle for you to "stick to your guns" and attempt to get what you believe is right.

3. **The other person.** Win–win is a fine ideal, but sometimes the other person isn't willing or able to collaborate. You probably know communicators who are so competitive that they put winning on even minor issues ahead of the well-being of your relationship. In such cases, your efforts to collaborate may have a low chance of success.

4. **Your goals.** Sometimes your overriding concern may be to calm down an enraged or upset person. Accommodating an outburst from your crotchety and sick neighbor, for example, is probably better than standing up for yourself and triggering a stroke. In still other cases, your moral principles might compel an aggressive statement even though it might not get you what you originally sought: "I've had enough of your racist jokes. I've tried to explain why they're so offensive, but you obviously haven't listened. I'm leaving!"

TABLE 11.1 FACTORS TO CONSIDER WHEN CHOOSING THE MOST APPROPRIATE CONFLICT STYLE

AVOIDING (LOSE–LOSE)	ACCOMMODATING (LOSE–WIN)	COMPETING (WIN–LOSE)	COMPROMISING (PARTIAL LOSE–LOSE)	COLLABORATING (WIN–WIN)
When the issue is of little importance	When you discover you are wrong	When there is not enough time to seek a win–win outcome	To achieve quick, temporary solutions to complex problems	When the issue is too important for a compromise
When the costs of confrontation outweigh the benefits	When the issue is more important to the other person than it is to you	When the issue is not important enough to negotiate at length	When opponents are strongly committed to mutually exclusive goals	When a long-term relationship between you and the other person is important
To cool down and gain perspective	When the long-term cost of winning isn't worth the short-term gain	When the other person is not willing to cooperate	When the issues are moderately important but not enough for a stalemate	To merge insights with someone who has a different perspective on the problem
	To build up credits for later conflicts	When you are convinced that your position is right and necessary	As a backup mode when collaboration doesn't work	To develop a relationship by showing commitment to the concerns of both parties
	To let others learn by making their own mistakes	To protect yourself against a person who takes advantage of noncompetitive people	To come up with creative and unique solutions to problems	

© Cengage Learning

SELF-ASSESSMENT

Your Conflict Style

Assess your conflict style by taking the self-test at the website for the Peace and Justice Support Network of the Mennonite Church. This instrument measures the way you deal with issues in both "calm" and "stormy" situations. Visit CengageBrain .com to access the Speech Communication CourseMate for *Looking Out/ Looking In* to find the link to this site. 🖥

Conflict in Relational Systems

So far we have focused on individual conflict styles. Even though the style you choose in a conflict is important, your style isn't the only factor that will determine how a conflict unfolds. In reality, conflict is relational: Its character usually is determined by the way the parties interact with each other.[32] You might, for example, be determined to handle a conflict with your neighbor assertively only to be driven to aggression by his uncooperative nature—or even to avoidance by his physical threats. Likewise, you might plan to hint to a professor that you are bothered by her apparent indifference but wind up discussing the matter in an open, assertive way in reaction to her constructive response.

Examples like these suggest that conflict doesn't depend on just individual choice. Rather, it depends on how the partners interact. When two or more people are in a long-term relationship, they develop their own **relational conflict style**—a pattern of managing disagreements. The mutual influence that parties have on each other is so powerful that it can overcome the disposition to handle conflicts in the manner that comes most easily to one or the other.[33] As we will soon see, some relational conflict styles are constructive, whereas others can make life miserable and threaten relationships.

COMPLEMENTARY, SYMMETRICAL, AND PARALLEL STYLES

Partners in interpersonal relationships—and impersonal ones, too—can use one of three styles to manage their conflicts. In relationships with a **complementary conflict style**, the partners use different but mutually reinforcing behaviors. In a **symmetrical conflict style**, both partners use the same behaviors. In a **parallel conflict style**, both partners shift between complementary and symmetrical patterns from one issue to another. Table 11.2 illustrates how the same conflict can unfold in very different ways, depending on whether the partners' communication is symmetrical or complementary. A parallel style would alternate between these two patterns, depending on the situation.

Research shows that a complementary *fight–flight* style is common in many unhappy marriages. One partner—most commonly the wife—addresses the conflict directly, whereas the other—usually the husband—withdraws.[34] It's easy to see how this pattern can lead to a cycle of increasing hostility and isolation, because each partner punctuates the conflict differently, blaming the other for making matters worse. "I withdraw because she's so critical," a husband might say. The wife wouldn't organize the sequence in the same way, however. "I criticize because he withdraws" would be her perception.

Complementary styles aren't the only ones that can lead to problems. Some distressed marriages suffer from destructively symmetrical communication. If both partners treat each other with matching hostility, one threat or insult leads to another in an escalatory spiral. If the partners both withdraw from each other instead of facing their problems, a de-escalatory spiral results in which the satisfaction and vitality ebb from the relationship, leaving it a shell of its former self.

As Table 11.2 shows, complementary and symmetrical behaviors can produce both "good" and "bad" results. If the complementary behaviors are positive, then a positive spiral results and the conflict stands a good chance of being resolved. This is the case in Example 2 in Table 11.2, where the boss is open to hearing the employee's concerns, listening willingly as the employee talks. Here, a complementary talk–listen pattern works well.

Symmetrical styles can also be beneficial. The clearest example of constructive symmetry occurs when both parties communicate assertively, listening to each other's concerns and working together to resolve them. The potential for this sort of solution occurs in Example 3, in the parent teenager conflict. With enough mutual respect and careful listening, both the parents and their teenager can understand one another's concerns and very possibly find a way to give both parties what they want.

TABLE 11.2 COMPLEMENTARY AND SYMMETRICAL CONFLICT STYLES

SITUATION	COMPLEMENTARY STYLES	SYMMETRICAL STYLES
EXAMPLE 1: Wife upset because husband is spending little time at home.	Wife complains; husband withdraws, spending even less time at home. *(Destructive)*	Wife complains. Husband responds angrily and defensively. *(Destructive)*
EXAMPLE 2: Female employee offended when male boss calls her "sweetie."	Employee objects to boss, explaining her reasons for being offended. Boss apologizes for his unintentional insult. *(Constructive)*	Employee maliciously "jokes" about boss at company party. *(Destructive)*
EXAMPLE 3: Parents uncomfortable with teenager's new friends.	Parents express concerns. Teen dismisses them, saying "There's nothing to worry about." *(Destructive)*	Teen expresses discomfort with parents' protectiveness. Parents and teen negotiate a mutually agreeable solution. *(Constructive)*

© Cengage Learning

PAUSE AND REFLECT

UNDERSTANDING CONFLICT STYLES

You can gain a clearer idea of how conflict styles differ by completing the following exercise.

1. Join a partner and choose one of the following conflicts to work on. If you prefer, you may substitute a conflict of your own.
   a. Roommates disagree about the noise level in their apartment.
   b. Parents want their college sophomore son or daughter to stay home for the winter vacation. The son or daughter wants to travel with friends.
   c. One person in a couple wants to spend free time socializing with friends. The other wants to stay at home together.
2. Role play the conflict four times, reflecting each of the following styles:
   a. Complementary (constructive)
   b. Complementary (destructive)
   c. Symmetrical (constructive)
   d. Symmetrical (destructive)
3. After experiencing each style, determine which of them characterizes the way conflict is managed in one of your interpersonal relationships. Are you satisfied with this approach? If not, describe what style would be more appropriate.

 You can complete this activity by visiting CengageBrain.com to access the Speech Communication CourseMate for *Looking Out/ Looking In*, and, if requested, email your responses to your instructor.

DESTRUCTIVE CONFLICT PATTERNS: THE FOUR HORSEMEN

Some conflict styles are so destructive that they are almost guaranteed to wreak havoc on relationships. These toxic forms of communication include what John Gottman calls "The Four Horsemen of the Apocalypse."[35]

Gottman has gathered decades of data about newlywed couples and their communication patterns. By observing their interactions, he has been able to predict with more than 90 percent accuracy whether the newlyweds will end up divorcing. Here are the four destructive signs he looks for:

1. **Criticism.** These are attacks on a person's character. As you read in Chapters 5 and 10, there's a significant difference between legitimate complaints about behavior phrased in descriptive "I" language ("I wish you had been on time—we're going to be late to the movie") and critical character assaults stated as evaluative "you" messages ("You're so thoughtless—you never think of anyone but yourself").

2. **Defensiveness.** As Chapter 10 explained, defensiveness is a reaction that aims to protect one's presenting self by denying responsibility ("You're crazy—I never do that") and counterattacking ("You're worse about that than I am"). Although some self-protection is understandable, problems arise when a person refuses to listen to or even acknowledge another's concerns.

3. **Contempt.** A contemptuous comment belittles and demeans. It can take the form of name-calling putdowns ("You're a real jerk") or sarcastic barbs ("Oh, *that* was brilliant"). Contempt can also be communicated nonverbally through dramatic eye rolls or disgusted sighs. (Try doing both of those at the same time and imagine how dismissive they can be.)

4. **Stonewalling.** Stonewalling occurs when one person in a relationship withdraws from the interaction, shutting down dialogue—and any chance of resolving the problem in a mutually satisfactory way. It sends a disconfirming "You don't matter" message to the other person.

Here's a brief exchange illustrating how the "four horsemen" can lead to a destructive spiral of aggression:

"You overdrew our account again—can't you do *anything* right?" (*Criticism*)

"Hey, don't blame me—you're the one who spends most of the money." (*Defensiveness*)

"At least I have better math skills than a first grader. Way to go, Einstein." (*Contempt*)

"Whatever." (*said while walking out of the room*) (*Stonewalling*)

It's easy to see how this kind of communication can be destructive in any relationship, not just a marriage. It's also easy to see how these kinds of comments can feed off each other and develop into destructive conflict rituals, as we'll discuss now.

CONFLICT RITUALS

When people have been in a relationship for some time, their communication often develops into **conflict rituals**—usually unacknowledged but very real patterns of interlocking behavior.[36] Consider the following common rituals.

- A young child interrupts her parents, demanding to be included in their conversation. At first the parents tell the child to wait, but she whines and cries until the parents find it easier to listen than to ignore the fussing.
- A couple fights. One partner leaves. The other accepts the blame for the problem and begs forgiveness. The first partner returns, and a happy reunion takes place. Soon they fight again.

- A boss flies into rage when the pressure builds at work. Recognizing this, the employees avoid him as much as possible. When the crisis is over, the boss compensates for his outbursts by being especially receptive to employee requests.
- Roommates have a blowout over housekeeping responsibilities. One roommate gives the other the "silent treatment" for several days, then begins picking up around the house without admitting being wrong.

There's nothing inherently wrong with the interaction in many rituals, especially when everybody involved accepts them as ways of managing conflict.[37] Consider the preceding examples. In the first, the little girl's whining may be the only way she can get the parents' attention. In the second, both partners might use the fighting as a way to blow off steam, and both might find that the joy of a reunion is worth the grief of the separation. In the third, the ritual might work well for the boss (as a way of releasing pressure) and for employees (as a way of getting their requests met). And in the fourth, at least the house gets cleaned—eventually.

"I'm not yelling *at* you, I'm yelling *with* you."

Rituals can cause problems, though, when they become the *only* way relational partners handle their conflicts. As you learned in Chapter 1, competent communicators have a large repertoire of behaviors, and they are able to choose the most effective response for a given situation. Relying on one ritual pattern to handle all conflicts is no more effective than using a screwdriver to handle every home repair or putting the same seasoning on every dish you cook. Conflict rituals may be familiar and comfortable, but they aren't always the best way to resolve the various conflicts that are part of any relationship.

PAUSE AND REFLECT

YOUR CONFLICT RITUALS

Describe two conflict rituals in one of your important relationships. One of your examples should consist of a positive ritual and the other of a negative ritual. For each example, explain:

1. a subject that is likely to trigger the conflict (such as, money, leisure time, affection);
2. the behavior of one partner that initiates the ritual;
3. the series of responses by both partners that follows the initiating event; and
4. how the ritual ends.

Based on your description, explain an alternative to the unsatisfying ritual, and describe how you might be able to manage the conflict in a more satisfying way.

 You can complete this activity by visiting CengageBrain.com to access the Speech Communication CourseMate for *Looking Out/ Looking In*, and, if requested, email your responses to your instructor.

Variables in Conflict Styles

By now you can see that every relational system is unique. The communication patterns in one family, business, or classroom are likely to be very different from those in any other. But along with the differences that arise in individual relationships, two powerful variables affect the way people manage conflict: gender and culture. We will now look at each variable and see how it affects how conflict is managed.

GENDER

Men and women often approach conflicts differently. Even in childhood, males are more likely to be aggressive, demanding, and competitive, whereas females are more likely to be cooperative. Studies of children from preschool to early adolescence have shown that boys try to get their way by ordering one another around: "Lie down." "Get off my steps." "Gimme your arm." By contrast, girls are more likely to make proposals for action, beginning with the verb *let's*: "Let's go find some." "Let's ask her, 'Do you have any bottles?'" "Let's move these out first."[38] Whereas boys tell each other what role to take in pretend play ("Come on, be a doctor"), girls more commonly ask each other what role they want ("Will you be the patient for a few minutes?") or make a joint proposal ("We can both be doctors"). Furthermore, boys often make demands without offering an explanation ("Look, man. I want the wire cutters right now"). By contrast, girls often give reasons for their suggestions ("We gotta clean 'em first . . . 'cause they got germs").[39]

Adolescent girls use aggression in conflicts, but their methods are usually more indirect than those of boys. Whereas teenage boys often engage in verbal showdowns, and may even engage in physical fights, teenage girls typically use gossip, backbiting, and social exclusion.[40] This is not to suggest that girls' aggression is any less destructive than boys'. The film *Mean Girls* (based on the book *Queen Bees and Wannabes*[41]) offers a vivid depiction of just how injurious these indirect assaults can be on the self-concepts and relationships of young women.

Gender differences in dealing with conflict often persist into adulthood. One survey of college students revealed that men and women viewed conflicts in contrasting ways.[42] Regardless of their cultural background, female students described men as being concerned with power and more interested in content than relational issues. Phrases used to describe male conflict styles included: "The most important thing to males in conflict is their egos." "Men don't worry about feelings." "Men are more direct." By contrast, women were described as being more concerned with maintaining the relationship during a conflict. Phrases used to describe female conflict styles included: "Women are better listeners." "Women try to solve problems without controlling the other person." "Females are more concerned with others' feelings."

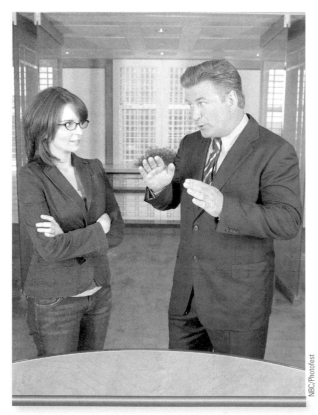

Tina Fey plays head writer Liz Lemon on the TV show *30 Rock*. Her conflict-management style typically involves placating, accommodating, cajoling, and harmonizing as she tries to get characters with large egos to work together. (See the TV summary at the end of this chapter.)

These sorts of differences don't mean that men are incapable of forming good relationships. Instead, their notions of what makes a good relationship are different. For some men, friendship and aggression aren't mutually exclusive. In fact, many strong male relationships are built around competition (e.g., at work or in athletics). Women can be competitive, too, but they also are more likely to use logical reasoning and bargaining than aggression.[43] And when it comes to avoidance, women tend to view withdrawal from conflict as more injurious to a relationship than do men (which is why women are more likely to say, "We *have* to talk about this").[44]

A look at the entire body of research on gender and conflict suggests that the differences in how the two sexes handle conflict are relatively small and sometimes different from the stereotypical picture of aggressive men and passive women.[45] It would appear that people may *think* there are greater differences in male and female ways of handling conflicts than there actually are.[46] People who assume that men are aggressive and women are accommodating may notice behavior that fits these stereotypes ("See how much he bosses her around. A typical man!"). On the other hand, behavior that doesn't fit these stereotypes (accommodating men, pushy women) goes unnoticed.

While men and women do have characteristically different conflict styles, the reasons may have little to do with gender. The situation at hand has a greater influence on shaping the way a person handles conflict.[47] For example, both men and women are more likely to respond aggressively when attacked by the other person. (Recall the discussion of defensive spirals in Chapter 10.) In fact, researchers exploring how married couples handle disagreements found that the importance of gender in determining conflict style is "dwarfed" by the behavior of the other person.[48]

What, then, can we conclude about the influence of gender on conflict? Research has demonstrated that there are, indeed, some small but measurable differences in the two sexes. But, although men and women may have characteristically different conflict styles, the individual style of each communicator—regardless of gender—and the nature of the relationship are more important than gender in shaping the way he or she handles conflict.

CULTURE

The way in which people manage conflict varies tremendously depending on their cultural background. The straight-talking, assertive approach that characterizes many North Americans is not the universal norm.[49]

Perhaps the most important cultural factor in shaping attitudes toward conflict is an orientation toward individualism or collectivism.[50] In individualistic cultures like the United States, the goals, rights, and needs of each person are considered important, and most people would agree that it is an individual's right to stand up for him- or herself. By contrast, collectivist cultures (more common in Latin America and Asia) consider the concerns of the group to be more important than those of any individual. In these cultures, the kind of assertive behavior that might seem perfectly appropriate to a North American would be regarded as rude and insensitive.

Another factor that affects conflict is the difference between high- and low-context cultural styles.[51] Recall from our discussion in Chapter 6 that low-context cultures like the United States place a premium on being direct and literal. By contrast, high-context cultures like Japan value self-restraint and avoiding confrontation. For this reason, what seems like "beating around the bush" to an American would seem polite to an Asian. In Japan, for example, even a simple request like "Close the door" would be too straightforward.[52] A more indirect statement such as "It is somewhat cold today" would be more appropriate. Perhaps more important, Japanese are reluctant to say "No" to a request. A more likely answer would be "Let me think about it for awhile," which anyone familiar with Japanese culture would recognize as a refusal.

When indirect communication is a cultural norm, it is unreasonable to expect more straightforward approaches to succeed. When people from different cultures face a conflict, their habitual communication patterns may not mesh smoothly. The challenge faced by an American husband and his Taiwanese wife illustrates this sort of problem. The husband would try to confront his wife verbally and directly (as is typical in the United States), leading her to either become defensive or withdraw completely from the discussion. She, on the other hand, would attempt to indicate her displeasure by changes in mood and eye contact (typical of Chinese culture) that were either not noticed or were uninterpretable by her husband. Thus, neither "his way" nor "her way" was working, and they could not see any realistic way to "compromise."[53]

It isn't necessary to look only at Asia to encounter cultural differences in conflict. Americans visiting Greece, for example, often think they are witnessing an argument when they are overhearing a friendly conversation.[54] A comparative study of American and Italian nursery-school children showed that one of the Italian childrens' favorite pastimes was a kind of heated debating that Italians call *discussione* but that Americans would call *arguing*. Likewise, research has shown that the conversations of working-class Jewish people of eastern European origin used arguments as a means of being sociable.

Even within the United States, the ethnic background of communicators plays a role in their ideas about conflict. When members of a group of Mexican American and Anglo American college students were asked about their views regarding conflict, some important differences emerged.[55] For example, Anglo Americans seemed more willing to accept conflict as a natural part of relationships, whereas Mexican Americans were more concerned about the short- and long-term dangers of conflict. It's not surprising that people from collectivist, high-context cultures emphasizing harmony tend to handle conflicts in less-direct ways. With differences like these, it's easy to imagine how two friends, lovers, or fellow workers from different cultural backgrounds might have trouble finding a conflict style that is comfortable for them both.

Despite these differences, it's important to realize that culture isn't the only factor that influences the way people approach conflict or how they behave when they disagree. Some research suggests that our approach to conflict may be part of our biological makeup.[56] Furthermore, scholarship suggests that a person's self-concept is more powerful than his or her culture in determining conflict style.[57] For example, an assertive person raised in an environment that downplays conflict is still likely to be more aggressive than an unassertive person who grew up in a culture where conflicts are common. You might handle conflicts calmly in a job where rationality and civility are the norm but shriek like a banshee at home if that's the way you and a relational partner handle conflicts. Finally, the way each of us deals with conflict is a matter of personal choice. We can choose to follow unproductive patterns or we can choose more constructive approaches.

 ## Constructive Conflict Skills

The collaborative, win–win conflict style described earlier in this chapter has many advantages over win–lose and lose–lose approaches. Why, then, is it so rarely used? There are three reasons. The first is lack of awareness. Some people are so used to competition that they mistakenly think that winning requires them to defeat their "opponent."

Even when they know better, there is another factor that prevents many people from seeking win–win solutions. Conflicts are often emotional affairs in which people react combatively without stopping to think of better alternatives. Because this kind

LOOKING AT DIVERSITY

Marilynn Jorgensen: Conflict and Cultural Style

Marilynn Jorgensen conducts workshops around the world for Six Seconds, an international organization that helps clients improve performance by dealing effectively with the emotion-related side of work.

I work with clients from a variety of cultures. At one recent workshop in Dubai, we hosted attendees from countries including Sweden, India, Brazil, Germany, China, Iraq, Iran, Israel, South Africa, Poland, Japan, and Canada.

People all around the world have the same powerful emotions: pride, concern, fear, and anger. But the way they *deal* with those emotions is often shaped by their background. For example, some cultures deal with conflict head on, while others handle it much more indirectly. Some cultures are open to change, while others resist changing communication patterns that have been practiced for centuries.

When working with people from a different background, a lot of behavior can seem odd, disturbing, or even offensive. "Why won't she speak up?" one person might think. "Why is he so loud and aggressive?" the other might wonder.

A major part of my training is to help people from different cultural backgrounds slow down when they encounter others with different conflict styles so they don't overreact. Instead of responding before you understand the other person's personal style and cultural background, it's better to adopt an attitude of curiosity. Be an observer and a listener: Try to find out how that stranger feels, and why. Get in the habit of saying "Please help me understand . . . ." Being genuinely interested in the other person is a sign of respect, and that's very disarming. Once you understand why people are behaving as they do, their "strange" actions usually make more sense.

Techniques like these won't resolve every conflict, but they can make working together more smooth, satisfying, and productive.

of emotional reflex prevents constructive solutions, it's often necessary to stop yourself from speaking out aggressively during a conflict and starting an escalating spiral of defensiveness. The time-honored advice of "stopping and counting to ten" applies here. After you've thought about the matter a bit, you'll be able to *act* constructively instead of *reacting* in a way that's likely to produce a lose–lose outcome.

A third reason win–win solutions are rare is that they require the other person's cooperation. It's difficult to negotiate constructively with someone who insists on trying to defeat you. In this case, use your best persuasive skills to explain that by working together you can find a solution that satisfies both of you.

COLLABORATIVE PROBLEM SOLVING

Despite these challenges, it is definitely possible to become better at resolving conflicts. In the following pages, we will outline a method to increase your chances of being able to handle your conflicts in a collaborative, win–win manner. In a longitudinal study following one hundred couples who had conflict skills training, researchers found that the method *works* for couples willing to focus on improving their relationships.[58] As you read the following steps, try to imagine yourself applying them to a problem that's bothering you now.

Identify Your Problem and Unmet Needs Before you speak out, it's important to realize that the problem that is causing conflict is yours. Whether you want to return an unsatisfactory piece of merchandise, complain to noisy neighbors because your sleep is being disturbed by their barking dog, or request a change in working conditions from your employer, the problem is yours. Why? Because in each case you are the person who "owns" the problem—the one who is dissatisfied. You are the one who has paid for the unsatisfactory merchandise; the merchant who sold it to you has the use of your good money. You are the one who is losing sleep as a result of your neighbors' dog; they are content to go on as before. You are the one who is unhappy with your working conditions, not your employer.

Realizing that the problem is yours will make a big difference when the time comes to approach the other party. Instead of feeling and acting in an evaluative way, you'll be more likely to state your problem in a descriptive way, which will not only be more accurate but also reduce the chance of a defensive reaction.

After you realize that the problem is yours, the next step is to identify the unmet needs that make you dissatisfied. For instance, in the barking dog example, your need may be to get some sleep or to study without interruptions. In the case of a friend who teases you in public, your need would probably be to avoid embarrassment.

Sometimes the task of identifying your needs isn't as simple as it first seems. Behind the apparent content of an issue is often a relational need. Consider this example: A friend hasn't returned some money you lent long ago. Your apparent need in this situation might be to get the money back. But a little thought will probably show that this isn't the only, or even the main, thing you want. Even if you were rolling in money, you'd probably want the loan repaid because of a more important need: *to avoid feeling victimized by your friend's taking advantage of you.*

As you'll soon see, the ability to identify your real needs plays a key role in solving interpersonal problems. For now, the point to remember is that before you voice your problem to your partner, you ought to be clear about which of your needs aren't being met.

Make a Date Destructive fights often start because the initiator confronts a partner who isn't ready. There are many times when a person isn't in the right frame of mind to face a conflict, perhaps owing to fatigue, being in too much of a hurry to take the necessary time, being upset over another problem, or not feeling well. At times like these, it's unfair to "jump" a person without notice and expect to get full attention for your problem. If you do persist, you'll probably have an ugly fight on your hands.

After you have a clear idea of the problem, approach your partner with a request to try to solve it. For example, "Something's been bothering me. Can we talk about it?" If the answer is "Yes," then you're ready to go further. If it isn't the right time to confront your partner, then find a time that's agreeable to both of you.

Describe Your Problem and Needs Your partner can't possibly meet your needs without knowing why you're upset and what you want. Therefore, it's up to you to describe your problem as specifically as possible. The best way to deliver a complete, accurate message is to use the assertive message format discussed in Chapter 10. Notice how well this approach works in the following examples:

"Is this a good time to have a big fight?"

Example 1

"I have a problem. It's about your leaving dirty clothes around the house after I've told you how much it bothers me *(behavior)*. It's a problem because I have to run around like crazy and pick things up whenever guests come, which is no fun at all *(consequence)*. I'm starting to think that either you're not paying attention to my requests or you're trying to drive me crazy *(thoughts)*, and either way I'm getting more and more resentful *(feeling)*. I'd like to find some way to have a neat place without my having to be a maid or a nag."

Example 2

"I have a problem. When you drop by without calling ahead, and I'm studying *(behavior)*, I don't know whether to visit or ask you to leave *(thought)*. Either way, I get uncomfortable *(feeling)*, and it seems like whatever I do, I lose: Either I have to put you off or get behind in my work *(consequences)*. I'd like to find a way to get my studying done and still socialize with you *(intention)*."

Example 3

"Something is bothering me. When you tell me you love me and yet spend almost all your free time with your other friends *(behavior)*, I wonder whether you mean it *(thought)*. I get insecure *(feeling)*, and then I start acting moody *(consequence)*. I need some way of finding out for sure how you feel about me *(intention)*."

After stating your problem and describing what you need, it's important to make sure that your partner has understood what you've said. As you can remember from the discussion of listening in Chapter 7, there's a good chance—especially in a stressful conflict—that your words will be misinterpreted.

It's usually unrealistic to insist that your partner paraphrase your statement, and fortunately there are more tactful and subtle ways to make sure that you've been understood. For instance, you might try saying, "I'm not sure I expressed myself very well just now—maybe you should tell what you heard me say so I can be sure I got it right." In any case, be absolutely sure that your partner understands your whole message before going any further. Legitimate agreements are tough enough without getting upset about a conflict that doesn't even exist.

Consider Your Partner's Point of View After you have made your position clear, it's time to find out what your partner needs to feel satisfied about this issue. There are two reasons why it's important to discover your partner's needs. First, it's fair: Your partner has just as much right as you to feel satisfied, and if you expect help in meeting your needs, then it's reasonable that you behave in the same way. But in addition to fairness, there's another practical reason for concerning yourself with what your partner wants. Just as an unhappy partner will make it hard for you to become satisfied, a happy partner will be more likely to cooperate in letting you reach your goals. Thus, it's in your own self-interest to discover and meet your partner's needs.

You can learn about your partner's needs simply by asking about them: "Now I've told you what I want and why. Tell me what you need to feel okay about this." After your partner begins to talk, your job is to use the listening skills discussed earlier in this book to make sure that you understand.

Negotiate a Solution Now that you and your partner understand each other's needs, the goal becomes finding a way to meet them. This is done by developing as many potential solutions as possible and then evaluating them to decide which one best meets everyone's needs. Probably the best description of the win–win approach was written by Thomas Gordon in his book *Parent Effectiveness Training*.[59] The following steps are a modification of this approach.

1. Identify and define the conflict. We've discussed identifying and defining the conflict in the preceding pages. These consist of discovering each person's problem and needs, setting the stage for meeting all of them.

2. Generate a number of possible solutions. In this step, the partners work together to think of as many means as possible to reach their stated ends. The key concept here is quantity: It's important to generate as many ideas as you can think of without worrying about which ones are good or bad. Write down every thought that comes up, no matter how unworkable. Sometimes a far-fetched idea will lead to a more workable one.

3. Evaluate the alternative solutions. This is the time to talk about which solutions will work and which ones won't. It's important for all parties to be honest about their willingness to accept an idea. If a solution is going to work, everyone involved has to support it.

4. Decide on the best solution. Now that you've looked at all the alternatives, pick the one that looks best to everyone. It's important to be sure that everybody understands the solution and is willing to try it out. Remember that your decision doesn't have to be final, but it should look potentially successful.

Follow Up the Solution You can't be sure that the solution will work until you try it. After you've tested it for awhile, it's a good idea to set aside some time to talk over its progress. You may find that you need to make some changes or even rethink the whole problem. The idea is to keep on top of the problem, and to keep using creativity to solve it.

You can expect and prepare for a certain amount of resistance from the other person. When a step doesn't meet with success, simply move back and repeat the preceding ones as necessary.

Win–win solutions aren't always possible. There will be times when even the best-intentioned people simply won't be able to find a way of meeting all their needs. In times like these, the process of negotiation has to include some compromises, but even then the preceding steps haven't been wasted. The genuine desire to learn what the other person wants and to try to satisfy those wants will build a climate of goodwill that can help you find the best solution to the present problem and also improve your relationship in the future.

CONSTRUCTIVE CONFLICT: QUESTIONS AND ANSWERS

After learning about win–win negotiating, people often express doubts about how well it can work. "It sounds like a good idea," they say, "but. . . ." Four questions arise more than any others, and they deserve answers.

Isn't the Win–Win Approach Too Good To Be True? Research shows that seeking mutual benefit is not just a good idea—it actually works. In fact, the win–win approach produces better results than a win–lose approach. In a series of experiments, researchers presented subjects with a bargaining situation called "the prisoner's dilemma," in which they could choose either to cooperate or betray a confederate.[60] There are three types of outcomes in prisoner's dilemma: One partner can win big by betraying a confederate, both can win by cooperating, or

NBC/Photofest

On reality shows that feature house hunting and home design, couples try to create a more ideal lifestyle—although they often have conflicting ideas about what constitutes "ideal." Experts often help partners find win–win solutions to their disagreements.

both can lose by betraying each other. Although cynics might assume that the most effective strategy is to betray a partner (a win–lose approach), researchers found that cooperation is actually the best hard-nosed strategy. Players who demonstrated their willingness to support the other person and not hold grudges did better than those using a more competitive approach.

Isn't the Win–Win Approach Too Elaborate? The win–win approach is detailed and highly structured. In everyday life, you may rarely use every step. Sometimes the problem at hand won't justify the effort, and at other times you and your partner might not need to be so deliberate to take care of the problem. Nonetheless, while learning to use the approach, try to follow all of the steps carefully. After you have become familiar with and skillful at using them all, you will be able to use whichever ones prove necessary in a given situation. For important issues, you are likely to find that every step of the win–win approach is important. If this process seems time consuming, just consider the time and energy that will likely be required if you don't resolve the issue at hand.

Isn't Win–Win Negotiating Too Rational? Frustrated readers often complain that the win–win approach is so sensible that only a saint could use it successfully. "Sometimes I'm so angry that I don't care about being supportive or empathetic or anything else," they say. "I just want to blow my top!"

At times like this, you might need to temporarily remove yourself from the situation so you don't say or do something you'll later regret. You might feel better confiding in a third party. Or you might blow off steam with physical exercise. There are even cases when an understanding partner might allow you to have what has been called a "Vesuvius"—an uncontrolled, spontaneous explosion. Before you blow your top, though, be sure that your partner understands what you're doing and realizes that whatever you say doesn't call for a response. Your partner should let you rant and rave for as long as you want without getting defensive or "tying in." Then when your eruption subsides, you can take steps to work through whatever still troubles you.

Is It Possible to Change Others? Readers often agree that win–win problem solving would be terrific—if everyone had read *Looking Out/Looking In* and understood the method. "How can I get the other person to cooperate?" the question goes. Though you won't always be able to gain your partner's cooperation, a good job of selling can do the trick most of the time. The key lies in showing that it's in your partner's self-interest to work together with you: "Look, if we can't settle this, we'll both feel miserable. But if we can find an answer, think how much better off we'll be." Notice that this sort of explanation projects both the favorable consequences of cooperating and the unfavorable consequences of competing.

You can also boost the odds of getting your partner's cooperation by modeling the communication skills described in this book. You've read that defense-arousing behavior is reciprocal, but so is supportive communication. If you can listen sincerely, avoid evaluative attacks, and empathize with your partner's concerns, for example, there's a good chance that you'll get the same kind of behavior in return. And even if your cooperative attitude doesn't succeed, you'll gain self-respect from knowing that at least you behaved honorably and constructively.

IN REAL LIFE

Win–Win Problem Solving

It is 7:15 A.M. on a typical school day. Chris enters the kitchen and finds the sink full of dirty dishes. It was her roommate Terry's turn to do them. She sighs in disgust and begins to clean up, slamming pots and pans.

Terry: Can't you be a little more quiet? I don't have a class till 10:00, and I want to catch up on sleep.

Chris: *(Expressing her aggression indirectly in a sarcastic tone of voice)* Sorry to bother you. I was cleaning up last night's dinner dishes.

Terry: *(Misses the message)* Well, I wish you'd do it a little more quietly. I was up late studying last night, and I'm beat.

Chris: *(Decides to communicate her irritation more directly, if aggressively)* Well, if you'd done the dishes last night, I wouldn't have had to wash them now.

Terry: *(Finally realizes that Chris is mad at her, responds defensively)* I was going to do them when I got up. I've got two midterms this week, and I was studying until midnight last night. What's more important—grades or a spotless kitchen?

Chris: *(Perpetuating the growing defensive spiral)* I've got classes, too, you know. But that doesn't mean we have to live like pigs!

Terry: *(Angrily)* Forget it. If it's such a big deal, I'll never leave another dirty dish!

Chris and Terry avoid each other as they get ready for school. During the day, Chris realizes that attacking Terry will only make matters worse. She decides on a more constructive approach that evening.

Chris: That wasn't much fun this morning. Want to talk about it?

Terry: I suppose so. But I'm going out to study with Kim and Alisa in a few minutes.

Chris: *(Realizing that it's important to talk at a good time)* If you have to leave soon, let's not get into it now. How about talking when you get back?

Terry: Okay, if I'm not too tired.

Chris: Or we could talk tomorrow before class.

Terry: Okay.

Later that evening Terry and Chris continue their conversation.

Chris: *(Defines the issue as her problem by using the assertive message format)* I hated to start the day with a fight. But I also hate having to do the dishes when it's not my turn *(behavior)*. It doesn't seem fair for me to do my job and yours *(interpretation)*, and that's why I got so mad *(feeling)* and nagged at you *(consequence)*.

Terry: But I was studying! You know how much I have to do. It's not like I was partying.

Chris: *(Avoids attacking Terry by sincerely agreeing with the facts and explaining further why she was upset)* I know. It wasn't just doing the dishes that got me upset. It seems like there have been a lot of times when I've done your jobs and mine, too.

Terry: *(Defensively)* Like when?

Chris: *(Gives specific descriptions of Terry's behavior)* Well, this was the third time this week that I've done the dishes when it's your turn, and I can think of a couple of times lately when I've had to clean up your stuff before people came over.

Terry: I don't see why it's such a big deal. If you just leave the stuff there, I'll clean it up.

Chris: *(Still trying to explain herself, she continues to use "I" language)* I know you would. I guess it's harder for me to put up with a messy place than it is for you.

Terry: Yeah. If you'd just relax, living together would be a lot easier!

Chris: *(Resenting Terry's judgmental accusation that the problem is all hers)* Hey, wait a second! Don't blame the whole thing on me. It's just that we have different standards. It looks to you like I'm too hung up on keeping the place clean . . .

Terry: Right.

Chris: . . . and if we do it your way, then I'd be giving up. I'd have to either live with the place messier than I like it or clean everything up myself. Then I'd get mad at you, and things would be pretty tense around here. *(Describes the unpleasant consequences of not solving the problem in a mutually satisfactory way)*

Terry: I suppose so.

Chris: We need to figure out how to take care of the apartment in a way that we can both live with. *(Describes the broad outline of a win–win solution)*

Terry: Yeah.

Chris: So what could we do?

Terry: *(Sounding resigned)* Look, from now on I'll just do the dishes right away. It isn't worth arguing about.

Chris: Sure it is. If you're sore, the apartment may be clean, but it won't be worth it.

Terry: *(Skeptically)* Okay, what do you suggest?

Chris: Well, I'm not sure. You don't want the pressure of having to clean up right away, and I don't want to have to do my jobs and yours, too. Right?

Terry: Yeah. *(Still sounding skeptical)* So what are we going to do—hire a housekeeper to clean up?

Chris: *(Refusing to let Terry sidetrack the discussion)* That would be great if we could afford it. How about using paper plates? That would make cleaning up from meals easier.

Terry: Yeah, but there would still be pots and pans.

Chris: Well, it's not a perfect fix, but it might help a little. *(Goes on to suggest other ideas)* How about cooking meals that don't take a lot of work to clean up—maybe more salads and less fried stuff that sticks to pans? That would be a better diet, too.

Terry: Yeah. I do hate to scrub crusty frying pans. But that doesn't do anything about your wanting the living room picked up all the time, and I bet I still wouldn't keep the kitchen as clean as you like it. Keeping the place super clean just isn't as big a deal to me as it is for you.

Chris: That's true, and I don't want to have to nag you! *(Clarifies the end she's seeking)* You know, it's not really cleaning up that bothers me. It's doing more than my share of work. I wonder if there's a way I could be responsible for keeping the kitchen

clean and picking up if you could do something else to keep the workload even.

Terry: Are you serious? I'd love to get out of doing the dishes! You mean you'd do them . . . and keep the place picked up . . . if I did something else?

Chris: As long as the work was equal and you really did your jobs without me having to remind you.

Terry: What kind of work would you want me to do?

Chris: How about cleaning up the bathroom?

Terry: Forget it. That's worse than doing the dishes.

Chris: Okay. How about cooking?

Terry: That might work, but then we'd have to eat together all the time. It's nice to do our own cooking when we want to. It's more flexible that way.

Chris: Okay. But what about shopping? I hate the time it takes, and you don't mind it that much, do you?

Terry: You mean shop for groceries? You'd trade that for cleaning the kitchen?

Chris: Sure. And picking up the living room. It takes an hour each time we shop, and we make two trips every week. Doing the dishes would be much quicker.

Terry: All right!

The plan didn't work perfectly. At first Terry put off shopping until all the food was gone, and Chris took advantage by asking Terry to run other errands during her shopping trips. But their new arrangement proved much more successful than the old arrangement. The apartment was cleaner and the workload more even, which satisfied Chris. Terry was less frequently the object of Chris's nagging, and she had no kitchen chores, which made her happier. Just as important, the relationship between Chris and Terry was more comfortable—thanks to win–win problem solving.

Communication Scenarios

 To watch and analyze a video related to this feature and this topic, visit CengageBrain .com to access the Speech Communication CourseMate for Looking Out/Looking In.

SUMMARY

Conflict is a fact of life in every interpersonal relationship. The way in which conflicts are handled plays a major role in the quality of a relationship. When managed constructively, conflicts can lead to stronger and more satisfying interaction; but when they are handled poorly, relationships will suffer.

Communicators can respond to conflicts in a variety of ways: avoiding, accommodating, competing, compromising, or collaborating. Each approach can be justified in certain circumstances. The way a conflict is handled is not always the choice of a single person: The parties influence each other as they develop a relational conflict style. This style may be complementary, symmetrical, or parallel, and it can involve constructive or destructive rituals. The "four horsemen" of criticism, defensiveness, contempt, and stonewalling are counterproductive ways to communicate during conflict.

Besides being shaped by the relationship, a conflict style is also shaped by a person's gender and cultural background. In most circumstances a collaborative, win–win outcome is the ideal, and it can be achieved by following the guidelines on pages 364–368.

KEY TERMS

accommodating (350)
avoiding (349)
collaborating (356)
competing (351)
complementary conflict style (358)
compromising (354)
conflict (346)

conflict ritual (360)
crazymaking (353)
direct aggression (352)
parallel conflict style (358)
passive aggression (353)
relational conflict style (358)
symmetrical conflict style (358)

ONLINE RESOURCES

Now that you have read this chapter, visit CengageBrain.com to access the Speech Communication CourseMate for *Looking Out/Looking In* for quick access to the electronic resources that accompany this text. Your CourseMate offers:

- **Study tools** that will help you assess your learning and prepare for exams (*digital glossary, key term flash cards, interactive quizzes*).
- **Activities and assignments** that will help you hone your knowledge, understand how theory and research applies to your own life (*Self-Assessment, Pause and Reflect*), consider ethical challenges in interpersonal communication (*Ethical Challenge*), and build your interpersonal communication skills throughout the course (*Skill Builder*). If requested, you can submit your answers to your instructor.
- **Media resources** that will allow you to watch and critique videos of interpersonal communication situations (*In Real Life, interpersonal video simulations, and interactive video activities*).
- In addition to interactive teaching and learning tools, CourseMate includes an **interactive eBook.** Take notes, highlight, search, and interact with embedded media specific to *Looking Out/Looking In*.

SEARCH TERMS

When searching online databases to research topics in this chapter, use the following terms (along with this chapter's key terms) to maximize the chances of finding useful information:

competition	negotiation
conflict management	problem solving
culture conflict	social conflict
interpersonal conflict	

FILM AND TELEVISION

You can see the communication principles described in this chapter portrayed in the following films and television programs.

THE NATURE OF CONFLICT

The Hunger Games (2012) Rated PG-13

In this tale set in a dystopian future, adolescents are pitted against each other in a large forested arena and told to fight to the death. These "games" are staged by a malevolent government and have all of the features of conflict noted in this chapter: an expressed struggle, incompatible goals (one person's win means death for the others), scarce resources (particularly food and water), and interdependence (the contestants' fates are linked).

Katniss Everdeen (Jennifer Lawrence) doesn't like the win–lose nature of the game, especially since the default winner is the government that holds this contest for entertainment and a means of control. She form alliances with other participants, and ultimately she emerges with what some might call a compromise—but most would regard as the only possible win–win solution.

CONFLICT STYLES

Win Win (2011) Rated R

FOX Searchlight/The Kobal Collection

At the outset of this movie, everyone seems to be losing. Mike (Paul Giamatti) is a down-on-his-luck lawyer and the coach of a winless high school wrestling team. Kyle (Alex Shaffer) is a runaway teenager who feels abandoned by his mother, Cindy (Melanie Lynskey). She's a recovering drug addict who has recently lost her boyfriend. And her elderly father, Leo (Burt Young), has been placed in assisted care against his will.

But each of these people has resources the others need, such as money, athletic talent, a house, and a home. At first, the characters try to gain these resources from each other through aggression or compromise. Ultimately, they recognize their interdependence and strive for mutually satisfying solutions. As its title suggests, the movie demonstrates that collaborative problem solving can help turn losing into winning.

30 Rock (2006–) Rated TV-PG

TV comedy writer Liz Lemon (Tina Fey) and her boss Jack Donaghy (Alec Baldwin) are "frienemies." They obviously value their relationship, yet they constantly struggle over both work-related issues and personal matters. Jack obviously enjoys provoking Liz—not out of malice, but because he relishes conflict. By contrast, Liz is an accommodator: Keeping everyone around her happy is her goal, and she'll punish herself to keep the peace.

Many episodes of this popular series revolve around the complications that arise from Jack's confrontational style and Liz's obsession with harmony. The results are amusing, but in real life each character would profit from adopting some of the other's approach.

CULTURE AND CONFLICT
Borat (2008) Rated R

This over-the-top mockumentary chronicles the misadventures of Kazakhstani TV personality Borat Sagdiyev (Sacha Baron Cohen) as he travels across the United States to learn about American culture. One critic aptly described Borat as the "village idiot for the global village." His efforts to reach out to Americans are stunningly incompetent and offensive. Viewers who appreciate the satire in this film recognize that the outrageousness pictured is less about Borat's shocking but fictional prejudices than about how those attitudes go unchallenged by the Americans he meets.

CHAPTER ELEVEN

Managing Interpersonal Conflicts

CHAPTER OUTLINE

Use this outline to take notes as you read the chapter in the text and/or as your instructor lectures in class.

I.   **THE NATURE OF CONFLICT**
   A. **Conflict Defined**
     1. Expressed struggle
     2. Perceived incompatible goals
     3. Perceived scarce resources
     4. Interdependence
     5. Interference from the other party
   B. **Conflict Is Natural**
   C. **Conflict Can Be Beneficial**

II. **CONFLICT STYLES**
   A. **Avoiding (Lose–Lose)**
   B. **Accommodating (Lose–Win)**
   C. **Competing (Win–Lose, May Degenerate to Lose–Lose)**
     1. Direct aggression
     2. Passive aggression
   D. **Compromising (Partial Lose–Lose)**
   E. **Collaborating (Win–Win)**
   F. **Which Style to Use?**
     1. Relationship
     2. Situation

3. Other person
4. Your goals

III. **CONFLICT IN RELATIONAL SYSTEMS**

    A. **Complementary, Symmetrical, and Parallel Styles**
       1. Complementary
       2. Symmetrical
       3. Parallel

    B. **Destructive Conflict Patterns: The Four Horsemen**
       1. Criticism
       2. Defensiveness
       3. Contempt
       4. Stonewalling

    C. **Conflict Rituals**
       1. Patterns of behavior
       2. Problematic if the *only* pattern

IV. **VARIABLES IN CONFLICT STYLES**

    A. **Gender**
       1. Socialization
       2. Situation

    B. **Culture**
       1. Individualism versus collectivism
       2. Low-context versus high-context
       3. Indirect and direct
       4. Ethnic background
       5. Personal choice

V. **CONSTRUCTIVE CONFLICT SKILLS**

    A. **Collaborative Problem Solving**
       1. Identify your unmet needs
       2. Make a date

3. Describe your problem and needs
   a. Clear messages
   b. Listening and paraphrasing
4. Consider your partner's point of view
5. Negotiate a solution
   a. Identify and define the conflict
   b. Generate a number of possible solutions
   c. Evaluate the alternative solutions
   d. Decide on the best solution
6. Follow up the solution

B. **Constructive Conflict: Questions and Answers**
1. Isn't Win–Win too good to be true?
2. Isn't Win–Win too elaborate?
3. Isn't Win–Win negotiating too rational?
4. Is it possible to change others?

_____

_____

_____

_____

_____

_____

_____

_____

_____

_____

_____

_____

KEY TERMS

accommodating
avoiding
collaborating
competing
complementary conflict style
compromising
conflict

conflict ritual
crazymaking
direct aggression
parallel conflict style
passive aggression
relational conflict style
symmetrical conflict style

ACTIVITIES

11.1 UNDERSTANDING CONFLICT STYLES

LEARNING OBJECTIVES

- Identify the relational conflict styles, patterns of behavior, and conflict rituals that define a given relationship.

INSTRUCTIONS

1. For each of the conflicts described below, write responses illustrating the five types of conflict styles.
2. Describe the probable consequences of each style.

_____

1. Your dad wants and expects you to spend every Thanksgiving with his whole extended family. You and some close friends who don't have large families want to get away for those four days and do something different. Your dad already arranged your transportation home.

Avoiding (lose–lose) response _____

_____

Probable consequences _____

_____

Accommodating (lose–win) response _____

_____

Probable consequences _____

_____

Competing (win–lose) response _____

_____

Probable consequences _____

_____

Compromising (partial lose–lose) response _____

_____

Probable consequences _____

_____

Collaborating (win–win) response _____

_____

Probable consequences _____

_____

2. A fan behind you at a ballgame toots a loud air horn every time the home team makes any progress. The noise is spoiling your enjoyment of the game.

Avoiding (lose–lose) response_____

_____

Probable consequences _____

_____

Accommodating (lose–win) response _____

_____

Probable consequences _____

_____

Competing (win–lose) response _____

_____

Probable consequences _____

_____

Compromising (partial lose–lose) response _____

_____

Probable consequences _____

_____

Collaborating (win–win) response _____

_____

Probable consequences _____

_____

3. Earlier in the day you asked your roommate to stop by the store and pick up snacks for a party you are both hosting this evening. Your roommate arrives home without the food.

Avoiding (lose–lose) response _____

_____

Probable consequences _____

_____

Accommodating (lose–win) response _____

_____

Probable consequences _____

_____

Competing (win–lose) response _____

_____

Probable consequences _____

_____

Compromising (partial lose–lose) response _____

_____

Probable consequences _____

_____

Collaborating (win–win) response _____

_____

Probable consequences _____

_____

4. You and Marc share a cubicle and a computer at work and you are both responsible
    for the same amount and type of work. Marc arrives a few minutes earlier than you
    and stays on the computer for several hours, then begins his non-computer work.
    You would be able to work more efficiently if you had some time on the computer
    early in the day.

    Avoiding (lose–lose) response_____

    _____

    Probable consequences _____

    _____

    Accommodating (lose–win) response _____

    _____

    Probable consequences _____

    _____

    Competing (win–lose) response _____

    _____

    Probable consequences _____

    _____

    Compromising (partial lose–lose) response _____

    _____

Probable consequences _____

_____

Collaborating (win–win) response _____

_____

Probable consequences _____

_____

5. You and your spouse have to make a decision about your five-year olds' schooling. You believe strongly in supporting public schools and having children attend the neighborhood school. Your husband believes he didn't get a good education in public school and since you can afford to, you should send your child to private school.

Avoiding (lose–lose) response _____

_____

Probable consequences _____

_____

Accommodating (lose–win) response _____

_____

Probable consequences _____

_____

Competing (win–lose) response _____

_____

Probable consequences _____

_____

Compromising (partial lose–lose) response _____

_____

Probable consequences _____

_____

Collaborating (win–win) response _____

_____

Probable consequences _____

_____

_____

What styles are easiest to use with family? With friends? At work? With strangers? Why?

_____

_____

_____

11.2 YOUR CONFLICT STYLES

LEARNING OBJECTIVES

- Identify the conflicts in your important relationships and how satisfied you are with the way they have been handled.
- Describe your personal conflict styles, evaluate their effectiveness, and suggest alternatives as appropriate.

INSTRUCTIONS

1. Use the following form to record three conflicts that occur in your life that you are comfortable analyzing.
2. For each, describe your behavior, show how it fits the definition of conflict, classify your conflict style, and describe the consequences of your behaviors.
3. Summarize your findings in the space provided.

Class _____   Name_____

INCIDENT	YOUR BEHAVIOR	HOW IT MEETS THE DEFINITION OF CONFLICT Expressed struggle Perceived compatible goals Perceived scarce resources Interdependence Interference of other party	YOUR CONFLICT STYLE Avoid Accommodate Compete Compromise Collaborate	CONSEQUENCES
EXAMPLE *My friend accused me of being too negative about the possibility of finding rewarding, well-paying work.*	*I became defensive and angrily denied his claim. In turn I accused him of being too critical.*	*This was clearly an expressed struggle and I perceived interference in my choice of jobs. Possibly we both perceived scarcity of the reward of feeling good about ourselves.*	*Competing*	*After arguing for some time, we left each other, both feeling upset. I'm sure we'll both feel awkward around each other for a while.*
1.				
2.				
3.				

Class _____   Name_____

CONCLUSIONS

1. Are there any individuals or issues that repeatedly arouse conflicts?

   _____

   _____

2. What conflict style(s) do you most commonly use? Do you use different styles with different people or in different situations? Why or why not?

   _____

   _____

   _____

   _____

3. You can go online to http://jeffcoweb.jeffco.k12.co.us/high/wotc/confli1.htm and take a brief quiz about your approaches to conflict (are you a turtle, shark, bear, fox, or owl?). How do these animals compare to the labels used in the text?

   _____

   _____

   _____

   _____

4. Choose one or more of the conflicts you described in which you did not use a collaborative style and explain how you could have used a collaborative style. Predict what would have happened.

_____

_____

_____

_____

5. Are you satisfied with your usual way(s) of approaching conflict? Why or why not?

_____

_____

_____

_____

11.3 THE END VERSUS THE MEANS

LEARNING OBJECTIVES

- Identify the conflicts in your important relationships and how satisfied you are with the way they have been handled.
- Describe your personal conflict styles, evaluate their effectiveness, and suggest alternatives as appropriate.
- To distinguish the ends from the means in a personal conflict.

INSTRUCTIONS

1. In each of the conflict situations on the next page, identify the <u>ends</u> each party seems to be seeking. There may be ends that the relationship shares as well as individual ends for each of the parties involved. Ends in a conflict are the overall, general (often relational) goals that the dyad has.
2. Brainstorm a series of possible <u>means</u> that could achieve each person's (and the relationship's) ends. Means are the many possible ways to reach the end state.
3. Record conflict situations of your own, identifying ends and means.

CONFLICT SITUATION	SHARED ENDS	SPEAKER'S ENDS	OTHER'S ENDS	POSSIBLE MEANS
EXAMPLE *My friend wants me to visit her in Washington and meet her family. I'd like to visit, but it would cost a lot, and I'd rather save the money for something else.*	*We both want to maintain the affection in the relationship. We both want one another to know we are important to one another and that we care about one another and our families.*	*I want to spend as little money as possible while still letting my friend know how important she is to me. I don't want to lose her friendship.*	*She wants to show her family what a good friend I am and have some companionship while she has to stay in Washington.*	*She/her family sends me money to go to Washington. We share the cost. I combine whatever else I want to do with a short trip to Washington. We arrange for the family to meet me when they next come to our city. My friend comes back with her sister or mother to spend time with me.*

Class _____   Name_____

CONFLICT SITUATION	SHARED ENDS	SPEAKER'S ENDS	OTHER'S ENDS	POSSIBLE MEANS
1. My roommate wants a friend (whom I dislike) to sublease a room in our apartment.				
2. I'm dating a person who's of a different race than I am, and my family thinks this is a mistake.				
3. My older sister thinks that I'll turn into an alcoholic when I have a few beers (there are a few alcohol problems in our family). I tell her not to worry, but she won't get off my case.				
4. My mom keeps asking me about my grades and nagging me on the issue of my boyfriend. She thinks I'm going to make the same mistakes she did.				

CONFLICT SITUATION	SHARED ENDS	SPEAKER'S ENDS	OTHER'S ENDS	POSSIBLE MEANS
5. Some people in my office listen to country music all day. I've got nothing against it, but it gets old. I'd like more variety.				
6. (Your example)				

11.4 WIN–WIN PROBLEM SOLVING

LEARNING OBJECTIVES

- Identify the relational conflict styles, patterns of behavior, and conflict rituals that define a given relationship.
- Demonstrate how you could use the win–win approach in a given conflict.

INSTRUCTIONS

1. Follow the instructions below as a guide to dealing with an interpersonal conflict facing you now.
2. After completing the win–win steps, record your conclusions in the space provided.

Step 1: Identify your unmet needs (i.e., the situation, the person(s) involved, the history, etc.).

_____

_____

Step 2: Make a date. (Choose a time and place that will make it easiest for both parties to work constructively on the issue.)

_____

Step 3: Describe your problem and needs (behavior, interpretation, feeling, consequence, intention). Avoid proposing specific means or solutions at this point.

_____

_____

Step 3A: Ask your partner to show that s/he understands you (paraphrase or perception check).

_____

_____

Step 3B: Solicit your partner's point of view/clear message (behavior, interpretation, feeling, consequence, intention).

_____

_____

_____

Step 4: Clarify your partner's point of view (paraphrase or perception check as necessary).

_____

_____

Step 5: Negotiate a solution.

a. Restate the needs of both parties (what both have in common).

_____

_____

b. Work together to generate a number of possible solutions that might satisfy these needs. Don't criticize any suggestions here!

_____

_____

_____

_____

_____

_____

c. Evaluate the solutions you just listed, considering the advantages and problems of each. If you think of any new solutions, record them above.

_____

_____

_____

d. Decide on the best solution, listing it here.

_____

Step 6: Follow up the solution. Set a trial period, and then plan to meet with your partner and see if your agreement is satisfying both your needs. If not, return to step 3 and use this procedure to refine your solution.

_____

_____

CONCLUSIONS

In what ways is this procedure similar to or different from the way in which you usually deal with interpersonal conflicts?

_____

_____

_____

Was the outcome of your problem-solving session different from what it might have been if you had communicated in your usual style? How?

_____

_____

_____

In what ways can you use the no-lose methods in your interpersonal conflicts? With whom? On what issues? What kinds of behavior will be especially important?

_____

_____

_____

What concerns or hesitations do you have about using the win–win approach? Why?

_____

_____

_____

11.5 MEDIATED MESSAGES—CONFLICT MANAGEMENT

LEARNING OBJECTIVES

- Identify the conflicts in your important relationships and how satisfied you are with the way they have been handled.
- To manage conflict in mediated contexts.

INSTRUCTIONS

Discuss each of the questions below in your group. Prepare written answers for your instructor, or be prepared to contribute to a large group discussion, comparing your experiences with those of others in your class.

1. In your experience, does conflict occur more rapidly or less rapidly in mediated contexts (e.g., email, instant messaging/chat, telephone)?

   _____

   _____

   _____

2. Describe how mediated communication channels might help or hinder the brainstorming process (an important aspect of win–win problem solving). Would the level of emotion involved make a difference? Why or why not?

   _____

   _____

   _____

3. Describe gender and/or cultural differences in conflict management that might occur in mediated contexts.

   _____

   _____

   _____

4. Describe whether, in your experience, certain mediated contexts tend to promote the use of particular conflict styles and whether or not conflict is easier or harder to manage using particular mediated channels.

_____

_____

_____

11.6 CONFLICT MANAGEMENT

LEARNING OBJECTIVES

- Identify the relational conflict styles, patterns of behavior, and conflict rituals that define a given relationship.

INSTRUCTIONS

Use the case below and the discussion questions that follow to discuss the variety of communication issues involved in effective communication. Make notes on this page, add other pages on your own, or prepare a group report/analysis based on your discussion. Add your own experiences to individualize the analysis.

CASE

Klaus and Drew have been roommates for two years, and they have had very few problems. But this term Klaus has a difficult and early class schedule, and he has taken on more hours at work to make ends meet. Drew's parents support him completely and he has a very light schedule this term. Klaus and Drew's friends continue to come to their house to party, and Drew is very irritated with Klaus because he's always studying and is a big bore all of a sudden. Klaus thinks Drew is a spoiled brat and insensitive to his needs. Neither Klaus nor Drew has said anything at this point.

1. Should Klaus and Drew bring this conflict out in the open? Would airing their differences be beneficial or harmful to the relationship?

_____

_____

2. What are the unmet needs of Klaus and Drew in this situation? Should they keep those unmet needs to themselves and use an avoidance style or should they use one of the other personal conflict styles?

_____

_____

_____

3. Evaluate the potential of the win–win problem-solving method to solve this situation.

_____

_____

Class _____   Name_____

11.7 ASSESSING YOUR CONFLICT STYLE

LEARNING OBJECTIVES

- Identify the conflicts in your important relationships and how satisfied you are with the way they have been handled.
- Describe your personal conflict styles, evaluate their effectiveness, and suggest alternatives as appropriate.

INSTRUCTIONS

Describe three conflicts that you have been in that did not have a successful resolution for you. Identify your conflict style in each and then describe what you could have done differently in this conflict.

Conflict 1 Description:

_____

_____

_____

Conflict Style: _____

What you would have done differently?

_____

_____

_____

Conflict 2 Description:

_____

_____

_____

Class _____   Name_____

Conflict Style: _____

What you would have done differently?

_____

_____

_____

Conflict 3 Description:

_____

_____

_____

Conflict Style: _____

What you would have done differently?

_____

_____

_____

11.8 REPAIRING RELATIONSHIPS AFTER CONFLICT

LEARNING OBJECTIVES

- Describe the possible strategies for repairing a given relational transgression.
- Identify the content and relational dimensions of communication in a given transaction.

INSTRUCTIONS

1. Consider the various situations listed below.
2. Identify the type of transgression for each set of categories (columns 2 and 3) and give your reasons for classifying it as you do.
3. Evaluate the options for repair along with the reasons you'd make the choice you do.
4. Record and analyze relational situations after conflict from your experience, your observations, films, or books.

SITUATION	TYPE OF TRANSGRESSION	IMPACT OF TRANSGRESSION	STRATEGIES FOR REPAIR
1. Your sibling works for the same company you do. You were applying for a promotion and really wanted the job. Unknown to you, your sibling also applied and got the job.			

SITUATION	TYPE OF TRANSGRESSION	IMPACT OF TRANSGRESSION	STRATEGIES FOR REPAIR
2. You and your (friend/partner/ roommate—you choose) make plans to travel to Mexico together next summer. Each of you agrees to ask for the same weeks of vacation and sign up for the same flights. You request your time off, pay for your flights, and mentally prepare for the trip. Five weeks before the trip, the other person tells you he/she has decided not to "waste" a week of vacation in Mexico.			

Class _____   Name_____

STUDY GUIDE

CHECK YOUR UNDERSTANDING

TRUE/FALSE

Mark the statements below as true or false. Correct statements that are false on the lines below to create a true statement.

_____   1. Gender and culture rarely have an impact on the types and styles of conflict.

_____   2. Partners of self-silencers experience more frustration and discomfort when dealing with the avoiding partner.

_____   3. It is best to adopt the attitude of curiosity when encountering a conflict with someone from another culture.

_____   4. Effective communication during conflicts can actually keep good relationships strong.

_____   5. Conflicts can never be constructive.

_____   6. Passive aggressive styles can be seen as a type of competing.

_____   7. Competing is clearly superior to other conflict styles to get what you want.

_____   8. Crazymaking is just another name for passive aggression.

_____   9. "It takes two to tango"—in conflict, as in dancing, men and women behave in totally similar ways.

_____ 10. The first step in win–win problem solving is to make a follow-up plan.

COMPLETION

Fill in the blanks with the crazymaker terms listed below.

avoiders   pseudoaccommodators   guiltmakers   subject changers   distractors
mind readers   trivial tyrannizers   gunnysackers   beltliners   trappers

1. _____ don't respond immediately when they get angry. Instead, they let conflicts build up until they all pour out at once.

2. _____ do things they know will irritate their conflict partner rather than honestly sharing their resentments.

3. _____ engage in character analyses, explaining what the other person *really* means, instead of allowing their partners to express feelings honestly.

4. _____ set up a desired behavior for their partners and then when the behavior is met, they attack the very thing they requested.

5. _____ refuse to fight by leaving, falling asleep, or pretending to be busy.

6. _____ try to make their partners feel responsible for causing their pain even though they won't come right out and say what they feel or want.

7. _____ refuse to face up to a conflict either by giving in or by pretending that there's nothing at all wrong.

8. _____ use intimate knowledge of their partners to get them "where it hurts."

9. _____ attack other parts of their partner's life rather than express their feelings about the object of their dissatisfaction.

10. _____ escape facing up to aggression by shifting the conversation whenever it approaches an area of conflict.

MULTIPLE CHOICE

Match the terms below with their definitions.

_____   1. win–lose

_____   2. indirect communication

_____   3. "Vesuvius"

_____   4. conflict style

_____   5. passive aggression

a. an indirect expression of aggression, delivered in a way that allows the sender to maintain a façade of kindness
b. an oblique way of expressing wants or needs in order to save face for the recipient
c. an uncontrolled, spontaneous explosion involved in conflict
d. an approach to conflict resolution in which one party reaches its goal at the expense of the other
e. a pattern of managing disagreements that repeats itself over time in a relationship

Choose the letter of the personal conflict style that is best illustrated by the behavior found below.

a. avoidance
b. accommodation
c. compete/direct aggression
d. compete/passive aggression
e. compromise
f. collaborate/win–win

_____   6.   Stan keeps joking around to keep us from talking about commitment.

_____   7.   "I can't believe you were so stupid as to have deleted the report."

_____   8.   Even though he wanted to go to the party, Allen stayed home with Sara rather than hear her complain.

_____   9.   Alternating bicycling and using a car, roommates are able to share expenses for only one car.

_____   10.   A smoker and nonsmoker agree that smoking on the balcony meets both their needs.

_____   11.   Rather than tell Nick about his frustration over Nick's not meeting the deadline, Howard complained to others about Nick's unreliability while maintaining a smiling front to Nick.

_____ 12. Carol wouldn't answer the phone after their disagreement because she was afraid it would be Nancy on the other end.

_____ 13. Seeing John's obvious distress, Terrell put aside his work to listen to John for a half-hour. This didn't totally meet either's needs, but did partially meet each person's needs.

_____ 14. Even though Sage could see Kham's distress, she told him she had a deadline to meet in one hour and asked if they could talk then.

_____ 15. (Sarcastically) "Oh, sure, I *loved* having dinner with your parents instead of going to the party Saturday night."

Choose the best answer for each statement below.

16. When partners use different but mutually reinforcing behaviors, they illustrate a

   a. complementary conflict style.
   b. symmetrical conflict style.
   c. parallel conflict style.
   d. supportive conflict style.

17. Research suggests that partners of "self-silencers" (people who avoid conflict) often feel
   a. relieved that they never fight.
   b. encouraged to be more honest.
   c. frustrated and uncomfortable.
   d. none of the above

18. Partners who fight but are unsuccessful at satisfying important content and relational goals have a _____ style.

   a. intimate-aggressive
   b. intimate-nonaggressive
   c. nonintimate-nonaggressive
   d. nonintimate-aggressive

19. Partners who avoid conflicts — and one another — instead of facing issues head-on have a(n) _____ style.

   a. intimate-aggressive
   b. intimate-nonaggressive
   c. nonintimate-nonaggressive
   d. nonintimate-aggressive

20. Partners who have a low amount of attacking or blaming, who confront one another either directly or indirectly, but manage to prevent issues from interfering with their relationship have a _____ style.

   a.   intimate-aggressive
   b.   intimate-nonaggressive
   c.   nonintimate-nonaggressive
   d.   nonintimate-aggressive

CHAPTER ELEVEN STUDY GUIDE ANSWERS

TRUE/FALSE

| 1. F | 3. T | 5. F | 7. F | 9. F |
| 2. T | 4. T | 6. T | 8. T | 10. F |

COMPLETION

1. gunnysackers	5. avoiders	9. distractors
2. trivial tyrannizers	6. guiltmakers	10. subject changers
3. mind readers	7. pseudoaccomodators	
4. trappers	8. beltliners	

MULTIPLE CHOICE

1. d	5. a	9. f	13. e	17. c
2. b	6. a	10. f	14. f	18. d
3. c	7. d	11. d	15. c	19. c
4. e	8. b	12. a	16. a	20. b

Endnotes

CHAPTER ONE

1. Williams, K. D. (2001). *Ostracism: The power of silence* (pp. 7–11). New York, NY: Guilford.
2. Schachter, S. (1959). *The psychology of affiliation* (pp. 9–10). Stanford, CA: Stanford University Press.
3. Gawande, A. (2009, March 30). Hellhole. *The New Yorker*, 36–45.
4. Holt-Lunstad, J., Smith, T. B., & Layton, J. B. (2010). Social relationships and mortality risk: A meta-analytic review. *PLoS Med*, 7(7), e1000316. Retrieved from http://www.plosmedicine.org/article/info%3Adoi%2F10.1371%2Fjournal.pmed.1000316
5. Three articles in the *Journal of the American Medical Association (JAMA)* 267 (January 22/29, 1992) discuss the link between psychosocial influences and coronary heart disease: Case, R. B., Moss, A. J., Case, N., McDermott, M., & Eberly, S. (1992, January 22/29). Living alone after myocardial infarction. *JAMA, 267*, 515–519; Williams, R. B., Barefoot, J. C., Califf, R. M., Haney, T. L., Saunders, W. B., Pryon, D. B., . . . & Mark, D. B. (1992, January 22/29). Prognostic importance of social and economic resources among medically treated patients with angiographically documented coronary artery disease. *JAMA, 267*, 520–524; and Ruberman, R. (1992, January 22/29). Psychosocial influences on mortality of patients with coronary heart disease. *JAMA, 267*, 559–560; Cacioppo, J. T., Ernst, J. M., Burleson, M. H., McClintock, M. K., Malarkey, W. B., Hawkley, L. C., . . . & Berntson G. G. (2000). Lonely traits and concomitant physiological processes: The MacArthur social neuroscience studies. *International Journal of Psychophysiology, 35*, 143–154.
6. Cohen, S., Doyle, W. J., Skoner, D. P., Rabin, B. S., & Gwaltney, J. M. (1997). Social ties and susceptibility to the common cold. *Journal of the American Medical Association, 277*, 1940–1944.
7. Parker-Pope, T. (2010). *For better: The science of a good marriage.* New York, NY: Dutton.
8. Ybarra, O., Burnstein, O. E., Winkielman, P., Keller, M. C., Manis, M., Chan, E., & Rodriguez, J. (2008). Mental exercising through simple socializing: Social interaction promotes general cognitive functioning. *Personality and Social Psychology Bulletin, 34*, 248–259.
9. Bell, R. A. (2010). Conversational involvement and loneliness. In M. L. Knapp & J. A. Daly (Eds.), *Interpersonal communication* (pp. 99–120). Thousand Oaks, CA: Sage.
10. Floyd, K., & Riforgiate, S. (2006). Human affection exchange: XII. Affectionate communication is related to diurnal variation in salivary free cortisol. *Western Journal of Communication, 75*, 351–368.
11. Shattuck, R. (1980). *The forbidden experiment: The story of the wild boy of Aveyron* (p. 37). New York, NY: Farrar, Straus & Giroux.
12. Rubin, R. B., Perse, E. M., & Barbato, C. A. (1988). Conceptualization and measurement of interpersonal communication motives. *Human Communication Research, 14*, 602–628.
13. Diener, E., & Seligman, M. E. P. (2002). Very happy people. *Psychological Science, 13*, 81–84.
14. Kahneman, D., Krueger, A. B., Schkade, D. A., Schwartz, N., & Stone, A. A. (2004). A daily measure. *Science, 306*, 1645.
15. Rehman, U. S., & Holtzworth-Munroe, A. (2007). A cross-cultural examination of the relation of marital communication behavior to marital satisfaction. *Journal of Family Psychology, 21*, 759–763.
16. Rochmis, J. (2000). Humans do many things. *Wired Magazine* online. Retrieved from http://www.wired.com/culture/lifestyle/news/2000/02/34387
17. McPherson, M., Smith-Lovin, L., & Brashears, M. E. (2006). Social isolation in America: Changes in core discussion networks over two decades. *American Sociological Review, 71*, 353–375; McPherson, M., Smith-Lovin, L., & Brashears, M. E. (2008). The ties that bind are fraying. *Contexts, 7*, 32–36.
18. Reis, H. T., & Gable, S. L. (2003). Toward a positive psychology of relationships. In C. L. Keyes & J. Haidt (Eds.), *Flourishing: The positive person and the good life* (pp. 129–159). Washington, DC: American Psychological Association.
19. Harper's index. (1994, December). *Harper's*, 13.
20. Mauksch, L. B., Dugdale, D. C., Dodsonb, S., & Epstein, R. (2007). Relationship, communication, and efficiency in the medical encounter. *Archives of Internal Medicine, 168*, 1387–1395; Holmes, F. (2007). If you listen, the patient will tell you the diagnosis. *International Journal of Listening, 21*, 156–161.
21. Joint Commission on the Accreditation of Healthcare Organizations. (2008). *Sentinel event statistics.* Oakbrook Terrace, IL: Author.
22. Levinson, W., Roter, D., & Mullooly J. P. (1997). Physician-patient communication: The relationship with malpractice claims among primary care physicians and surgeons. *Journal of the American Medical Association, 277*, 553–59; Rodriguez, H. P., Rodday, A. C., Marshall, R. E., Nelson, K. L., Rogers, W. H., & Safran, D. G. (2008). Relation of patients' experiences with individual physicians to malpractice risk. *International Journal for Quality in Health Care, 20*, 5–12.

23. Maslow, A. H. (1968). *Toward a psychology of being*. New York, NY: Van Nostrand Reinhold.

24. Korn, C. J., Morreale, S. P., and Boileau, D. M. (2000). Defining the field: Revisiting the ACA 1995 definition of communication studies. *Journal of the Association for Communication Administration, 29*, 40–52.

25. Mychalcewycz, P. (2009, February 12). Breaking up via text message becoming commonplace, poll finds. Retrieved from http://www.switched.com/2009/02/12/breaking-up-via-text-message-becoming-commonplace-poll-finds/

26. Shelly, R. K. (1997). Sequences and cycles in social interaction. *Small Group Research, 28*, 333–356.

27. Redmond, M. V. (1995). Interpersonal communication: Definitions and conceptual approaches. In M. V. Redmond (Ed.), *Interpersonal communication: Readings in theory and research* (pp. 4–11). Fort Worth, TX: Harcourt Brace.

28. Miller, G. R., & Steinberg, M. (1975). *Between people: A new analysis of interpersonal communication*. Chicago, IL: SRA; and Stewart, J., & Logan, C. (1998). *Together: Communicating interpersonally* (5th ed.). New York, NY: McGraw-Hill.

29. Bochner, A. P. (1984). The functions of human communication in interpersonal bonding. In C. C. Arnold & J. W. Bowers (Eds.), *Handbook of rhetorical and communication theory* (p. 550). Boston, MA: Allyn and Bacon; Trenholm, S., & Jensen, A. (1992). *Interpersonal communication* (2nd ed., pp. 27–33). Belmont, CA: Wadsworth; and Stewart, J., & D'Angelo, G. (1998). *Together: Communicating interpersonally* (5th ed., p. 5). New York, NY: McGraw-Hill.

30. Wood, J. (1997). *Relational communication* (2nd ed.). Belmont, CA: Wadsworth.

31. Gergen, K. J. (1991). *The saturated self: Dilemmas of identity in contemporary life* (p. 158). New York, NY: Basic Books.

32. Daum, M. (2009, March 7). The age of friendaholism. *Los Angeles Times*, B13.

33. Buck, R., & VanLear, C. A. (2002). Verbal and nonverbal communication: Distinguishing symbolic, spontaneous, and pseudo-spontaneous nonverbal behavior. *Journal of Communication, 52*, 522–541; and Clevenger, T., Jr. (1991). Can one not communicate? A conflict of models. *Communication Studies, 42*, 340–353; Stamp, G. H., & Knapp, M. L. (1990). The construct of intent in interpersonal communication. *Quarterly Journal of Speech, 76*, 282–299.

34. Coupland, N., Giles, H., & Wiemann, J. M. (Eds.). (1991). *Miscommunication and problematic talk*. Newbury Park, CA: Sage.

35. Dillard, J. P., Solomon, D. H., & Palmer, M. T. (1999). Structuring the concept of relational communication. *Communication Monographs, 66*, 49–65; and Watzlawick, P., Beavin, J., & Jackson, D. (1967). *Pragmatics of human communication*. New York, NY: Norton.

36. McCroskey, J. C., & Richmond, V. P. (1996). *Fundamentals of human communication: An interpersonal perspective*. Prospect Heights, IL: Waveland.

37. Sillars, A. (1998). (Mis)Understanding. In B. H. Spitzberg & W. R. Cupach (Eds.), *The dark side of close relationships* (pp. 73–102). Mahwah, NJ: Erlbaum.

38. Keysar, B. & Henley, A. S. (2002). Speakers' overestimation of their effectiveness. *Psychological Science, 13*, 207–212.

39. Wu, S. & Keysar, B. (2007). The effect of information overlap on communication effectiveness. *Cognitive Science, 31*, 169–181.

40. Powers, W. G. & Witt, P. L. (2008). Expanding the framework of communication fidelity theory. *Communication Quarterly, 56*, 247–267.

41. McCroskey, J. C., & Wheeless, L. (1976). *Introduction to human communication* (p. 5). Boston, MA: Allyn and Bacon; Cloven, D. H., & Roloff, M. E. (1991). Sense-making activities and interpersonal conflict: communicative cures for the mulling blues. *Western Journal of Speech Communication, 55*, 134–158; and Stiebel, D. (1997). *When talking makes things worse! Resolving problems when communication fails*. Kansas City, MO: Andrews McMeel.

42. Rainie, L. & Anderson, J. (2008). *The future of the Internet III: How experts see it*. Washington, DC: Pew Internet & American Life Project.

43. See pewinternet.org. The site updates regularly with current studies.

44. Anderson, J. (2010, July 2). *The future of social relations*. Washington, DC: Pew Internet & American Life Project.

45. Smith, A. (2011, November 15). *Why Americans use social media*. Washington, DC: Pew Internet & American Life Project.

46. Hampton, K. (2009, November 4). *Social isolation and new technology*. Washington, DC: Pew Internet & American Life Project.

47. Rainie, L. (2011, January 18). *The social side of the Internet*. Washington, DC: Pew Internet & American Life Project.

48. Hampton, K. (2011, June 16). *Social networking sites and our lives*. Washington, DC: Pew Internet & American Life Project.

49. Flanagin, A. J. (2005). IM online: Instant messaging use among college students. *Communication Research Reports, 22*, 175–187.

50. Boase, J., Horrigan, J. B., Wellman, B., & Rainie, L. (2006, January). *The strength of Internet ties*. Washington, DC: Pew Internet & American Life Project.

51. Dainton, M., & Aylor, B. (2002). Patterns of communication channel use in the maintenance of long-distance relationships. *Communication Research Reports, 19*, 118–129.

52. Kirkpatrick, D. (1992, March 23). Here comes the payoff from PCs. *Fortune*, 93–102.

53. Surinder, K. S., & Cooper, R. B. (2003). Exploring the core concepts of media richness theory: The impact of cue multiplicity and feedback immediacy on decision quality. *Journal of Management Information Systems, 20*, 263–299.

54. Atheunis, L. M., Valkenburg, P. M., & Peter, J. (2007). Computer-social media and interpersonal attraction: An experimental test of two explanatory hypotheses. *Cyber-Psychology & Behavior, 10*, 831–835.

55. Walther, J., & Ramirez, A. (2010). New technologies and new directions in online relating. In S. W. Smith & S. R. Wilson (Eds.), *New directions in interpersonal communication research* (pp. 264–284). Los Angeles, CA: Sage.

56. Ramirez, A., & Zhang, S. (2007). When online meets offline: The effect of modality switching on relational communication. *Communication Monographs, 74,* 287–310.

57. Watts, S. A. (2007). Evaluative feedback: perspectives on media effects. *Journal of Computer-Social Media, 12.* Retrieved from http://jcmc.indiana.edu/vol12/issue2/watts.html

58. Spitzberg, B. H. (2010). Communication competence as knowledge, skill, and impressions. In M. L. Knapp & J. A. Daly (Eds.), *Interpersonal communication* (pp. 203–210). Thousand Oaks, CA: Sage; and Wilson, S. R., & Sabee, C. M. (2003). Explicating communicative competence as a theoretical term. In J. O. Greene & B. R. Burleson (Eds.), *Handbook of communication and social interaction skills.* Mahwah, NJ: Erlbaum.

59. Ames, D. R., & Flynn, F. J. (2007). What breaks a leader: The curvilinear relation between assertiveness and leadership. *Journal of Personality and Social Psychology, 92,* 307–324.

60. Spitzberg, B. H. (1991). An examination of trait measures of interpersonal competence. *Communication Reports, 4,* 22–29.

61. Teven, J. J., Richmond, V. P., McCroskey, J. C., & McCroskey, L. L. (2010). Updating relationships between communication traits and communication competence. *Communication Research Reports, 27,* 263–270.

62. Hullman, G. A., Planisek, A., McNally, J. S., & Rubin, R. B. (2010). Competence, personality, and self-efficacy: Relationships in an undergraduate interpersonal course. *Atlantic Journal of Communication, 18,* 36–49.

63. Brown, R. F., Bylund, C. L., Gueguen, J. A., Diamond, C., Eddington, J., & Kissane, D. (2010). Developing patient-centered communication skills training for oncologists: Describing the content and efficacy of training. *Communication Education, 59,* 235–248; Hyvarinen, L., Tanskanen, P., Katajavuori, N., & Isotalus, P. (2010). A method for teaching communication in pharmacy in authentic work situations. *Communication Education, 59,* 124–145.

64. Rubin, R. B., Perse, E. M., & Barbato, C. A. (1988). Conceptualization and measurement of interpersonal communication motives. *Human Communication Research, 14,* 602–628.

65. Morreale, S. P., & Pearson, J. C. (2008). Why communication education is important: The centrality of the discipline in the 21st century. *Communication Education, 57,* 224–240.

66. Hample, D. (2005). Invitational capacity. In F. van Emeren & P. Houtlosser, *The practice of argumentation* (pp. 337–348). Amsterdam, The Netherlands: John Benjamins.

67. Braithwaite, D. O., & Eckstein, N. (2003). Reconceptualizing supportive interactions: How persons with disabilities communicatively manage assistance. *Journal of Applied Communication Research, 31,* 1–26.

68. Stephens, K. K., Houser, M. L., & Cowan, R. L. (2009). R U able to meat me: The impact of students' overly casual email messages to instructors. *Communication Education, 58,* 303–326.

69. Burleson, B. R. (2007). Constructivism: A general theory of communication skill. In B. B. Whaley & W. Samter (Eds.), *Explaining communication: Contemporary theories and exemplars* (pp. 105–128). Mahwah, NJ: Erlbaum.

70. Wackman, D. B., Miller, S., & Nunnally, E. W. (1976). *Student workbook: Increasing awareness and communication skills* (p. 6). Minneapolis, MN: Interpersonal Communication Programs.

71. Burleson, B. R., & Caplan, S. E. (1998). Cognitive complexity. In J. C. McCroskey, J. A. Daly, M. M. Martin, & M. J. Beatty (Eds.), *Communication and personality: Trait perspectives* (pp. 233–286). Creskill, NJ: Hampton Press.

72. Wiemann, J. M., & Backlund, P. M. (1980). Current theory and research in communication competence. *Review of Educational Research, 50,* 185–199; and Lakey, S. G., & Canary, D. J. (2002). Actor goal achievement and sensitivity to partner as critical factors in understanding interpersonal communication competence and conflict strategies. *Communication Monographs, 69,* 217–235; Redmond, M. V. (1985, December). The relationship between perceived communication competence and perceived empathy. *Communication Monographs, 52,* 377–382; and Redmond, M. V. (1989). The functions of empathy (decentering) in human relations. *Human Relations, 42,* 593–605.

73. Hamachek, D. E. (1987). *Encounters with the self* (2nd ed., p. 8). Fort Worth, TX: Holt, Rinehart and Winston; Daly, J. A., Vangelisti, A. L., & Daughton, S. M. (1995). The nature and correlates of conversational sensitivity. In M. V. Redmond (Ed.), *Interpersonal communication: Readings in theory and research.* Fort Worth, TX: Harcourt Brace.

74. Dunning, D. A., & Kruger, J. (1999, December). Unskilled and unaware of it: How difficulties in recognizing one's own incompetence lead to inflated self-assessments. *Journal of Personality and Social Psychology, 77,* 1121–1134.

75. Executive Office of the President, Council of Economic Advisers. (2009, July). *Preparing the workers of today for the jobs of tomorrow* (p. 10). Retrieved from http://www.whitehouse.gov/administration/eop/cea/Jobs-of-the-Future/

76. Hart, R. P., as reported by Knapp, M. L. (1984). In *Interpersonal communication and human relationships* (pp. 342–344). Boston, MA: Allyn and Bacon; Hart, R. P., & Burks, D. M. (1972). Rhetorical sensitivity and social interaction. *Speech Monographs, 39,* 75–91; and Hart, R. P., Carlson, R. E., & Eadie, W. F. (1980). Attitudes toward communication and the assessment of rhetorical sensitivity. *Communication Monographs, 47,* 1–22.

77. Kim, Y. Y. (1991). Intercultural communication competence: A systems-theoretic view. In S. Ting-Toomey & F. Korzenny (Eds.), *Cross-cultural interpersonal communication.* Newbury Park, CA: Sage; and Chen, G. M., & Sarosta, W. J. (1996). Intercultural communication competence: A synthesis. In B. R. Burleson & A. W. Kunkel (Eds.), *Communication yearbook 19.* Thousand Oaks, CA: Sage.

78. Burgoon, J. K., & Dunbar, N. E. (2000). An interactionist perspective on dominance-submission: Interpersonal dominance as a dynamic, situationally contingent social skill. *Communication Monographs, 67,* 96–121.

79. Collier, M. J. (1996). Communication competence problematics in ethnic relationships. *Communication Monographs, 63,* 314–336.

80. Chen, L. (1997). Verbal adaptive strategies in U.S. American dyadic interactions with U.S. American or East-Asian partners. *Communication Monographs, 64,* 302–323.

81. Mulac, A., Bradac, J., & Gibbons, P. (2001). Empirical support for the gender-as-culture hypothesis. *Human Communication Research, 27,* 121–152.

82. Hajek, C. & Giles, H. (2003). New directions in intercultural communication competence: The process model. In B. R. Burleson & J. O. Greene (Eds.), *Handbook of communication and social interaction skills.* Mahwah, NJ: Erlbaum; and Ting-Toomey, S., & Chung, L. C. (2005). *Understanding intercultural communication.* Los Angeles, CA: Roxbury.

83. Kalliny, M., Cruthirds, K., & Minor, M. (2006). Differences between American, Egyptian and Lebanese humor styles: Implications for international management. *International Journal of Cross-Cultural Management, 6,* 121–134.

84. Samovar, L. A., & Porter, R. E. (2004). *Communication between cultures* (5th ed.). Belmont, CA: Wadsworth.

85. Kassing, J. W. (1997). Development of the intercultural willingness to communicate scale. *Communication Research Reports, 14,* 399–407.

86. Burgoon, J. K., Berger, C. R., & Waldron, V. R. (2000). Mindfulness and interpersonal communication. *Journal of Social Issues, 56,* 105–128.

87. Berger, C. R. (1979). Beyond initial interactions: Uncertainty, understanding, and the development of interpersonal relationships. In H. Giles & R. St. Clair (Eds.), *Language and social psychology* (pp. 122–144). Oxford, England: Blackwell.

88. Carrell, L. J. (1997). Diversity in the communication curriculum: Impact on student empathy. *Communication Education, 46,* 234–244.

89. Mayer-Schönberger, V. (2011). *Delete: The virtue of forgetting in the digital age.* Princeton, NJ: Princeton University Press.

90. Sheppard, S. (2010, October). Cyber screening. *HR Management, 15.* Retrieved from http://www.hrmreport.com/article/Cyber-screening/#

91. Rosen, J. (2010, July 25). The web means the end of forgetting. *New York Times Magazine,* 30–35.

92. Bauerlein, M. (2009, September 4). Why Gen-Y Johnny can't read nonverbal cues. *Wall Street Journal.* Retrieved from http://online.wsj.com/article/SB10001424052970203863204574348493483201758.html

CHAPTER TWO

1. Baumeister, R. F. (2005). *The cultural animal: Human nature, meaning, and social life.* New York, NY: Oxford University Press; Baumeister, R. F., Campbell, J. D., Krueger, J. I., & Vohs, K. D. (2003). Does high self-esteem cause better performance, interpersonal success, happiness, or healthier lifestyles? *Psychological Science in the Public Interest, 4,* 1–44.

2. Vohs, K. D., & Heatherton, T. F. (2004). Ego threats elicits different social comparison process among high and low self-esteem people: Implications for interpersonal perceptions. *Social Cognition, 22,* 168–191.

3. Daly, J. A. (2010). Personality and interpersonal communication. In M. L. Knapp & J. A. Daly (Eds.), *Interpersonal communication* (Vol. I, pp. 41–98). Thousand Oaks, CA: Sage; Soldz, W., & Vaillant, G. E. (1999). The big five personality traits and the life course: A 45-year longitudinal study. *Journal of Research in Personality, 33,* 208–232.

4. Wright, W. (1998). *Born that way: Genes, behavior, personality.* New York, NY: Knopf.

5. Schwartz, C. E., Wright, C. I., Shin, L. M., Kagan, J., & Rauch, S. L. (2003, June 20). Inhibited and uninhibited infants 'grown up': Adult amygdalar response to novelty. *Science,* 1952–1953.

6. Cole, J. G., & McCroskey, J. C. (2000). Temperament and socio-communicative orientation. *Communication Research Reports, 17,* 105–114.

7. Heisel, A. D., McCroskey, J. C., & Richmond, V. P. (1999). Testing theoretical relationships and non-relationships of genetically based predictors: getting started with communibiology. *Communication Research Reports, 16,* 1–9.

8. Cole, J. G., & McCroskey, J. C. (2000). Temperament and socio-communicative orientation. *Communication Research Reports, 17,* 105–114.

9. Wigley, C. J. (1998). Verbal Aggressiveness. In J. C. McCroskey, J. A. Daly, M. M. Martin, & M. J. Beatty (Eds.), *Personality and communication: Trait perspectives.* New York, NY: Hampton.

10. McCroskey, J. C., Heisel, A. D., & Richmond, V. P. (2001). Eysenck's big three and communication traits: Three correlational studies. *Communication Monographs, 68,* 360–366.

11. Dweck, C. (2008). Can personality be changed? The role of beliefs in personality and change. *Current Directions in Psychological Science, 6,* 391–394.

12. Begney, S. (2008, December 1). When DNA is not destiny. *Newsweek, 152,* 14.

13. Jaret, C., Reitzes, D., & Shapkina, N. (2005). Reflected appraisals and self-esteem. *Sociological Perspectives, 48,* 403–419.

14. Salimi, S., Mirzamani, S., & Shahiri-Tabarestani, M. (2005). Association of parental self-esteem and expectations with adolescents' anxiety about career and education. *Psychological Reports, 96,* 569–578; Vangelisti, A. L., & Crumley, L. P. (1998). Reactions to messages that hurt: The influence of relational contexts. *Communication Monographs, 65,* 173–196.

15. Rill, L., Baiocchi, E., Hopper, M., Denker, K., & Olson, L. N. (2009). Exploration of the relationship between self-esteem, commitment, and verbal aggressiveness in romantic dating relationships. *Communication Reports, 22,* 102–113.

16. Leets, L., & Sunwolf. (2004). Being left out: Rejecting outsiders and communicating group boundaries in childhood and adolescent peer groups. *Journal of Applied Communication Research, 32,* 195–223.

17. Sillars, A., Koerner, A., & Fitzpatrick, M. A. (2005). Communication and understanding in parent-adolescent relationships. *Human Communication Research, 31,* 107–128.

18. Adler, T. (1992, October). Personality, like plaster, is pretty stable over time. *APA Monitor,* 18.

19. Brown, J. D., Novick, N. J., Lord, K. A., & Richards, J. M. (1992). When Gulliver travels: Social context, psychological closeness, and self-appraisals. *Journal of Personality and Social Psychology, 62,* 717–734.

20. Krcmar, M., Giles, S., & Helme, D. (2008). Understanding the process: How mediated and peer norms affect young women's body esteem. *Communication Quarterly, 56,* 111–130.

21. Myers, P. N., & Biocca, F. A. (1992). The elastic body image: The effect of television advertising and programming on body image distortions in young women. *Journal of Communication, 42*, 108–134.

22. Strong, C. M. (2005). The role of exposure to media idealized male physiques on men's body image. *Dissertation Abstracts International, 65*, 4306.

23. Haferkamp, N., & Kramer, N. C. (2011). Social comparison 2.0: Examining the effects of online profiles on social-networking sites. *Cyberpsychology, Behavior, and Social Networking, 14*(5), 309–314.

24. Grodin, D., & Lindolf, T. R. (1995). *Constructing the self in a mediated world*. Newbury Park, CA: Sage.

25. Sheldon, P. (2010). Pressure to be perfect: Influences on college students' body esteem. *Southern Communication Journal, 75*, 277–298.

26. Han, M. (2003). Body image dissatisfaction and eating disturbance among Korean college female students: Relationships to media exposure, upward comparison, and perceived reality. *Communication Studies, 34*, 65–78; Harrison, K., & Cantor, J. (1997). The relationship between media consumption and eating disorders. *Journal of Communication, 47*, 40–67.

27. Carrell, L. J., & Willmington, S. C. (1996). A comparison of self-report and performance data in assessing speaking and listening competence. *Communication Reports, 9*, 185–191.

28. Meyers, D. (1980, May). The inflated self. *Psychology Today, 14*, 16.

29. Ellison, N., Heino, R., & Gibbs, J. (2006). Managing impressions online: Self-presentation processes in the online dating environment. *Journal of Computer-Mediated Communication 11*: Article 2. Retrieved from http://jcmc.indiana.edu/vol11/issue2/ellison.html

30. Sturman, E. D., & Mongrain, M. (2008). The role of personality in defeat: A revised social rank model. *European Journal of Personality, 22*, 55–79; Brown, J. D., & Mankowski, T. A. (1993). Self-esteem, mood, and self-evaluation: Changes in mood and the way you see you. *Journal of Personality and Social Psychology, 64*, 421–430.

31. Gara, M. A., Woolfolk, R. L., Cohen, B. D., & Goldston, R. B. (1993). Perception of self and other in major depression. *Journal of Abnormal Psychology, 102*, 93–100.

32. Miller, L. C., Cooke, L. L., Tsang, J., & Morgan, F. (1992). Should I brag? Nature and impact of positive and boastful disclosures for women and men. *Human Communication Research, 18*, 364–399.

33. Bower, B. (1992, August 15). Truth aches: People who view themselves poorly may seek the 'truth' and find despair. *Science News*, 110–111; Swann, W. B. (2005). The self and identity negotiation. *Interaction Studies, 6*, 69–83.

34. Wilmot, W. W. (1995). *Relational communication* (pp. 35–54). New York, NY: McGraw-Hill.

35. Servaes, J. (1989). Cultural identity and modes of communication. In J. A. Anderson (Ed.), *Communication yearbook 12* (p. 396). Newbury Park, CA: Sage.

36. Bharti, A. (1985). The self in Hindu thought and action. In A. J. Marsella, G. Devos, & F. Hsu (Eds.), *Culture and self: Asian and Western perspectives* (pp. 185–230). New York, NY: Tavistock.

37. Bochner, S. (1994). Cross-cultural differences in the self-concept: A test of Hofstede's individualism/collectivism distinction. *Journal of Cross-Cultural Psychology, 25*, 273–283.

38. Gudykunst, W. B., & Ting-Toomey, S. (1988). *Culture and interpersonal communication*. Newbury Park, CA: Sage.

39. Samovar, L. A., & Porter, R. E. (1991). *Communication between cultures* (p. 91). Belmont, CA: Wadsworth.

40. Ting-Toomey, S. (1988). A face-negotiation theory. In Y. Kim & W. Gudykunst (Eds.), *Theory in interpersonal communication*. Newbury Park, CA: Sage.

41. Lederman, L. C. (1993). Gender and the self. In L. P. Arliss & D. J. Borisoff (Eds.), *Women and men communicating: Challenges and changes* (pp. 41–42). Fort Worth, TX: Harcourt Brace.

42. Wittels, A. (1978). *I wonder . . . A satirical study of sexist semantics*. Los Angeles, CA: Price Stern Sloan.

43. Knox, M., Funk, J., Elliott, R., & Bush, E. G. (2000). Gender differences in adolescents' possible selves. *Youth and Society, 31*, 287–309.

44. Robins, J., & Robins, R. W. (1993). A longitudinal study of consistency and change in self-esteem from early adolescence to early childhood. *Child Development, 64*, 909–923.

45. Smith, C. J., Noll, J. A., & Bryant, J. B. (1999). The effect of social context on gender self-concept. *Sex Roles, 40*, 499–512.

46. Rosenthal, R., & Rubin, D. B. (2010). Interpersonal expectancy effects: The first 345 studies. In M. L. Knapp & J. A. Daly (Eds.), *Interpersonal communication* (Vol. II, pp. 75–98). Thousand Oaks, CA: Sage.

47. Dweck, C. S. (2006). *Mindset: The new psychology of success*. New York, NY: Random House.

48. Kolligan, J., Jr. (1990). Perceived fraudulence as a dimension of perceived incompetence. In R. J. Sternberg & J. Kolligen, Jr. (Eds.), *Competence considered* (pp. 261–285). New Haven, CT: Yale University Press; Vangelisti, A. L., Corbin, S. D., Lucchetti, A. E., & Sprague, R. J. (1999). Couples' concurrent cognitions: The influence of relational satisfaction on the thoughts couples have as they converse. *Human Communication Research, 25*, 370–398.

49. Zimmerman, B., Bandura, A., & Martinez-Pons, M. (1992). Self-motivation for academic attainment: The role of self-efficacy beliefs and personal goal setting. *American Educational Research Journal, 29*, 663–676.

50. Downey, G., & Feldman, S. I. (1996). Implications of rejection sensitivity for intimate relationships. *Journal of Personality and Social Psychology, 70*, 1327–1343.

51. MacIntyre, P. D., & Thivierge, K. A. (1995). The effects of speaker personality on anticipated reactions to public speaking. *Communication Research Reports, 12*, 125–133.

52. Rosenthal, R., & Jacobson, L. (1968). *Pygmalion in the classroom*. New York, NY: Holt, Rinehart and Winston.

53. Blank, P. D. (Ed.). (1993). *Interpersonal expectations: Theory, research, and applications*. Cambridge, England: Cambridge University Press.

54. Turk, W. (2009). Let's go for self-fulfilling prophecies. *Defense AT&L, 38*, 56–59.

55. Johnson, E. (2006). *Ethics in the workplace: Tools and tactics for organizational transformation*. Thousand Oaks, CA: Sage.

56. Schlenker, B. R., & Weigold, M. F. (2010). Interpersonal processes involving impression regulation and manage-

ment. In M. L. Knapp & J. A. Daly (Eds.), *Interpersonal communication* (Vol. II, pp. 160–194). Thousand Oaks, CA: Sage.

57. Shaw, C. M., & Edwards, R. (1997). Self-concepts and self-presentations of males and females: Similarities and differences. *Communication Reports, 10,* 55–62.

58. Goffman, E. (1959). *The presentation of self in everyday life.* Garden City, NY: Doubleday; Goffman, E. (1971). *Relations in public.* New York, NY: Basic Books.

59. Stewart, J., & Logan, C. (1998). *Together: Communicating interpersonally* (5th ed., p. 120). New York, NY: McGraw-Hill.

60. Leary, M. R., & Kowalski, R. M. (1990). Impression management: A literature review and two-component model. *Psychological Bulletin, 107,* 34–47.

61. Brightman, V., Segal, A., Werther, P., & Steiner, J. (1975). Ethological study of facial expression in response to taste stimuli. *Journal of Dental Research, 54,* 141.

62. Chovil, N. (1991). Social determinants of facial displays. *Journal of Nonverbal Behavior, 15,* 141–154.

63. Metts, S., & Grohskopf, E. (2003). Impression management: Goals, strategies, and skills. In J. O. Greene and B. R. Burleson (Eds.), *Handbook of communication and social skills* (pp. 357–399). Mahwah, NJ: Erlbaum.

64. Coleman, L. M., & DePaulo, B. M. (1991). Uncovering the human spirit: Moving beyond disability and "missed" communications. In N. Coupland, H. Giles, & J. M. Wiemann (Eds.), *"Miscommunication" and problematic talk* (pp. 61–84). Newbury Park, CA: Sage.

65. Valkenburg, P. M., & Peter, J. (2008). Adolescents' identity experiments on the Internet: Consequences for social competence and self-concept unity. *Communication Research, 35,* 208–231.

66. Vander Zanden, J. W. (1984). *Social psychology* (3rd ed., pp. 235–237). New York, NY: Random House.

67. DePaulo, B. M. (2010). Nonverbal behavior and self-presentation. In M. L. Knapp & J. A. Daly (Eds.), *Interpersonal communication* (Vol. II, pp. 251–336). Thousand Oaks, CA: Sage.

68. Brouwer. D. (1998). The precarious visibility politics of self-stigmatization: The case of HIV/AIDS tattoos. *Text and Performance Quarterly, 18,* 114–136.

69. O'Sullivan, P. B. (2000). What you don't know won't hurt me: Impression management functions of communication channels in relationships. *Communication Monographs, 26,* 403–432; Barnes, S. B. (2003). *Computer-mediated communication: Human-to-human communication across the Internet* (pp. 136–162). Boston, MA: Allyn and Bacon.

70. Sanderson, J. (2008). The blog is serving its purpose: Self-presentation strategies on 38Pitches.com. *Journal of Computer-Mediated Communication, 13,* 912–936.

71. Suler, J. R. (2002). Identity management in cyberspace. *Journal of Applied Psychoanalytic Studies, 4,* 455–459.

72. Gibbs, J. L., Ellison, N. B., & Heino, R. D. (2006). Self-presentation in online personals: The role of anticipated future interaction, self-disclosure, and perceived success in Internet dating. *Communication Research, 33,* 1–26.

73. Toma, C. L., Hancock, J. T., & Ellison, N. B. (2008). Separating fact from fiction: An examination of deceptive self-presentation in online dating profiles. *Personality and Social Psychology Bulletin, 34,* 1023–1036.

74. Salimkhan, G., Manago, A., & Greenfield, P. (2010). The construction of the virtual self on MySpace. *Cyberpsychology: Journal of Psychosocial Research on Cyberspace, 4,* article 1.

75. Bennett, R. (2008, April 4). Revealed: Secrets of choosing an online dating name. *Times Online.* Retrieved from http://technology.timesonline.co.uk/tol/news/tech_and _web/the_web/article3677778.ece

76. Gonzales, A. L., & Hancock, J. T. (2011). Mirror, mirror on my Facebook wall: Effects of exposure to Facebook on self-esteem. *Cyberpsychology, Behavior, and Social Networking, 11,* 79–83.

77. Madden, M., & Smith, A. (2010, May 26). *Reputation management and social media.* Pew Internet & American Life Project. Retrieved from http://www.pewinternet.org /Reports/2010/Reputation-Management.aspx

78. Altman, I., & Taylor, D. A. (1973). *Social penetration: The development of interpersonal relationships.* New York, NY: Holt, Rinehart and Winston; Taylor, D. A., & Altman, I. (1987). Communication in interpersonal relationships: Social penetration processes. In M. E. Roloff & G. R. Miller (Eds.), *Interpersonal processes: New directions in communication research* (pp. 257–277). Newbury Park, CA: Sage.

79. Luft, J. (1969). *Of human interaction.* Palo Alto, CA: National Press Books.

80. Petronio, S. (2007). Translational research endeavors and the practices of communication privacy management. *Journal of Applied Communication Research, 35,* 218–22.

81. Affifi, T. D., & Steuber, K. (2009). The revelation risk model (RRM): Factors that predict the revelation of secrets and the strategies used to reveal them. *Communication Monographs, 76,* 144–176; Affifi, T. D., & Steuber, K. (2009). Keeping and revealing secrets. *Communication Currents, 4,* 1–2.

82. Dindia, K. (2002). Self-disclosure research: Advances through meta-analysis. In M. Allen & R. W. Preiss (Eds.), *Interpersonal communication research: Advances through meta-analysis* (pp. 169–185). Mahwah, NJ: Erlbaum; Derlega, V. J., & Chaikin, A. L. (1975). *Sharing intimacy: What we reveal to others and why.* Englewood Cliffs, NJ: Prentice-Hall.

83. Savin-Williams, R. C. (2001). *Mom, Dad. I'm gay: How families negotiate coming out.* Washington, DC: American Psychological Association.

84. Hess, J. A., Fannin, A. D., & Pollom, L. H. (2007). Creating closeness: Discerning and measuring strategies for fostering closer relationships. *Personal Relationships, 14,* 25–44; Mitchell, A. E., et al. (2008). Predictors of intimacy in couples' discussions of relationship injuries: An observational study. *Journal of Family Psychology, 22,* 21–29.

85. MacNeil, S., & Byers, E. S. (2009). Role of sexual self-disclosure in the sexual satisfaction of long-term heterosexual couples. *Journal of Sex Research, 46,* 3–14; Fincham, F. D., & Bradbury, T. N. (1989). The impact of attributions in marriage: An individual difference analysis. *Journal of Social and Personal Relationships, 6,* 69–85.

86. Derlega, V., Winstead, B. A., Mathews, A., & Braitman, A. L. (2008). Why does someone reveal highly personal information? Attributions for and against self-disclosure in close relationships. *Communication Research Reports, 25,*

115–130; Niederhoffer, K. G., & Pennebaker, J. W. (2002). Sharing one's story: On the benefits of writing or talking about emotional experience. In C. R. Snyder & S. J. Lopez (Eds.), *Handbook of positive psychology* (pp. 573–583). London, England: Oxford University Press.

87. Greene, K., Derlega, V. J., & Mathews, A. (2006). Self-disclosure in personal relationships. In A. Vangelisti & D. Perlman (Eds.), *The Cambridge handbook of personal relationships* (pp. 409–427). New York, NY: Cambridge University Press; Rosenfeld, L. B. (2000). Overview of the ways privacy, secrecy, and disclosure are balanced in today's society. In S. Petronio (Ed.), *Balancing the secrets of private disclosures* (pp. 3–17). Mahwah, NJ: Erlbaum.

88. Powell, J. (1969). *Why am I afraid to tell you who I am?* Niles, IL: Argus Communications.

89. Alter, A. L., & Oppenheimer, D. M. (2009). Suppressing secrecy through metacognitive ease: Cognitive fluency encourages self-disclosure. *Psychological Science, 20,* 1414–1420.

90. Myers, S., & Brann, M. (2009). College students' perceptions of how instructors establish and enhance credibility through self-disclosure. *Qualitative Research Reports in Communication, 10,* 9–16.

91. Rosenfeld, L. B., & Gilbert, J. R. (1989). The measurement of cohesion and its relationship to dimensions of self-disclosure in classroom settings. *Small Group Behavior, 20,* 291–301.

92. Rosenfeld, L. B., & Bowen, G. I. (1991). Marital disclosure and marital satisfaction: Direct-effect versus interaction-effect models. *Western Journal of Speech Communication, 55,* 69–84.

93. McDaniel, S. H., et al. (2007). Physician self-disclosure in primary care visits: Enough about you, what about me? *Archives of Internal Medicine, 167,* 1321–1326.

94. Agne, R., Thompson, T. L., & Cusella, L. P. (2000). Stigma in the line of face: Self-disclosure of patients' HIV status to health care providers. *Journal of Applied Communication Research, 28,* 235–261; Derlega, V. J., Winstead, B. A., & Folk-Barron, L. (2000). Reasons for and against disclosing HIV-seropositive test results to an intimate partner: A functional perspective. In S. Petronio (Ed.), *Balancing the secrets of private disclosures* (pp. 71–82). Mahwah, NJ: Erlbaum; Caughlin, J. P., et al. (2009). Do message features influence reactions to HIV disclosures? A multiple-goals perspective. *Health Communication, 24,* 270–283.

95. Allen, M., et al. (2008). Persons living with HIV: Disclosure to sexual partners. *Communication Research Reports, 25,* 192–199.

96. O'Hair, D., & Cody, M. J. (1993). Interpersonal deception: The dark side of interpersonal communication? In B. H. Spitzberg & W. R. Cupach (Eds.), *The dark side of interpersonal communication* (pp. 181–213). Hillsdale, NJ: Erlbaum.

97. Spranca, M., Minsk, E., & Baron, J. (1991). Omission and commission in judgement and choice. *Journal of Experimental Social Psychology, 27,* 76–105.

98. Dunleavy, K. N., Chory, R. M., & Goodboy, A. K. (2010). Responses to deception in the workplace: Perceptions of credibility, power, and trustworthiness. *Communication Studies, 61,* 239–255.

99. George, J. F. & Robb, A. (2008). Deception and computer-mediated communication in daily life. *Communication Reports, 21,* 92–103.

100. Knapp, M. L. (2006). Lying and deception in close relationships. In A. Vangelisti & D. Perlman (Eds.), *The Cambridge handbook of personal relationships* (pp. 517–532). New York, NY: Cambridge University Press.

101. Turner, R. E., Edgely, C., & Olmstead, G. (1975). Information control in conversation: Honesty is not always the best policy. *Kansas Journal of Sociology, 11,* 69–89.

102. Feldman, R. S., Forrest, J. A., & Happ, B. R. (2002). Self-presentation and verbal deception: Do self-presenters lie more? *Basic and Applied Social Psychology, 24,* 163–170.

103. Hample, D. (1980). Purposes and effects of lying. *Southern Speech Communication Journal, 46,* 33–47.

104. McCornack, S. A., & Levine, T. R. (1990). When lies are uncovered: Emotional and relational outcomes of discovered deception. *Communication Monographs, 57,* 119–138.

105. Seiter, J. S., Bruschke, J., & Bai, C. (2002). The acceptability of deception as a function of perceivers' culture, deceiver's intention, and deceiver-deceived relationship. *Western Journal of Communication, 66,* 158–181.

106. Bavelas, J. B., Black, A., Chovil, N., & Mullett, J. (2010). Truths, lies, and equivocations: The effects of conflicting goals on discourse. In M. L. Knapp & J. A. Daly (Eds.), *Interpersonal communication* (Vol. II, pp. 379–408). Thousand Oaks, CA: Sage.

107. Bavelas, J. B., Black, A., Chovil, N., & Mullett, J. (1990). *Equivocal communication* (p. 171). Newbury Park, CA: Sage.

108. Bavelas, J. B., Black, A., Chovil, N., & Mullett, J. (1990). *Equivocal communication* (p. 171). Newbury Park, CA: Sage.

109. Robinson, W. P., Shepherd, A., & Heywood, J. (1998). Truth, equivocation/concealment, and lies in job applications & doctor-patient communication. *Journal of Language & Social Psychology, 17,* 149–164.

110. Motley, M. T. (1992). Mindfulness in solving communicators' dilemmas. *Communication Monographs, 59,* 306–314.

111. Shimanoff, S. B. (1988). Degree of emotional expressiveness as a function of face-needs, gender, and interpersonal relationship. *Communication Reports, 1*(2), 1–8.

CHAPTER THREE

1. The graphic demonstrations of factors influencing perception in this and the following paragraph are borrowed from Coon, D., & Mitterer, J. (2013). *Introduction to psychology* (13th ed.). Belmont, CA: Cengage Wadsworth.

2. Simons, D. J. (2011). *The invisible gorilla: How our intuitions deceive us.* New York, NY: Broadway.

3. Nelson, T. D. (2009). *Handbook of prejudice, stereotyping, and discrimination.* London, England: Psychology Press.

4. Allen, M. (1998). Methodological considerations when examining a gendered world. In D. Canary and K. Dindia (Eds.), *Handbook of sex differences and similarities in communication* (pp. 427–444). Mahwah, NJ: Erlbaum.

5. Allen, B. (1995). Diversity and organizational communication. *Journal of Applied Communication Research, 23,* 143–155; Buttny, R. (1997). Reported speech in talking race on campus. *Human Communication Research, 23,* 477–506; Hughes, P. C., & Baldwin, J. R. (2002). Communication and stereotypical impressions. *Howard Journal of Communications, 13,* 113–128

6. Perloff, R. M., Bonder, B., Ray, G. B., Ray, E. B., & Siminoff, L. A. (2006). Doctor-patient communication, cultural competence, and minority health: Theoretical and empirical perspectives. *American Behavioral Scientist, 49,* 835–852; Oliver, M. N., Goodwin, M. A., Gotler, R. S., & Strange, K. C. (2001). Time use in clinical encounters: Are African-American patients treated differently? *Journal of the National Medical Association, 93,* 380–385.

7. Oetzel, J. (1998). The effects of self-construals and ethnicity on self-reported conflict styles. *Communication Reports, 11,* 133–144.

8. Nishizawa, N. (2004). The 'self' of Japanese teenagers: Growing up in the flux of a changing culture and society. *Dissertation Abstracts International, 65,* 2642.

9. Watzlawick, P., Beavin, J., & Jackson, D. D. (1967). *Pragmatics of human communication* (p. 65). New York, NY: Norton.

10. Reznick, R. M., & Roloff, M. E. (2011). Getting off to a bad start: The relationship between communication during an initial episode of a serial argument and argument frequency. *Communication Studies, 62,* 291–306.

11. Floyd, K., & Morman, M. T. (2000). Reacting to the verbal expression of affection in same-sex interaction. *Southern Communication Journal, 65,* 287–299.

12. Rosenthal, R., & Rubin, D. B. (2010). Interpersonal expectancy effects: The first 345 studies. In M. L. Knapp & J. A. Daly (Eds.), *Interpersonal communication* (pp. 297–338). Thousand Oaks, CA: Sage.

13. Alberts, J. K., Kellar-Guenther, U., & Corman, S. R. (1996). That's not funny: Understanding recipients' responses to teasing. *Western Journal of Communication, 60,* 337–357; Edwards, R., Bello, R., Brandau-Brown, F., & Hollems, D. (2001). The effects of loneliness and verbal aggressiveness on message interpretation. *Southern Communication Journal, 66,* 139–150.

14. Bradbury, T. N. & Fincham, F. D. (1990). Attributions in marriage: Review and critique. *Psychological Bulletin, 107,* 3–33; Manusov, V. (1990). An application of attribution principles to nonverbal behavior in romantic dyads. *Communication Monographs, 57,* 104–118.

15. Reissmann, C. K. (2008). *Narrative methods for the human sciences.* Thousand Oaks, CA: Sage.

16. Kellas, J. K. (2005). Family ties: Communicating identity through jointly told family stories. *Communication Monographs, 72,* 365–389.

17. Flora, J. & Segrin, C. (2000). Relationship development in dating couples: Implications for relational satisfaction and loneliness. *Journal of Social and Personal Relationships, 17,* 811–825.

18. Baxter, L. A. & Pittman, G. (2001). Communicatively remembering turning points of relational development in heterosexual romantic relationships. *Communication Reports, 14,* 1–17.

19. Murray, S. L., Holmes, J. G., & Griffin D. W. (2004). The benefits of positive illusions: Idealization and the construction of satisfaction in close relationships. In H. T. Reis & C. E. Rusbult, *Close relationships: Key readings* (pp. 317–338). Philadelphia, PA: Taylor & Francis; Martz, J. M., Verette, J., Arriaga, X. B., Slovik, L. F., Cox, C. L., & Rosbult, C. E. (1998). Positive illusion in close relationships. *Personal Relationships, 5,* 159–181.

20. For a detailed description of how the senses affect perception, see Ackerman, N. (1990). *A natural history of the senses.* New York, NY: Random House.

21. For descriptions of various psychological disorders and their treatments, visit the National Institute of Mental Health website at http://www.nimh.nih.gov/.

22. Seidman, B. (2011, June 25). *Do not operate this marriage while drowsy.* Retrieved from http://www.pbs.org/wnet/need-to-know/the-daily-need/do-not-operate-this-marriage-while-drowsy/9839/

23. Alaimo, K., Olson, C. M., & Frongillo, E. A. (2001). Food insufficiency and American school-aged children's cognitive, academic, and psychosocial development. *Pediatrics, 108,* 44–53.

24. Maguire, M. (2005). Biological cycles and cognitive performance. In A. Esgate et al., *An introduction to applied cognitive psychology* (pp. 137–161). New York, NY: Psychology Press; Cooper, C., & McConville, C. (1990). Interpreting mood scores: Clinical implications of individual differences in mood variability. *British Journal of Medical Psychology, 63,* 215–225.

25. Giles, H., Coupland, N., & Wiemann, J. M. (1992). Talk is cheap . . . but 'my word is my bond': Beliefs about talk. In K. Bolton & H. Kwok (Eds.), *Sociolinguistics today: International perspectives* (pp. 218–243). London, England: Routledge & Kegan Paul.

26. Manusov, V., Winchatz, M. R., & Manning, L. M. (1997). Acting out of our minds: Incorporating behavior into models of stereotype-based expectancies for cross-cultural interactions. *Communication Monographs, 64,* 119–139.

27. Becker, J. B., Berkley, K. J., Geary, N., Hampson, E., Herman, J. P., & Young, E. (2007). *Sex differences in the brain: From genes to behavior.* New York, NY: Oxford University Press.

28. Halpern, D. F. (2000). *Sex differences in cognitive abilities* (3rd ed.). Mahwah, NJ: Erlbaum.

29. Rathus, S. A. (1993). *Psychology* (5th ed.; pp. 640–643). Fort Worth, TX: Harcourt Brace Jovanovich;Wade, C., & Tavris, C. (1987). *Psychology* (pp. 488–490). New York, NY: Harper & Row.

30. Bem, S. L. (1985). Androgyny and gender schema theory: A conceptual and empirical integration. In T. B. Sonderegger (Ed.), *Nebraska symposium on motivation: Psychology and gender* (pp. 179–226). Lincoln: University of Nebraska Press.

31. Swami, V., & Furnham, A. (2008). Is love really so blind? *The Psychologist, 21,* 108–111.

32. Gonzaga, G. C., Haselton, M. G., Smurda, J., Davies, M., & Poore, J. C. (2008). Love, desire, and the suppression of thoughts of romantic alternatives. *Evolution and Human Behavior, 29,* 119–126.

33. Seibold, D. R., & Spitzberg, B. H. (2010). Attribution theory and research: Review and implications for communication. In M. L. Knapp & J. A. Daly (Eds.), *Interpersonal communication* (pp. 297–338). Thousand Oaks, CA: Sage.

34. Hamachek, D. (1992). *Encounters with the self* (3rd ed.). Fort Worth, TX: Harcourt Brace Jovanovich.

35. For a review of these perceptual biases, see Hamachek, D. (1992). *Encounters with the self* (3rd ed.). Fort Worth, TX: Harcourt Brace Jovanovich.; Bradbury, T. N. & Fincham, F. D. (1990). Attributions in marriage: Review and critique. *Psychological Bulletin, 107,* 3–33. For an example of

the self-serving bias in action, see Buttny, R. (1997). Reported speech in talking race on campus. *Human Communication Research, 23*, 477–506.

36. Young, S. L. (2004). What the _____ is your problem?: Attribution theory and perceived reasons for profanity usage during conflict. *Communication Research Reports, 21*, 338–347.

37. Zhang, S. (2009). Sender-recipient perspectives of honest but hurtful evaluative messages in romantic relationships. *Communication Reports, 22*, 89–101.

38. Dion, K., Berscheid, E., & Walster, E. (1972). What is beautiful is good. *Journal of Personality and Social Psychology, 24*, 285–290.

39. Watkins, L., & Johnston, L. (2000). Screening job applicants: The impact of physical attractiveness and application quality. *International Journal of Selection and Assessment, 8*, 76–84.

40. Dougherty, T., Turban, D., & Collander, J. (1994). Confirming first impressions in the employment interview. *Journal of Applied Psychology, 79*, 659–665.

41. Cook, G. I., Marsh, R. L., & Hicks, J. L. (2003). Halo and devil effects demonstrate valence-based influences on source-mentoring decisions. *Consciousness and Cognition, 12*, 257–278.

42. Marek, C. I., Wanzer, M. B., & Knapp, J. L. (2004). An exploratory investigation of the relationship between roommates' first impressions and subsequent communication patterns. *Communication Research Reports, 21*, 210–220.

43. Keysar, B. (2007). Communication and miscommunication: The role of egocentric processes. *Intercultural Pragmatics, 4*, 71–84.

44. Edwards, C., Edwards, A., Qingmei, Q., & Wahl, S. T. (2007). The influence of computer-mediated word-of-mouth communication on student perceptions of instructors and attitudes toward learning course content. *Communication Education, 56*, 255–277.

45. DiPaola, B. M., Roloff, M. E., & Peters, K. M. (2010). College students' expectations of conflict intensity: A self-fulfilling prophecy. *Communication Quarterly, 58*, 59–76.

46. Sillars, A., Shellen, W., McIntosh, A., & Pomegranate, M. (1997). Relational characteristics of language: Elaboration and differentiation in marital conversations. *Western Journal of Communication, 61*, 403–422.

47. Stiff, J. B., Dillard, J. P., Somera, L., Kim, H., & Sleight, C. (1988). Empathy, communication, and prosocial behavior. *Communication Monographs, 55*, 198–213.

48. Goleman, D. (2006). *Social intelligence*. New York, NY: Bantam; Decety, J., Michalska, K., & Aktsuki, Y. (2008). Who caused the pain? An fMRI investigation of empathy and intentionality in children. *Neuropsychologia, 46*, 2607–2614.

49. Goleman, D. (2006). *Social intelligence*. New York, NY: Bantam.

50. Davis, M. (1994). The heritability of characteristics associated with dispositional empathy. *Journal of Personality, 62*, 369–391.

51. Burleson, B., Delia, J., & Applegate, J. (1995). The socialization of person-centered communication: Parental contributions to the social-cognitive and communication skills of their children. In M. A. Fitzpatrick & A. Vangelisti

(Eds.), *Perspectives in family communication* (pp. 34–76). Thousand Oaks, CA: Sage.

52. Tucker, D. M., Luu, P., & Derryberry, D. (2005). Love hurts: The evolution of empathic concern through the encephalization of nociceptive capacity. *Development and Psychopathology, 17*, 699–713.

53. Wu, S., & Keysar, B. (2007). Cultural effects on perspective taking. *Psychological Science, 18*, 600–606.

54. Martin, R. (1992). Relational cognition complexity and relational communication in personal relationships. *Communication Monographs, 59*, 150–163; Burleson, B. R., & Caplan, S. E. (1998). Cognitive complexity. In J. C. McCroskey, J. A. Daly, M. M. Martin, & M. J. Beatty (Eds.), *Communication and personality: Trait perspectives* (pp. 233–286). Creskill, NY: Hampton Press.

55. Burleson, B. R., & Caplan, S. E. (1998). Cognitive complexity. In J. C. McCroskey, J. A. Daly, M. M. Martin, & M. J. Beatty (Eds.), *Communication and personality: Trait perspectives* (p. 22). Creskill, NY: Hampton Press.

56. Burleson, B. R. (1989). The constructivist approach to person centered communication: Analysis of a research exemplar. In B. Dervin, L. Grossberg, B. J. O'Keefe, & E. Wartella (Eds.), *Rethinking communication: Paradigm exemplars* (pp. 33–72). Newbury Park, CA: Sage.

57. Sypher, B. D., & Zorn, T. (1986). Communication-related abilities and upward mobility: A longitudinal investigation. *Human Communication Research, 12*, 420–431.

58. Joireman, J. (2004). Relationships between attributional complexity and empathy. *Individual Differences Research, 2*, 197–202.

59. Medvene, L., Grosch, K., & Swink, N. (2006). Interpersonal complexity: A cognitive component of person-centered care. *The Gerontologist, 46*, 220–226.

60. Rockwell, P. (2007). The effects of cognitive complexity and communication apprehension on the expression and recognition of sarcasm. In A. M. Columbus (Ed.), *Advances in psychology research* (pp. 185–196). Hauppauge, NY: Nova Science Publishers.

61. Little, C., Packman, J., Smaby, M. H., & Maddux, C. D. (2005). The skilled counselor training model: Skills acquisition, self-assessment, and cognitive complexity. *Counselor Education & Supervision, 44*, 189–200.

62. Reps, P. (1967). Pillow education in rural Japan. In *Square sun, square moon* (pp. 17–19). New York, NY: Tuttle.

CHAPTER FOUR

1. Goleman, D. (1995). *Emotional intelligence: Why it can matter more than I.Q.* New York, NY: Bantam; Goleman, D. (2006). *Social intelligence: The new science of human relationships*. New York, NY: Bantam.

2. Carmeli, A., Yitzhak-Halevy, M., & Weisberg, J. (2009). The relationship between emotional intelligence and psychological wellbeing. *Journal of Managerial Psychology, 24*, 66–78.

3. Smith, L., Heaven, P. C., & Ciarrochi, J. (2008). Trait emotional intelligence, conflict communication patterns, and relationship satisfaction. *Personality and Individual Differences, 44*, 1314–1325.

4. Planalp, S., Fitness, J., & Fehr, B. (2006). Emotion in theories of close relationships. In A. L. Vangelisti & D. Perlman

(Eds.), *The Cambridge handbook of personal relationships* (pp. 369–384). New York, NY: Cambridge University Press; Baumeister, R. F. (2005). *The human animal*. New York, NY: Oxford University Press.

5. Rochman, G. M., & Diamond, G. M. (2008). From unresolved anger to sadness: Identifying physiological correlates. *Journal of Counseling Psychology, 55*, 96–105.

6. Gottman, J. M., & Silver, N. (1999). *The seven principles for making marriages work*. New York, NY: Three Rivers Press.

7. Samp, J. A., & Monahan, J. L. (2009). Alcohol-influenced nonverbal behaviors during discussions about a relationship problem. *Journal of Nonverbal Behavior, 33*, 193–211.

8. Ekman, P., Levenson, R. W., & Friesen, W. V. (1983, September 16). Autonomic nervous system activity distinguishes among emotions. *Science, 221*, 1208–1210.

9. Kleinke, C. L., Peterson, T. R., & Rutledge, T. R. (1998). Effects of self-generated facial expressions on mood. *Journal of Personality and Social Psychology, 74*, 272–279.

10. Oosterwijk, S., Rotteveel, M., Fischer, A. H., & Hess, U. (2009). Embodied emotion concepts: How generating words about pride and disappointment influences posture. *European Journal of Social Psychology, 39*, 457–466.

11. Valins, S. (1966). Cognitive effects of false heart-rate feedback. *Journal of Personality and Social Psychology, 4*, 400–408.

12. Berger, C. R., & Lee, K. J. (2011). Second thoughts, second feelings: Attenuating the impact of threatening narratives through rational reappraisal. *Communication Research, 38*, 3–26.

13. Wallace, J. C., Edwards, B. D., Shull, A., & Finch, D. M. (2009). Examining the consequences in the tendency to suppress and reappraise emotions on task-related job performance. *Human Performance, 22*, 23–43; Moore, S. A., Zoellner, L. A., & Mollenholt, N. (2008). Are expressive suppression and cognitive reappraisal associated with stress-related symptoms? *Behaviour Research and Therapy, 46*, 993–1000; Nezlek, J. B., & Kuppens, P. (2008). Regulating positive and negative emotions in daily life. *Journal of Personality, 76*, 561–580.

14. Plutchik, R. (1980). *Emotion: A psychoevolutionary synthesis*. New York, NY: Harper & Row; Shaver, P. R., Wu, S., & Schwartz, J. C. (1992). Cross-cultural similarities and differences in emotion and its representation: A prototype approach. In M. S. Clark (Ed.), *Emotion* (pp. 175–212). Newbury Park, CA: Sage.

15. Ekman, P. (1999). Basic emotions. In T. Dalgleish & T. Power (Eds.), *The handbook of cognition and emotion* (pp. 45–60). Sussex, England: Wiley; Ortony, A., & Turner, T. J. (1990). What's basic about basic emotions? *Psychological Review, 97*, 315–331.

16. Ferrari, M., & Koyama, E. (2002). Meta-emotions about anger and amae: A cross-cultural comparison. *Consciousness and Emotion, 3*, 197–211.

17. Shaver, P. R., Wu, S., & Schwartz, J. C. (1992). Cross-cultural similarities and differences in emotion and its representation: A prototype approach. In M. S. Clark (Ed.), *Emotion* (pp. 175–212). Newbury Park, CA: Sage.

18. Goleman, D. (1995). *Emotional intelligence: Why it can matter more than I.Q.* New York, NY: Bantam.

19. Gottman, J. M., Katz, L. F., & Hooven, C. (1997). *Meta-emotion: How families communicate emotionally*. Mahwah,

NJ: Erlbaum; Young, S. L. (2009). The function of parental communication patterns: Reflection-enhancing and reflection-discouraging approaches. *Communication Quarterly, 57*, 379–394.

20. Lunkenheimer, E. S., Shields, A. M., & Kortina, K. S. (2007). Parental emotion coaching and dismissing in family interaction. *Social Development, 16*, 232–248.

21. McCroskey, J. C., Richmond, V. P., Heisel, A. D., & Hayhurst, J. L. (2004). Eysenck's big three and communication traits: Communication traits as manifestations of temperament. *Communication Research Reports, 21*, 404–410; Gross, J. J., Sutton, S. K., & Ketelaar, T. V. (1998). Relations between affect and personality: Support for the affect-level and affective-reactivity views. *Personality and Social Psychology Bulletin, 24*, 279–288.

22. Costa, P. T., & McCrae, R. R. (1980). Influence of extraversion and neuroticism on subjective well-being: Happy and unhappy people. *Journal of Personality and Social Psychology, 38*, 668–678.

23. Yen, J., Yen, C., Chen, C., Wang, P., Chang, Y., & Ko, C. (2012). Social anxiety in online and real-life interaction and their associated factors. *Cyberpsychology, Behavior, and Social Networking, 15*, 7–12.

24. Kelly, L., Duran, R. L., & Zolten, J. J. (2001). The effect of reticence on college students' use of electronic mail to communicate with faculty. *Communication Education, 50*, 170–176; Scharlott, B. W., & Christ, W. G. (2001). Overcoming relationship-initiation barriers: The impact of a computer-dating system on sex role, shyness, and appearance inhibitions. *Computers in Human Behavior, 11*, 191–204.

25. Goddard, C. (2002). Explicating emotions across languages and cultures: A semantic approach. In S. R. Fussell (Ed.), *The verbal communication of emotions* (pp. 18–49). Mahwah, NJ: Erlbaum.

26. Tsai, J. L., Knutson, B., & Fung, H. H. (2006). Cultural variation in affect valuation. *Journal of Personality and Social Psychology, 90*, 288–307.

27. Kotchemidova, C. (2010). Emotion culture and cognitive constructions of reality. *Communication Quarterly, 58*, 207–234.

28. Pennebaker, J. W., Rime, B., & Blankenship, V. E. (1996). Stereotypes of emotional expressiveness of northerners and southerners: A cross-cultural test of Montesquieu's hypotheses. *Journal of Personality and Social Psychology, 70*, 372–380.

29. Mortenson, S. T. (2009). Interpersonal trust and social skill in seeking social support among Chinese and Americans. *Communication Research, 36*, 32–53.

30. Wilkins, R., & Gareis, E. (2006). Emotion expression and the locution 'I love you': A cross-cultural study. *International Journal of Intercultural Relations, 30*, 51–75.

31. Guerrero, L. K., Jones, S. M., & Boburka, R. R. (2006). Sex differences in emotional communication. In K. Dindia & D. J. Canary (Eds.), *Sex differences and similarities in communication* (2nd ed., pp. 242–261). Mahwah, NJ: Erlbaum; Wester, S. R., Vogel, D. L., Pressly, P. K., & Heesacker M. (2002). Sex differences in emotion: A critical review of the literature and implications for counseling psychology. *Counseling Psychologist, 30*, 630–652.

32. Swenson, J., & Casmir, F. L. (1998). The impact of culture-sameness, gender, foreign travel, and academic

background on the ability to interpret facial expression of emotion in others. *Communication Quarterly, 46*, 214–230.

33. Canli, T., Desmond, J. E., Zhao, Z., & Gabrieli, J. D. E. (2002). Sex differences in the neural basis of emotional memories. *Proceedings of the National Academy of Sciences, 10*, 10789–10794.

34. Merten, J. (2005). Culture, gender and the recognition of the basic emotions. *Psychologia: An International Journal of Psychology in the Orient, 48*, 306–316.

35. Kunkel, A. W., & Burleson, B. R. (1999). Assessing explanations for sex differences in emotional support: A test of the different cultures and skill specialization accounts. *Human Communication Research, 25*, 307–340.

36. Dunsmore, J., Her, P., Halberstadt, A., & Perez-Rivera, M. (2009). Parents' beliefs about emotions and children's recognition of parents' emotions. *Journal of Nonverbal Behavior, 33*, 121–140.

37. Witmer, D. F., & Katzman, S. L. (1999). On-line smiles: Does gender make a difference in the use of graphic accents? *Journal of Computer-Mediated Communication, 2* (online, domain name expired).

38. Mansson, D. H., & Myers, S. A. (2011). An initial examination of college students' expressions of affection through Facebook. *Southern Communication Journal, 76*, 155–168.

39. Brody, L, R., & Hall, J. A. (2008). Gender and emotion in context. In M. Lewis, J. M. Haviland-Jones, & L. F. Barrett (Eds.), *Handbook of emotions* (3rd ed., pp. 395–408). New York, NY: Guilford.

40. Shimanoff, S. B. (1984). Commonly named emotions in everyday conversations. *Perceptual and Motor Skills, 58*, 514; Gottman, J. M. (1982). Emotional responsiveness in marital conversations. *Journal of Communication, 32*, 108–120.

41. Haybe, J. G., & Metts, S. (2008). Managing the expression of emotion. *Western Journal of Communication, 72*, 374–396; Shimanoff, S. B. (1988). Degree of emotional expressiveness as a function of face-needs, gender, and interpersonal relationship. *Communication Reports, 1*, 43–53.

42. Waugh, C. E., & Fredericson, B. L. (2006). Nice to know you: Positive emotions, self-other overlap, and complex understanding in the formation of a new relationship. *The Journal of Positive Psychology, 1*, 93–106.

43. Shimanoff, S. B. (1985). Rules governing the verbal expression of emotions between married couples. *Western Journal of Speech Communication, 49*, 149–165.

44. Rosenfeld, L. B. (1979). Self-disclosure avoidance: Why I am afraid to tell you who I am. *Communication Monographs, 46*, 63–74.

45. Erbert, L. A., & Floyd, K. (2004). Affectionate expressions as face-threatening acts: Receiver assessments. *Journal of Social and Personal Relationships, 17*, 230–246.

46. Hatfield, E., Cacioppo, J. T., Rapson, R. L., & Oatley, K. (1984). *Emotional contagion*. Cambridge, England: Cambridge University Press; Colino, S. (2006, May 30). That look—It's catching. *The Washington Post*, HE01.

47. Goleman, D. (2006). *Social intelligence: The new science of human relationships* (p. 115). New York, NY: Bantam.

48. Bakker, A. B. (2005). Flow among music teachers and their students: The crossover of peak experiences. *Journal of Vocational Behavior, 66*, 822–833.

49. Jiangang, D., Xiucheng, F., & Tianjun, F. (2011). Multiple emotional contagions in service encounters. *Journal of the Academy of Marketing Science, 39*, 449–466.

50. Goodman C. R., & Shippy, R. A. (2002). Is it contagious? Affect similarity among spouses. *Aging and Mental Health, 6*, 266–274.

51. Belluck, P. (2008, December 5). Strangers may cheer you up, study says. *The New York Times*, A12.

52. Sullins, E. S. (1991). Emotional contagion revisited: Effects of social comparison and expressive style on mood convergence. *Personality and Social Psychology Bulletin, 17*, 166–174.

53. Anderson, C., Keltner, D., & John, O. P. (2003, May). Emotional convergence between people over time. *Journal of Personality and Social Psychology, 84*, 1054–1068.

54. DeAngelis, T. (1992). Illness linked with repressive style of coping. *APA Monitor, 23(12)*, 14–15.

55. Seigman, A. W., & Smith, T. W. (1994). *Anger, hostility, and the heart*. Hillsdale, NJ: Erlbaum.

56. Graham, S., Huang, J. Y., Clark, M. S., & Helgeson, V. S. (2008). The positives of negative emotions: Willingness to express negative emotions promotes relationships. *Personality and Social Psychology Bulletin, 34*, 394–406; Kennedy-Moore, E., & Watson, J. C. (1999). *Expressing emotion: Myths, realities, and therapeutic strategies*. New York, NY: Guilford.

57. Nelton, S. (1996, February). Emotions in the workplace. *Nation's Business*, 25–30.

58. Kramer, M. W., & Hess, J. A. (2002). Communication rules for the display of emotions in organizational settings. *Management Communication Quarterly, 16*, 66–80.

59. Booth-Butterfield, M., & Booth-Butterfield, S. (1998). Emotionality and affective orientation. In J. C. McCroskey, J. A. Daly, M. M. Martin, & M. J. Beatty (Eds.), *Communication and personality: Trait perspectives* (pp. 171–189). Creskill, NY: Hampton.

60. Barrett, L. F., Gross, J., Christensen, T., & Benvenuto, M. (2001). Knowing what you're feeling and knowing what to do about it: Mapping the relation between emotion differentiation and emotion regulation. *Cognition and Emotion, 15*, 713–724.

61. Grewal, D., & Salovey, P. (2005). Feeling smart: The science of emotional intelligence. *American Scientist, 93*, 330–339; Yoo, S. H., Matsumoto, D., & LeRoux, J. (2006). The influence of emotion recognition and emotion regulation on intercultural adjustment. *International Journal of Intercultural Relations, 30*, 345–363.

62. Bushman, B. J., Baumeister, R. F., & Stack, A. D. (1999). Catharsis, aggression, and persuasive influence: Self-fulfilling or self-defeating prophecies? *Journal of Personality and Social Psychology, 76*, 367–376.

63. For an extensive discussion of ways to express emotions, see Fussell, S. R. (2002). *The verbal communication of emotions*. Mahwah, NJ: Erlbaum.

64. Honeycutt, J. M. (2003). *Imagined interactions: Daydreaming about communication*. Cresskill, NJ: Hampton Press; Honeycutt, J. M., & Ford, S. G. (2001). Mental imagery and intrapersonal communication: A review of research on imagined interactions (IIs) and current developments. *Communication Yearbook 25* (pp. 315–338). Thousand Oaks, CA: Sage.

65. Pennebaker, J. (2004). *Writing to heal: A guided journal for recovering from trauma and emotional upheaval*. Oakland, CA: Harbinger.

66. Floyd, K., Mikkelson, A. C., Hesse, C., & Pauley, P. M. (2007). Affectionate writing reduces total cholesterol: Two randomized, controlled studies. *Human Communication Research, 33*, 119–142.

67. Metts, S., & Wood, B. (2008). Interpersonal emotional competence. In M. T. Motley (Ed.), *Studies in applied interpersonal communication* (pp. 267–285). Thousand Oaks, CA: Sage.

68. Spitzberg, B. H. (2006). Preliminary development of a model and measure of computer-mediated communication (CMC) competence. *Journal of Computer-Mediated Communcation, 11*, article 12. Retrieved from http://jcmc.indiana.edu/vol11/issue2/spitzberg.html

69. O'Sullivan, P. B. (2000). What you don't know won't hurt me: Impression management functions of communication channels in relationships. *Human Communication Research, 26*, 403–431.

70. Galovski, T. E., Malta, L. S., & Blanchard, E. B. (2005). *Road rage: Assessment and treatment of the angry, aggressive driver*. Washington, DC: American Psychological Association.

71. Mallalieu, S. D., Hanton, S., & Jones, G. (2003). Emotional labeling and competitive anxiety in preparation and competition. *The Sports Psychologist, 17*, 157–174.

72. Bourhis, J., & Allen, M. (1992). Meta-analysis of the relationship between communication apprehension and cognitive performance. *Communication Education, 41*, 68–76.

73. Patterson, M. L., & Ritts, V. (1997). Social and communicative anxiety: A review and meta-analysis. In B. R. Burleson (Ed.), *Communication yearbook 20*. Thousand Oaks, CA: Sage.

74. Smith, J. M., & Alloy, L. B. (2009). A roadmap to rumination: A review of the definition, assessment, and conceptualization of this multifaceted construct. *Clinical Psychology Review, 29*, 116–128.

75. Bushman, B. J., Bonacci, A. M., Pedersen, W. C., Vasquez, E. A., & Miller, N. (2005). Chewing on it can chew you up: Effects of rumination on triggered displaced aggression. *Journal of Personality and Social Psychology, 88*, 969–983.

76. For a thorough discussion of how neurobiology shapes feelings, see LeDoux, J. E. (1996). *The emotional brain*. New York, NY: Simon and Schuster.

77. Vocate, D. R. (1994). Self-talk and inner speech. In D. R. Vocate (Ed.), *Intrapersonal communication: Different voices, different minds* (pp. 3–32). Hillsdale, NJ: Erlbaum.

78. Ayers, J., Keereetaweep, T., Chen, P., & Edwards, P. A. (1998). Communication apprehension and employment interviews. *Communication Education, 47*, 1–17.

79. Booth-Butterfield, M., & Trotta, M. R. (1994). Attributional patterns for expressions of love. *Communication Reports, 7*, 119–129.

80. Vangelisti, A. L., Corgin, S. D., Lucchetti, A. E., & Sprague, R. J. (1999). Couples' concurrent cognitions: The influence of relational satisfaction on the thoughts couples have as they converse. *Human Communication Research, 25*, 370–398.

81. Bargh, J. A. (1988). Automatic information processing: Implications for communication and affect. In H. E. Sypher & E. T. Higgins (Eds.), *Communication, social cognition, and affect* (pp. 9–32). Hillsdale, NJ: Erlbaum.

82. Beck, A. (1976). *Cognitive therapy and the emotional disorders*. New York, NY: International Universities Press.

83. Metts, S., & Cupach, W. R. (1990). The influence of relationship beliefs and problem-solving relationships on satisfaction in romantic relationships. *Human Communication Research, 17*, 170–185.

84. Meichenbaum, A. (1977). *Cognitive behavior modification*. New York, NY: Plenum; Ellis, A., & Greiger, R. (1977). *Handbook for rational-emotive therapy*. New York, NY: Springer; Wirga, M., & DeBernardi, M. (2002, March). The ABCs of cognition, emotion, and action. *Archives of Psychiatry and Psychotherapy, 1*, 5–16.

85. Elphinston, R. A., & Noller, P. (2011). Time to face it! Facebook intrusion and the implications for romantic jealousy and relationship satisfaction. *Cyberpsychology, Behavior, and Social Networking, 14*, 631–635; Muise, A., Christofides, E., & Desmarais, S. (2009). More information than you ever wanted: Does Facebook bring out the green-eyed monster of jealousy? *CyberPsychology & Behavior, 12*, 441–444.

86. Chatham-Carpenter, A., & DeFrancisco, V. (1997). Pulling yourself up again: Women's choices and strategies for recovering and maintaining self-esteem. *Western Journal of Communication, 61*, 164–187.

CHAPTER FIVE

1. Sacks, O. W. (1989). *Seeing voices: A journey into the world of the deaf* (p. 17). Berkeley: University of California Press.

2. Henneberger, M. (1999, January 29). Misunderstanding of word embarrasses Washington's new mayor. *The New York Times* online. Retrieved from http://www.nyt.com

3. Keysar, B., & Henly, A. S. (2002). Speakers' overestimation of their effectiveness. *Psychological Science, 13*, 207–212; Wyer, R. S., & Adava, R. (2003). Message reception skills in social communication. In J. O. Greene & B. R. Burleson (Eds.), *Handbook of communication and social interaction skills* (pp. 291–355). Mahwah, NJ: Erlbaum.

4. Scott, T. L. (2000, November 27). Teens before their time. *Time*, 22.

5. Wallsten, T. (1986). Measuring the vague meanings of probability terms. *Journal of Experimental Psychology, 115*, 348–365.

6. Prentice, W. E. (2005). *Therapeutic modalities in rehabilitation*. New York: McGraw-Hill.

7. Wolfram, W., & Schilling-Estes, N. (2005). *American English: Dialects and variation* (2nd ed.). Malden, MA: Blackwell.

8. Coupland, N., Wiemann, J. M., & Giles, H. (1991). Talk as "problem" and communication as "miscommunication": An integrative analysis. In N. Coupland, J. M. Wiemann, & H. Giles (Eds.), *"Miscommunication" and problematic talk* (pp. 1–17). Newbury Park, CA: Sage.

9. Pearce, W. B., & Cronen, V. (1980). *Communication, action, and meaning*. New York: Praeger; Cronen, V., Chen, V., & Pearce, W. B. (1988). Coordinated management of meaning: A critical theory. In Y. Y. Kim & W. B. Gudykunst (Eds.), *Theories in intercultural communication* (pp. 66–98). Newbury Park, CA: Sage.

10. Graham, E. K. E., Papa, M., & Brooks, G. P. (1992). Functions of humor in conversation: Conceptualization and measurement. *Western Journal of Communication, 56,* 161–183.

11. O'Sullivan, P. B., & Flanagin, A. (2003). Reconceptualizing "flaming" and other problematic communication. *New Media and Society, 5,* 67–93.

12. Christenfeld, N., & Larsen, B. (2008). The name game. *The Psychologist, 21,* 210–213.

13. Mehrabian, A. (2001). Characteristics attributed to individuals on the basis of their first names. *Genetic, Social, and General Psychology Monographs, 127,* 59–88.

14. Social Security Administration. (2012). *Popular baby names.* Retrieved from http://www.ssa.gov/OACT /babynames/

15. Fryer, R. G., & Levitt, S. D. (2004). The causes and consequences of distinctively black names. *Quarterly Journal of Economics, 119,* 767–805.

16. Aune, R. K., & Kikuchi, T. (1993). Effects of language intensity similarity on perceptions of credibility, relational attributions, and persuasion. *Journal of Language and Social Psychology, 12,* 224–238.

17. Giles, H., Mulac, A., Bradac, J. J., & Johnson, P. (2010). Speech accommodation theory: The first decade and beyond. In M. L. Knapp & J. A. Daly (Eds.), *Interpersonal communication* (pp. 39–74). Thousand Oaks, CA: Sage.

18. Baruch, Y., & Jenkins, S. (2006). Swearing at work and permissive leadership culture: When anti-social becomes social and incivility is acceptable. *Leadership & Organization Development Journal, 28,* 492–507.

19. Ireland, M. E., Slatcher, R. B., Eastwick, P. W., Scissors, L. E., Finkel, E. J., & Pennebaker, J. W. (2011). Language style matching predicts relationship initiation and stability. *Psychological Science, 22,* 39–44.

20. Cassell, J., & Tversky, D. (2005). The language of online intercultural community formation. *Journal of Computer-Mediated Communication, 10,* article 2.

21. Reyes, A. (2005). Appropriation of African American slang by Asian American youth. *Journal of Sociolinguistics, 9,* 509–532.

22. Ng, S. H., & Bradac, J. J. (1993). *Power in language: Verbal communication and social influence* (p. 27). Newbury Park, CA: Sage.

23. Parton, S., Siltanen, S. A., Hosman, L. A., & Langenderfer, J. (2002). Employment interview outcomes and speech style effects. *Journal of Language and Social Psychology, 21,* 144–161.

24. Hosman, L. A. (1989). The evaluative consequences of hedges, hesitations, and intensifiers: Powerful and powerless speech styles. *Human Communication Research, 15,* 383–406.

25. El-Alayli, A., Myers, C. J., Petersen, T. L., & Lystad, A. L. (2008). "I don't mean to sound arrogant, but . . .": The effects of using disclaimers on person perception. *Personality and Social Psychology Bulletin, 34,* 130–143.

26. Samovar, L. A., & Porter, R. E. (2001). *Communication between cultures* (4th ed., pp. 58–59). Belmont, CA: Wadsworth.

27. Bradac, J., & Mulac, A. (1984). Attributional consequences of powerful and powerless speech styles in a crisis-intervention context. *Journal of Language and Social Psychology, 3,* 1–19.

28. Bradac, J. J. (1983). The language of lovers, flovers [sic], and friends: Communicating in social and personal relationships. *Journal of Language and Social Psychology, 2,* 141–162.

29. Geddes, D. (1992). Sex roles in management: The impact of varying power of speech style on union members' perception of satisfaction and effectiveness. *Journal of Psychology, 126,* 589–607.

30. Kubany, E. S., Richard, D. C., Bauer, G. B., & Muraoka, M. Y. (1992). Impact of assertive and accusatory communication of distress and anger: A verbal component analysis. *Aggressive Behavior, 18,* 337–347.

31. Gordon, T. (1974). *T.E.T.: Teacher Effectiveness Training* (p. 74). New York: Wyden.

32. Raskin, R., & Shaw, R. (1988). Narcissism and the use of personal pronouns. *Journal of Personality, 56,* 393–404; Vangelisti, A. L., Knapp, M. L., & Daly, J. A. (1990). Conversational narcissism. *Communication Monographs, 57,* 251–274.

33. Dreyer, A. S., Dreyer, C. A., & Davis, J. E. (1987). Individuality and mutuality in the language of families of field-dependent and field-independent children. *Journal of Genetic Psychology, 148,* 105–117.

34. Seider, B. H., Hirschberger, G., Nelson, K. L., & Levenson, R. W. (2009). We can work it out: Age differences in relational pronouns, physiology, and behavior in marital conflict. *Psychology and Aging, 24,* 604–613; Honeycutt, J. M. (1999). Typological differences in predicting marital happiness from oral history behaviors and imagined interactions. *Communication Monographs, 66,* 276–291.

35. Slatcher, R. B., Vazire, S., & Pennebaker, J. W. (2008). Am "I" more important than "we"? Couples' word use in instant messages. *Personal Relationships, 15,* 407–424; Proctor, R. F., & Wilcox, J. R.. (1993). An exploratory analysis of responses to owned messages in inter-personal communication. *ETC: A Review of General Semantics, 50,* 201–220.

36. Tannen, D. (1990). *You just don't understand: Women and men in conversation.* New York: William Morrow; Gray, J. (1992). *Men are from Mars, women are from Venus.* New York: HarperCollins.

37. Dindia, K. (2006). Men are from North Dakota, women are from South Dakota. In K. Dindia & D. J. Canary (Eds.), *Sex differences and similarities in communication: Critical essays and empirical investigations of sex and gender in interaction* (2nd ed., pp. 3–18). Mahwah, NJ: Erlbaum; Goldsmith, D. J., & Fulfs, P. A. (1999). "You just don't have the evidence": An analysis of claims and evidence in Deborah Tannen's *You just don't understand.* In M. E. Roloff (Ed.), *Communication yearbook 22* (pp. 1–49). Thousand Oaks, CA: Sage.

38. Haas, A., & Sherman, M. A. (1982). Conversational topic as a function of role and gender. *Psychological Reports, 51,* 453–454; Fehr, B. (1996). *Friendship processes.* Thousand Oaks, CA: Sage.

39. Clark, R. A. (1998). A comparison of topics and objectives in a cross section of young men's and women's everyday conversations. In D. J. Canary & K. Dindia (Eds.), *Sex differences and similarities in communication: Critical essays and*

empirical investigations of sex and gender in interaction (pp. 303–319). Mahwah, NJ: Erlbaum.

40. DeCapua, A., Berkowitz, D., & Boxer, D. (2006). Women talk revisited: Personal disclosures and alignment development. *Multilingua, 25,* 393–412.

41. Wood, J. T. (1994). *Gendered lives: Communication, gender, and culture* (p. 141). Belmont, CA: Wadsworth.

42. Sherman, M. A., & Haas, A. (1984, June). Man to man, woman to woman. *Psychology Today, 17,* 72–73.

43. Ragsdale, J. D. (1996). Gender, satisfaction level, and the use of relational maintenance strategies in marriage. *Communication Monographs, 63,* 354–371.

44. Giles, H., & Street, R. L., Jr. (1985). Communication characteristics and behavior. In M. L. Knapp & G. R. Miller (Eds.), *Handbook of interpersonal communication* (pp. 205–261). Beverly Hills, CA: Sage; Kohn, A. (1988, February). Girl talk, guy talk. *Psychology Today, 22,* 65–66.

45. Mehl, M. R., Vazire, S., Ramírez-Esparza, N., Slatcher, R. B., & Pennebaker, J. W. (2007). Are women really more talkative than men? *Science, 317,* 82.

46. Mulac, A. (2006). The gender-linked language effect: Do language differences really make a difference? In K. Dindia & D. J. Canary (Eds.), *Sex differences and similarities in communication: Critical essays and empirical investigations of sex and gender in interaction* (2nd ed., pp. 127–153). Mahwah, NJ: Erlbaum.

47. Clark, R. A. (1998). A comparison of topics and objectives in a cross section of young men's and women's everyday conversations. In D. J. Canary & K. Dindia (Eds.), *Sex differences and similarities in communication: Critical essays and empirical investigations of sex and gender in interaction* (pp. 303–319). Mahwah, NJ: Erlbaum.

48. Fandrich, A. M., & Beck, S. J. (2012). Powerless language in health media: The influence of biological sex and magazine type on health language. *Communication Studies, 63,* 36–53.

49. Carli, L. L. (1990). Gender, language, and influence. *Journal of Personality and Social Psychology, 59,* 941–951.

50. Canary, D. J., & Hause, K. S. (1993). Is there any reason to research sex differences in communication? *Communication Quarterly, 41,* 129–144.

51. Zahn, C. J. (1989). The bases for differing evaluations of male and female speech: Evidence from ratings of transcribed conversation. *Communication Monographs, 56,* 59–74; Grob, L. M., Meyers, R. A., & Schuh, R. (1997). Powerful/powerless language use in group interactions: Sex differences or similarities? *Communication Quarterly, 45,* 282–303.

52. Precht, K. (2008). Sex similarities and differences in stance in informal American conversation. *Journal of Sociolinguistics, 12,* 89–111.

53. Dindia, K. (2006). Men are from North Dakota, women are from South Dakota. In K. Dindia & D. J. Canary (Eds.), *Sex differences and similarities in communication: Critical essays and empirical investigations of sex and gender in interaction* (2nd ed., pp. 3–20). Mahwah, NJ: Erlbaum.

54. Zahn, C. J. (1989). The bases for differing evaluations of male and female speech: Evidence from ratings of transcribed conversation. *Communication Monographs, 56,* 59–74.

55. Fisher, B. A. (1983). Differential effects of sexual composition and interactional content on interaction patterns in dyads. *Human Communication Research, 9,* 225–238.

56. Pilgeram, R. (2007). "Ass-kicking" women: Doing and undoing gender in a US livestock auction. *Gender, Work and Organization, 14,* 572–595.

57. Ellis, D. G., & McCallister, L. (1980). Relational control sequences in sex-typed and androgynous groups. *Western Journal of Speech Communication, 44,* 35–49.

58. Steen, S., & Schwarz, P. (1995). Communication, gender, and power: Homosexual couples as a case study. In M. A. Fitzpatrick & A. L. Vangelisti (Eds.), *Explaining family interactions* (pp. 310–343). Thousand Oaks, CA: Sage.

59. Samovar, L. A., & Porter, R. E. (1991). *Communication between cultures* (pp. 165–169). Dubuque, IA: W. C. Brown.

60. Ricks, D. (1983). *Big business blunders: Mistakes in international marketing* (p. 41). Homewood, IL: Dow Jones-Irwin.

61. Sugimoto, N. (1991, March). *"Excuse me" and "I'm sorry": Apologetic behaviors of Americans and Japanese.* Paper presented at the Conference on Communication in Japan and the United States, California State University, Fullerton.

62. Gudykunst, W. B., & Ting-Toomey, S. (1988). *Culture and interpersonal communication.* Newbury Park, CA: Sage.

63. Hall, E. (1959). *Beyond culture.* New York: Doubleday.

64. Basso, K. (1970). To give up on words: Silence in Western Apache culture. *Southern Journal of Anthropology, 26,* 213–230.

65. Yum, J. (1987). The practice of Uye-ri in interpersonal relationships in Korea. In D. Kincaid (Ed.), *Communication theory from Eastern and Western perspectives* (pp. 87–100). New York: Academic Press.

66. Boroditsky, L. (2009). How does our language shape the way we think? In M. Brockman (Ed.), *What's next? Dispatches on the future of science* (pp. 116–129). New York: Vintage; Deutscher, G. (2010). *Through the language glass: Why the world looks different in other languages.* New York: Metropolitan Books.

67. Martin, L., & Pullum, G. (1991). *The great Eskimo vocabulary hoax.* Chicago: University of Chicago Press.

68. Giles, H., & Franklyn-Stokes, A. (1989). Communicator characteristics. In M. K. Asante & W. B. Gudykunst (Eds.), *Handbook of international and intercultural communication* (pp. 117–144). Newbury Park, CA: Sage.

69. Whorf, B. (1956). The relation of habitual thought and behavior to language. In J. B. Carroll (Ed.), *Language, thought, and reality* (pp. 134–159). Cambridge, MA: MIT Press.

70. Rheingold, H. (1988). *They have a word for it.* Los Angeles: Jeremy P. Tarcher.

71. Bowers, J. S., & Pleydell-Pearce, C. W. (2011). Swearing, euphemisms, and linguistic relativity. *PLoS ONE, 6,* e22341. doi:10.1371/journal.pone.0022341

CHAPTER SIX

1. Burgoon, J. K. (1994). Nonverbal signals. In M. L. Knapp & G. R. Miller (Eds.), *Handbook of interpersonal communication* (p. 235). Newbury Park, CA: Sage.

2. Riggio, R. E. (2006). Nonverbal skills and abilities. In V. Manusov & M. L. Patterson (Eds.), *The Sage handbook of*

nonverbal communication (pp. 79–86). Thousand Oaks, CA: Sage.

3. Burgoon, J. K., Guerrero, L., & Manusov, V. (2011). Nonverbal signals. In M. L. Knapp & J. A. Daly (Eds.), *The Sage handbook of interpersonal communication* (4th ed., pp. 239–282). Thousand Oaks, CA: Sage.

4. Jones, S. E., & LeBaron, C. D. (2002). Research on the relationship between verbal and nonverbal communication: Emerging interactions. *Journal of Communication, 52,* 499–521.

5. DePaulo, B. M. (1994). Spotting lies: Can humans learn to do better? *Current Directions in Psychological Science, 3,* 83–86.

6. Burgoon, J. K. (1994). Nonverbal signals. In M. L. Knapp & G. R. Miller (Eds.), *Handbook of interpersonal communication* (pp. 229–232). Newbury Park, CA: Sage.

7. Manusov, F. (1991, Summer). Perceiving nonverbal messages: Effects of immediacy and encoded intent on receiver judgments. *Western Journal of Speech Communication, 55,* 235–253; Buck, R., & VanLear, C. A. (2002). Verbal and nonverbal communication: Distinguishing symbolic, spontaneous, and pseudo-spontaneous nonverbal behavior. *Journal of Communication, 52,* 522–541.

8. Clevenger, T., Jr. (1991). Can one not communicate? A conflict of models. *Communication Studies, 42,* 340–353.

9. Burgoon, J. K., & LePoire, B. A. (1999). Nonverbal cues and interpersonal judgments: Participant and observer perceptions of intimacy, dominance, composure, and formality. *Communication Monographs, 66,* 105–124.

10. Keating, C. F. (2006). Why and how the silent self speak volumes: Functional approaches to nonverbal impression management. In V. Manusov & M. L. Patterson (Eds.), *The Sage handbook of nonverbal communication* (pp. 321–340). Thousand Oaks, CA: Sage.

11. Horan, S. M., & Booth-Butterfield, M. (2010). Investing in affection: An investigation of affection exchange theory and relational qualities. *Communication Quarterly, 58,* 394–413.

12. Ramirez, A., & Burgoon, J. K. (2004). The effect of interactivity on initial interactions: The influence of information valence and modality and information richness on computer-mediated interaction. *Communication Monographs, 71,* 442–447.

13. Derks, D., Bos, A. E. R., & von Grumbkow, J. (2007). Emoticons and social interaction on the Internet: The importance of social context. *Computers in Human Behavior, 23,* 442–879; Byron, K., & Baldridge, D. (2007). E-mail recipients' impressions of senders' likeability: The interactive effect of nonverbal cues and recipients' personality." *Journal of Business Communication, 44,* 137.

14. Cross, E. S., & Franz, E. A. (2003, April). *Talking hands: Observation of bimanual gestures as a facilitative working memory mechanism.* Paper presented at the Cognitive Neuroscience Society 10th Annual Meeting, New York.

15. Motley, M. T. (1993). Facial affect and verbal context in conversation: Facial expression as interjection. *Human Communication Research, 20,* 3–40.

16. Capella, J. N., & Schreiber, D. M. (2006). The interaction management function of nonverbal cues. In V. Manusov & M. L. Patterson (Eds.), *The Sage handbook of nonverbal communication* (pp 361–379). Thousand Oaks, CA: Sage.

17. Giles, H., & LePoire, B. A. (2006). The ubiquity of social meaningfulness of nonverbal communication. In V. Manusov & M. L. Patterson (Eds.), *The Sage handbook of nonverbal communication* (pp. xv–xxvii). Thousand Oaks, CA: Sage.

18. Ekman, P. (2003). *Emotions revealed: Recognizing faces and feelings to improve communication and emotional life.* New York: Holt.

19. Vrig, A. (2006). Nonverbal communication and deception. In V. Manusov & M. L. Patterson (Eds.), *The Sage handbook of nonverbal communication* (pp. 341–360). Thousand Oaks, CA: Sage.

20. Guerrero, L. K., & Floyd, K. (2006). *Nonverbal communication in close relationships.* Mahwah, NJ: Erlbaum; DePaulo, B. M.(1980). Detecting deception modality effects. In L. Wheeler (Ed.), *Review of personality and social psychology* (Vol. 1, pp. 125–162). Beverly Hills, CA: Sage; Greene, J., O'Hair, D., Cody, M., & Yen, C. (1985). Planning and control of behavior during deception. *Human Communication Research, 11,* 335–364.

21. Burgoon, J. K., & Levine, T. R. (2010). Advances in deception detection. In S. W. Smith & S. R. Wilson (Eds.), *New directions in interpersonal communication research* (pp. 201–220). Thousand Oaks, CA: Sage.

22. Lock, C. (2004). Deception detection: Psychologists try to learn how to spot a liar. *Science News Online, 166,* 72.

23. Caso, L., Vrij, A., Mann, S., & DeLeo, G. (2006). Deceptive responses: The impact of verbal and non-verbal countermeasures. *Legal and Criminological Psychology, 11,* 99–111; Vrig, A. (2004). Why professionals fail to catch liars and how they can improve. *Legal and Criminological Psychology, 9,* 159–181.

24. Harwig, M., & Bond, C. F. (2011). Why do lie-catchers fail? A lens model meta-analysis of human lie judgments. *Psychological Bulletin, 137,* 643–659.

25. Lindsey, A. E., & Vigil, V. (1999). The interpretation and evaluation of winking in stranger dyads. *Communication Research Reports, 16,* 256–265.

26. Smiling through the artichokes. (1998, September 9). *San Francisco Examiner.* Retrieved from http://www.sfgate.com /cgi-bin/article.cgi?f=/e/a/1998/09/09/EDITORIAL4056.dtl

27. Simon, R. (1995, March 20). Proceed with caution if using hand signals. *Los Angeles Times.* Retrieved from http:// articles.latimes.com/1995–03–20/local/me-44877_1 _hand-signals

28. Lim, G. Y., & Roloff, M. E. (1999). Attributing sexual consent. *Journal of Applied Communication Research, 27,* 1–23.

29. Rourke, B. P. (1989). *Nonverbal learning disabilities: The syndrome and the model.* New York: Guilford.

30. Fudge, E. S. (n.d.). *Nonverbal learning disorder syndrome?* Retrieved from http://www.nldontheweb.org/fudge.htm

31. Rosip, J. C., & Hall, J. A. (2004). Knowledge of nonverbal cues, gender, and nonverbal decoding accuracy. *Journal of Nonverbal Behavior, 28,* 267–286; Hall, J. A. (1985). Male and female nonverbal behavior. In A. W. Siegman & S. Feldstein (Eds.), *Multichannel integrations of nonverbal behavior* (pp.69–103). Hillsdale, NJ: Erlbaum.

32. Hall, J. A. (2006). Women and men's nonverbal communication. In V. Manusov & M. L. Patterson (Eds.), *The Sage handbook of nonverbal communication* (pp. 201–218). Thousand Oaks, CA: Sage.

33. Canary, D. J., & Emmers-Sommer, T. M. (1997). *Sex and gender differences in personal relationships*. New York: Guilford.

34. Knofler, T., & Imhof, M. (2007). Does sexual orientation have an impact on nonverbal behavior in interpersonal communication? *Journal of Nonverbal Behavior, 31,* 189–204.

35. Matsumoto, D., & Yoo, S. H. (2005). Culture and applied nonverbal communication. In R. S. Feldman & R. E. Riggio (Eds.), *Applications of nonverbal communication* (pp. 255–277). Mahwah, NJ: Erlbaum.

36. Birdwhistell, R. (1970). *Kinesics and context*. Philadelphia: University of Pennsylvania Press.

37. Ekman, P., Friesen, W. V., & Baer, J. (1984, May). The international language of gestures. *Psychology Today, 18,* 64–69.

38. Hall, E. (1969). *The hidden dimension*. Garden City, NY: Anchor Books.

39. Matsumoto, D. (2006). Culture and nonverbal behavior. In V. Manusov & M. L. Patterson (Eds.), *The Sage handbook of nonverbal communication* (pp. 219–235). Thousand Oaks, CA: Sage.

40. Bavelas, J. B., Coates, L., & Johnson, T. (2002). Listener responses as a collaborative process: The role of gaze. *Journal of Communication, 52,* 566–579.

41. Levine, R. (1988). The pace of life across cultures. In J. E. McGrath (Ed.), *The social psychology of time* (pp. 39–60). Newbury Park, CA: Sage.

42. Hall, E. T., & Hall, M. R. (1987). *Hidden differences: Doing business with the Japanese*. Garden City, NY: Anchor Press.

43. Levine, R., & Wolff, E. (1985, March). Social time: The heartbeat of culture. *Psychology Today, 19,* 28–35.

44. Booth-Butterfield, M., & Jordan, F. (1998). *"Act like us": Communication adaptation among racially homogeneous and heterogeneous groups*. Paper presented at the Speech Communication Association meeting, New Orleans.

45. Ekman, P. (2003). *Emotions revealed*. New York: Holt.

46. Eibl-Eibesfeldt, J. (1972). Universals and cultural differences in facial expressions of emotions. In J. Cole (Ed.), *Nebraska symposium on motivation* (pp. 297–314). Lincoln: University of Nebraska Press.

47. Coulson, M. (2004). Attributing emotion to static body postures: Recognition accuracy, confusions, and viewpoint dependence. *Journal of Nonverbal Behavior, 28,* 117–139.

48. Mehrabian, A. (1981). *Silent messages* (2nd ed., pp. 47–48, 61–62). Belmont, CA: Wadsworth.

49. Carney, D. R., Cuddy, A. J., & Yap, A. J. (2010). Power posing: Brief nonverbal displays affect neuroendocrine levels and risk tolerance. *Psychological Science, 21,* 1363–1368.

50. Corballis, M. C. (2002). *From hand to mouth: The origins of language*. Princeton, NJ: Princeton University Press.

51. Andersen, P. A. (2008). *Nonverbal communication: Forms and functions* (2nd ed., p. 37). Long Grove, IL: Waveland Press.

52. Ekman, P., & Friesen, W. V. (1969). The repertoire of nonverbal behavior: Categories, origins, usage, and coding. *Semiotica, 1,* 49–98.

53. Sueyoshi, A., & Hardison, D. M. (2005). The role of gestures and facial cues in second language listening comprehension. *Language Learning, 55,* 661–699.

54. Koerner, B. I. (2003, March 28). What does a "thumbs up" mean in Iraq? *Slate*. Retrieved from http://www.slate.com/id/2080812

55. Ekman, P., & Friesen, W. V. (1974). Nonverbal behavior and psychopathology. In R. J. Friedman & M. N. Katz (Eds.), *The psychology of depression: Contemporary theory and research* (pp. 3–31). Washington, DC: J. Winston.

56. Ekman, P. (2001). *Telling lies*. New York: Norton.

57. Ekman, P., & Friesen, W. V. (1975). *Unmasking the face: A guide to recognizing emotions from facial clues*. Englewood Cliffs, NJ: Prentice-Hall.

58. Ekman, P., & Friesen, W. V. (1975). *Unmasking the face: A guide to recognizing emotions from facial clues* (p. 150). Englewood Cliffs, NJ: Prentice-Hall.

59. Krumhuber, E., & Kappas, A. (2005). Moving smiles: The role of dynamic components for the perception of the genuineness of smiles. *Journal of Nonverbal Behavior, 29,* 3–24.

60. Davis, S. F., & Kieffer, J. C. (1998). Restaurant servers influence tipping behavior. *Psychological Reports, 83,* 223–226.

61. Gueguen, N., & Jacob, C. (2002). Direct look versus evasive glance and compliance with a request. *Journal of Social Psychology, 142,* 393–396.

62. Andersen, P. A., Guerrero, L. K., & Jones, S. M. (2006). Nonverbal behavior in intimate interactions and intimate relationships. In V. Manusov & M. L. Patterson (Eds.), *The Sage handbook of nonverbal communication* (pp. 259–278). Thousand Oaks, CA: Sage.

63. Burgoon, J. K., & Dunbar, N. E. (2006). Nonverbal skills and abilities. In V. Manusov & M. L. Patterson (Eds.), *The Sage handbook of nonverbal communication* (pp. 279–298). Thousand Oaks, CA: Sage.

64. Guerrero, L. K., & Floyd, K. (2006). *Nonverbal communication in close relationships*. Mahwah, NJ: Erlbaum.

65. Davis, M., Markus, K. A., & Walters, S. B. (2006). Judging the credibility of criminal suspect statements: Does mode of presentation matter? *Journal of Nonverbal Behavior, 30,* 181–198.

66. Einhorn, L. J. (1981). An inner view of the job interview: An investigation of successful communicative behaviors. *Communication Education, 30,* 217–228.

67. Bone, J. (2009, January 23). Caroline Kennedy says no to Senate but may become London envoy. *London Times*. Retrieved from http://www.timesonline.co.uk

68. Knapp, M. L., & Hall, J. A. (2010). *Nonverbal communication in human interaction* (7th ed., pp. 344–346). Boston: Wadsworth.

69. Trees, A. R. (2000). Nonverbal communication and the support process: Interactional sensitivity in interactions between mothers and young adult children. *Communication Monographs, 67,* 239–261.

70. Buller, D., & Aune, K. (1992). The effects of speech rate similarity on compliance: Application of communication accommodation theory. *Western Journal of Communication, 56,* 37–53; Buller, D., LePoire, B. A., Aune, K., & Eloy, S. V. (1992). Social perceptions as mediators of the effect of speech rate similarity on compliance. *Human Communication Research, 19,* 286–311; Buller, D. B., & Aune, R. K. (1988). The effects of vocalics and nonverbal sensitivity on compliance: A speech accommodation theory explanation. *Human Communication Research, 14,* 301–332.

71. Andersen, P. A. (1984). Nonverbal communication in the small group. In R. S. Cathcart & L. A. Samovar (Eds.), *Small group communication: A reader* (4th ed., pp. 258–270). Dubuque, IA: W. C. Brown.

72. Harris, M., Ivanko, S., Jungen, S., Hala, S., & Pexman, P. (2001, October). *You're really nice: Children's understanding of sarcasm and personality traits.* Poster presented at 2nd Biennial Meeting of the Cognitive Development Society, Virginia Beach.

73. Tusing, K. J., & Dillard, J. P. (2000). The sounds of dominance: Vocal precursors of perceived dominance during interpersonal influence. *Human Communication Research, 26,* 148–171.

74. Zuckerman, M., & Driver, R. E. (1989). What sounds beautiful is good: The vocal attractiveness stereotype. *Journal of Nonverbal Behavior, 13,* 67–82.

75. Ng, S. H., & Bradac, J. J. (1993). *Power in language: Verbal communication and social influence* (p. 40). Newbury Park, CA: Sage.

76. Heslin, R., & Alper, T. (1983). Touch: A bonding gesture. In J. M. Wiemann & R. P. Harrison (Eds.), *Nonverbal interaction* (pp. 47–75). Beverly Hills, CA: Sage.

77. Heslin, R., & Alper, T. (1983). Touch: A bonding gesture. In J. M. Wiemann & R. P. Harrison (Eds.), *Nonverbal interaction* (pp. 47–75). Beverly Hills, CA: Sage.

78. Burgoon, J., Walther, J., & Baesler, E. (1992). Interpretations, evaluations, and consequences of interpersonal touch. *Human Communication Research, 19,* 237–263.

79. Crusco, A. H., & Wetzel, C. G. (1984). The Midas touch: Effects of interpersonal touch on restaurant tipping. *Personality and Social Psychology Bulletin, 10,* 512–517.

80. Hornik, J. (1992). Effects of physical contact on customers' shopping time and behavior. *Marketing Letters, 3,* 49–55.

81. Smith, D. E., Gier, J. A., & Willis, F. N. (1982). Interpersonal touch and compliance with a marketing request. *Basic and Applied Social Psychology, 3,* 35–38.

82. Gueguen, N., & Vion, M. (2009). The effect of a practitioner's touch on a patient's medication compliance. *Psychology, Health & Medicine, 14,* 689–694.

83. Adler, T. (1993, February). Congressional staffers witness miracle of touch. *APA Monitor,* 12–13.

84. Driscoll, M. S., Newman, D. L., & Seal, J. M. (1988). The effect of touch on the perception of counselors. *Counselor Education and Supervision, 27,* 344–354; Wilson, J. M. (1982). The value of touch in psychotherapy. *American Journal of Orthopsychiatry, 52,* 65–72.

85. Field, T., Lasko, D., Mundy, P., Henteleff, T., Kabat, S., Talpins, S., & Dowling, M. (1997). Brief report: Autistic children's attentiveness and responsivity improve after touch therapy. *Journal of Autism and Developmental Disorders, 27,* 333–338.

86. Kraus, M. W., Huang, C., & Keltner, D. (2010). Tactile communication, cooperation, and performance: An ethological study of the NBA. *Emotion, 10,* 745–749.

87. Patzer, G. (2008). *Looks: Why they matter more than you ever imagined.* New York: Amacon.

88. Hosoda, M., Stone-Romero, E. F., & Coats, G. (2003). The effects of physical attractiveness on job-related outcomes: A meta-analysis of experimental studies. *Personnel Psychology, 56,* 431–462.

89. Agthe, M., Sporrle, M., & Maner, J. K. (2011). Does being attractive always help? Positive and negative effects of attractiveness on social decision making. *Personality and Social Psychology Bulletin, 37,* 1042–1054.

90. Dion, K. K. (1973). Young children's stereotyping of facial attractiveness. *Developmental Psychology, 9,* 183–188.

91. Ritts, V., Patterson, M. L., & Tubbs, M. E. (1992). Expectations, impressions, and judgments of physically attractive students: A review. *Review of Educational Research, 62,* 413–426.

92. Riniolo, T. C., Johnson, K. C., & Sherman, T. R. (2006). Hot or not: Do professors perceived as physically attractive receive higher student evaluations? *Journal of General Psychology, 133,* 19–35.

93. Albada, K. F., Knapp, M. L., & Theune, K. E. (2002). Interaction appearance theory: Changing perceptions of physical attractiveness through social interaction. *Communication Theory, 12,* 8–40.

94. Thourlby, W. (1978). *You are what you wear* (p. 1). New York: New American Library.

95. Knapp, M. L., & Hall, J. A. (2010). *Nonverbal communication in human interaction* (7th ed., pp. 201–207). Boston: Wadsworth.

96. Hall, E. (1969). *The hidden dimension.* Garden City, NY: Anchor Books.

97. Hackman, M., & Walker, K. (1990). Instructional communication in the televised classroom: The effects of system design and teacher immediacy. *Communication Education, 39,* 196–206; McCroskey, J. C., & Richmond, V. P. (1992). Increasing teacher influence through immediacy. In V. P. Richmond & J. C. McCroskey (Eds.), *Power in the classroom: Communication, control, and concern* (pp. 101–119). Hillsdale, NJ: Erlbaum.

98. Conlee, C., Olvera, J., & Vagim, N. (1993). The relationships among physician nonverbal immediacy and measures of patient satisfaction with physician care. *Communication Reports, 6,* 25–33.

99. Brown, G., Lawrence, T. B., & Robinson, S. L. (2005). Territoriality in organizations. *Academy of Management Review, 30,* 577–594.

100. Sadalla, E. (1987). Identity and symbolism in housing. *Environment and Behavior, 19,* 569–587.

101. Maslow, A., & Mintz, N. (1956). Effects of aesthetic surroundings: Initial effects of those aesthetic surroundings upon perceiving "energy" and "well-being" in faces. *Journal of Psychology, 41,* 247–254.

102. Teven, J. J., & Comadena, M. E. (1996). The effects of office aesthetic quality on students' perceptions of teacher credibility and communicator style. *Communication Research Reports, 13,* 101–108.

103. Sommer, R. (1969). *Personal space: The behavioral basis of design.* Englewood Cliffs, NJ: Prentice-Hall.

104. Sommer, R., & Augustin, S. (2007). Spatial orientation in the cubicle. *Journal of Facilities Management, 5,* 205–214.

105. Ballard, D. I., & Seibold, D. R. (2000). Time orientation and temporal variation across work groups: Implications for group and organizational communication. *Western Journal of Communication, 64,* 218–242.

106. Kalman, Y. M., & Rafaeli, S. (2011). Online pauses and silence: Chronemic expectancy violations in written computer-mediated communication. *Communication Research, 38,* 54–69.

107. Andersen, P. A., Guerrero, L. K., & Jones, S. M. (2006). Nonverbal behavior in intimate interactions and intimate relationships. In V. Manusov & M. L. Patterson (Eds.), *The Sage handbook of nonverbal communication* (pp. 259–278). Thousand Oaks, CA: Sage.

108. Egland, K. I., Stelzner, M. A., Andersen, P. A., & Spitzberg, B. S. (1997). Perceived understanding, nonverbal communication, and relational satisfaction. In J. E. Aitken & L. J. Shedletsky (Eds.), *Intrapersonal communication processes* (pp. 386–396). Annandale, VA: Speech Communication Association.

109. Walther, J. B. (2006). Nonverbal dynamics in computer-mediated communication. In V. Manusov & M. L. Patterson (Eds.), *The Sage handbook of nonverbal communication* (pp. 461–479). Thousand Oaks, CA: Sage.

110. Walther, J. B., & Bunz, U. (2005). The rules of virtual groups: Trust, liking, and performance in computer-mediated communication. *Journal of Communication, 55*, 828–846.

CHAPTER SEVEN

1. Emanuel, R., Adams, J., Baker, K., Daufin, E. K., Ellington, C., Fitts, E., Himsel, J., Holladay, L., & Okeowo, D. (2008). How college students spend their time communicating. *International Journal of Listening, 22*, 13–28; Barker, L., Edwards, R., Gaines, C., Gladney, K., & Holley, R. (1981). An investigation of proportional time spent in various communication activities by college students. *Journal of Applied Communication Research, 8*, 101–109.

2. Wolvin, A. D., & Coakley, C. G. (1981). A survey of the status of listening training in some Fortune 500 corporations. *Communication Education, 40*, 152–164.

3. Prager, K. J., & Buhrmester, D. (1998). Intimacy and need fulfillment in couple relationships. *Journal of Social and Personal Relationships, 15*, 435–469.

4. Vangelisti, A. L. (1994). Couples' communication problems: The counselor's perspective. *Journal of Applied Communication Research, 22*, 106–126.

5. Wolvin, A. D. (1984). Meeting the communication needs of the adult learners. *Communication Education, 33*, 267–271.

6. Beall, M. L., Gill-Rosier, J., Tate, J., & Matten, A. (2008). State of the context: Listening in education. *International Journal of Listening, 22*, 123–132.

7. Davis, J., Foley, A., Crigger, N., & Brannigan, M. C. (2008). Healthcare and listening: A relationship for caring. *International Journal of Listening, 22*, 168–175; Davis, J., Thompson, C. R., Foley, A., Bond, C. D., & DeWitt, J. (2008). An examination of listening concepts in the healthcare context: Differences among nurses, physicians, and administrators. *International Journal of Listening, 22*, 152–167.

8. Schnapp, D. C. (2008). Listening in context: Religion and spirituality. *International Journal of Listening, 22*, 133–140.

9. Flynn, J., Valikoski, T., & Grau, J. (2008). Listening in the business context: Reviewing the state of research. *International Journal of Listening, 22*, 141–151.

10. Fernald, A. (2001). Hearing, listening, and understanding: Auditory development in infancy. In G. Bemner & A. Fogel (Eds.), *Blackwell handbook of infant development* (pp. 35–70). Malden, MA: Blackwell.

11. Burleson, B. R. (2010). Explaining recipient responses to supportive messages: Development and tests of a dual-process theory. In S. W. Smith & S. R. Wilson (Eds.), *New directions in interpersonal communication research* (pp. 159–179). Los Angeles: Sage; Bodie, G. D., & Burleson, B. R. (2008). Explaining variations in the effects of supportive messages: A dual-process framework. In C. S. Beck (Ed.), *Communication yearbook 32* (pp. 355–398). New York: Routledge.

12. Langer, E. (1990). *Mindfulness*. Reading, MA: Addison-Wesley; Burgoon, J. K., Berger, C. R., & Waldron, V. R. (2000). Mindfulness and interpersonal communication. *Journal of Social Issues, 56*, 105–127.

13. Burgoon, J. K., Berger, C. R., & Waldron, V. R. (2000). Mindfulness and interpersonal communication. *Journal of Social Issues, 56*, 105–127.

14. Langer, E. (1990). *Mindfulness* (p. 90). Reading, MA: Addison-Wesley.

15. Cooper, L. O., & Buchanan, T. (2010). Listening competency on campus: A psychometric analysis of student listening. *The International Journal of Listening, 24*, 141–163.

16. Kochkin, S. (2005). MarkeTrak VII: Hearing loss population tops 31 million. *Hearing Review, 12*, 16–29.

17. Flexer, C. (1997, February). Commonly asked questions about children with minimal hearing loss in the classroom. *Hearing Loss*, 8–12.

18. Smeltzer, L. R., & Watson, K. W. (1984). Listening: An empirical comparison of discussion length and level of incentive. *Central States Speech Journal, 35*, 166–170.

19. Pasupathi, M., Stallworth, L. M., & Murdoch, K. (1998). How what we tell becomes what we know: Listener effects on speakers' long-term memory for events. *Discourse Processes, 26*, 1–25.

20. Powers, W. G., & Witt, P. L. (2008). Expanding the theoretical framework of communication fidelity. *Communication Quarterly, 56*, 247–267; Fitch-Hauser, M., Powers, W. G., O'Brien, K., & Hanson, S. (2007). Extending the conceptualization of listening fidelity. *International Journal of Listening, 21*, 81–91; Powers, W. G., & Bodie, G. D. (2003). Listening fidelity: Seeking congruence between cognitions of the listener and the sender. *International Journal of Listening, 17*, 19–31.

21. Lewis, M. H., & Reinsch, N. L., Jr. (1988). Listening in organizational environments. *Journal of Business Communication, 23*, 49–67.

22. Imhof, M. (2002). In the eye of the beholder: Children's perception of good and poor listening behavior. *International Journal of Listening, 16*, 40–57.

23. Barker, L. L. (1971). *Listening behavior*. Englewood Cliffs, NJ: Prentice-Hall.

24. Vangelisti, A. L., Knapp, M. L., & Daly, J. A. (1990). Conversational narcissism. *Communication Monographs, 57*, 251–274; McCroskey, J. C., & Richmond, V. P. (1993). Identifying compulsive communicators: The talkaholic scale. *Communication Research Reports, 10*, 107–114.

25. McComb, K. B., & Jablin, F. M. (1984). Verbal correlates of interviewer empathic listening and employment interview outcomes. *Communication Monographs, 51*, 367.

26. Hansen, J. (2007). *24/7: How cell phones and the Internet change the way we live, work, and play*. New York: Praeger; Turner, J. W., & Reinsch, N. L. (2007). The business

communicator as presence allocator: Multicommunicating, equivocality, and status at work. *Journal of Business Communication*, *44*, 36–58.

27. Wolvin, A., & Coakley, C. G. (1988). *Listening* (3rd ed., p. 208). Dubuque, IA: W. C. Brown.

28. Nichols, R. (1987, September). Listening is a ten-part skill. *Nation's Business*, *75*, 40.

29. Golen, S. (1990). A factor analysis of barriers to effective listening. *Journal of Business Communication*, *27*, 25–36.

30. Nelson, P., Kohnert, K., Sabur, S., & Shaw, D. (2005). Noise and children learning through a second language: Double jeopardy? *Language, Speech, & Hearing Services in Schools*, *36*, 219–229.

31. Kline, N. (1999). *Time to think: Listening to ignite the human mind* (p. 21). London: Ward Lock.

32. Carrell, L. J., & Willmington, S. C. (1996). A comparison of self-report and performance data in assessing speaking and listening competence. *Communication Reports*, *9*, 185–191.

33. Nichols, R. G., Brown, J. I., & Keller, R. J. (2006). Measurement of communication skills. *International Journal of Listening*, *20*, 13–17; Spinks, N., & Wells, B. (1991). Improving listening power: The payoff. *Bulletin of the Association for Business Communication*, *54*, 75–77.

34. Listen to this: Hearing problems can stress relationships. (2008). Retrieved from http://www.energizer.com/livehealthy/#listentothis; Shafer, D. N. (2007). Hearing loss hinders relationships. *ASHA Leader*, *12*, 5–7.

35. Carbaugh, D. (1999). "Just listen": "Listening" and landscape among the Blackfeet. *Western Journal of Communication*, *63*, 250–270.

36. Bippus, A. M. (2001). Recipients' criteria for evaluating the skillfulness of comforting communication and the outcomes of comforting interactions. *Communication Monographs*, *68*, 301–313.

37. Goodman, G., & Esterly, G. (1990). Questions—The most popular piece of language. In J. Stewart (Ed.), *Bridges not walls* (5th ed., pp. 69–77). New York: McGraw-Hill.

38. Burleson, B. R. (1994). Comforting messages: Features, functions, and outcomes. In J. A. Daly & J. M. Wiemann (Eds.), *Strategic interpersonal communication* (p. 140). Hillsdale, NJ: Erlbaum.

39. Myers, S. (2000). Empathic listening: Reports on the experience of being heard. *Journal of Humanistic Psychology*, *40*, 148–173; Grant, S. G. (1998). A principal's active listening skills and teachers' perceptions of the principal's leader behaviors. *Dissertation Abstracts International Section A: Humanities and Social Sciences*, *58*, 2933; Van Hasselt, V. B., Baker, M. T., & Romano, S. J. (2006). Crisis (hostage) negotiation training: A preliminary evaluation of program efficacy. *Criminal Justice and Behavior*, *33*, 56–69.

40. Bruneau, J. (1989). Empathy and listening: A conceptual review and theoretical directions. *Journal of the International Listening Association*, *3*, 1–20; Cissna, K. N., & Anderson, R. (1990). The contributions of Carl R. Rogers to a philosophical praxis of dialogue. *Western Journal of Speech Communication*, *54*, 137–147.

41. Burleson, B. R. (2003). Emotional support skills. In J. O. Greene and B. R. Burleson (Eds.), *Handbook of communication and social interaction skills* (p. 552). Mahwah, NJ: Erlbaum.

42. Hample, D. (2006). Anti-comforting messages. In K. M. Galvin & P. J. Cooper (Eds.), *Making connections: Readings in relational communication* (4th ed., pp. 222–227). Los Angeles: Roxbury; Burleson, B. R., & MacGeorge, E. L. (2002). Supportive communication. In M. L. Knapp & J. A. Daly (Eds.), *Handbook of interpersonal communication* (3rd ed., pp. 374–422). Thousand Oaks, CA: Sage.

43. Samter, W., Burleson, B. R., & Murphy, L. B. (1987). Comforting conversations: The effects of strategy type on evaluations of messages and message producers. *Southern Speech Communication Journal*, *52*, 263–284.

44. Burleson, B. (2008). What counts as effective emotional support? In M. T. Motley (Ed.), *Studies in applied interpersonal communication* (pp. 207–227). Thousand Oaks, CA: Sage.

45. Davidowitz, M., & Myrick, R. D. (1984). Responding to the bereaved: An analysis of "helping" statements. *Death Education*, *8*, 1–10; Servaty-Seib, H. L., & Burleson, B. R. (2007). Bereaved adolescents' evaluations of the helpfulness of support-intended statements. *Journal of Social and Personal Relationships*, *24*, 207–223; Toller, P. (2011). Bereaved parents' experiences of supportive and unsupportive communication. *Southern Communication Journal*, *76*, 17–34.

46. Miczo, N., & Burgoon, J. K. (2008). Facework and nonverbal behavior in social support interactions within romantic dyads. In M. T. Motley (Ed.), *Studies in applied interpersonal communication* (pp. 245–266). Thousand Oaks, CA: Sage.

47. Clark, R. A., & Delia, J. G. (1997). Individuals' preferences for friends' approaches to providing support in distressing situations. *Communication Reports*, *10*, 115–121.

48. Lewis, T., & Manusov, V. (2009). Listening to another's distress in everyday relationships. *Communication Quarterly*, *57*, 282–301.

49. MacGeorge, E. L., Feng, B., & Thompson, E. R. (2008). "Good" and "bad" advice: How to advise more effectively." In M. T. Motley (Ed.), *Studies in applied interpersonal communication* (pp. 145–164). Thousand Oaks, CA: Sage; Notarius, C. J., & Herrick, L. R. (1988). Listener response strategies to a distressed other. *Journal of Social and Personal Relationships*, *5*, 97–108.

50. Messman, S. J., Canary, D. J., & Hause, K. S. (2000). Motives to remain platonic, equity, and the use of maintenance strategies in opposite-sex friendships. *Journal of Social and Personal Relationships*, *17*, 67–94.

51. Goldsmith, D. J., & Fitch, K. (1997). The normative context of advice as social support. *Human Communication Research*, *23*, 454–476; Goldsmith, D. J., & MacGeorge, E. L. (2000). The impact of politeness and relationship on perceived quality of advice about a problem. *Human Communication Research*, *26*, 234–263.

52. MacGeorge, E. L., Feng, B., & Thompson, E. R. (2008). "Good" and "bad" advice: How to advise more effectively." In M. T. Motley (Ed.), *Studies in applied interpersonal communication* (pp. 145–164). Thousand Oaks, CA: Sage.

53. Miczo, N., & Burgoon, J. K. (2008). Facework and nonverbal behavior in social support interactions within romantic dyads. In M. T. Motley (Ed.), *Studies in applied interpersonal communication* (pp. 245–266). Thousand Oaks, CA: Sage.

54. Silver, R., & Wortman, C. (1981). Coping with undesirable life events. In J. Garber & M. Seligman (Eds.), *Human helplessness: Theory and applications* (pp. 279–340). New York: Academic Press; Young, C. R., Giles, D. E., & Plantz, M. C. (1982). Natural networks: Help-giving and help-seeking in two rural communities. *American Journal of Community Psychology, 10*, 457–469.

55. Clark, R. A., & Delia, J. G. (1997). Individuals' preferences for friends' approaches to providing support in distressing situations. *Communication Reports, 10*, 115–121.

56. Burleson, B. (1994). Comforting messages: Their significance and effects. In J. A. Daly & J. M. Wiemann (Eds.), *Communicating strategically: Strategies in interpersonal communication* (pp. 135–161). Hillside, NJ: Erlbaum; Chesbro, J. L. (1999). The relationship between listening styles and conversational sensitivity. *Communication Research Reports, 16*, 233–238.

57. Sargent, S. L., & Weaver, J. B. (2003). Listening styles: Sex differences in perceptions of self and others. *International Journal of Listening, 17*, 5–18; Johnston, M. K., Weaver, J. B., Watson, K., & Barker, L. (2000). Listening styles: Biological or psychological differences? *International Journal of Listening, 14*, 32–47.

58. Samter, W. (2002). How gender and cognitive complexity influence the provision of emotional support: A study of indirect effects. *Communication Reports, 15*, 5–17; Hale, J. L., Tighe, M. R., & Mongeau, P. A. (1997). Effects of event type and sex on comforting messages. *Communication Research Reports, 14*, 214–220.

59. Burleson, B. R. (1982). The development of comforting communication skills in childhood and adolescence. *Child Development, 53*, 1578–1588.

60. Lemieux, R., & Tighe, M. R. (2004). Attachment styles and the evaluation of comforting responses: A receiver perspective. *Communication Research Reports, 21*, 144–153.

61. Burleson, B. R., Holmstrom, A. J., & Gilstrap, C. M. (2005). "Guys can't say that to guys:" Four experiments assessing the normative motivation account for deficiencies in the emotional support provided by men. *Communication Monographs, 72*, 468–501.

62. Woodward, M. S., Rosenfeld, L. B., & May, S. K. (1996). Sex differences in social support in sororities and fraternities. *Journal of Applied Communication Research, 24*, 260–272.

63. Burleson, B. R., & Kunkel, A. (2006). Revisiting the different cultures thesis: An assessment of sex differences and similarities in supportive communication. In K. Dindia & D. J. Canary (Eds.), *Sex differences and similarities in communication* (2nd ed., pp. 137–159). Mahwah, NJ: Erlbaum.

64. Horowitz, L. M., Krasnoperova, E. N., & Tatar, D. G. (2001). The way to console may depend on the goal: Experimental studies of social support. *Journal of Experimental Social Psychology, 37*, 49–61.

65. MacGeorge, E. L., Feng, B., & Thompson, E. R. (2008). "Good" and "bad" advice: How to advise more effectively. In M. T. Motley (Ed.), *Studies in applied interpersonal communication* (pp. 145–164). Thousand Oaks, CA: Sage; Young, R. W., & Cates, C. M. (2004). Emotional and directive listening in peer mentoring. *International Journal of Listening, 18*, 21–33.

66. Feng, B., & Lee, K. J. (2010). The influence of thinking styles on responses to supportive messages. *Communication Studies, 61*, 224–238.

CHAPTER EIGHT

1. Byrne, D. (2010). An overview (and underview) of research and theory within the attraction paradigm. In M. L. Knapp & J. A. Daly (Eds.), *Interpersonal communication* (pp. 77–94). Thousand Oaks, CA: Sage.

2. Hatfield, E., & Sprecher, S. (1986). *Mirror, mirror: The importance of looks in everyday life*. Albany: State University of New York Press.

3. Walster, E., Aronson, E., Abrahams, D., & Rottmann, L. (1966). Importance of physical attractiveness in dating behavior. *Journal of Personality and Social Psychology, 4*, 508–516.

4. Luo, S., & Zhang, G. (2009). What leads to romantic attraction: Similarity, reciprocity, security, or beauty? Evidence from a speed-dating study. *Journal of Personality, 77*, 933–964.

5. Hancock, J. T., & Toma, C. L. (2009). Putting your best face forward: The accuracy of online dating profile photographs. *Journal of Communication, 59*, 367–386.

6. Antheunis, M. L., & Schouten, A. P. (2011). The effects of other-generated and system-generated cues on adolescents' perceived attractiveness on social network sites. *Journal of Computer-Mediated Communication, 16*, 391–406.

7. Lewandowski, G. W., Aron, A., & Gee, J. (2007). Personality goes a long way: The malleability of opposite-sex physical attractiveness. *Personal Relationships, 14*, 571–585.

8. Albada, K. F. (2010). Interaction appearance theory: Changing perceptions of physical attractiveness through social interaction. In M. L. Knapp & J. A. Daly (Eds.), *Interpersonal communication* (pp. 99–130). Thousand Oaks, CA: Sage.

9. Barelds, D., & Dijkstra, P. (2009). Positive illusions about a partner's physical attractiveness and relationship quality. *Personal Relationships, 16*, 263–283.

10. Hamachek, D. (1982). *Encounters with others: Interpersonal relationships and you*. New York: Holt, Rinehart & Winston.

11. Yun, K. A. (2002). Similarity and attraction. In M. Allen, N. Burrell, B. M. Eayle, & R. W. Preiss (Eds.), *Interpersonal communication research: Advances through meta-analysis* (pp. 145–168). Mahwah, NJ: Erlbaum.

12. Luo, S., & Klohnen, E. (2005). Assortative mating and marital quality in newlyweds: A couple-centered approach. *Journal of Personality and Social Psychology, 88*, 304–326; Amodio, D. M., & Showers, C. J. (2005). Similarity breeds liking revisited: The moderating role of commitment. *Journal of Social and Personal Relationships, 22*, 817–836.

13. Aboud, F. E., & Mendelson, M. J. (1998). Determinants of friendship selection and quality: Developmental perspectives. In W. M. Bukowski & A. F. Newcomb (Eds.), *The company they keep: Friendship in childhood and adolescence* (pp. 87–112). New York: Cambridge University Press.

14. Ledbetter, A. M., Griffin, E., & Sparks, G. G. (2007). Forecasting friends forever: A longitudinal investigation of

sustained closeness between best friends. *Personal Relationships, 14*, 343–350.

15. Burleson, B. R., & Samter, W. (1996). Similarity in the communication skills of young adults: Foundations of attraction, friendship, and relationship satisfaction. *Communication Reports, 9*, 127–139.

16. Jones, J. T., Pelham, B. W., & Carvallo, M. (2004). How do I love thee? Let me count the J's: Implicit egotism and interpersonal attraction. *Journal of Personality and Social Psychology, 87*, 665–683.

17. Ireland, M. E., Slatcher, R. B., Eastwick, P. W., Scissors, L. E., Finkel, E. J., & Pennebaker, J. W. (2011). Language style matching predicts relationship initiation and stability. *Psychological Science, 22*, 39–44; Scissors, L. E., Gill, A. J., Geraghty, K., & Gergle, D. (2009). In CMC we trust: The role of similarity. *Proceedings of CHI 2009*, 527–536. New York: ACM Press.

18. Alford, J. R., Hatemi, P. K., Hibbing, J. R., Martin, N. G., & Eaves, L. J. (2011). The politics of mate choice. *The Journal of Politics, 73*, 362–379.

19. Mette, D., & Taylor, S. (1971). When similarity breeds contempt. *Journal of Personality and Social Psychology, 20*, 75–81.

20. Fisher, H. (2007, May/June). The laws of chemistry. *Psychology Today, 40*, 76–81.

21. Heatherington, L., Escudero, V., & Friedlander, M. L. (2005). Couple interaction during problem discussions: Toward an integrative methodology. *Journal of Family Communication, 5*, 191–207.

22. Rick, S. I., Small, D. A., & Finkel, E. J. (2011). Fatal (fiscal) attraction: Spendthrifts and tightwads in marriage. *Journal of Marketing Research, 48*, 228–237.

23. Specher, S. (1998). Insiders' perspectives on reasons for attraction to a close other. *Social Psychology Quarterly, 61*, 287–300.

24. Aronson, E. (2004). *The social animal* (9th ed.). New York: Bedford, Freeman, & Worth.

25. Fiske, S. T., Cuddy, A. J. C., & Glick, P. (2007). Universal dimensions of social cognition: Warmth and competence. *Trends in Cognitive Sciences, 11*, 77–83.

26. Dindia, K. (2002). Self-disclosure research: Knowledge through meta-analysis. In M. Allen & R. W. Preiss (Eds.), *Interpersonal communication research: Advances through meta-analysis* (pp. 169–185). Mahwah, NJ: Erlbaum.

27. Ledbetter, A. M., Mazer, J. P., DeGroot, J. M., & Meyer, K. R. (2011). Attitudes toward online social connection and self-disclosure as predictors of Facebook communication and relational closeness. *Communication Research, 38*, 27–53; Sheldon, P. (2009). "I'll poke you. You'll poke me!" Self-disclosure, social attraction, predictability and trust as important predictors of Facebook relationships. *Cyberpsychology: Journal of Psychosocial Research on Cyberspace, 3*(2), article 1.

28. Dindia, K. (2002). Self-disclosure research: Knowledge through meta-analysis. In M. Allen & R. W. Preiss (Eds.), *Interpersonal communication research: Advances through meta-analysis* (pp. 169–185). Mahwah, NJ: Erlbaum.

29. Shirley, J. A., Powers, W. G., & Sawyer, C. R. (2007). Psychologically abusive relationships and self-disclosure orientations. *Human Communication, 10*, 289–301.

30. Flora, C. (2004, January/February). Close quarters. *Psychology Today, 37*, 15–16.

31. Haythornthwaite, C., Kazmer, M. M., & Robbins, J. (2000). Community development among distance learners: Temporal and technological dimensions. *Journal of Computer-Mediated Communication, 6*(1), article 2. Retrieved from http://jcmc.indiana.edu/vol6/issue1/haythornthwaite.html

32. Stafford, L. (2008). Social exchange theories. In L. A. Baxter & D. O. Braithewaite (Eds.), *Engaging theories in interpersonal communication: Multiple perspectives* (pp. 377–389). Thousand Oaks, CA: Sage.

33. DeMaris, A. (2007). The role of relationship inequity in marital disruption. *Journal of Social and Personal Relationships, 24*, 177–195.

34. Knapp, M. L., & Vangelisti, A. L. (2006). *Interpersonal communication and human relationships* (6th ed.). Boston: Allyn & Bacon; Avtgis, T. A., West, D. V., & Anderson, T. L. (1998). Relationship stages: An inductive analysis identifying cognitive, affective, and behavioral dimensions of Knapp's relational stages model. *Communication Research Reports, 15*, 280–287; Welch, S. A., & Rubin, R. B. (2002). Development of relationship stage measures. *Communication Quarterly, 50*, 34–40.

35. Dindia, K. (2003). Definitions and perspectives on relational maintenance communication. In D. J. Canary and M. Dainton (Eds.), *Maintaining relationships through communication* (pp. 1–30). Mahwah, NJ: Erlbaum.

36. Johnson, A. J., Wittenberg, E., Haigh, M., Wigley, S., Becker, J., Brown, K., & Craig, E. (2004). The process of relationship development and deterioration: Turning points in friendships that have terminated. *Communication Quarterly, 52*, 54–67.

37. Scharlott, B. W., & Christ, W. G. (1995). Overcoming relationship-initiation barriers: The impact of a computer-dating system on sex role, shyness, and appearance inhibitions. *Computers in Human Behavior, 11*, 191–204.

38. Urista, M. A., Dong, Q., & Day, K. D. (2009). Explaining why young adults use MySpace and Facebook through uses and gratifications theory. *Human Communication, 12*, 215–230.

39. Berger, C. R. (1987). Communicating under uncertainty. In M. E. Roloff & G. R. Miller (Eds.), *Interpersonal processes: New directions in communication research* (pp. 39–62). Newbury Park, CA: Sage; Berger, C. R., & Calabrese, R. J. (1975). Some explorations in initial interaction and beyond: Toward a developmental theory of interpersonal communication. *Human Communication Research, 1*, 99–112.

40. Pratt, L., Wiseman, R. L., Cody, M. J., & Wendt, P. F. (1999). Interrogative strategies and information exchange in computer-mediated communication. *Communication Quarterly, 47*, 46–66.

41. Tolhuizen, J. H. (1989). Communication strategies for intensifying dating relationships: Identification, use and structure. *Journal of Social and Personal Relationships, 6*, 413–434.

42. Johnson, A. J., Wittenberg, E., Haigh, M., Wigley, S., Becker, J., Brown, K., & Craig, E. (2004). The process of relationship development and deterioration: Turning points in friendships that have terminated. *Communication Quarterly, 52*, 54–67.

43. Johnson, K. R., & Holmes, B. M. (2009). Contradictory messages: A content analysis of Hollywood-produced

romantic comedy feature films. *Communication Quarterly, 57*, 352–373.

44. Baxter, L. A. (1987). Symbols of relationship identity in relationship culture. *Journal of Social and Personal Relationships, 4*, 261–280.

45. Buress, C. J. S., & Pearson, J. C. (1997). Interpersonal rituals in marriage and adult friendship. *Communication Monographs, 64*, 25–46.

46. Dunleavy, K. N., & Booth-Butterfield, M. (2009). Idiomatic communication in the stages of coming together and falling apart. *Communication Quarterly, 57*, 416–432; Bell, R. A., & Healey, J. G. (1992). Idiomatic communication and interpersonal solidarity in friends' relational cultures. *Human Communication Research, 18*, 307–335.

47. Papp, L. M., Danielewicz, J., & Cayemberg, C. (2012). Are we Facebook Official? Implications of dating partners' Facebook use and profiles for intimate relationship satisfaction. *CyberPsychology, Behavior & Social Networking, 15*, 85–90.

48. Foster, E. (2008). Commitment, communication, and contending with heteronormativity: An invitation to greater reflexivity in interpersonal research. *Southern Communication Journal, 73*, 84–101.

49. Skowron, E., Stanley, K., & Shapiro, M. (2009). A longitudinal perspective on differentiation of self, interpersonal and psychological well-being in young adulthood. *Contemporary Family Therapy: An International Journal, 31*, 3–18.

50. Courtright, J. A., Miller, F. E., Rogers, L. E., & Bagarozzi, D. (1990). Interaction dynamics of relational negotiation: Reconciliation versus termination of distressed relationships. *Western Journal of Speech Communication, 54*, 429–453.

51. Battaglia, D. M., Richard, F. D., Datteri, D. L., & Lord, C. G. (1998). Breaking up is (relatively) easy to do: A script for the dissolution of close relationships. *Journal of Social and Personal Relationships, 15*, 829–845.

52. Metts, S., Cupach, W. R., & Bejllovec, R. A. (1989). "I love you too much to ever start liking you": Redefining romantic relationships. *Journal of Social and Personal Relationships, 6*, 259–274.

53. Duck, S. (1982). A topography of relationship disengagement and dissolution. In S. Duck (Ed.), *Personal relationships 4: Dissolving personal relationships* (pp. 1–30). New York: Academic Press.

54. Weber, A. L., Harvey, J. H., & Orbuch, T. L. (1992). What went wrong: Communicating accounts of relationship conflict. In M. L. McLaughlin, M. J. Cody, & S. J. Read (Eds.), *Explaining one's self to others: Reason-giving in a social context* (pp. 261–280). Hillsdale, NJ: Erlbaum.

55. Johnson, A. J., Wittenberg, E., Haigh, M., Wigley, S., Becker, J., Brown, K., & Craig, E. (2004). The process of relationship development and deterioration: Turning points in friendships that have terminated. *Communication Quarterly, 52*, 54–67.

56. Baxter, L. A., & Montgomery, B. M. (1992). *Relating: Dialogues and dialectics*. New York: Guilford; Rawlins, W. K. (1996). *Friendship matters: Communication, dialectics, and the life course*. New York: Aldine de Gruyter.

57. Baxter, L. A. (1994). A dialogic approach to relationship maintenance. In D. J. Canary & L. Stafford (Eds.), *Communication and relational maintenance* (pp. 233–254). San Diego, CA: Academic Press; Sahlstein, E., & Dun, T. (2008). "I wanted time to myself and he wanted to be together all the time": Constructing breakups as managing autonomy-connection. *Qualitative Research Reports in Communication, 9*, 37–45.

58. Sahlstein, E., & Dun, T. (2008). "I wanted time to myself and he wanted to be together all the time": Constructing breakups as managing autonomy-connection. *Qualitative Research Reports in Communication, 9*, 37–45.

59. Buunk, A. P. (2005). How do people respond to others with high commitment or autonomy in their relationships? *Journal of Social and Personal Relationships, 22*, 653–672.

60. Morris, D. (1997). *Intimate behavior* (pp. 21–29). New York: Kodansha USA.

61. Golish, T. D. (2000). Changes in closeness between adult children and their parents: A turning point analysis. *Communication Reports, 13*, 78–97.

62. Baxter, L. A., & Erbert, L. A. (1999). Perceptions of dialectical contradictions in turning points of development in heterosexual romantic relationships. *Journal of Social and Personal Relationships, 16*, 547–569.

63. Miller-Ott, A. E., Kelly, L., & Duran, R. L. (2012). The effects of cell phone usage rules on satisfaction in romantic relationships. *Communication Quarterly, 60*, 17–34; Duran, R. L., Kelly, L., & Rotaru, T. (2011). Mobile phones in romantic relationships and the dialectic of autonomy versus connection. *Communication Quarterly, 59*, 19–36.

64. Graham, E. E. (2003). Dialectic contradictions in postmarital relationships. *Journal of Family Communication, 3*, 193–215.

65. Baxter, L. A., Braithwaite, D. O., Golish, T. D., & Olson, L. N. (2002). Contradictions of interaction for wives of elderly husbands with adult dementia. *Journal of Applied Communication Research, 30*, 1–20.

66. Petronio, S. (2000). The boundaries of privacy: Praxis of everyday life. In S. Petronio (Ed.), *Balancing the secrets of private disclosures* (pp. 37–49). Mahwah, NJ: Erlbaum.

67. Debatin, B., Lovejoy, J. P., Horn, A., & Hughes, B. N. (2009). Facebook and online privacy: Attitudes, behaviors, and unintended consequences. *Journal of Computer-Mediated Communication, 15*, 83–108.

68. Pawlowski, D. R. (1998). Dialectical tensions in marital partners' accounts of their relationships. *Communication Quarterly, 46*, 396–416.

69. Griffin, E. M. (2000). *A first look at communication theory* (4th ed.). New York: McGraw-Hill.

70. Braithwaite, D. O., & Baxter, L. (2006). "You're my parent but you're not": Dialectical tensions in stepchildren's perceptions about communicating with the nonresident parent. *Journal of Applied Communication Research, 34*, 30–48.

71. Montgomery, B. M. (1993). Relationship maintenance versus relationship change: A dialectical dilemma. *Journal of Social and Personal Relationships, 10*, 205–223.

72. Braithwaite, D. O., Baxter, L. A., & Harper, A. M. (1998). The role of rituals in the management of the dialectical tension of "old" and "new" in blended families. *Communication Studies, 49*, 101–120.

73. Christensen, A., & Jacobson, J. (2000). *Reconcilable differences*. New York: Guilford.

74. Baxter, L. A., & Braithwaite, D. O. (2006). Social dialectics: The contradictions of relating. In B. Whaley & W.

Samter (Eds.), *Explaining communication: Contemporary communication theories and exemplars* (pp. 305–324). Mahwah, NJ: Erlbaum.

75. Sahlstein, E., & Dun, T. (2008). "I wanted time to myself and he wanted to be together all the time": Constructing breakups as managing autonomy-connection. *Qualitative Research Reports in Communication, 9,* 37–45.

76. Conville, R. L. (1991). *Relational transitions: The evolution of personal relationships* (p. 80). New York: Praeger.

77. Brown, D. E. (1991). *Human universals.* New York: McGraw-Hill.

78. Hamon, R. R., & Ingoldsby, B. B. (Eds.). (2003). *Mate selection across cultures.* Thousand Oaks, CA: Sage.

79. Myers, J. E., Madathil, J., & Tingle, L. R. (2005). Marriage satisfaction and wellness in India and the United States: A preliminary comparison of arranged marriages and marriages of choice. *Journal of Counseling & Development, 83,* 183–190; Yelsma, P., & Athappilly, K. (1988). Marriage satisfaction and communication practices: Comparisons among Indian and American couples. *Journal of Comparative Family Studies, 19,* 37–54.

80. Kim, M. S. (2002). *Non-Western perspectives on human communication: Implications for theory and practice.* Thousand Oaks, CA: Sage.

81. Breitman, P., & Hatch, C. (2000). *How to say no without feeling guilty.* New York: Broadway Books.

82. Imami, M. (1981). *16 ways to avoid saying no.* Tokyo: Nihon Keizai Shimbun.

83. Watzlawick, P., Beavin, J. H., & Jackson, D. D. (1967). *Pragmatics of human communication.* New York: Norton; Lederer, W. J., & Jackson, D. D. (1968). *The mirages of marriage.* New York: Norton.

84. Bell, R. A., & Daly, J. A. (1995). The affinity-seeking function of communication. In M. V. Redmond (Ed.), *Interpersonal communication: Readings in theory and research* (pp. 155–192). Fort Worth, TX: Harcourt Brace.

85. Dainton, M. (1998). Everyday interaction in marital relationships: Variations in relative importance and event duration. *Communication Reports, 11,* 101–143.

86. Myers, S. A., & Avtgis, T. A. (1997). The association of socio-communicative style and relational types on perceptions of nonverbal immediacy. *Communication Research Reports, 14,* 339–349.

87. Richmond, V. P., & McCroskey, J. C. (2004). *Nonverbal behavior in interpersonal relationships* (5th ed., chapter 11). Boston: Allyn and Bacon.

88. Lim, T. S., & Bowers, J. W. (1991). Facework: Solidarity, approbation, and tact. *Human Communication Research, 17,* 415–450.

89. Frei, J. R., & Shaver, P. R. (2002). Respect in close relationships: Prototype, definition, self-report assessment, and initial correlates. *Personal Relationships, 9,* 121–139.

90. Palmer, M. T. (1989). Controlling conversations: Turns, topics, and interpersonal control. *Communication Monographs, 56,* 1–18.

91. Watzlawick, P., Beavin, J. H., & Jackson, D. D. (1967). *Pragmatics of human communication.* New York: Norton.

92. Tannen, D. (1986). *That's not what I meant! How conversational style makes or breaks your relations with others* (p. 190). New York: Morrow.

CHAPTER NINE

1. Crowther, C. E., & Stone, G. (1986). *Intimacy: Strategies for successful relationships* (p. 13). Santa Barbara: Capra Press.

2. Peterson, C. (2006). *A primer in positive psychology.* New York: Oxford.

3. Berscheid, E., Schneider, M., & Omoto, A. M. (1989). Issues in studying close relationships: Conceptualizing and measuring closeness. In C. Hendrick (Ed.), *Close relationships* (pp. 63–91). Newbury Park, CA: Sage.

4. Morris, D. (1973). *Intimate behavior* (p. 7). New York: Bantam.

5. Manning, W. D., Giordano, P. C., & Longmore, M. A. (2006). Hooking up: The relationship contexts of "nonrelationship" sex. *Journal of Adolescent Research, 21,* 459–483.

6. Baxter, L. A. (1994). A dialogic approach to relationship maintenance. In D. Canary & L. Stafford (Eds.), *Communication and relational maintenance* (pp. 233–254). San Diego: Academic Press.

7. Vangelisti, A. L., & Beck, G. (2007). Intimacy and the fear of intimacy. In L. L'Abate (Ed.), *Low-cost approaches to promote physical and mental health: Theory, research, and practice* (pp. 395–414). New York: Springer.

8. Wood, J. T., & Inman, C. C. (1993). In a different mode: Masculine styles of communicating closeness. *Applied Communication Research, 21,* 279–295; Floyd, K. (1995). Gender and closeness among friends and siblings. *Journal of Psychology, 129,* 193–202.

9. Dindia, K. (2000). Sex differences in self-disclosure, reciprocity of self-disclosure, and self-disclosure and liking: Three meta-analyses reviewed. In S. Petronio (Ed.), *Balancing disclosure, privacy and secrecy* (pp. 21–37). Mahwah, NJ: Erlbaum.

10. Balswick, J. O. (1988). *The inexpressive male: A tragedy of American society.* Lexington, MA: Lexington Books.

11. Morman, M. T., & Floyd, K. (1999). Affection communication between fathers and young adult sons: Individual and relational-level correlates. *Communication Studies, 50,* 294–309.

12. Stafford, L., Dainton, M., & Haas, S. (2000). Measuring routine and strategic relational maintenance: Scale revision, sex versus gender roles, and the prediction of relational characteristics. *Communication Monographs, 67,* 306–323.

13. Reissman, C. K. (1990). *Divorce talk: Women and men make sense of personal relationships.* New Brunswick, NJ: Rutgers University Press.

14. Bowman, J. M. (2008). Gender role orientation and relational closeness: Self-disclosive behavior in same-sex male friendships. *Journal of Men's Studies, 16,* 316–330.

15. Good, G. E., Porter, M. J., & Dillon, M. G. (2002). When men divulge: Men's self-disclosure on prime time situation comedies. *Sex Roles, 46,* 419–427.

16. Morman, M. T., & Floyd, K. (2002). A "changing culture of fatherhood": Effects of affectionate communication, closeness, and satisfaction in men's relationships with their fathers and their sons. *Western Journal of Communication, 66,* 395–411.

17. Adamopoulos, J. (1991). The emergence of interpersonal behavior: Diachronic and cross-cultural processes in the

evolution of intimacy. In S. Ting-Toomey & F. Korzenny (Eds.), *Cross-cultural interpersonal communication* (pp. 155–170). Newbury Park, CA: Sage; Fontaine, G. (1990). Cultural diversity in intimate intercultural relationships. In D. D. Cahn (Ed.), *Intimates in conflict: A communication perspective* (pp. 209–224). Hillsdale, NJ: Erlbaum.

18. Adamopoulos, J., & Bontempo, R. N. (1986). Diachronic universals in interpersonal structures. *Journal of Cross-Cultural Psychology, 17,* 169–189.

19. Argyle, M., & Henderson, M. (1985). The rules of relationships. In S. Duck & D. Perlman (Eds.), *Understanding personal relationships* (pp. 63–84). Beverly Hills, CA: Sage.

20. Triandis, H. C. (1994). *Culture and social behavior* (p. 230). New York: McGraw-Hill.

21. Lewin, K. (1936). *Principles of topological psychology.* New York: McGraw-Hill.

22 Hatfield, E., & Rapson, R. L. (2006). Passionate love, sexual desire, and mate selection: Cross-cultural and historical perspectives. In P. Noller & J. A. Feeney (Eds.), *Close relationships: Functions, forms, and processes* (pp. 227–243). Hove, England: Psychology Press/Taylor & Francis.

23. Hian, L. B., Chuan, S. L., Trevor, T. M. K., & Detenber, B. H. (2004). Getting to know you: Exploring the development of relational intimacy in computer-mediated communication. *Journal of Computer-Mediated Communication, 9*(3), 1–24.

24. Valkenberg, P., & Peter, J. (2009). The effects of instant messaging on the quality of adolescents' existing friendships: A longitudinal study. *Journal of Communication, 59,* 79–97; Ko, H., & Kuo, F. (2009). Can blogging enhance subjective well-being through self-disclosure? *CyberPsychology & Behavior, 12,* 75–79; Mazer, J. P., Murphy, R. E., & Simonds, C. J. (2008). The effects of teacher self-disclosure via "Facebook" on teacher credibility. *RCA Vestnik (Russian Communication Association),* 30–37; Hu, Y., Wood, J. F., Smith, V., & Westbrook, N. (2004). Friendships through IM: Examining the relationship between instant messaging and intimacy. *Journal of Computer-Mediated Communication, 10*(1), 38–48.

25. Rosen, L. D., et al. (2008). The impact of emotionality and self-disclosure on online dating versus traditional dating. *Computers in Human Behavior, 24,* 2124–2157; Ben-Ze'ev, A. (2003). Privacy, emotional closeness, and openness in cyberspace. *Computers in Human Behavior, 19,* 451–467.

26. Boase, J., Horrigan, J. B., Wellman, B., & Rainie, L. (2006). The strength of Internet ties. *Pew Internet & American Life Project.* Retrieved from http://www.pewinternet.org/pdfs/PIP_Internet_ties.pdf

27. Henderson, S., & Gilding, M. (2004). "I've never clicked this much with anyone in my life": Trust and hyperpersonal communication in online friendships. *New Media & Society, 6,* 487–506.

28. Henline, B. H., Lamke, L. K., & Howard, M. D. (2007). Exploring perceptions of online infidelity. *Personal Relationships, 14,* 113–128; Whitty, M. T. (2005). The realness of cybercheating: Men's and women's representations of unfaithful Internet relationships. *Social Science Computer Review, 23,* 57–67.

29. Lewis, K., Kaufman, J., & Christakis, N. (2008). The taste for privacy: An analysis of college student privacy settings in an online social network. *Journal of Computer-Mediated Communication, 14,* 79–100; Tufekei, Z. (2008). Can you see me now? Audience and disclosure regulation in online social network sites. *Bulletin of Science, Technology & Society, 28,* 20–36.

30. Baumeister, R. F. (2005). *The cultural animal: Human nature, meaning, and social life.* New York: Oxford.

31. Bellah, R., Madsen, W. M., Sullivan, A., & Tipton, S. M. (1985). *Habits of the heart: Individualism and commitment in American life.* Berkeley: University of California Press; Sennett, R. (1974). *The fall of public man: On the social psychology of capitalism.* New York: Random House; Trenholm, S., & Jensen, A. (1990). *The guarded self: Toward a social history of interpersonal styles.* Paper presented at the Speech Communication Association meeting, San Juan, Puerto Rico.

32. Sillars, A. (1995). Communication and family culture. In M. A. Fitzpatrick & A. L. Vangelisti (Eds.), *Explaining family interactions* (pp. 375–399). Thousand Oaks, CA: Sage.

33. Kellas, J. (2010). Transmitting relational worldviews: The relationship between mother-daughter memorable messages and adult daughters' romantic relational schemata. *Communication Quarterly, 58,* 458–479.

34. Strom, R. E., & Boster, F. J. (2011). Dropping out of high school: Assessing the relationship between supportive messages from family and educational attainment. *Communication Reports, 24,* 25–37.

35. Simon, E. P., & Baxter, L. A. (1993). Attachment-style differences in relationship maintenance strategies. *Western Journal Of Communication, 57,* 416–430.

36. Fowler, C., & Dillow, M. R. (2011). Attachment dimensions and the Four Horsemen of the Apocalypse. *Communication Research Reports, 28,* 16–26.

37. Shochet, I. M., Smyth, T., & Homel, R. (2007). The impact of parental attachment on adolescent perception of the school environment and school connectedness. *Australian & New Zealand Journal of Family Therapy, 28,* 109–118.

38. Domingue, R., & Mollen, D. (2009). Attachment and conflict communication in adult romantic relationships. *Journal of Social & Personal Relationships, 26,* 678–696.

39. Rocca, K. A, Martin, M. M., & Dunleavy, K. N. (2010). Siblings' motives for talking to each other. *Journal of Psychology, 144,* 205–219.

40. Brody, L. R., Copeland, A. P., Sutton, L. S., Richardson, D. R., & Guyer, M. (1998). Mommy and daddy like you best: Perceived family favoritism in relation to affect, adjustment, and family process. *Journal of Family Therapy, 20,* 269–291.

41. Gillies, V., & Lucey, H. (2006). "It's a connection you can't get away from": Brothers, sisters, and social capital. *Journal of Youth Studies, 9,* 479–493.

42. Peisah, C., Brodaty, H., & Quadrio, C. (2006). Family conflict in dementia: Prodigal sons and black sheep. *International Journal of Geriatric Psychiatry, 21,* 485–492.

43. Suitor, J. J., Sechrist, J., Plikuhn, M., Pardo, S. T., Gilligan, M., & Pillemer, K. (2009). The role of perceived maternal favoritism in sibling relations in midlife. *Journal of Marriage and Family, 71,* 1026–1038.

44. Pyke, K. (2005). Generational deserters and "black sheep": Acculturative differences among siblings in Asian immigrant families. *Journal of Family Issues, 26,* 491–517.

45. Goetting, A. (1986). The developmental tasks of sibling-ship over the life cycle. *Journal of Marriage and the Family, 48,* 703–714.

46. Rittenour, C. E., Myers, S. A., & Brann, M. (2007). Commitment and emotional closeness in the sibling relationship. *Southern Communication Journal, 72,* 169–183.

47. Bryant, C. M., Conger, R. D., & Meehan, J. M. (2001). The influence of in-laws on change in marital success. *Journal of Marriage and Family, 63,* 614–626.

48. Ahrons, C. R. (1980). Divorce: A crisis of family transition and change. *Family Relations, 29,* 533–540.

49. Watzlawick, P., Beavin, J., & Jackson, D. (1967). *Pragmatics of human communication: A study of interactional patterns, pathologies, and paradoxes.* New York: Norton.

50. Sabourin, T. (2006). Theories and metatheories to explain family communication: An overview. In L. H. Turner & R. West (Eds.), *Family communication sourcebook* (pp. 43–60). Thousand Oaks, CA: Sage.

51. Thompson, E. H., & Trice-Black, S. (2012). School-based group interventions for children exposed to domestic violence. *Journal of Family Violence, 27,* 233–241.

52. Wahl, K., & Metzner, C. (2012). Parental influences on the prevalence and development of child aggressiveness. *Journal of Child & Family Studies, 21,* 344–355.

53. Barboza, G., Schiamberg, L. B., Oehmke, J., Korzeniewski, S. J., Post, L. A., & Heraux, C. G. (2009). Individual characteristics and the multiple contexts of adolescent bullying: An ecological perspective. *Journal of Youth & Adolescence, 38,* 101–121.

54. Whitchurch, G. G., & Constantine, L. L. (1993). Systems theory. In P. G. Boss, W. J. Doherty, R. LaRossa, W. R. Schumm, & S. K. Steinmetz (Eds.), *Sourcebook of family theories and methods: A contextual approach* (pp. 325–349). New York: Plenum Press.

55. Koerner, A. F., & Fitzpatrick, M. A. (2002). Toward a theory of family communication. *Communication Theory, 12,* 70–91.

56. Barbato, C. A., Graham, E. E., & Perse, E. M. (2003). Communicating in the family: An examination of the relationship of family communication climate and interpersonal communication motives. *Journal of Family Communication, 3,* 123–148.

57. Sherman, S. M., & Dumlao, R. (2008). A cross-cultural comparison of family communication patterns and conflict between young adults and parents. *Journal of Family Communication, 8,* 186–211.

58. Avtgis, T. A. (1999). The relationship between unwillingness to communicate and family communication patterns. *Communication Research Reports, 16,* 333–338.

59. Koesten, J. (2004). Family communication patterns, sex of subject, and communication competence. *Communication Monographs, 71,* 226–244.

60. Petronio, S. (1991). Communication boundary management: A theoretical model of managing disclosure of private information between marital couples. *Communication Theory, 1,* 311–335.

61. Thorson, A. R. (2009). Adult children's experiences with their parent's infidelity: Communicative protection and access rules in the absence of divorce. *Communication Studies, 60,* 32–48. doi:10.1080/10510970802623591

62. Sherman, S. M., & Dumlao, R. (2008). A cross-cultural comparison of family communication patterns and conflict between young adults and parents. *Journal of Family Communication, 8,* 186–211.

63. Schrodt, P., Witt, P. L., & Messersmith, A. S. (2008). A meta-analytical review of family communication patterns and their associations with information processing, behavioral, and psychosocial outcomes. *Communication Monographs, 75,* 248–269.

64. Ledbetter, A. M., & Schrodt, P. (2008). Family communication patterns and cognitive processing: Conversation and conformity orientations as predictors of informational reception apprehension. *Communication Studies, 59,* 388–401.

65. Schrodt, P., & Carr, K. (2012). Trait verbal aggressiveness as a function of family communication patterns. *Communication Research Reports, 29,* 54–63.

66. Ledbetter, A. M., & Vik, T. A. (2012). Parental invasive behaviors and emerging adults' privacy defenses: Instrument development and validation. *Journal of Family Communication, 12,* 227–217.

67. Johnson, A., Wittenberg, E., Haigh, M., Wigley, S., Becker, J., Brown, K., & Craig, E. (2004). The process of relationship development and deterioration: Turning points in friendships that have terminated. *Communication Quarterly, 52,* 54–67.

68. Hartup, W. W., & Stevens, N. (1997). Friendships and adaptation in the life course. *Psychological Bulletin, 121,* 355–370.

69. Pecchioni, L. (2005). Friendship throughout the life span. In L. Pecchioni, K. B. Wright, & J. F. Nussbaum (Eds.), *Life-span communication* (pp. 97–116). Hillsdale, NJ: Erlbaum; Samter, W. (2003). Friendship interaction skills across the life-span. In J. O. Greene & B. R. Burleson (Eds.), *Handbook of communication and social interaction skills* (pp. 637–684). Mahwah, NJ: Erlbaum.

70. Rawlins, W. K. (1992). *Friendship matters, communication, dialectics, and the life course* (p. 105). New York: De Gruyter.

71. Kalmijn, M. (2003). Shared friendship networks and the life course: An analysis of survey data on married and cohabiting couples. *Social Networks, 25,* 231–249.

72. Nussbaum, J. F., Pecchioni, L., Baringer, D., & Kundrat, A. (2002). Lifespan communication. In W. B. Gudykunst (Ed.), *Communication yearbook 26* (pp. 366–389). Mahwah, NJ: Erlbaum.

73. Utz, S. (2007). Media use in long-distance friendships. *Information, Communication & Society, 10,* 694–713.

74. Solomon, S., & Knafo, A. (2007). Value similarity in adolescent friendships. In T. C. Rhodes (Ed.), *Focus on adolescent behavior research* (pp. 133–155). Hauppauge, NY: Nova Science Publishers.

75. Swain, S. (1989). Covert intimacy: Closeness in the same-sex friendships of men. In B. Risman & P. Schwartz (Eds.), *Gender in intimate relations: A microstructural approach* (pp. 75–87). Belmont, CA: Wadsworth.

76. Swain, S. (1989). Covert intimacy: Closeness in the same-sex friendships of men. In B. Risman & P. Schwartz (Eds.), *Gender in intimate relations: A microstructural approach* (pp. 75–87). Belmont, CA: Wadsworth.

77. Dindia, K., & Allen, M. (1992). Sex differences in self-disclosure: A meta-analysis. *Psychological Bulletin, 112*, 106–124.

78. Bond, B. J. (2009). He posted, she posted: Gender differences in self-disclosure on social network sites. *Rocky Mountain Communicator, 6*(2), 29–37.

79. Holmstrom, A. J. (2009). Sex and gender similarities and differences in communication values in same-sex and cross-sex friendships. *Communication Quarterly, 57*, 224–238.

80. Sapadin, L. A. (1988). Friendship and gender: Perspectives of professional men and women. *Journal of Social and Personal Relationships, 5*, 387–403.

81. Holmstrom, A. J. (2009). Sex and gender similarities and differences in communication values in same-sex and cross-sex friendships. *Communication Quarterly, 57*, 224–238.

82. Halatsis, P., & Christakis, N. (2009). The challenge of sexual attraction within heterosexuals' cross-sex friendship. *Journal of Social and Personal Relationships, 26*, 919–937.

83. Sapadin, L. A. (1988). Friendship and gender: Perspectives of professional men and women. *Journal of Social and Personal Relationships, 5*, 387–403.

84. Ledbetter, A. M., Mazer, J. P., DeGroot, J. M., & Meyer, K. R. (2011). Attitudes toward online social connection and self-disclosure as predictors of Facebook communication and relational closeness. *Communication Research, 38*, 27–53.

85. Guerrero, L. K., & Chavez, A. (2005). Relational maintenance in cross-sex friendships characterized by different types of romantic intent: An exploratory study. *Western Journal of Communication, 69*, 339–358.

86. Wyndol, F., & Shaffer, L. (2011). Romantic partners, friends, friends with benefits, and casual acquaintances as sexual partners. *Journal of Sex Research, 48*, 554–564.

87. Bisson, M. A., & Levine, T. R. (2009). Negotiating a friends with benefits relationship. *Archives of Sexual Behavior, 38*, 66–73.

88. Lehmiller, J., VanderDrift, L. E., & Kelly, J. R. (2011). Sex differences in approaching friends with benefits relationships. *Journal of Sex Research, 48*, 275–284.

89. Bisson, M. A., & Levine, T. R. (2009). Negotiating a friends with benefits relationship. *Archives of Sexual Behavior, 38*, 66–73.

90. Hopcke, R. H., & Rafaty, L. (2001). *Straight women, gay men: Absolutely fabulous friendships.* Tulsa: Council Oak Books.

91. Bartlett, N. H., Patterson, H. M., VanderLaan, D. P., & Vasey, P. L. (2009). The relation between women's body esteem and friendships with gay men. *Body Image, 6*, 235–241.

92. Ellison, N. B., Steinfield, C., & Lampe, C. (2007). The benefits of Facebook "friends": Social capital and college students' use of online social networks sites. *Journal of Computer-Mediated Communication, 12*, 1143–1168.

93. More than half of online friends go on to meet in person. (2008, December 17). *Daily Mail Reporter.* Retrieved from http://www.dailymail.co.uk/sciencetech/article-1096664/More-half-online-friends-meet-person.html

94. Ellison, N. B., Steinfield, C., & Lampe, C. (2007). The benefits of Facebook "friends": Social capital and college students' use of online social networks sites. *Journal of Computer-Mediated Communication, 12*, 1143–1168.

95. Hampton, K. N., Sessions Goulet, L., Marlow, C., & Rainie, L. (2012). *Why most Facebook users get more than they give.* Washington, DC: Pew Internet and American Life Project. Retrieved from http://www.pewinternet.org/Reports/2012/Facebookusers/Summary/Power-Users.aspx

96. Tong, S. T., Van Der Heide, B., Langwell, L., & Walther, J. B. (2008). Too much of a good thing? The relationship between number of friends and interpersonal impressions on Facebook. *Journal of Computer-Mediated Communication, 13*, 531–549; Kim, J., & Lee, J. R. (2011). The Facebook paths to happiness: Effects of the number of Facebook friends and self-presentation on subjective well-being. *CyberPsychology, Behavior & Social Networking, 14*, 59–364.

97. Dunbar, R. I. M. (1992, June). Neocortex size as a constraint on group size in primates. *Journal of Human Evolution, 22*(6), 469–493.

98. Hendrick, S. S., & Hendrick, C. (1992). *Romantic love.* Thousand Oaks, CA: Sage; Lee, J. A. (1977). A typology of the styles of loving. *Personality and Social Psychology Bulletin, 3*, 173–182.

99. Baxter, L. A. (2001). Communicatively remembering turning points of relational development in heterosexual romantic relationships. *Communication Reports, 14*, 1–17.

100. Becker, J. A. J., Johnson, A. J., Craig, E. A., Gilchrist, E. S., Haigh, M. M., & Lane, L. T. (2009). Friendships are flexible, not fragile: Turning points in geographically-close and long-distance friendships. *Journal of Social & Personal Relationships, 4*, 347–369.

101. Mongeau, P. A., Serewicz, M. C. M., Henningsen, M. L. M., & Davis, K. L. (2006). Sex differences in the transition to a heterosexual romantic relationship. In K. Dindia & D. J. Canary (Eds.), *Sex differences and similarities in communication* (2nd ed., pp. 337–358). Mahwah, NJ: Erlbaum.

102. Papp, L. M., Danielewicz, J., & Cayemberg, C. (2012). Are we Facebook Official? Implications of dating partners' Facebook use and profiles for intimate relationship satisfaction. *CyberPsychology, Behavior & Social Networking, 15*, 85–90.

103. Theiss, J. A., & Solomon, D. H. (2007). Communication and the emotional, cognitive, and relational consequences of first sexual encounters between partners. *Communication Quarterly, 55*, 179–206.

104. Siegert, J. R., & Stamp, G. H. (1994). "Our first big fight" as a milestone in the development of close relationships. *Communication Monographs, 61*, 345–361.

105. Dailey, R. M., Rossetto, K. R., McCracken, A. A., Jin, B., & Green, E. W. (2012). Negotiating breakups and renewals in on-again/off-again dating relationships: Traversing the transitions. *Communication Quarterly, 60*, 165–189.

106. Baxter, L. A., & Bullis, C. (1986). Turning points in developing romantic relationships. *Human Communication Research, 12*, 469–493.

107. Gottman, J. (1994). *Why marriages succeed or fail.* New York: Simon & Schuster.

108. Holman, T. B., & Jarvis, M. O. (2003). Hostile, volatile, avoiding, and validating couple-conflict types: An investigation of Gottman's couple-conflict types. *Personal Relationships, 10*, 267–282.

109. Chapman, G. (2010). *The 5 love languages.* Chicago: Northfield.

110. Egbert, N., & Polk, D. (2006). Speaking the language of relational maintenance: A validity test of Chapman's (1992) five love languages. *Communication Research Reports, 23,* 19–26.

111. Weigel, D. J., Brown, C., & O'Riordan, C. K. (2011). Everyday expressions of commitment and relational uncertainty as predictors of relationship quality and stability over time. *Communication Reports, 24,* 38–50; Weigel, D. J. (2008). Mutuality and the communication of commitment in romantic relationships. *Southern Communication Journal, 73,* 24–41.

112. Rabby, M. K. (2007). Relational maintenance and the influence of commitment in online and offline relationships. *Communication Studies, 58,* 315–337.

113. Canary, D. J., & Stafford, L. (1992). Relational maintenance strategies and equity in marriage. *Communication Monographs, 59,* 243–267; Stafford, L., & Canary, D. J. (1991). Maintenance strategies and romantic relationship type, gender, and relational characteristics. *Journal of Personality and Social Psychology, 7,* 217–242.

114. Egbert, N., & Polk, D. (2006). Speaking the language of relational maintenance: A validity test of Chapman's (1992) five love languages. *Communication Research Reports, 23,* 19–26.

115. Johnson, A. J., Haigh, M. M., Becker, J. A. H., Craig, E. A., & Wigley, S. (2008). College students' use of relational management strategies in email in long-distance and geographically close relationships. *Journal of Computer-Mediated Communication, 13,* 381–404.

116. Ledbetter, A. M. (2010). Assessing the measurement invariance of relational maintenance behavior when face-to-face and online. *Communication Research Reports, 27,* 30–37.

117. Craig, E., & Wright, B. (2012). Computer-mediated relational development and maintenance on Facebook. *Communication Research Reports, 29,* 119–129.

118. Utz, S. (2007). Media use in long-distance friendships. *Information, Communication & Society, 10,* 694–713.

119. Houser, M. L., Fleuriet, C., & Estrada, D. (2012). The cyber factor: An analysis of relational maintenance through the use of computer-mediated communication. *Communication Research Reports, 29,* 34–43.

120. Hall, J. A., Larson, K. A., & Watts, A. (2011). Satisfying friendship maintenance expectations: The role of friendship standards and biological sex. *Human Communication Research, 37,* 529–552.

121. Merolla, A. J. (2010). Relational maintenance and noncopresence reconsidered: Conceptualizing geographic separation in close relationships. *Communication Theory, 20,* 169–193; Stafford, L. (2005). *Maintaining long-distance and cross residential relationships.* Mahwah, NJ: Erlbaum.

122. Johnson, A. J., Becker, J. A. H., Craig, E. A., Gilchrist, E. S., & Haigh, M. M. (2009). Changes in friendship commitment: Comparing geographically close and long-distance young-adult friendships. *Communication Quarterly, 57,* 395–415.

123. McGuire, K. C., & Kinnery, T. A. (2010). When distance is problematic: Communication, coping, and relational satisfaction in female college students' long-distance dating

relationships. *Journal of Applied Communication Research, 38,* 27–46.

124. Johnson, A. J., Craig, E. A., Haigh, M. M., Becker, J. A. H., & Craig, E. A. (2009). Relational closeness: Comparing undergraduate college students' geographically close and long-distance friendships. *Personal Relationships, 16,* 631–646.

125. MacGeorge, E. L., Feng, B., & Burleson, B. R. (2011). Supportive communication. In M. L. Knapp & J. A. Daly (Eds.), *The Sage handbook of interpersonal communication* (4th ed., pp. 317–354). Thousand Oaks, CA: Sage.

126. High, A. C., & Dillard, J. P. (2012). A review and meta-analysis of person-centered messages and social support outcomes. *Communication Studies, 53,* 99–118.

127. Semmer, N. K., Elfering, A., Jacobshagen, N., Perrot, T., Beehr, T. A., & Boos, N. (2008). The emotional meaning of instrumental social support. *International Journal of Stress Management, 15,* 235–251.

128. Rains, S. A., & Keating, D. M. (2011). The social dimension of blogging about health: Health blogging, social support, and well-being. *Communication Monographs, 78,* 511–553.

129. Fox, S. (2011, June). *Peer-to-peer healthcare.* Washington, DC: Pew Internet & American Life Project. Retrieved from http://www.pewinternet.org/Reports/2011/P2PHealthcare.aspx

130. Sanford, A. A. (2010). "I can air my feelings instead of eating them": Blogging as social support for the morbidly obese. *Communication Studies, 61,* 567–584.

131. Rusbult, C. E., Hannon, P. A., Stocker, S. L., & Finkel, E. J. (2005). Forgiveness and relational repair. In E. L. Worthington (Ed.), *Handbook of forgiveness* (pp. 185–206). New York: Routledge.

132. Emmers-Sommer, T. M. (2003). When partners falter: Repair after a transgression. In D. J. Canary & M. Dainton (Eds.), *Maintaining relationships through communication* (pp. 185–205). Mahwah, NJ: Erlbaum.

133. Dindia, K., & Baxter, L. A. (1987). Strategies for maintaining and repairing marital relationships. *Journal of Social and Personal Relationships, 4,* 143–159.

134. Waldron, V. R., Kelley, D. L., & Harvey, J. (2008). Forgiving communication and relational consequence. In M. T. Motley (Ed.), *Studies in applied interpersonal communication* (pp. 165–184). Thousand Oaks, CA: Sage.

135. Park, H. S. (2009). Cross-cultural comparison of verbal and nonverbal strategies of apologizing. *Journal of International and Intercultural Communication, 2,* 66–87; Park, H. S., & Guan, X. (2006). The effects of national culture and face concerns on intention to apologize: A comparison of the USA and China. *Journal of Intercultural Communication Research, 35,* 183–204.

136. Exline, J. J., Deshea, L., & Holeman, V. T. (2007). Is apology worth the risk? Predictors, outcomes, and ways to avoid regret. *Journal of Social & Clinical Psychology, 26,* 479–504.

137. Wallace, H. M., Exline, J. J., & Baumeister, R. F. (2008). Interpersonal consequences of forgiveness: Does forgiveness deter or encourage repeat offenses? *Journal of Experimental Social Psychology, 44,* 453–460.

138. Chapman, G. D., & Thomas, J. M. (2006). *The five languages of apology.* Chicago: Northfield; Kelley, D. L., &

Waldron, V. R. (2005). An investigation of forgiveness-seeking communication and relational outcomes. *Communication Quarterly, 53*, 339–359.

139. Merolla, A. J. (2008). Communicating forgiveness in friendships and dating relationships. *Communication Studies, 59*, 114–131.

140. Orcutt, H. K. (2006). The prospective relationship of interpersonal forgiveness and psychological distress symptoms among college women. *Journal of Counseling Psychology, 53*, 350–361; Eaton, J., & Struthers, C. W. (2006). The reduction of psychological aggression across varied interpersonal contexts through repentance and forgiveness. *Aggressive Behavior, 32*, 195–206.

141. Lawler, K. A., Younger, J. W., Piferi, R. L., et al. (2003). A change of heart: Cardiovascular correlates of forgiveness in response to interpersonal conflict. *Journal of Behavioral Medicine, 26*, 373–393.

142. Waldron, V. R., & Kelley, D. L. (2005). Forgiving communication as a response to relational transgressions. *Journal of Social and Personal Relationships, 22*, 723–742.

143. Waldron, V. R., & Kelley, D. L. (2008). *Communicating forgiveness.* Thousand Oaks, CA: Sage.

144. Guerrero, L. K., & Bachman, G. F. (2010). Forgiveness and forgiving communication in dating relationships: An expectancy-investment explanation. *Journal of Social and Personal Relationships, 27*, 801–823.

145. Bachman, G. F., & Guerrero, L. K. (2006). Forgiveness, apology, and communicative responses to hurtful events. *Communication Reports, 19*, 45–56.

146. Henline, B. H., Lamke, L. K., & Howard, M. D. (2007). Exploring perceptions of online infidelity. *Personal Relationships, 14*, 113–129.

147. Takaku, S., Weiner, B., & Ohbuchi, K. (2001). A cross-cultural examination of the effects of apology and perspective-taking on forgiveness. *Journal of Language & Social Psychology, 20*, 144–167.

148. Kelley, D. (1998). The communication of forgiveness. *Communication Studies, 49*, 255–272.

CHAPTER TEN

1. Barbato, C. A., Graham, E. E., & Perse, E. M. (2003). Communicating in the family: An examination of the relationship of family communication climate and interpersonal communication motives. *Journal of Family Communication, 3*, 123–148.

2. Dailey, R. M. (2006). Confirmation in parent–adolescent relationships and adolescent openness: Toward extending confirmation theory. *Communication Monographs, 73*, 434–458.

3. Teven, J. J., Martin, M. M., & Neupauer, N. C. (1998). Sibling relationships: Verbally aggressive messages and their effect on relational satisfaction. *Communication Reports, 11*, 179–186.

4. Vangelisti, A. L., & Young, S. L. (2000). When words hurt: The effects of perceived intentionality on interpersonal relationships. *Journal of Social & Personal Relationships, 17*, 393–424.

5. Seiberg, E. (1976). Confirming and disconfirming communication in an organizational setting. In J. Owen, P. Page, & G. Zimmerman (Eds.), *Communication in organizations* (pp. 129–149). St. Paul, MN: West.

6. Sieberg, E., & Larson, C. (1971). *Dimensions of interpersonal response.* Paper presented at the meeting of the International Communication Association, Phoenix.

7. Cox, S. A. (1999). Group communication and employee turnover: How coworkers encourage peers to voluntarily exit. *Southern Communication Journal, 64*, 181–192.

8. Gottman, J. M., & Levenson, R. W. (2000). The timing of divorce: Predicting when a couple will divorce over a 14-year period. *Journal of Marriage and the Family, 62*, 737–745.

9. Rancer, A. S., & Avtgis, T. A. (2006). *Argumentative and aggressive communication: Theory, research, and application.* Thousand Oaks, CA: Sage.

10. Wade, A., & Beran, T. (2011). Cyberbullying: The new era of bullying. *Canadian Journal of School Psychology, 26*, 44–61; Dempsey, A. G., Sulkowski, M. L., Dempsey, J., & Storch, E. A. (2011). Has cyber technology produced a new group of peer aggressors? *Cyberpsychology, Behavior, and Social Networking, 14*, 297–302.

11. Alberts, J. K. (1988). An analysis of couples' conversational complaints. *Communication Monographs, 55*, 184–197.

12. Alberts, J. K., & Driscoll, G. (1992). Containment versus escalation: The trajectory of couples' conversational complaints. *Western Journal of Communication, 56*, 394–412.

13. Gottman, J. M., & Silver, N. (1999). *The seven principles for making marriage work.* New York: Random House.

14. Rancer, A. S., & Avtgis, T. A. (2006). *Argumentative and aggressive communication: Theory, research, and application.* Thousand Oaks, CA: Sage.

15. Jordan-Jackson, F. F., Lin, Y., Rancer, A. S., & Infante, D. A. (2008). Perceptions of males and females' use of aggressive and nonaffirming messages in an interpersonal dispute: You've come a long way baby? *Western Journal of Communication, 72*, 239–258.

16. Cissna, K., & Seiberg, E. (1995). Patterns of interactional confirmation and disconfirmation. In M. V. Redmond (Ed.), *Interpersonal communication: Readings in theory and research* (pp. 301–317—AU). Fort Worth, TX: Harcourt Brace.

17. Allen, M. W. (1995). Communication concepts related to perceived organizational support. *Western Journal of Communication, 59*, 326–346.

18. Dailey, R. M. (2008). Assessing the contribution of nonverbal behaviors in displays of confirmation during parent–adolescent interactions: An actor–partner interdependence model. *Journal of Family Communication, 8*, 62–91.

19. Wilmot, W. W. (1987). *Dyadic communication* (pp. 149–158). New York: Random House.

20. Burggraf, C., & Sillars, A. L. (1987). A critical examination of sex differences in marital communication. *Communication Monographs, 54*, 276–294; Newton, D. A., & Burgoon, J. K. (1990). The use and consequences of verbal strategies during interpersonal disagreements. *Human Communication Research, 16*, 477–518.

21. Hocker, J. L., & Wilmot, W. W. (1995). *Interpersonal conflict* (4th ed., p. 34). Dubuque, IA: Brown & Benchmark.

22. Hocker, J. L., & Wilmot, W. W. (1995). *Interpersonal conflict* (4th ed., p. 36). Dubuque, IA: Brown & Benchmark.

23. Gottman, J. M., & Levenson, R. W. (1999). Rebound for marital conflict and divorce prediction. *Family Process, 38*, 387–292.

24. Domenici, K., & Littlejohn, S. (2006). *Facework: Bridging theory and practice*. Thousand Oaks, CA: Sage; Lapinski, M. K., & Boster, F. J. (2001). Modeling the ego-defensive function of attitudes. *Communication Monographs, 68,* 314–324.

25. Becker, J. A. H., Ellevold, B., & Stamp, G. H. (2008). The creation of defensiveness in social interaction II: A model of defensive communication among romantic couples. *Communication Monographs, 75,* 86–110; Stamp, G. H., Vangelisti, A. L., & Daly, J. A. (1992). The creation of defensiveness in social interaction. *Communication Quarterly, 40,* 177–190.

26. Turk, D. R., & Monahan, J. L. (1999). "Here I go again": An examination of repetitive behaviors during interpersonal conflicts. *Southern Communication Journal, 64,* 232–244.

27. Cupach, W. R., & Messman, S. J. (1999). Face predilections and friendship solidarity. *Communication Reports, 12,* 117–124.

28. Trees, A. R., Kerssen-Griefp, J., & Hess, J. A. (2009). Earning influence by communicating respect: Facework's contributions to effective instructional feedback. *Communication Education, 58,* 397–416.

29. Kingsley Westerman, C. Y., & Westerman, D. (2010). Supervisor impression management: Message content and channel effects on impressions. *Communication Studies, 61,* 585–601.

30. Gibb, J. (1961, September). Defensive communication. *Journal of Communication, 11,* 141–148; Robertson, E. (2005). Placing leaders at the heart of organizational communication. *Communication Management, 9,* 34–37.

31. Proctor, R. F., & Wilcox, J. R. (1993). An exploratory analysis of responses to owned messages in interpersonal communication. *ETC: A Review of General Semantics, 50,* 201–220.

32. Seider, B. H., Hirschberger, G., Nelson, K. L., & Levenson, R. W. (2009). We can work it out: Age differences in relational pronouns, physiology, and behavior in marital conflict. *Psychology and Aging, 24,* 604–613.

33. Czech, K., & Forward, G. L. (2010). Leader communication: Faculty perceptions of the department chair. *Communication Quarterly, 58,* 431–457.

34. Harwood, J., Ryan, E. B., Giles, H., & Tysoski, S. (1997). Evaluations of patronizing speech and three response styles in a non-service-providing context. *Journal of Applied Communication Research, 25,* 170–195.

35. Miller, S., Nunnally, E. W., & Wackman, D. B. (1975). *Alive and aware: How to improve your relationships through better communication*. Minneapolis, MN: International Communication Programs; Remer, R., & deMesquita, P. (1990). Teaching and learning the skills of interpersonal confrontation. In D. D. Cahn (Ed.), *Intimates in conflict: A communication perspective* (pp. 225–252). Hillsdale, NJ: Erlbaum.

36. Smith, M. (1975). *When I say no, I feel guilty* (pp. 93–110). New York: Dial Press.

37. Benoit, W. L., & Drew, S. (1997). Appropriateness and effectiveness of image repair strategies. *Communication Reports, 10,* 153–163; Stamp, G. H., Vangelisti, A. L., & Daly, J. A. (1992). The creation of defensiveness in social interaction. *Communication Quarterly, 40,* 177–190.

CHAPTER ELEVEN

1. Wilmot, W., & Hocker, J. L. (2010). *Interpersonal conflict* (8th ed., pp. 44–56). New York: McGraw-Hill; Buzzanell, P. M., & Burrell, N. A. (1997). Family and workplace conflict: Examining metaphorical conflict schemas and expressions across context and sex. *Human Communication Research, 24,* 109–146.

2. Metts, S., & Cupach, W. (1990). The influence of relationship beliefs and problem-solving responses on satisfaction in romantic relationships. *Human Communication Research, 17,* 170–185.

3. Wilmot, W., & Hocker, J. L. (2010). *Interpersonal conflict* (8th ed., pp. 11–19). New York: McGraw-Hill.

4. Cupach, W. R., & Canary, D. J. (1997). *Competence in interpersonal conflict* (pp. 5–6). New York: McGraw-Hill.

5. Benoit, W. L., & Benoit, P. J. (1987). Everyday argument practices of naive social actors. In J. Wenzel (Ed.), *Argument and critical practices* (pp. 465–474). Annandale, VA: Speech Communication Association.

6. Samter, W., & Cupach, W. R. (1998). Friendly fire: Topical variations in conflict among same- and cross-sex friends. *Communication Studies, 49,* 121–138.

7. Vuchinich, S. (1987). Starting and stopping spontaneous family conflicts. *Journal of Marriage and Family, 49,* 591–601.

8. Gottman, J. M. (1982). Emotional responsiveness in marital conversations. *Journal of Communication, 32,* 108–120; Cupach, W. R. (1982, May). *Communication satisfaction and interpersonal solidarity as outcomes of conflict message strategy use*. Paper presented at the International Communication Association conference, Boston.

9. Koren, K., Carlton, K., & Shaw, D. (1980). Marital conflict: Relations among behaviors, outcomes, and distress. *Journal of Consulting and Clinical Psychology, 48,* 460–468.

10. Wilmot, W., & Hocker, J. L. (2010). *Interpersonal conflict* (8th ed., p. 37). New York: McGraw-Hill.

11. Gottman, J. M. (1979). *Marital interaction: Experimental investigations*. New York: Academic Press; Infante, D. A., Myers, S. A., & Buerkel, R. A. (1994). Argument and verbal aggression in constructive and destructive family and organizational disagreements. *Western Journal of Communication, 58,* 73–84.

12. Crohan, S. E. (1992). Marital happiness and spousal consensus on beliefs about marital conflict: A longitudinal investigation. *Journal of Science and Personal Relationships, 9,* 89–102.

13. Canary, D. J., Weger, H., Jr., & Stafford, L. (1991). Couples' argument sequences and their associations with relational characteristics. *Western Journal of Speech Communication, 55,* 159–179.

14. Harper, M. S., & Welsh, D. P. (2007). Keeping quiet: Self-silencing and its association with relational and individual functioning among adolescent romantic couples. *Journal of Social and Personal Relationships, 24,* 99–116.

15. Afifi, T. D., McManus, T., Steuber, K., & Coho, A. (2009). Verbal avoidance and dissatisfaction in intimate conflict situations. *Human Communication Research, 35,* 357–383; Caughlin, J. P., & Golish, T. D. (2002). An analysis of the association between topic avoidance and dissatisfaction: Comparing perceptual and interpersonal explanations. *Communication Monographs, 69,* 275–295.

16. Caughlin, J. P., & Arr, T. D. (2004). When is topic avoidance unsatisfying? Examining moderators of the association between avoidance and dissatisfaction. *Human Communication Research, 30,* 479–513.

17. Cahn, D. D. (1992). *Conflict in intimate relationships* (p. 100). New York: Guilford.

18. Wilmot, W., & Hocker, J. L. (2010). *Interpersonal conflict* (8th ed., p. 159). New York: McGraw-Hill.

19. Oetzel, J. G., & Ting-Toomey, S. (2003). Face concerns in interpersonal conflict: A cross-cultural empirical test of the face negotiation theory. *Communication Research, 30,* 599–625; Dsilva, M. U., & Whyte, L. O. (1998). Cultural differences in conflict styles: Vietnamese refugees and established residents. *Howard Journal of Communication, 9,* 57–68.

20. Messman, S. J., & Mikesell, R. L. (2000). Competition and interpersonal conflict in dating relationships. *Communication Reports, 13,* 21–34.

21. Olson, L. N., & Braithwaite, D. O. (2004). "If you hit me again, I'll hit you back": Conflict management strategies of individuals experiencing aggression during conflicts. *Communication Studies, 55,* 271–285.

22. Warren, K., Schoppelrey, S., & Moberg, D. (2005). A model of contagion through competition in the aggressive behaviors of elementary school students. *Journal of Abnormal Child Psychology, 33,* 283–292.

23. Infante, D. A. (1987). Aggressiveness. In J. C. McCroskey & J. A. Daly (Eds.), *Personality and interpersonal communication* (pp. 157–191). Newbury Park, CA: Sage.

24. Roloff, M. E., & Reznick, R. M. (2008). Communication during serial arguments: Connections with individuals' mental and physical well-being. In M. T. Motley (Ed.), *Studies in applied interpersonal communication* (pp. 97–120). Thousand Oaks, CA: Sage.

25. Infante, D. A., Rancer, A. S., & Jordan, F. F. (1996). Affirming and nonaffirming style, dyad sex, and the perception of argumentation and verbal aggression in an interpersonal dispute. *Human Communication Research, 22,* 315–334.

26. Infante, D. A., Chandler, T. A., & Rudd, J. E. (1989). Test of an argumentative skill deficiency model of interspousal violence. *Communication Monographs, 56,* 163–177.

27. Martin, M. M., Anderson, C. M., Burant, P. A., & Weber, K. (1997). Verbal aggression in sibling relationships. *Communication Quarterly, 45,* 304–317.

28. Kassing, J. W., & Infante, D. A. (1999). Aggressive communication in the coach-athlete relationship. *Communication Research Reports, 16,* 110–120.

29. Beatty, M. J., Valencic, K. M., Rudd, J. E., & Dobos, J. A. (1999). A "dark side" of communication avoidance: Indirect interpersonal aggressiveness. *Communication Research Reports, 16,* 103–109.

30. Filley, A. C. (1975). *Interpersonal conflict resolution* (p. 23). Glenview, IL: Scott, Foresman.

31. Canary, D. (2003). Managing interpersonal conflict: A model of events related to strategic choices. In J. O. Greene & B. R. Burleson (Eds.), *Handbook of communication and social interaction skills* (pp. 515–549). Mahwah, NJ: Erlbaum.

32. Wilmot, W., & Hocker, J. L. (2010). *Interpersonal conflict* (8th ed., pp. 13–16). New York: McGraw-Hill; Knapp, M. L.,

Putnam, L. L., & Davis, L. J. (1988). Measuring interpersonal conflict in organizations: Where do we go from here? *Management Communication Quarterly, 1,* 414–429.

33. Burggraf, C. S., & Sillars, A. L. (1987). A critical examination of sex differences in marital communication. *Communication Monographs, 53,* 276–294.

34. McGinn, M. M., McFarland, P. T., & Christensen, A. (2009). Antecedents and consequences of demand/withdraw. *Journal of Family Psychology, 23,* 749–757.

35. Gottman, J. (1994). *Why marriages succeed or fail.* New York: Simon & Schuster; Fowler, C., & Dillow, M. R. (2011). Attachment dimensions and the Four Horsemen of the Apocalypse. *Communication Research Reports, 28,* 16–26; Holman, T. B., & Jarvis, M. O. (2003). Hostile, volatile, avoiding, and validating couple-conflict types: An investigation of Gottman's couple-conflict types. *Personal Relationships, 10,* 267–282.

36. Rossel, J., & Collins, R. (2006). Conflict theory and interaction rituals: The microfoundations of conflict theory. In J. H. Turner (Ed.), *Handbook of sociological theory* (pp. 509–532). New York: Springer.

37. Cupach, W. R., & Canary, D. J. (1997). *Competence in interpersonal conflict* (p. 109). New York: McGraw-Hill.

38. Tannen, D. (1989). *You just don't understand: Women and men in conversation* (pp. 152–157, 162–165). New York: William Morrow.

39. Tannen, D. (1989). *You just don't understand: Women and men in conversation* (pp. 152–157, 162–165). New York: William Morrow.

40. Hess, N. H., & Hagen, E. H. (2006). Sex differences in indirect aggression: Psychological evidence from young adults. *Evolution and Human Behavior, 27,* 231–245; Underwood, M. K. (2003). *Social aggression among girls.* New York: Guilford.

41. Wiseman, R. (2003). *Queen bees and wannabes: Helping your daughter survive cliques, gossip, boyfriends, and other realities of adolescence.* New York: Three Rivers Press.

42. Collier, M. J. (1991). Conflict competence within African, Mexican, and Anglo-American friendships. In S. Ting-Toomey & F. Korzenny (Eds.), *Cross-cultural interpersonal communication* (pp. 132–154). Newbury Park, CA: Sage.

43. Papa, M. J., & Natalle, E. J. (1989). Gender, strategy selection, and discussion satisfaction in interpersonal conflict. *Western Journal of Speech Communication, 52,* 260–272.

44. Afifi, T. D., Joseph, A., & Aldeis, D. (2012). The "standards for openness hypothesis": Why women find (conflict) avoidance more dissatisfying than men. *Journal of Social and Personal Relationships, 29,* 102–125.

45. Gayle, B. M., Preiss, R. W., & Allen, M. A. (2001). A meta-analytic interpretation of intimate and non-intimate interpersonal conflict. In M. A. Allen, R. W. Preiss, B. M. Gayle, & N. Burrell (Eds.), *Interpersonal communication: Advances through meta-analysis* (pp. 345–368). New York: Erlbaum.

46. Allen, M. (1998). Methodological considerations when examining a gendered world. In D. Canary & K. Dindia (Eds.), *Handbook of sex differences and similarities in communication* (pp. 427–444). Mahwah, NJ: Erlbaum.

47. Cupach, W. R., & Canary, D. J. (1997). *Competence in interpersonal conflict* (p. 63–65). New York: McGraw-Hill.

48. Burggraf, C. S., & Sillars, A. L. (1987). A critical examination of sex differences in marital communication. *Communication Monographs, 54*, 276–294.

49. Gudykunst, W. B., & Ting-Toomey, S. (1988). *Culture and interpersonal communication* (pp. 153–160). Newbury Park, CA: Sage.

50. Holt, J. L., & DeVore, C. J. (2005). Culture, gender, organizational role, and styles of conflict resolution: A meta-analysis. *International Journal of Intercultural Relations, 29,* 165–196.

51. Ting-Toomey, S. (1988). Rhetorical sensitivity style in three cultures: France, Japan, and the United States. *Central States Speech Journal, 39,* 28–36.

52. Okabe, K. (1987). Indirect speech acts of the Japanese. In L. Kincaid (Ed.), *Communication theory: Eastern and Western perspectives* (pp. 127–136). San Diego: Academic Press.

53. Fontaine, G. (1991). Cultural diversity in intimate intercultural relationships. In D. D. Cahn (Ed.), *Intimates in conflict: A communication perspective* (pp. 209–224). Hillsdale, NJ: Erlbaum.

54. Tannen, D. (1989). *You just don't understand: Women and men in conversation* (p. 160). New York: William Morrow.

55. Collier, M. J. (1991). Conflict competence within African, Mexican, and Anglo-American friendships. In S. Ting-Toomey & F. Korzenny (Eds.), *Cross-cultural interpersonal communication* (pp. 132–154). Newbury Park, CA: Sage.

56. Beatty, K. J., & McCroskey, J. C. (1997). It's in our nature: Verbal aggressiveness as temperamental expression. *Communication Quarterly, 45,* 446–460.

57. Oetzel, J. G. (1998). Explaining individual communication processes in homogeneous and heterogeneous groups through individualism-collectivism and self-construal. *Human Communication Research, 25,* 202–224.

58. Hahlweg, K., & Richter, D. (2010). Prevention of marital instability and distress: Results of an 11-year longitudinal follow-up study. *Behaviour Research and Therapy, 48,* 377–383.

59. Gordon, T. (1970). *Parent effectiveness training* (pp. 236–264). New York: Wyden.

60. Axelrod, R. (1984). *The evolution of cooperation.* New York: Basic Books.

Feature Box Notes

CHAPTER ONE, ON THE JOB

a. National Association of Colleges and Employers. (2012). *Job outlook 2012*. Retrieved from http://www.naceweb.org/Research/Job_Outlook/Purchase_Job_Outlook_2012.aspx

b. Winsor, J. L., Curtis, D. B., & Stephens, R. D. (1997). National preferences in business and communication education: An update. *Journal of the Association for Communication Administration, 3*, 170–179; Peterson, M. S. (1997). Personnel interviewers' perceptions of the importance and adequacy of applicants' communication skills. *Communication Education, 46*, 287–291.

c. Endicott, F. S. (1979). *The Endicott report: Trends in the employment of college and university graduates in business and industry.* Evanston, IL: Placement Center, Northwestern University.

d. Hindi, N. M., Miller, D. S., & Catt, S. E. (2004). Communication and miscommunication in corporate America: Evidence from Fortune 200 firms. *Journal of Organizational Culture, 8*, 13–26.

e. Darling, A. L., & Dannels, D. P. (2003). Practicing engineers talk about the importance of talk: A report on the role of oral communication in the workplace. *Communication Education, 52*, 1–16.

f. Gray, E. F. (2010). Specific oral communication skills desired in new accountancy graduates. *Business Communication Quarterly, 73*, 40–67.

g. Communication skills deemed vital. (1999, August 22). *Santa Barbara News-Press*, J1.

h. Richman, J. (2002, September 16). The news journal of the life scientist. *The Scientist, 16*, 42.

CHAPTER ONE, ETHICAL CHALLENGE

a. An English translation of Martin Buber's *I and Thou* was published in 1970 by Scribner's. For useful descriptions of its central themes, see Stewart, J. (2006). A philosopher's approach. In J. Stewart (Ed.), *Bridges not walls* (9th ed., pp. 679–696). New York: McGraw-Hill; Paton, H. J. (1955). *The modern predicament*. London: Allen & Unwin.

CHAPTER TWO, ETHICAL CHALLENGE

a. Read Kant's own words on truth telling in the following works: On a supposed right to lie from altruistic motives. (1964). In L. W. Beck (Trans. and Ed.), *Critique of practical reason and other writings in moral philosophy*. Chicago: University of Chicago Press; Paton, H. J. (Trans.). (1964). *Groundwork of the metaphysics of morals*. New York: Harper Torchbooks.

b. Fried, C. (1978). *Right and wrong*. Cambridge, MA: Harvard University Press; Bok, S. (1979). *Lying: Moral choice in public and private life*. New York: Vintage.

CHAPTER THREE, ON THE JOB

a. Equal Employment Opportunity Commission. (2010). *Sexual harassment charges EEOC & FEPAs combined: FY 1997–FY 2010*. Retrieved from http://www.eeoc.gov/eeoc/statistics/enforcement/sexual_harassment.cfm

b. Ohse, D. M., & Stockwell, M. S. (2008). Age comparisons in workplace sexual harassment perceptions. *Sex Roles, 59*, 240–253.

c. Fiedler, A. M., & Blanco, R. I. (2006). The challenge of varying perceptions of sexual harassment: An international study. *Journal of Behavioral and Applied Management, 7*, 274–292.

CHAPTER THREE, ETHICAL CHALLENGE

a. For a discussion of the Golden and Platinum rules, see Bennett, M. (1979). Overcoming the Golden Rule: Sympathy and empathy. In D. Nimmo (Ed.), *Communication yearbook 3* (pp. 407–422). New Brunswick, NJ: Transaction Books; Johannesen, R. L. (2002). *Ethics in human communication*. Prospect Heights, IL: Waveland Press.

CHAPTER FOUR, ON THE JOB

a. Scott, C., & Myers, K. K. (2005). The socialization of emotion: Learning emotion management at the fire station. *Journal of Applied Communication Research, 33*, 67–92.

b. Miller, K. I., & Koesten, J. (2008). Financial feeling: An investigation of emotion and communication in the workplace. *Journal of Applied Communication Research, 36*, 8–32.

c. Tracy, S. J. (2005). Locking up emotion: Moving beyond dissonance for understanding emotion labor discomfort. *Communication Monographs, 72*, 261–283.

CHAPTER FIVE, ON THE JOB

a. Jay, T. B., & Janschewitz, K. (2008). The pragmatics of swearing. *Journal of Politeness Research: Language, Behavior, Culture, 4*, 267–288.

b. Johnson, D. I., & Lewis, N. (2010). Perceptions of swearing in the work setting: An expectancy violations theory perspective. *Communication Reports, 23*, 106–118.

c. Sutton, R. I. (2010, June 18). Is it sometimes useful to cuss when you are at work?: The strategic use of swear words. *Psychology Today*. Retrieved from http://www.psychologytoday.com/blog/work-matters/201006/is-it-sometimes-useful-cuss-when-you-are-work

CHAPTER SIX, ON THE JOB

a. Goldberg, C., & Cohen, D. J. (2004). Walking the walk and talking the talk: Gender differences in the impact of interviewing skills on applicant assessments. *Group & Organization Management, 29*, 369–384.

b. Stewart, G. L., Dustin, S. L., Barrick, M. R., & Darnold, T. C. (2008). Exploring the handshake in employment interviews. *Journal of Applied Psychology, 93*, 1139–1146.

c. Riggio, R. E., & Throckmorton, B. (1988). The relative effects of verbal and nonverbal behavior, appearance, and social skills on evaluation made in hiring interviews. *Journal of Applied Social Psychology, 18*, 331–348; Gifford, R., Ng, C. F., & Wilkinson, M. (1985). Nonverbal cues in the employment interview: Links between applicant qualities and interviewer judgments. *Journal of Applied Psychology, 70*, 729–736.

d. Krumhuber, E., Manstead, A., Cosker, D., Marshall, D., & Rosin, P. (2009). Effects of dynamic attributes of smiles in human and synthetic faces: A simulated job interview setting. *Journal of Nonverbal Behavior, 33,* 1–15.

CHAPTER SEVEN, ON THE JOB

a. Sypher, B. D., Bostrom, R. N., & Seibert, J. H. (1989). Listening communication abilities and success at work. *Journal of Business Communication, 26,* 293–303; Alexander, E. R., Penley, L. E., & Jernigan, I. E. (1992). The relationship of basic decoding skills to managerial effectiveness. *Management Communication Quarterly, 6,* 58–73.

b. Winsor, J. L., Curtis, D. B., & Stephens, R. D. (1999). National preferences in business and communication education: An update. *Journal of the Association for Communication Administration, 3,* 170–179.

c. Johnson, S., & Bechler, C. (1998). Examining the relationship between listening effectiveness and leadership emergence: Perceptions, behaviors, and recall. *Small Group Research, 29,* 452–471.

d. Christensen, D., & Rees, D. (2002, October). Communication skills needed by entry-level accountants. *The CPA letter, 82.* Retrieved from http://www.aicpa.org/pubs/cpaltr/Oct2002/AUDIT/audit.htm

e. Marchant, V. (1999, June 28). Listen up! *Time, 153,* 74; *Job Outlook 2006.* (2006). Retrieved from http://www.naceweb.org/press/display.asp?year=&prid=235

f. Brownell, J. (1990). Perceptions of effective listeners: A management study. *Journal of Business Communication, 27,* 401–415.

CHAPTER SEVEN, ETHICAL CHALLENGE

a. Rogers, C. (1961). *On becoming a person.* Boston: Houghton Mifflin.

b. High, A. C., & Dillard, J. P. (2012). A review and meta-analysis of person-centered messages and social support outcomes. *Communication Studies, 63,* 99–118.

CHAPTER EIGHT, ON THE JOB

a. Waldeck, J. H., & Myers, K. K. (2007). Organizational assimilation theory, research, and implications for multiple areas of the discipline: A state of the art review. *Communication Yearbook, 31,* 322–367; Hart, Z. P., & Miller, V. D. (2005). Context and message content during organizational socialization: A research note. *Human Communication Research, 31,* 295–309; Madlock, P. E., & Horan, S. M. (2009). Predicted outcome value of organizational commitment. *Communication Research Reports, 26,* 40–49.

b. Barge, J. K., & Schlueter, D. W. (2004). Memorable messages and newcomer socialization. *Western Journal of Communication, 68,* 233–256.

CHAPTER NINE, ON THE JOB

a. Studies summarized in More confident, less careful: Why office romances are hard to manage. (2007, March 21). *Knowledge@Wharton.* Retrieved from http://knowledge.wharton.upenn.edu/article.cfm?articleid=1686; How to handle an office romance. (2007, August 29). *CNN.* Retrieved from http://articles.cnn.com/2007-08-29/living/office.romance_1_office-romance-workplace-romances-personal-relationship?_s=PM:LIVING

b. More confident, less careful: Why office romances are hard to manage. (2007, March 21). *Knowledge@Wharton.* Retrieved from http://knowledge.wharton.upenn.edu/article.cfm?articleid=1686

CHAPTER TEN, ON THE JOB

a. Cooil, B., Aksoy, L., Keiningham, T. L., & Maryott, K. M. (2009). The relationship of employee perceptions of organizational climate to business-unit outcomes: An MPLS approach. *Journal of Service Research, 11,* 277–294; Pincus, D. (1986). Communication satisfaction, job satisfaction, and job performance. *Human Communication Research, 12,* 395–419.

b. Sopow, E. (2008). The communication climate change at RCMP. *Strategic Communication Management, 12,* 20–23; Kassing, J. W. (2008). Consider this: A comparison of factors contributing to employees' expressions of dissent. *Communication Quarterly, 56,* 342–355; Saunders, D. (2008). Create an open climate for communication. *Supervision, 69,* 6–8; Beck, C. E., & Beck, E. A. (1996). The manager's open door and the communication climate. In K. M. Galvin & P. Cooper (Eds.), *Making connections: Readings in relational communication* (pp. 286–290). Los Angeles: Roxbury.

c. Goleman, D. (2006). *Social intelligence* (p. 279). New York: Random House.

d. Akkirman, A. D., & Harris, D. L. (2005). Organizational communication satisfaction in the virtual workplace. *Journal of Management Development, 24,* 397–409.

e. Waldvogel, J. (2007). Greetings and closings in workplace email. *Journal of Computer-Mediated Communication, 12,* 456–477.

CHAPTER TEN, ETHICAL CHALLENGE

For more information on nonviolent strategies, see Ackerman, P., & Kruegler, C. (1994). *Strategic nonviolent conflict: The dynamics of people power in the twentieth century.* Westport, CT: Praeger; Holmes, R. L. (Ed.). (1990). *Nonviolence in theory and practice.* Belmont, CA: Wadsworth.

CHAPTER ELEVEN, ON THE JOB

a. Lutgen-Sandvik, P. (2003). The communicative cycle of employee emotional abuse: Generation and regeneration of workplace mistreatment. *Management Communication Quarterly, 16,* 471–501.

b. Namie, G., & Namie, R. (2009). *The bully at work: What you can do to stop the hurt and reclaim your dignity on the job.* Naperville, IL: Sourcebooks.

c. Pearson, C., & Porath, C. (2009). *The cost of bad behaviour.* New York: Portfolio.

CHAPTER ELEVEN, ETHICAL CHALLENGE

For more information about crazymaking, see Bach, G., & Wyden, P. (1968). *The intimate enemy.* New York: Avon; Bach, G. (1971). *Aggression lab: The fair fight manual.* Dubuque, IA: Kendall-Hunt.

Glossary

abstraction ladder A range of more to less abstract terms describing an event or object.

abstract language Language that is vague and general rather than concrete and specific. *See also* behavioral language.

accenting Nonverbal behaviors that emphasize part of a verbal message.

accommodating A lose–win conflict style in which the communicator submits to a situation rather than attempts to have his or her needs met.

adaptors Unconscious bodily movements in response to the environment.

advising A listening response in which the receiver offers suggestions about how the speaker should deal with a problem.

affinity The degree to which persons like or appreciate one another.

aggressiveness Verbal attacks that demean another's self-concept and inflict psychological pain.

ambiguous response A disconfirming response with more than one meaning, leaving the other party unsure of the responder's position.

ambushing A style in which the receiver listens carefully in order to gather information to use in an attack on the speaker.

analyzing A listening response in which the receiver offers an interpretation of a speaker's message.

androgynous Possessing both masculine and feminine traits.

argumentativeness Presenting and defending positions on issues while attacking positions taken by others.

assertive message format A direct expression of the sender's needs and thoughts delivered in a way that does not attack the receiver's dignity. A complete assertive message describes behavior, interpretation, feeling, consequence, and intention.

attending The process of filtering out some messages and focusing on others.

attribution The process of attaching meaning to behavior. *See also* interpretation statement.

avoiding (conflict style) A lose–lose conflict style in which the parties ignore the problem at hand.

avoiding (relational stage) A stage of relational deterioration immediately before terminating in which the parties minimize contact with one another.

behavioral description An account that refers only to observable phenomena.

behavioral language Language that describes observable behavior. *See also* abstract language.

benevolent lie A lie defined by the teller as not malicious, or even helpful, to the person to whom it is told.

body orientation A type of nonverbal communication characterized by the degree to which we face forward or away from someone.

bonding A stage of relational development in which the parties make symbolic public gestures to show that their relationship exists.

breadth A dimension of self-disclosure involving the range of subjects being discussed.

"but" statement A statement in which the word *but* cancels out the expression preceding it.

certainty An attitude behind messages that dogmatically implies that the speaker's position is correct and that the other person's ideas are not worth considering. Likely to generate a defensive response.

channel The medium through which a message passes from sender to receiver.

chronemics The study of how humans use and structure time.

circumscribing A stage of relational deterioration in which partners begin to reduce the scope of their contact and commitment to one another.

clichés Ritualized, stock statements delivered in response to a social situation.

co-culture A culture that exists within the larger culture of a country or society, such as subgroups defined by age, race or ethnicity, occupation, sexual orientation, physical disability, religion, avocation, and so on.

cognitive complexity The ability to construct a variety of frameworks for viewing an issue.

cognitive conservatism The tendency to seek and attend to information that conforms to an existing self-concept.

collaborating A conflict management style that seeks win–win solutions.

communication climate The emotional tone of a relationship between two or more individuals.

communication competence The ability to accomplish one's personal goals in a manner that maintains a relationship on terms that are acceptable to all parties.

competing A win–lose approach to conflicts that seeks to resolve them in one's own way.

complaining A disagreeing message that directly or indirectly communicates dissatisfaction with another person.

complementary conflict style A relational conflict style in which partners use different but mutually reinforcing behaviors.

complementing Nonverbal behavior that reinforces a verbal message.

compromising An approach to conflict resolution in which both parties attain at least part of what they wanted through self-sacrifice.

confirming communication A message that expresses caring or respect for another person.

conflict An expressed struggle between at least two interdependent parties who perceive incompatible goals, scarce resources, and interference from the other party in achieving their goals.

conflict ritual An unacknowledged repeating pattern of interlocking behavior used by participants in a conflict.

conformity orientation The degree to which a family enforces a uniformity of attitudes, values, and beliefs.

connection-autonomy dialectic The tension between the need for integration and the need for independence in a relationship.

consequence statement An explanation of the results that follow from either the behavior of the person to whom the message is addressed or the speaker's interpretation of the addressee's behavior. Consequence statements can describe what happens to the speaker, the addressee, or others.

content dimension The part of a message that communicates information about the subject being discussed. *See also* relational dimension.

contradicting Nonverbal behavior that is inconsistent with a verbal message.

control The social need to influence others.

controlling communication Messages in which the sender tries to impose some sort of outcome on the receiver, usually resulting in a defensive reaction.

convergence The process of adapting one's speech style to match that of others with whom the communicator wants to identify. *See also* divergence.

conversation orientation The degree of openness a family has in discussing a range of topics.

counterfeit questions Questions that disguise the speaker's true motives, which do not include a genuine desire to understand the other person. *See also* sincere questions.

crazymaking *See* passive aggression.

debilitative emotions Emotions that prevent a person from functioning effectively.

decode The process in which a receiver attaches meaning to a message.

de-escalatory conflict spiral A communication pattern in which the parties slowly lessen their dependence on one another, withdraw, and become less invested in the relationship. *See also* spiral.

defensive listening A response style in which the receiver perceives a speaker's comments as an attack.

defensiveness The attempt to protect a presenting image that a person believes is being attacked.

depth A dimension of self-disclosure involving a shift from relatively nonrevealing messages to more personal ones.

description Gibb's term for language that describes a complaint in behavioral terms rather than being judgmental, thereby creating a supportive communication climate. *See also* evaluation, "I" language.

dialectical tensions Inherent conflicts that arise when two opposing or incompatible forces exist simultaneously.

differentiating A relational stage in which the parties reestablish their individual identities after having bonded together.

direct aggression A criticism or demand that threatens the face of the person at whom it is directed.

disagreeing messages Messages that communicate to the other person, "You are wrong." Includes aggressiveness, complaining, and argumentativeness.

disconfirming communication A message that expresses a lack of caring or respect for another person.

disinhibition The tendency to transmit messages without considering their consequences; occurs more frequently in mediated communication.

divergence Language mannerisms that emphasize a communicator's differences from others. *See also* convergence.

dyad Two individuals communicating. The interaction may or may not be interpersonal in nature.

emblems Deliberate nonverbal behaviors with precise meanings that are known to virtually all members of a cultural group.

emotional contagion The process by which emotions are transferred from one person to another.

emotional intelligence The ability to understand and manage one's own emotions and be sensitive to others' feelings.

emotion labor Managing and even suppressing emotions when doing so is both appropriate and necessary.

emotive language Language that conveys the sender's attitude rather than simply offers an objective description.

empathy The ability to project oneself into another person's point of view so as to experience the other's thoughts and feelings. *See also* sympathy.

encode The process of putting thoughts into symbols, most commonly words.

environment The field of experiences that leads a person to make sense of another's behavior. Environments consist of physical characteristics, personal experiences, relational history, and cultural background.

equality A type of supportive communication described by Gibb that suggests that the sender regards the receiver as worthy of respect.

equivocal language Ambiguous language that has two or more equally plausible meanings.

escalatory conflict spiral A communication pattern in which one attack leads to another until the initial skirmish escalates into a full-fledged battle. *See also* spiral.

ethnocentrism The attitude that one's own culture is superior to others.

evaluation Gibb's term for judgmental assessments of another person's behavior, thereby increasing the odds of creating a defensive communication climate. *See also* description, "I" language.

experimenting An early stage in relational development consisting of a search for common ground. If the experimentation is successful, then the relationship will progress to intensifying. If not, it may go no further.

face The socially approved identity that a communicator tries to present. *See also* identity management.

face-threatening act Behavior by another that is perceived as attacking an individual's presenting image, or face.

facilitative emotions Emotions that contribute to effective functioning.

fallacy of approval The irrational belief that it is vital to win the approval of virtually every person a communicator deals with.

fallacy of catastrophic expectations The irrational belief that the worst possible outcome will probably occur.

fallacy of causation The irrational belief that emotions are caused by others and not by the person who has them.

fallacy of helplessness The irrational belief that satisfaction in life is determined by forces beyond one's control.

fallacy of overgeneralization Irrational beliefs in which (1) conclusions (usually negative) are based on limited evidence, or (2) communicators exaggerate their shortcomings.

fallacy of perfection The irrational belief that a worthwhile communicator should be able to handle every situation with complete confidence and skill.

fallacy of shoulds The irrational belief that people should behave in the most desirable way.

family communication pattern A mode of family interaction that involves a blending of conversation and conformity orientations. These include consensual, pluralistic, protective, and laissez-faire patterns.

family system A group of interdependent individuals who interact and adapt together as a whole.

feeling statement An expression of the sender's emotions that results from interpretation of sense data.

friends with benefits (FWB) A popular term for non-romantic heterosexual friendships that include sexual activity.

gender role Socially approved ways that men and women are expected to behave.

gestures Motions of the body, usually hands or arms, that have communicative value.

Gibb categories Six sets of contrasting styles of verbal and nonverbal behavior. Each set describes a communication style that is likely to arouse defensiveness and a contrasting style that is likely to prevent or reduce it. Developed by Jack Gibb.

halo effect The power of a first impression to influence subsequent perceptions.

haptics The study of touching.

hearing The physiological dimension of listening.

high-context cultures Cultures that avoid direct use of language, relying instead on the context of a message to convey meaning.

identity management The communication strategies people use to influence how others view them. *See also* face.

"I" language A statement that clearly identifies the speaker as the source of a message. *See also* "you" language, description.

illustrators Nonverbal behaviors that accompany and support verbal messages.

immediacy The degree of interest and attention that we feel toward and communicate to others.

impersonal communication Behavior that treats others as objects rather than individuals. *See also* interpersonal communication.

impersonal response A disconfirming response that is superficial or trite.

impervious response A disconfirming response that ignores another person's attempt to communicate.

impression management *See* identity management.

incongruous response A disconfirming response in which two messages, one of which is usually nonverbal, contradict each other.

initiating The first stage in relational development in which the parties express interest in one another.

insensitive listening Failure to recognize the thoughts or feelings that are not directly expressed by a speaker.

instrumental goals Goals aimed at getting others to behave in desired ways.

insulated listening A style in which the receiver ignores undesirable information.

integrating A stage of relational development in which the parties begin to take on a single identity.

intensifying A stage of relational development that precedes integrating in which the parties move toward integration by increasing the amount of contact and the breadth and depth of self-disclosure.

intention statement A description of where the speaker stands on an issue, what he or she wants, or how he or she plans to act in the future.

interpersonal communication A continuous, transactional process involving participants who occupy different but overlapping environments and create relationships through the exchange of messages, many of which are affected by external, physiological, and psychological noise.

interpretation The process of attaching meaning to sense data.

interpretation statement A statement that describes the speaker's interpretation of the meaning of another person's behavior. *See also* attribution.

interrupting response A disconfirming response in which one communicator interrupts another.

intimacy A state of closeness arising from physical, intellectual, or emotional contact or sometimes from shared activities.

intimate distance One of Hall's four distance zones, ranging from skin contact to 18 inches.

irrelevant response A disconfirming response in which one communicator's comments bear no relationship to the previous speaker's ideas.

"it" statements Statements that replace the personal pronoun "I" with the less immediate word "it," often reducing the speaker's acceptance of responsibility for the statement.

Johari Window A model that describes the relationship between self-disclosure and self-awareness.

judging A listening response in which the receiver evaluates the sender's message either favorably or unfavorably.

kinesics The study of body position and motion.

leakage Nonverbal behaviors that reveal information a communicator does not disclose verbally.

leanness Messages (usually electronic) that are stark from a lack of nonverbal information; opposite of richness.

linear communication model A characterization of communication as a one-way event in which a message flows from sender to receiver.

linguistic relativism The notion that the worldview of a culture is shaped and reflected by the language its members speak. *See also* Sapir-Whorf hypothesis.

listening Process that consists of hearing, attending, understanding, responding, and remembering an aural message.

listening fidelity The degree of congruence between what a listener understands and what the message sender was attempting to communicate.

love languages Modes of communicating affection in romantic relationships. These include words of affirmation, quality time, gifts, acts of service, and physical touch.

low-context cultures Cultures that use language primarily to express thoughts, feelings, and ideas as directly as possible.

manipulators A type of nonverbal adaptors involving self-touching behaviors.

mediated communication Communication between individuals that is conducted via technological channels such as email, chat rooms, texting, and instant messaging.

message Information sent from a sender to a receiver.

metacommunication Messages (usually relational) that refer to other messages; communication about communication.

microexpression A brief facial expression.

mindful listening Giving careful and thoughtful attention and responses to the messages we receive.

mindless listening Reacting to others' messages automatically and routinely without much mental investment.

mixed message Situation in which a person's words are incongruent with his or her nonverbal behavior.

monochronic Behavior emphasizing punctuality, schedules, and completing one task at a time.

narrative The stories used to describe one's personal world.

negotiation The sense making that occurs between and among people as they influence one another's perceptions and try to achieve a shared perspective. Fourth stage in the perception process.

neutrality A defense-arousing behavior described by Gibb in which the sender expresses indifference toward a receiver.

noise External, physiological, and psychological distractions that interfere with the accurate transmission and reception of a message.

nonverbal communication Messages expressed by other than linguistic means.

openness-privacy dialectic The tension between the need for disclosure and the need for secrecy in a relationship.

organization The second stage in the perception process in which selected information is arranged in some meaningful way.

paralanguage Nonlinguistic means of vocal expression: rate, pitch, tone, and so on.

parallel conflict style A relational conflict style in which the approach of the partners varies from one situation to another.

paraphrasing Restating a speaker's thoughts or feelings in the listener's own words.

passive aggression An indirect expression of aggression delivered in a way that allows the sender to maintain a façade of kindness.

perceived self The person we believe ourselves to be in moments of candor. It may be identical with or different from the presenting and ideal self.

perception checking A three-part method for verifying the accuracy of interpretations, including a description of the sense data, two possible interpretations, and a request for confirmation of the interpretations.

personal distance One of Hall's four distance zones, ranging from 18 inches to 4 feet.

personality A relatively consistent set of traits exhibited by a person across a variety of situations.

pillow method A method for understanding an issue from several perspectives rather than with an egocentric "I'm right and you're wrong" attitude.

polychronic An approach to the use of time that emphasizes flexibility and pursuing multiple tasks.

posture The way in which individuals carry themselves—erect, slumping, and so on.

powerless speech mannerisms Ways of speaking that may reduce perceptions of a communicator's power.

pragmatic rules Linguistic rules that help communicators understand how messages may be used and interpreted in a given context.

predictability-novelty dialectic The tension between the need for stability and the need for change in a relationship.

presenting self The image a person presents to others. It may be identical with or different from the perceived and ideal self.

privacy management The choices people make to reveal or conceal information about themselves.

problem orientation A supportive style of communication described by Gibb in which the communicators focus on working together to solve their problems instead of trying to impose their own solutions on one another.

prompting Using silences and brief statements of encouragement to draw out a speaker.

provisionalism A supportive style of communication described by Gibb in which the sender expresses a willingness to consider the other person's position.

proxemics The study of how people use interpersonal space and distance.

pseudolistening An imitation of true listening in which the receiver's mind is elsewhere.

public distance One of Hall's four distance zones, extending outward from 12 feet.

punctuation The process of determining the causal order of events.

questioning A listening response in which the receiver seeks additional information from the sender.

reappraisal Rethinking the meaning of emotionally charged events in ways that alter their emotional impact.

receiver One who notices and attends to a message.

reference groups Groups against which we compare ourselves, thereby influencing our self-concept and self-esteem.

reflected appraisal The theory that a person's self-concept mirrors the way the person believes others regard him or her.

regulating One function of nonverbal communication in which nonverbal cues control the flow of verbal communication among individuals.

relational commitment A promise—sometimes implied and sometimes explicit—to remain in a relationship and to make that relationship successful.

relational conflict style A pattern of managing disagreements that repeats itself over time in a relationship.

relational dimension The part of a message that expresses the social relationship between two or more individuals. *See also* content dimension.

relational maintenance Communication aimed at keeping relationships operating smoothly and satisfactorily.

relational transgression One partner's violation of the explicit or implicit terms of the relationship, letting the other one down in some important way.

relational turning point Transformative event that alters a relationship in a fundamental way.

relative words Words that gain their meaning by comparison.

remembering Ability to recall information.

repeating Nonverbal behaviors that duplicate the content of a verbal message.

respect The social need to be held in esteem by others.

responding Giving observable feedback to the speaker.

richness An abundance of nonverbal cues that add clarity to a verbal message; opposite of leanness.

role A set of expectations about how to communicate.

rumination Dwelling persistently on negative thoughts that, in turn, intensifies negative feelings.

Sapir-Whorf hypothesis Theory of linguistic relativity in which language shapes a culture's perceived reality. *See also* linguistic relativism.

selection The first stage in the perception process in which some data are chosen to attend to and others to ignore.

selective listening A listening style in which the receiver responds only to messages that interest him or her.

self-concept The relatively stable set of perceptions each individual holds of himself or herself.

self-disclosure The process of deliberately revealing information about oneself that is significant and that would not normally be known by others.

self-esteem The part of the self-concept that involves an individual's evaluations of his or her self-worth.

self-fulfilling prophecy An expectation of an event, followed by behaviors based on that expectation, that makes the outcome more likely to occur than would have been the case otherwise.

self-monitoring The process of attending to one's behavior and using these observations to shape the way one behaves.

self-serving bias The tendency to interpret and explain information in a way that casts the perceiver in the most favorable manner.

self-talk The nonvocal process of thinking; sometimes referred to as *intrapersonal communication*.

semantic rules Rules that govern the meaning of language as opposed to its structure. *See also* syntactic rules.

sender The creator of a message.

significant others People whose opinion is important enough to affect one's self-concept strongly.

sincere questions Attempts to elicit information that enable the asker to understand the other person. *See also* counterfeit questions.

social comparison Evaluation of oneself in terms of or by comparison to others.

social distance One of Hall's distance zones, ranging from 4 to 12 feet.

social media All of the many channels that make remote personal communication possible, including email, text messages, tweets, and social networking sites.

social penetration A model that describes relationships in terms of their breadth and depth.

social support Assistance for others provided through emotional, informational, or instrumental resources.

spiral A reciprocal communication pattern in which each person's message reinforces the other's. *See also* de-escalatory conflict spiral, escalatory conflict spiral.

spontaneity A supportive communication behavior described by Gibb in which the sender expresses a message without any attempt to manipulate the receiver.

stage-hogging A listening style in which the receiver is more concerned with making his or her own point than in understanding the speaker.

stagnating A stage of relational deterioration characterized by declining enthusiasm and by standardized forms of behavior.

static evaluation The tendency to view people or relationships as unchanging.

stereotyping Categorizing individuals according to a set of characteristics assumed to belong to all members of a group.

strategy A defense-arousing style of communication described by Gibb in which the sender tries to manipulate or deceive a receiver.

substituting Nonverbal behavior that takes the place of a verbal message.

superiority A defense-arousing style of communication described by Gibb in which the sender states or implies that the receiver is not worthy of respect.

supporting A listening response that demonstrates solidarity with a speaker's situation.

symmetrical conflict style A relational conflict style in which both partners use the same tactics.

sympathy Compassion for another's situation. *See also* empathy.

syntactic rules Rules that govern the ways symbols can be arranged, as opposed to the meanings of those symbols. *See also* semantic rules.

tangential response A disconfirming response that uses the speaker's remark as a starting point for a shift to a new topic.

terminating The concluding stage of relational deterioration, characterized by the acknowledgement of one or both parties that the relationship is over.

territory A stationary area claimed by an individual.

transactional communication model A characterization of communication as the simultaneous sending and receiving of messages in an ongoing, irreversible process.

understanding Occurs when sense is made of a message.

"we" language Statement that implies that the issue is the concern and responsibility of both the speaker and receiver of a message. *See also* "I" language, "you" language.

"you" language A statement that expresses or implies a judgment of the other person. *See also* "I" language.

Name Index

Subject Index

Note: page references followed by *f* indicate figures; those followed by *t* indicate tables.

distance and, 208–9
    territory and, 209–10
physiological noise, 10
physiology of perception, 86, 88–89
    age and, 88
    biological cycles and, 89
    health and fatigue and, 88
    hunger and, 88–89
    psychological changes and, 88
    senses, 86, 88
pillow method, 104, 104f, 107–9
Platinum Rule, 105
polychronic, 197
posture, 198, 199–200
powerless speech mannerisms, 165–66, 165t
pragmatic rules, 160–61, 160t
predictability-novelty dialectic, 264
presenting self, 52, 319–20
privacy management, 61
private self, 51–52
problem orientation, 321–22
problem-solving, 18
prompting, 229–30
provisionalism, 323, 324–25
proxemics, 208
proximity in relationships, 254
pseudolistening, 224
psychological noise, 10
public distance, 209
public self, 51–52
punctuation, 82–83, 83f
Pygmalion in the Classroom, 50, 74

Q
questioning, 230–31

R
rankism, 324
rational-emotive therapy, 136
rational thinking, 138–43, 145–36
reaffirmation, 266
reappraisal, 119
recalibration, 266
receiver (*See* listening), 8, 9f
reciprocity
    attraction in relationships and, 253
    communication patterns and, 317–19, 318t
    self-disclosure and, 61–62
recognition, 316
reference groups, 42
reflected appraisal, 41

regulating, 191
rejection, self-disclosure and, 62
relational commitment, 299, 299t
relational communication, 268–71
    communication climate of (*See* communication climate)
    content messages in, 268–69
    films/television shows depicting, 274–75
    metacommunication, 271
    nonverbal communication and, 189–90
    relational messages in, 268–71
    stages of, 255–61
relational conflict styles, 358–61
relational cycles, 267, 267f
relational development, 255–66, 256f
    assessment of, 262
    developmental perspective, 255–61
    dialectical perspective, 262–66
relational dimension, 16–17
relational maintenance, 255–56, 256f, 299–300, 301
relational messages, 268–71
    affinity in, 269
    content of, 268–69
    control in, 270–71
    immediacy in, 269–70
    metacommunication and, 271
    respect in, 270
    types of, 269–71
relational roles, 92, 93
relational stages, 255–61
    avoiding, 260
    bonding, 258–59
    circumscribing, 259–60
    differentiating, 259
    experimenting, 256, 257
    initiating, 256, 257
    integrating, 258
    intensifying, 258
    stagnating, 260
    terminating, 260–61
relational transgressions, 302–5
    assessment of, 303
    forgiving, 304–5
    repair, strategies for, 303, 304
    types of, 302, 302t
relational turning points, 295, 296
relationships. *See also* interpersonal communication; self-disclosure
    appearance and, 250–51, 253
    building and maintaining, 54, 62